Educational Psychology

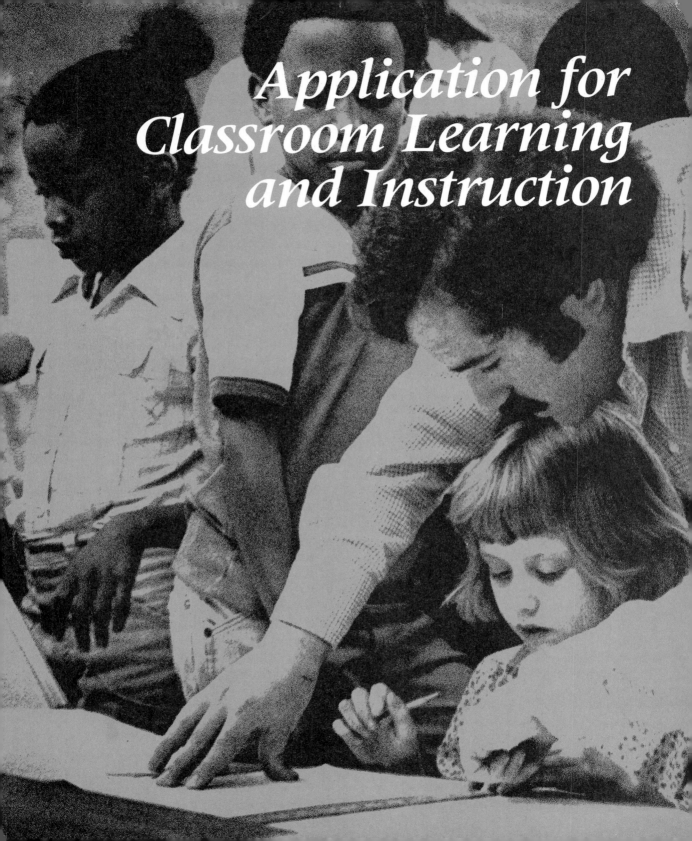

Application for Classroom Learning and Instruction

Educational Psychology

Robert R. Reilly
University of Arkansas

Ernest L. Lewis
Southern Illinois University at Carbondale

Consultant for Instructional Applications

Laurel Tanner
Temple University

Macmillan Publishing Co., Inc.
NEW YORK

Collier Macmillan Publishers
LONDON

Macmillan Publishing Co., Inc.
866 Third Avenue, New York, New York 10022

Collier Macmillan Canada, Inc.

Library of Congress Cataloging in Publication Data

Reilly, Robert R.
  Educational psychology.

  Bibliography: p.
  Includes index.
  1. Educational psychology.   I. Lewis, Ernest L.
II. Title.
LB1051.R44   370.15   82-15169
ISBN 0-02-399250-6   AACR2

Printing: 1 2 3 4 5 6 7 8   Year: 3 4 5 6 7 8 9 0

ISBN   0-02-399250-6

To our students, from whom
we have learned and continue to learn

Preface
to the Student

The textbook you are about to read is an introduction to educational psychology for prospective teachers. A problem of many educational psychology texts is that they are so broad, and therefore so long, sometimes even including material from philosophy, history, sociology, and literature, that students see the field as a vast smorgasbord, a hodgepodge that overloads and confuses rather than enlightens.

This book provides a focus that is both reasonable and practical. Educational psychology is seen as an applied discipline dealing with the nature, outcomes, and evaluation of classroom learning and instruction. It is limited to those findings, concepts, and principles from psychology that are *actually helpful* in understanding and facilitating classroom learning. A major goal of the book is to present the material in clear, readable prose, without the numerous references and quotes that sometimes serve only to confuse the student, and to present practical applications for teaching throughout the book.

There are four parts to this text. Part I is essential background for teaching, namely, the understanding of basic processes of development and learning. Terminology and principles that are crucial throughout the book appear here first, the rationale being to proceed from more covert and theoretical variables to more overt and practical applications later in the book.

Part II is devoted to the child's personal and social development. A humanistic approach is outlined, and the affective domain is explored in detail, with particular attention given to motivation, values, moral development, and emotions.

Part III focuses on important student variables, crucial areas of individual differences that influence classroom behavior. Intelligence, creativity, social class, race, sex, and exceptionality are all presented in terms of the essential knowledge and understanding that a teacher needs in these areas.

Part IV explores practical and applied dimensions of improving classroom instruction. Classroom climate is analyzed in searching for effective learning environments, and procedures for planning and evaluating instruction follow. Particular attention is directed toward constructing and using classroom tests. Discipline is seen as a highly important topic, with specific suggestions, and the book closes with a description of a first-year teacher's experiences and her recommendations on how to survive in today's classroom.

As you read the book, you will find frequent anecdotal examples that are presented in boxes to separate them from the text material. These informal examples are meant to illustrate the concepts and principles in specific, concrete situations that the reader can understand. It is hoped that you will find these examples to be both educational and entertaining.

You will also find a list of questions that serve as a preview of each chapter, a detailed summary at the end of each chapter, study questions, and a few key references. These aids are intended to help you assimilate and apply the content of each chapter.

R. R. R.
E. L. L.

Preface
to the Instructor

The first priority of the book you are about to read is that of having high student readability. It is written in a style designed for easy assimilation by students, and its informality and wealth of examples are meant to be helpful in this regard. Although it is consistent with the latest concepts and research in the field, the authors have chosen to hold listings of references and quotations to a minimum and to make clear where they stand on important issues. This approach is intended to help the student in synthesizing the material in the book and applying it to teaching. It is also meant to avoid the excessive length of most educational psychology textbooks.

The book is eclectic, presenting a synthesis of psychological theories, concepts, and research applied to classroom learning and instruction. At the same time, the authors favor a cognitive-humanistic approach to many of education's problems, and this approach is often highlighted. The goal is to present the student with a variety of principles and approaches and to indicate how each of these has implications for the classroom. The book is *not* a methods book, however, but an applied psychology textbook for teachers and other educational practitioners.

The organization of the book is described in the Preface for students. The five basic areas of educational psychology are included, but only insofar as they are seen to be relevant to classroom learning and instruction. These areas are (1) development, (2) learning, (3) instruction, (4) evaluation, and (5) personal and social adjustment.

In its simplest form, the philosophy of this textbook could be stated as the "traditional" idea that teachers must understand cognitive development and the nature of the mind and learn how to foster intellectual skills, combined with the "progressive" idea that this must be done in a truly

ix

humanistic fashion. This means with concern for self-concept, attitudes, values, and all the facets of developing the whole person and not just the intellect.

The authors, Robert Reilly and Ernest Lewis, have taught a total of forty-one years between them, including public school teaching and college and graduate teaching, both in education and in psychology. Reilly, a professor of education and psychology at the University of Arkansas, received his Ph.D. from the University of Illinois in 1963 with an emphasis in classroom learning and instruction. His teaching and research have included all five basic areas of educational psychology described, but especially the areas of development and learning. Originally a public school music teacher, he has taught at the university level for nineteen years with the introductory educational psychology course always a part of his varied assignments.

Lewis is chairman and professor of guidance and educational psychology at Southern Illinois University at Carbondale. Originally a junior high school mathematics teacher, he has served as a school administrator and as a member of a federally funded mathematics curriculum development program. He received his Ph.D. in educational psychology from Southern Illinois University in 1971 with specialization in statistics and measurement. He has taught educational statistics, measurement, evaluation, and educational psychology at the university level for thirteen years. The major focus of his research has been in educational measurement and evaluation.

Several pedagogical techniques that the book employs are incisive questions as a preview to each chapter, numerous anecdotal examples to illustrate the concepts presented, thorough and concise chapter summaries, study questions at the end of each chapter, and a few key references for each chapter. A student study guide is available as well as an instructor's manual. The chapters are written at a level that college undergraduates can read and understand the contents with a minimum of aid from the instructor, leaving you free to augment the text with other research findings, theories, concepts, and learning experiences.

Sincere appreciation is extended to numerous individuals whose encouragement and support were essential to the development of this book. To name just a few: Stew Jones and George Kaluger, successful authors themselves, whose early encouragement was invaluable. Also we would like to thank Norman Gronlund and Laurel Tanner for their wise counsel and suggestions throughout the project. Lloyd Chilton, who is a most competent and humanistic editor, was extremely supportive throughout the project. Susan Tracz and Roy Sumner provided valuable contributions throughout the manuscript revision. Jeannie Wyant, Joyce Lewis, Mary Dueker, and Karen Woodmansee provided efficient and flawless typing. Finally, we would like to thank the many students in Fayetteville, Little Rock, and Carbondale for their thoughtful and enthusiastic reactions to the developing manuscript. Most of all, thanks to our wives and families for their patience and support throughout the long and sometimes painful preparation of this book.

R. R. R.
E. L. L.

Contents

I
Development and Learning: The Basis of Educational Psychology

xiii

II

Personal and Social Development: The Whole Person

III
Student Variables:
Looking at the Individual

IV

Classroom Instruction: Doing a Better Job

Educational
Psychology

Educational Psychology in Today's World

PREVIEW

What is educational psychology?

What is the traditional versus progressive argument?

What is the basic goal of the schools?

What is the cognitive-humanistic approach to educational psychology?

Why do schools receive so much criticism?

Why have schools taken on so many goals?

How have changes in the birth rate affected education?

How have inflation and a tight economy affected education?

What are some recent changes in how teachers are educated?

What is the "Back to Basics" movement?

How do conservation and the limits of growth affect education?

How has mainstreaming affected education?

How has affirmative action affected education?

What is the cognitive-humanistic approach?

Teaching is the largest profession there is in the United States today: It employs the greatest number of individuals and services the largest population group in our society. Some 3.3 million people are already employed in teaching and another 200,000 enter the field each year. Its clients number 60 million on a daily basis, which, despite the decline in numbers of students in recent years, represents 88% of all Americans in the 5- to 18-year-old age group.

If we ask, "What is teaching?" many would answer that the purpose of teaching is "to instruct" or "to give instruction." Such a simple definition or concept of teaching presents several difficulties, however. First, we all know that teachers are expected to do a lot more than give instruction. They must handle discipline problems, prepare tests, supervise playgrounds and study halls, serve as counselors, prepare report cards, and so on. A second difficulty of such a simple definition of teaching is that it does not refer to learning. Any student or teacher knows that instruction can be given but that little or no learning on the part of the person being taught may take place. A third difficulty is that, because teaching is so familiar to everyone in our society, most people have strong feelings as to how it can be done best. As a result, teachers and schools are open to considerable criticism. The list of problems can be extended. Let us look at some of them in more detail.

Traditional Versus Progressive: A False Dichotomy

Today's world is loaded with false dichotomies, the artificial either/or arguments that do *not* really reflect the complexity of reality. Education, too, is plagued with such false dichotomies, which can easily act as obstacles to progress (Combs, 1979). A good example of one such troublesome dichotomy is the idea of "traditional versus progressive." This outlook holds that anything labeled "traditional" in education is old, shopworn, disproven, irrelevant, and relatively useless, whereas anything labeled "progressive" is new, vital, proven, innovative, relevant, and definitely worthwhile. This is not the case, however, not only because something really new in education is extremely rare, but also because the job of education is to *identify* and *preserve* that which is of value and at the same time facilitate orderly change. In addition, many "new" or "progressive" ideas are not new at all. An approach to educational psychology that encompasses only the progressive or new will necessarily omit many important and valuable traditional ideas, whereas a traditional approach will tend to ignore innovations and new ideas. An outlook that encompasses both the traditional and the progressive is called for, and this is what this textbook is designed to accomplish.

The School's Basic Goal: Development of Cognitive Skills

In this book, teaching is seen as the facilitating and guiding of classroom learning and motivation. But what is the nature of this classroom learning and motivation? Although the schools are expected to foster learning and development in virtually all areas of human traits and endeavors, there is a *basic* goal underlying the creation of the schools, a specific, primary purpose that led to the development of this social institution, just as there is a basic primary purpose for hospitals, churches, courts, and prisons. This *raison d'être* for the school is the *development of the intellect*, the powers of thinking, reasoning, and utilizing knowledge. It is from this concern for the intellect that part of the approach of this textbook—the *cognitive*—comes.

The Importance of Humanizing Education

At the same time that the cognitive skills of thinking, reasoning, problem solving, and understanding are seen as basic, the widespread concerns about attitudes, values, morals, mental and physical health, and personal and social adjustment are also seen as vital problems in our society, prob-

Concern for cognitive goals might lead to overregimentation. (CEMREL, Inc.)

lems that require the attention of many, if not all, of our social institutions. Although many educators would disagree, Carl R. Rogers made the following statement several years ago about public schools in the United States:

It is probable that our schools are more damaging than helpful to personality development and are a negative influence on creative thinking. They are primarily institutions for incarcerating or taking care of the young to keep them out of the adult world. [Carl Rogers in Evans, 1975, p. 150]

It is hoped that this view does not hold. Schools that turn their backs on such problems would be indeed remiss, and this is the area of prime concern with which humanists such as Rogers deal. It is from humanistic psychology that the second half of the approach of this book comes, that is, a *cognitive-humanistic* approach to educational psychology.

Why Schools Are Criticized

At present, we find that schools have taken on so many goals from so many different facets of society that they appear to be trying to be all things to all people. This expansion of goals to include such a broad array from so many different areas appears to be one of the major causes for the criticism that is presently being leveled against schools. The school cannot take on the goals of the family, the church, the courts, government, business, medicine, law, and so on and do a decent job with more than a few of these goals, to say nothing of the basic goals of education. Add to this the fact that the various goals of the social institutions are in a state of flux and are seen differently by different segments of society, and it is no wonder schools are criticized.

Of course, there are other reasons that education is vulnerable to criticism, and these will become readily apparent when you join the ranks of teachers. These include the fact of the field's high visibility, the chronic shortage of funds, the basic conservative nature of the enterprise, the tendency for everyone to believe they are "experts" when it comes to schools and what they do, confusion as to who *should* control education, and the tendency to measure everything in materialistic terms—the list is almost endless.

The extent of the public's expectations for the schools can be seen in the responses reported in the thirteenth annual Gallup Poll of the public's attitudes toward the public schools (1981). When asked whether the schools devoted enough attention toward several educational objectives, 62% said that not enough attention was given to "Developing students' moral and ethical character," 59% said that not enough attention was given to

4

"Teaching students how to think," 56% said that not enough attention was given to "Preparing students to become informed citizens," and 43% said that not enough attention was given to "Preparing students for college." Clearly the American public sets high standards for its public schools.

Teachers cannot be oblivious to such criticisms, but they also must avoid becoming unduly pessimistic and cynical about their jobs. After all, teachers in America have much to be proud of. Few nations have *even attempted* to offer education to all as a birthright, to utilize education as the major vehicle for social mobility, to extend education even to the seriously handicapped, or to include all of the long list of goals that the people of the United States tend to expect of their schools.

Current Problems and Their Impact on Education

The Passing of the "Baby Boom"

One area of serious concern to educators can be summed up with some population statistics. During the postwar period from 1946 through the late 1950s, the United States experienced a "baby boom," an unprecedented increase in the number of infants born each year. As this large crop

Adult learners can help fill empty classroom seats. (Arkansas State Department of Education.)

of children grew up, schools expanded to accommodate them, more teachers were trained and employed, and a big part of education in the 1950s and 1960s related to the "tooling up" for this great increase in numbers. Today, the "baby boom" crop has completed college, has married, and has established careers and can be seen in the employment figures—more persons are employed in the United States today than ever before in the nation's history.

For a number of reasons, the birth rate has dropped since 1960, especially in the 1970s, and the United States is now experiencing its *lowest* birth rate in history. This situation is seen as relatively permanent, what with the changes in philosophy concerning parenthood, increased expenses in raising a family, and pressure for zero population growth. As a result, the projections for the 1980s are that there will be a steady *decrease* in the number of school-aged children. This decline in the number of students has already hit many elementary and secondary schools. After steady growth for years, such a decline, of course, produces a climate of belt tightening, anxiety, retrenchment, and insecurity and raises questions about entering an overcrowded field.

Given this situation, some argue that the reduction of students could result in better use of our teachers, reduced class sizes, and more remedial help. But because declining enrollment is generally accompanied by declining funds, these suggestions tend not to get carried out. Buried in these statistics is the fact that an increasing proportion of the population is *older* each year; for example, that baby boom population of the late 1940s is now moving into the 30-year-old and older range and soon will invade the middle-aged range. Coupled with the fact that people are living longer due to medical advances, nutrition, and other factors, we can see a whole new clientele for education—the older or adult learner. If the empty seats in the classrooms of the 1980s and 1990s are taken up by adult learners in their thirties, forties, and beyond, then a "crisis" due to a shortage of students may be averted.

Inflation and a Tight Economy

Another problem for the schools is economic. The United States has experienced a high rate of inflation and declining value of the dollar on a worldwide basis for most of the 1970s, and economists predict continuing problems in this area in the years immediately ahead. This means that schools face escalating costs at a time when budgets are being trimmed; salary increments cannot keep up with inflation, and teachers go on strike. Programs that were accepted in former years are questioned as "frills," and we hear of decisions based on "retrenchment" and "belt-tightening" philosophies.

Partly as a result of these economic factors, the *accountability movement* has spread throughout the country, with varying impact on the schools.

Although difficult to define exactly, the key element in accountability seems to be a desire to have clear evidence of the effects of a school program and to relate these effects to the cost of the program in dollars, time, and resources. While there is controversy over just who should be held accountable for what, and over just how to go about gathering data, it is accurate to say that accountability has hit the schools and that nobody is immune from its effects. In a given school, accountability may take the form of program planning budgeting system, performance-based evaluation, minimal competency testing, competency-based certification, or some other system.

Changes in the Educational Process of Teachers

While it is often said that some things never really change or that "the more things change, the more they stay the same," there really *have* been some significant changes in how teachers are educated in recent years. Let us take a brief look at some of these changes and analyze their effects.

One widespread change is a trend toward increasing amounts of *laboratory experiences* and *practical applications* in teacher education courses. Laboratory experiences in teacher education usually consist of such things as observing and working with children in classroom, extracurricular, and community settings; tutoring students; doing case studies; preparing instructional materials; microteaching; attending school board meetings—anything that gets the prospective teacher involved in components of his or her future job. In the past, the one laboratory experience common to all programs was student or practice teaching for six, eight, or more weeks. Now the tendency is to insist on a number of laboratory experiences, including working with real live children, long before student teaching. Accompanying this laboratory experience trend is the tendency for all education courses to spend more time on practical applications of the subject being taught. So long as this does not lead to a sort of "cult of practicality" in which only what is immediately practical is taught, one can hardly take issue with such a trend.

A natural outgrowth of this desire for more laboratory and practical type experiences is the development of *teacher centers*. A teacher center is a place away from a college or university in which a significant part of a teacher's in-service training is carried out. Such centers usually contain resource materials, such as books, curriculum materials, media supplies and equipment, and personnel who supply instruction in these important areas. Since such centers are often funded by sources other than a college of education, they represent an increase in involvement and control of teacher education by sources outside the university, that is, more involvement by practitioners in the profession. So long as colleges of education and teacher centers work cooperatively, this seems to be a healthy trend.

Another trend that affects teachers is that of increasing *specificity in*

7

certification. Rather than a general certificate that would allow a teacher to work in a wide variety of subjects across a broad range of ages, the tendency now is to specify more precisely just what a teacher can teach, and at what grade level. Thus, we see more teachers prepared specifically for primary grades, middle school, and junior high or specifically for instrumental music, physical sciences, social sciences, math, and so on. In addition to specifying more clearly the subjects and grade level and requirements for such certification, there is also a tendency to require periodic upgrading to maintain one's certification. Such a tightening of certification standards should have beneficial effects on the profession, but it will also interact with other factors that may increase competition for getting and keeping jobs.

The "Back to Basics" Movement

In the ninth annual Gallup Poll on education (1977), a question was asked concerning the so-called Back to Basics movement. While 60% of the respondents indicated initially that they did not know about this movement, almost all of that 60% agreed with "Back to Basics" once it was explained to them. Of the 40% who were already familiar with it, approximately 83% agreed wholeheartedly with the "Back to Basics" idea. Thus, we see an overwhelming grass-roots support for this recent trend, even though the majority did not even realize that there was such a movement.

By "Back to Basics," the public generally means reading, writing, and mathematics—the subjects generally included in the "Three R's." However, some respondents to the ninth annual Gallup Poll also mentioned other subjects such as history, citizenship, science, and spelling. Back to Basics supporters are usually troubled by declining achievement test scores of high school students and by reports of high school graduates with insufficient skills in reading, writing, science, and math.

Another part of the Back to Basics idea concerns the general climate and atmosphere of the schools. Respondents to the Gallup Polls mentioned manners, morals, discipline, order, a return to basic values, and a dropping of modern fads and frills as being important. Back to Basics is presently having a great influence on the schools, as can be seen in the move to minimal competency testing. It does not appear to be a time for radical innovation in the public schools.

Conservation and the Limits of Growth

Another factor impinging on the work of the teacher is the new awareness of the limited nature of physical resources and the need to control pollution, care for the environment, and limit industrial growth. After decades of encouragement to use more energy, spend more money, expand the standard of living, and measure the quality of life in terms of economic growth, we now see a new outlook in which we are told to stop wasting energy, cut back on our life-styles, accept a stable or declining standard of living, and appreciate the merits of a stable economy in tune with the environment. Growth for its own sake is no longer seen as good and is limited by long-term economic problems. Such a climate not only is a challenge to teachers in terms of helping students understand these underlying forces in a changing world, but affects the schools in terms of conservation of the schools' own resources and limits in the schools' growth. It sometimes seems that the "anything is possible" attitude of the early 1960s has been replaced by a "little is possible" attitude in the early 1980s.

This "little is possible" attitude—when joined with the facts about population statistics, inflation and the struggling economy, the accountability movement, changes in how teachers are educated, and the Back to Basics movement—can easily make teachers feel that their jobs are pretty hopeless, that there is no use in hoping for progress and innovation. Nothing could be farther from the truth. The climate today is excellent for changes and innovation in education, the only catch being that these changes and innovations must *not* be expensive, both in terms of money and other resources. In other words, it is a time not for million-dollar solutions but rather a time for two-dollar solutions.

Mainstreaming

As if the problems and trends noted already were not enough, Public Law 94-142, passed by the U.S. Congress in 1975, has spurred a deluge of changes and actions relating to education for the handicapped. Although not entirely fitting, the term often used to summarize all these activities is *mainstreaming*. The essence of PL 94-142 is that it serves as an educational Bill of Rights for the handicapped, making it clear that all handicapped persons are entitled to full access to public education in the least restrictive setting without undue hardship or inconvenience for their families. This means that the handicapped must have physical access to buildings and resources, that they must be educated in the least restrictive environment with their peers in the regular classroom whenever appropriate, that special classes and services must be provided when necessary, and that all teachers must have information and skills relating to the handicapped. The implications are staggering and will be explored in greater detail in Chapter 12.

What mainstreaming is *not* intended to be is a dumping of all handicapped into regular classes, saving money and creating chaos for teachers. Although the implementation of PL 94-142 and the various state laws relating to it has already demonstrated some confusion over what the laws require, the end result should be not only help for the handicapped, but

9

also an improvement in the ability of the schools to identify and respond to the needs of *all* students.

Affirmative Action

The drive to prohibit unequal opportunities and treatment of minority group members and women in the United States is analogous to the mainstreaming movement in many respects. In this case, the "Bill of Rights" is for all citizens in that affirmative action is based on the principle that nobody can be discriminated against in housing, jobs, education, or other areas because of race, creed, sex, nationality, religion, and so on. In the area of education, schools must demonstrate evidence that definite action is taking place to equalize educational opportunities.

How does this affect a public school? Teachers cannot be hired on the basis of sex, and if its staff were predominantly male, the school would be expected to recruit more females. Male faculty cannot be paid more than female faculty of the same ability, training, and experience. Positions must be advertised widely so that they are open to all potential applicants. The curriculum cannot be slanted unfairly against any minority group, and tests cannot be used unfairly against minority groups. If a school has predominantly or totally white enrollment, steps might be taken to achieve a better balance of students from different racial groups.

As any reader knows, the various steps taken in the name of affirmative action have sometimes proven controversial, with disputes over busing, quotas, scholarships, admissions, test scores, women's sports, and many other issues arousing intense emotional reactions. Occasionally, the resulting turmoil has made it very difficult for classroom teachers to carry out their tasks, and teachers in these cases have probably asked themselves why they ever chose such a way to earn a living. Nevertheless, affirmative action represents the ideal of the "common school" that is basic in American public education, and teachers must meet the challenge of facilitating these ideals at the same time that they strive to raise the quality of education for all students.

Why Study Educational Psychology?

This brief review of current issues and trends should make it apparent that it is not a boring time to be entering the field of teaching. The study of educational psychology is intended to help you to understand the nature of the learner and the learning process, the many variables that interact as learning and development take place in the classroom, the role that the teacher plays in the classroom, the social interaction within the classroom, and many other psychological variables that affect school behavior. As the book proceeds from Part One, Development and Learning: The Basis of Educational Psychology, to Part Two, Personal and Social Development, to Part Three, Important Student Variables, to Part Four, Improving Classroom Instruction, it is hoped that you will be able to integrate what has been presented into the development of your own unique teaching style, remembering that only the "real you" can succeed in the classroom. The study of educational psychology is intended to help develop that "real you" into an effective classroom teacher and at the same time help you to enjoy to the fullest your chosen profession of teaching.

Teaching is much more than giving instruction. The field of educational psychology, which can be thought of simply as the application of psychology to teaching, has much to offer in helping teachers deal with the myriad expectations placed on them each day. Because the teaching profession encompasses so many roles, the field of educational psychology is also very broad. In addition, even though educational psychology is considered a science, much of what is written and proposed in this field is still at the theory stage, and there are often several different theories for each subject being considered. As a result, any textbook on educational psychology will of necessity present ideas that sometimes seem contradictory.

We have attempted to minimize the contradictions to the extent possible by adopting a cognitive-humanistic approach to educational psychology. The cognitive aspect of our philosophy is described best by David Ausubel et al.:

The subject matter of educational psychology, therefore, can be inferred directly from the problems facing the classroom teacher. The latter must generate interest in subject matter, inspire commitment to learning, motivate pupils, and help induce realistic aspirations for educational achievement. Teachers must decide what is important for pupils to learn, ascertain what learnings they are ready for, pace instruction properly, and decide on the appropriate size and difficulty level of learning tasks. They are expected to organize subject matter expeditiously, present materials clearly, simplify learning tasks at initial stages of mastery, and integrate current and past learnings. . . . Finally, since teachers are concerned with teaching groups of students in a social environment, they must grapple with problems of group instruction, individualization, communication, and discipline. [Ausubel et al., 1978, pp. 10–11]

While Ausubel et al. contend that educational psychology must focus on classroom learning and resist the "something for everyone" syndrome, we have shown that the array of factors that influence classroom learning is vast and complex. Somewhere between the "smorgasbord" approach of something for everyone and the "elitist" approach of a purist, there must be a happy medium. We have attempted to strike that balance by combining the cognitive approach with humanism. This philosophy simply means that skill development must be done with concern for self-concept,

11

Unusual classroom environments may contribute to enhanced learning. (CEMREL, Inc.)

attitudes, and values (Rogers, 1974). We believe that teachers must understand cognitive development to foster intellectual skills. They must also consider emotional development to develop the whole person.

In working toward this cognitive-humanistic approach to educational psychology, we have divided this book into four parts. Part One is devoted to what we see as essential background for classroom instruction, namely, the understanding of basic processes of development and learning. Terminology and principles that are crucial throughout the book are introduced; we proceed from more covert and theoretical variables to the more overt and practical applications later in the book.

In Part Two, the focus is on the child's personal and social development, a highly important secondary goal of schools today. A humanistic approach is outlined, and the affective domain is explored in detail, with particular attention to values, moral development, emotions, and alienation. This part ends with a discussion of motivational theory and its implications for classroom instruction.

Part Three is devoted to important student variables, exploring some of the crucial areas of individual differences that influence classroom behavior. Intelligence, creativity, social class, race, sex, and exceptionality are all presented in terms of the essential knowledge and understanding that a teacher needs in these areas.

Part Four deals with more practical and applied aspects of improving classroom instruction. Classroom climate is analyzed in searching for effective learning environments and the conceptual background and specific procedures for planning and evaluating instruction follow. Particular attention is given to constructing and using classroom as well as standardized tests. Discipline is seen as a highly important topic, and specific suggestions are presented; the discussion closes with a description of a first-year teacher's experiences and recommendations on how to survive in today's classroom.

Our attempt to combine cognitive and humanistic psychology will help you to integrate the information provided in each part of the book. However, be prepared for the fact that we still must present ideas that at times seem contradictory and that a vast amount of information is presented. Both of these are necessary, if not desirable, facets of any textbook on educational psychology. It is hoped that the cognitive-humanistic approach we have adopted—that is, the tempering of concentration on thinking, understanding, and reasoning with the development of healthy self-concepts, feelings, and values—will provide a framework for reconciling the information presented. By combining the two, we hope to avoid the cold, analytic outcome of concentrating on the brain above all else, as well as the soft, ill-defined outcome of an overly zealous humanism.

To aid you in your study of the material in the book, we have included major questions to be covered, study questions, and a thorough and concise summary at the end of each chapter. We have minimized references and quotations and have provided a number of examples to illustrate the concepts presented. We have attempted to minimize the use of jargon and to explain various principles and theories with clarity. You must do the rest!

Summary

Although the format of the present text is broad and eclectic, it emphasizes the cognitive and the humanistic approaches to educational psychology. In this the cognitive processes of thinking and reasoning are seen as the primary goal of the school, but at the same time, this and all the other goals of the school must be pursued in a humanistic manner. The individual's self-esteem and growth toward self-actualization are important considerations, and a blending of the cognitive and affective domains is essential.

The educational enterprise is described as the largest profession, with over 3 million teachers serving 60 million students every day. This vast enterprise receives considerable criticism, but an underlying reason for this is that far too many goals are assigned to the schools, goals for which other social institutions should be responsible. Under pressure to be all things to all people, schools understandably fail at some of these goals.

The reader is studying educational psychology in a national climate of difficulty and turmoil. The decline in the birth rate following the postwar baby boom has led to a declining enrollment. Inflation and a tight economy, worldwide energy problems, adjustment to an economy of scarcity, and chronic unemployment are all part of today's reality. Phrases such as *accountability, retrenchment,* and *back to basics* reflect a concern with getting the most out of the educational dollar. The rights of all groups in society, reflected in the affirmative action and mainstreaming movements, present a special challenge to the classroom teacher.

In this climate of challenge accompanied by limited resources, the teacher has a great need to know as much as possible about the applications of psychology to education in order to carry out the goal of cognitive development and all the other legitimate goals of the school in a humanistic fashion.

Study Questions

1. In this chapter it is stated that far too many goals are pursued by the schools. What other social institutions can you name that achieve important goals that affect the young? Can you list the primary goals of these institutions?

2. It is the authors' view that the development of cognitive skills is the primary goal of the schools. Do you agree with this, or do you see some other goal as more important? What do you see as the most important secondary goals of the schools?

3. With the nation facing many serious problems and given the decreasing need for teachers, many observers believe that it is not a good time to enter the profession of teaching. Can you think of a number of reasons why today is an excellent and exciting time to become a teacher?

4. One of the answers to the problem of a declining enrollment is to recruit more adult learners, to make education continue throughout life. Are there some subjects that could be learned more readily and appreciated by older learners? Are there any advantages in waiting until you are older before studying some topics? Do older learners require a different type of teacher or a different approach in the classroom?

5. One of the effects of the mainstreaming movement has been the placing of handicapped students in the regular classroom who might have been excluded formerly. What sort of problems does a teacher face in teaching a large class that includes several handicapped children, and what must be known to do a good job?

References

Ausubel, D. P., Novak, J. D., and Hanesian, H. *Educational Psychology: A Cognitive View,* 2nd ed. New York: Holt, Rinehart and Winston, 1978.

Combs, A. *Myths in Education: Beliefs That Hinder Progress and Their Alternatives.* Boston: Allyn & Bacon, 1979.

Gallup, G. H. "The Ninth Annual Gallup Poll of the Public's Attitudes Toward the Public Schools," *Phi Delta Kappan,* 59(1), September 1977, pp. 33–48.

———— ''The Thirteenth Annual Gallup Poll of the Public's Attitudes Toward the
    Public Schools,'' *Phi Delta Kappan,* 63(1), September 1981, pp. 33–47.
Rogers, C. R. ''Can Learning Encompass Both Ideas and Feelings,'' *Education,*
    95(2), 1974, pp. 103–114.
———— ''The Emerging Person: A New Revolution,'' in R. I. Evans, *Carl Rogers:
    The Man and His Ideas.* New York: E. P. Dutton, 1975, pp. 147–175.

I
Development and Learning: The Basis of Educational Psychology

In this first part, the reader is introduced to the basic principles of development and learning that form the basis of educational psychology. After the broad principles of development are presented, the developmental task approach of Robert Havighurst and the psychosocial theory of Erik Erikson are reviewed. An important area of development—intellectual development—is explored in detail, focusing on the work of the eminent Swiss psychologist, Jean Piaget. Learning principles, both from a conditioning and from a cognitive point of view, are discussed, and classroom implications are explored.

The principles of development and learning that are presented in this section are crucial for understanding the rest of the book. The reader is urged to study Chapters 2 through 6 thoroughly before going on to succeeding chapters. The more covert factors that affect classroom behavior, such as the principles of development and learning, are presented first; the more overt factors, such as discipline and tests and measurement, follow. It is important to understand these covert factors before proceeding to the later chapters.

Principles of Human Development

2

Sam, age 11 months, walks, albeit somewhat precariously, without any help. John, age 13 months, is unable to walk and stands only with someone holding his hand. Judy, age 6 years, can read and recite poetry, whereas Jane, also age 6 years, has developed no such skills. Leroy, age 12, is intensely interested in athletics and furiously impatient as he awaits some signs of growth, voice change, and the beginnings of manhood; his sister at age 11, on the other hand, is already a young woman in appearance and is taller and heavier than Leroy.

Unusual? Not at all. Such differences are observed every day throughout North America and, in fact, throughout the world. Rather than illustrating the work of a capricious deity, they are explained and understood in the field of developmental psychology, which studies growth and change over time to find principles that explain this growth and facts about behavior at each stage of development. Some of the major issues and principles of development and their relation to classroom teaching are reviewed in this chapter.

*Developmental principles explain growth
and behavior differences among
individuals. (Joyce Lewis.)*

One of the oldest and most bitterly contested controversies about human development focuses on the source of developmental changes: Is development the result of innate, inborn, and inherited factors (the nature view), or is it the result of experience, practice, and environmental influences (the nurture view)?

The Earliest Views

Until the twentieth century, the predominance of opinion lined up heavily on the nature side of this argument. A view that was dominant for centuries was that of the *preformationists,* so labeled because they believed that all traits and characteristics of a person were preformed, that everything one is is inborn. Such an outlook actually denies the whole idea of development, since, if everything is already there, preformed, then one only grows bigger and older, rather than truly changing. This view is seen in literature from early centuries until the 1800s as children are not only referred to and understood purely on adult terms but even pictured as miniature adults. In a sense, the preformationists denied childhood, and it was not until the late 1800s, when child labor laws were passed, that distinctions were made between children and adults.

Not quite so extreme as the preformationists was another group labeled *predeterminists,* who did acknowledge that development takes place and even admitted some environmental influence, but a closer look at their theories revealed that the whole course of development was predetermined by genetic factors. Thus, John Calvin saw the child's behavior as predetermined by his or her innate sinful nature. Other predeterminists agreed that human evolution was recapitulated in each child's growth through predetermined stages and that the course of development was predetermined by maturational factors.

The Kallikaks and Their Descendants

A famous attempt at demonstrating the preponderance of heredity over environment was the study of the descendants of a Revolutionary War veteran, Arnold Kallikak (Goddard, 1912). Kallikak had children by two different women, one his wife of "blueblood" New England descent and the other a woman of questionable lineage and intelligence. A study of the descendants of both liaisons over several generations found that on the blueblood side the incidence of crime, mental retardation, physical and psychological illnesses, poverty, and deviance in general was remarkably less than on the questionable side. This was hailed at first as dramatic

21

proof that heredity (nature) had far more influence on development than
environment (nurture). It was not until several years later that someone
pointed out that these claims did not really resolve anything since the
environments of the two groups of descendants were drastically different.

The Nurture View

On the nurture side, one of the most famous proponents was John Locke,
who claimed that an infant was born a *tabula rasa* (blank slate) upon
which the environment would have its effects and determine the traits
and characteristics of that individual. Jean Jacques Rousseau, who cham-
pioned the idea of innate goodness, carried his argument to the level of
politics and government, pleading that the criminal or deviate was a result
of the society that spawned him and that only by having a good society
could we hope to have good individuals. His famous *Émile* (1762) is an
account of how he taught an orphaned child, given up by society as hopelessly primitive and stupid, and changed him into a civilized human being.

Also well known on the nurture side is Carl Rogers (1980) whose
conception of human nature as extremely plastic and malleable is now
famous as the basis of his nondirective person-centered therapy. In fact,
it would appear difficult for any proponent of a verbal approach to psychotherapy to operate unless it were felt that the environment was extremely important. Belief in an approach such as Rogers's requires both
the acceptance of the idea of the effects of experience and an optimistic
belief in the human being's desire to change and improve.

The Interaction Compromise

You might conclude at this point that the nature-nurture controversy is a
thing of the past, since everyone now accepts the idea that both heredity
and environment interact to determine human traits and characteristics.
The solution is not quite so simple, however, even though it is correct to
say that the heredity-environment issue has been settled by an "interaction
compromise" in which nature and nurture interacting are seen as the
cause of development. The problem is one of questions such as, How much
heredity, and how much environment? Specifically what heredity and
what environmental factors interact for any one area or trait? What is the
nature of this interaction, and can it be regulated? Is intelligence 60%
heredity and 40% environment? Is 90% of personality the result of environment? Are *all* traits and characteristics determined by interaction?

Illustrations of some of these problems are discussed in later chapters
of this book. For example, Jean Piaget (1970) saw the course of cognitive
development as an interaction of the individual with the environment, but
gave important emphasis to maturational or internal factors, whereas Jer-

The information provided in the following table represents the correlation that exists between the intelligence test scores of individuals with varying genetic and environmental backgrounds. Each of the decimal fractions in the table is called a *correlation coefficient*. A correlation coefficient represents the magnitude and direction of relationships that exist between two variables. In the table the variables correlated were the intelligence test scores of individuals reared under different circumstances.

Intelligence Test Correlations for Persons with Varying Degrees of Genetic Similarity and Environmental Similarity*

	Median Correlation
Identical twins reared together	.87
Identical twins reared apart	.75
Fraternal twins reared together	.53
Siblings reared together	.49
Parents and their children	.50
Foster parents and their children	.20

*Adapted from L. Erlenmeyer-Kimling and L. F. Jarvik, "Genetics and Intelligence: A Review." *Science,* 142(3598), December 1963, pp. 1477–1479. Copyright 1963 by the American Association for the Advancement of Science.

Two things are said to be correlated if they vary together. That is, if people who are tallest also tend to be the heaviest, we say that height and weight are correlated positively. If people who have the highest intelligence test scores take the shortest amount of time to complete a test, we say that intelligence test scores and time to complete a test are correlated negatively. The correlation has a plus sign if the correlation is positive and a value of 1.0 if the correlation is perfect. The correlation has a minus sign if the correlation is negative and a value of -1.0 if the correlation is perfect. All other correlations lie somewhere between $+1.0$ and -1.0. The closer the coefficient is to $+1$ or -1, the stronger the correlation; the closer the coefficient is to 0, the weaker the correlation.

Notice in the table how genetic similarity leads to similarity in IQ. Identical twins show more positive correlation between their IQs than do fraternal twins, who in turn show more correlation than do siblings. But note also how the table illustrates the importance of environment. Identical twins reared together have a very high similarity of IQ, but this is because *both* their heredity and environment are similar. The correlation is less when they are raised apart.

Thus, the table demonstrates two facts: heredity influences IQ scores and environment does also, thus supporting the interaction explanation of heredity and environment.

ome Bruner (1966) has placed a much heavier emphasis on external, experiential factors. Arthur Jensen (1969, 1981) studied intelligence in children and concluded that approximately 20% of what we call intelligence can be influenced by environment and that the other 80% is determined by heredity.

WHAT CAUSED TOMMY'S PROBLEMS?

Tommy's mother died when he was 2 years old, and it would have to be said that he had a lonely childhood. The fact that he wet the bed did not help either. By the time he started school, he was so shy that he would hide behind a tree if he saw another student coming down the street. He had not done well at all in kindergarten, and an IQ test in second grade yielded a score of 90.

Tommy's poor performance in school led to his not trying, and his lack of effort irritated his teachers. Their attempts to force some effort from him led to his being more defensive, and he was soon labeled a behavior problem. His social withdrawal prompted other children to tease and ridicule him, so that he gradually became a chronic "loner." By the time he reached eighth grade he was fairly large and strong and had become a bully, getting what little joys in life he could out of picking on smaller children.

Tommy's performance in school had deteriorated to almost certain failure in every class by tenth grade. He was always in trouble and felt that the teachers picked on him. It was not surprising that he dropped out of school early in the year. After a series of low-paying jobs, he quit working entirely and collected unemployment compensation for a while. Just before Christmas, he was caught stealing narcotics from a drugstore. Due partly to his age and partly to it being his first offense, he was given a suspended sentence and told that he must see a counselor. The counselor had no illusions about the difficulty of a case such as Tommy's because she could see the cumulative nature of Tommy's development from early childhood. He did not just suddenly fall into his present state but instead had gotten there gradually through failures to resolve problems and achieve important developmental tasks from early childhood on. Tommy's case is not hopeless, but he does need considerable help in the unraveling of his developmental problems.

So even with the interaction compromise, questions about the relative influence of nature versus nurture on development still abound. In addition, there are questions as to how hereditary factors and environmental factors interact. Since hereditary factors set limits for an individual that cannot be exceeded while the environment can limit an individual's ability to achieve his or her inherited potential, both must be taken into account. The school should provide an environment that allows inherited potential to be achieved (Salkind, 1981).

Development Is Continuous

An important principle of human development is that it is continuous. Most developmental changes are not dramatic, drastic changes, but rather slight and gradual changes from day to day that go unnoticed. The child who knew a small number of words last year knows twice as many now;

24

Intelligence results from an interaction of genetic and environmental factors. (CEMREL, Inc.)

the little girl is "suddenly" a young lady (but when did it happen?); the boy's aunt and uncle say, "My, how much you've grown," but the parents had hardly noticed. The bulk of developmental change involves smooth, continuous development within stages rather than abrupt, qualitative changes.

A related concept is that development is *cumulative:* those slight changes from day to day add up to important differences. Moreover, each phase of development builds on what has happened previously, and problems that are not solved contribute to later problems.

Early Measures as Predictors

As illustrations of the continuity in development, let us look at some examples from psychological research. In the physical realm, Nancy Bayley (1946) is famous for her studies of infants and measures of infant characteristics as predictors of later growth and development. Even though children grow at different rates, and spurts and plateaus are obvious, these differences are not random. It might surprise the reader to know that the height, weight, body build, and strength of an adult are predictable to some extent from measures taken during the first years of life. Bayley worked out simple formulas for predicting just about everything that was measurable in infancy, and from these formulas, she was able to prepare tables that estimated the adult heights of children when they were still very young (see Table 2.1). By using Bayley's tables, physicians or parents could tell whether a child was progressing normally by comparing the child with these figures and could predict the child's future growth.

This tendency for continuity in development is not restricted to the physical; it extends also to areas such as personality and intelligence. Psychologists have found that characteristics of temperament and personality type can be identified early in life and that these basic traits are remarkably stable throughout life. In other words, if you are rather compulsive, are a perfectionist at heart, and drive yourself to do more and more, these traits were probably identifiable early in life and had been developing and consolidating throughout childhood. A friend of yours might be very relaxed, mild-mannered, and easygoing and would likewise have exhibited these traits very early. In each case, a trained psychologist could see these traits gradually developing in the individual's growth to maturity.

Table 2.1. *Estimates of Mature Height of Boys with Skeletal Ages Within One Year of Their Chronological Ages, Skeletal Ages 7 to 13 Years**

Skeletal Age	7-0	7-3	7-6	7-9	8-0	8-3	8-6	8-9	9-0	9-3	9-6	9.9	10-0	10-3	10-6	10.9	11.0	11-3	11-6	11-9	12-0	12-3	12-6	12-9
% of mature height	69.3	70.1	70.6	71.3	71.8	72.5	73.4	74.3	75.0	75.8	76.5	77.4	78.1	78.9	79.7	80.3	81.0	81.4	82.7	83.0	83.8	84.4	85.5	86.4
Present Height (inches)																								
42																								
43	62.0	61.3																						
44	63.5	62.8	62.3	61.7	61.3																			
45	64.9	64.2	63.7	63.1	62.7																			
46	66.4	65.6	65.2	64.5	64.1	63.4	62.7	61.9	61.3															
47	67.8	67.0	66.6	65.9	65.4	64.8	64.0	63.3	62.7	62.0	61.4	60.7												
48	69.3	68.5	68.0	67.3	66.9	66.2	65.4	64.6	64.0	63.3	62.7	62.0												
49	70.7	69.9	69.4	68.7	68.2	67.6	66.8	65.9	65.3	64.6	64.0	63.3	62.7	62.1	61.5	61.0	60.5							
50	72.2	71.3	70.8	70.1	69.6	69.0	68.1	67.3	66.7	66.0	65.4	64.6	64.1	63.4	62.7	62.3	61.7							
51	73.6	72.8	72.2	71.5	71.0	70.3	69.5	68.6	68.0	67.3	66.7	65.9	65.4	64.6	64.0	63.5	63.0	62.7	61.7	61.4	60.9			
52	75.0	74.2	73.7	72.9	72.4	71.7	70.8	70.0	69.3	68.6	68.0	67.2	66.7	65.9	65.2	64.8	64.2	63.9	62.9	62.6	62.1	61.6		
53	76.5	75.6	75.1	74.3	73.8	73.1	72.2	71.3	70.7	69.9	69.3	68.5	67.9	67.2	66.5	66.0	65.4	65.1	64.1	63.9	63.2	62.8		
54				75.7	75.2	74.5	73.6	72.7	72.0	71.2	70.6	69.8	69.2	68.4	67.8	67.2	66.7	66.3	65.3	65.1	64.4	64.0	63.2	62.5
55				77.1	76.6	75.9	74.9	74.0	73.3	72.6	71.9	71.1	70.5	69.7	69.0	68.5	67.9	67.6	66.5	66.3	65.6	65.2	64.3	63.7
56				78.5	78.0	77.2	76.3	75.4	74.7	73.9	73.2	72.4	71.8	71.0	70.3	69.7	69.1	68.8	67.7	67.5	66.8	66.4	65.5	64.8
57								76.7	76.0	75.2	74.5	73.6	73.1	72.2	71.5	71.0	70.4	70.0	68.9	68.7	68.0	67.5	66.7	66.0
58								78.1	77.3	76.5	75.8	74.9	74.4	73.5	72.7	72.2	71.6	71.3	70.1	69.9	69.2	68.7	67.8	67.1
59												76.2	75.6	74.8	74.0	73.5	72.8	72.5	71.3	71.1	70.4	69.9	69.0	68.3
60												77.5	76.8	76.1	75.3	74.7	74.1	73.7	72.6	72.3	71.6	71.1	70.2	69.4
61															76.5	76.0	75.3	74.9	73.8	73.5	72.8	72.3	71.3	70.6
62																	76.5	76.2	75.0	74.7	74.0	73.5	72.5	71.8
63																			76.2	75.9	75.2	74.6	73.7	72.9
64																				77.1	76.4	75.8	74.9	74.1
65																				78.3	77.6	77.0	76.0	75.2
66																				79.5	78.8	78.2	77.2	76.4

*From N. Bayley, "Tables for Predicting Adult Height from Skeletal Age and Present Age," *Journal of Pediatrics*, 28(1), January 1946, p. 53. Reprinted with permission.

DIVERSITY IN DEVELOPMENT

Let us look at two young ladies—Carolyn and Sue—who grew up in the same neighborhood at the same time. At age 3 they were both cute toddlers, the only noticeable difference between them being that Carolyn was more active and more talkative. Outside of this, they both played a lot together and seemed very much alike.

By age 7, we see some noticeable differences. Carolyn spends more time at artwork and is usually quite good at it; she also participates more in class and seems to like school better. Sue does all right in her artwork and gets by in school, but she shows no flair for it; she remains quiet and shows little enthusiasm for school, except on the playground, where she comes to life. Sue is very strong for a 7-year-old and plays softball and tackle tag with the boys during recess.

By age 11, it is easy to tell Carolyn and Sue apart. Carolyn can be found studying and working on her creative writing and art projects late into the night, while Sue spends her spare time playing ball, ice skating, and practicing gymnastics. Carolyn now makes straight "A's" in school, whereas Sue makes "C's" in most of her subjects. Sue is such an outstanding softball player that the junior high physical education teacher has checked to see if she can play on the school team, all boys, next year.

Both Carolyn and Sue are normal, healthy children. Their development illustrates how diversity increases as developmental effects accumulate and how experience builds on existing differences to make them even greater over time.

A study that illustrates this was conducted by M. E. Smith in 1952. In this study, three judges were asked to rate five adults on thirty-five personality characteristics such as affectionate, brave, persevering, careless, and nervous. These ratings were then compared to ratings the adults had received on the same personality factors when they were children. The ratings of the characteristics from childhood and adulthood were remarkably similar, with only five of the personality characteristics showing no tendency to remain constant from childhood to adulthood.

A thoroughly studied area of development that illustrates the continuity and predictability of development is that of intelligence. If a child is bright at age 3, that child will most likely continue to develop at a faster pace and be bright in comparison with other children at ages 7, 11, 16, and 23 also. The slow child at age 5 will probably be behind at age 10, even though much development has taken place. In fact, differences between bright and dull children are greater as time passes, illustrating that the child of higher intelligence makes greater gains as time passes.

Increasing Divergence

An interesting claim, in relation to the discussion here, is that there is a *law of compensation* for component aspects of development. According to this view, one with outstanding abilities in some areas will be very poor in others as the result of nature's desire to compensate. Thus, a star athlete will probably be dull or unartistic, a brilliant child will be clumsy or sickly, and a talented artist will be weak or weird. Such a law is comforting when we face some area in which we are inept because it implies that we must be outstanding in some other area to compensate.

Unfortunately (at least if you have just found something in which you exhibit no ability and are looking for the law of compensation to rescue you), this so-called "law" did not stand up to scientific scrutiny. When Louis Terman and Melita Oden studied hundreds of gifted children, a study begun by Terman in 1921, they looked for evidence of the compensation hypothesis but found absolutely none (Terman and Oden, 1959). In fact, Terman and Oden found that these gifted children tended to score *above* rather than below average when other variables were examined, and when traced on through high school, college, and into adult life, they were found to be a healthy, happy, productive group, with no evidence of any compensation law at work.

While Terman and Oden's work was successful in challenging the inaccurate beliefs concerning a law of compensation, ironically it contributed to another belief that represents the reverse of the compensation hypothesis. According to the *law of correlation,* a claim was made that a gifted person in one area (such as intelligence) would most likely be bigger, stronger, handsomer, nicer, happier, and healthier. In other words, some looked at Terman and Oden's findings and were pleased to hear that the law of compensation was dead, but they immediately replaced it with an equally inaccurate law of correlation, saying that, if you are outstanding in one area, you are probably outstanding in other areas also.

What is the truth? Without getting bogged down in a discussion of statistics, the best way of describing the facts in relation to component aspects is simply to point out that, if you know where a person stands on one trait or characteristic, you don't really know *anything* about where that person stands on any other trait. Gifted children are just as variable when it comes to size, looks, interests, temperament, and health as are other children. Actually, the law of nature that seems to function here is neither compensation nor correlation but, instead, the law of increasing divergence of component aspects of development. This simply means that the variability and complexity of individuals *increases* with age and experience.

Norms Versus Normality

A discussion of similarities and differences in human beings would not be complete without addressing the problem of "what is normal"? There are a number of different ways of defining what is normal, none of which is really satisfactory, and one must be careful not to confuse these. A common meaning of normal comes from looking at averages. Anything that

THINGS ARE NOT ALWAYS AS THEY SEEM

Mr. Roberts knew that first impressions weren't always accurate, but the four new teachers they sent him during the flu epidemic sure took the cake. First, there was the tall blonde who wore too much makeup, swung her hips when she walked, and chewed gum. There was no doubt she was a home economics teacher and a real dingbat. He hoped that she could at least find her classroom and speak a coherent sentence.

The handsome, broad-shouldered fellow was obviously the substitute physical education teacher. The girls would swoon over him and the boys would obey him, but since he probably couldn't read, Mr. Roberts made a note to check in on his class first.

The third was a woman about one foot short for her weight, in other words, *fat*. She was obviously the frustrated spinster he had heard about, who ate compulsively to offset her loneliness, was jolly and good-natured in spite of it all, and taught English literature with a passion that made you believe she must have been there.

Finally, there was the skinny fellow with glasses. He was obviously an introvert, neurotic, and withdrawn, and Mr. Roberts wondered why they couldn't send him a math teacher the kids would like. This absent-minded professor would probably have chaos in his class within an hour, if he wasn't too far off in his ivory tower to even notice.

Mr. Roberts was wrong on every count! The ''dumb blonde'' turned out to be the math teacher, and one of the finest he had ever seen. She had a master's degree in math with a straight ''A'' average. The handsome, broad-shouldered fellow was the English teacher, although by trade he was a writer. He was a very sensitive person, having published three books of poetry, and only taught occasionally as a break from his work as a professional writer.

The skinny fellow with glasses was the physical education teacher and had been an outstanding athlete in both tumbling and track and field. His enthusiasm and sense of humor were contagious, and Mr. Roberts managed to hire him the next year as a full-time teacher and track coach. Finally, the stout lady was happily married and the mother of eight and an excellent home economics teacher. She was serious but had a gentle nature, and the work she managed to inspire in the dressmaking class that year was amazing.

Mr. Roberts had made the mistake of assuming that real people would fit popular stereotypes. He forgot that every human being is a unique individual with a unique developmental history and that most stereotypes are highly inaccurate. People might occasionally fit by accident (some blondes, like any other group, *will* turn out to be dumb, for example), but more often than not they won't.

can be measured—height, weight, attitudes, beliefs, behaviors, abilities— can lead to a *statistical* average. For example, a widely used measure of pubescence (i.e., just when someone has changed into an adult physiologically), reports that on the average boys reach pubescence at age 13.6 and girls at age 12.8. If we were to stop there, we might conclude that most boys and girls are abnormal because very few reach pubescence at exactly these ages. A closer inspection indicates the range of normality for this particular variable is extremely broad, so that a girl reaching pubescence at age 9 or at age 16 is still normal. Height is another example, with an average of 60 inches for 12-year-olds, but a wide variability around this average is normal.

Adolescents, of course, do not have such statistical considerations in mind when they worry about whether or not they are normal. One teacher handled such problems in an unusual way. If a student expressed concerns about being normal, Mr. Blake would whip out impressive charts and graphs, ask the student a number of questions about the student's age, height, weight, and whatever else was under scrutiny. Suddenly a smile of relief would spread over Mr. Blake's face, and he would show the student an elaborate chart. The chart was the familiar bell-shaped normal curve, with numerous entries under it, and he would inform the student, "I have good news. You come under the normal curve. You are normal." Of course, anyone comes under the normal curve since the tails of the curve never end, but in this case a slight bit of deception was used in a constructive fashion to allay the gnawing fears of an adolescent that somehow he wasn't "normal."

Another problem with the statistical definition of normality is that, just because many people think or do certain things, this really doesn't mean that these behaviors are healthy or good. If most of your group smokes cigarettes, then statistically this is "normal," but it is absurd to imply that somebody who does not smoke is somehow "abnormal."

What *is* a reasonable conception of normality, or must the term be thrown out altogether? Certainly the idea that whatever the teacher, or parent, or expert of some sort *says* is normal is hardly any better than the statistical definition, and behaviors that any society has condoned or forbidden hardly lead to a consistent theory of normality. It is tempting to discard the concept completely and adopt an "anything goes" attitude. As we will see in Chapter 7, there is a *humanistic* definition of normality, which says that any behavior that is not harmful to the individual or to others, and contributes to positive growth motivation, can be considered normal. This definition leaves room for the fact that in a psychological sense a person may be "sick" even though well adjusted and another may be perfectly healthy even though "different." It seems reasonable to argue that such a view of normality is most useful for teachers.

The Miracle of Biology

Have you ever noticed that, even though you have known hundreds or even thousands of people in your lifetime, no two are exactly alike? In fact, as you get to know people well, it is fascinating how their uniqueness becomes striking. Given the very limited number of components that make up the human face, isn't it surprising that no two faces are ever *exactly* alike? There is no such thing as "identity" (i.e., exact sameness) in nature, not even "identical twins" are born exactly alike, and each of us can rest comfortably in the assurance that we are truly unique.

At the same time, however, we are all the same in that we share so many experiences, abilities, limitations, perceptions, and outlooks as human beings. As one grows older, one can't help but be impressed by the myriad ways in which we all share the same humanity, the same world. This is what is meant by the phrase *the miracle of biology*. The fact that, with all the sameness, all the characteristics and laws that a species shares, each individual is still unique is truly amazing.

Teachers must keep this fact in mind when they work with children, colleagues, or parents of any age. They share the traits and characteristics of human beings, and more specifically of their culture and age level, but at the same time each one is a unique individual. The teacher must try to get the children to appreciate their belongingness and fellowship with others, but at the same time help them to appreciate their own special skills and uniqueness. They must be helped to overcome their fear of being seen as strange, different, or unacceptable. This is especially difficult at certain age levels, such as junior high age, where the child's chief concern seems to be one of erasing any differences, melting into a crowd, and being accepted by one's peers.

To accomplish this, the teacher must be able to do two things: (1) accept children in general, and all the behaviors and traits that are characteristic of their age level, and (2) recognize and encourage individuality and uniqueness, even at times when it is troublesome or irritating. Remember also that accepting a trait or behavior *does not* necessarily mean you like it or encourage it.

Some Key Concepts in Development

Before pursuing other principles of development, let us look at some important terms and what they mean. Three concepts that are crucial for understanding development are examined now.

Maturation: The "Internal Ripening" Idea

Why can Pat learn to walk with ease at 12 months of age when all the instruction in the world failed to teach her to walk two months ago? Why are 8-year-olds interested in different things than 5-year olds? Why does a 4-year-old think that the sun follows him wherever he goes? Why does a 12-year-old, long a good friend of dirt, suddenly start spending hours each day grooming before the bathroom mirror?

Each of these questions can be answered by relating them to the con-

31

cept of *maturation*. This view says that a certain amount of developmental change is controlled from within, unaffected by environment or experience. We might imagine a sort of "nature's clock" within us that regulates growth and development and is completely oblivious to what is happening outside. Thus, the 12-month-old can walk primarily because she is ready; the growth and development of the muscles, bones, nervous system, and coordination is such that she can learn at 12 months what she could not yet learn at 10 months.

The concept of maturation is often referred to as the "internal ripening" hypothesis. This says that certain internal changes must take place before an individual is ready for any particular behavior or experience. The internal ripening idea is illustrated best in the work of noted psychologist Arnold Gesell, who studied thousands of children over the years with his colleagues at the famous Gesell Institute in New Haven, Connecticut. Gesell (1928, 1954) described the characteristics and behaviors of children at each age level, becoming famous for his "ages and stages" approach. A considerable part of his explanation for the changes and differences he observed hinged on the internal ripening (maturation) idea. No specific training or experience is necessary to explain the questions we have raised. The explanation lies in the internal maturational process.

CAN YOU TEACH A 3-YEAR-OLD TO ROLLER SKATE?

Gary and Barry were both 3 years old, and their fathers were teaching them to roller skate. Gary seemed to take to it quite well, improving steadily as his father cheered him on, and by the third day he was skating down the sidewalk easily, smiling and relaxed and hardly ever falling.

Barry, on the other hand, could not seem to get the hang of it. He fell almost every step he took, and couldn't seem to balance or coordinate his movements; it did not help to see how well Gary was doing. Barry's father did everything he could to help and encourage him, but his efforts were futile. Barry did not improve, and by the third day he just stood and cried while his father put the skates on. He was either a nonathlete or just a sissy, his father concluded, as he gave up in disgust.

Barry did not touch the skates until three months later, when he put them on and learned to skate with ease. He soon surpassed Gary with his skating skills and went on to become a roller derby champion. The factors that impeded Barry three months earlier were maturational: he simply was not ready yet in terms of the "internal ripening" process, and it had nothing to do with his courage or the quality of his father's instruction. Gary was slightly ahead of Barry in terms of these maturational factors, so he was able to learn to skate with ease, but once Barry was ready maturationally, he not only learned to skate but quickly had more skill than Gary. Teachers should remember this example when working with children on any new task. Their lack of progress at first could be due to internal maturational factors, and it might be a poor indicator of their future potential.

Learning: Influence from the Environment

Certainly all of development and behavior *cannot* be explained by the "internal ripening" idea. An important part of development involves interaction with the environment, learning about the world and developing skills and habits through training and experience. Learning has been defined as "the process of acquiring relatively permanent change in understanding, attitude, knowledge, information, ability and skill through experience" (Wittrock, 1977, p. ix). Learning defined in this way is obvious in areas such as language development or psychomotor learning. It is no coincidence that American children speak English rather than French; this is the language that they have experienced, and all the internal ripening in the world will not cause them to speak French. Likewise, you do not become a champion figure skater or violinist without a tremendous amount of learning through experience.

So, if maturation represents the internal and learning represents the external, how do we link these two terms with development? Simply by stating that development is essentially the interaction of the two processes—maturation and learning—and virtually any developmental sequence involves both. This interaction of maturation and learning is discussed in relation to cognitive development in the next chapter.

Readiness: Sum Total of All Factors

Maturation and learning interact to determine the course of development. Readiness is a term for the sum total of a person's development, experience, motivation, ability, and interest in relation to a particular learning task. Is this child ready to learn square root? This depends on (1) the child's level of general cognitive maturity, (2) the child's past learning in math, (3) the child's motivation and interest, (4) the child's anxiety, and (5) the quality of instruction available. A major mistake often made in relation to the term readiness is to assume that it refers only to maturation. This is *not* true and frequently causes many problems in relation to doing anything about readiness. The term refers to the *sum total* of a child's maturation, development, and learning; that is, it is a composite of all factors relevant to the new learning task.

An important concept in relation to the idea of readiness is the concept of *critical periods*. This view states that there are certain times in a child's development when it is important to do or learn certain things, that the child is ripe for particular experiences during these critical periods, and that learning will be easier and more effective at this time. Let us look at a few examples of this.

Very early in life, the infant forms an attachment to a specific person, usually the mother, and this relationship is crucial for everything that happens later. If nobody is available with whom the child can make the attachment, or if the mother is removed before attachment is completed, the child will be affected emotionally. If this attachment is not formed during the critical period, it is much more difficult to form later. In extreme cases, infants have been known to die in foundling homes, in spite of reasonable care and nutrition, for no apparent reason other than the lack of a close personal attachment (Gardner, 1972).

Languages, particularly the spoken sounds, can be learned with relative ease early in life. A young child learning to speak a second language in a U.S. school, for example, will be able to reproduce the patterns and sounds of the second language without too much effort. An adult American will have considerable trouble doing this, and usually even though the adult might become very adept at the new language, he or she will not be able to make some of the sounds correctly. The critical period for developing certain speech patterns and movements is long since past for the adult, and in this sense the old cliché, "You can't teach an old dog new tricks," is appropriate.

Although somewhat controversial, since some psychologists believe that the critical periods hypothesis implies the idea of patterned instincts, the critical periods principle has been applied to education in terms of finding

A DUCKLING FINDS ITS MOTHER

At age 5, Dennis loved animals, as do so many children at his age, but he was also conscious of the need to be a boy and not a "sissy." He was thus appalled when the newborn duckling his uncle had given him started to follow him everywhere. No matter what he did to discourage it, the duckling was always right there behind him, as if Dennis were its mother, and the other kids started calling him "Donald Duck," quacking and waddling whenever they saw him. He even tried hitting the duckling and throwing pebbles at it to discourage it, but it stubbornly refused to stop following him. He finally took to keeping it in a pen and only letting it out when nobody was around, and he never did figure out why the duckling followed only him and not his sister, who spent more time with it than he did.

What Dennis did not realize was that the duckling had *imprinted* on him. Imprinting is an instinctual behavior that comes about within a brief period immediately after the birth of a duckling. It is an extreme example of the importance of critical periods in learning, and it is unlikely that any such example exists in humans. The duckling focuses on whoever is present—which is usually the mother duck—and that stimulus object is literally *imprinted* on the duckling's brain. He will now follow that object, we might call it a "mother figure." anywhere. Dennis just happened to be the object that was present, rather than the mother duck, when the imprinting took place in this case. Now, regardless what Dennis did, he was imprinted in the duckling's mind as the stimulus object to follow, and its instinct was to follow Dennis everywhere, completely oblivious to Dennis's annoyance.

the ideal time for learning each aspect of the curriculum and making sure it is taught during that period. Most psychologists feel that humans do not have instincts in the same way as animals do or that if they do they are extremely weak and vague. The idea that particular experiences might "take" best during a certain period in a child's development, that at certain times children are ripe for certain types of learning, seems to be a reasonable one, and one that is consistent with what we know about maturation, learning, and development. It appears that you would be well advised as a teacher to try to discover these critical periods for the various subjects and students that you teach.

General Trends in Development

Some trends in development, in a very broad sense, are clear and predictable. When one is aware of these trends, many of the observations we make of children and adults are quite understandable.

General to Specific Development

First, development proceeds from the *general* to *specific*, which means that children learn the more gross movements, skills, and ideas first and only later proceed to the more specific and detailed. This principle has been

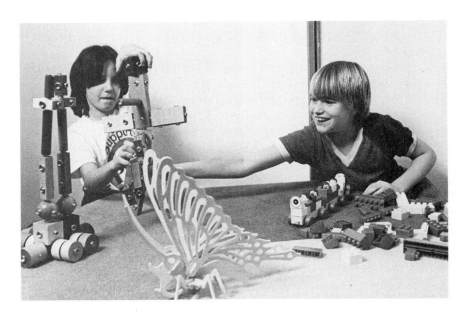

Development proceeds from general to specific. (CEMREL, Inc.)

noticed more in recent years, as evidenced in some of the toys and materials that you will find in today's nursery schools, kindergartens, or on playgrounds. Have you ever seen a 3-year-old trying to play with very detailed toys, figures, intricate games, or small blocks? The child will usually have trouble manipulating these objects and will soon lose interest. When the toddler is given large blocks, easily manipulated figures, and toys that make use of the general to specific principle, however, we notice an immediate change in behavior. Most young children love these large objects and activities, and gradually they work up to more intricate toys and specific tasks.

Head to Extremities Development

A second trend that is noticeable is the principle of *head to extremities*, which says that development takes place first at the head and the parts of the body nearest the head and gradually proceeds on down to the arms, legs, and toes. As the infant grows, development gradually spreads on down, until the adult figure emerges in which all parts of the body are developed fully.

GRANDMA KNOWS BEST

Marilyn sincerely wanted to be a good mother. She had saved her money while she was working, and she was happy to spend some of it to assure that her baby would have lots of educational toys with which to play. She had acquired quite a collection of toys and games while awaiting her baby's birth, and when it turned out to be a boy, she quickly bought a supply of trucks, soldiers, and other boyish things to augment her collection. Little Timmy would have plenty of toys.

She smiled smugly when her mother, who had come to see the new addition, put several old pots, pans, and cooking utensils in little Timmy's crib. Grandmothers were like that, and she could remove them after Grandma left since Timmy obviously would want to play with all of his expensive toys. She was startled when Timmy cried angrily at her removing the pots and pans and was amazed over the next week to find that Timmy preferred to play with the much larger pans and cooking utensils, handling them and banging them together, rather than the much more sophisticated (and also smaller and intricate) toys and games she had provided.

Grandma may not have known the textbook words for it, but she understood the principle that development proceeds from the *general* to the *specific,* from the gross to the more intricate muscular movement. Timmy would appreciate and no doubt play with all his sophisticated, delicate little toys some day, but first he had to master gross coordination and large muscle movement. The pots and pans and cooking utensils that Grandma had presented him were perfect for this.

Structure Before Function Development

The junior high football team is practicing. We watch with disbelief as the smaller boy, who looks much younger, pushes the larger boy back. He is undoubtedly stronger, faster, and better coordinated than the larger boy.

The larger boy might look considerably different if we check back a year later. The example illustrates the principle that *structure precedes function*, in this case the structure of the muscles and body growing ahead of the ability to coordinate and use this improved structure. The coach, if he understood this principle, might not be so upset about the situation, knowing that there is a lag between the tremendous growth of pubescence and the ability to coordinate the results of this growth.

Irregular but Orderly Development

We have already noted the fact that development is cumulative and continuous. Unfortunately, in trying to predict the path of development, it is often anything but orderly and regular. We see spurts and plateaus, changes in the rate of development, one area jumping ahead rapidly while another stands still, and it might appear that the path of development is virtually random. Such is not the case, however. The primary reason for what appears (but really isn't) as chaos in development is the fact that it involves the complex interaction of a large number of factors. The reason that a child's social development is temporarily at a standstill involves much more than the social area alone. The physical, emotional, intellectual, and

---

IS DEVELOPMENT PREDICTABLE?

Mabel had been teaching for only two years, but already she could see the amazing variations in development in her students. Sam was spurting ahead physically but at a standstill mentally, and yet his physical growth seemed to be a big boost to him socially. Hugo, meanwhile, was very small for his age, and although this seemed to be no problem last year, it appeared to be disrupting his school work and social adjustment this year. Frank had gone from a general picture of standing still in all areas two years ago to a tremendous improvement socially last year and was now blossoming intellectually. Amos, who appeared to have it made two years ago, has somehow slipped into a rut that he shows no signs of escaping at present.

In her first year of teaching, Mabel looked at such facts and concluded that the course of development was completely unpredictable and chaotic, but by now she was beginning to see that this was not so. The different aspects of development—physical, mental, emotional, social—did not proceed perfectly smoothly and at the same pace. Still, the results were explainable and, if you had known enough about the child, predictable.

social areas are intertwined, and problems in one area will affect other areas also. The adolescent who is so upset about his peer group relations that he cannot study and even develops somatic complaints is a case in point.

Don't be fooled by the apparent chaos in development, however. Development *is* orderly, even if irregular, and it is somewhat predictable if you know something of the factors involved.

Developmental Tasks and Education

With these basic terms and principles of development in mind, let us turn to the work of a famous educator, Robert Havighurst. Havighurst was one of the first scholars to try to break down development at each age level into important tasks to be accomplished and relate these to education. He defined a developmental task as a task "which arises at or about a certain period in the life of the individual, successful achievement of which leads to his happiness and to success with later tasks, while failure leads to unhappiness in the individual, disapproval by the society, and difficulty with later tasks" (Havighurst, 1972, p. 2). In other words, Havighurst believed that there were critical periods in the development of a person at which certain things must be accomplished. These tasks may be in the area of the physical such as walking, the cognitive such as learning to read, or the social such as in relationships with the opposite sex. In whatever area, the successful accomplishment of a developmental task provides the basis for achieving future developmental tasks and for a person to view himself or herself positively. The failure to achieve a given developmental task leads to a negative view of oneself and to difficulty with later developmental tasks.

Havighurst provided a list of the developmental tasks for each of several developmental stages. The importance of these tasks for the teacher relates to a concept that Havighurst called *teachable moments*, when certain maturations and experiences have been combined and a person is ready to learn certain things. Until conditions are right, no amount of teaching will be successful. As Havighurst said, "When the body is ripe, and society requires, and the self is ready to achieve a certain task, the teachable moment has come. Efforts at teaching, which would have been largely wasted if they had come earlier, give gratifying results when they come at the teachable moment, when the task should be learned" (Havighurst, 1972, p. 7).

To provide some idea of what Havighurst thought were the important developmental tasks of some of his various stages, we list them now. The listing includes tasks that you will be expected to teach at whatever level you plan to work and several tasks that you can expect to have to achieve as you continue in your personal development. The statements after each task are ours.

Early childhood requires that one learn to relate to others. (CEMREL, Inc.)

Early-Childhood Tasks

1. *Learning to walk* depends upon maturation.
2. *Learning to talk* depends upon maturation, but experience will play an important role.
3. *Learning sex differences and sexual modesty* is the beginning of sex-role identification, which we discuss at length in Chapter 11.
4. *Learning to relate oneself emotionally to parents, siblings, and other people* is accomplished largely by modeling the behaviors of others. Thus, parents see and hear their children reflecting their behaviors.
5. *Learning to distinguish right and wrong and developing a conscience* is the beginning of social development and responsibility. We discuss this at length in Chapter 7.

Middle-Childhood Tasks

1. *Building wholesome attitudes toward self* is extremely important in all aspects of learning. The teacher must do what is possible to enhance one's image of self.
2. *Learning to get along with peers* marks the continuation of social development. Relationships with others need to be enhanced.

3. *Developing fundamental skills, such as reading, writing, and calculating* form the major skills and are viewed as the basic goal of the school and of elementary education.
4. *Learning an appropriate masculine and feminine role* is accomplished to a large extent by modeling important individuals in the child's life. It is discussed at length in Chapter 11.
5. *Developing conscience, morality, and a scale of values* is discussed in Chapter 7.
6. *Achieving personal independence* involves allowing the child to make decisions, within reason, independently.

Adolescence Tasks

1. *Achieving new and more mature relations with agemates of both sexes* represents the continuation of development of social behavior. The teacher can enhance this by allowing opportunities for students to work together.
2. *Achieving a masculine or feminine social role* is covered in Chapter 11.
3. *Achieving emotional independence of parents and other adults* can be a trying experience for parents and teenagers. Teachers and parents must provide students with opportunities to make decisions for themselves.
4. *Selecting and preparing for an occupation* requires providing guidance in career decision making in high schools.
5. *Developing intellectual skills and concepts necessary for civic competence* is the basic goal of the school.
6. *Preparing for marriage and family life* includes taking courses in marriage, family, and effective parenting.
7. *Desiring and achieving socially responsible behavior* is the goal of many schools that have begun to provide specific instruction in the areas of morals and responsibility to help students achieve this task.

Early-Adulthood Tasks

Most of the readers of this book are likely to be in the developmental stage of early adulthood, roughly ages 18 to 28. It is generally at this age that you are "on your own." According to Havighurst, people in early adulthood face the following developmental tasks:

1. Selecting a mate.
2. Learning to live with a marriage partner.
3. Starting a family.
4. Rearing children.
5. Managing a home.

6. Getting started in an occupation.
7. Taking on civic responsibility.
8. Finding a congenial social group.

These may be the most important tasks an individual faces. You will face most of them, if you haven't already, with very little help from society.

There are important developmental tasks to be accomplished by middle-aged and older people, indicating that development is a continuous process from birth to death. We have not listed the specific tasks presented by Havighurst for these last two age groups because they are not generally seen as responsibilities of the schools. It should be noted, however, that, if concern for adult education continues to grow in America, this may change in the not too distant future.

Psychosocial Development

Just as Havighurst described the important tasks that must be achieved at various stages of development, Erik Erikson (1968) proposed a stage theory of development that was based upon the concept of critical periods. Erikson, however, concentrated primarily on the personality development of an individual. According to Erikson, the motivating factor of an individual at a particular point interacts with demands that society places on him or her at the same time to create certain conflicts. The resolution of these conflicts determine the individual's psychosocial development. In other words, motivation of an individual brings about conditions that present a critical period for the development of certain personality characteristics. The way in which these conflicts are resolved with the demands of society during this critical period determine the individual's personality and the way in which he or she approaches the conflicts encountered in later developmental stages.

Such a theory of psychosocial development is of particular concern to the teacher who is interested in developing the whole person. If teachers recognize that they are observing and influencing not only the cognitive but also the personality development of a student, their approaches and demands may be different. The following are the stages of psychosocial development that Erikson proposed, along with the major conflicts that are encountered during that stage and the potential outcomes.

1. *Trust versus mistrust* (birth to age 1½). During this stage the child will learn whether to trust people in general or whether to mistrust. Erikson believes that, if a child's needs during this period are met in a consistent manner, the child will develop trust in others. If, on the other hand, the child's needs are not met or are met in an inconsistent manner, the

41

Allowing children to explore will develop autonomy. (CEMREL, Inc.)

child will develop a general mistrust of others. The child who resolves this conflict with a general feeling of trust will have *faith* in others in attempting to resolve the conflicts of later developmental stages and will be able to *hope* for successful attainment of wishes.

2. *Autonomy versus doubt* (age 1½ to age 3). In Erikson's second stage, the child is seen as developing personal autonomy or as having doubts about his or her abilities to cope with the surrounding world. Children who are allowed independence and the ability to explore during this time will develop a feeling of autonomy. The child who is not allowed this independence, and suffers from too many demands, will learn to doubt his or her abilities. If the conflict of this stage is resolved in favor of autonomy, the foundation is laid for a positive self-concept and the development of a free *will*.

3. *Initiative versus guilt* (age 3 to age 6). During this stage, children will test their independence. If these attempts at new behavior are met with encouragement, they will develop initiative. If, on the other hand, these attempts at independence are discouraged, a feeling of guilt will result. Initiative is encouraged by providing opportunities to test new behavior. Guilt will result if opportunities are limited or if attempts at independence are punished. If the conflicts of this stage are resolved in favor of willingness to take action independently, the individual will develop a sense of *purpose* for later developmental stages.

4. *Industry versus inferiority* (age 6 to age 12). Erikson believes that children in this stage will either be successful in achieving skills and abilities that the society expects of them or they will not. Those who are suc-

42

cessful develop a general good feeling about their ability to learn important skills and to deal with their peers. This is called *industry*. Those who meet with failure in attempting to achieve these skills and in dealing with their peer group develop a feeling of inferiority or worthlessness. In either case, the result could become a self-fulfilling prophecy in dealing with conflicts encountered in later stages. The industrious child has a self-view of being *competent* to resolve these later conflicts and will be successful. The child who has developed inferiority will have a self-view of being incompetent and, thus, will be unsuccessful. Success, therefore, is critical in this stage, and each child should be provided with ample opportunity to be successful.

5. *Identity versus identity confusion* (age 12 to age 18). This period of adolescence is one of the most trying in psychosocial development. It is the time during which the individual searches for the answer to the question, "Who am I?" If the child's environment is supportive in allowing the identification of a role, the result will be the definition of self or an identity. If the environment is nonsupportive, the result will be a poor definition of self or identity confusion. Erikson says that an individual who develops a clear personal identity possesses *fidelity*, or loyalty.

6. *Intimacy versus isolation* (young adulthood—age 18 to age 35). During this period, the individual attempts to establish close meaningful relationships with others, as evidenced by the high percentage of people who marry during this period. But this need for close relationships is not limited to marriage relationships; rather, it is an attempt to establish intimate relationships with other people in general. The importance of development in previous stages can be seen easily in this stage, for persons who feel guilty, are not trusting of others, or have poor definitions of themselves will have a difficult time establishing close relationships with others. Failure to establish a close relationship results in isolation. The person who develops intimacy with others can know *love*. The person who develops isolation during this stage will have a very poor self-concept and will be unable to experience love as mutual devotion.

7. *Generativity versus stagnation* (adulthood—age 35 to age 60). It is during this stage that Erikson believes the individual will do those things that are consistent with his or her self-image and role expectations. It is because this consistency between one's expectations as to life-style and actual life-style is under the control of the individual that Erikson called the outcome *generativity*. The individual who develops generativity *cares* about the development of the next generation and the world in general. Individuals who are incapable of such caring will become overly concerned with their personal needs and tend toward stagnation.

8. *Integrity versus despair* (aging—after age 60). According to Erikson, people who develop through the seven previous stages successfully will be able to look back on their lives in this final stage with the realization

43

A positive view of life indicates integrity. (CEMREL, Inc.)

that they have led fairly productive, successful, and happy lives. Such a view of one's life allows one to adjust to coming death. Such a person, one with integrity, Erikson characterized as having true *wisdom*. On the other hand, a person who has not developed successfully through the seven previous stages will view his or her life as meaningless and unsuccessful. Such a negative view of one's life would bring about a state of despair. [Derived from Erikson, 1968, pp. 91–141].

Stages in Adult Development

According to both Havighurst and Erikson, human development does not end when people graduate from high school or college; it continues throughout life. It is important for the teacher to have an understanding of what happens in adult development so that he or she will better recognize and deal with developmental crises of his or her own. The following discussions present some of the current thinking on adult development.

The Twenties

Following adolescence, the young adult moves into a period in which his or her major problems stem from getting established in a career, achieving in that career, establishing relationships with others, and starting a family.

A close relationship with another person, quite often including marriage, is an important part of this stage. As Erikson states, the major conflict during this period is one of intimacy versus isolation, with the desire to be really close to at least one other person at the top of the list of motives during this period. The search for personal identity and the ability to develop intimacy overshadow any other tasks during the twenties.

Other writers, such as Gould (1978), Levinson (1978), and Sheehy (1977), speak of a "reaching out" to others during this decade. The young adult is expansive, devoted to mastering the world. The young husband and wife work closely in establishing a home and career and tend not to examine commitments closely or engage in introspection. This is the period during which the young man often acquires a "mentor," a patron and supporter who is somewhat older and who "takes him under his wing" to help him up the career ladder and helps interpret life for him.

The Thirties

There is widespread agreement that something significant in development happens at around age 30. It usually takes the form of a personality crisis, in which the former beliefs and assurances waiver, life begins to look more confusing and painful, and self-reflection churns up new doubts and questions. "What am I doing in this field? Why do I have to meet everyone else's expectations? Is this what I really want out of life? Did I marry the right woman? I'm tired of working so hard to get ahead in my job."

The first real crisis in a marriage often takes place at about this time, sometimes in the form of infidelity, sometimes in conflicts over money, life-style, or children. The first major job dissatisfactions often arise at this point. Social life tends to decline during the 29–34 age period.

Gail Sheehy (1977) calls this period "Catch 30" as the individual suddenly asks himself what he is doing and why. He was too busy getting established and getting ahead in his twenties, but now he is suddenly aware that he may be in a rut, and he wants to break away from these restrictions, to escape the rut. Choices that were made during the twenties are now questioned. This is often a period of separation, divorce, and discontentment and a desire for change. After focusing on the externals, finding a notch, starting a marriage in the twenties, the focus now shifts to the self, to more self-concern.

After the crisis of "Catch 30," the individual settles down to a period of what Sheehy calls "rooting and extending." Perhaps a few changes within the career or marriage have taken place, and the crisis has passed. Now a more rational and orderly period follows, in which the family digs in (sometimes literally in a new house) and the breadwinner climbs the career ladder in earnest. Satisfaction with life almost always goes downhill in the thirties, with less social life, more work, increasing expenses and conflicts in raising a family, and a circle of fewer but closer friends. There

is a desire for order and stability, but at the same time a wrenching struggle
to get ahead. It is in the mid-30s that most men feel a real desire to "settle
down," and some writers believe that if steps toward settling down in
terms of a community and a job haven't been taken by age 35, chances
of forming a reasonable satisfying life structure are quite small.

The Forties

The part of adult development that has been researched and written about
the most is that around age 40, referred to by various frightening names
such as "midlife crisis," "midlife explosion," or "midlife transition."
Somewhere around age 37 to 43 comes the first awareness that death will
come and time is running out. This is seen as an unstable, explosive time
resembling a second adolescence. All values and commitments are open
to question, and the man of 40 wonders "Is there time to change?"

Levinson (1978) labels this the "BOOM" period, "Becoming One's
Own Man." It appears that the 40-year-old looks back on life and eval-
uates it, trying to decide if it has all been worthwhile. If it hasn't, time is
running out, and changes must be made right away. Unresolved personality problems are blamed on parents. There is one last chance to make it
big in one's career. Everyone who has studied the midlife crisis period
agrees that it is a time of both danger and opportunity.

According to Gail Sheehy, midlife crisis begins

with a vague feeling: "I have reached some sort of meridian in my life. I had better
take a survey, reexamine where I have been, and reevaluate how I am going to
spend my resources from now on. Why am I doing all this? What do I really
believe in?" [Sheehy, 1977, p. 350]

Sheehy sees this as interrupting the continuity of the life cycle. Age
35–45 is labeled the "deadline decade," and somewhere in this decade
each of us has a full-blown authenticity crisis. The steps in this crisis are
described by Sheehy (1977, pp. 351–364) as follows:

1. *Seeing the dark at the end of the tunnel.* You notice weaknesses in the
   physical self, you realize that you are getting older. You won't live
   forever and won't achieve all that you had planned. There is an awareness of people divorcing and dying and of old friendships ending. There
   is only so much time left. You feel as if the fourth quarter is about to
   begin, and you are behind in the game.
2. *A change in time sense.* It is "that apostrophe in time between the end
   of growing up and the beginning of growing old." Time is running out.
   Men worry, "Can I do it before it's too late?" Women worry, "What
   will I do with all this time?" Women often see new opportunities
   opening up; men see them closing.

3. *A change in the sense of aliveness versus stagnation.* This feels like boredom, but it is really time diffusion. There is a sudden, drastic lack of trust in the future. Trust can no longer come from anyone else; it must come from within. The feeling of stagnation is followed by a sense of redefined purpose, a real change in outlook.

4. *A change in the sense of self and others.* A man's son beats him at tennis; his daughter sees him as getting old. His youthful picture of himself is now romantic fantasy. Parents are now growing old and are in need of help. You are now at the head of the generational train, with the children gaining on you. Various physical complaints arise.

5. *Deillusioning the dream.* You see that it is reality versus the dreams of age 25. You ask "Is this all there is?" Concern with age is very important in a culture that practices "the planned obsolescence of people." If the ideal self is not attainable and you refuse to lower ideals, the result is chronic depression. Often, the solution is found outside of work. If dreams have been realized, then you must find a new dream.

6. *Groping toward authenticity.* The existing role and life structure seems too confining. The husband sees wife, children, family, and friends as hemming him in. There is physical slippage, loss of youth, a fading purpose of roles, and a shortage of answers. Women assert themselves more, men start facing their own emotions. Loose ends from previous stages come back to haunt us. This can lead to severe depression, sexual promiscuity, power chasing, hypochondria, alchohol abuse, drugs, reckless driving, and so on. It can also lead to new insights and a new intimacy.

7. *From disassembling to renewal.* As he strives for this new authenticity, the man moves through a disassembling, then finally to renewal. There is a reintegration of an identity truly his own, a new uniqueness.

8. *Riding out the down side.* The best thing is to go into the darkness and explore it rather than deny it. Only by going through it does one get on by. Otherwise, one can become phony and superficial. One must let the changes happen: if delayed, it will be harder to change later.

The result of all this, if you are lucky, is to emerge reborn, authentically new, and with enlarged love for self and others. If not so lucky, you emerge sad and bitter, feeling that you had your chances and blew them, and resigned to a basically unhappy life. It should not require much imagination to see the importance of recognizing the midlife crisis if it is happening to a colleague, supervisor, parent, or especially to oneself.

After the Midlife Crisis

The process of growing and changing does *not* end even after the midlife crisis, which ends about age 45. After this crisis is resolved, it is followed by a period of settling down. This is a stable time, marked by a feeling that the die is cast, that one must live with the decisions that were made; there is a desire to get on with life. Money is less important. During this period, husband and wife turn to each other for sympathy as they once did their parents.

After about age 50, researchers see a sort of mellowing, in which there is a softening of feelings and relationships. There is a tendency to avoid emotion-laden issues, a preoccupation with everyday joys, triumphs, and irritations. Parents are no longer blamed for personal problems. There is a willingness to live in the present rather than a preoccupation with either past or future.

Seeker Self Versus Merger Self

A concept from Sheehy's work that is of particular interest to teachers is that of the *seeker self* and the *merger self*. Everyone has both components. The *seeker self* wants to grow, change, achieve, and experience the world. The *merger self* wants to relate to others, share affection and love, join with another in closeness and intimacy.

During the twenties, the seeker self is usually very much predominant in the male, with his energy focused on achieving, getting ahead, fulfilling his dreams in his career. His merger self is sort of "on hold" as he devotes his efforts to getting established and climbing the career ladder.

For the woman during the twenties, the picture is exactly the opposite. Most of the woman's energy goes into the merger self, as she strives to be a wife, mother, and homemaker. Her seeker self is placed on a back burner, as she literally has no time to develop this part of herself. She is too busy with all the tasks of running a household and raising a family.

During the thirties, this picture often changes. For the man, striving for success and achievement may become less important, and he turns toward his wife and family to develop that part of him that was neglected during the twenties, his merger self. At the same time, the wife may be moving in exactly the opposite direction, with her neglected seeker self now coming to the fore. She is tiring of a life defined by relationships with others, and she is anxious to find new parts of herself, to see what she can do, to grow and develop and change. This newfound ambition in the woman may be disturbing to the husband, particularly if it comes at the time when he is looking for his merger self and trying to strengthen ties with his wife and family. It may be a significant cause of marital discord and divorce.

Conclusions

Before closing this discussion of developmental problems in adulthood, it should be pointed out that the findings to date are incomplete. So far, it is primarily middle-class males who have been studied, usually males in the professions. The data on women are limited, and the data on minority groups and working-class men and women are almost nonexistent. Even so, the stages of adulthood as described would seem to be significant for teachers in working with colleagues and with parents and other adults encountered in their work. Above all, it is important for teachers to realize what is happening to themselves as they progress through the many stages of adulthood.

Problems in Development

In a perfect world, all children would grow and develop in a healthy, "normal" fashion, and no problems of arrested or abnormal development would occur. Such a world is not the world in which we live, however, and various forms of developmental problems occur with some frequency. Sometimes these problems have a physiological or even hereditary basis, sometimes they are due to psychological or social factors, sometimes they have an economic basis, but usually they are due to a combination of two or more of these causes. Other chapters in this book deal with some of these problems, such as Chapter 12, on special education. Without going into these details, now we would like to comment on some of the implications when teachers must deal with children with developmental problems.

The first suggestion for teachers is to remember the "tyranny of the average." Don't be guilty of forgetting that the range of normality is usually very broad. In recognizing this, you would logically accept and encourage differences and uniquenesses, not punishing those who are different, but instead implying a philosophy of "dare to be different." Children can tolerate a wide variety of individual differences if they see parents and other adults as accepting and encouraging these differences.

In accepting and encouraging differences, teachers must become adept at distinguishing between the typical, everyday developmental problems that children face and overcome and the more unusual or serious problems that require special attention. Contrary to the old saying, "you'll outgrow it," children frequently do *not* outgrow such problems, and without help, the problems become worse.

For example, the class bully later becomes a delinquent and then a criminal; the anxious little boy becomes a neurotic adult; the shy and withdrawn little girl goes on to become an alcoholic; and the poor reader drops out of school and is unable to find a job. These are all cases in which special attention, the right kind of help at the right time, may have led to changes for the better and the avoidance of such a bad outcome.

In recognizing problems that are serious or require special attention, the teacher must be careful not to exaggerate the problem or to invite the

49

WHY DID GUS TURN OUT AS HE DID?

Gus was born and raised in one of the poorest areas in town. His father was an unskilled worker who was unemployed a good deal of the time, and since Gus had two brothers and three sisters, they had a hard time making ends meet. His father took to drinking more heavily as time passed, and his parents fought constantly and showed few signs of affection. Gus got along fairly well with his mother, not with his father, and his best relationship was with his older brother.

Gus was a sickly child and missed school often. He was in an accident at age 6 that left him with a permanent limp. His oldest brother got mixed up in a drug ring and was sent to prison when Gus was 11. At age 12, his mother died, and life grew even worse. He worked at various odd jobs while completing high school but had to turn over most of what he earned to his father to help pay expenses. He looked forward to the day he could leave his unhappy home.

At this point, you might be expecting to hear how Gus ran away from home, became a delinquent or a school dropout, or even how he went berserk and beat up his father. But none of these things happened. In fact, Gus graduated from high school with excellent grades, went to college on a scholarship plus a job for board and room, earned a "B-plus" average, went to law school and then on to a distinguished career as a lawyer. He also had great compassion for the poor and helped not only his own family but a wider community by organizing and helping to run a series of free legal clinics in inner-city neighborhoods. At present, he is considering running for Congress.

Unusual? Perhaps, but not really all that unusual. Gus represents an outcome that defies explanation based on our present knowledge of psychology. Why is it that thousands of children who grow up in the worst possible conditions go on to lead healthy, normal, productive lives in spite of it all? It is not too surprising when a child from Gus's background grows up to be deviant or criminal as an adult, but what about all those who do *not* end up that way? Something about human nature, or some unknown environmental variables, interact to cause some individuals to develop into normal, healthy human beings while others in the same circumstances become criminals. Still others in what appear to be ideal circumstances sometimes grow up with all sorts of personal or social problems. Psychology still has a long way to go in understanding all the factors involved in human behavior.

use of the problem as an excuse for lack of effort or cooperation. It is one thing for a child with eye problems to know that he or she has problems and must adapt to them, but it is something else to conclude that one cannot study, compete, or even try because of vision problems.

Teachers should be willing to talk about developmental problems with other teachers, counselors, and parents but especially with the person who has the problem. Ignoring problems is not likely to bring comfort to the child involved. Be it physical, emotional, intellectual, social, or a combination of these, it is helpful for children to be able to talk with someone who accepts them, but recognizes the problem, sees them as worthwhile persons in spite of problems, and has some helpful suggestions. Teachers need to be sympathetic, but they must also be careful that this sympathy is not interpreted as condoning all forms of behavior.

One thing a teacher *is* in a position to do with respect to the child with a serious developmental problem is to aid the child in securing help. Be it a counselor, physician, clinical psychologist, physical therapist, or minister, the child might benefit greatly from professional consultation. Sometimes all that is necessary is to point out the problem to parents, who will then seek aid. One of the most effective forms of therapy for developmental problems is knowledge—merely finding out the facts about a problem area is in itself reassuring, even if it can also contain elements of threat. The child who is developing curvature of the spine and might need to wear a brace is still better off to know this now than to wait until the condition is far more serious.

In recognizing developmental problems, keep in mind that the course of development is seldom smooth, that there are spurts and plateaus rather than straight lines of progress, and that occasional regressions to earlier behavior are not uncommon. Although disturbing at the time, the plateaus will most likely not last forever, and the child will move ahead. Also, many internal changes, not obvious yet at the external level, may be taking place during an apparent plateau.

Finally, we come to the oft-repeated phrase, "You must recognize your *own* problems before you can be of any help to others." Teachers need to be aware of any unresolved problems from their own childhood, as these have a way of hanging on and causing mischief long after childhood. In addition, the developmental tasks you face at your present stage of development are important and can interfere with your ability to recognize and help children with their own problems. Knowing about the development of adulthood is helpful not only in understanding yourself but also in understanding and helping your colleagues and friends with their problems.

Summary

This chapter presents a broad summary of the field of developmental psychology as it applies to teaching. Traditional controversies in the field, such as the nature-nurture controversy, the discrete stages versus continuous development argument, the law of compensation, and norms versus normality are discussed in the context of their implications for education. The "miracle of biology," the fact that we are all the same and yet all different, is the most important general principle of development.

Three key concepts of development—maturation, readiness, and learning—are explored. Maturation is that portion of development that is controlled from within, the "internal ripening" aspect. Learning is that portion of development that is a result of experience, the interaction with the environment. Readiness refers to all aspects of development that add up to whether or not the learner is ready to undertake a specific task.

General trends in development are reviewed briefly. Development proceeds from the general to the specific and also from the head to the extremities. Another trend is that structure precedes function. The interaction of many factors in development make it appear that this is a chaotic process, but underneath it all, development is orderly and predictable.

A large portion of the chapter is devoted to the topic of developmental tasks and education. Robert Havighurst's outlining of the tasks for age levels is presented. Havighurst stated that his developmental tasks represented teachable moments that, if missed, would cause the individual difficulty in later developmental stages.

Erikson, whose theory of psychosocial development is presented in this chapter, postulated that each person's personality is determined by the resolution of conflicts that occur at various stages in development. His eight stages are presented along with a discussion of the conflicts to be resolved in each stage.

In dealing with problems in development, the teacher must remember that most problems result from an interaction of many factors. We must avoid the "tyranny of the mean" and remember that the range of normality is very broad. Parents and teachers should accept and encourage individual differences in children.

At the same time, teachers should be alert for important developmental problems and see to it that children receive help when it is needed. The cumulative nature of development and the ways in which early experience and problems affect whatever follows is crucial.

Finally, teachers must recognize the ongoing developmental stages of adulthood that they are experiencing themselves and how they affect the attitudes and behavior of parents and colleagues as they come to grips with their own developmental problems. As we now know, development never ends, and we all continue to grow and change throughout our lives.

Study Questions

1. We hear such phrases as "he gets that from his mother" or "he's just like his father" in everyday conversations. What are the implications of such statements, and what assumptions about human nature are being made? Are these assumptions accurate?

2. Make a list of several things that you do well. Decide in each case what percentage of the skill is due to heredity and what percentage is due to environment. Are any of the skills close to 100% heredity or environment? Are any close to a 50:50 interaction? Is it difficult to decide how much heredity or environment contributes to a particular skill?

3. What accounts for the fact that traits and characteristics from early childhood can be seen readily later in the adult? Can you think of any of your own unique traits or behaviors that were already present at age 5? Why is it important for a teacher to recognize the principle of continuity?

4. The big, husky athlete who must be slow intellectually, the plain-looking woman who of course has a wonderful personality, the gifted child next door who obviously is neurotic, each of these can be seen as an example of the law of compensation. How many other examples of this so-called law can you think of? Can you think of examples of the law of correlation? Would a belief in either one of these laws affect how a teacher would function in the classroom?

5. As adults, teachers are subject to the same problems as are other adults in progressing through the stages of adult development. Describe how the "Catch 30" period of development might influence a teacher's functioning in the classroom. How might the "midlife crisis" affect the work of a teacher?

References

Bayley, N. "Tables for Predicting Adult Height from Skeletal Age and Present Height." *Journal of Pediatrics*, 28(1), January 1946, pp. 49–64.

Bruner, J. S. *Toward a Theory of Instruction*. Cambridge, Mass.: Belknap Press of Harvard University Press, 1966.

Erikson, E. *Identity, Youth and Crisis*. New York: W. W. Norton, 1968.

Erlenmeyer-Kimling, L., and Jarvik, L. F. "Genetics and Intelligence: A Review" *Science*, 146 (3598), December 1963, pp. 1477–1479.

Gardner, L. "Deprivation Dwarfism." *Scientific American*, 227(1), July 1972, pp. 76–82.

Gesell, A. *Infancy and Human Growth*. New York: Macmillan, 1928.

——— "The Ontogenesis of Infant Behavior," in L. Carmichael ed. *Manual of Child Psychology*, 2nd ed. New York: John Wiley & Sons, 1954, pp. 335–373.

Goddard, H. H. *The Kallikak Family: A Study in Heredity of Feeble-mindedness*, New York: Macmillan, 1912.

Gould, R. L. *Transformations: Growth and Change in Adult Life*. New York: Simon and Schuster, 1978.

Havighurst, R. *Developmental Tasks and Education*, 3rd ed. New York: David McKay, 1972.

Jensen, A. R. "Reducing the Heredity-Environment Uncertainty: A reply." *Harvard Educational Review*, 39(1), Winter 1969, pp. 449–483.

——— *Straight Talk About Mental Tests*. New York: The Free Press, 1981.

Levinson, D. S. *The Seasons of a Man's Life*. New York: A. A. Knopf, 1978.

Piaget, J. *Science of Education and the Psychology of the Child*. New York: Orion, 1970.

Rogers, C. R. *A Way of Being*. Boston: Houghton Mifflin, 1980.

Rousseau, J. J. *Emile*. New York: E. P. Dutton, 1974.

Salkind, N. J. *Theories of Human Development*. New York: D. Van Nostrand, 1981.

Sheehy, G. *Passages: Predictable Crises of Adult Life*. New York: Bantam, 1977.

Smith, M. E. "A Comparison of Certain Personality Traits as Rated in the Same Individuals in Childhood and Fifty Years Later," *Child Development*, 23(3), September 1951, pp. 159–180.

Terman, L., and Oden, M. *Genetic Studies of Genius V, The Gifted Group at Mid-life*. Stanford, Calif.: Stanford University Press, 1959.

Wittrock, M. ed. *Learning and Instruction*. Berkeley, Calif.: McCutchan, 1977.

Jean Piaget: A View of Cognitive Development

3

PREVIEW

What is cognitive development?

What are Piaget's contributions to psychology and education?

What is the semiclinical interview?

Why were Americans slow in accepting Piaget's contributions?

How do maturation and experience interact as the child develops?

What does adaptation mean?

Why is the interaction of assimilation and accommodation important?

What is equilibration, and why is it an important concept?

What is conservation, and how does it come about in the child's thinking?

What are cognitive structures, and why are they important?

What are mental operations, schemes, and schemas, and what is their role in thinking?

What are the four stages of cognitive development as defined by Piaget?

What is the sensorimotor stage?

What is the preoperational stage?

What is the concrete operations stage?

What is the formal operations stage?

How are cognitive problems solved at the concrete level?

What are some examples of formal reasoning patterns?

What are the crucial differences between concrete and formal operations?

What are combinatorial, proportional, probabilistic, and correlational reasoning, and why are they important?

What is the difference between moral realism and moral relativism?

What implications for teachers can be found in Piaget's work?

What can teachers do to help children move through Piaget's stages?

It seems reasonable to say that the most important area of development for the teacher to study is that of *cognitive development*. Assimilating and applying knowledge, thinking and reasoning, using the mind to solve problems—these are the behaviors that are central to learning in the classroom. What is the nature of such processes, and how does the mind develop from infancy to adulthood? The psychologist who is generally believed to have contributed the most toward understanding the stages of thought that a child goes through in progressing from the limited thinking of the infant or young child to the complex, abstract reasoning of the adult is the Swiss psychologist, Jean Piaget.

A Genius Is Finally Recognized

Even though much of his work was done in the 1930s and 1940s, and published widely in both articles and books, Jean Piaget was relatively unknown in the United States until fairly recently. The explanation for this is spelled out succinctly by Meyer and Dusek:

There is a general consensus that the work of Jean Piaget has had a greater impact on developmental psychology than that of any other single theorist. His work is probably at least somewhat familiar to both psychologists and informed laymen. It is a curious fact that had we written this book 15 or 20 years ago, we might not have mentioned Piaget at all, or at most we would have described him as something of a curiosity.

Piaget suffered this neglect in part because he writes in French and it is probably something of an understatement to describe the work, and Piaget's prose, even in translation, as less than clear. More importantly, the general philosophical atmosphere pervading American psychology was mechanistic, as opposed to organismic, and good research dictated the operationalizing of the philosophy of logical positivism. Thus, theories that employed terms like "stage," "schemas," or "structure" and referred to physiological structures were simply not accepted as science. [Meyer and Dusek, 1979, p. 180]

The facts about Piaget's life give no clear answer as to why he became such a unique and productive scholar. Born in 1896 in the small village of Neuchātel, Switzerland, Piaget was the son of a history professor. Biographers claim that there was considerable conflict between his devoutly religious mother and his free-thinking professor father and that Piaget turned to intellectual pursuits partly as an escape from these conflicts. At age 10, his fascination at observing an albino sparrow led to his first publication in a scientific journal. He continued to publish articles and books for over seventy years.

Several interesting themes are illustrated in Piaget's life. One is the almost accidental component of adaptation. Piaget described himself as clumsy, and not at all athletic, and this probably encouraged intellectual pursuits as compensation. There just happened to be a museum available where Piaget spent considerable time as a child, and the curator had a collection of mollusks. Piaget started collecting mollusks and writing articles about them, which led to an international reputation as an expert on mollusks and the start of a career in biology. At age 16 he was offered the job of curator of a museum in Geneva, but he turned it down.

Other interesting facts were his interests cutting across disciplines and thus not exactly fitting one (e.g., biology, philosophy, psychology, education, epistemology), so that in a way he invented his own unique field and made his contribution. Until his death in September 1980, Piaget called himself a *genetic epistemologist* investigating the origins of human knowledge.

The influence of Aristotle, who saw logic and reason as the unifying force underlying all of nature, on Piaget's theories is obvious.

Not surprisingly, Piaget came to regard human intelligence, man's rational function, as providing the unifying principle of all the sciences, including the social, biological and natural disciplines. It was a point of view that was to guide him during his entire career. [Elkind, 1976, p. 62]

Piaget's rigid self-discipline (rise very early every day, five publishable pages before doing anything else, simple schedule, followed daily all his life) is intriguing, along with his tremendous love of working and avoidance of modern complications. Such discipline and energy seem almost universal among outstanding scientists and scholars.

Piaget may have been not only the world's greatest developmental psychologist but also the one who offered the most useful knowledge for teachers. Piaget saw the study of children as the true basic science for teachers, and his analysis of the development of thought in the child is the central core of what a teacher needs to know. Without this, all the methodology in the world may be of little use.

Each summer Piaget disappeared into the Alps to a secret hideaway where he wrote a number of articles and often a book based on the year's work in the Center for Genetic Epistemology at the University of Geneva. Over the years, this formula produced an amazing amount of information about development and thinking, and although Piaget's work was overlooked in the United States until the 1960s, Piaget is now recognized worldwide as a giant in the field of developmental psychology.

David Elkind (1981), an American psychologist who is recognized as a leading expert in interpreting Piaget, divides Piaget's career into three periods. During the first (roughly 1922 to 1929), Piaget became aware of and explored children's ideas about the physical world. An important experience in this period was Piaget's going to work as a young man, having just completed his education, for Alfred Binet in Paris. Binet, you may recall, developed the first modern intelligence test in 1908, and Piaget was employed in interviewing and evaluating children on the various types of tasks that go into intelligence tests. Although he was supposed to score answers and record the results, Piaget was fascinated by the *wrong* answers that occurred and started pursuing these misconceptions. In these interviews, he became convinced that children's minds do not work in the same way as adults' and that the nature of children's thought processes could be inferred by listening and observing closely.

A procedure of questioning and exploring, called the "semiclinical interview," became an important part of Piaget's later work. Piaget found not only that children reasoned differently from adults but also that they had different world views and philosophies and ideas quite foreign to the adult mind. He found that young children believe that the sun and moon follow them when they walk, that anything that moves is alive, that animals and objects have human motives, and that dreams come in through the window at night. He was also impressed with the fact that children can only see the world from their own view and cannot construct another or a hypothetical viewpoint.

Elkind places the beginning of Piaget's second period as 1929, continuing for about a decade. Using his own three children as his main subjects, Piaget observed and listened very closely and traced the child's spontaneous mental growth from infancy. He was ingenious at asking questions and inventing games that brought out the structure and functions of the small child's mind. He kept detailed records of all these episodes, and they were a major source of three books that have become classics: *The Origins of Intelligence in Children; Play, Dreams, and Imitation in Children;* and *The Construction of Reality in the Child.* The original publication of these works in the late 1930s stimulated a scurry of research activity concerning infant behavior and marked the end of this second period in Piaget's career.

The third and major phase of Piaget's career began around 1940 and continued until 1980. During this period, Piaget studied the development of those mental abilities in children that gradually enable the child to construct a realistic view of the world (Elkind, 1981). Piaget and his colleagues studied hundreds of children, both in the "semiclinical interview" setting and in more carefully controlled experiments and amassed an astounding amount of information about thinking and stages of cognitive development in children and adolescents. Most of the publications of Piaget (he wrote over thirty books and hundreds of articles) came from this third phase of Piaget's career.

Important in this third phase was Piaget's realization that a considerable part of cognitive growth involves the interaction of constancy and change. The child lives in a dynamic, changing world, but there is also constancy and stability in this world. The child must learn to distinguish between apparent change and real change, between appearance and fact, to see the world as "always changing, yet always the same." The child

PIAGET QUESTIONS A CHILD

The open-ended questioning procedure that Piaget (1929, p. 278) relied on so heavily in his study of children is illustrated in the following excerpts. Notice how the examiner asks leading questions but then follows up each answer the child gives in exploring how their minds work. Each question yields further elaboration, and new directions also emerge. Psychologists refer to this as the "semiclinical interview procedure."

Child, age 9 yrs., 5 mo. *E.* How did the sun begin? *C.* I don't know, it's not possible to say. *E.* You are right there, but we can guess. Has there always been a sun? *C.* No. It's the electricity which has always been growing more and more. *E.* Where does this electricity come from? *C.* From the earth, from water. *E.* What is electricity? *C.* It's the current. *E.* Can a current of water make electricity? *C.* Yes. *E.* What is this current made of? *C.* It's made of steam. . .

Child age 8 yrs., 8 mo. *E.* How did the sun begin? *C.* With fire, it's a ball of fire which gives light. *E.* Where does the fire come from? *C.* From the clouds. *E.* How does that happen? *C.* It's electricity in the clouds. *E.* Do you think that somebody made the sun? *C.* No, it came all alone. . . .

Such discussions allow the examiner to explore any tangent in trying to get a picture of the workings of the child's mind. While such interviews have been a valuable source of Piaget's insight concerning thought in the child, it is easy to see why American psychologists, with their emphasis on the environment, conditioning, controlled experiments, and statistical data, for many years shunned Piaget's work as "unscientific."

receives a static formal education and yet must interpret a dynamic world. An example of this is teaching the child the details of what an apple is, but not when an apple is no longer an apple, when it has been transformed into something else, or the conditions under which it changes or only appears to change.

For example, a child is shown an apple and learns the details of the apple such as reddish-colored skin, shape, and texture, but when the apple has been baked or sliced, the child may not be able to accept this changed form as being still an apple. Likewise, an apple that has been treated and changed into hard cider is no longer an apple but an alcoholic beverage.

Piaget's Basic Concepts

The work of Piaget is a perfect example of the modern *interactionist* view of development described in Chapter 2. The child does not understand the nature of the world totally as a maturational process from within, but neither does the child learn it entirely from without, from experience.

A CHILD'S LOGIC

Adults typically smile at the "silly" mistakes that children make in their descriptions of the world. The child who thinks there is an animal called "Gladly the crosseyed bear" or that thunder is caused by two clouds bumping together is a great source of humor. Consider the little girl who said "Holy Mary, mother of God, pray for us *cinders* . . ." in her mistaken version of the Hail Mary; the little boy who insisted that dreams come in the window at night; the little girl who was convinced that sand fell faster through an hour glass when she worked faster; the little boy who was convinced that dogs knew exactly what he was thinking because they could smell his thoughts; the little girl who insisted that babies come from something you ate and made their exit through mother's belly button; and the little boy who acknowledged that a father could be an athlete, an Episcopalian, and a Democrat, but "not all at the same time, unless he moved."

Each of these examples is more than a cute misperception, however. The young child is busy perceiving the world in ways that are consistent with his or her cognitive stage of development, and while these may seem inaccurate and humorous to an adult, they are perfectly logical and reasonable to the child. They are revealing of the child's level of thinking, and they demonstrate that a child does not reason in the same fashion as an adult.

As Piaget explains repeatedly, it is only through a complex interaction of experience with the necessary internal maturation that the child is able to *invent* or *structure* the nature of reality. No amount of instruction will cause this before the child is ready, but it will not come in a vacuum without experience either. It is through experience that the structure of reality is formed and modified (Cross, 1976).

The details of how the child invents, through the force of his or her own logic, the nature of reality was the central focus of Piaget's work. In the remainder of this chapter, we look closely at a number of Piaget's key concepts and at the four major stages of cognitive development in an attempt to achieve an understanding of Piaget's formulations and their implications for education.

Adaptation

Biologists and others have known for over one hundred years that organisms adapt to their environment, so we could hardly claim something new in Piaget's understanding that a child adapts to the environment. Piaget's contribution here was in describing the *nature* of this adaptation process and breaking it down into *assimilation* and *accommodation*, two dynamic and interacting parts of adaptation.

Assimilation

Assimilation is defined as the use or classifying of an object into existing mental categories or operations. Thus, when the infant takes an object and puts it into his mouth, he is *assimilating* the object to the familiar process of eating. If the object happens to be a dollar bill, this assimilation may not be pleasing to the infant's mother or even to the infant, but it still satisfies our definition of using or classifying the object into existing categories or operations.

Another example of assimilation is the young child who knows what "dog" means, but then calls cats, squirrels, and rabbits "dogs." In this case also, the example happens to be one of incorrect assimilation, but it is assimilation nonetheless. The child has assimilated the new object (squirrel) into the existing category (dog). Most of the time, the assimilation will be accurate, such as the child learning how to hold a pencil and then assimilating other tools—crayons, brush, knife—into this same operation.

Accommodation

There are other times when the child changes the existing categories to adjust to reality. When this happens, the child is *accommodating*. In the dog example, when the child learns that squirrels, cats, and rabbits are not dogs and refines his vocabulary to identify dogs, cats, squirrels, and rabbits accurately, he is accommodating. Thus, we see that *assimilation* and *accommodation* interact as the child adapts to the environment and that these two contrasting aspects of adaptation are very important.

If you understand these two concepts, you should be able to apply them to the following example. The child sees a Basenji for the first time (the Basenji is a breed of dog that doesn't bark). He pets the dog, plays with it, says "Nice doggie," and is puzzled by the fact that the dog doesn't bark. Finally, he smiles and says "Some dogs say 'woof, woof,' some say 'bow, wow,' and some dogs don't say anything at all." In this example, the child is *assimilating* when he identifies the Basenji as a dog, fitting it into his existing concept where it seems to fit. When it fails to bark, he is puzzled and confused, because this does not fit his understanding of what a dog does. Finally, he *accommodates* to this new information from the environment by refining his concept of dog to include dogs who never bark!

Equilibration

A concept that is closely related to that of adaptation is what Piaget refers to as *equilibration*. This is the process that balances both assimilation and accommodation as they interact with each other. Equilibration is a self-regulatory process, determined primarily from within, and if the word *self-regulation* is kept in mind, it helps to understand the concept of equilibration.

As the child explores and learns, he encounters situations in which existing concepts and procedures do not work, and a state of dissonance or disequilibrium is created. If he is ready, he will resolve this disequilibrium by inventing the new operation or concept that is needed. Thus, accommodation to the realities of the world comes when existing knowledge is inadequate *if* the child is ready to accommodate. Since this process is primarily self-regulating, the child must do this on his own, and it will not be speeded up by special instruction.

Consider the child who is confronted with two pieces of cake. At age 3, he concludes that his piece is bigger because he *wants* it to be bigger. At 5, it is bigger because it *appears* to be bigger. At age 7, he realizes it is not bigger, even though it might appear to be, because it weighs the same as the other piece. This progression from an egocentric view (it is what I want it to be) to appearance (it looks or seems bigger) to objective reality results from accommodation, but it is self-regulatory primarily from within the child.

Conservation

This is probably the one idea of Piaget's that has been discussed and researched more than any other. When a child understands conservation, he understands both constancy and transition. He can distinguish between how things look and how they really are. Piaget described this as "always changing, always the same."

Understanding conservation applies to many different areas. The child who has this concept will recognize that the number of buttons remains constant although you rearrange them, the length is the same even when the boxes look different. Size, order, substance, weight, all these remain the same even when the appearance is changed. On the other hand, the child will also recognize when any of these have *actually* changed, regardless of whether they appear different. He must be ready for the logic required in doing this, and no amount of instruction will cause him to understand conservation before he is ready.

In a typical conservation experiment, the child is presented with two pieces of plasticine or Playdoh. The two pieces are roughly round blobs that the child sees as two equal pieces. Without adding any material or taking any away, one blob is molded into a long, skinny piece, while the other is fashioned into a compact little cube. The child who understands conservation will recognize immediately that both pieces still contain the same amount of clay, while the child who has not yet mastered this concept will identify incorrectly the long piece as containing more clay.

Cognitive Structures

The mental organizations or abilities of any particular child are his cognitive structures. The unique mental abilities that distinguish a 7-year-old from those younger children who do not yet possess these mental abilities

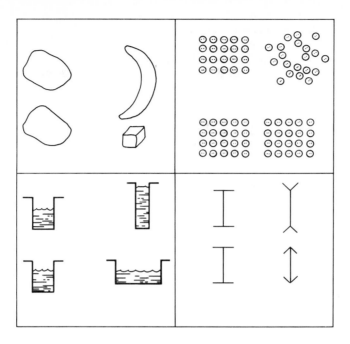

These figure panels illustrate some of the tasks used by psychologists in testing whether a child understands the concept of conservation. In the upper left, two pieces of Playdoh are seen to be the same size. One is then molded into a banana, and the other into a compact cube. A child without conservation, judging on appearance, will say that the banana has more Playdoh.

In the upper right, two piles of twenty buttons each are used, and they are counted carefully to assure that they have the same number. Then, one pile is spread out while the other is left in a tight array, and the child is asked "Now which pile has more buttons?" The child who understands conservation of number can see that both piles still contain the same number of buttons.

In the lower left is the famous beaker experiment. Both containers have the same amount of Koolaid. Then one is poured into the tall beaker, while the other is poured into the fat-bottomed one. A child, judging by appearance, will see the tall beaker as containing more, while the child who grasps conservation will realize that they both still contain the same amount.

In the lower right is another illustration of conservation in which a rod with arms on the end is used. The child can see that both rods are the same length, but when the arms are changed as they are at the right, the illusion is created that the top bar is longer. The child who understands conservation will realize that both bars are still the same length.

are essentially cognitive structures. These vary with the stages of cognitive functioning. The cognitive structures of a child also determine what can be assimilated at any particular time and are a part of the process of accommodation. Part of Piaget's contribution was his recognition that these structures could be *inferred* if you observed and listened to a child carefully.

As an example, suppose that a 3-year-old said, "The sun follows me wherever I go. It goes faster if I'm in a car, and slower if I'm walking." Upon further study, you note that he believes it is much steeper going up a hill than it is going down and that the sand in an hour glass moves faster when he is working fast and slower when he is working slow. These ideas should not be upsetting, since they fit the cognitive structures of a typical 3-year-old who is still in an egocentric cognitive stage. If you tried to correct him and teach him that these things were not true, he would be unable to understand, since he lacks the necessary cognitive structures for taking a point of view not central about himself. That ability to take a different point of view (socialized thought) does not develop until about 7 or 8 years of age.

Mental Operations

Mental operations are defined as *cognitive structures in action*, the tools of thinking. Whenever a child reasons, he is performing a mental operation, applying a cognitive structure to the world as he sees it. In Piaget's analysis, performing mental operations requires the use of symbols, so that this aspect of thinking is reserved for children beyond the preoperational or intuitive stages. We might say that mental operations are similar to physically operating on the environment, except that in mental operations the activity is in the mind, in thinking. A most important characteristic of an operation is that it can be reversed. That is, since the operation is mental, the individual can perform operations and then imagine what things were like before the operation was performed. This reversibility of an operation is very important in understanding Piaget's stages of thought.

Schemes

A scheme is an organized pattern of behavior. When we get up in the morning and brush our teeth, dress, and tie our shoes, this could be called a *scheme*, an organized pattern of behavior that is repeated easily. There is a similarity to the actions, and it is possible to recognize the critical elements of the behavior pattern. The relationship of *behavioral schemes* to *mental operations* should now be obvious. The schemes are the observable evidence of mental operations or thought put into action. Thus, when a child in school is solving problems, he is using his existing *cognitive structures* to perform *mental operations* that enable him to carry out the *behavioral schemes* that get the work done or solve the problems.

A researcher asks a child to move one colored seat of a toy ferris wheel from one position to another. (Bernie Weithorn/SIUC Photographic Service.)

To assess reversibility the researcher then asks the child to put the seat back in its original position. (Bernie Weithorn/SIUC Photographic Service.)

The tendency to fall back on familiar schemes is illustrated in the story of the immigrant, just landed in New York, who could speak no English. On the boat, a friend had explained to him that if he went into a restaurant and said "Ham sandwich and a cup of coffee" he could eat. This went on for a week, and then the friend explained that he could say "Bean soup and a piece of pie" to get something different. He went into the restaurant and said "Bean soup and a piece of pie" and the following dialogue ensued:

Waiter: "Apple, cherry, or banana?"
Immigrant: "Bean soup and a piece of pie."
Waiter: "You want ice cream on it?"
Immigrant: "Ham sandwich and a cup of coffee."

Just like the immigrant in this story, we all tend to revert to familiar schemes in new situations when something doesn't work or when anxious or threatened.

Schema

Another important concept of Piaget, which unfortunately has caused confusion due to its similarity to the word *scheme,* is the concept of *schema.* A schema is a mental structure that is capable of generalization. It is similar to what other psychologists mean by the word *concept,* but in Piaget's model, schema is tied to mental operations and cognitive structures. Schemas occur at many different levels of abstraction. They form a kind of framework into which incoming sensory data can fit, and they also change (accommodate) to assimilate the data better.

Decentration

Decentration refers to the ability to consider more than one factor at the same time. In the discussion of conservation, the child must be able to consider both shape and volume at the same time. Until this is possible, conservation is not possible. Similarly, classification on more than one variable is not possible until decentration is achieved. A child without decentration may be able to classify animals as dogs or cats. It is not until he can consider more than one attribute that he can classify them into white dogs, black dogs, white cats, and black cats.

Four Stages of Cognitive Development

With these concepts in mind, let us look at the four stages of cognitive development defined by Piaget. By *cognitive stage,* Piaget means a characteristic pattern of cognitive structures, mental operations, and schema that are exhibited by children in a given age range and that are *qualitatively different* from those of children in another age range. In other words, most

A child's mental imagery is assessed by asking him "If the snail moves along the track, will it be inside or outside? What direction will it face?" (Bernie Weithorn/SIUC Photographic Service.)

The problem is made more difficult by increasing the complexity of the track. (Bernie Weithorn/SIUC Photographic Service.)

5-year-olds really do think differently from most 7-year-olds, even though the age at which an individual child reaches the next stage varies. The *order* of the stages is the same for all children, even though some progress faster and some slower. A child cannot get to stage 3 without passing through stage 2 or to stage 4 without passing through 3. Finally, progress through these stages is determined by adaptation to the environment (as-

67

simeilation and accommodation in action), which means interaction of maturation with experience. The rate of progress through these stages cannot be changed appreciably by specific instruction.

Stage 1: Sensorimotor Period— The Conquest of Objects

From birth to age 2 (these ages are only approximations and vary from child to child), the infant's mental functioning consists of what is called the *sensorimotor stage.* Exploring the world physically, learning to identify objects, grasping things (and usually trying to study them by putting them in the mouth), finding out where self ends and the outside world begins

---

THROUGH THE EYES OF A 1-YEAR-OLD

Did you ever try to imagine what the world looks like to a 1-year-old? Looking up to a world of giants, lost in a sea of kneecaps, the world must indeed be a threatening place. Everyone else gets around fine, even including the family dog, while you, at the age of 1, are just beginning to walk. Even standing up without help is precarious.

And all the things in the world you don't know about! Everybody talks and nods and listens and smiles, but you know very little about what the talk means. You know how to smile, which you do at every opportunity, especially when anyone gives you some attention. But you don't really understand what they're saying. And all the objects— furniture, toys, magazines, clothes, tools, you name it—are all a fascinating mystery to you. You spend a good deal of time just trying to touch things, putting them in your mouth if possible, to see what they're like.

Eating is difficult for you, as your parents are trying to get you to use a little spoon and not make a mess, but you are hungry about six times a day. The subject of "toilet training" is a mystery to you also, although you are vaguely aware of the diapers you wear, your mother changing them several times a day, and the little potty seat they place you on, showering you with attention. You enjoy sitting on that potty seat and getting all that attention, although you wonder what on earth all the fuss is about.

To you, the most important goal in life is to explore the world around you physically. You know nothing about concepts or theories or someone else's point of view, so you see the world strictly from your vantage point.

Everything is related to your body, the center of your universe, and the only thing that registers is physical reality. The seeds of thought are being planted, but real thinking, in terms of any sort of activities beyond the purely physical, await the advanced age of 2 or so, when you will move beyond the sensorimotor to the preoperational, intuitive stage of thinking, naming objects, and so on. At that point, as life becomes more complex and awareness increases, you will probably say to yourself, "Oh, to be 1 again, without a care in the world!"

are all common activities at this stage. Sensorimotor behavior is very physical as the infant discovers basic facts about the world. Objects move, fall, disappear, and reappear, are hard, soft, hot, cold—all sorts of interesting facts are discovered. Since the infant has not acquired concepts as yet, he is fascinated with such simple games as "peekaboo." Without a concept of object permanence, it must be exciting for the child to see mother's face cease to exist and then have it recreated as it appears again out of nowhere! At first, when an infant drops a toy from its crib, it just cries or ignores it, not realizing that he can look down and see it on the floor. Later, he learns to look down, and even to drop things deliberately to see someone pick them up and return them.

While it may not appear to have much to do with thought, the sensorimotor stage is very important in cognitive development, for in this stage, the infant develops a basic understanding of the world around him and forms habits of exploring and learning. Although he needs to be protected from harm, the infant must have ample opportunity to interact with the physical world, explore, and adapt through assimilation and accommodation. The example of infants in extremely deprived orphanages who fail to develop physically as well as intellectually and emotionally illustrates what happens when ample opportunity to interact with the physical world is not available during the sensorimotor stage.

The newborn infant can see, hear, and feel far more than may be realized. It is only his *apparent* helplessness that has led observers in the past to conclude that the infant can see, hear, smell, taste, or feel very little.

Just how great *is* the infant's capacity for interacting with the world in this stage? Recent research tells us that the newborn can perceive color and shapes, even though muscular control of the eyes is poor. The sense of hearing functions immediately after birth also, as well as reaction to touch and movement. Feeling pain, temperature, and humidity and reacting to smell are all present at birth. Even taste becomes an active sense within days after birth, and the many reflexes that are inborn are well known to most readers. Thus, the infant comes well equipped to interact and learn from the world around him.

Within the sensorimotor period, a series of distinct stages has been identified. These are the modification of reflexes (first month), primary circular reactions (1–4 months), secondary circular reactions (4–10 months), coordination of secondary reactions (10–12 months), tertiary circular reactions (12–18 months), and the beginning of representational thought (18–24 months). These are mentioned only to illustrate the precision and detail with which each period of cognitive development has been analyzed.

Although physical, this period does include an understanding of certain concepts. The concept of object permanence is an example. This is defined as the knowledge that objects continue to exist even when one is not perceiving them. If you place a book on the desk and tomorrow it is gone, you would wonder were it is and may have some ideas as to who moved

69

it, but it is doubtful that you would believe that it had vanished into thin air. However, an infant must have considerable interaction with the environment before acquiring the concept of object permanence.

Another way of describing the sensorimotor period is to say that, in infancy, the major task is the "conquest of the object." The infant is living in a world of bits and pieces and has to "create from scratch" the facts about the world around him. He learns to associate touch, taste, sound, and sight with objects, and through this association he learns that objects are constant and have a life of their own. He discovers how to interact with these objects and to determine just where his body ends and the object world begins. He even begins to develop some rudimentary concepts of time and space, and a simple, if not always accurate, concept of causality.

Stage 2: Preoperational Thought—
The Conquest of Symbols

The period from about age 2 to approximately age 7 constitutes what Piaget called *preoperational thought.* If infancy can be described as the "conquest of the object," then the preoperational period can be summarized as the "conquest of the symbol." It is during this period that the young child learns that everything has a name and that names stand for the many properties of objects. At first, the child believes that the object *is* the name, that the name has some magical property that confers objecthood, and that if you change the name you have changed its properties. (A piece of wood *is* a gun if you name it that.)

This period is so important in the child's mental development because it marks the beginning of language and vocabulary, the development of true human language. It is during this period also that images of "good" and "bad" are first learned. Piaget describes children as moral realists at this stage; that is, the child considers only the rule and the consequences of behavior. He is incapable of considering motives in judging "good" and "bad." The first attempts at drawing are seen during this period, and the child recognizes parts of a picture and other details. Piaget concluded that a child must be in this stage to experience a true "nightmare" because, prior to this, the child does not have the necessary images and concepts.

The newly acquired ability to use symbolization is basic to the fascination that 3- and 4-year-olds show for "pretending" and other games. As in the anecdote, two sticks are an airplane, a row of chairs is a train, the dog becomes a baby, and pots and pans can be almost anything. The child dons mom's shoes or dad's hat and becomes the parent. Adults sometimes forget the depth of such symbolization, the extent to which this is reality for the child. The symbolization includes objects and events not present and subconscious symbols as well.

BUT YOU BROKE MY AIRPLANE

The children had been playing on the floor, apparently having a good time and not complaining. I was curious as to what was holding their attention so well, so I peaked around the corner to see what they were doing. To my surprise, they were sitting on the floor, playing with several popsicle sticks. David had several sticks in a stack and referred to this as his house. Emily, meanwhile, had two sticks crossed and held together by a piece of string. They seemed engrossed in this simplest of make-believe games, but before I could observe any more the phone rang.

In crossing the floor where they were playing to answer the phone, I accidentally stepped on Emily's sticks. She immediately started screaming, and I tried to convince her that it was OK, I'd fix it. But she continued crying her eyes out after I answered the phone, and I finally cut my conversation short because of all this wailing.

At first, when she told me the sticks were her airplane, I told her I would make her another one. This didn't seem to help, even after I *did* fashion her a new plane. There was something special about the two sticks I had broken.

I was getting a little irritated, thinking she was just acting spoiled, when it dawned on me that this illustrated one of Piaget's points. Emily was 3 years old. In the early stages of naming, she, of course, saw a one-to-one correspondence between the thing and its name. Symbols could never again in life be more powerful than this; the thing *was* its name. She not only *called* the two popsicle sticks her airplane, in her eyes they *were* an airplane. I had unwittingly destroyed not two sticks that were temporarily her airplane, but something that was real in her mind as an airplane because the name "airplane" had decided that.

I managed to alleviate the situation by getting down on my hands and knees and becoming her horse, which she rode in appropriate joy for one who perceives a father on all fours as a *real horse*. I hoped, as she rode on my back, that the phone wouldn't ring and destroy her horse and that she'd had enough before my back gave out.

Stage 3: Concrete Operations— The Conquest of Reasoning

The period in which logical reasoning patterns emerge is during the *concrete operations* stage from about age 7 through age 11. The child now has both the necessary structure (schema, operations) and the necessary experience to perform logical processes of thought. He now possesses internalized actions that permit him to do "in his head" what before he had to do by actually manipulating objects. He is performing reasoning operations, but these must be *related* to things. His thinking needs reference to familiar actions, objects, and observable properties.

Students sometimes make the mistake of assuming that "concrete operations" means an actual "hands-on" manipulation of objects. Such manipulation may be helpful, but it is not essential. Concrete thinking *is* limited to the physical world as it has been experienced.

71

This child clearly demonstrates concrete operations. (CEMREL, Inc.)

Some of the mental abilities that the child displays in this period are the use of class inclusion, conservation, and serial ordering. He is able to understand concepts and simple hypotheses that make direct reference to familiar actions and objects, he can follow step-by-step instructions, provided that each step is completely specified, and he can relate his viewpoint to that of another in a simple situation.

After reading the description of concrete operations, you may be wondering why the child needs to progress beyond this stage. What important cognitive skills does he not yet possess? Concrete reasoning is limited, as seen by the following example of an 8-year-old trying to solve a problem in science. The child

1. Searches for and identifies some of the variables causing the phenomenon, but does so unsystematically and incompletely.
2. Makes observations and draws inferences from them, but does not consider all possibilities.
3. Responds to difficult problems by applying a related but not necessarily correct solution.
4. Processes information but is not spontaneously aware of his own reasoning, inconsistencies, or contradictions with other known facts.

If you were a science teacher, these limitations would obviously influence what you could and could not do in your science class, and you would have to orient your teaching toward the reasoning abilities of the students, with the thought of helping them move toward the next stage.

WHEN IN DOUBT, DO SOMETHING CONCRETE

Albert was given the following math problem:

Homer and Jethro are playing blackjack. They agree that at the end of each round, the loser shall pay the winner one fourth of his (the loser's) holdings at that point. Homer has $24 to start and Jethro has $18. Homer loses the first round; Jethro loses the second and the third. How much does each have at the end of three rounds?

Albert's reasoning was as follows: "Let's see, Homer has $24 and Jethro $18. Eighteen is three fourths of $24. Homer has lost one fourth of his money, but Jethro has lost two fourths of his. This means that Jethro lost $9, because that's half of 18, and Homer lost $6, because that's one fourth of 24. That means Homer gained $9 from Jethro, but lost $6, so he gained $3. Twenty-four plus $3, that's $27 for Homer.

"Jethro lost $9, but gained $6, so he lost $3, and $3 from $18 is $15. So Homer had $27 at the end and Jethro $15.

"No, wait, if Homer gave Jethro $6 then Jethro had $24. If he then lost half, he lost $12, so he ended up with $12 and Homer with $24. No, wait, that's not right. If Homer had $24 and gained $12, that's $36. . . . Shoot, I don't know!"

This example is typical of concrete reasoning. Albert is doing something familiar, and almost correct in that he sees the problem as one involving fractions and addition and subtraction. But he cannot think through each step, and he cannot review his thinking to be sure if he is right or not.

Stage 4: Formal Operations—
The Nature of Abstract Thought

We come finally to the goal that so many parents and teachers are hoping their children will soon reach, the goal of formal logical reasoning. Most children acquire the skills of this type of thought at ages 11 to 15, although it is important to keep in mind that many do *not* show clear evidence of this stage until later.

In formal operational thought, one can reason with concepts, relationships, abstract properties, axioms, and theories. Ideas can be expressed in symbols that need not be tied to the physical world or to experience. Some key patterns at this stage are combinatorial reasoning, proportional reasoning, probabilistic reasoning, and correlational reasoning. The student with these skills can recognize reasonable hypotheses, see implicit assumptions, reason hypothetically, verify the results of his reasoning, and review his own reasoning process.

The advantages that these mental abilities give the student should be obvious, but they do not come quickly or easily. Much of what is described is already partly present in the concrete thinker, but only intuitively and unsystematically and only in familiar situations. When these have become explicitly understood and useful as general problem-solving procedures, the student is reaching the formal operational stage.

In the ensuing pages, problems that illustrate formal reasoning patterns are presented in boxes along with dialogues from typical student responses. These are discussed with emphasis on how they illustrate Piaget's theory. Then some recent research findings are presented.

Read each of the problems and try to answer all the questions carefully before proceeding to a discussion of the problem. This will get you more involved in the reasoning processes that the problems are meant to illustrate.

The islands puzzle, shown in the box, illustrates a number of important facts about the logical reasoning process. In answering the questions, the student must be able not only to understand the information as it is given but also to interpret what this information means and tie it together in solving the problem. When given the first two clues, he knows not only that you *can* go by plane between island C and D and you *cannot* go by

In formal operational thought, one can deal with hypotheses and theories. (Darrell Barry/ Little Rock School District.)

THE ISLANDS PUZZLE

The puzzle is about islands A, B, C, and D in the ocean. People have been traveling among these islands by boat for many years, but recently an airline started in business. The clues about possible plane trips are given below. The trips may be direct or include stops and plane changes on an island. When a trip is possible, it can be made in either direction between the islands. You may want to make marks on the map to help remember the clues.

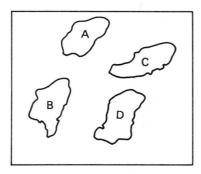

First Clue: People *can* go by plane between islands C and D.

Second Clue: People *cannot* go by plane between islands A and B. Use these two clues to answer question I. Do not read the next clue until *after* you answer the question.

Question I: Can people go by plane between islands B and D?

_____Yes _____No _____Can't tell from the two clues

Third Clue: People *can* go by plane between islands B and D. Use all three clues to answer questions II and III.

Question II: Can people go by plane between islands B and C?

_____ Yes _____No _____Can't tell from the three clues

Question III: Can people go by plane between islands A and C?

_____ Yes _____No _____Can't tell from the three clues

From E. F. Karplus and R. Karplus, "Intellectual Development Beyond Elementary School I. Deductive Logic," *School Science and Mathematics*, 70(619), May 1970, p. 398.

plane between islands A and B, but also that you don't know yet whether or not you can go by plane between islands B and D. The two clues do not state this specifically, but logical reasoning applied to the map of the four islands (or just in your head if the concrete prop isn't needed) tells you that you cannot be sure from the clues whether you can make a connection between B and D; that is, the A–B and the C–D connections, or lack of connections, don't really tell you anything about the B–D connection.

When you are given the third clue, that people *can* go by plane between islands B and D, you now can tie together these three clues and logically conclude that you know about connections among *all four* islands. How do you know this? Because of the rules (a trip can be made in either direction and can include going to one island and then on to another) coupled with the clues you have been given. If you *can* go between B and D and you *can* go between C and D, then obviously you *can* go between B and C (B to D and then D to C). Similarly, if you *can* go from B to D to C, but you *cannot* go from A to B, then logically you *cannot* go from A to C either, becase if you could, then you could get from A to B by going A to C to D to B! A most important element in this problem is keeping in mind the clues that you have been given, putting these clues together, and inferring the conclusions they add up to and also seeing what the clues imply about connections you have *not* been told about specifically. A student who is unable to perform this reasoning process will conclude that you cannot tell about B to C or A to C from the information given.

To understand more about the stages of cognitive development as they would appear in solving the frogs puzzle (see the box), let us analyze some typical student responses. To do this, it is necessary to add another category to the stages we have already described. This new category is "transitional," which simply means that the student shows some of the reasoning patterns of formal operations, but cannot function consistently in that stage. Such a student is in a transition from concrete to formal operations, and since this transition is not completed over night, it is almost like a

---

THE FROGS PUZZLE

Professor Thistlebush, an ecologist, conducted an experiment to determine the number of frogs that live in a pond near the field station. Since he could not catch all the frogs, he caught as many as he could, put a white band on their left hindlegs, and then put them back in the pond. The next day he sent his graduate assistant out to catch as many frogs as he could from the pond. Here are the data from the two trips:

First trip to the pond: 55 frogs caught, banded, and released.
Second trip to the pond: 72 frogs caught; of those 72 frogs, 12 had bands.

What is the total number of frogs in the pond? *Answer* _____

How was the professor able to make an estimate of the number of frogs from these data? What assumptions was he making about the frogs? What would be your line of reasoning in arriving at an estimate of the number of frogs in the pond?

From A. E. Lawson et al. *Biology Teaching and the Development of Reasoning* (Berkeley Calif.: The Regents of the University of California, 1976), pp. 1–6.

substage of its own. Thus we look at three types of reasoning examples: (1) concrete operations, (2) transitional operations, (3) formal operations. The examples are presented as dialogues between an experimenter and a student responding to the question, "What is the total number of frogs?"

Jean Piaget: A View of Cognitive Development

Fred, Age 15

"I can't do it. I don't know."

Exper.: "Just make a guess."

Fred: "Well, there were 72. Twelve were banded, so I guess I would subtract that. No, I don't think this is right. That leaves 60. . . . I can't think. Multiply 60 times 55? No, that's too many. How about divide?"

Exper.: "OK, what is your answer?"

Fred: "Well, I don't know. Is it 6? No, there must be more. Fifty-five banded plus 60 not banded. That's 115. I'll say 115."

Exper.: "Are you sure?"

Fred: "Well, I guess. No, I don't understand the problem."

Analysis. Fred tries valiantly, but he cannot solve the problem. He either does not understand proportionality, or else just does not see it in relation to this problem. He tries several concrete operations, such as adding, multiplying and dividing, but they are really just stabs in the dark. He cannot examine his own thought process and verify if it is correct. He is just guessing, using the concrete operations with which he is familiar.

Priscilla, Age 18

"I don't know. That's playing with numbers too much. Sixty frogs not banded? I'd have to catch a third group and band them."

Exper.: "Why?"

Prisc.: "To get better data."

Exper.: "Can you make an estimate from what is given?"

Prisc.: "I don't know. 60 and 55 together? No, that won't work. . . . I wouldn't try to make a guess. If the sample were bigger, I might try. I could guess, based on the first two tries, about 200?"

Exper.: "Could you explain that?"

Prisc.: "Well, it's sort of a progression. Fifty-five caught and banded the first time, and then 72 caught the second time, so 55 plus 72 are 127. On the third time, it should jump to about 200. I'll guess 200."

Analysis. This is a good example of transitional thinking. Priscilla exhibits some fairly sophisticated reasoning patterns, such as the idea of a progression, and she definitely experiences the disequilibration Piaget talks about. She knows that a concrete response, such as 60 plus 55, won't work and can see that familiar concrete patterns are inadequate. She is searching, and, with some helpful suggestions and experience on a number of problems, she can be helped through the transition into formal operational thought.

Cathy, Age 18

"Seventy-two were caught and 12 were banded. That is, 1 out of 6 were banded. If the 55 mingled with the rest of the frogs, they should be about one-sixth of the pond. Six times 55 is 330. . . . Let's see, this is saying that out of 330 frogs, 55 were caught and banded. Once they mingled again with the rest, we caught a small sample of 72. One-sixth of them were banded. We're assuming that they were mingled fairly evenly, and that death or reproduction wasn't significant in one day. . . . Yes, I'll go with the 330— that's a reasonable estimate."

Analysis. This is a beautiful example of formal logical reasoning. Cathy sees the problem immediately as one of proportion. She reasons it through, based on the number of banded and unbanded frogs in the second sample compared with the total banded the first day, and solves the equation $72/12 = X/55$ correctly. She then reviews her thinking, checks on what assumptions she is making and concludes with a high degree of certainty that her answer is reasonable. She is using proportional and probabilistic reasoning, and she is making clear the logic of her conclusion. She can pick up the implicit assumptions and reason hypothetically without needing objects to manipulate. The advantages for a student who is able to reason in this fashion should be obvious.

Summary of Concrete Versus Formal Reasoning Skills

A closer look at what the learner can do at the concrete and formal stages should help to clarify just what is involved in thought patterns during these stages. Since the first two stages—sensorimotor and preoperational thought—are completed by most children at ages 7 or 8, the stages of concrete and formal operations are of most interest to teachers.

Concrete Reasoning Patterns

A child at the concrete stage demonstrates such reasoning patterns as *class inclusion, conservation,* and *serial ordering,* which include such operations as counting, negation, reciprocation, and identity. In *class inclusion,* the child understands simple classification and generalizations. If you understand that all dogs are animals, but only some animals are dogs, you are applying class inclusion.

In *conservation,* the individual understands that, if nothing is added or taken away, then the amount, length, number, weight, and so on remain the same. The individual can distinguish between apparent differences and real differences and can apply this to a wide variety of situations.

In *serial ordering,* the child arranges a set of objects or data in serial order and establishes a one-to-one correspondence. For example, if a child is shown three plants that are one, two, and three feet tall, respectively, and is asked how old they are, he will assume that the smallest plant is the youngest and the largest plant is the oldest. He will probably also assume that young plants have smaller leaves. If he is told that the plants are the same age, but have grown at different rates, he will be confused.

Possessing concrete reasoning patterns enables the child to do school work that includes the following behaviors:

1. Understands concepts and simple hypotheses that make a direct reference to familiar actions and objects and can be explained in terms of simple associations (e.g., the plants in this container are taller because they got more fertilizer).
2. Follows step-by-step instructions as in a recipe, provided that each step is specified completely (e.g., identifying organisms with the use of a taxonomic key or finding an element in a chemical solution using a standard procedure).
3. Relates one's viewpoint to that of another in a simple situation (e.g., a girl is aware that she is her sister's sister).

However, limitations in concrete reasoning lead to such phenomena as the child who explores the effect of fertilizer on plants but forgets to hold the age and species constant; or the child who concludes that it is the sun that made one plant bigger while overlooking the difference in type of soil and moisture; or the adolescent who computes subgroups in a set and ignores the fact that the subgroup total is much larger than the set total.

Because of limitations such as these, there is good reason for teachers to strive to move children ahead toward the use of formal reasoning patterns, also keeping in mind that developing formal reasoning abilities is a long and gradual process that begins far before the stage itself.

Formal Reasoning Patterns

An individual at the formal operational stage displays the reasoning patterns of combinatorial, proportional, propositional, probabilistic, and correlational reasoning (Inhelder and Piaget, 1958).

In *combinatorial* reasoning, the individual considers all possible relations of experimental or theoretical conditions in a systematic manner.

In *proportional* reasoning, the individual recognizes and interprets relationships in situations described by observable or abstract variables (e.g., in the frogs puzzle, for every 12 banded frogs there are 72 total frogs; therefore, for every 55 banded frogs, there should be 330 total frogs). Proportional reasoning is very important in understanding scientific principles.

79

In *propositional* reasoning, the individual can consider hypothesized propositions, recognizing the necessity of taking into consideration all the known variables and designing a test that controls all variables but the one being investigated. The mealworm puzzle following requires such reasoning. The student who understands this problem recognizes the need for all four situations, what is learned in each instance, and how all four situations combined allow the conclusion that the worms must be affected by both light and moisture.

In *probabilistic* reasoning, the individual recognizes the fact that natural phenomena themselves are probabilistic and that any conclusions or explanatory model must involve probabilistic considerations. Again, in the mealworms puzzle, this means recognizing that the few worms at the opposite end are not really important and that the "effect" is not perfect or 100%. In the frogs puzzle, it implies recognizing the assumptions of the frogs mingling, birth or death being negligible, even though not necessarily perfectly accurate, and the fact that 330 is an approximation and not necessarily precise. Even such mundane events as the daily weather report contain some probabilistic reasoning, and the conclusion that the weathercaster was wrong because he said "20% chance of rain" and then it rained shows that this type of reasoning is not always understood.

In *correlational* reasoning, the individual is able to decide whether phenomena or events are related, whether they tend to go together. This requires awareness that chance fluctuations matter little and that the relationship doesn't always hold true. When the child recognizes that dark clouds and rain usually go together, but occasionally one happens without the other, he is getting into this type of reasoning. Counting the number of blue-eyed blondes and brown-eyed brunettes and then subtracting the number of brown-eyed blondes and blue-eyed brunettes to see if there is a relationship of hair color to eye color is a more advanced example of correlational reasoning.

These patterns are not completely absent at the concrete level, and they are gradually increasing during that period. But they are understood only intuitively (the child cannot explain the reasoning), and they are used partially and unsystematically. The concrete thinker needs reference to familiar actions, objects, and observable properties. Class inclusion, conservation, and serial ordering are used consistently, but combinatorial, propositional, proportional, probabilistic, and correlational reasoning are either not used or are used only partially by the concrete reasoner. To carry out a particular procedure, the concrete thinker needs specific, step-by-step or "cookbook" instructions. Also, he is not aware of his own reasoning, inconsistencies among various statements he makes, or contradictions with other known facts.

The formal thinker, on the other hand, can reason with concepts, relationships, abstract properties, axioms, and theories. He uses symbols to express abstract ideas. He uses combinatorial, propositional, proportional, probabilistic, and correlational reasoning consistently and appropriately,

THE MEALWORMS PUZZLE

Professor Snarff wanted to find out if mealworms respond to light and/or moisture. He set up four boxes containing worms with a light bulb by each box as a light source and wet newspaper on the bottom as a source of moisture. Twenty-four hours later he found the following results. What should he conclude from these results about mealworms' response to light and/or moisture? ("Response" means any movement toward or away from.)

1. Mealworms respond to light only.
2. Mealworms respond to moisture only.
3. Mealworms respond to both light and moisture.
4. Mealworms respond to neither light nor moisture.

   You should be able to select one of the answers, explain it clearly in view of the results, show how the findings combine to support your answer, and re-examine your thinking if you are operating at the formal operations stage.

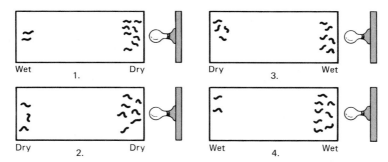

Analysis. If you answered (3), both light and moisture, you are probably using formal reasoning patterns. Condition 1, with most of the worms on the light, dry end, indicates they may be responding to light, or moisture, or both. Condition 2 indicates that, in the absence of moisture, they respond to light *alone* since both ends are dry. Put this together with condition 3, and it looks as if they must respond to moisture also, since the large number crawling toward the light were offset by those crawling *away from* the moisture, and we have about the same number on both ends. Condition 4 further supports the fact that they crawl toward light, with moisture constant in this case, so, by putting the results of all four conditions together, we would have to conclude that mealworms respond to (crawl toward) light but respond also (crawl away from) moisture.

   Notice in the problem that we have *not* determined if the response to light is stronger than to moisture or if the response to moisture changes in the absence of light. We would need more conditions, some with light at both ends and some with no light present, to answer such questions, but in the four conditions presented, we are able to conclude that mealworms *do respond* to both light and moisture.

Adapted from A. E. Lawson et al. *Biology Teaching and the Development of Reasoning* (Berkeley, Calif.: The Regents of the University of California, 1976), pp. 1–2.

and can explain the process. He does not need specific "cookbook" instructions but can plan a lengthy procedure given overall goals and resources. And, finally, he is aware and critical of his own thought processes; he can check his thinking, evaluate its validity, recognize errors, be certain of his conclusions—he can literally think *about* thinking! This last point is, of course, extremely important for teachers to keep in mind as a difference between concrete and abstract thinkers.

Moral Development

Piaget (1965) theorized that, as the child moves through the cognitive stages, his judgment of good and bad or right and wrong also changes. The young child in the preoperational stage is able to see the world only from his viewpoint, which Piaget called *egocentric thought.* He is unable to take the view of another individual and is not even aware that such a view could be different from his own. In addition, he is able to think of only one aspect of a problem or situation. That is, he is unable to decenter or to consider several aspects simultaneously. Because of these limitations, Piaget says that a child in the preoperational stage is a *moral realist.* The child considers only the rule in determining "good" or "bad." If the rule is broken, the child is bad. Egocentric thought prevents the child from perceiving that, in the view of others, the rule may not be a good one. The inability to decenter prevents the child from considering the rule, the consequences of breaking it, and the motive for breaking it simultaneously.

As children move into the formal operation stage, they have developed socialized thought. That is, they are able to understand that different people have different viewpoints and that these other viewpoints may be different from their own. They have also developed decentration. This latter quality allows them to consider rules, motives, and consequences in making moral judgments. When they reach this stage, they have become *moral relativists.* They make judgments of behavior based not only on rules but also on motivation and circumstances. Behavior is no longer right or wrong because the rule says it is. Rather, the intent of the individual and the conditions under which the individual is functioning are considered along with the rule in determining right and wrong.

Some Recent Research Findings

The relevance of Piaget's work may be more apparent if we look at research findings in this area. One of the strongest findings is that the infant and young child must interact physically with the world for cognitive development to progress (Brainerd, 1978). Infants whose parents allow a high degree of activity, encouraging exploration and interaction with the world, tend to progress through the sensorimotor and preoperational periods more effectively. Although there is insufficient research to support completely the generalization that this is true at all levels, it seems reasonable to make such a suggestion. Active exploration, adapting to the environment and it to you, seem to be important for learning at all age levels.

A second area of findings has to do with what Piaget called the "American question." This label arose from the repeated queries by Americans as to whether or not progress through the stages could be "speeded up" in some way by the right type of training and experiences—the European attitude seemed to be a more naturalistic one of understanding the stages as they exist.

Much research has been done concerning this question, some with positive findings and some not, but the general conclusion seems to be that you cannot *teach* the basic mental operations of these stages to someone who is not yet ready (Kamii, 1973). For example, a 6-year-old who is not ready to understand conservation cannot be made to understand it, even if he is taught how to solve various problems in this area. This would seem to say that generally, the answer to the "American question" is "no." But as usual, life is not that simple, and other findings indicate that a general range of experiences relating to the mental operations or cognitive stage in question is helpful (Engelmann, 1967). The child who has a broad range of experience and activities, many of which are related directly or indirectly to conservation (of length, substance, volume, weight, number), will progress more smoothly and efficiently through this stage as he becomes maturationally ready.

The age range at which children move into the different stages is very broad, and parents and teachers are urged to avoid being misled by this. A child who is still in preoperational thought at age 7 or 8 is not abnormal or even necessarily less intelligent than the 7- or 8-year-old who is clearly in concrete operations. The stage in which a child is at a particular age is not an accurate index of IQ. Of special interest is the age 11–15 estimate of formal operations made by Piaget. It is apparent from recent research that a large number of adolescents do *not* display formal operational thought at this age level or even beyond this age level (Dale, 1970, Jackson, 1965). Studies have also found that at least 50% of college freshmen in a number of American universities studied do *not* show evidence of formal operations on problems similar to those presented in this chapter (Thornton and Fuller, 1981; Killian, 1979).

This finding is highly relevant for secondary teachers. It means that possibly half or more of the students being taught are probably not yet fully established at the formal reasoning level. It means that you must include concrete illustrations in your teaching and bridge the gap between the concrete and the abstract. It means that you cannot assume that students, regardless how bright they are, can automatically understand material presented in an abstract way. It is becoming apparent that many adults *never* reach the formal reasoning stage, and even so are able to function quite effectively in life (Graves, 1972). Yet it is the teacher's objective to help all students progress toward formal reasoning by teaching in terms of possibilities, not limitations.

Some additional discoveries reveal why so many students beyond the age of 15 do not display formal operations. A student may be capable of this type of reasoning but may revert back to a lower level (concrete reasoning) under certain circumstances (Duckworth, 1973). Anxiety, stress, an unfamiliar situation, new and unusual material, and low interest level are all circumstances in which students may operate at the concrete level even though potentially capable of formal reasoning. A student might use formal reasoning in his major field and courses where he feels confident but resort to concrete patterns in other courses. For example, many mature, healthy, intelligent college students will resort to the concrete level or below if presented with *anything* mathematical.

Implications for Teachers

Piaget's analysis of cognitive development has many implications for parents and teachers, and most of these are really just simple and straightforward applications of his ideas. It is crucial that anyone working with a student knows the cognitive stage at which that student is functioning, the schemas and operations that individual is capable of performing. Unless you have some idea of this, you do not know the level and type of material that this student is capable of understanding, nor do you know the instructional technique that is likely to be effective. To acknowledge this fully, the teacher has a need to know this for any group of students in general but also for individual students in the group.

A second clear implication is the need to bridge the gap between the concrete and the abstract in your teaching. Beyond the third or fourth grade level, it can be safely assumed that some of the students are already getting into the formal operations stage, some are doing well in the logic of concrete operations and developing the rudiments of formal operations, some are struggling along in concrete reasoning, and some perhaps are still preoperational. Even at the twelfth grade level or beyond, some students are *not* employing formal abstract reasoning processes. Thus, you must include concrete referents and examples, and even objects to manipulate at times, to give all students the opportunity to follow what you are teaching. Remember, too, that even the most advanced formal operational thinker *enjoys* some concrete examples and activities.

Findings about the *transitional period* between concrete and formal operations are also important for parents and teachers. The student who is in this transition is the one who can be helped the most by exploration and problem solving, since it helps to consolidate their skills and provides the experience necessary to move on into the formal stage. This transitional period is almost like a stage in itself, but one in which the student correctly applies formal operations at times and at other times is strictly concrete in performance. Bridging the gap between concrete and abstract is helpful to this type of student. So, also, is providing problems to solve, encouraging formal reasoning, rewarding attempts at it, discussing it, and examining one's own reasoning patterns.

Remember that students *do* regress at times. Material that is threatening or unfamiliar, stressful situations, and the like may cause such reverting back to earlier levels or thinking. Proceeding more slowly, giving more examples, and rewarding formal reasoning are all helpful in this regard. It even appears that some students fail to use formal operations because they are not *required* to do so. Focusing on the reasoning process, making sure that students understand this process, and asking questions that require formal reasoning will help to stimulate this in students who have the potential but are failing to use these patterns.

It should be most obvious that students need continuous opportunities to explore and to interact with the environment if cognitive growth resulting from assimilation and accommodation is to take place. Piaget's theories do *not* encourage the idea of the student passively absorbing knowledge from the outside world. The teacher who takes Piaget seriously will have a classroom in which the students are actively exploring, experimenting, solving puzzles and problems, perhaps even arguing and agonizing over dilemmas that they are trying to resolve.

Another reason for the agonizing and dilemmas is found in Piaget's concept of *equilibration*. The student, when faced with a problem or situation that seems insoluble when past procedures are applied, is thrown into a stage of disequilibrium. The dissonance this creates forces the student to try new approaches, modify past procedures, and discover new solutions or ideas. It is this *disequilibration*, in relation to the student's self-regulatory maturation from within, that leads to accommodation and cognitive growth. One might say that part of the teacher's task is to avoid making it so easy for the student; rather, encourage constructive dilemmas and dissonance so that the students will struggle to accommodate and move ahead in their cognitive functioning.

Piaget's inclusion of a theory of moral development within his theory of cognitive development should be of particular interest to the teacher who adopts a cognitive-humanistic viewpoint, for it shows that, as a child develops such cognitive abilities as socialized thought and decentration, his ability to judge his own behavior and that of others develops. The teacher concerned with the whole child will attempt to work with this developing morality. Students should be provided opportunities to practice their increasing ability to make relative decisions regarding right and wrong.

It should be noted also that, as students move into the formal operations stage, they become fascinated with the thought process itself. They become more interested in what can be generated from that process than with what is realistic. Therefore, you may find that, when a student is given an exercise to help expand his formal reasoning abilities, he generates ideas and suggestions that, while possible, are unrealistic. As a teacher, you will need to work toward helping the student see the difference between "possible" and "possible and realistic."

A final note is that Piaget's work carries the strong implication that teachers should be *child development specialists.* To see the world from the child's point of view, appreciate his line of reasoning, and create a child-centered environment to foster growth and development, the teacher must know a great deal about child development. It seems reasonable to add that it helps to like children and to enjoy working with them. Piaget's work provides a basis for those who like and enjoy working with children to become more effective in their jobs and also should help others preparing to teach children to learn to like and enjoy working with them.

Summary

Cognitive development is the most important area of development for the teacher to understand. The psychologist who contributed the most toward understanding cognitive development was Jean Piaget, whose theories are the principal focus of this chapter.

After some biographical facts that help to place Piaget's work in perspective, especially in terms of his own adaptation to the world, the theories of this man who called himself a *genetic epistemologist* are presented.

Piaget's contributions are divided into three periods. In his first period, he became aware of and explored children's ideas about the physical world. He was particularly fascinated by children's misconceptions and their explanations for the world as they perceive it.

In his second period, he studied his own three children intensely and published three books based primarily on these observations. In his third phase, he continued to study children and adults to trace the path of development of their mental abilities.

Piaget's model for mental development stressed the interaction of heredity and environment. The child adapts to the environment by assimilating what is there into his existing mental structures and abilities, but he also accommodates by modifying his thinking to fit existing reality. It is through a complex interaction of experience with the necessary internal maturation that the child is able to invent or structure the nature of reality. The interaction of assimilation with accommodation is regulated through equilibration, a self-regulatory process.

Other important concepts of Piaget are conservation, the understanding and recognition of both constancy and change in the environment and the ability to distinguish change in substance from change in appearance; cognitive structures, the mental organizations or abilities that distinguish a child at one age from a child at another; mental operations, the cognitive structures in action that have the capability of being reversed mentally; schemes, which are organized patterns of behavior; and schemas, which are particular mental structures that are capable of generalization and transfer. This last term, *schema,* is similar to what other psychologists mean by the word *concept.*

With these basic terms in mind, Piaget's four stages of cognitive development are explored. The cognitive stage is a characteristic pattern of cognitive structures, mental operations, and schemas that are exhibited by children in a given age range. The order of these stages is the same for all children even though speed of progression through them may vary.

Stage 1, the sensorimotor stage, is described as the "conquest of objects." Exploring the world physically, learning to identify objects, grasping things, and finding out where self ends and the outside world begins are all common activities at this stage. It is in this stage that the infant develops a basic understanding of the world around him and forms habits of exploring and learning. This period continues through about age 2.

In stage 2, preoperational thought, from about ages 2 through 7, the young child is engaged in the conquest of the symbol. Learning to name objects, the beginning of language and vocabulary, and images such as "good" and "bad" develop during this stage. The newly acquired ability to use symbolization enables the child to use past experience to deal with the present and the future. The child is a moral realist and engages primarily in egocentric thought and speech.

In stage 3, concrete operations, logical reasoning patterns emerge. This takes place from about ages 7 to 11. The child can now do "in his head" what before he had to do by actually manipulating objects. The use of class inclusion, conservation, and serial ordering comes about in this stage. Although concrete operations represents a major breakthrough as the beginning of logical reasoning, it has limitations, one of which is that the child is still unable to study and be aware of his own reasoning process. The ability to center on more than one aspect of a situation develops during this stage and allows one to develop socialized thought and speech.

Stage 4, formal operations, is reached between the ages of 11 and 15, although many persons do not give evidence of this stage until later. In formal operations, true abstract thought is taking place, without the need to relate it to experience of the physical world. The student can reason with concepts, relationships, abstract properties, axioms, and theories. He can recognize reasonable hypotheses, see implicit assumptions, reason hypothetically and deductively, and verify the results of his reasoning, and what is especially important, he can review his own reasoning process critically. At this stage, he develops moral relativism in which he can consider motives in determining "good" or "bad" in addition to considering the rules or laws that may have been violated.

Examples of concrete and formal operational thought are presented, and a number of problems that illustrate formal reasoning are explored. Keep in mind also that the transition from one stage to the next is gradual, with overlapping, so that the child might be in a transitional stage. The model of the four stages of cognitive development and the detailed description of each type of thinking are important for the teacher to know in understanding and working with children of any age.

Study Questions

1. Piaget emphasized the importance of equilibration, the self-regulatory process whereby the child develops new conceptions of the world around him. Why is it important for teachers to understand this concept? Can you present some examples of situations in which the teacher utilizes this concept in planning a lesson?
2. Many high school students and even some adults do not exhibit thinking beyond Piaget's stage 3, concrete operations. What are the advantages for a student who is able to function at stage 4, formal operations? What sort of problems arise when the teacher cannot function beyond stage 3?
3. Piaget labeled the desire of American educators to learn how to "speed up" the child's progress through the four stages of reasoning the "American question." In what ways might it be an advantage for a child to progress more quickly than average to stage 4, formal operations? How might such rapid progress lead to some problems or difficulties?
4. The period of preoperational thought, from ages 2 to 7, is the period in which the child learns to use symbols, the beginning of language and vocabulary. How many examples can you think of that illustrate how a child from a deprived background would fall behind during this period?
5. How many ways can you specify in which a student who is well into formal operations has an advantage over a student who is still in concrete operations in a twelfth-grade science class?

References

Brainerd, C. *Piaget's Theory of Intelligence*. Englewood Cliffs, N.J.: Prentice-Hall, 1978.

Cross, K. P. *Accent on Learning*. San Francisco: Jossey-Bass, 1976.

Dale, L. S. "The Growth of Systematic Thinking: Replication and Analysis of Piaget's First Chemical Experiment," *Australian Journal of Psychology*, 22(3), December 1970, pp. 277–286.

Duckworth, E. "The Having of Wonderful Ideas." In M. Schwebel and J. Raph, eds. *Piaget in the Classroom*. New York: Basic Books, 1973, pp. 258–277.

Elkind, D. *Child Development and Education: A Piagetian Perspective*. New York: Oxford University Press, 1976.

——— *Children and Adolescents: Interpretive Essays on Jean Piaget*, 3rd ed. New York: Oxford University Press, 1981.

Englemann, S. "Teaching Formal Operations to Preschool Advantaged and Disadvantaged Children," *Ontario Journal of Educational Research*, 9(3), Spring 1967, pp. 193–207.

Graves, A. J. "Attainment of Mass, Weight, and Volume in Minimally Educated Adults," *Developmental Psychology*, 7(2), September 1972, p. 223.

Inhelder, B., and Piaget, J. *The Growth of Logical Thinking from Childhood to Adolescence*. New York: Basic Books, 1958.

Jackson, S. "The Growth of Logical Thinking in Normal and Subnormal Children," *British Journal of Educational Psychology*, 35(2), June 1965, pp. 255–258.

Kamii, C. "Pedagogical Principles Derived from Piaget's Theory: Relevance for Educational Practice," in M. Schwebel and J. Raph, eds. *Piaget in the Classroom*. New York: Basic Books, 1973, pp. 199–215.

Karplus, A. E., and Karplus, R. "Intellectual Development Beyond Elementary School I. Deductive Logic," *School Science and Mathematics*, 70(619), May 1970, pp. 398–406.

Killian, C. R. "Cognitive Development of College Freshmen," *Journal of Research in Science Teaching*, 16(4), July 1979, pp. 347–350.

Lawson, A. E., Carlson, E., Sullivan, F., Wilcox, R. S., and Wollman, W. *Biology Teaching and the Development of Reasoning*. Berkeley, Calif.: The Regents of the University of California, 1976.

Meyer, W. J., and Dusek, J. B. *Child Psychology: A Developmental Perspective*. Lexington, Mass.: D. C. Heath, 1979.

Piaget, J. *The Child's Conception of the World*. New York: Harcourt, Brace, 1929.

———— *Play, Dreams, and Imitation in Childhood*. New York: W. W. Norton, 1951.

———— *The Origins of Intelligence in the Child*. New York: International Universities Press, 1952.

———— *The Construction of Reality in the Child*. New York: Basic Books, 1954.

———— *The Moral Judgment of the Child*. New York: The Free Press, 1965.

Thornton, M. C., and Fuller, R. G. "How Do Students Solve Proportion Problems?" *Journal of Research in Science Teaching*, 18(4) July 1981, pp. 335–340.

Learning Principles: Conditioning Approaches

4

PREVIEW

Why is it important for teachers to study learning theories?

How is learning defined by psychologists?

What are some implications for teachers in the way that learning is defined by psychologists?

What is the relationship between learning and change in behavior?

What was the conditioning model presented by Pavlov?

What is the stimulus-response language of the conditioning model?

How did John Watson extend Pavlov's model?

What was the behaviorist movement headed by Watson?

What is classical conditioning?

How is classical conditioning a part of everyday life?

What is Thorndike's instrumental conditioning?

How does the law of effect explain problem-solving behavior?

What is the identical elements explanation of transfer?

What was Thorndike's contribution to progressive education?

What is B. F. Skinner's operant conditioning model?

How is behavior shaped by its results?

What is the role of reinforcement in learning?

What was Skinner's contribution to teaching machines and programmed instruction?

What are Skinner's criticisms of teaching in the schools?

How would a teacher proceed from Skinner's operant conditioning point of view?

What are the advantages of positive reinforcement?

When does operant conditioning work best?

What are the shortcomings of the operant conditioning approach?

"Why should we need a chapter on learning? After all, all teachers know what learning is, that's their job." This point of view might sound reasonable, since this *is* the stuff of which a teacher's job is made, what he or she is paid to do. In fact, "Talking about teaching without mentioning learning is like talking about farming without mentioning crops."

Even though the teacher has spent many hours fostering learning, and probably has considerable insight into the process, it is still difficult to present a precise definition of learning. And when asked, teachers often respond with phrases such as "acquiring knowledge," "solving problems," "increasing insight," "improving one's skills," or "coping with the environment." None of these captures the meaning of the construct as studied by psychologists.

A Definition of Learning

Although psychologists disagree on many details, they do agree on the basic definition: *learning is a change in behavior.* If psychology is the science that studies behavior, then learning is the area of psychology that focuses on change in behavior. But do we mean *all* changes in behavior? No, because we know that some changes in behavior can be accounted for on the basis of growth and development, or maturation, or physical injury. So we must add to our definition the qualification that we are referring to changes in behavior that result from practice or experience. We must also point out that we do not mean purely temporary or transitional changes, but that we mean changes with some degree of permanence, some ability to last. When we tie these ideas together, we have a more complete definition of learning as *a retainable change in behavior resulting from practice or experience.* Note that this definition says nothing about the behavior change being good or bad—any type of change in behavior that results from practice or experience fits our definition. Students learn useless, maladaptive, or "wrong" behaviors as well as right ones; students learn many other responses in addition to or instead of what the teacher wants them to learn.

We note also that there is nothing in the definition that limits it to intellectual or "book learning," or what the psychologist calls the "cognitive domain." We learn attitudes, emotions, feelings, motor skills, and phobias as well as facts, concepts, and principles. Learning thus takes on a sort of universal quality in that it refers to *any* change in behavior resulting from practice or experience. The idea that "you are what you have learned to be" takes on real meaning here, since it is difficult to see any area of human behavior that is not affected by learning as we have defined it. The child learns not only that 2 + 2 = 4, but also that he hates school, likes the girl next to him, is smart in math, knows how to make spitballs, knows how to get away with pranks, and knows shortcuts for learning arithmetic faster.

An important aspect of this definition is that it *does* insist on *change in behavior* as evidence that learning has taken place. The teacher cannot assume that students have learned just because a good presentation has been made. The teacher cannot even assume that students have learned because they have answered correctly on a test, since learning implies change in behavior. *The teacher cannot really say that learning has taken place unless there is evidence that behavior has changed as a result of instruction.* If behavior after an instructional experience can be shown to be different, in some relatively permanent fashion, from what it was before instruction took place, then learning took place as a result of teaching. An examination of teaching practices indicates that these requirements are not often satisfied; teachers seldom have pretests to compare with posttests to see how much student behavior has changed, and they seldom have proof when behavior does change that is resulted from their teaching.

Some Discrepancies

Now that we have defined learning and explained some of the details of our definition, we must confuse the issue by pointing out that learning is actually somewhat more complex than our definition. Psychologists do not *really* believe that learning is a "change in behavior" any more than they believe that anxiety is a deflection of the needle on a lie detector. Words such as *learning, anxiety, fear,* and *motivation* are hypothetical constructs, words invented by psychologists to describe events that take place inside a person. Nobody has ever really seen learning take place; they have seen behavior change and have used the word *learning* to describe it. They have *inferred* that learning has taken place by observing the *behavior change* that is evidence of this learning in the same way that we infer that someone is anxious when we observe that the individual paces the floor, bites his or her nails, and speaks in a shaky voice.

Thus we have defined learning in terms of the conditions under which we infer that it has taken place. Table 4.1 illustrates what is meant. In this

	A	B	C
Table 4.1 *Change in Behavior**	Antecedent conditions (the "before" behavior)	The experimental condition (practice or experience, instruction)	Consequent conditions (the "after" behavior)
	Example: Child cannot tie his shoe.	Example: You deliver a brilliant lecture on hand-eye coordination.	Example: Child can now tie his shoe!

*The experimental paradigm that illustrates learning. If behavior changes from A to C as a result of B, we infer that learning has taken place inside the organism.

simple paradigm, we are measuring behavior, then exposing the organism to some practice or experience, then measuring behavior again. If the experiment is well controlled and we can see that behavior changed from A to C, then we can infer that learning has taken place. The word *learning* is the hypothetical construct used as the label for all types of changes in behavior that fit this paradigm. Most psychologists would agree that something takes place inside the organism, that there is a chemical change in the brain that someday may be measured and understood to account for learning. But at present, the psychologist must limit the definition to that which he or she can observe, overt behavior.

Another discrepancy in our definition concerns the insistence on change in behavior as evidence of learning. Although this is the usual definition, it does not satisfy all psychologists, for a number of reasons. As we see in the next chapter, some psychologists stress the fact that learning is a change in how we see things, and they use phrases such as *change in disposition* rather than *change in behavior.* The discrepancy here goes beyond the question of what we infer; it concerns the claim that learning may take place without change in behavior and that change in behavior is not always evidence that learning has taken place.

Pavlov and the Conditioning Model

The basic language of psychology in the United States since the early 1900s has been the language of stimulus-response. This vocabulary stems from the classical conditioning model that was developed by Ivan Pavlov in Russia (1927). By pairing a buzzer with food, Pavlov demonstrated that a dog could be conditioned to salivate automatically when the buzzer was sounded. Pavlov called the food the *unconditioned stimulus* and the dog's salivating at the sight of food the *unconditioned response.* This was because salivating at the sight of the food was already a part of the dog's behavior. The reason that Pavlov called the buzzer the *conditioned stimulus* is that the buzzer did *not* cause salivation at the start of the experiment—the dog was being conditioned to salivate to the buzzer.

WHICH STUDENT HAD ACTUALLY LEARNED?

Consider the case of Frank and Elmer. Both boys had been placed in the remedial English class after scoring low on the English abilities test. During the course of the semester, Frank's behavior definitely changed. Although shy and retiring at first, he began to raise his hand and join discussions more and more as the semester unfolded. His frown changed to a smile, and he was one of the most involved and active students in the class after two months had passed. He paid attention, raised his hand, asked and answered questions, laughed at jokes, and in general was a pleasure to have around.

Elmer, on the other hand, showed no such changes in his behavior. He was shy and retiring, just like Frank, only he stayed that way. His look was generally one of sullenness, and he appeared to be unhappy throughout the course. His general glumness led the teacher to conclude that he must be learning little if anything in this remedial class.

But the results of the final exam presented a different picture. Frank scored 64 on the exam, right in the middle of the "D's." This surprised the teacher, who had thought that Frank must be doing well because of the change she had seen in his attention and participation in class. Meanwhile, Elmer scored 79 on the exam, a good solid "B." This also surprised the teacher, as she had concluded from the absence of change in his classroom behavior that Elmer was learning very little. Now, the question arises: Who had learned the most? Was it Frank, whose classroom behavior had changed remarkably, or was it Elmer, who had shown little change in classroom behavior? If the desired change in behavior were an increase in the score on the English test, we would have to say that Elmer had learned the most, since his score had shown a dramatic upward leap.

In this example, what one concludes depends on what type of change in behavior is desired. If attention and class participation is desired, then Frank clearly learned the most, but if a high test score is desired, it was Elmer who had shown the greatest change. Another interpretation was that Elmer had learned a lot, even though there was little change in his observable behavior, while Frank had learned very little, even though there was a dramatic change in his classroom behavior. It is often difficult to tell who is listening most carefully and getting the most out of classroom discussions.

Pavlov's model described learning as a gradual conditioning process, with stimulus-response (S-R) bonds built up through contiguity (meaning "close to" or "together") and repetition. The rationale behind this model is simple. Psychologists can only observe events that happen in the environment ("*stimuli*"), the behavior of the organism (*responses*), and the fact that behavior changes as a result of the interaction of the individual with his or her environment (*conditioning*). The psychologist cannot see inside a person's mind; cannot observe thoughts, feeling, insights, attitudes; and should be very careful about making inferences about things that cannot be observed. Pavlov's conditioning model is an objective, clear-cut description of observable behavior.

A Closer Look at the Conditioned Response

Imagine that you are helping Pavlov in his lab. You see a dog making the automatic or reflex response of salivating at the sight of food. You are not teaching him this response—it is already built in, so there is no need to condition it. This explains why it is called the *unconditioned response*, and the food the *unconditioned stimulus*, because this S-R association is already there: food elicits salivation *unconditionally*.

But what about the dog's salivating at the sound of the buzzer? It did *not* do this at the start of the experiment; we had to teach the dog to do this. How? By presenting the buzzer along with the food, of course. This causes the buzzer, which was originally a neutral stimulus, to take on the power of the food and elicit the "reflex"-type response of salivation. You have conditioned the dog to salivate at the mere sound of a buzzer, which explains why the buzzer is called the *conditioned stimulus* and salivation to the bell the *conditioned response.*

When Pavlov presented the buzzer repeatedly, without any food present, and the dog's salivation to the sound of the buzzer gradually faded out, Pavlov called this "extinction," since the conditioned response was being extinguished. Pavlov went on to develop various *laws of classical conditioning* that describe how responses are conditioned, strengthened, weakened, and extinguished and the effects of such variables as repetition, intensity of stimuli, interval between conditioned stimulus and unconditioned stimulus, and generalization to other stimuli.

The procedure described works also for conditioning a dog to withdraw its paw to the sound of a bell by pairing the bell with an electric shock or a human to blink his or her eye at a certain word by pairing it with an air puff. In each case, we see just two essential ingredients: contiguity and repetition. Notice that no concepts of reward, punishment, goal, intent, awareness, imitation, are proposed. This makes the classical conditioning model extremely simple. In paraphrasing, "you learn to associate what you do with whatever stimuli are present at the time, and repeating it strengthens the associations."

John Watson and "So What?"

All this may not seem to have much to do with youngsters or with school. But John Watson came along in the early 1900s and saw Pavlov's model as highly significant. He claimed that it explained not only how dogs learned to salivate or humans to blink their eyes but that it explained *all* learning. And since psychology until then had been so concerned with intangibles such as thoughts and feelings, he saw this as a major break-

THE HAZARDS OF LISTENING TO THE RADIO

Sometimes an expectant mother experiences what is called "morning sickness." Because of the change in metabolism and hormone imbalances, feelings of nausea and extreme discomfort are the major symptoms. In some women, these feelings take place any time of the day, while others experience it just in the morning. Jane had severe symptoms of morning sickness that lasted until an hour or so after breakfast.

Many months after giving birth to her first child, and long after the morning sickness had been forgotten, Jane was listening to the radio one afternoon and realized that she felt nauseated and uncomfortable. She recognized the symptoms of morning sickness but could not understand what was causing these symptoms. After three days in a row with these symptoms appearing, she consulted her doctor. Tests showed that she was definitely *not* pregnant, and her doctor suggested that she examine closely what she was doing just before these symptoms appeared.

At first, Jane could come up with nothing, until one day, as she sat listening to the radio, it dawned on her that the program she was listening to was the "Mary Merryfield" show. This was a program in which a monologue on housekeeping tips, cooking hints, and various thoughts for the day were delivered by an enthusiastic announcer named Mary Merryfield. Jane realized that the symptoms appeared each day when she listened to this radio broadcast. Yet she could think of no reason why the show had this effect; it was certainly a trivial stimulus, with nothing nauseous or upsetting about it, and yet here were the familiar symptoms of morning sickness each time she listened to this show.

Finally, it occurred to Jane that it was the Mary Merryfield show that she had listened to every morning in the early stages of her pregnancy. She had developed an association between a stimulus—the voice of Mary Merryfield—and a response that occurred in the presence of that stimulus—the morning sickness. Without any real cause and effect relationship, still the two had become associated through classical conditioning. Long after there was any real reason to have these feelings, they occurred as a result of classical conditioning, the voice of Mary Merryfield having become associated with the response of nausea and discomfort. If she would continue to listen to this show every day for a short period, the response would probably extinguish eventually, since the real unconditioned stimulus of hormone and metabolism imbalance was no longer present. (Presentation of the conditioned stimulus without the unconditioned stimulus should lead to extinction.) In this case, however, Jane simply stopped listening to Mary Merryfield. Jane had been the victim of accidental classical conditioning.

through. Psychology now had a scientific, measurable, observable model to allow it to join the ranks of the physical sciences. The movement that Watson (1925) spawned was called *behaviorism* (he is still called the father of this movement today), and its basic tenet was that psychologists should study only what could be defined and measured operationally.

Watson went on to claim that complex skills such as walking, running, and kicking a ball were chains of stimulus-response connections, learned in the same classical conditioning fashion as learning to salivate. He also claimed that talking and singing were learned this way and that, in fact everything, even thinking, could be analyzed as fitting the laws of classical conditioning.

"Give Me Ten Healthy Infants . . ."

The import of Watson's ideas was not lost on the educators of his time. If everything a person did, even the hallowed act of thinking, is a result of conditioning, then the school had better learn how to do this! But another aspect of Watson's work had an even greater impact—the claim that *all* human traits and characteristics were a result of conditioning. Watson patently rejected the emphasis on heredity in explaining human characteristics and instead placed it all on environment. He even boasted that, if he were given ten healthy infants and allowed complete control over their environments, he could make any one of them a baker, banker, thief, carpenter, you name it.

Watson and Li'l Albert

A famous experiment designed to show how everyday emotional behavior follows the laws of classical conditioning involved an 11-month-old child in a hospital. Watson received permission to use Little Albert as a subject, and the experiment went something like this.

Li'l Albert was sitting on the floor, apparently contented and happy. A white laboratory rat (actually a cute, friendly little creature) was placed on the floor in front of him. Just as Albert smiled and reached toward the rat, a loud gong just behind Albert was struck. Albert jumped about a foot and started crying.

You can see that the gong was the unconditioned stimulus (US) eliciting an automatic startle response (UR) as it would to anyone. The rat, on the other hand, was the conditioned stimulus (CS), since it was *not* the original source of any startle or fear response, and Albert had been conditioned so that the rat now elicited the same fear response (CR) as the gong. In other words, Albert learned through a simple classical conditioning process, with contiguity and repetition as the key ingredients.

Watson then went on with Li'l Albert to show how transfer or generalization takes place. A rabbit was placed in front of Albert, and he screwed up his face and cried, but *not* as much as he had for the rat. Then a dog, then a white scarf, and finally some Santa Claus whiskers were presented to Albert. The fear that Albert had associated with the rat generalized to these other stimuli, but only in relation to the similarity of each stimulus to the original conditioned stimulus, that is, the rat. Watson noted that this illustrated how transfer is a function of the similarity of the original conditioned stimulus to the stimulus in the transfer situation; for example, the rabbit aroused more fear than the scarf because the rabbit was more similar to the rat.

Classical Conditioning in Everyday Life

If you are thinking that classical conditioning went the way of hooped skirts and the passenger pigeon, you are wrong. This simple model and the laws connected with it are still useful in explaining certain types of learning in everyday life today. Let us look at just a few examples.

Emotional Learning

What is your reaction if an instructor says "Clear your desks; we're having a pop quiz"? Does your stomach tighten, heart accelerate, hands start shaking? Do you have a definite feeling of unease and discomfort? If so, you are exhibiting a common classical conditioning response known as *test anxiety.* You weren't born with it, and it didn't descend on you mysteriously or emerge somehow from your subconscious. And strangely enough, you probably do *not* habitually flunk tests or face some sort of dire consequences if you do score low. All that is necessary for a student to develop test anxiety is to experience the anxiety response in the presence of the test stimulus and the two become associated. Once the two are associated, then every time you face a test and respond with anxiety, the association is strengthened, regardless of how you score on the test. A psychologist could work with you to extinguish this response and replace it with other responses by simply applying the laws of conditioning.

The same laws apply to other emotions, be they positive (joy, affection, elation, pride, awe) or negative (jealousy, fear, anger, envy, guilt). All that is required is that the response happen in the presence of a certain stimulus on several occasions and you have learned a new association.

Phobias

A phobia is an exaggerated or unreasonable fear response to a relatively harmless object or situation. Although other explanations are possible, phobias can be explained and dealt with as simple classical conditioning phenomena. Take the case of canine phobia (fear of dogs). The person experiencing this phobia feels upset, shaky, cold, clammy, all sorts of fear symptoms at the mere sight of a dog. He may tell himself that this is ridiculous, but he cannot will these feelings to go away. If we examine his past, we may find that he has never even been bitten or attacked by

99

a dog. A therapist might use a step-by-step extinction procedure to cure this phobia, first getting the patient to talk about dogs until he is able to do this comfortably, then looking at pictures of dogs, then perhaps films of dogs, then real live dogs at a safe distance, and so on. Such a desensitization procedure might take months, but if the phobia is really bothering the person, it is worth it.

A type of phobia that you will see as a teacher, though far less often than the test phobia mentioned earlier, is a general fear and panic reaction to school or to certain stimuli connected with school. This phobia might manifest itself through various symptoms such as stomachaches, dizziness, and nausea as well as the usual fear symptoms. When approached from a simple conditioning point of view, the task is to extinguish or "unlearn" the anxiety responses and replace them with other responses. This cannot be done by punishing the child, even though it is tempting to conclude that he or she is faking or seeking attention.

Instead, the procedure is to reduce the source of the phobia to smaller, more manageable bits. One 10-year-old was so fearful of school that she suffered dizziness, nausea, and vomiting soon after entering the building. This had gradually become worse until the mere sight of school, or even the school bus pulling up in front of her house, would result in these symptoms, until finally just getting up in the morning was enough to produce nausea and vomiting.

After her parents had eliminated physical disease or emotional disorders as possible causes, the school psychologist decided to take a simple conditioning approach. The child was allowed to stay home from school in the morning, but each afternoon she was driven to school. At first, she was allowed to go to the art room and did not have to go to any classes, and the psychologist explained to her that the only requirement was that she spend one hour at school. After a week of this, she was doing well, and this requirement was extended to two hours each day. The next step was to require her to spend one hour of that time in her own classroom, and then two hours. The last step to be added was the school bus, at first just to go home, but eventually to ride it to school also. This 10-year-old still has some qualms about school, and she did not change magically into an outstanding student, but the fact that she could now go to school and spend the whole day there and even participate in the day's events without the previous severe symptoms was quite a change in what had looked like a hopeless case six weeks earlier.

Advertising and Conditioning

The scene begins with an athlete sprinting, then pole vaulting, then broad jumping. The crowd roars its approval. The announcer raves about how

Bruce Jenner has just won the Olympic decathlon—Bruce Jenner is number one, a champion.

The scene shifts immediately to the Jenner breakfast table. Bruce is commenting on all the hours of training that led up to his Olympic achievement—and on all the boxes of Wheaties he consumed. The scene ends with Jenner and Wheaties in center camera, both obviously winners.

Can you see the classical conditioning in the ad? No deep level of meaning, insight, or reasoning is involved. The ad is an example of simple classical conditioning in which the unconditioned response of pride, respect, and general "good feeling" generated by the unconditioned stimulus of an athlete winning the success, recognition, and acclaim is linked deliberately with the conditioned stimulus of Wheaties. Why? So that the same "good feeling" of pride and respect are elicited by the stimulus Wheaties; in other words, this reaction has become a conditioned response. This need not even be conscious to the viewer; the ad does not attempt to argue brilliantly and convince you through logical inference that Wheaties will help you win decathlon championships. It only hopes that, through simple contiguity and repetition, you will just happen to reach for Wheaties rather than brand X when you are grabbing some breakfast cereal in the supermarket (see Table 4.2).

Much of the advertising that bombards us in America can be seen as simple classical conditioning, with nothing deep or mysterious about it. Examples abound: ads attempting to link soft drinks with youth, fun, freedom; liquor ads that link sex, romance, and sophistication with a bottle of gin; the famous "Gusto" beer ads; deodorants and popularity; toothpaste and sex appeal; security and coffee; soap and social approval. All these examples can be analyzed for deeper meanings, unconscious human motivations, appeal to narcissism, and sexual symbolism. But a classical conditioning theorist would claim this is unnecessary; the laws of contiguity and repetition explain it all. Recall also that Pavlov was Russian and that the very effective propaganda techniques employed by the Soviet government today are based on Pavlov's model of classical conditioning. So, whether it is selling deodorant or selling national loyalty, classical conditioning works!

Table 4.2
Advertising as Classical
Conditioning*

Unconditioned stimulus ⟶	Unconditioned response
(Jenner winning decathlon; success, achievement, status, prestige)	(respect, pride, awe, general "good feeling")
Conditioned stimulus ⟶	Conditioned response
(box of Wheaties)	(respect, pride, awe, general "good feeling")

*The linking of the general good feeling described at the right to the stimulus Wheaties should, of course, lead to a tendency to buy Wheaties over brand X.

101

In spite of its usefulness, some conditioning theorists began to question simple classical conditioning as an explanation for *all* human behavior. What about response modification or the appearance of new responses? What about situations in which *no* stimulus can be identified as eliciting a response? What about problem solving, total complex situations; what about the results of behavior? Such questions as these led Edward Lee Thorndike to his proposal of another type of conditioning, in which the learner behaves within a total situation and learns on the basis of what *follows* his response. He saw learning more as a type of problem solving in which the learner tried a number of different responses until finally one was successful in solving the problem. The successful response was instrumental to success, so Thorndike called this type of trial and error learning "instrumental conditioning" (1932).

The Law of Effect

A famous example of Thorndike's work was his research on cats in puzzle boxes. If you place a cat, any cat, inside a cage and close the door, it will try to get out. If the latch on the door has a lever that will cause the door to swing open when pressed, we can observe the cat and see how it learns to escape from the cage. Thorndike reported that cats tried all sorts of things in attempting to get out, from scratching in the corners to running, jumping, or chewing on the bars. Eventually, however, the cat would push the lever and the door would open, and this was what it learned. If a string were used and pulling the string had the effect of opening the door, then the cat became an expert string puller. In fact, if Thorndike opened the door whenever the cat scratched its ear, then this is precisely what the cat learned: it would scratch its ear whenever it was placed in the cage. Thorndike concluded that the cat learned to do whatever led to a "satisfying state of affairs," and any behavior that did not lead to a satisfying state of affairs just faded out. This principle he called the *law of effect,* and it was central to his entire model of instrumental conditioning.

In Thorndike's analysis, the learner tries out various responses in a situation, until finding one that works, that is effective. One way this can be expressed, and in fact a powerful statement about human behavior, is that "You learn to do what gets results." Just as the family dog will sit and beg, "speak", shake hands, or whatever gets the result of a morsel of food, so also will the child cry, beg, say "please," or do whatever is effective in getting attention, money, dessert, or whatever result is desired.

How does the dog or the child (or perhaps we had better return to Thorndike's cats in the puzzle boxes) decide what behaviors are appropriate? Thorndike used the phrase "trial and error" to describe how the cat learned to pull a string and release the latch. Whatever the cat tried that didn't work (an "error") would just tend to fade away, whereas responses that got results would increase, until the cat became an expert at pulling the string, pressing the latch, or whatever resulted in its escape from the cage. Notice in this situation that *repetition* is important, just as it is in Pavlov's model, but that it is repetition of the *response* coupled with the *results* that is crucial to Thorndike. Cats, or children, learn to associate what they do with the results that follow, and the more they do it, the stronger the associations become.

From Puzzle Boxes to Progressive Education

Thorndike was also known for his theories and research on transfer, and clearly his "identical elements" model was one of the theoretical underpinnings in the progressive education movement. Thorndike challenged the "mental discipline" ideas that were predominant at that time and argued that transfer did not take place automatically as a result of the training of the mind "muscle" through rigorous discipline; rather, he asserted that transfer depended on the number of identical stimulus elements in the transfer situation as compared with the original learning situation. Thus, Thorndike reasoned that studying Latin, Greek, and the classics would *not* automatically cause the student to be a better thinker, nor would it automatically transfer to real life. His research on transfer in school led him to conclude that *any* subject might have considerable transfer if taught in a way that had many identical elements to the transfer situation, or it could have very little transfer if taught with few identical elements. The progressive education movement seized on this evidence that school must be as identical to real life as possible, and the more the classroom could be engineered to resemble the real world outside, the more effective the learning. Thus, the projects, field trips, and activity curriculum of the progressive school.

B. F. Skinner: Conditioning Today

Beyond its significant influence in the history of the behavioral sciences, conditioning theory is very much alive and well in the United States today. The most famous proponent of modern-day conditioning theory is B. F. Skinner of Harvard University, whose writings on operant conditioning, programmed instruction, and the experimental analysis of behavior have given him lofty status among psychologists and caused much controversy in other circles.

Essentially, Skinner (1968) has elaborated a detailed model that is a modern version of Thorndike's law of effect. Skinner says if we observe behavior closely, we see that the organism learns to do *whatever gets results.* In other words, if we make some reward (Skinner prefers the word "reinforcement") contingent upon certain behavior, then we observe that behavior increases in frequency and other behaviors that were *not* rewarded decrease. Thus, behavior is shaped or molded by what happens *after* the response, and Skinner calls this *reinforcement.* By controlling the reinforcement and by carefully reinforcing those responses that lead toward improvement while merely ignoring wrong responses, the experimenter can teach rats to press bars, pigeons to play Ping-Pong, or children to read.

Although starting with the same basic idea as Thorndike, Skinner added a systematic, step-by-step procedure for changing behavior. He calls this *operant conditioning.*

Operant conditioning can be distinguished from classical conditioning by looking at the behaviors being conditioned. In classical conditioning, a stimulus elicits a particular response from the individual; for example, in Pavlov's dogs, food brought about the automatic response of salivation. In operant conditioning, the behavior to be conditioned is generally an emitted one. That is, a stimulus does not cause the response. Rather, the stimulus is presented, one waits for the animal or person to demonstrate the desired behavior, and that behavior is then reinforced. Operant conditioning then depends upon the consequences of a response, whereas classical conditioning is based upon the association of a stimulus and response. As we have shown, classical conditioning is diagrammed as simple S-R. Operant conditioning, on the other hand, must be diagrammed as S-R reinforcement, since a response will only occur in the presence of a stimulus if the consequences tend to strengthen (reinforce) the response to the stimulus. According to Skinner, most learning, particularly at the higher levels, follows the operant conditioning model. The learner is in a complex situation, with many stimuli present, and emits a response rather than the stimulus eliciting one. The responses that are reinforced are then seen to increase, and responses that are not reinforced decrease, so that reinforcement becomes the major variable in behavioral change (note the similarity to Thorndike's law of effect).

The Importance of Reinforcement

A key to the success of Skinner's interpretation is found in his detailed analysis of the nature of reinforcement. There are four things that can happen after a learner makes a response: (1) some positive stimulus can follow the response (we might call this "reward"), (2) some negative stimulus can follow the response, (3) the response can lead to escape from or avoidance of some negative stimulus, or (4) the response can be followed by absolutely nothing.

The Premack Principle indicates that a desirable activity may be used as a reinforcer for a less desirable behavior. (Darrell Barry/Little Rock School District.)

Let us look at examples of each of these and also add the technical labels. A child who says "please," with the result that some cookies are awarded, is happy and says "please" next time and receives a piece of cake, is being conditioned through *positive reinforcement*. The response—"please"—is followed by a positive stimulus—cake, cookies—and the child is learning that in this type of situation the response "please" gets the desired results.

Positive reinforcement is illustrated in what has been labeled the *Premack principle* (Premack, 1965). Stated simply, this is the principle that a desired behavior (to the person doing the behaving) is made contingent on his or her first performing a less desired behavior. For instance, it may be that going out and playing at recess is a much desired behavior. If the child is required first to work the math problems for the day and is then allowed to go out to recess, then working math problems correctly becomes a more common behavior. The more desired behavior (playing during recess) has made the less desired behavior (doing math problems) a stronger behavior.

In another example, a boy is being held face down with his arm twisted painfully behind him. He finally quits struggling and says "uncle," at which point his arm is released. The next day he is attacked again, and says

105

"uncle" more quickly. He is learning to say "uncle" to escape from the pain this bully is inflicting upon him, and finally if he learns how to run fast enough or finds another path home, he may learn how to avoid the bully entirely. In either case, *negative reinforcement* is taking place, as responses are followed by escape from or avoidance of some negative consequence—in this case, pain. Note that both negative and positive reinforcement have the same effect: they both strengthen a response.

In still another situation, a 3-year-old takes a toy away from her baby sister, Sue, and her mother scolds her, takes the toy back, and slaps her hand. She soon learns not to take toys away from sister Sue, at least while mother is around, and *punishment* has taken place since a stimulus (scolding) has followed the response (toy snatching) and led to a decrease in the response. Note, however, that punishment is not punishment, in this interpretation, unless it does cause a decrease in response.

With both positive and negative reinforcement, a behavior is strengthened by its consequences. For punishment to occur, a behavior must be weakened by its consequences. If nothing follows a behavior, then it will not be strengthened. Rather, the probability of the behavior recurring will be weakened or will remain unchanged. Individuals who wish to bring about desirable behavior through reinforcement theory can make use of this principle. They can simply ignore undesired behavior while reinforcing desired behavior. The reinforcement will increase the probability that desired behavior will occur again, while the undesired behavior will remain unchanged. Such a process should lead to replacement of ignored undesirable behavior by reinforced desirable behavior.

How to Shape Behavior

Since the behavior that an operant conditioner wishes to reinforce must first be emitted, the conditioner must wait until the organism sees fit to respond appropriately. It is possible, of course, especially if the desired behavior is complex or out of the ordinary repertoire of the animal being conditioned, that the desired behavior might never occur spontaneously. In such cases, the operant conditioner may choose to build or shape the behavior by reinforcing successive approximations to it.

Skinner's prescriptions for shaping behavior can be seen in the famous Skinner box (Figure 4.1) as well as in the typical school example that follows. In the first instance, an albino rat is placed in an open-topped box with a little lever at one end. Just below the lever is a slot where pellets of rat food can be delivered. The trick is to teach the rat to press the bar with its right front paw. (The Skinner box is famous in experimental research in psychology.)

The box is used frequently in introductory courses in experimental psychology, with a student controlling the chute that releases the pellets and a rat learning to press the bar. The student drops a pellet (positive

WHY DOES LUCY KEEP MISBEHAVING?

Mrs. Smith, despite being a very busy person and on a tight schedule, tried to give Lucy the necessary love and affection while at the same time giving her the proper guidelines and discipline.

The first time the bridge group met at the Smith house, Lucy remained in the background for a while but then astounded the group by walking into the room and firing off several four-letter words. This raised some eyebrows and also led to Mrs. Smith taking Lucy out into the kitchen and earnestly explaining to her why she must not use such words.

The next week, Lucy again fired off several choice words for the bridge group, and her mother took her to her room and spanked her. A little while later, Lucy appeared in the room naked, swinging her wet diaper over her head. This broke up the entire group, and Mrs. Smith had quite a long talk with Lucy about this.

What Mrs. Smith failed to realize was that Lucy, being just a little child and having a very busy mother, had a strong desire to get attention from her mother. When behaving and doing as she was supposed to failed to lead to any attention, she resorted to other means, which *did* attain the desired attention. Her mother's attempts to punish her—verbally or physically—were actually serving as positive reinforcement. Lucy was getting the much desired attention each week by using four-letter words, toddling through the room naked, and performing any other activity she could devise.

The secret to this problem was for the mother to provide the desired attention *before* Lucy resorted to her desperation measures. Also, if Lucy did use a "cuss word" or try the naked routine, her mother should ignore such behavior completely.

reinforcement) when the rat faces the end of the box where the lever is and does nothing when the rat faces the other end. Before long, the rat faces the right end most of the time. The student then "raises the stakes" and drops a pellet only when the rat moves toward that end of the box.

The next step in reinforcing successive approximations or "shaping" behavior is to drop a pellet only when the rat is in some way touching or sniffing at the bar. The rat now pays increasing attention to the bar. The shaping continues in this fashion—reinforcing responses that gradually move in the right direction, ignoring other responses, shaping behavior through a series of successive approximations—until we see a rat that walks up to the bar, skillfully presses it with its right front paw, and munches the little pellet. Furthermore, it presses the bar now *without* the pellet being added and will continue to do so for quite some time.

Switch the scene to a child in school. Tammy is learning to play the clarinet in beginner's band. At first, her instructor shows approval if she holds the instrument approximately correctly and produces any sound at all. Gradually, however, the teacher raises the stakes and Tammy must learn to sit properly, form her lips and blow correctly, use the right fin-

Figure 4.1
Two examples of operant conditioning.

gerings, count accurately, breathe correctly, follow the dynamic signs, and so on. Although this is far more complex than the rat pressing the bar, Skinner maintains that the same laws apply. The instructor shows approval after Tammy does something right (positive reinforcement). The teacher also complains, nags, and stops the band at times for the same reason—to play it right, in tune, and in rhythm. If doing it right results in escape from the teacher's nagging and complaining, *negative reinforcement* is said to occur. At times, although he or she usually just ignores mistakes,

The pleasant sound of playing it right can become the reinforcer. (Bernie Weithorn/SIUC Photographic Service.)

the instructor will scold, frown, or even "tear his hair" at a particular violation to help to assure it won't occur next time (punishment). The other students also receive a boost when Tammy is praised which is called vicarious reinforcement (Bandura, 1969). A large part of the feedback—both positive and negative—that Tammy receives is built into the task; she can *hear* when it sounds good and when it sounds wrong, and as she progresses, the task becomes more and more self-reinforcing.

Teaching Machines and Programmed Learning

Skinner did not invent teaching machines and programmed instruction, but he added so much to both the rationale and the technology of these two related areas that his name is usually the first to come to mind when these terms are mentioned. A brief sample of a linear program, one that each student proceeds through in exactly the same manner, is given in Figure 4.2. Note the following characteristics of this program and how they illustrate operant conditioning or the shaping of behavior.

1. Material proceeds in small steps, moving gradually and sequentially toward goals of knowledge and understanding.
2. These small steps assure that the reader will make almost 100% correct responses.
3. Responses are followed by immediate feedback. This is usually in the form of positive reinforcement, since the response is almost always correct.
4. Prompts are used to help guarantee correct responses, but the answer is still produced freely or "emitted" by the learner.
5. Negative reinforcement or punishment is not used. Mistakes are corrected immediately when the student turns to the next frame.
6. The learner is participating actively, making frequent responses, as he or she learns primarily from positive reinforcement (i.e., experiences success).

Although some modern teaching machines are highly sophisticated and complex, they utilize the same basic components as the simple program just described. Small sequential steps, active participation, immediate feedback, numerous correct responses, all these factors tend to be a part of even the most sophisticated machine. To Skinner, these illustrate the laws of operant conditioning.

Skinner's Criticisms of Education

Unlike some psychologists, Skinner has been willing to write in detail about how his work applies to the public school classroom. His descriptions of just how to go about controlling and changing behavior in the

Figure 4.2
*Linear program.**

Directions: (1) Cover the answer portion of the page with a piece of paper or a marker. (2) After you have written your answer in the appropriate blank, slide the paper down to expose the correct answer. (3) Read each frame carefully. Easy frames lead to more advanced learnings.

11. Linguistics is the scientific study of language. Certain information from the scientific study of language or _____ is applicable to reading instruction.	**linguistics**
12. Phonology and phonetics, which are concerned with the study of speech sounds, are part of _____ study. Phonics refers to the application of information about the sounds of _____ to the teaching of reading. In reading, phonics refers to the use of knowledge about how _____ are represented by letters or letter combinations in written language to figure out unknown words. The English language does not have a completely predictable correspondence between sounds and written _____, thus making _____an incomplete word attack system.	**linguistic** **language** **sounds** **symbols** **phonics**
13. Orthography is the term used to refer to the writing system of a language. The writing system, or _____, of English is a complex one. English _____ is based on an alphabetic system.	**orthography** **orthography**
14. A phoneme is the smallest single unit of sound in the language which distinguishes one morpheme from another. For example, when the words *bit* and *sit* are spoken only the first phoneme is different. The spoken word *at* has two _____ while the spoken word *cat* has three _____.	**phonemes** **phonemes**

*From R. M. Wilson and M. Hall, *Programmed Word Attack for Teachers* (Columbus, Ohio: Charles E. Merrill, 1979), pp. vii, 3. Reprinted with permission.

schools have been an underlying influence in a set of techniques referred to as "behavior modification," which are described in Chapter 16.

Some of Skinner's operant conditioning ideas can be seen by looking at a few of his key criticisms of traditional education.

Too Much Aversive Stimulation

What is it that causes students to do all the things expected of them in school? (Most of the students, most of the time, that is.) Why do they arrive on time to classes, pay attention, do their homework, study for tests, work on projects, and cooperate and conform to myriad rules and demands? Skinner declares that far too often it is avoidance and escape conditioning (negative reinforcement) that governs these behaviors. What is it that students are trying to avoid or escape? The following quote from Skinner's *Technology of Teaching* gives some clues:

Ridicule (now largely verbalized, but once symbolized by the dunce cap or by forcing the student to sit facing a wall), scolding, sarcasm, criticism, incarceration (''being kept after school''), extra school or homework, the withdrawal of privileges, forced labor, ostracism, being put on silence, and fines—these are some of the devices which have permitted the teacher to spare the rod without spoiling the child. In some respects they are less objectionable than corporal punishment, but the pattern remains: the student spends a great part of his day doing things he does not want to do. [Skinner, 1968, p. 96]

One way in which to test this contention is to tell a group of students you are going to assign a term paper. What goes through *your* mind when such a project is mentioned? Are you overcome with positive feelings as you anticipate the rewards that are in store, the compliments, approval, high grade, and other positive reinforcers that may be forthcoming? Or do your heartbeats quicken and your innards tighten, in anticipation of all the negative consequences that you hope somehow to escape or avoid? Skinner argues that the vast majority of students have the latter reaction and that this is all too often the major ingredient in controlling and changing behavior in the traditional school. (Note also that we have not even

Teaching machines have increased greatly in capability as indicated by the PLATO system of the University of Illinois. (Bernie Weithorn/SIUC Photographic Service.)

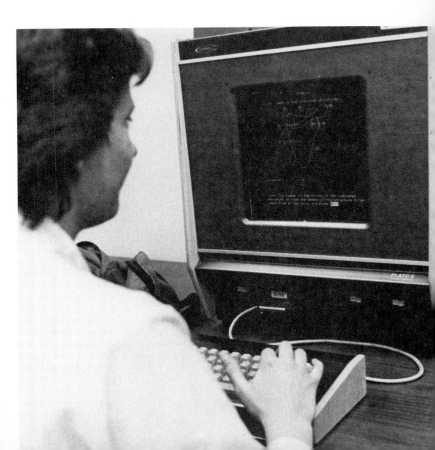

mentioned the obvious aversive stimulation of punishment, the purpose of which is to decrease certain behaviors. Without getting into a long technical argument, we can safely conclude that research indicates that punishment is *not* the safest, most effective, or most predictable way to change behavior.)

Skinner proposes the following test to see if you are an "aversive-control" type of teacher:

If a teacher is in any doubt about his own methods, he should ask himself a few questions. Do my students stop work immediately when I dismiss class? (If so, dismissal is obviously a release from a threat.) Do they welcome rather than regret vacations and unscheduled days of no school? Do I reward them for good behavior by excusing them from other assignments? Do I punish them by giving additional assignments? Do I frequently say "Pay attention," "Now remember," or otherwise gently "admonish them"? Do I find it necessary from time to time to "get tough" and threaten some form of punishment? [Skinner, 1968, pp. 96–97]

Infrequent Positive Reinforcement

The second major criticism of the schools that Skinner presents is closely related to the first. This is the complaint that true positive reinforcement is far too infrequent. Even when the student is *not* on the aversive stimulation merry-go-round, he or she seldom receives effective positive reinforcement. How often do you recall doing something in school that was followed by praise, acclaim, reward, approval, prizes, encouragement, recognition? Again, Skinner would guess that your answer is probably "not too often," and yet here is the one paradigm certified in so many studies as the safest, most predictable, effective, and durable way in which to change and control behavior.

Skinner agreed that positive reinforcement may be used so seldom because of the difficulty of defining or identifying reinforcers. For example, food may be a reinforcer to the hungry child but not to one who has just finished lunch. If one were to attempt to use food as a positive reinforcer in the classroom, the students would first have to be made hungry, which would raise ethical issues (Skinner, 1968). The awards, grades, and other incentives that the school has defined as reinforcers, Skinner argues, are contrived. In addition, not all students can get awards or high grades. Thus, you may reinforce some with these contrived reinforcers but what about the others?

Time Lag Between Behavior and Feedback

A third criticism of the schools concerns all three forms of feedback mentioned thus far: namely, positive reinforcement, negative reinforcement, and punishment. In all three cases, the feedback becomes *less* effective when there is a time lag between the behavior and the feedback. To be effective, with certain rare exceptions, feedback should follow behavior as immediately as possible.

When looking at simple situations, this generalization is easy to see. If the cow in the pasture touched the wire fence that it was to stay inside and then received a shock five minutes later, it would experience difficulty learning to avoid the fence. If a dog were rewarded for "shaking hands" by giving it a dog biscuit an hour later, hard telling what it would learn; probably it would learn whatever it did immediately before receiving the dog biscuit.

How much different is this from the mother who continues to nag long after the child has corrected an error? Or the teacher who returns a test two weeks after the class has taken it? Or the student who finds out that her solution was wrong three days after she has worked six pages of problems! You can guess Skinner's response in each case; the feedback is of little use because the time lag between the response and the feedback is too long.

There is no easy answer to the problem of providing feedback. However, by using such procedures as *vicarious reinforcement* (several students observing and reacting to reinforcement of *another* student) and *self-reinforcement* (either intrinsic to the task or involving a standard that has been internalized), immediate feedback can be provided in the classroom.

Absence of a Step-by-Step Sequence

Notice in operant conditioning how the learner proceeds in small, sequential steps as his or her behavior is gradually shaped, through a series of successive approximations, from the initial behavior to the particular skill being taught. Whether it is a pigeon pecking at a disc or a child learning to read, these small steps, with many correct responses and much reinforcement, are essential to learning.

In the traditional classroom, such a step-by-step sequence is usually missing. The teacher explains a problem, and a student does not understand one of the early points. But the student is not forced to make numerous responses as in a linear program, so he or she does not understand anything that follows and is even unsure of where he or she "missed the boat." The youngster will either remain confused and perhaps give up or, if he or she is lucky, will work it out independently and make a large leap to where the teacher is later. But the point is that some students are not so lucky and are easily lost or discouraged in the absence of a step-by-step sequence; even those who survive find the lack of such a sequence annoying and frustrating, to say nothing of the squandering of valuable time. Skinner sees effective and economical sequencing as an important part of the curriculum. As a result, he views the teaching machine and the linear program as effective pedagogical devices.

To summarize, the broad generalizations Skinner makes for teachers are (1) using positive reinforcement as much as possible, within practical limits, (2) at the same time, holding aversive stimulation (both negative reinforcement and punishment) to a minimum, (3) being sure that all

113

three of these—positive reinforcement, negative reinforcement, and punishment—follow the particular target behavior as immediately as possible, and (4) attempting to build a step-by-step sequence, with numerous responses and feedback, into everything you teach.

Teaching from Skinner's Operant Conditioning Approach

Upon studying a theory such as Skinner's operant conditioning theory, students usually ask, "Yes, but how can this be applied in the classroom?" In answer, we follow a teacher in a specific learning situation who is applying operant conditioning techniques in the classroom. The teacher described is a real teacher of a fifth grade class, but the reader should be able to extend the example, with appropriate modification, to any age level or subject.

Ms. Clark's class appears to be a bit disorganized, but upon closer inspection we see that this is really not the case. Students are working on a variety of tasks, some in groups, some individually. Ms. Clark moves around the room, answering questions, asking also, giving feedback, dispensing reinforcement. The class is indeed a very active class. Let us list the elements of operant conditioning that Ms. Clark is using.

Close Observation of Behavior. Ms. Clark knows all the students in the class and their present levels of performance. She identifies strengths and weaknesses and from this is able to decide just what the student is ready to tackle next. Without such close observation and awareness, the remaining steps in the conditioning process would not be possible.

Baselines and Target Behaviors. The first measure to be made in operant conditioning is called the *baseline*. In watching Sammy improve his math skills, Ms. Clark notes that he has difficulty with long division. He can divide a six-digit number, but he averages five and a half minutes on such a problem. He gets only 50% of such problems right and expresses anger or a desire to give up three times in each five-minute period. He crosses out or erases ten times in a five-minute period.

With such a baseline measure, Ms. Clark can work with Sammy and tell what kind of progress he is making. She can check periodically to monitor his speed, accuracy, frustration behaviors, and mistakes, and she can also set goals in these areas. A further payoff is that she can use such evidence to show Sammy that he is improving, since students often struggle along with the illusion that they are getting absolutely nowhere.

Starting with Available Behaviors. As we watch Ms. Clark, we note that different students are doing different things. One is working on a model, another is discussing a problem with another student, a third is reading, a fourth is writing an essay. In each case, Ms. Clark starts with where the child is, the present behaviors, and proceeds from there. If a child can barely write a sentence, then this is where she starts. If Joe's

Elementary teachers often employ the techniques of operant conditioning in small groups. (CEMREL, Inc.)

reading is at the second grade level, even though he is in fifth grade, she does *not* berate him for being behind, nor does she force him to read material at which he consistently fails. She starts with material at his level, rewards him for success, gradually increases the difficulty of the material, and works on up to fifth grade level.

Identifying Potential Reinforcers. One of the toughest problems in applying operant conditioning is to identify just what will be reinforcing for the child or group. The saying "different strokes for different folks" applies here, as what is an effective reinforcer for one child may not affect the next and might even have a negative effect on the third child. As we watch Ms. Clark, we notice that she reinforces different children in different ways; one gets a smile, the next a nod, the next a strong word of encouragement, and the next a hug. We also notice that she often uses the group as a reinforcer by announcing a child's achievement or by having the children show what they have done. This also serves as vicarious reinforcement, as other children put themselves in the place of the one being reinforced and feel good about it also. To do all this, Ms. Clark must know and understand quite a bit about each of the children she is teaching, as well as the characteristics of that age level in general.

The Importance of Success. One of the most potent of all reinforcers is the importance of success itself. Succeeding at any task, so long as one has knowledge of success, spurs the learner to attempting further tasks, as well as being useful information and making one feel good. Success begets success. Some psychologists feel that this is the most important of all possible reinforcers and that many of the problems in school could be solved if the children could be led through successful behavior. However, it must be success on a task of some importance to the student, the student must be aware of the success, and the student must attribute the success to his or her own efforts and not see it as just an accident or a ploy. The problem is to bring about a *perception* of success. We note that Ms. Clark is pointing out to her students constantly where each is making progress, where they have done something nice, just where improvement has taken place, even to the point of comparing it with past papers or tapes or other evidence.

Importance of Immediate Feedback. In dispensing feedback, Ms. Clark does so as soon as possible after any behavior. If Johnny has finally spelled a troublesome word correctly, he needs to know this *right now,* not next week or even ten minutes from now. Papers or projects are hung on the wall or demonstrated to the class immediately, and where it is important to be aware of a mistake, she points it out right now. Of course, she cannot be all places at once, but immediate feedback is built into many of the materials she is using, and all her students are being taught to dispense immediate reinforcement constantly to the learner.

Advantages of Positive Reinforcement. The general climate of Ms. Clark's class is very positive, with much praise, encouragement, and support and very little anxiety, blame, or criticism. This is because positive reinforcement has been found to be the safest way to change behavior, the most predictable, with the fewest side effects, and it is therefore recommended over negative reinforcement or punishment. This does *not* mean that negative reinforcement or punishment are "outlawed," however, as this would probably be impossible as well as unwarranted, but simply that positive reinforcement should be emphasized and the other two used sparingly. This is quite a change from the typical class in which much of the behavior is based on avoidance of or escape from painful results. Positive reinforcement encourages achievement motivation; negative reinforcement and punishment foster failure and avoidance motivation. The differences between these two types of motivation, and the reasons achievement motivation is better, are explored in Chapter 8.

Probably the most important side effect of negative reinforcement and punishment is that they teach students to avoid sticking their neck out, to "play it safe," to do whatever is necessary to *avoid* the painful consequences that are actually controlling behavior. Such cautious and safe behavior is not conducive to the exploration and risk taking that learning requires. The side effects of negative reinforcers and punishment are mainly

Teachers provide positive reinforcement in many different ways. (Darrell Barry/Little Rock School District.)

in the area of feelings, attitudes, and beliefs. Ms. Clark does not believe in controlling students in ways that foster negative feeling and attitudes, and she finds that most inappropriate behaviors disappear on their own if ignored.

Reinforcement Schedule. Another thing we notice in observing Ms. Clark is that she seems to vary the amount of reinforcement. When a student is starting a task, she provides a lot of reinforcement, sometimes appearing to reinforce every response—almost to the point of overdoing it. But as the student progresses, she provides less and less reinforcement, until as the student becomes proficient at the task, she rarely reinforces the performance. Some students seem to require more reinforcement than do others, and this she attempts to provide, but the general idea seems to be that of providing a lot of reinforcement in the early stages of learning and then tapering off as the learner progresses.

We also notice, in relation to the reinforcement schedule, that Ms. Clark tries to get students to proceed in small steps and to follow a smooth, step-by-step sequence as they learn a skill. All these techniques are in keeping with research findings on operant conditioning. She is shaping

117

behavior through a series of successive approximations and fading the reinforcement as the learning progresses.

The Need for an Active Classroom. Of all the things that stand out in Ms. Clark's classroom, none is more obvious than the fact that her class is very active. Children are doing things all the time in her room, and there are often so many different things going on at once that we marvel at how she can keep track of things. The activity is not chaos, however; it is merely the necessary activity for children to learn. To give positive reinforcements to good responses, there must be responses to begin with. Ms. Clark could hardly follow an operant conditioning model if the class sat in straight rows, listening silently, unless this is the only response she believes is appropriate in the classroom.

In all, we must conclude that Ms. Clark's class is a happy place. Students are enjoying themselves in her class, and they are all pursuing things that interest them. She does not seem to be forcing anyone to learn; instead the students really appear to do it on their own. The children obviously like her, but even more important, they like each other, and they like themselves. She has developed a positive learning environment built on operant conditioning principles.

Some Guidelines as to When Operant Conditioning Works Best

Although the operant conditioning techniques advocated by Skinner are effective when used appropriately, they are *not* the best techniques for all educational problems. As is true for any tool, they are useful for certain jobs, but not for others. First, operant conditioning appears to work best in certain content areas, but not as well in others. The linear programs that follow Skinner's guidelines have worked well in math, logic, the physical sciences, and to some extent the social sciences, as evidenced by the large number of programmed materials and textbooks in these areas, but we find relatively few such materials in the humanities, fine arts, philosophy, and the more complex aspects of the social sciences.

Operant conditioning techniques work best at the lower levels of cognitive functioning (i.e., the learning of vocabulary, facts, knowledge, and understanding of a set body of material). Math, the physical sciences, logic, and parts of the social sciences are loaded with such materials, which often have to be internalized in a sequential fashion before progressing to a higher level. Operant conditioning, as illustrated in Figure 4.2, does a good job of presenting such factual material in logical order. But when it comes to tasks higher up in the hierarchy, tasks such as applying, analyzing, synthesizing, judging values, and creative responses, operant conditioning is less appropriate. It is probably the type of cognitive task more than the field of study that determines this, and operant conditioning techniques

Psychomotor skills such as tying a shoe can be shaped through the use of positive reinforcement. (Darrell Barry/ Little Rock School District.)

are quite appropriate for teaching vocabulary, specific knowledge, and basic concepts in any field.

Operant conditioning also works quite well in the area of psychomotor learning. Whether you are learning to ski, or to knit, or to play a trombone, the general approach of shaping behavior through selective reinforcement seems to work quite well. It works well in shaping social behavior also, in terms of learning to conform to rules and adapt to situations, but it certainly is questionable as to whether operant conditioning can develop novel social behavior.

One area in which Skinner's ideas have been rejected pretty clearly is that of language, for it appears that the operant conditioning model falls far short of explaining the complexities of either spoken or written language. It is also of limited use in explaining moral or ethical behavior.

There are really no age limitations for the application of operant conditioning, but it appears to be more useful at younger age levels. This is because more vocabulary, knowledge, and facts are necessary in the early stages of learning a discipline before the student is ready to apply, analyze, synthesize, extend, and create in a more complex way. However, so much needs to be learned in terms of facts and sequential knowledge at any age level that it hardly makes sense to limit it based on age. Whether you are 4 or 40, operant conditioning works if it is done appropriately for the right type of learning task. In summary, if you are trying to learn the basic facts about a new and involved law just passed by Congress, then operant conditioning might be appropriate. But if you are trying to exchange views and insights to appreciate the reactions of various groups to such a law, some less structured approach may make more sense.

Criticisms of the Operant Conditioning Approach

Operant conditioning seems to operate from a philosophy that environment determines behavior, that people do not really have freedom of choice, that behavior can be understood as a machine, and that all behavior follows conditioning rules. This philosophy is seen by critics as dehumanizing. Skinner is accused of overlooking motivation from within, of ignoring individual differences, of espousing a materialistic philosophy, of stressing technology, and of encouraging manipulation of people. Some critics have reacted so strongly to Skinner's writings that they have seen him as advocating something truly evil, as somehow leading to the totalitarian state.

It is not really necessary to go into a lengthy exploration of these criticisms here, since this book's focus is on psychology applied to teaching, not on philosophy. It is important to note, however, that operant conditioning is a *tool,* and the question of whether a tool is good or bad depends on its use. If you as a teacher use operant conditioning to create a favorable learning environment and further worthy goals of teaching, then you are making good use of the tool. On the other hand, if your use of operant conditioning techniques stifles children's personalities, encourages blind conformity, creates young hedonists, causes increased dependence, or undermines the uniqueness and dignity of each individual, then you are misusing this tool. As with any potentially powerful tool, teachers must be careful how they use it and continually re-examine their goals, techniques, and results.

Summary

Learning is defined as change in behavior, capable of being retained, resulting from practice or experience, and not attributable to other causes. This definition is both broad and limiting. The teacher must be aware of all the different types of change in behavior that are taking place in the classroom but at the same time cannot really say that learning has taken place in the class unless there is evidence that behavior has changed as a result of instruction.

The origins of the conditioning model are traced to Pavlov at the turn of the century. Pavlov's famous experiments with dogs illustrated classical conditioning in which a stimulus and response become associated with each other through contiguity and repetition. The language of this model became the basic language of psychology in America, with a strong behaviorist orientation clear to the present. John Watson extended Pavlov's model to cover virtually all human behavior, as illustrated in his experiment with Little Albert. This demonstration, in which an infant was conditioned to fear a white rat in simple classical conditioning fashion, illustrates how everyday emotional responses are conditioned classically and how these responses generalize to other situations.

Classical conditioning is still a useful model for explaining behavior today, as evidenced in emotional responses. We learn fear, anger, jealousy, envy, and anxiety, not necessarily by making a response that is punished, but often just by making the particular response in the presence of a stimulus and associating the two. Phobias can be explained in this fashion, and a simple classical conditioning approach can be used to unlearn a phobia. A common classical conditioning response is test anxiety. Classical conditioning is also illustrated in much of the advertising that we see in newspapers and magazines and on television.

With the work of E. L. Thorndike, another type of conditioning was illustrated. Thorndike's cats attempting to escape from puzzle boxes were engaged in trial and error learning, a type of problem solving in which learning was based on the results of what they did. If the cat's pulling the string was instrumental in getting the door to open so it could escape, then it would learn to pull the string. If the latch would not open unless the cat scratched its ear, the cat would stop pulling the string and eventually learn to scratch its ear and escape from the box.

Thorndike's basic law—that the learner will learn to do whatever leads to a satisfying state of affairs—is called the law of effect. In Thorndike's model, repetition and reward were the two key ingredients in learning. He also explained transfer through an identical elements model that was one of the theories used in progressive education. This approach suggested that school learning be made as similar to life outside the classroom as possible to maximize transfer.

B. F. Skinner and his operant conditioning represent a modern-day elaboration of Thorndike's law of effect. In Skinner's explanation, one learns to do what gets results, what pays off. Learning is governed by its consequences. The key concept in Skinner's model is the concept of reinforcement. If a desired result is made contingent upon a particular behavior, then we observe that behavior increase in frequency, while other behaviors that were not reinforced decrease.

What Skinner added to Thorndike's law of effect was a detailed terminology and a systematic step-by-step system for controlling and changing behavior. His ideas were adapted to the teaching machine and programmed instruction and to the system of behavior modification that had been applied to a wide variety of institutional and therapeutic settings. Skinner believes that linear programming illustrates all the steps in operant conditioning in the shaping of behavior.

Skinner has written extensively about education and teaching, and his criticisms of the schools reflect several major themes: (1) too much aversive stimulation, (2) the infrequency of positive reinforcement, (3) the time lag between behavior and feedback, and (4) the absence of a step-by-step sequence.

121

*Study
Questions*

1. Suppose that you are a third grade teacher and that you have adopted the definition of learning as presented in this chapter. How many changes in behavior can you list that you would look for in relation to the goal of "good citizenship"? What if you wanted evidence that the students had developed better attitudes about personal hygiene?
2. A true behaviorist would insist that no learning has taken place unless it is evidenced by change in behavior. Can you think of several examples in which learning may have taken place even though no change in behavior is apparent? How about instances in which there is an observed change in behavior but no true learning has taken place?
3. Dr. Reilly has a dog that will sit, speak, shake hands, roll over, and climb the ladder and slide down the slide when commanded to do so. Describe, from a classical conditioning point of view, the step-by-step sequence of events that took place in the dog learning these tricks.
4. Select several of your favorite ads from newspaper or television commercials and identify the different components in each ad that explain it from a classical conditioning point of view. Can you explain these same ads from the point of view of Thorndike's law of effect or in Skinner's operant conditioning terminology?
5. Take the subject that you plan to teach as an example. In what ways could Skinner's operant conditioning model be of use to you in teaching your subject? What disadvantages do you see in teaching your subject from Skinner's point of view?
6. How many ways can you think of in which aversive stimulation was used on you as a student? How did you react to this stimulation? What were the results? Can you think of positive ways in which the teacher *could* have proceeded in each instance?

References

Bandura, A. *Principles of Behavior Modification.* New York: Holt, Rinehart and Winston, 1969.

Pavlov, I. P. *Conditioned Reflexes: An Investigation of the Physiological Activity of the Cerebral Cortex.* London: Oxford University Press, 1927.

Premack, D. "Reinforcement Theory." In D. Levine, ed. *Nebraska Symposium on Motivation: 1965.* Lincoln, Neb.: University of Nebraska Press, 1965, pp. 123–180.

Skinner, B. F. *The Technology of Teaching.* New York: Appleton-Century-Crofts, 1968.

Thorndike, E. L. *The Fundamentals of Learning.* New York: Teachers College, Columbia University, 1932.

Watson, J. B. *Behaviorism.* New York: W. W. Norton, 1925.

Wilson, R. M., and Hall, M. *Programmed Word Attack for Teachers.* Columbus, Ohio: Charles E. Merrill, 1979.

Learning Principles: Cognitive Approaches

5

PREVIEW

What is the cognitive or perceptual model for explaining learning?

What was Wertheimer's classical Gestalt model?

What did Kohler find in studying problem solving in apes?

What is the importance of understanding and relationships?

What are the basic principles of Lewin's field theory?

Why are the learner's purpose and the present situation important in learning?

What sort of changes in perception take place in learning in the cognitive model?

What was Bruner's contribution to understanding school learning?

What is meant by intuitive learning?

Why is it important to understand the underlying principles in studying a subject?

What is the nature of meaningful discovery learning?

Why is relevance important in classroom learning?

What was Bruner's view concerning readiness?

How does the spiral curriculum function in classroom learning?

Why is it important to learn generic concepts?

Why is it important for the learner to be an active participant?

What are Bruner's suggestions for improving teaching and learning in the schools?

What is Ausubel's subsumption theory of meaningful verbal learning?

What are the meanings of inductive and deductive processes in learning?

How do Ausubel and Bruner differ, and how are they the same?

What are the prerequisites for meaningful verbal learning in the classroom?

What is the difference between reception learning and discovery learning?

What is cognitive structure, and why is it important?

What are the basic goals of the school, according to Ausubel?

How can the teacher use both Ausubel's and Bruner's approaches in the classroom?

Unlike the conditioning models, but with a history just as long and rich in ideas, is a second family of theories based on what is usually referred to as the *cognitive* or *perceptual* model. This model has a number of differences when compared with the conditioning model, the most basic being that in the cognitive approach behavior is determined by the learner's perception and understanding of the situation relative to his or her goals or purpose and that learning is change in perception and understanding rather than change in behavior.

While conditioning theorists emphasize environment and overt behavior, cognitive theorists focus on the individual and internal drives and motives. The individual's perception of self as well as the outside world is the important thing. Behavior is seen in cognitive theories as a symptom of one's perception—how one *feels* about what one does is just as important as what is done. Cognitive psychologists use labels such as "perceptual field," "cognitive field," and "phenomenological field" to indicate the individual's perception of the world.

The cognitive psychologist is concerned about what is going on inside the individual. (Darrell Barry/Little Rock School District.)

To a cognitive theorist, learning is a change in how a person *sees* or *understands* a situation and need not be linked to S-R bonds or even to behavior. A burst of insight or understanding might take place along with behavioral change or be relatively separate from it.

The global approach of cognitive theories also stresses the idea that different parts of a situation are interrelated and that they can only be studied in the context of the total situation, namely, that "the whole is greater than the sum of its parts." To break down a situation into its component parts and study them separately is to lose something. The cognitive theorist attempts to design complex everyday situations to study and understand at that level rather than reduce them to a simple level and study each component separately.

Cognitive theorists also reject the idea that behavior can be random, passive, or just a response to environmental stimulation. *All behavior is purposeful, it makes sense, if seen through the eyes of the person exhibiting the behavior.* If we want to understand behavior, we must understand how the person sees the situation, what his or her purpose or goal is (Combs and Snygg, 1959).

THE EYE OF THE BEHOLDER

Mr. Snarff, the school principal, was in favor of holding the school's Christmas party at night at the local country club. He was almost finished saying this to the November faculty meeting when Tom Brainerd walked in. Because of his tardiness, Tom thought Mr. Snarff was arguing against rather than for the country club format. Tom immediately rose and argued for holding the Christmas party on a Friday afternoon in the school cafeteria. The reactions of several of the teachers in attendance were as follows.

1. *Fred, Tom's friend.* "Good old Tom. He's calling the old man right in front of the faculty. What guts, what coolness. Tom is indeed brave."
2. *Cynthia, Tom's fiancée.* "Oh my gosh, Tom's making an awful mistake. He doesn't realize that Mr. Snarff can't stand disagreements. I wish he'd be more careful. He is far too naïve for his own good."
3. *John, another teacher.* "What a jerk. A grandstand play just to impress his peers. Tom really doesn't have any moxie, and he'll be buttering up old Snarff first chance he gets. What a phony display this is."

Who was right? Was Tom highly brave, innocent and naïve, or putting on a phony show of courage? Each observer saw Tom differently, and the motives for Tom's actions were actually in the eye of each beholder. In this case, none of them was right, for Tom was motivated to agree with the "boss" based on his own perception of the situation, which happened to be inaccurate.

The Origins of the Cognitive Model

Wertheimer's Classical Gestalt Model

While Ivan Pavlov and John Watson were developing the conditioned reflex model, Max Wertheimer and others, primarily in Germany, were spelling out a theory, the basis for which lay in the visual perception laboratory. Usually referred to as *classical Gestalt psychology,* which means "configuration," the basic theory is that the learner sees a total picture, with all its parts interrelated. The way in which a learner sees any part of the picture or "field" depends on its relationships with other parts. Items in the field that can be differentiated or seen clearly are said to be in "figure," and parts of the field that serve as background are called "ground." Learning is then defined as changes in figure-ground relationships, or the development of a better Gestalt.

An understanding of how the learner organizes and groups the different parts of his or her field can be seen in several of Wertheimer's (1938) *laws of perception.* The key law is the *law of pragnanz,* which states that the organism imposes order on the field or situation; that is, we tend to perceive any situation not as isolated, meaningless bits, but as some sort of an organized whole or Gestalt (Wertheimer, 1959). How this organizing and grouping takes place is summed up by the following laws:

Law of proximity: an item in the field will be grouped with items that are near it.

Law of similarity: an item in the field will be grouped with items that are similar to it in any way.

Law of closure: incomplete figures will be seen as complete—they will be closed in some way.

Law of continuity: figures in the field will be completed in the same form that they began—curved lines will continue as curves and straight lines as straight lines.

Wertheimer believed that the basic ideas in this visual perception model could be extended to all behavior and life in general. The field is not just the visual field but, rather, that part of the situation that the individual "sees" or understands—the world as the individual experiences it. Whether we are talking about studying geometry, experiencing emotional reactions, or learning to kick a football, we do so on the basis of our perception of the total situation, how the parts are related to each other and how this total perception improves over time. Wertheimer also described perceptual change as more like a burst of insight or understanding than as a gradual conditioning process.

HOW MANY ANIMALS DO YOU SEE?

If you study this Currier and Ives lithograph, which was published in 1872, you will be able to identify a hidden horse, a wild boar, and several human faces. Once identified, these hidden figures become so obvious that you probably wonder why you could not see them earlier. This is an example of changing figure-ground relationships. The hidden animals can be seen when they are brought into figure and other aspects of the picture remain in the background. According to Wertheimer, distinguishing figure-ground relationships develops a better Gestalt, and these changes in perception, rather than changes in behavior, are the essence of learning.

Kohler and His Apes

Another aspect of focusing on relationships can be seen in the work of one of Wertheimer's colleagues, Wolfgang Kohler. Kohler (1925) studied problem solving in apes on the Canary Islands from 1913 to 1918. A typical Kohler problem was to place an ape in a large cage with a bunch of bananas hanging from the ceiling (see Figure 5.1). The ape could not reach the bananas, but if it stacked two wooden boxes together, it could climb up and reach them. Kohler observed how apes learned to stack the boxes and climb up and pick the bananas, and he saw little evidence of a

127

Figure 5.1
Kohler's apes were able to stack boxes or to telescope bamboo poles to reach bananas.

gradual conditioning process, trial and error, or any of the S-R-type explanations. Instead, he saw evidence that the ape perceived a problem situation and tried to find a solution. Finding a solution usually resembled a burst of insight or understanding, often occurring as it sat pondering over the problem, and the burst of insight might be followed immediately by the correct behavior.

Note in the problems that the ape perceives a situation, but at first its Gestalt is such that it does not *understand* the relationships of the boxes, the ceiling, and the bananas. As it ponders this problem, the ape restructures the situation (in its mind, of course) and sees a solution to its problem *in the relationship* of boxes to ceiling. It is this new perception, this "better Gestalt" that allows the ape to stack the boxes and reach the bananas. Learning has taken place internally, whether you prefer to call it "in its mind" or "in its perception" or even "in its nervous system." The crucial point here is how the different elements are seen relative to the total picture. In other experiments, Kohler engineered situations in which apes learned to use bamboo poles to reach up and knock down the bananas, to telescope poles together for this purpose, and even to reach through the bars and use one pole to roll another one over and into the cage and make use of it.

Lewin's Field Theory

A third variation of the cognitive approach is illustrated by the topological theory of Kurt Lewin (1936), the basic idea being that behavior is a result of the situation as perceived by the individual, as the individual relates it to his or her own needs and purpose. The individual's perception of a situation is called his or her "cognitive field," and the world as he or she sees it and experiences it, including goals as well as barriers to them, is his or her "life space." Lewin used the techniques of topology, or rubber-band geometry,* to draw life spaces complete with vectors (forces pushing in a direction) and valences (positive and negative values); he believed that this was the key to understanding the individual and his behavior.

Another interesting aspect of Lewin's (1935) work is seen in his analysis of conflicts. As the individual seeks to reach goals that he or she sees in this life space, the individual also finds that there are barriers to reaching these goals and that there are forces pushing him or her in different directions. The goal of college, for example, might have a high positive valence, but at the same time the cost in money and effort, the possibility of failure, and the desire to travel and have fun all interfere with the positive part. An individual in such a predicament is described by Lewin as having an *approach-avoidance conflict*. If the positive valences are strong

*Topological geometry is the general mathematical science of nonmetric spatial relationships. The size and shape of figures is not important, but their relationships are, such as part to whole or the properties of objects and figures that are not affected by distortion.

SO YOU DON'T LIKE SPINACH

Lewin used vectors and valences to describe conflicts and life spaces. The following is his explanation as to how an adult induces a child to eat an undesired food:

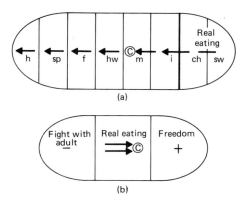

(a)

(b)

If a particular kind of food is not desired, the otherwise unified action of eating usually breaks up into a series of separate steps such as: putting the hand on the table (h); taking the spoon (sp); putting the food on the spoon (f); bringing the spoon halfway to the mouth (hw); bringing it to the mouth (m); taking the food into the mouth (i); chewing (ch); swallowing (sw). The procedure of the adult is sometimes to bring the child (C) step by step through these regions closer to the region of the "real eating" (chewing and swallowing). In doing so he usually meets with increasing resistance in accordance with the fact that with approach to the undesired action the repulsive forces (represented as arrows in the figure) increase. However, as soon as the food is once in the mouth it is often not spit out, even when the adult has fed the child against its will. Instead the child goes on to chewing and swallowing the food.

From K. Lewin. *Principles of Topological Psychology* (New York: McGraw-Hill, 1936), p. 97. Reprinted with permission.

enough, the individual will overcome the barriers and attend college anyway, but not without some anxiety; if the negative valences are strong enough, the individual will find some reason *not* to attend college or perhaps will drop out soon after beginning.

Lewin described other types of conflict also—for example, the *approach-approach conflict* and the *avoidance-avoidance conflict*—and he conducted research on all three types. A person who must make a choice between several positive activities, such as playing bridge, attending a concert, or going shopping, is faced with an approach-approach conflict and might agonize considerably before making a decision. In a similar manner, the student who must choose among French, German, and Russian, none of which is desired, or face the fourth choice of not graduating, is faced with an avoidance-avoidance conflict: the student must do something, but each

GET ME TO THE CHURCH ON TIME

Sam and Barbara announced their engagement in the spring, with plans to marry in September. They worked busily on the arrangements for the wedding until July and then surprised everyone by postponing the wedding until Christmas vacation. They then went ahead with arrangements and everything seemed fine until Thanksgiving, when they announced that Christmas vacation was no time to have a wedding, with all the snow and cold weather and difficulty in traveling. They said that spring would be a much better time, and set the date for the Saturday before Easter.

When the day finally arrived, the church was filled with friends and relatives enthusiastically awaiting a wedding. The organist played a number of songs, but nothing happened. It was past time for the wedding to start, and the organist was playing songs a second or third time, but still no wedding.

At first, the crowd paid little attention, since it was not unusual for a wedding to start a little late. By the time the wedding was a half-hour late, everyone became uncomfortable and wondered what was wrong. After they waited for forty minutes, the minister stepped out and announced that there would be no wedding, since they did not know the whereabouts of the groom. He added that he prayed there had been no accident or injury that prevented the groom from showing up.

In reconstructing what happened that day, it was found that the groom had seen the bride on the night before the wedding and, although somewhat nervous, had indicated no problems or misgivings. He then proceeded to the airport, where he climbed aboard a flight to California to join his mother.

This situation seems to fit Lewin's concept of an approach-avoidance conflict. A serious step such as matrimony can involve both positive and negative components. Sam was aware of both the positive and negative feelings about getting married, but when the goal was a long way off, the positive feelings far outweighed the negative, and the couple went ahead with plans to be married. As the day came closer, however, the negative aspects—losing one's freedom, financial difficulties, etc.—loomed larger, and this led to postponing the marriage until Christmas. With the marriage far off in the future, the positive aspects again outweighed the negative, and plans for the marriage proceeded smoothly.

Once again, as Sam's approach-avoidance conflict moved close to the wedding day, the avoidance gradient became so strong that he vacillated once again, and the wedding was postponed until spring. Finally, when the goal of the wedding day again loomed close on the horizon, Sam was overwhelmed by the negative aspects.

In an approach-avoidance conflict, the person experiencing the conflict often vacillates between approaching the goal and moving away from it, and this can repeat itself several times. One of the resolutions of the conflict is to leave the field completely, to escape from the scene and avoid the conflict altogether. This is what Sam ultimately did. He began to panic several days before the wedding, but this time postponement was out of the question. The negative aspects became so strong on the night before the wedding that they clearly outweighed the positive, but Sam did not have the courage to tell his fiancée and face all the problems of canceling the wedding. He panicked and fled to his mother in California.

alternative is distasteful. Persons faced with such conflicts often look for an escape, a chance to "cop out."

An important aspect of any field theory is the way in which it deals with the present situation. The individual's behavior can be understood and predicted if we can just find out how the person perceives the situation and what it is that he or she expects. Likewise, any attempts at changing someone's behavior will probably fail unless we can change the person's perceptual field, which is the cause of behavior. In each of these theories—Wertheimer's, Kohler's, and Lewin's—the key to behavior is found in the present situation as perceived by the individual and as it relates to his or her goals.

Present-day Cognitive Theories

Jerome Bruner

The cognitive theory advanced by Jerome Bruner of Harvard University is a broad and articulate argument for changes in the schools so that students understand the basis of what they are studying. Bruner's description of this in *The Process of Education* became an instant classic (Bruner, 1960).

The Importance of Intuitive Understanding

Have you ever known immediately that something was right, without knowing why? Or understood a principle but found yourself unable to explain it to someone else? Or perceived a promising solution to a problem that you could not prove until later? Jerome Bruner sees each of these as instances of "intuitive understanding," an important but neglected aspect of education.

Intuitive thinking, the training of hunches, is a much neglected and essential feature of productive thinking not only in formal academic disciplines, but also in everyday life. The shrewd guess, the fertile hypothesis, the courageous leap to a tentative conclusion—these are the most valuable coins of the thinker at work, whatever his line of work.

For a working definition of intuition, we do well to begin with *Webster*: "immediate apprehension or cognition." "Immediate" in this context is contrasted with "mediated"—apprehension or cognition that depends on the intervention of formal methods of analysis and proof. Intuition implies the act of grasping the meaning, significance, or structure of a problem or situation without explicit reliance on the analytic apparatus of one's craft. [Bruner, 1960, pp. 13–14,60]

Not only is intuitive understanding *not* always encouraged in school but it seems to be *actively discouraged*. Knowing something intuitively somehow violates the goal of the traditional school. The student is expected to reproduce verbal statements or numerical formulas. The student who reveals a deep grasp of a subject but not much ability to put it into words is often overlooked in favor of the student who has an abundance of seemingly appropriate words. Most teachers do not know much about the nature of intuitive thinking, and Bruner believes that this is as much a problem as improving its use by students.

Intuitive thinking is highly important to mathematicians, physicists, biologists, and others. Indeed, a scientist's reputation often seems a reflection of his *intuitiveness* as perceived by his colleagues. Bruner sees outstanding teachers in these fields as recognizing this, but not the majority of more ordinary teachers.

In contrast to intuitive thinking is *analytic* thinking, which is highly stressed in the traditional classroom. Analytic thinking characteristically proceeds a step at a time. The steps are usually explicit and can be reported by one learner to another. This type of thinking proceeds with considerable awareness of the information and operations involved.

Intuitive thinking, meanwhile, takes a back seat in formal schooling. It does not advance in careful, well-defined steps. When they have arrived at an answer, intuitive thinkers have little awareness of the process by which they reached it. They cannot explain how they obtained their answer, or to what aspects of the problem they were reacting. Bruner concluded that the school has somehow devalued intuition.

The Underlying Principles in a Discipline

Another key concept in Bruner's thinking is that of each discipline having certain concepts, principles, and procedures that must be understood before one can make sense out of all the facts one might learn. At first, Bruner called this idea the *structure* of a discipline, but later he abandoned this term since nobody was certain just what "structure" meant.

Bruner contends that every subject has a basic structure and that it is the understanding of this structure that is really crucial in school learning. This idea was one of the underlying principles of the experimental curricula that were tried out in the late 1950s and on through the 1960s. These curricula, called "new math," "new science," "new biology," and "new physics" at the time all attempted to get the student to learn the basic concepts and principles underlying the subject. Bruner saw the approach as practical, since students have only a limited amount of exposure to the material they are to learn.

Indeed, there were shortcomings in these "new" curricula. They often seemed to work best in classes of highy motivated, college-bound students or in the advanced as compared with the average classes. Average and below average students seemed to have difficulty in making the logical leaps from specific examples to general principles that the inductive approach of the "new curricula" required. But the idea of learning the basic concepts and principles of a subject, rather than just stringing together facts, seems to be a reasonable suggestion.

133

THE IMPORTANCE OF GENERIC CONCEPTS

Shirley had a headache, and her brother, who is a doctor, recommended that she take Tylenol. When Shirley arrived at the drugstore, she asked for Tylenol, and the druggist suggested that possibly she would like to take Wal-Mart's pain reliever, which was on sale. In both cases, she would be getting tablets that contained 3.25 milligrams of acetaminophen, so why pay considerably more just for the brand-name Tylenol.

"No," Shirley responded, "My brother told me to take Tylenol, and that's what I'll take." Shirley did not mind paying 50% more for the Tylenol, because she believed that this was what the doctor ordered.

This illustration is analogous to Bruner's idea of generic concept. Acetaminophen, the active ingredient in Tylenol and similar pain relievers, is the same material regardless what brand is purchased. By knowing the generic term for a medication, the purchaser is free to look at a wide variety of name brands and purchase the one that is the best bargain. The generic name for the drug is analogous to a generic concept, one that has a broad generalizability and that applies to a wide variety of situations. The specific brand Tylenol is analogous to a concept that has far less generalizability. A concept that applies to only one or a few situations is far less useful than one that has wide applicability, just as knowing the brand Tylenol is much more limiting than knowing the highly generalizable active ingredient, acetaminophen.

The Importance of Discovery Learning

Bruner also suggests that the best way in which to make sure that students learn the most basic and significant things in school is to take pains to assure that knowledge is self-discovered. Students must discover concepts, meanings, and relationships, and they must do it through an inductive process of exploring problems and reaching their own conclusions. Bruner calls for nothing less than the classroom becoming a miniature laboratory with the students "discovering science":

> Just what it takes to bring off such teaching is something on which a great deal or research is needed, but it would seem that an important ingredient is a sense of excitement about discovery of regularities of previously unrecognized relations and similarities between ideas, with a resulting sense of self-confidence in one's abilities. Various people who have worked on curricula in science and mathematics have urged that it is possible to present the fundamental structure of a discipline in such a way as to preserve some of the exciting sequences that lead a student to discover for himself [Bruner, 1960, p.20]

There is some research support for the idea that knowledge that is self-discovered seems more significant to the learner and is remembered better. But, of course, discovery learning is time consuming, and it is unlikely that a teacher could expect to teach everything in this way. On the other

According to Bruner, students must discover concepts for themselves. (CEMREL, Inc.)

hand, a class in which *no* self-discovered learning is taking place is a class that is missing some of the most basic principles of learning itself, as well as the subject being studied, according to Bruner.

The Importance of Relevance

Bruner sees the most important goal of school learing to be that it "serve us in the future," that is, take us somewhere, that it be useful. Although the word *relevance* has been so overused in the past decade that one shies away from using it in the 1980s, relevance was exactly what Bruner meant. In his book, *The Relevance of Education* (1971), Bruner argued that there are essentially two kinds of relevance: social relevance and personal relevance. He suggested that school learning should lead to both but that it was the second, *personal* relevance that Bruner found to be most wanting in the public schools of the 1970s. Unless education could lead to effective convictions for the individual, it was missing this most important form of relevance. Education must be relevant not only to the skills and tasks but also in terms of principles.

A Different View of Readiness

Another important idea in Bruner's writing is that of approaching readiness from a different direction. Instead of the set curriculum for each grade, and forcing all children to fit that curriculum, Bruner concluded that *"any subject can be taught effectively in some intellectualy honest form to any child at any stage of development"* [emphasis added] (Bruner, 1960, p. 33). With this in mind, the task of the teacher becomes one of adapting the curriculum to the child rather than of adjusting the child to fit the curriculum.

You may recall from Chapter 3 that this does not appear consistent with Piaget's ideas about the importance of cognitive stages and the child's inability to learn something until he or she is cognitively ready. Bruner does not see his readiness as contradictory to Piaget, as he is suggesting that teachers adapt their approach to the readiness level of the child.

Bruner's ideas about readiness were the stimulus for some amazing experiments in which such topics as calculus, physics, and biology were taught to children as young as 5 years old. A reasonable conclusion here seems to be that teaching at any level must be approached from the standpoint of the learner and his or her background, goals, capacities, and experience rather than sticking to a lockstep curriculum.

Another concept that ties in closely with this readiness idea is that of the *spiral curriculum.* In the usual classroom, learning consists of a series of episodes, which Bruner feels are like pieces of content that are not very well related to each other. In the spiral curriculum, students are introduced to basic ideas early, in a way that fits their readiness, and then exposed repeatedly to the same ideas in the future, but in increasing complexity (Bruner, 1966). It is the teacher's job to bring out relationships as the class proceeds on up the spiral.

Bruner also stresses the importance of learning concepts, especially the key, highly generalizable "generic concepts" that are so crucial in any discipline, rather than just learning isolated facts. A concept is a way of classifying, a set of rules for determining whether or not something fits into a certain category. In this way, *mammal* is a concept, and a child who understands this concept can tell whether any animal, even a hypothetical one, is a mammal. The really broad and highly generalizable generic concepts are the most important to learn both in understanding a subject and in transferring this knowledge to future situations. Part of what Bruner meant by learning a generic concept is simply learning a general principle or attitude rather than a specific skill:

The early teaching of science, mathematics, social studies, and literature should be designed to teach these subjects with scrupulous intellectual honesty, but with an emphasis upon the intuitive grasp of ideas and upon the use of these basic ideas.

A second way in which earlier learning renders later performance more effi-cient is through what is conveniently called nonspecific transfer or, more accu-rately, the transfer of principles and attitudes. In essence, it consists of learning initially not a skill but a general idea, which can then be used as a basis for recognizing subsequent problems as special cases of the ideas originally mastered. [Bruner, 1960, p. 13, 16]

The Importance of Doing

An aspect of Bruner's writings that has been remarkably consistent over the past twenty years is his insistence on the importance of the learner's *doing things* in education. Active involvement of the student, not just as an end in itself, but as necessary step toward true understanding, has always been part of Bruner's message.

But just what is it that the child must do if we are to improve educa-tion? Bruner suggested in *The Relevance of Education* that the following changes needed to be made to involve students in doing things that have relevance to their lives:

1. *Education must no longer strike an exclusive posture of neutrality and objectivity.* Bruner suggested that the skills of problem solving had to be given a chance to develop on problems that have an"inherent passion." For example, it is a fact that the United States is first in the world in gross national product and yet ninth in infant mortality. Bruner would argue that the school should explore facts such and these and encourage the students to take a stand based on values, beliefs, morals. Reasons for the United States being ninth in infant mortality could be discovered by the students, and steps to erase this fact could be recommended as a result of such deliberations.

2. *Education must concentrate more on the unknown and the speculative, using the known and established as a basis for extrapolation.* Bruner claimed that there are two types of scholars, the *knowers* and the *seekers*. The know-ers already know the answers to existing problems and are looking to the past. The seekers, on the other hand, are trying to find solutions to new problems, looking at problems for which there are no clearly known so-lutions. Instead of being taught to be knowers, Bruner believed that stu-dents, along with their teachers, should be encouraged to be seekers. Using what is already known to project a possible solution to a newly defined problem would do students more good than giving them clear-cut answers to problems from the past. Defining problems in itself is an important educational venture.

3. *The teacher must share the process of education with the learner.* In encouraging students to take responsibility for their learning, the teacher must risk the possibility of wasting time. One of the ways of trying to get students to be responsible for what they do in school is to tie what is done in school to money, occupations, and prestige—"Do this so that some day you may be rich and successful." But Bruner believes it is important that the reward for mastering something is the mastery, rather than any ulterior

137

To discover principles, Bruner says students must be involved in doing. (CEMREL, Inc.)

motive. We must let students experience the joy of mastery, and to do this we must share some of the responsibility with the students.

4. *Divide the curriculum into M-W-F "best of what we had" and T-Th "wild blue yonder experimentation."* Bruner is a great believer in seminars, political analyses, the development of position papers on school problems, problem finding, and all sorts of relevant activities in the local community. He is willing to admit that a large part of school must be devoted to passing on the culture, to learning from our past experiences. But he argues that we also need to devote time to innovations, brainstorming, "what if" experiments, and new problems that we haven't solved yet. It is difficult to do both at the same time; hence Bruner's suggestion that we deliberately devote two days each week to this function. It is probably true that in many schools today not even two hours a week are spent in such an activity.

David Ausubel

Another modern-day cognitive theory, with both similarities to and differences from Bruner's, is that of David P. Ausubel. Ausubel restricts his theory to meaningful learning of verbal materials, the type of subject matter learning that takes place in the classroom. Ausubel, like Bruner, is concerned with basic understanding and meaning, but unlike Bruner, he does *not* conclude that this must be done in an inductive discovery learning fashion.

Ausubel's theory, an elegant one, is far too detailed for presentation here, but a look at several key elements of it should suffice for comparison with Bruner's ideas.

Two Distinct Types of Learning

Ausubel sees part of the failure of learning theories to contribute successfully to solving educational problems in the tendency to focus on just one type of learning. This one type of learning, in which bits of material or "associations" are memorized arbitrarily and verbatim, is the well-known rote learning. Letter-number pairs, nonsense syllables, pairs of words, and serial lists are common examples of this type of learning, and they follow all the laws of associative learning identified in the experimental laboratory. Some school learning (e.g., memorizing vocabulary words, multiplication tables, scientific symbols) undoubtedly fits this description.

Another type of learning, far more important for teachers, is what Ausubel calls *meaningful assimilation*. In this type of learning, the *substance* of the material is assimilated *nonarbitrarily* and is related to the individual's past knowledge. This is a different learning process from that of rote learning and most likely does not follow the same laws.

Prerequisites for Meaningful Learning

For meaningful assimilation to take place, two things are necessary: *potentially meaningful material* and a *meaningful learning set.* The first of these is obviously a factor about which the teacher can do something, since the selection, organization, and presentation of material in a meaningful fashion seems self-evidently a part of the teacher's job. However, the "potentially" here suggests that the teacher cannot guarantee meaning, but only that the material is consistent with the child's developmental level and past experience.

The second prerequisite, a motivational one, is just as important. Students will *not* assimilate the new material in a meaningful fashion unless they have the desire and the know-how for doing so; that is, the teacher might present potentially *meaningful* material, but the student at the same time might insist on learning it in a *rote* fashion anyway! This second prerequisite, a "meaningful learning set" in the student, is also one that the teacher can influence, since motivational variables *are* subject to outside influences. (See Chapter 8 for a discussion of motivational variables.)

One obvious reason for students sometimes learning in a rote fashion is that they are not really rewarded for meaningful learning:

In the course of meaningful learning, a student must relate the component elements to his or her idiosyncratic cognitive structure. The result is almost always some minor variation between how the learner internalizes the information and

139

Ausubel contends that reception learning can be meaningful. (Bernie Weithorn/SIUC Photographic Service.)

how the teacher perceives the information. Thus in later recall of statements or propositions, the student's answer may vary somewhat from that expected by the teacher even when the student's answer is substantively correct. Unfortunately, such responses often are scored wrong and students learn to use rote (verbatim) learning approaches rather than to learn meaningfully. [Ausubel et al., 1978, pp. 50–51]

The Goal of Meaningful Learning

The idea of helping students learn in a meaningful rather than by a rote process is not an end in itself. The real reason for this is the outcome: *meaning*. Ausubel describes the nature of such learning, which he calls *meaningful reception learning*, as essentially the acquisition of new meanings. For this type of learning to be successful, the learner must have an intentional goal of learning in a meaningful way (meaningful learning set), and the material must also be such that it is *potentially* meaningful to the learner. This means that it can be assimilated nonarbitrarily and substantively into the learner's cognitive structure and that there are relevant ideas in cognitive structure to which it can be related. Since each learner's cognitive structure is unique, then to some extent all material that is learned meaningfully is unique. In spite of the individualized nature of learning, there are still certain things that any concepts have in common, which explains the dimension of social or shared meanings. According to Ausubel, there is sufficient similarity between the individual meanings that learners place on concepts to permit communication between individuals.

Reception Learning Versus Discovery Learning

In his analysis of how the learner assimilates new material and ties it to his existing knowledge, Ausubel concludes that most of this is done in what he calls *reception learning* situations. Reception learning is that type of learning in which the material is presented, either in written or spoken form, and the learner simply internalizes it. Unfortunately, many educators make the assumption that all learning of this type (reception learning) is rote learning.

In contrast, in situations in which the learner must actively discover the concept or new idea, we see a different situation that has caused many educators to assume that *all* discovery learning is meaningful. Ausubel, however, has made the important contribution of separating these two dimensions—the rote meaningful dimension and the reception discovery dimension—and pointing out that they are independent of each other.

Ausubel et al. notes that "Although the distinction between reception and discovery learning . . . has absolutely nothing to do with the rote-meaningful dimension of the learning process, the two dimensions of learning were commonly confused. This confusion is partly responsible for the widespread but unwarranted twin beliefs that reception learning is invaribly rote and that discovery learning is inherently and necessarily meaningful" (Ausubel et al., 1978, p. 27). In other words, old-fashioned practices such as lectures were denounced as worthless because by definition they led to rote learning, while any sort of discovery technique was automatically accepted as good, because discovery learning by definition was meaningful. Ausubel helped to demonstrate that lectures and other reception learning techniques *could* be meaningful and that discovery methods *could* result in rote learning.

A look at Figure 5.2 helps to explain these ideas. The vertical line represents the rote meaningful dimension, and learning can be anywhere on this continuum. The horizontal line represents the discovery reception dimension, and a teaching technique can fall anywhere on this continuum. The type of learning so often criticized in traditional schools has been *rote*

Figure 5.2
Schema showing how rote meaningful and reception discovery can be seen as two separate dimensions and the types of learning seen in each quadrant.

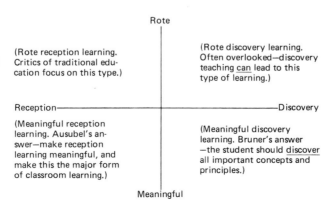

Rote

(Rote reception learning. Critics of traditional education focus on this type.)

(Rote discovery learning. Often overlooked—discovery teaching <u>can</u> lead to this type of learning.)

Reception————————————————Discovery

(Meaningful reception learning. Ausubel's answer—make reception learning meaningful, and make this the major form of classroom learning.)

(Meaningful discovery learning. Bruner's answer—the student should <u>discover</u> all important concepts and principles.)

Meaningful

reception learning, which is represented in the upper left quadrant, but it is only one type of reception learning. In the upper right quadrant, we have *rote discovery* learning, in which students are engaged in a discovery experience but are not really aware of any meaningful ideas or concepts that are being learned. (They might be having a great time in the laboratory and enhancing their social lives, but their actual knowledge of the subject may be increasing only in rote fashion.) In the lower left quadrant, we find *meaningful reception* learning, the type that Ausubel advocates and sees as the appropriate process for most classroom learning. In the lower right quadrant, we find *meaningful discovery* learning, which is obviously the type of learning that discovery enthusiasts have in mind.

Importance of Cognitive Structure

Ausubel calls his theory a *cognitive* theory, since its major goal is to describe what happens *inside* individuals as they learn, particularly what happens to new material as they relate it to what they already know. As learners add more knowledge to their ''cognitive structures'' (the sum total of their knowledge in an area and how that knowledge is organized within them), this structure constantly changes and grows, and any new material is related to many different points in this structure. Instead of new material being crammed into one's brain in an arbitrary, verbatim fashion, as in rote learning, Ausubel sees meaningful learning as the assimilation of new material into one's cognitive structure in a nonarbitrary, substantive way, and the anchoring of the new material into key elements of this structure. Such assimilation obviously implies that the exact nature of what is learned and how it relates to cognitive structure is unique to each individual.

Types of Assimilation

In analyzing specifically how new material is subsumed into cognitive structure, Ausubel describes four types of assimilation. The first, *combinatorial learning*, involves the learning of new ideas that do *not* ''fit in'' under existing ideas and, at the same time, do *not* serve as broad, organizing principles for further learning either. In combinatorial learning, ''sensible combinations of previously learned ideas can be nonarbitrarily related to a *broad background* of *generally relevant* content in cognitive structure by virtue of their *general congruence* with such content as a whole'' (Ausubel et al., 1978, p. 59). Examples of this type of learning abound in the classroom, since most of the new generalizations that students learn in science, math, social studies, and the humanities are really combinatorial concepts, for example, relationships between mass and energy, heat and volume, genetic structure and variability, demand and price.

The second type of assimilation, *subordinate learning*, involves the subsuming of new knowledge under a more general principle or idea. Actually, Ausubel refers to this as ''derivative subsumption'' and says that it ''takes place when learning material is understood as a specific example of an established concept in cognitive structure or is supportive or illustrative of a previously learned general proposition'' (Ausubel et al., 1978, p. 58). An example here would be to recognize that scarlet, aqua, and lavender are names for colors but not as easily recognized as are the names red, blue, and purple that designate the same colors.

The third type of assimilation, *correlative learning,* is a common way for new material to be learned in which the new knowledge is ''an extension, elaboration, modification, or qualification of previously learned propositions'' (Ausubel et al., 1978, pp. 58–59). This illustrates an important relationship between new knowledge and past experience. An example here would be a person who knew what patriotism was and understood acts of patriotism such as defending the flag and now assimilates the new idea that conserving energy is also an act of patriotism.

The fourth type of assimilation is extremely important in meaningful learning, even though it is probably not as common as the other three. This is *superordinate learning,* in which ''one learns an inclusive new proposition under which several established ideas may be subsumed'' (Ausubel et al., 1978, p. 59). In other words, whenever you put several concepts together to form a new principle under which further knowledge can be subsumed, you are engaged in *superordinate learning.* When you discover the idea that ties together a number of facts, this is superordinate learning also, and the inductive leaps that are so much a part of discovery learning are obviously part of superordinate learning. Thus, this is the one type of assimilation in which Ausubel is willing to acknowledge that discovery learning is probably best, even though only a small part of what is learned in school.

The Goals of the School

There is no question in Ausubel's mind as to the basic goals of schooling. Schools exist ''to foster intellectual growth and to transmit subject-matter knowledge'' (Ausubel et al., 1978, p. 33). Ausubel sees a number of recent trends as supporting his view. Among these are the increasing concern for basic skills, intellectual content, and quality of curriculum in schools. Along with these concerns, Ausubel sees a greater stress on learning as an end in itself and an increased willingness on the part of the school to accept responsibility for the preparation of instructional goals and the fostering of motivation as support for his contention that the ultimate goal of the school is to further intellectual growth. According to Ausubel, the criterion for determining whether a school meets this ultimate goal comes after the student has left school. That is, whether the student has the ability and desire to learn and apply knowledge in adult life.

Bruner and Ausubel: More Alike than Different

Although much is made of the ''controversy'' between Bruner and Ausubel over reception versus discovery learning, a closer look reveals that the two are far more alike than different. The overwhelming message of

143

both views is that *meaning and understanding* are the essence of classroom learning, and they both reject the mechanistic rote model of the behaviorists. In fact, a moment's reflection turns up at least the following ten similarities in the two viewpoints:

1. Both stress meaning and understanding. Even though Bruner believes that such meaning and understanding must be discovered inductively and Ausubel believes that it can be assimilated deductively, they both share the same goals.
2. Both emphasize learning the *substance* of the material rather than verbatim recall. In each case, if the substance is understood, the material will have wide transfer and utility for further use.
3. Both stress relationships, Bruner in emphasizing how anything learned must be related to other things and how one finds meaning in these relationships and Ausubel in describing how newly learned material is related or "anchored" to existing ideas in cognitive structure.
4. Both accent the importance of learning broad concepts and principles. Bruner calls these "generic" concepts, with a high degree of generalizability, and they seem remarkably similar to Ausubel's "anchoring ideas" or "organizers" that aid in assimilating new material.
5. Both talk about organization or "structure," Bruner in advocating learning and the underlying structure of the discipline and Ausubel in describing how material is organized in cognitive structure.
6. Both agree that school learning must be studied at the everyday level of complexity and not reduced to oversimplified laboratory situations.
7. Both are *cognitive* theories, attempting to understand processes in the mind rather than just studying the external physical world.
8. Both stress the importance of language as basic in human thought and communication and the chief tool in school learning.
9. Both see readiness as extremely important and the starting point for *any* type of meaningful learning.
10. Both agree on the basic need for improving instruction, that is, to make classroom learning meaningful to the student. (You are advised to take a close look at this list, because it not only summarizes similarities between these two theorists but it also presents most of the features of *any* cognitive approach to classroom learning.)

With such a list of agreements, it may sound strange to say that Bruner and Ausubel are seen as controversial. The major source of conflict can be seen in relation to point 10—just how do you make classroom learning meaningful? Bruner's answer is that meaning comes from what the student discovers independently, namely, that concepts are the crucial outcomes of discovery and that the teacher's job is to engineer situations in which self-discovery takes place in an inductive fashion through problems that capture the student's interest.

Ausubel, on the other hand, believes that the majority of classroom instruction must be receptive-type learning, with material presented to students in a deductive fashion, and that the most important part of this goes beyond concepts to ideas, principles, or "proposition learning."

Teaching for Reasoning and Understanding

As with Skinner's theory of operant conditioning discussed in Chapter 4, you may be asking, "How do I apply these cognitive theories?" The remainder of the chapter will address the application of these theories to teaching toward understanding. To begin, four points are common to the application of both Bruner and Ausubel.

1. *Starting where the learner is.* The first and certainly one of the most important implications of cognitive theory concerns the concept of readiness and its importance in relation to each individual learner. This means that the teacher should devote considerable effort to identifying the knowledge that the students already have, their skills and abilities, motives, and experiences, so that this can be the starting point in teaching them. Literally, the teacher must find out just where the students are and start there in teaching them. And because of the individual nature of cognitive structure, or any other aspect of readiness, it also means that the teacher must know something about each student's readiness individually. In the final analysis, readiness and learning are each individual and unique.

2. *Planning in the cognitive realm.* A second implication of the cognitive approach concerns the nature of planning and organization. In conditioning approaches, which tend to be atomistic or reductionist (study each specific part, break the problem down to its simplest components, etc.), the implication is for teachers to proceed in small steps, presenting the material bit by bit, so that the learner gradually puts together an understanding of the topic piece by piece. Cognitive approaches imply exactly the opposite. In the cognitive approach, the student starts with a general picture or overview, even if it might be fuzzy, and moves gradually to the details, proceeding from the general to the specific. It is only much later that the student gets down to understanding specific details and relationships.

You may be able to think of teachers who fit either one or the other of these approaches. It is usually easy to remember teachers who followed the specific-to-general approach, because this seems to be the more common. You learned facts, concepts, and events day by day, chapter by chapter, and eventually (it was hoped) you could put it all together and understand it as an organized whole. The problem, however, is that all too often the learner ends up with the bits and pieces, but fails to com-

145

prehend on a broader scale. When this situation occurs, the learner is apt to forget the "bits and pieces" rather quickly or to be unable to fit them together.

You may be able to recall an occasional teacher who used the cognitive approach. This teacher began with a general outline or overview of the whole subject. Once the students had a fair understanding of this overview, this teacher proceeded gradually to more specific details and relationships. It was not until late in the course that the fine points and details came into sharp focus. The advantage of this approach is that, even if students fail to grasp the fine points, they will have an overview or general understanding of the subject, which is far more resistant to extinction than are the details. Actually, neither approach is 100% "best," and both should be used in the classroom. Be sure that your students *do* get a broad, general picture of each topic as well as the subject as a whole but, at the same time, present some details from the beginning. The number and specificity of precise details can increase as the course proceeds, enabling the student to have the best of both worlds—a broad, general understanding of the unit or subject, combined with detailed knowledge and understanding of the finer points.

3. *Teaching for insight and understanding.* Another implication of the cognitive approach is that saying the correct answer or emitting the appropriate behavior are *not* sufficient evidence of learning. Cognitive theorists seek a real depth of comprehension of the substance and relationships in material that is learned. They speak of insight into a problem, meaning and relationships, and understanding underlying principles rather than merely of memorizing facts. In teaching for this type of learning, one must move away from memorization of isolated bits of information and rote drill. The teacher must take the time to make certain that students have progressed beyond the superficial. To this end, ask thoughtful and penetrating questions, require students to convert what they have learned into their own words, and have them apply what they learn to new situations. In short, make every attempt to get beyond simple verbalisms. We explore two approaches to this in detail in the ensuing pages: the "discovery approach," which follows from the writings of Piaget and Bruner, and the "deductive approach," which follows from the writings of Ausubel. Although quite different in some respects, both approaches share the goal of striving for substantive, in-depth learning and retention on a long-term basis.

4. *Importance of the learner's intent.* A key factor in teaching for insight and understanding is the *intent of the learner.* Ausubel referred to this as "meaningful learning set" or a real desire on the student's part to assimilate the substance of the material in a meaningful fashion rather than just cram in some terms and key points to pass an exam. The importance of the intent of the learner in this regard cannot be overemphasized. If the student is striving for rote memorization of facts and details, this is all that will be learned, no matter how much potential for meaning the lesson

has. Although teachers cannot force students to have an intent to learn meaningfully, they are a major factor in determining whether or not students develop such a learning set. Teachers who set insight and understanding high in their goals model the importance of this in their own behavior, find ways of emphasizing this in their planning, take the time necessary to pursue in depth, ask questions, and listen to students. All these techniques get across to students the importance of pursuing meaning and understanding in what they learn. Another important factor in developing intent to learn is the teacher's method of testing and determining grades. Students are not apt to develop a strong desire to pursue insight and understanding if the teacher tests only factual recall information.

Guided Discovery Learning: Bruner

To Bruner, most significant learning is *inductive*: one starts with particular facts and information, puts together what is known about these things, and makes a logical leap to a general principle or idea that underlies or explains all the facts and information. For Bruner, the classroom should be structured so that the children apply what they already know to the solving of a problem that is important to them. In the course of solving this problem, students discover an important concept or principle. If possible, the concepts discovered should be broad and general, and students should be given immediate practice in applying them to new problems.

For the desired results to take place, however, several things seem to be necessary. First, discovery seems to work best if it is *guided* discovery in which the situation is structured with enough guidance that it is almost guaranteed that the desired discovery will occur. Second, it is important to verbalize what has been discovered—to assure that the learner has discovered what was supposed to have been discovered and to make certain that what has been discovered is understood. Finally, it seems to be helpful to apply the newly acquired principle or concept immediately. Such application expands the principle and helps the student to remember it.

Guided discovery, as described, seems to have a motivational effect for students; that is, the students feel good about themselves, get a kick out of it, and feel satisfied when a discovery is made. In addition, self-discovered knowledge tends to "stick with us" or be more resistant to extinction.

However, there are drawbacks to the guided discovery method. The most obvious is the great amount of time the discovery process takes. Also, since no one knows how long it will take some students to discover some principles, it is very difficult to adhere to a teaching schedule. For this reason, many critics of discovery learning feel that it should be used sparingly.

147

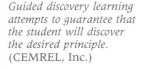

Development and Learning: The Basis of Educational Psychology

Another criticism is that discovery learning techniques tend to work best with bright, interested students. A discovery lesson might work very well with a class of high-achieving, highly motivated students. But what if the class is average or below and doesn't really want to be in school? The informal discovery situation might only confuse these students as they approach the problem with a conviction that they cannot do it. This approach could also lead to discipline problems. With a low-achieving class, great care must be applied to select discovery situations that are both easy and interesting. As a pattern of success develops, more complicated problems and concepts can be introduced.

A third problem with discovery learning is that students might not understand what it is that they have discovered! Take for example the biology class that spends many hours roaming the fields collecting leaves, worms, frogs, twigs, apparently "discovering biology." It is possible that nobody in the class has the slightest idea what they are discovering.

Discovery learning is *not necessarily* meaningful. Unless the teacher makes an effort to be sure that students understand and can explain what is discovered, this type of learning can be just as rote as any other.

One way of summing up the problems involved in discovery teaching is the statement that "the results are not always predictable." The class

Guided discovery learning attempts to guarantee that the student will discover the desired principle. (CEMREL, Inc.)

Without planning, discovery learning may not be effective. (Darrell Barry/Little Rock School District.)

may fail to complete the task in the time available, it may be too difficult or even too easy, discipline problems may develop, or the students may be unable to understand the principle they are pursuing. All these possibilities might tempt you to conclude that this type of teaching is not for you. But keep in mind that the payoff involved—the satisfaction, ego boost, individual learning, memory enhancement—far outweighs any risk involved in a discovery learning situation. We urge the incorporation of this method of teaching into the classroom on a regular basis, even though it is impractical to attempt to use it all the time.

Classroom Presentation: Ausubel

We now come to that part of teaching that has received so much criticism in some quarters that you might believe it is downright sinful—the ageless lecture. The abuses of this practice, in which the lecturer rambles on for an hour while the audience sits politely and doesn't understand a word of what is being said, are probably familiar to the reader and certainly cannot be justified. But to throw out all lectures because some are bad is tantamount to "throwing out the baby with the bath water." Teacher presentation to the class *can* be a meaningful, effective, economical, and enjoyable method of instruction. The fact that it is still used so widely despite strong criticism suggests that it is a necessary part of instruction for most teachers. The solution seems to lie in making lectures meaningful rather than in eliminating lectures entirely.

Teacher presentation can be effective and economical. (Bernie Weithorn/SIUC Photographic Service.)

Here are some suggestions for making passive, reception-type learning (lectures) meaningful, based on Ausubel's model of long-term meaningful verbal learning. Keep in mind that Ausubel advocated deductive learning, going from general to specific, rather than the inductive learning advocated by Bruner.

1. *Assessing readiness.* Before you can present material in a style that captures student motivation, builds on past experience, fits current abilities, and can be assimilated into cognitive structure, you must determine these variables for the students you are teaching. This requires an awareness of the characteristics of that age level in general, as well as knowing specific details about this group and the individuals in it. As Ausubel says, the most important single principle is what the student already knows—"ascertain this and teach accordingly."

There is no easy or magical way to assess readiness, and usually few tests are available to assist the teacher. Most of this assessment is done informally, on a day-to-day basis, as the teacher listens closely to student responses, observes carefully, and records progress and weaknesses. Pretests (to see what the students already know) are an obvious but seldom-used technique for assessing readiness. An openness to questions, discussions, review, and a willingness to pursue student problems are other aspects of this.

2. *Selecting material.* When you know about the interests, abilities, and cognitive structures of your class and are continually getting more information about this, the next step in planning a presentation is deciding on what to present. Don't try to pack too much into a classroom presentation. Condense the presentation into a small number of key points, and make sure that you get those points across. Try to start with concrete examples that fit the students' experience. Do not be afraid to include humor, controversy, or absurd examples.

Where do you find material for classroom presentations? One source is the textbook the class is using, but don't make the mistake of "teaching the text." Since most of you will be teaching students who already know how to read, don't make the mistake of reading the textbook for them. If you select material from the textbook for your lecture, it should be presented somewhat differently, with special goals in mind. The lecture can augment and clarify the text, but it should be more than mere repetition.

Alternate sources are textbooks other than what the class is using, magazines, newspapers, even personal experiences. Actually, it is amazing how many things you can find that relate to what you are teaching in the classroom if you really look for it. A magazine article as written might be too complex for a fourth grade class, for example, but the material could be presented by the teacher in a form that fits the abilities of this age group.

3. *Identifying organizing principles.* A third step in planning your presentation is to identify the broad, general principles that underly the material you want to present. Ausubel calls these "organizing principles," and says they act as a scaffolding on which other facts, concepts, and principles can be hung. Teachers *cannot* assume that students will discover these on their own or that they are obvious. No matter how obvious an implicit principle might seem to the teacher, it most likely is not at all clear to some of the students.

Once you have identified the broad, organizing principles underlying your material, you must then determine how you can emphasize these principles before, during, and after the main body of your presentation. The most important part of planning a presentation is to assure that the students gain a basic understanding of the organizing principles. Also, you should realize that writers don't always state these underlying principles, and it is important for you to infer what the basic principles are before presenting material from written sources.

4. *Presenting an overview: The general to the specific.* One important conclusion from Ausubel's analysis is the effectiveness of presenting an overview or a preview of new material. Remember, in Ausubel's deductive approach, that the general concept or principle is presented first and that the specific examples come later. Some teachers call this the "big-picture" approach, in which students are told that what they are studying fits into a much larger picture, why it is important, and what it relates to before getting down to specific details.

151

The idea of an overview and the suggestion to proceed from the general to the specific apply to teaching a complete course as well as to the planning of a specific lecture. The cognitive approach suggests that the teacher present an overview of the entire course in the first days of the semester and gradually proceed to more specific details. It also suggests that the teacher keep referring to this overview and relating new material to it.

5. *Using advance organizers.* Present broad, general organizing principles in advance of new material—the advance organizer technique. Let us look at a few examples of this technique.

In one of his studies, Ausubel (1960) used a learning passage that focused on the metallurgical properties of plain carbon steel. This 2,500-word passage focused on the structure of metal as it relates to temperature, carbon content, and rate of cooling, with various factual details about critical temperatures and technological processes. This was basically unfamiliar material for the college students involved in the study. The advance organizer in this study consisted of a 500-word passage that presented some basic principles about alloys without presenting any of the actual learning material.

In a second study (Ausubel and Youssef, 1963), students were learning a number of facts, concepts, and principles about Zen Buddhism, a topic about which most American students know nothing. The advance organizer in this study was a brief passage reviewing the basic principles of Christianity that were part of the past experience of the students, the idea being that students will learn new material (Zen Buddhism) more readily if they can anchor it to existing organizing principles in their cognitive structure (Christianity).

In another study (Ausubel and Fitzgerald, 1962), the new learning passage was one dealing with specific hormonal changes in pubescence, and the advance organizer was a brief passage of general facts about uniformity and variability in sex characteristics.

In all these studies, the students were presented with a brief passage written at a much higher level of abstraction, generality, and inclusiveness than the learning passage itself, which was then followed by the learning passage. This was done to call to mind any organizing conepts that the students already possessed, so that they would use them in learning the new material. In each case, the organizers were helpul in assimilating and understanding the new material. Any teacher can use this approach by thinking of broad, general organizing principles that will help in learning new material, presenting this clearly *before* presenting the material, and then making sure that the new material is tied to the organizer. These are especially helpful when they deal with situations that are already familiar and of interest to students: for example, a history teacher used an example of children squabbling and learning to get along on the playground as an advance organizer for the teaching of economic laws and relations among nations. In this particular case, the students not only learned the new material much better because of the organizing principles, but they did not even realize that the discussion of children on the playground was a history lesson—they thought it was just an enjoyable digression.

6. *Stressing principles and concepts.* Stress principles and concepts in your teaching! This may seem self-evident, but when one compares the complaints of teachers that their students just don't understand the material with observations of how those same teachers are *presenting* the material, it is clear that the idea is not so self-evident in practice. Students will tend to memorize, learn superficial facts, and develop glib verbal knowledge devoid of real understanding unless the teacher stresses the understanding of concepts and principles in the teaching process. This assumes that the teacher understands the concepts and principles and knows how to get these across. A true intent to teach for understanding is a large part of the battle, coupled with patience and the flexibility to question, discuss, explain, and review until one is satisfied that this goal has been accomplished.

7. *Focusing on relationships.* In the discussion of transfer earlier in the chapter, the importance of pointing out relationships between what was learned yesterday and what is learned today, what is learned in physics to what is learned in math, and what is learned in school and life outside of school was noted. This is even more important to a cognitive theorist than it is to a behaviorist, because understanding relationships is the basis of any cognitive explanation of learning. Students do *not* automatically see relationships, and it is helpful to point out obvious relationships that we might mistakenly take for granted as well as more subtle or even questionable ones. What better way to encourage understanding than to argue over the claim that Democratic presidents tend to get us into wars while Republican presidents tend to get us into recessions or to argue about whether there really is a relationship between a full moon and the incidence of violent crimes? Students must learn to see relationships, and they must learn to examine them critically to discern which relationships are really cause and effect, which are only accidental, and which are only apparent. Some students find this difficult to do without continuous encouragement and practice.

Keeping these seven steps in mind—assessing cognitive structure, selecting appropriate material, identifying organizing principles, presenting an overview and proceeding from the general to the specific, using advance organizers, stressing principles and concepts, and focusing on relationships—the novice as well as the experienced teacher should be able to develop meaningful classroom presentations for any subject. It is obvious that there are no shortcuts or easy solutions to this problem, and no cookbook recipes, but if the basic concepts and principles from the preceding discussion are understood, applying them to the task of making teaching meaningful should be rewarding.

Another factor that is extremely helpful in making learning meaningful is teacher enthusiasm. Somehow, if the teacher is enthusiastic, it is helpful in getting students to go beyond simple memory and into the more subtle meanings of a subject. Devising clever tasks for the students, presenting them with an air of suspense, using humor when appropriate, and supplementing other teaching techniques with media presentations are all ways of capturing student attention and encouraging meaningful learning.

Summary

The cognitive or perceptual approach to explaining learning, which has been around as long as the conditioning approach, stresses the idea that behavior is determined by the learner's perception and understanding of the situation relative to his or her goals or purpose. How a person *feels* about what he or she does is just as important as what that person does. Since learning is a change in how a person *sees* or understands a situation, it need not be linked to S-R bonds or even to behavior.

Cognitive approaches focus on the individual, are global in nature, and are based on the belief that all behavior is purposeful. The basic laws of learning in classical Gestalt psychology, as spelled out by Max Wertheimer, illustrate the nature of the perceptual approach. The field is the world as the individual perceives it. Relationships as perceived are an important part of this. Perceptual changes are more like bursts of insight or understanding than like a conditioning process.

Classical Gestalt psychology was advanced further by the work of Wolfgang Kohler, who studied problem solving in apes. In learning how to utilize objects in his environment to get bananas down from the top of his cage, the ape behaved more as if learning were a burst of insight, a change in the perception of relationships in the situation, rather than a gradual process of conditioning or trial and error.

Lewin's field theory is another example of cognitive theory, although it gets away from the visual perception model. Lewin's basic idea was that behavior is a result of the situation as perceived by the individual, as the individual relates it to his or her own needs and purposes. The individual's perception of the environment is his or her *cognitive field,* which has in it various goals, purposes, vectors, and valences. As the individual works to reach goals within his or her field, conflict situations result. Part of Lewin's contribution was his understanding of approach-approach, approach-avoidance, and avoidance-avoidance conflicts. Lewin borrowed concepts from math and science to illustrate his theory by drawing life spaces as experienced by individuals. His work was instrumental in advancing the field of social psychology by studying everyday complex situations in the laboratory.

Current examples of cognitive theory are the works of Jerome Bruner and David Ausubel. Although both have basic goals in common—an emphasis on the importance of meaning and understanding, a rejection of rote memorization, the importance of understanding the substance of the material, an emphasis on broad concepts and principles, an emphasis on relationships, and the importance of readiness and language development—they differ on how these cognitive goals can be achieved in the classroom. Bruner advocates an inductive, discovery-type process in which learners discover important concepts and principles through problem solving, in similar fashion to a scientific researcher; Ausubel et al. suggest that such discovery learning is extremely time-consuming and not really necessary for learners beyond the age of 12. Ausubel advocates a reception learning process, deductive in nature, in which the learner assimilates the material by reading or listening to presentations.

Bruner's advice for meaningful learning stresses the importance of intuitive understanding and inductive leaps. He believes that intuitive thought is shunned in the classroom in favor of analytical thinking. He talks about the importance of learning broad, highly generalizable concepts, and constantly relating what is learned to what one already knows. A different look at readiness, the spiral curriculum, and the importance of doing are all parts of Bruner's approach to classroom learning.

Ausubel's theory is limited to long-term meaningful verbal learning and the retention and use of this material over a long period of time. But Ausubel argues that this is the most important type of learning that takes place in the classroom. In this type of learning, the substance and meaning of the material is related to what is already part of the learner's cognitive structure. Potentially meaningful material and a meaningful learning set are the prerequisites for this type of learning to take place.

Unlike Bruner's model for the classroom, in which meaningful material is discovered in an inductive fashion, Ausubel stresses the deductive process of finding meaning in material that is presented to the student. This he calls meaningful reception learning. He argues that both reception learning and discovery learning can be either meaningful or rote. Ausubel explores the laws of assimilation of new material into existing cognitive structure as the basis of school learning.

We see, then, that both Ausubel and Bruner are interested in meaningful learning, relating new material to what is already known, the importance of broad concepts and principles, the study of school learning at the complex, everyday level, and the need for improving existing classroom instruction. Their chief difference is in how to do this, with Bruner advocating inductive, discovery techniques and Ausubel advocating deductive, reception techniques.

1. Watch a dog or a young child as they learn to do something they could not do earlier. Is there any validity to the claim that they are learning about relationships rather than just a simple conditioning process? Is it any easier to see the role of perception and understanding in the case of the child's learning than it is in the dog's learning?
2. Why is intuitive understanding so important in the early stages of learning a new subject? How can a teacher encourage such intuitive learning to take place? What can a teacher look for as evidence of such intuitive learning?

3. What are the advantages of an inductive, discovery learning approach in the classroom? What is particularly satisfying to the student in such an approach? Why is it practical to use discovery learning methods for only a part of what is learned in the classroom?

4. Can you use the subject of English as an example of the "spiral curriculum"? What facts and principles, such as those involved in grammatical usage, are taught again and again, but each time at a higher level of understanding? Can you think of any factors in human nature that interfere with the success of the spiral curriculum?

5. Bruner says that "any subject can be taught effectively in some intellectually honest form to any child at any stage of development" (Bruner, 1960, p. 33). What does this imply regarding such things as sex education for first-graders, engineering for third-graders, creative writing in kindergarten, or trigonometry for second-graders? Is there a need to qualify Bruner's statement?

6. What can the teacher do to assure that material is learned meaningfully in the classroom, in terms of Ausubel's theory? How does one make material potentially meaningful? What can be done to get the students to have a meaningful learning set?

References

Ausubel, D. P. "The Use of Advance Organizers in the Learning and Retention of Meaningful Verbal Material." *Journal of Educational Psychology*, 51(5), October 1960, pp. 267–272.

Ausubel, D. P., and Fitzgerald, D. "Organizer, General Background, and Antecedent Learning Variables in Sequential Verbal Learning." *Journal of Educational Psychology*, 53(6), December 1962, pp. 243–249.

Ausubel, D. P., & Youssef, M. "Role of Discriminability in Meaningful Parallel Learning." *Journal of Educational Psychology*, 54(6), December 1963, pp. 331–336.

Ausubel, D. P., Novak, J., and Hanesian, H. *Educational Psychology: A Cognitive View.* 2nd ed. New York: Holt, Rinehart and Winston, 1978.

Bruner, J. S. *The Process of Education.* Cambridge, Mass.: Harvard University Press, 1960.

———. *Toward a Theory of Instruction.* Cambridge, Mass.: Belknap Press of Harvard University Press, 1966.

———. *The Relevance of Education.* New York: W. W. Norton, 1971.

Combs, A. W., & Snygg, D. *Individual Behavior: A Perceptual Approach to Behavior.* Rev. Ed. New York: Harper & Row, 1959.

Kohler, W. *The Mentality of Apes.* 2nd Ed. London: Routledge & Kegan Paul Limited, 1927.

Lewin, K. *A Dynamic Theory of Personality.* New York: McGraw-Hill, 1935.

———. *Principles of Topological Psychology.* New York: McGraw-Hill, 1936.

Wertheimer, M. "Laws of Organization in Perceptual Forms," In Ellis, W. D., ed. *A Sourcebook of Gestalt Psychology.* London: Kegan Paul, Trench, Trubner & Co., 1938, pp. 71–88.

———. *Productive Thinking.* Enlarged ed.; Michael Wertheimer, ed. New York: Harper & Row, 1959.

Skill Building in the Classroom

6

PREVIEW

What is the central purpose of any program of education?

What are Gagné's types of learning, and how are they related?

What role does the teacher play in instruction?

How does the information processing model explain complex human behavior?

What are five learning outcomes described by Gagné?

How are Gagné's suggestions useful to teacher?

What is the significance of working backward in planning a lesson?

Where does each learning theory fit in Gagné's hierarchy of eight types of learning?

How does Gagné recommend that teachers use various media in instruction?

What are the different types of motivation that affect learning in the classroom?

What are the three different ways to explain extinction or forgetting?

What are the differences between short-term and long-term memory?

How can teachers help students to get material into long-term memory?

What are the roles of repetition, recitation, and review?

What is Robinson's SQ3R method?

How can teachers help students to develop study habits?

What are mnemonic devices that aid in memory?

What are the roles of generalization and discrimination in the transfer of learning?

What are lateral and vertical transfer, and why are they important in the classroom?

What are some guidelines for developing effective study skills?

How can the teacher encourage transfer?

When we look at theories such as Skinner's operant conditioning or Bruner's cognitive theory, we are not particularly interested in determining whether the theory is true or false. Rather, we examine such theories to determine whether they are useful in the classroom. Assuming, as we have stated earlier, that the central purpose of classroom instruction is to promote learning, one needs to ask regarding any theory of instruction "How can this be applied in the classroom?" If the answer is that the theory cannot be applied, the theory may reasonably be discarded. If, in the other hand, the theory can be applied effectively, it meets the crtiterion of usefulness and may be used when appropriate. Whether or not a theory can be applied effectively depends on a number of considerations. The learning styles of students, the teaching styles of the teacher, the content to be taught, and the number of students in the class and their backgrounds all would have to be considered in assessing whether or not a theory of instruction is useful. When one considers all factors, the conclusion most likely to be reached is that parts of a theory may be applied at times, and at other times, parts of other theories should be applied.

In Chapter 4 we showed how the theory of operant conditioning might be applied. In Chapter 5, we demonstrated ways in which cognitive theory might be applied. Certainly, the nature of the content under consideration and the goals of instruction are important in deciding whether to use operant conditioning or cognitive theory.

In this chapter, we present a discussion of a number of different skills and learning that a teacher may wish to teach. We also make suggestions as to how these might be taught. Before engaging in that discussion, a detailed discussion of different types and levels of learning as set forth by Robert Gagné is presented as these help to determine whether a particular method of instruction is appropriate.

Gagné's Hierarchy: Different Types of Learning

Beginning with his first book on *The Conditions of Learning* in 1965, Gagné made an important contribution to teachers by eliminating some of the confusion caused by opposing theories. Is learning a gradual thing, or can it take place suddenly? Is reinforcement important, or isn't it? How important is language in the learning of concepts? Is repetition crucial, or isn't it? An answer to questions such as those just offered, which may

Robert M. Gagné

sound like a dodge, is that it all depends on the *particular type* of learning. Rather than there being just one set of universal laws that applies to all instances of change in behavior (learning), Gagné concluded that there are at least eight *different types* of learning. There are conditions within the learner and conditions in the enviroment that are important for each of these, and these eight types of learning are related to each other in a hierarchy; that is, types 1 and 2 are prerequisites for types 3 and 4, and so on.

If the sight of a spider causes Wendy to have an involuntary emotional response, a reflex type of reaction, this was probably learned through association of the stimulus (spider) and the response (anxiety). No reinforcement was needed. Repetition of the association strenghtened it, and now Wendy is plagued with this same general anxiety response whenever she sees a spider. Gagné calls this *signal learning*, and you will note that it is at the bottom of the hierarchy in Figure 6.1. This type of learning is essentially the same as the *classical conditioning* of Pavlov and Watson.

The second type of learning in the hierarchy requires signal learning as a basic prerequisite and is clearly different. It is intentional and is the

159

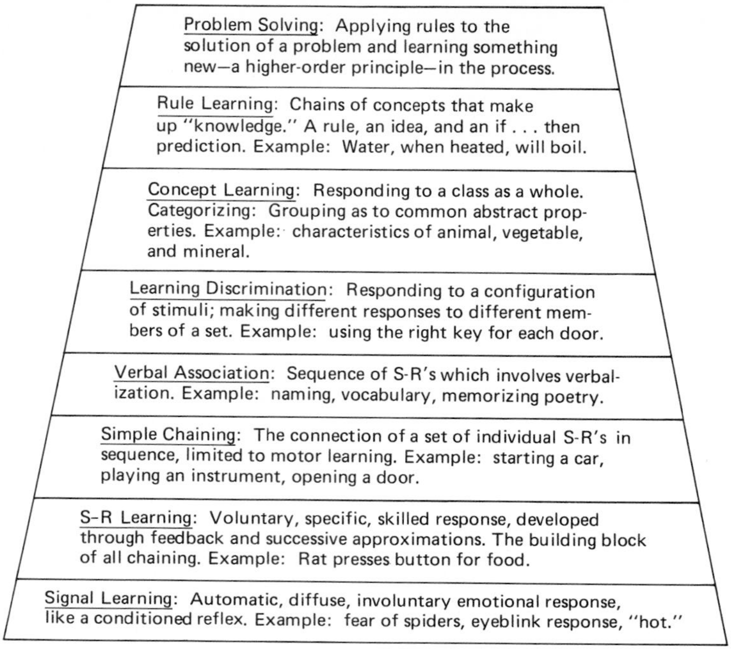

Figure 6.1
Gagné's hierarchy of eight types of learning. [Derived from R. M. Gagné, The Conditions of Learning, *3rd ed. (New York: Holt, Rinehart and Winston, 1977, pp. 73–180).]*

beginning of the development of specific, skilled responses. *S-R learning* requires the use of reinforcement and the shaping of behavior and is obviously similar to the operant conditioning explanations of Thorndike and Skinner. We can already see our hierarchy or "pyramid" growing, as type 1—signal learning—feeds into type 2—S-R learning—which in turn feeds into type 3, the *chaining of S-R links.*

The significance of Gagné's model for teachers really begins at type 4, *verbal association*, even though levels 1 through 3 lead up to this type of learning. The reason for this is that most classroom instruction involves levels 4 through 8, so these are the levels on which teachers will concentrate most of the time.

The Teacher's Role in Instruction

In Gagné's analysis, the teacher has three major tasks in classroom instruction, and learning theory can help the teacher only as it relates to these tasks. The teacher must (1) *design instruction*, selecting, planning, sequencing, and organizing learning experiences for the classroom; (2) *manage instruction*, actually carrying out those experiences planned, be it by oral presentation, reading, discussion, or some other medium; and (3) *evaluate instruction*. "On a day-to-day or even minute-to-minute basis, the effective teacher maintains a concern about what each student has learned"

160

and uses various forms of feedback to plan the next step in instruction (Gagné, 1975, p. 4)

With these three tasks in mind, let us look further at Gagné's terminology and what he says the teacher must know about human learning. In a break with the earlier S-R theorists, Gagné (1975) admits that learning is only inferred from overt behavior. Learning, itself, takes place inside an individual's head—in his brain. He believes that we must try to understand what is going on inside the learner and that the best model for understanding this at present is the *information processing* model. In other words, Gagné is essentially a behaviorist using the conditioning model, but he attempts to provide an explanation of what happens *between* the stimulus and the response inside the learner. He believes it is essential that teachers have some understanding of this and also that the information processing model (as outlined in Figure 6.2) is of greatest importance today in learning theory.

In Figure 6.2, the learning process begins when some stimulus from the *environment* is perceived by one of the *sense receptors* (sight, hearing, touch, taste, smell). Awareness of the stimulus enters the *sensory register*, a sort of ''echo chamber'' in which it is available to be processed for a very brief time, about one second or even less. If it doesn't get beyond the sensory register, then it does not get into memory at all, and there is no recollection of the stimulus input. This would be like being introduced to someone, definitely hearing his name, but five seconds later ''forgetting'' it. It did not make it even to short-term memory!

When the stimulus gets beyond the sensory register and into short-term memory, the learner is aware of the stimulus and can respond to it.

Gagné believes that the teacher must try to understand what is going on inside the student. (CEMREL, Inc.)

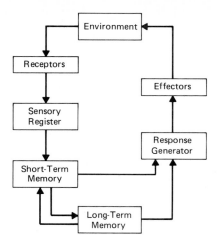

Figure 6.2
Basic information processing modeling proposed by Gagné. [*Adapted from R.M. Gagné,* Essentials of Learning for Instruction *(Hinsdale, Ill.: Dryden Press, 1975).*]

It is also possible, at this point, to code the information and enter it into long-term memory. Short-term memory is usually explained as sort of an electrical circuit, in which the stimulus acts as a "switch" that triggers the firing of the circuit. It is very strong for a brief period, but it fades out in a matter of minutes. This would be similar to being introduced to a couple at a party, introducing the couple to several other persons, and then ten minutes later having no idea as to their names. Another example that is often used is that of looking up a telephone number and dialing it. Unless some special effort is made to get the number into long-term memory, it is forgotten shortly after dialing.

When a stimulus input gets into long-term memory, it is somehow entered into the cortex chemically, literally stored in the brain cells. This is the really crucial part of memory, the part that we usually have in mind when we talk about remembering something. A memory trace in long-term memory is permanent, but this does *not* mean that it can always be retrieved readily. You might think of it as a book in the library—the book is stored on the shelf and is definitely there, but finding it is another story. Usually you look it up in the card catalogue first, by title, or by author, or by subject. Long-term memory works the same way, but sometimes finding the right cue to jog memory isn't so easy! For example, have you ever found that you couldn't recall something on an exam even though you *knew* you knew the right answer and yet could "remember" it easily after the test?

Gagné summarizes the information processing model as follows:

Stimulation from the learner's environment activates receptors to produce *patterns of neural impulses*. These patterns persist in the sensory register for a brief interval (some hundredths of a second), from which they may be processed by *selective perception* into perceived objects and object qualities, or features. This "information" may then be stored in short-memory as auditory, articulatory, or visual

TEACHER PLANNING MORNING'S LESSONS

As she got ready for work, Joyce reviewed in her mind what she would be doing in her fourth-grade class this morning. First, she knew there would be a fire drill, and she wanted to emphasize to the students that they should automatically drop whatever they were doing and file quickly and quietly out the appropriate door whenever the fire alarm sounds. Next, she knew she would have to spend some time drilling on spelling words and also on multiplication, and she planned to use the flash cards she had made and lots of repetition to get these across. She also had some clever devices she wanted to use to try to help students remember the names of the states.

She planned her history lesson for right after recess, when the class would be fresh and energetic. She had invented several riddles that were clues to important historical events, and she wanted an open, informal situation to give every student the opportunity to discover the answers. This would be much different from the organized drill before recess, and she would be ready to go off on any tangent that might help to bring about insight into history and increase the desire to study it. The class would be ready for a quieter lesson (she hoped) by 11:00, at which time she would present a careful explanation of some principles of movement in her science lesson. To get immediate feedback and diagnose any difficulties, she would give a brief but difficult test just before lunch.

After lunch, students would be attempting to solve this week's "mind benders" she had given them Monday. They could work alone or in groups, while she circulated around, observing and asking questions, but she would not tell them any answers or show the solutions until Friday. This sometimes turned into a bit of a free-for-all, but she thought it important that they have the opportunity to solve some problems on their own. Since some of the problems were easier than others, every student had a chance to solve a few problems. She stressed strategies they learned in attacking the problems rather than the correct answer as a major goal. After art class, a very relaxed, low pressure period that she always enjoyed, she planned to show a film that sharpened the distinction between the various types of cloud formations as a good way to end the day.

Can you see any of Gagné's eight types of learning illustrated in these lesson plans? Notice how Joyce varied the type of situation, goals, and activities depending on the particular type of learning involved. The variations in activity and method not only made the class more interesting and fun for the students (and the teacher), but they were also consistent with the conditions within the learner and conditions in the environment that foster each particular type of learning.

images, which are subject to *rehearsal.* As input to the long-memory, the information is *semantically (or meaningfully) encoded,* and then stored in this form. Processes of *search* may be instituted, followed by the process of *retrieval.* At this point, the information may be returned to the short-term memory, which is conceived as a "working" or "conscious" memory. From this structure, or directly from long-term memory, the response generator is brought into play to generate a suitable *response organization.* The signal flow from this structure activates effectors which exhibit the human *performance.* Feedback is provided via the learner's observations of this performance and the phenomenon of *reinforcement* establishes the learned entities as capabilities available for future recall, exercise, and use. Since these events are displayed linearly in the figure, the feedback loop is not indicated as part of the diagram, but must be imagined by the reader. [Gagné, 1977, pp. 57–59]

The Outcomes of Learning

Five types of learning outcomes are important for teachers, according to Gagné: (1) *verbal information,* (2) *intellectual skills,* (3) *cognitive strategies,* (4) *attitudes,* and (5) *motor skills.* A quick look at Figure 6.1 will enable you to see that Gagné's original hierarchy of cognitive learning was different from this listing of five types of learning outcomes. This is partly because attitudes and motor skills were not addressed in Gagné's original hierarchy and partly because the five types of outcome are a broader description of learning than the specific types addressed in the hierarchy. Both these analyses of Gagné should be helpful to you in understanding the different varieties of learning in the classroom.

Gagné's Suggestions for Planning Instruction

There are numerous reasons why Gagné's work is useful to the teacher in planning instruction. First, the very fact that Gagné specifies different types of outcomes allows the teacher to plan specifically for the type of learning that he or she wants to foster. A vocabulary lesson at the verbal association level clearly calls for a different plan than the discovery of a higher-order principle, just as motor skills learning calls for a different plan than the learning of attitudes. Knowing specifically what type or types of learning are involved is a big step toward the planning of any particular lesson.

Second, Gagné's work clarifies the relationship of the different types of learning to each other and specifies the necessary prerequisites to learning at each level of his hierarchy. Thus, if a teacher is having problems at one level, let us say the level of concept learning, he or she can check to see if the prerequisites for learning at this level are present. The prerequisites for concept learning are that (1) the necessary verbal associations and learning discriminations must be present and understood; (2) the student must be capable of perceiving and understanding the situation and utilizing results of learning at lower levels; (3) ability to follow verbal instructions is important, and clear instructions must be present; (4) a variety of examples is necessary; (5) contiguity and reinforcement help, but rote repetition does not; and (6) testing assures that the learner can generalize the concept.

As illustrated in the example of Joyce, there are some definite places to turn if a lesson is not succeeding. Teachers can review the items of knowledge leading up to the concept to make sure that these are present and understood. They can check to see that all appropriate conditions in the situation are met. They can test to see if the students have the prerequisite capabilities. They can review their instructions and also provide examples. In short, they can go through an imaginery checklist to verify that all necessary prerequisites, all conditions in the learner, and all conditions in the environment have been satisfied.

A third contribution of Gagné's hierarchical approach is that it allows room for each of the different learning theories (Gage, 1978). This enables the teacher to make use of aspects of classical conditioning, operant conditioning, and cognitive theories, rather than being in search of who is "right" and all the rest wrong! This in turn gives something for other theorists to build on, in further defining different types of learning and their relationships, and in incorporating new findings with what is already known.

TEACHING THE CONCEPT "MAMMAL"

As the period ended, Peter felt that the lesson had gone well, with most of the eighth-grade class gaining a fairly clear understanding of the concept "mammal." He had begun by reviewing quickly the terms, definitions, and concepts that were involved. It would not help to talk about "bearing its young internally," "nursing its young," "breathing air," or "being warm blooded" if nobody knew what these terms meant.

The next step was to define mammal and then present several examples in which mammals had to be distinguished from other creatures. He took plenty of time in doing this to assure that students perceived and understood the situation. He then focused on a few unusual mammals, such as dolphins and whales, and went over the reasons why these mammals could be identified if the criteria were understood. Next, he presented examples of several creatures that were new to the class, listing their traits and characteristics, and having the class decide in each case if it was a mammal. He avoided rote repetition in doing this, knowing that it would not help, and was sure to include several animals that were *not* mammals. When he reached a point where they seemed to be doing very well at this, demonstrating their understanding of the concept, he then invented several creatures, giving them certain characteristics, to test if the class really understood the concept. This led to some spirited arguments, but it seemed to sharpen the distinction still further, and he concluded the lesson with a final, detailed review of just what was and what wasn't a mammal and how the key points could be retained in memory.

In all, it was an effective lesson, even though he had to admit it was hardly earth shaking. He believed in moving ahead a little each day, making sure that he taught each step in the topic as well as he could, and in the end all of those little steps, such as a clear and accurate concept of mammal, would add up to a broad understanding of the subject as a whole.

Finally, a unique idea that is implied by Gagné's model is that of starting at the end and working backward to the beginning in planning for instruction. The end is the final goal of the lesson or unit, the point in the hierarchy to be reached (say, the discovery of the principles underlying Boyle's laws). In looking at that final goal, the teacher decides just what

WORKING BACKWARD IN PLANNING A LESSON

Louise was teaching her twelfth-grade psychology class about a disorder called "obsessive-compulsive neurosis." She knew that this was her final target, an understanding of what this label meant, so she started there in her planning and asked herself what would lead into that. She recognized that an understanding of personality types in relation to behavior was important, as were the dynamics of defense mechanisms, neurosis, and psychosis. Distinguishing between obsessive thoughts and compulsive behaviors was also important.

As she worked back in her planning, she noted that the obsessive-compulsive neurosis has its roots in the need for security and control and that it has some similarities to phobias with which all the students were somewhat familiar. This led her back to thoughts about the infant in its insecure, helpless position and the attempts of all children to gain some feeling of security and control, and how this is reflected in society. She thought also of how myths, legends, and tradition can serve the same function.

When she was through jotting down her ideas, starting at the end as stated and working backward, she was happy to see a lesson readily emerging. She would begin the class with a discussion of how the infant views the world, emphasizing its helpless, insecure position. This would lead to a broader example of humanity as a whole and how habits, myths, legends, and superstitions provide the illusion of safety and control. She would then present a few familiar phobias (fear of heights, closed places, snakes) as examples and use this to lead into the concept of defense mechanisms.

The second day, she would get into more detailed discussion of defense mechanisms, especially repression and displacement, and a description of neurosis as a more extreme version of defense mechanisms. After some examples and a discussion of obsessive thoughts as distinguished from compulsive behaviors, she would get the class to "discover" that all this is an adult answer to the same problem of helplessness and insecurity that she started with two days ago. We all have the same problem of inadequate control of our world, and the obsessive-compulsive behavior pattern serves to solve this problem. A careful discussion would be necessary to assure that the class understood that a person is not necessarily sick if he exhibits this pattern and to get them to see the difference between a "healthy" person with this personality type and one who is unhealthy or "neurotic." Her final step would be to see if the class could handle the question of why an obsessive-compulsive neurosis would be so difficult to change.

Louise has followed a planning approach implied by Gagné's work, that of starting at the conclusion and working back step by step in her planning. This resulted in an effective and economical presentation and discussion, over several days, of some very difficult and important concepts and principles in her high school psychology class.

concepts and principles are necessary to get to the higher-level general principle. The teacher then works back through the facts and concepts leading to those principles and on back to the basic vocabulary needed. In doing this, the focus is on what is necessary to be learned to reach the final goal. The plan is sequential, logical, and economical, and once it has been decided just where the students are in terms of their existing knowledge and experience, the teacher can decide what classroom experiences will lead them to the goal.

Where Each Theory Fits

Let us take a closer look at one of the points just made, namely, the idea that the levels of the hierarchy imply different learning theories. Where do Watson and Pavlov fit? It should be obvious that this model fits very nicely at the signal learning level, and in fact "a diffuse, involuntary emotional response" sounds like a definition of the conditioning of Pavlov's dogs or Li'l Albert learning to fear the rat. This classical conditioning model fades out of the picture, quickly, however, as we move up the hierarchy, and we see that the operant conditioning of Skinner seems to fit S-R learning (level 2) and both simple and verbal chaining at levels 3 and 4. Thus, if you are teaching vocabulary, basic facts and terminology, or physical skills, you would look to the operant conditioning theories for help. You would be much concerned with reinforcement, repetition, the step-by-step sequencing of responses, and immediate feedback.

These conditioning theories are less appropriate, however, as we move on up the ladder through learning discriminations (level 5) to concept learning (level 6), rule learning (level 7), and problem solving (level 8). At these higher levels, learning involves insight and understanding. Repetition and reinforcement are not as productive in bringing about understanding of the substance of meaningful concepts and principles as with lower-level learning. As a result, we must look more and more to the cognitive theories of Bruner, Ausubel, and Piaget as we move into these higher-level skills. The teacher, therefore, should be eclectic, using the theory appropriate for the type and level of learning involved.

Gagné and the Uses of Media

Another example of the applications of Gagné's work is in the area of instructional media. Gagné and Briggs (1979) point out that there are a number of different media for instruction, and one of the most important practical decisions for the teacher is the choice of media for any particular lesson. Instruction may be delivered orally by the teacher, or it may come from printed material. Pictures, films, audiotapes, videotapes, and physical objects may also be used.

167

Most of the time, the teacher will be employing *language media*. Oral communication is the most adaptable of all media, but it is not always the most effective. It should be supplemented by other media when the task demands it. Oral communication is particularly helpful for channeling motivation toward instructional goals, for informing the learner of expected outcomes, and for providing guidance and procedural suggestions. It is also the chief form of interaction between student and teacher, as in class discussion.

Another important point is that oral communication can be greatly improved by adding other media in the right places. A model that shows the earth's movement around the sun clarifies something visually that is difficult to explain verbally. The concept of wave motion in physics can be explained verbally, but it is very difficult to understand unless a picture, preferably a moving one, is added. A town meeting can be described in social studies, but is better understood and has more impact if observed in action.

Gagné points out that the higher up the education ladder you go, the more dependence there is on printed media. Even at the highest levels, however, it is still important to discuss the ideas derived from books and articles. The teacher must be constantly aware of the need for students to discuss what they are reading. Learning to read adequately is the most important skill of early schooling, since without this the student is cut off from the increasingly important printed media.

Gagné sees problems in the most common printed media, textbooks, in that they often do not follow established findings in terms of ''properly supporting the processes involved in each learning phase'' (Gagné, 1977,

Teachers may employ a variety of media in providing instruction. (Bernie Weithorn/SIUC Photographic Service.)

The higher you go up the education ladder, the more dependence upon verbal media. (Darrell Barry/Little Rock School District.)

p. 306). In other words, if the printed material is not sequential, does not fit the conditions within the learner, and does not provide such things as feedback and reinforcement or encourage active involvement of the learner, then the reader has trouble learning what he or she is supposed to from the textbook. Since it is beyond the scope of teachers to train textbook writers, it becomes the teacher's duty to identify problems in the text, add the needed explanation and examples, reinforce the students' efforts, provide discussion time, and supplement the book with other appropriate media.

Nonverbal media that are used in instruction include pictures, diagrams, and actual objects. These are used because they are involved directly in the performance expected as a result of learning; for example, if the lesson pertains to map reading, then maps of some type should actually be read as part of the lesson.

A second and much broader reason for using such nonverbal media is that they are the means by which the learner can acquire the *visual images* that are a very important part of remembering and applying what is learned. Gagné uses the term *encoding schemes* to describe this memory and application function of pictures and objects. The images gained from such nonverbal illustrations enhance the recall of prerequisite skills for later learning,

169

Pictures used in conjunction with other media help provide visual images which are important for remembering. (Arkansas State Department of Education.)

add cues for retrieving a newly learned skill, aid in transfer, broaden and add detail to the context in which material is remembered, and have a favorable effect on feelings and attitudes.

It is not surprising that Gagné's analysis of media concludes with an explanation of the properties of verbal-picture combinations or of oral or printed media combined with illustrations. The teacher can enhance verbal instruction with pictures, diagrams or charts, and actual objects for the students to study. The textbook can also enhance both interest and learning by providing sample pictures, diagrams, or tables, although it obviously cannot contain actual objects to manipulate. The old saying, "a picture is worth a thousand words," applies here, although sometimes that saying may be reversed in that a good verbal explanation *can* be very helpful or "a good *word* is worth a thousand pictures." However, we must agree with Gagné that the judicious combination of both verbal and nonverbal media enhances student interest, learning, transfer, and memory.

Building a Desire to Learn

Gagné's analysis presents a multitude of ideas for the planning of instruction. The teacher must trigger some existing *motivation* in the students, and by informing them of the objective the teacher sets up an *expectancy* for learning. The teacher then *directs attention* to the relevant points so that selective perception will occur and provides guidance and rehearsal so that

Table 6.1. *A Lesson on Water Vapor and Air**

Instructional Event	Function
1. Teacher directs attention to clouding of windows on a cold day, the ring of water left by a glass of ice water, the cloud left by breathing on a mirror. Question students about why these events happen.	1. Establishment of *achievement* motivation, based on curiosity and the desire to display knowledge to other children and parents.
2. Children are given tin cans and ice cubes.	2. Providing *stimulus objects.*
3. Students are told to put the ice cubes in the cans, and to watch what happens to the outside of the cans.	3. Completion of stimulus situation. Directions to focus *attention, selective perception.*
4. Students are asked to describe what they see. "Fog," "drops of water," "large drops, running down," "a ring of water at base of can."	4. Verbal directions to stimulate *recall* of previously learned concepts.
5. Students are asked what they can infer from their observations. "Liquid is water from the air."	5. Learning of a rule by discovery; for some students, this may be *recall*. Feedback provided.
6. Other alternatives are presented to the students. Could it be some other liquid? Could it come from the metal of the can? How can one test an inference?	6. Verbal directions to inform the learners of the expected outcome of instruction (how to test this inference). Establishing an *expectancy.*
7. "How can we tell whether this liquid is water?" ("Taste it.")	7. Requiring *recall* of previously learned rule.
8. "If the water comes out of the metal, what should happen when it is wiped off?" ("Can should weigh less.")	8. Requiring *recall* of previously learned rule.
9. Students are asked, "If the water comes from the air, what should happen to the weight of the can after the water collects on it?" ("Can should increase in weight.") Can is weighed on an equal-arm balance for direct observation of increase in weight of can by ice.	9. Requiring *recall* of previously learned rules.
10. Students are asked to recall that steam consists of water droplets and water vapor (an invisible gas). Air can contain water vapor.	10. Requiring *recall* of previously learned rules.
11. Students are asked to state (a) what they observed; (b) what they inferred; and (c) how they checked their inference.	11. Verbal guidance to suggest *encoding* for concepts of observation and inference; and of rules for checking inferences. *Feedback* provided.
12. Students are asked to make and test inferences in two or three new situations, and to describe the operations and reasoning involved. These might be (a) water evaporation; (b) the extinguishing of a candle in a closed cylinder; (c) the displacement of water by gas in an inverted cylinder.	12. Additional *examples* of the concepts and rules learned, for the purpose of insuring *retention* and *learning transfer.*
13. Another new situation is presented to the students and they are asked to describe it in terms of (a) what they observed; (b) what they inferred; (c) how they checked their inferrence.	13. *Appraisal* providing feedback.

*From *The Conditions of Learning,* Third Edition, by Robert M. Gagné. Copyright © 1977 by Holt, Rinehart and Winston. Copyright © 1965, 1970 by Holt, Rinehart and Winston, Inc. Reprinted by permission of Holt, Rinehart and Winston.

what is learned can be coded into long-term memory. The teacher must tie in what is learned with what has been learned previously to encourage *transfer* and must use review and application for this same purpose.

Table 6.1 illustrates steps in the learning process and things that the teacher must do in relation to each step. Study the table and relate it to the eight types of learning to see if you really understand the model.

In describing motivation, Gagné identifies two important functions, that of *identifying* student's motives and that of *channeling* them into activities that accomplish educational goals. A basic type of extrinsic motive is *incentive motivation* (such things as approval, other types of reinforcement, social recognition, success). This type of motivation seems to follow the recommendations of reinforcement theorists in line with B. F. Skinner's work described in Chapter 4.

In relation to incentive motivation, Gagné points out that "if incentive motivation is to be used effectively for instructional design, the learner must be informed of the nature of the achievement expected as an outcome of learning. . . . The primary effect of providing learners with an expectancy of the learning outcome is to enable them to match their own performances with a class of performance they expect to be 'correct' " (Gagné, 1977, p. 291). In other words, the teacher tells the students what they are going to learn, what skill they are to attain, and then goes ahead and teaches it. This not only motivates the student, but also provides guidance and helps the student to utilize feedback.

A second type of motive is *task motivation*. In this type of motive, the affiliation aspects of approval and recognition are less important, but intrinsic aspects of the task itself become important. The motives of *mastery* and *achievement* have been explored in great detail by psychologists, and this is what Gagné is talking about. This type of motivation is superior to incentive motivation because it is satisfying in and of itself, and also because it directly affects the student's self-esteem without any need for reinforcement by others. Researchers such as David Ausubel et al. (1978), D. C. McClelland (1965), J. W. Atkinson (1964), and R. W. White (1959) have explored such motivation and found that programs designed deliberately to increase this type of motivation in students can be effective. This is certainly an important area in which teachers can have an impact and is discussed in detail in Chapter 8.

Remembering and Forgetting

Your personal educational experience has probably shown you that some things are remembered very well, that others are "there" but sometimes hard to find, and that others are sometimes lost completely. We now look at the dynamics of remembering and forgetting.

Three Models of Extinction (Forgetting)

Let us begin with a question students often ask—why do we forget things we have learned? One answer is that we forget those connections or associations made previously because they grow rusty or fade away through lack of use. This *disuse model* suggests that teachers should review often, and also tie in any new learning to previous learning, to continue to exercise and stamp in the S-R connections. The stress on repetition of the early conditioning theorists was due in part to the fear that any S-R connection would fade away from disuse.

Although this disuse model seems to fit commonsense notions about memory and has much folk wisdom to support it, it has failed to gain the backing of research findings in recent years. It may be an excellent idea for you to use repetition, review often, and tie in any new learnings with what is already known, but the reasons for doing so must be explained by something other than the disuse model of forgetting.

A second explanation for forgetting that follows from conditioning the-

---

INTERFERENCE IN LANGUAGE LEARNING

Bob had been studying French for two months and felt that he was making rapid progress. He was tossing around French words and phrases as if they were from his native tongue. He figured that he could pass the French reading exam that was required for graduation without waiting until spring. He was doing so well that he decided to get a head start on German, the other required langauge.

Bob thought that his rapid progress in French would help him in German. But instead the opposite occurred. The words in his French vocabulary kept conflicting with the German words he was trying to learn. Before long, he couldn't keep the French words straight either, so that he was getting a sort of combination of French and German when he translated. Even worse, he kept trying to apply French rules of grammar to German sentences and vice versa. It got to the point that he even had trouble writing an English sentence correctly. Finally, he gave up on German, spent several more months studying French, passed the exam, and *then* tackled German and did all right. He had learned that, although there is positive transfer from one language to another, especially related languages such as French and German, there is interference also.

Trying to start a second foreign language when one is still in the early stages of consolidating a first foreign language tends to maximize the amount of interference. He was getting both *proactive inhibition* (what he had previously learned in French was interfering with what he was currently learning in German) and *retroactive inhibition* (what he was currently learning in German was interfering with what he had previously learned in French). By dropping the second learning task until the first one was understood more clearly and overlearned, the second task became easier to keep separate from the first, and more positive transfer was allowed to take place.

ory is the idea that you forget what you learned previously because you learn new things that take their place. This is called the *interference model* because the new learning is interfering with what you already knew. This model suggests that the teacher must make any new learning very clear and bring out similarities and differences between what is already known and what is learned, so that interference can be held to a minimum. Also, research indicates that there will be less interference if a task is practiced even after one has already learned it. This process for preventing forgetting is called *overlearning* and is based upon the idea that partially learned tasks interfere more with other partially learned tasks than do tasks that are learned completely.

A third explanation for forgetting actually comes from the cognitive theories that we explored in Chapter 5. In this explanation, the key to memory is the way in which the material is coded and organized as it is assimilated. Remembered materials are modified and reorganized as new materials are added to memory, so that forgetting can be seen as a result of the *process of reorganization,* as a part of the same organizing process as learning itself.

But before we can achieve any understanding of memory, it is necessary that we take a close look at *two types* of memory as understood by psychologists and demonstrated in memory research.

Short-term and Long-term Memory

Earlier in this chapter, we discussed the information processing model for explaining the learning process and presented this model in Figure 6.2. In the figure, the *stimuli* from the environment enter the *sensory register* through the *sense receptors,* where they are available momentarily. If the brain chooses to use what gets into this sensory register, it is entered into *short-term memory* by merely focusing on it or rehearsing it briefly. Information stays in this short-term memory for only a brief period.

Researchers tell us that this short-term memory resembles an electrical circuit or feedback loop, the immediate memory of what we have heard or seen reverberating like an echo in a large room, but soon to be lost if we do not make use of it. Thus the examples given earlier of forgetting a phone number immediately after dialing it or forgetting names two minutes after being introduced, even after saying the names several times. Teachers in class can easily be fooled by this. If students respond correctly immediately after learning something new, we assume that they have it in memory only to find later that they have forgotten it completely.

It takes something special to get the new material beyond short-term memory and into long-term memory, where once again researchers tell us that the memory is somehow coded and stored chemically in the molecules of the brain (specifically, the cortex). The exact mechanism of this process is still a mystery, but it *is* clear that it is a chemical process, that

SO YOU WANT TO HAVE YOUR HEAD EXAMINED?

The patient was stretched out on the operating table, under the bright lights, with several surgeons, nurses, and anesthetists working over him. Part of the patient's skull was open, and the surgeons were probing directly in the patient's brain with their instruments. There was considerable conversation during the operation, but the most startling thing was that the patient himself was awake and participating in this conversation!

"What do you feel now?" the surgeon would ask, as he probed a particular point in the brain with his tiny electric instrument.

"I feel something in my left leg, something like a shock." With further probing, the left leg jumped, and the surgeon commented to the aide as to where they were in the brain.

It really became unbelievable when they started probing in the cortex. "What do you see now?" "I see a room. It's my Grandmother's living room. We're getting ready to eat Thanksgiving dinner. I can smell turkey and sweet potatoes cooking. Grandma is humming along with the radio. They are playing "Shine on Harvest Moon." Why it's so clear, it's like I am there right now!"

The patient was very excited as these memories were revived. They were so clear, it was just as if he were reliving them. Sometimes, an incident was remembered that had been long since forgotten.

Research such as this was conducted by Wilder Penfield, a brain surgeon, as he operated on the brains of epileptics in the 1930s (Penfield and Rasmussen, 1950). He was probing the brain to find out exactly how each part functioned, so that any brain tissue that he cut to relieve the "electric storms" that cause epileptic seizures would not also destroy important brain functions. The patient had to be awake during such surgery to report what was happening as the surgeon probed in the brain (the brain has no pain receptors, so the patient suffered no pain from this). In this type of surgery, it was found that memories seemed to be stored chemically, throughout the cortex, and events apparently forgotten for many years were still stored there. This supports the theory that *anything* that gets into long-term memory remains there permanently, stored in a chemical fashion in the cortex, and requires just the right stimulus to bring it back to consciousness.

it is different from short-term memory, and that new material cannot be retrieved and used later unless it gets into long-term memory. It is almost as if a special switch in the brain decides that certain things are worth preserving and then gives the signal "Now Print This" to the cortex, just like the "Print" button on a computer.

Since it is also becoming clear that *everything* that ever gets into long-term memory probably stays there permanently, for a lifetime (barring some disaster to the brain), it would seem quite important for a teacher to worry about what does and doesn't get into this amazing storage facility and to look for ways to improve both getting material into it and retrieving it for use later on. Let us look now at some of the ways that have been developed for improving memory.

175

Repetition, Recitation, and Review

Repetition has always been known to be helpful to memory, although it is important to take care just what it is that is being repeated. Repetition of correct responses, with awareness of what it is and what it relates to, is helpful, but repetition of wrong responses or mindless repetition without any awareness of meaning is useless or even counterproductive. Surveying the material to be learned, interacting with it by asking questions and reciting answers as you read, repeating important points, and reviewing immediately and again later have all proved to be helpful.

These techniques were found to be so effective that Francis P. Robinson combined them into a carefully organized and quite successful study system. This system was called the SQ3R method, the letters corresponding to key steps in the technique: survey, question, read, recite, and review (Robinson, 1970). If you were applying this method of studying to the reading of this chapter, it would go something like this.

First you would survey the chapter to see what you were about to encounter, noting the major divisions, headings, length, and general flow

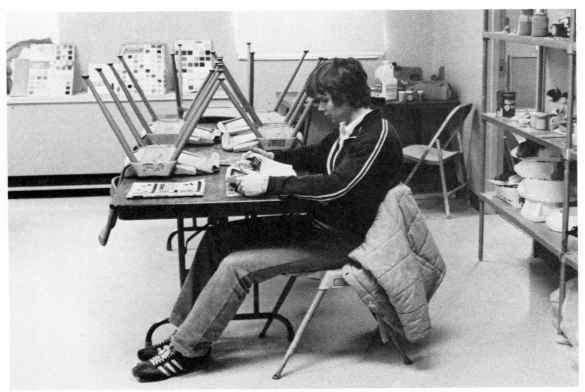

This student apparently has learned that he requires solitude when studying and seeks it where he can find it. (Bernie Weithorn/SIUC Photographic Service.)

of the material. As you were doing this, you would jot down (on paper or just in your mind) some key questions that you would want to answer as you read. Now you would be ready to read the chapter in detail, with a good idea of what you were looking for and specific questions to answer as you read.

Next you would read the entire chapter, noting the answers to your questions as you go, but not really stopping to record answers. You would be trying to get an entire reading of the chapter, but with a focus. Immediately after reading it, you would refer to your questions and recite what you had learned in relation to each question. For many people it helps to actually recite out loud or write down what has been learned, but the important thing is that you would be clarifying in your mind just what it is that you have learned and providing an opportunity for it to get into long-term memory. Finally, you would go back and review the chapter, skimming over it once again to make sure that you had gotten all the major points and ideas.

This system has proven successful for many hundreds of students over the years, although it will not automatically be successful for everyone. First, it is necessary to pursue such a system thoroughly enough and long enough to give it a chance to work. Second, study habits are an individualistic thing, so that what works well for some will not work for others. However, it appears reasonable to say that *any* student can improve his or her memory by developing some systematic ways of studying, both in the areas of what is chosen to commit to memory in the first place and also by improving its retrievability.

As an example of what we mean here, let us look at a student taking notes. (Whether or not this student could be called "typical" is uncertain, but let us say he is not unusual.) This student is feverishly trying to get down as much as he can of what the instructor is saying. In doing so, the resulting notes are a hodgepodge, and he doesn't know what to make of them later. Unfortunately, he has concentrated so much on taking notes that he has missed much of what the teacher has said. His notes are not really helpful in selecting the most important concepts and ideas to code into long-term memory, nor are they of much use in assuring retrieval later (such as final exam time).

In contrast, another student is taking notes in a much different fashion. She listens intently to what the professor says, and only occasionally writes something down. What she writes is often a question or comment to be followed up later, as well as key ideas or terms. We notice also that she jots things down while the professor pauses, or is perhaps reviewing something she already knows, and that she spends several minutes jotting down notes *after* the class is over. In fact, this is probably the best time to take notes or study, immediately *after* a class, while much of the material is still available and while what will get into long-term memory is being determined. Students usually do just the opposite, studying *before* class instead of right after class, which is far less helpful to memory.

177

Mnemonic Devices

Although you would do well to avoid placing too much hope in the efficacy of tricks or gimmicks, there *is* an area of memory research that deals with the use of special devices for improving memory. Such a special technique or device is called a *mnemonic device.* Some entertainers have developed these devices to the point where they can astound an audience with their feats of memory, such as being introduced to thirty people in rapid succession and then rattling off every one of their names. Let us look at two of the most common mnemonic devices and see how they work.

The first of these, the *mnemonic pegboard,* consists of a counting system in which each number has a rhyming term associated with it (e.g., one is bun, two is shoe, three is tree, four is door, five is hive, six is sticks, etc.). This list of numbers and terms is thoroughly ingrained in memory and is automatic. The trick, then, is to take any new ideas to be remembered and tie them to the sequential list of terms. In doing this, you also create a graphic picture in your mind of each item as part of the term, so when you count down your list of terms later, you will have a vivid image to help you remember each one. Thus if you needed to remember butter, milk, eggs, lettuce, and soap at the store, you might picture in your mind

Drill can produce overlearning, which aids memory. (Darrell Barry/Little Rock School District.)

a big bun with butter smeared all over it, a shoe with milk spilled upon it, a strange tree with eggs instead of leaves, a door with lettuce sticking out or growing above, below, and around it, and an unfortunate soul being stung all over by bees and trying to wash them off with a huge bar of soap. The image is supposed to be deliberately dramatic, strange, or even humorous, and when you get to the store and run through "one is bun, two is shoe, three is tree," you will most likely remember every one of the items you were to purchase and get a chuckle as a bonus. Try it the next time you need to remember a list of things.

The second type of device, called the *method of loci,* consists of a list of familiar places, and the things you want to remember are associated with each of these places. For example, in your house you may have a sink, pool table, piano, bathtub, and junk room. These become an automatic list of places in your mind. When committing a list of items to memory, you associate each one in turn with your automatic list of places and get a vivid and perhaps ridiculous picture in your mind of each thing in the particular place on the list. Later, when you need to remember you run through your automatic place list and each item springs vividly to mind. Try both of these and see which one works better for you.

In these two examples, the mnemonic device included a visual image. This is not necessarily part of a mnemonic device, but it often helps. Anybody can create his or her own mnemonic devices, some of which get pretty complicated; the only important consideration is that it be an automatic, repeatable system and that it work for *you.*

Overlearning

Another helpful memory technique is that of *overlearning.* A technical description of this specifies that it means the learning of a response or association "beyond criterion," which means that you continue to rehearse the association far beyond the point at which you get it correct. The reason that overlearning is useful is because it makes the response or association far more resistant to extinction. This provides a meaningful rationale for drill, a practice resisted by students and even by many educators as "old-fashioned." If students understood that you were simply pursuing a certain degree of overlearning to assure that the learning would stick (establishing a specific goal here, such as "twenty trials past criterion," might help), perhaps they would see a reason for drill.

Finally, we can sum up the question of improving memory in this way: yes, memory *can* be improved; all people can increase their powers of memory if they attack it systematically and on a daily basis, but it is a highly individualistic undertaking. You must experiment and find what works for you, and if you are helping students to improve their memories, you must show them how to experiment, practice, and find what works for them.

179

Transfer

The hope that what is learned in the classroom will transfer to life outside the classroom is basic in teaching, for if we could not demonstrate transfer, we would be unable to justify school at all. What the student learns in a specific classroom situation *must* be useful in other situations, both within and outside of school, and teachers must work constantly to assure that this happens.

There are two basic aspects to transfer: discrimination and generalization. The student must be able to see what he or she has learned as *generalizing* to a wide variety of situations but, at the same time, must be able to *discriminate* those situations where it is inappropriate. Take, as an example, the child who learns in Scouts that it is fun to call others by humorous nicknames and then generalizes this to other social situations and finds that it works there also, that others approve and reciprocate; he then has a handy new tool for popularity. When he extends this learning to the classroom, however, calls other students nicknames in class, and

Much of what is learned in vocational studies can be transferred directly outside the classroom. (Bernie Weithorn/SIUC Photographic Service.)

TEACHING FOR TRANSFER

George had intended to take general psychology last semester, but he dropped it after a few weeks. All those facts about correlations, significant statistics, the parts of the brain, and the terminology baffled him. It did not seem to have anything to do with real life, certainly not his life.

He still remembered the last lecture before he dropped the course. The professor was listing all the parts of the eye and the facts about vision. He was trying to memorize facts about the rods and cones, retina, afterimage, and such, but he had nothing to tie it to, and it just sort of went in one ear and out the other.

Now, a semester later, he was taking general psychology again, but from another instructor. This instructor was talking about vision also, but he had brought a large clear plastic model of an eye and passed it around the room. As he described the eye's function, he compared it with a camera and outlined on the board just how a camera worked. He had an antique camera that he took apart for the class and then reassembled, naming each part in terms of its function and comparing it with a part of the eye. After some discussion assured him that the students understood this, he then conducted a little experiment on "afterimage" that resulted in the students' being able to see an image of the American flag on the wall in *green and black.* This not only illustrated the afterimage effect, but got across some facts about color vision. The class concluded with an explanation and demonstration of how a movie projector works, how you see only the illusion of movement even though it is a series of still negatives, and how this illustrates the afterimage effect in the eye.

George could not believe that this was the same course, and indeed the same textbook as he had encountered last semester. The instructor was teaching the same facts, but doing it in a way that linked it to past experience and the outside world and dramatized the facts being taught. There was no transfer in the way these things were being taught the first time, and George had dropped the course. The second time, his interest was held because of the way in which the course was taught, maximizing transfer, and the material seemed entirely different. This same idea can be utilized in teaching *any* subject.

even refers to the teacher as "Shorty," he is stunned by the teacher's reprimand and the failure of others to respond. He has failed to discriminate between situations in which his "nickname" behavior generalized appropriately and other situations in which it is inappropriate.

Research on transfer indicates that there *are* guidelines for teachers to follow in maximizing transfer. One fact that needs emphasis immediately is that the "mental discipline" idea about transfer did not hold up under scientific scrutiny. The idea that the mind is like a muscle and you strengthen it through exercise, with certain subjects (usually the hard ones) strengthening the mind automatically because they are such good exercise, was challenged by research findings as early as the 1920s. Transfer does *not* take place automatically; no subject by itself assures transfer. The major determinant of transfer appears to be the way in which the subject is taught and learned.

A second idea, claiming to follow the "identical elements" transfer theory of Thorndike (1913), stressed the learning of things that were immediately useful and practical. The greater the number of "identical elements" you could incorporate into the classroom in terms of the lives of the students outside the classroom *right now*, the greater the transfer that would take place. Concepts, theories, and skills that were not immediately practical were shunned by some enthusiasts of this approach as not immediately useful. This approach was undermined by research also, however, since many things that are not immediately practical or useful prove to be very useful in the long run. Students actually like learning completely new things, and sometimes considerable transfer takes place in spite of *no* apparent identical elements. Transfer of principles, learning strategies, and even attitudes was found to be important. One generalization that seems to follow from research on transfer in the classroom is that transfer is enhanced if teachers consistently seek to achieve it by way of their instructional methods.

Lateral and Vertical Transfer

Two types of transfer are important in the classroom. When you learn something that transfers to other subjects and situations, but all at the same level, this is *lateral transfer*. When you learn something that transfers to other learnings at a higher level, either in the same subject or outside it, this is *vertical transfer*. In *vertical transfer*, the learning has generalized and is useful farther along in the learning process. Gagné likens it to climbing the rungs on a ladder—you are moving up, vertically, rather than out, horizontally.

Both types of transfer are important, and the teacher should have both in mind in the classroom. Tying something in with other learning at the same level aids memory and usefulness later on and helps the learner to clarify the new learning and makes it more interesting. Tying in previous learning as we move up the ladder is important also, both in terms of enhancing learning and in improving memory.

Suggestions for Teachers

To end this chapter, we present some suggestions for teaching to improve transfer in classroom learning. These are things that many teachers do naturally, as part of their teaching style, but any teacher can improve the amount of transfer by deliberately concentrating on such guidelines.

182

TWO TEACHERS TEAR THEIR HAIR IN FRUSTRATION

Joan had been teaching math at Center High School for six years, and Fred, the physics teacher, had been there for five. They liked each other and spent quite a bit of time together. One day at lunch Fred leveled an attack on Joan because he was teaching Boyle's laws concerning relationships of temperature, volume, and pressure in gases and the students could not even begin to work the problems. Since these students had taken Joan's math course, or were in it at present, he wanted to know how they could pass a sophomore math course and not be able to work problems involving proportions.

Now it was Joan's turn to attack. She had spent a month on proportions last year, until the class appeared to be experts at working fractions, percentages, and other proportions. She was working on that topic *right now* in math class, so some of Fred's students came directly from working proportion problems in her math class to studying about Boyle's laws in his physics class. She could not believe that she had not done her job and decided that Fred must just be a lousy teacher.

The sad thing in this story is that these breakdowns in learning are not uncommon. Students learn things in one class and assume that they have absolutely nothing to do with another class. This compartmentalization leads to using correct grammar only in English, applying math only in math class, and seeing no relationship between geography and history or psychology and economics.

The conflict between Joan and Fred highlights the fact that one cannot assume that students will see transfer among the different subjects they study. It must be encouraged and pointed out, continuously and often, by the teachers themselves.

1. *Stress transfer both inside and outside of school.* It appears that the first step in teaching for transfer is simply having it in mind, being conscious of its importance, and therefore stressing it whenever possible. Although transfer to life outside of school is important, it may be that transfer *inside* of school is more neglected in the long run. Many things that are learned in school are important primarily as they relate to more learning in school, and there is nothing wrong with this. Critics sometimes forget that school *is* part of life and in fact a very large part for most children, so that to imply that the only "real life" that exists is that outside of school is a serious error. It is better for a student to see the significance of what is being learned today in relation to what was learned yesterday, or will be learned later, or to some other class, than to attempt a weak or trivial tie-in to "real life" outside the classroom. But whenever learning can be related in an important or meaningful fashion to life outside of school, this is very helpful for transfer, memory, interest, and motivation.

2. *Deliberately point out relationships whenever possible.* As teachers, we all tend to take for granted many of the relationships in the subjects we teach. We forget that these relationships are not always obvious to stu-

dents, and it is sometimes painful to realize that relationships that are obvious to us are not apparent to our students. We really need not worry about pointing out a relationship that is already obvious, for in doing this the student will probably feel good that he or she has already recognized the relationship independently.

3. *Present overviews and frequent review.* If students are to see relationships in what they learn, they need to have the "big picture" presented to them repeatedly. An overview of a unit is helpful not only at the beginning but in the middle and at the end also. Reviews in the form of presentations, discussions, and even homework designed to stress transfer is helpful. Reviews should take place *not* just before a test, when students are anxious and see them only as help in cramming for the test, but at frequent points throughout the learning process. At times, review should look clear back into what was learned last semester or even last year. To fight the feeling of wasting time or getting behind, teachers can keep reminding themselves that without these frequent reviews not much transfer will take place, and most of what is learned will be forgotten quickly.

4. *Encourage students to apply what they learn.* Students can help considerably in solving the transfer problem if they are taught that transfer *is* important and if they are encouraged to seek it on their own and are given opportunities to apply their skills. When problems or questions arise, the teacher can encourage them to apply what they know themselves rather than serve as an answering service. Bringing examples from outside, discussing their relationship to the class, demonstrating the relationship, seeing the class in regard to other aspects of school are all ways that students can find transfer on their own. Such efforts must be rewarded, however, not just by smiles and social approval, but if possible in other ways that would be reflected in that area of such vital importance to students, *grades.*

5. *Deliberately test for transfer.* Students tend to learn whatever they *think* will be on the test. If they find that the test includes many transfer tasks, they will tend to look for transfer in their learning. If the examples of transfer discussed in class, the students' descriptions of their own experiences, are somehow included in quizzes or tests, they will tend to realize their importance and pay closer attention to such discussions. Also, the teacher can find out much more about the extent of transfer in the students' learning by testing it deliberately. The results of the test can then be used to make adjustments in the teaching program.

6. *Use specific, concrete examples from television, newspapers, school activities, current events, and life in general.* The concrete and formal operational stages of reasoning described in Chapter 3 are stages that many students have not yet reached. It isn't until about ages 8 to 10 that we can count on most students reasoning logically at the concrete operational level, and even in high school at least half the students still reason at the concrete rather than the abstract, formal level. Moreover, even for students at the formal operational level, the use of specific concrete examples from the world outside the classroom aids memory and transfer and makes learning

184

Concrete examples can be valuable in improving transfer. (Arkansas Gazette.)

more enjoyable. A dedicated teacher, even while watching television, reading, or in recreation, will constantly be looking for concrete examples that can be used in class.

7. *Provide opportunities for overlearning.* Material learned just barely well enough to pass a test, or to satisfy an assignment, will tend to have a minimal amount of transfer. Encouraging overlearning requires patience on the teacher's part, as well as inventiveness in finding ways to reduce boredom or make a ''game'' out of practice. An additional point here, in relation to not just overlearning but transfer in general, is that it is best to keep the anxiety level fairly low if you are concentrating on transfer. This means that overlearning sessions, while spirited and enthusiastic, need to be flexible and fun, not tense and confining.

8. *Encourage questions and comments and be willing to pursue them.* Every teacher has experienced that sinking feeling when the important concept or principle that has been the focus of the lesson is lost due to an irrelevant comment or question. But if transfer is a worthy goal, we have to risk such outcomes. While some questions lead nowhere, others lead to im-

185

portant points and ideas related to the topic, and we'll never know what the students' questions are without them being asked. To a considerable extent, students can be *taught* to ask intelligent questions, and asking questions is one of the best ways in which to find out how learning transfers beyond the immediate situation. Sometimes student discussion gives every appearance of "stalling," thereby avoiding further material or assignments, but this is far less important than the need to foster transfer. A careful analysis of how much is accomplished every classroom minute would indicate that a certain amount of stalling would be permissible anyway. The skillful teacher will find ways to turn a silly question or irrelevant comment into useful examples that are related to the subject.

9. *Be aware of what other teachers are doing and how their work could relate to your class.* The world is not really divided into separate little containers of knowledge that are completely isolated from each other. Math is an important part of any science, history relates to all the social sciences, English is part of almost every subject, and art relates to almost everything. Yet it is surprising how often teachers labor heroically in their own classrooms, apparently oblivious to the teaching going on in every other class. If teachers were more aware of what their colleagues were doing, many examples of transfer could be found right there, within school. A homework assignment in physics class might be a perfect example of a current math procedure, or a concept in sociology could explain a current event in history. The student, however, will often say, "You can't take off for grammar. This ain't English class!"

10. *Devise projects and competitive games that foster transfer.* Children of all ages, and even adults, like competition when it is a team effort and "just for fun." When the goal of a lesson is to encourage transfer, this can be built into a game-type situation, and the class can enjoy the game at the same time they discover ways to generalize their learning. Homework assignments, group and individual projects, extra-credit projects, demonstrations, guest speakers, and the "show and tell" procedure are all excellent vehicles for fostering transfer.

With ideas such as these, but more important with a real desire to maximize transfer, any teacher should be able to achieve a fair amount of transfer in the classroom and to discover new ways in which to increase the amount of transfer and generalization of classroom learning.

Summary

The way in which learning theories account for many different types of learning is spelled out in the work of Robert Gagné, who has presented a hierarchy of eight different types of learning, each one a prerequisite for the next. The various learning theorists fit in at different points in the hierarchy, with each theory working best at that particular level. Most classroom teaching takes place at the upper levels of the hierarchy—learning discriminations, concept learning, rule learning, and problem solving.

Gagné sees the three major tasks in classroom instruction as (1) designing instruction, (2) managing instruction, and (3) evaluating instruction. He believes that the best way in which to understand what goes on inside the learner at present is through the information processing model.

Teachers are responsible for learning outcomes in five areas of (1) verbal information, (2) intellectual skills, (3) cognitive strategies, (4) attitudes, and (5) motor skills. Gagné's model is helpful because it enables the teacher to specify the prerequisites for any particular learning task, it gives ideas as to what to look for when problems in learning occur, and it aids in planning by working backward from the final goal and planning only what is necessary to reach that goal.

Many different media are employed in classroom instruction. The teacher may present material orally or from printed material or from pictures, films, audiotapes, videotapes, or physical objects. Usually the teacher is utilizing the various language media, particularly oral communication. Oral communication is particularly helpful for channeling motivation toward instructional goals, for informing the learner of expected outcomes, and for providing guidance and procedural suggestions. Oral communications can be enhanced greatly by adding other media in the appropriate places.

In planning instruction, the teacher must trigger motivation in the students, set up an expectancy for learning, direct attention to the relevant points, provide for guidance and rehearsal, and work toward productive transfer of what is learned.

Three models of forgetting are presented: the disuse model, the interference model, and the coding and organizing model. Memory is better understood when one considers the differences between short-term and long-term memory. The information proccessing model aids in understanding this. Short-term memory is similar to an electrical circuit or feedback loop; long-term memory involves the chemical storage in the cells of the cortex. Once a stimulus has become a part of the long-term storage system, it is probably there permanently, if one can only find a way of retrieving it.

Repetition, recitation, and review are all helpful in getting material into the long-term memory. Robinson developed a specific system of improving study skills, the SQ3R method, which is built around the steps of survey, question, read, recite, review. Study skills are a highly individual thing, but it is likely that systematic effort will lead to improved study skills for any student.

Two examples of a mnemonic device are the mnemonic pegboard and the method of loci. Visual images are often a part of such devices. Overlearning is another technique for improving long-term memory. Ways of improving transfer are related to the two aspects of generalization and discrimination. It is important to work for both lateral and vertical transfer.

187

It is not enough to assume that such transfer will take place automatically; rather it must be pointed out and encouraged daily by the teacher. The chapter concludes with ten suggestions for improving transfer in teaching.

Study Questions

1. Specify an important concept that is taught in your field of teaching. Can you work backward from this concept and outline a lesson that follows Gagné's hierarchy of eight types of learning? What are the prerequisites for each step? How would you go about teaching the concept efficiently and effectively?
2. Following Gagné's advice, when would you use films in teaching your subject in the classroom? When would pictures, graphs, and other aids be useful? What part of your subject would require oral presentation, and what parts could students understand simply through reading about them?
3. What can teachers do to assure that what they are teaching gets beyond short-term memory and into the students' long-term memory? What kind of test items would you use to try to guarantee that the substance of what you have taught is firmly planted in the students' long-term memory?
4. A large part of instruction is still carried out by means of printed media, particularly in the form of textbooks. What does a successful textbook need to have, from your point of view? What makes some textbooks less desirable as a means of instruction?
5. The literature on operant conditioning emphasizes that positive reinforcement is the best means, in the long run, for bringing about favorable learning outcomes. In your own experience, what were some of the most potent positive reinforcers that helped you to learn, and what was the role of aversive stimulation when *you* were a student?
6. Think of the many subjects you have studied in your career as a student. Which subjects have the most transfer to life outside the school? Did the teachers in these subjects do anything you can remember that helped this transfer to take place?

References

Atkinson, J. W. *An Introduction to Motivation.* Princeton, N.J.: Van Nostrand, 1964.
Ausubel, D. P., Novak, J. D., and Hanesian, H. *Educational Psychology: A Cognitive View.* 2nd ed. New York: Holt, Rinehart and Winston, 1978.
Gage, N. *The Scientific Basis of the Art of Teaching.* New York: Columbia Teachers College Press, 1978.
Gagné, R. M. *Essentials of Learning for Instruction.* expanded ed. Hinsdale, Ill.: Dryden Press, 1975.
———. *The Conditions of Learning.* 3rd ed. New York: Holt, Rinehart and Winston, 1977.
Gagné, R. M., and Briggs, L. *Principles of Instructional Design.* 2nd ed. New York: Holt, Rinehart and Winston, 1979.
McClelland, D. C. "Toward a Theory of Motive Acquisition." *American Psychologist,* 20(5), May 1965, pp. 321–333.
Penfield, W., and Rasmussen, T. *The Cerebral Cortex of Man: A Clinical Study of Localization of Function.* New York: Macmillan, 1950.
Robinson, F. P. *Effective Study.* 4th ed. New York: Harper & Row, 1970.

Thorndike, E. L. *The Psychology of Learning: Educational Psychology (Vol. 2)*. New York: Columbia Teachers College Press, 1913.

White, R. W. "Motivation Reconsidered: The Concept of Competence." *Psychological Review*, 66(5), September 1959, pp. 297–333.

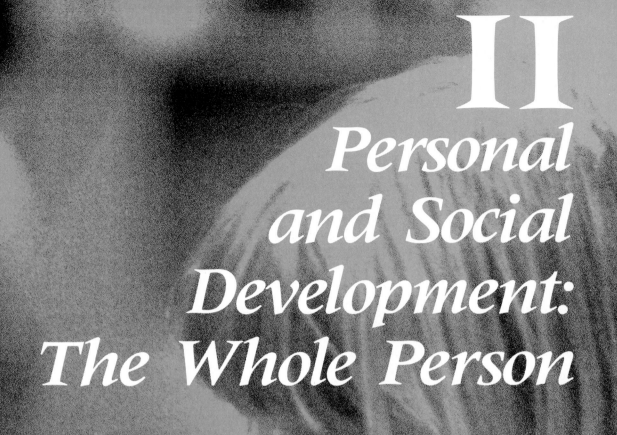

II
Personal and Social Development: The Whole Person

The reader is now introduced to basic principles of humanistic psychology. Humanistic psychology is concerned wih the personal and social development of a person. You have already read Erik Erikson's theory regarding social development of the person in Chapter 2. Erikson, you will recall, looked at stages in a person's psychosocial development. In this part, we discuss the theories of Carl Rogers and Abraham Maslow as a guiding framework for humanistic teaching.

The principles of humanistic psychology relate specifically to those goals and objectives of the school included in the *affective domain:* attitudes, beliefs, values, interests, appreciations, and responsibilities. It is argued in Chapter 7 that teachers have responsibility for these important areas as well as for the development of cognitive skills. Specific strategies for the development and clarification of values, responsibilities, and beliefs are presented.

An important factor influencing the success of teaching is the motivation of the student. Motivation originates within the individual and helps to determine his or her behavior in any situation. In Chapter 8, various theories of motivation are examined in detail. The teacher's role in the development of motivation is also examined and specific suggestions are made as to how teachers can best use motivational theory in their classrooms.

Humanistic Psychology and the Affective Domain

7

PREVIEW

What is humanistic psychology?

What is the humanist creed?

What are the cognitive, affective, and psychmotor domains?

Why should teachers study the affective domain?

What ideas form the basis of Rogers's person-centered therapy?

What is unconditional positive regard?

How is classroom teaching similar to counseling?

What are the dimensions of a healthy personality?

Why must teachers be open and authentic?

What is Maslow's motivational hierarchy?

What is self-actualization, and how is it attained?

What is a peak experience, and why is it a good thing?

What is the teacher's role in relation to Maslow's hierarchy?

How are deficiency needs different from being needs?

How do self-actualized teachers view the classroom?

What is a value system?

What is the behavioristic approach to the study of values?

What is the value sharing approach to studying values?

What is the value clarification approach?

How do schools violate the valuing process?

What type of classroom atmosphere encourages the development of values?

What is Rokeach's definition of a value?

What did Rokeach find in his research on human values?

What is measured on the Rokeach value survey?

How are values changed?

What is Kohlberg's model of moral development?

What stages of morality do most adults demonstrate?

What are the implications of Kohlberg's model for teachers?

How can teachers serve as models of moral reasoning?

In the introduction to this text, humanistic psychology was cited as the "other half" of the view of teaching adopted by the authors. As stated by the late Abraham Maslow,

Our first proposition states that the individual is an integrated, organized whole. I must confess that I have come to think of this humanist trend in psychology as a revolution in the truest, oldest sense of the word. . . . It is as if Freud supplied to us the sick half of psychology and we must now fill it out with the healthy half. . . . I think it fair to say that no theory of psychology will ever be complete which does not centrally incorporate the concept that man has his future within him, dynamically active at this present moment. [Maslow, 1970, p. 19; Maslow, 1968, pp. iii, 5, 15]

The Humanist Creed

Much of the work of humanistic psychologists can be combined into a statement about the nature of the individual and society and the goals of psychology, a statement of beliefs that we refer to as *the humanist creed*. In its briefest possible form, it declares that

1. Human beings are born to be wholesome, productive, creative persons. Human nature is good, not bad.
2. Although affected by the environment, important aspects of the personality come from within.
3. The goal of psychology should be to free up each individual to find his or her own inner self, to let each person become what he or she truly can be.
4. Psychology, then, must begin by focusing on individuals rather than on groups and normative data.
5. This requires a positive viewpoint of the nature of the individual and what he or she can become. It also suggests that we should study healthy, productive people, rather than the troubled and neurotic that are so often studied.

6. Freedom, an inner psychological freedom, is important in this view. While the many forces of society tend to subjugate individuality, the psychologist's job is to encourage it, to help it flourish.
7. In the final analysis, any social institution must be measured by this standard; to what extent does the institution foster healthy growth and selfhood to those involved? This is the ultimate criterion of schools as well.

This emphasis on the individual, development from within, the positive aspects of human nature, and the freedom to become all that one is constitutes a philosophical basis for a psychology that is considerably different from the behaviorist approaches (Shaffer, 1978).

The Taxonomy of Educational Objectives

Over the past thirty years, as educators have attempted to describe what can be learned in school, what goals can be established and carried out, and what behavioral changes can be achieved, a taxonomy of educational objectives has been developed. This taxonomy has three separate but interrelated domains: (1) the cognitive, (2) the affective, and (3) the psychomotor.

Taxonomy of Educational Objectives. Handbook I. Cognitive Domain, a milestone work in education, was published in 1956. Written by Benjamin

Cognitive objectives relate to the intellectual goals of the school. (Darrell Barry/Little Rock School District.)

Affective objectives relate to feelings and emotions. (Arkansas Gazette.)

Bloom and co-workers, it analyzed the cognitive or intellectual domain that is so obviously a part of schooling. This taxonomy not only mapped the domain; it also showed teachers how to develop learning objectives at each taxonomic level and how to evaluate pupil attainment. This first handbook was highly successful, and it led to an all-out effort to develop handbooks for the other two domains, the affective and the psychomotor.

A second taxonomy, *Handbook II. Affective Domain,* appeared in 1964, written by David Krathwohl and co-workers. Although not as famous as the first (possibly because most teachers are more aware of cognitive goals), this taxonomy of the affective domain is just as important.

The third handbook, on the psychomotor domain, has never materialized, although Harrow (1972) has developed a modest taxonomy in this area.

In the *cognitive domain,* objectives are related to the mind, to the results of attending, perceiving, remembering, associating, discriminating, analyzing, synthesizing, evaluating—in other words, to all forms of intellectual activity. Such activities are obviously important in school. The cognitive domain is discussed in detail in Chapter 14.

The third domain, the *psychomotor,* has to do with all behaviors involving body movements or muscular control. Teachers in fields such as music, physical education, coaching, certain vocational arts, typing, and dance are very much concerned with this type of learning. However, since one book cannot cover all things, we have decided to omit psychomotor skills from this text. Teachers with a special interest or need in this area are advised to consult such authors as Harrow (1972) and Kibler et al. (1970).

*Psychomotor objectives
relate to body movements.
(Darrell Barry/Little
Rock School District.)*

The Affective Domain

The *affective domain* includes all behaviors associated with feelings and emotions. Positive and negative feelings, emotions, attitudes, values, interests, appreciations, aspirations, morals, character—all are components of the affective domain. Clearly, the affective domain plays an important part in a young person's development. Even Piaget (1981), so well known for his work on cognitive development, argued that the affective and cognitive domains are inseparable and that each has important effects on the other. Yet, critics claim that affect is generally overlooked in school.

Affective learning, although it has not been completely neglected in the schools, has been slighted. There are reasons for this, of course. For one thing, although courses may have affective objectives, over time they tend to erode. This may be partly because it is difficult to evaluate the attainment of affective objectives. But furthermore, philosophical and perhaps political and legal difficulties are involved in evaluating pupils' attitudes and values, especially if such evaluation leads to grading and marking. Fear of indoctrination and a belief that democracy implies freedom of choice are factors. Another cause of erosion may lie in the frequently slow attainment of affective objectives, which are usually developed over time. [Ringness, 1975, pp. xi–xii]

197

Most teachers do not deliberately plan for affective learning experiences. In addition to the reasons just cited, this may stem from the belief of many people in our society that schools should teach "readin', writin', and 'rithmetic" and stay out of such areas as attitudes, morals, and values. This is unfortunate, because teachers *do* influence the affective domain, whether they are conscious of it or not, in almost everything they do.

The model of the affective domain developed by Krathwohl et al. (1964) is concerned with all aspects of this domain except emotions and personality development. The taxonomy portrays a continuum of affective behaviors in terms of degree of internalization. Early in this process, one can be only involved peripherally with a particular object or idea, aware of its existence but not investing strong affect in it. Farther along in the taxonomy, we see how one becomes more deeply involved, as in responding to the object or idea, developing positive feelings for it, or even making it a whole way of life.

Figure 7.1 presents a range of commonly used affective terms measured against the taxonomy continuum. In studying the figure note that it is neutral; that is, it applies to either positive or negative attitudes or values. Note also that it displays the entire continuum of receiving, responding, valuing, organizing, and characterizing in a value complex. It shows the dimensions encompassed by interests, appreciations, attitudes, values, and personal adjustment. This figure should clarify the fact that each aspect of affective behavior (attitude, value, interest) encompasses several dimensions of the continuum. What is not easily seen, but is true about the continuum, is that the divisions between the different steps in the continuum (receiving, responding, valuing, organizing, and characterizing) are actually somewhat vague. That is, it is often difficult to distinguish between one who has an "attitude" and one who has a "value." Nevertheless, the concepts of attitude, value, and appreciation are useful to the teacher, and the continuum helps us to understand how they are related.

To understand Figure 7.1 better, let us follow through with one concept—conservation. At first, students only become aware of what conservation is, some of the terms, and what it consists of, but they do not have a strong feeling for or against. They are willing to read, to learn more about it, to find out about pollution and its causes, to see some of the choices involved in conservation. But they are only at level 1, receiving, showing awareness, willingness to receive more information, to give selected attention to conservation material.

At level 2, responding, the students must form an opinion. At first, they may simply go along with the teacher's opinion, which is probably in favor of conservation. But later they will show that they are forming an internal conviction by willingly supporting conservation in public. Still later, they will even defend their position if attacked or in a conflict situation, when there might even be something to lose. They have moved through level 2—responding, at first with acquiescence in responding, then with willingness to respond, and finally with satisfaction in responding.

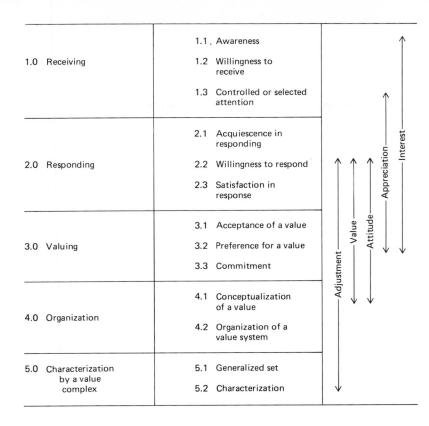

1.0 Receiving	1.1 Awareness
	1.2 Willingness to receive
	1.3 Controlled or selected attention
2.0 Responding	2.1 Acquiescence in responding
	2.2 Willingness to respond
	2.3 Satisfaction in response
3.0 Valuing	3.1 Acceptance of a value
	3.2 Preference for a value
	3.3 Commitment
4.0 Organization	4.1 Conceptualization of a value
	4.2 Organization of a value system
5.0 Characterization by a value complex	5.1 Generalized set
	5.2 Characterization

Figure 7.1
Range of meaning of commonly used affective terms measured against the taxonomy continuum. [Adapted from T. Ringness, The Affective Domain in Education *(Boston: Little, Brown, 1975), p. 21.]*

At level 3, valuing, students have broadened their opinions and have internalized them still further. They fully accept the need for conservation, they have internalized their opinions into their hierarchy of values, and they are becoming committed to them. The position has become an internalized belief and will govern the students' actions. They have moved through level 3, valuing, by first accepting the value, then showing preference for it, and finally developing a commitment to it.

Still later, a student may go beyond level 3 and organize his or her views on conservation into his or her total value system, along with views on politics, government, science, and related areas. It is possible even to reach level 5, in which conservation becomes an important part of the student's life in terms of a major in college or a career in life, thus moving to a generalized set and characterization by a value complex.

Why Study the Affective Domain?

An important part of what education in America attempts to do is to develop inner direction and self-control in students (Ringness, 1975). This means that we attempt to help students become capable of making decisions for themselves and to accept the responsibility for those decisions.

As we attempt to develop this inner direction and control, we cannot afford to ignore the affective domain. Decisions and responsibility in almost any area of life are based upon interests, beliefs, attitudes, and values—the affective domain. This is where humanistic psychology enters the picture and is most important, since it concentrates on the total person (Combs, 1973).

Humanistic Psychology

To any humanistic psychologist, the schools must be able to accomplish their goals in the cognitive area and at the same time (1) develop healthy self-concepts; (2) satisfy each child's needs for security and love; (3) foster respect for self and others; (4) encourage uniqueness and diversity; (5) allow each child to become what he or she truly can be; (6) allow freedom

Humanistic psychology is concerned with the development of the whole person. (CEMREL, Inc.)

of choice and individual responsibility; and (7) help each child feel that he or she is a decent, capable, lovable, worthwhile human being.

In addition, humanistic psychologists stress that the schools must avoid (1) pressures leading to cutthroat competition; (2) excessive rigidity and regimentation; (3) developing insincere persons who role play inappropriately; (4) feelings of failure and worthlessness; (5) separation of feelings and other parts of self from the intellectual self; (6) overprotecting students from the consequences of their own decisions; and (7) a climate that is devoid of values, beliefs, and feelings.

Accomplishing these goals is no small challenge. It summarizes the most central aspect of the teacher's dilemma in today's schools—how to bring about the "basics," the cognitive skills that almost everyone expects from the schools, and yet promote growth in these other areas. But it can be done and research indicates that it is being done (at least in some cases) (Combs, et al., 1969). Let us look at two contemporary versions of these humanistic goals in the schools.

Carl Rogers: Psychology of the Person

Carl Rogers is famous in psychology for a particular type of psychotherapy, often referred to as "Rogerian counseling." Therapy is very open and permissive, and the client is encouraged to talk about anything that he or she chooses. The counselor's job is to listen closely and try to reflect what the client says, to be an "active listener." In this type of client-centered therapy, the counselor does not interpret or solve the client's problems; rather, the client literally cures himself or herself. Rogers believes that the same qualities that enhance such therapy should logically enhance learning in the classroom also. He has summarized them as follows:

These same attitudinal changes would promote any whole-person learning—they would hold for the classroom as well as the therapist's office. . . .

Perhaps the most basic of these essential attitudes is realness or genuineness. When the facilitator is a real person, being what he or she is, entering into a relationship with the learner without presenting a front or façade, the facilitator is much more likely to be effective. . . .

There is another attitude which stands out in those who are successful in facilitating learning. . . . I think of this attitude as a prizing of each learner, a prizing of his or her feelings, opinions, and person. It is a caring for the learner, but a non-possessive caring. It is an acceptance of this other individual as a separate person, a respect for the other as having worth in his or her own right. It is a basic trust— a belief that this other person is somehow fundamentally trustworthy.

201

Carl Rogers. (Courtesy of Nozizwe S.)

A further element which establishes a climate for self-initiated experiential learning is empathic understanding. When the teacher has the ability to understand the student's reactions from the inside, has a sensitive awareness of the way the process of education and learning seems *to the student*, then again the likelihood that significant learning will take place is increased. [Rogers, 1980, pp. 270–272]

Rogers summarized his views on education in his 1969 book *Freedom to Learn*. He described the teacher as a facilitator, and even argued that it is doubtful that a teacher could "teach" a student anything in the traditional sense. In this work, Rogers stated that the classroom must be a very special, open, accepting climate in which students really are *free* to learn if they are to be prepared to live comfortably in the world. The teacher, rather than structuring the situation as completely as possible, should provide a bare minimal structure and encourage individual responsibility.

ROGERS'S THEORIES IN ACTION

Bob couldn't get over the attitude of the counselor. Bob had been sent to him for getting into trouble, as he had been sent to the principal and others before, always for the same reason. He expected to be punished, but instead this counselor listened intently as Bob told his version of what happened. He seemed sincerely interested in what he had to say, and especially in how he felt about it. As Bob talked, his tenseness and expectation of punishment gradually decreased, and he was surprised to find himself telling the counselor about his family, his father's unexpected death two years ago, and his inability to study. The session ended with no threats, advice, or punishment, and the counselor asked if he would like to come and see him again.

Bob went to see the counselor the next week, and in turn went back a number of times. The counselor allowed him to talk about anything he felt like mentioning, and always showed a genuine interest and concern for what Bob had to say. He had never experienced such complete acceptance. He did not understand why the counselor failed to nag, scold, or criticize and decided that perhaps the counselor just enjoyed talking with him and was bored with his job. At any rate, it was better than school, where it seemed that everyone was always finding fault with him. The people at school had acted as if they wanted to get rid of him when they first sent him to this counselor at the community guidance clinic.

As the sessions progressed, Bob found himself talking about things he had never discussed with anyone. One day, quite unexpectedly, as he was describing how he liked to go fishing with his father, he broke into tears and sobbed uncontrollably. The counselor did not get upset, tell him to stop crying, pat him on the back, or any of the things he might expect. The counselor merely handed him a tissue and stated that Bob loved his father and missed him very much. Bob talked for the next half-hour about the many things he had done with his father.

The counselor did not give Bob any advice, nor did he reprimand or punish him. Gradually, his visits to the counselor decreased in frequency, until one day near the end of the year the counselor asked if Bob would like to quit seeing him. He agreed, but they both also agreed that Bob could call and make an appointment to see him any time he felt like it. He never did quite understand what happened as a result of all those sessions with the counselor, except that he did feel much better about himself now, and his grades in school had improved considerably. He hadn't been in trouble for over six weeks, which made him feel good also. Bob understood himself much better now, although he wondered why the counselor had not just told him all of the things that he had to discover for himself. The counselor was one of the nicest people Bob had ever known, and he enjoyed the sessions with him, but this was one counselor who sure didn't do any counseling!

Without realizing it, Bob had participated successfully in nondirective, person-centered therapy, in which the therapist had provided an environment of warmth, empathy, and genuineness—unconditional positive regard—and in this climate Bob had utilized his own inner resources to discover his inner self and solve his own problems.

Such a classroom should reflect warmth, empathy, and genuineness, adding up to unconditional positive regard. Rogers acknowledged that such freedom is difficult, however, and suggested that the teacher evolve into it by gradually experimenting with the degree of freedom with which he or she is comfortable.

Another way of describing the goals of humanistic education as viewed by Rogers is to look at the positive changes he sees taking place in therapy and inferring that these same positive personality characteristics would be important in others also. In one of his most interesting books, *On Becoming a Person* (1961), Rogers delved into his experience as teacher, therapist, and counselor to describe the directions he has seen people take when

---

WHERE IS THAT NICE KID I USED TO KNOW?

Ms. Barnes did not like what she was seeing now in Paul. When she had taught him as a sophomore, he had been quiet and cooperative, completing his assignments on time and never causing any trouble. He responded whenever called on, paid attention, and followed directions well.

Now, as a senior, he had changed. He was no longer as quiet and certainly was not as cooperative. He sometimes didn't hand in an assignment at all and even raised questions and argued in class about assignments he did not like. He had challenged her several times in class and disagreed with her interpretation of history. He seemed to enjoy getting the class embroiled in an argument and almost always took the minority view or some unusual stance. He even ignored directions at times, apparently preferring to do things his own way and in his own good time.

She understood from his parents that they had noticed these changes also and were worried because Paul had announced that he had changed his mind about being a lawyer and instead planned to start in college without declaring a major. Certainly Paul could succeed in almost any field, he was such a fine student, but Ms. Barnes saw this as further evidence of how confused Paul was.

He had even stopped dating Linda, after all these years, and seemed to be "playing the field." He was planning a ski trip clear to Colorado over Christmas with a gang that she considered marginal and a bicycling trip clear to Maine in June that she considered to be ridiculous as well as dangerous. "What a shame," she thought to herself, "that such a nice boy as Paul has to go through such an awful stage."

Ms. Barnes needn't have worried. Paul was experiencing positive growth, moving away from "oughts," others' expectations, and façades and toward self-direction, openness, self-hood, and exploring the world and searching for his true inner self. These changes in Paul would be seen as very positive by Carl Rogers, Jean Piaget, or Abraham Maslow, who would have applauded Paul's growth toward maturity and authenticity. Such growth is often upsetting to parents and teachers, however, who interpret it as a sign of confusion, regression, or hostility. Do you see in this any conflict between Rogers's goals of healthy selfhood and the teacher's goals of order and control in the classroom?

Rogers argues that teachers must be very accepting so that students are free to learn.
(Bernie Weithorn/SIUC Photographic Service.)

they move closer to understanding and accepting themselves as individuals. Although it may not be reasonable to expect students to reach the sort of insights and understandings that adults eventually do, it is still logical to look at these changes that Rogers describes as eventual long-term goals of humanistic teaching.

Rogers sees the healthy personality as moving (1) away from façades, "ought to's," others' expectations, pleasing others, and other-directedness in general and (2) toward self-direction, complexity, openness to experience, trust of self, and acceptance of others. In general, the person becomes open to change, sees himself or herself as a process rather than a fixed product, accepts his or her own complexity, and at the same time becomes more accepting of others. (Seeing oneself as a process rather than as a product means realizing that one is always growing and changing, always experiencing new aspects of oneself. In seeing oneself as process, one is enabled to be open to new experiences and the changes embodied in psychological growth.) The individual moves "toward *being*, knowingly and acceptingly, the process which he inwardly and actually *is*. He moves *away* from being what he is not, from being a façade" (Rogers, 1961, p. 175).

The ideas just outlined raise numerous questions for teacher self-examination. Are you teaching students only from the neck up? Are you neglecting attitudes, values, perceptions, and feelings? Are you providing

205

an atmosphere of trust and acceptance in which students feel free to learn? Is it a climate of warmth, empathy, and genuineness? And, perhaps most important of all, are you a model of open, authentic selfhood yourself, rather than hiding behind the "role" of teacher?

Abraham Maslow: Psychology of the Healthy

We looked briefly at Maslow's basic assumptions about human nature at the beginning of this chapter. Maslow saw a unique core of individuality within each of us, this inner core being highly sensitive and easily subjugated. He saw the need for psychologists to study healthy persons rather than to focus on the unhealthy and neurotic. In addition, he saw the healthy personality engaged in a lifelong quest to find this true inner self.

Let us look more specifically at human motivation as described by

*Abraham Maslow.
(Courtesy of Office of Public
Affairs, Brandeis
University.)*

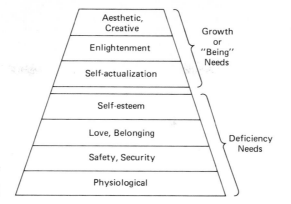

Figure 7.2
Maslow's hierarchy of needs.
[Derived from Maslow, A.
Motivation and Personality,
2nd ed. (New York: Harper
and Row, 1970), pp. 35–51.]

Maslow in his famous *needs hierarchy*. In Figure 7.2, you see what looks like a pyramid, with "physiological needs" at the bottom and "aesthetic and creative needs" at the top. This pyramid is designed to illustrate some of Maslow's ideas about a most central aspect of human nature, namely motivation.

The needs are placed in a pyramid or hierarchy to illustrate Maslow's contention that a person focuses on one level until reaching at least a minimal degree of satisfaction and then concentrates on the next level. Thus, the physical needs of hunger, thirst, and shelter must be satisfied before the individual moves on to the security needs, and these must in turn be satisfied before the individual can concentrate on the needs of love and belonging and so on.

The lowest four needs—physiological through self-esteem—are described as *deficiency needs*. This means that the individual reacts to a deficiency in food, security, affection, or esteem and, upon satisfying the need, restores a state of balance. The hungry person eats and is no longer hungry, the insecure person does something to restore a feeling of security, and the lonely person seeks affection. Once enough satisfaction in the area of affection is achieved, the person strives toward doing those things that give a greater feeling of esteem, boost self-concept, or give feelings of self-worth.

The top of the hierarchy, above the double line, represents a different type of need, which Maslow called *being needs* or *growth needs*, which suggests a distinctly different process from the deficiency needs just described. To reach this level of growth needs, the individual must have at least a reasonable degree of satisfaction of the deficiency needs, and Maslow concluded from his research that only a small number of adults in the United States had essentially reached this level of growth needs.

The following quotes from Maslow's writings should clarify and enrich your understanding of Maslow's hierarchy.

207

School lunch and breakfast programs are indicative of our understanding that education cannot proceed until physical needs are met. (Arkansas State Department of Education.)

1. *Physiological Needs.* "The physiological needs, when unsatisfied, dominate the organism, pressing all capacities into their service and organizing these capacities so that they may be most efficient in this service. . . . Undoubtedly these physiological needs are the most prepotent of all needs. What this means is that in the human being who is missing everything in life in an extreme fashion, it is most likely that the major motivation would be the physiological needs rather than any others."

2. *Safety Needs.* "If the physiological needs are relatively well gratified, there then emerges a new set of needs, which we may categorize roughly as the safety needs (security; stability; dependency; protection; freedom from fear, from anxiety and chaos; need for structure, order, law, limits; strength in the protector; and so on)."

3. *Love and Belongingness Needs.* "If both the physiological and the safety needs are fairly well gratified, there will emerge the love and affection and belongingness needs, and the whole cycle already described will repeat itself with this new center. Now the person will feel keenly, as never before, the absence of friends, or a sweetheart, or a wife, or children. . . . In our society the thwarting of these needs is the most commonly found core in cases of maladjustment and more severe pathology."

4. *Esteem Needs.* "All people in our society (with a few pathological ex-

ceptions) have a need or desire for a stable, firmly based, usually high evaluation of themselves, for self-respect, or self-esteem, and for the esteem of others. . . . These are, first, the desire for strength, for achievement, for adequacy, for mastery and competence, for confidence in the face of the world, and for independence and freedom. Second, we have what we may call the desire for reputation or prestige . . . status, fame and glory, dominance, recognition, attention, importance, dignity, or appreciation. . . . Satisfaction of the self-esteem needs leads to feelings of self-confidence, worth, strength, capability, and adequacy, of being useful and necessary in the world.''

WHICH CHILD WAS "SPOILED"?

Lou and Bud are as different as night and day. Both aged 21, and both from middle-class families and with college degrees, it is amazing how different their personalities are. Lou is very selfish and demanding, always wanting things his way and apparently fearful of being cheated or left out. He seems to want rewards constantly for anything he does, and he never appears to get enough affection. Always thinking of himself and his own comfort and satisfaction, it is not surprising that some who know him believe that he is the product of indulgent parents who showered him with rewards and affection.

Bud, on the other hand, is a very kind and generous person who appears unconcerned about his own satisfaction. Self-confident and secure, he does not indicate the need for physical pleasure, affection, attention, and reward that Lou has, and he is obviously more concerned about growth and achievement than about physical needs, acceptance, pleasure, and recognition. In Bud's case, it is not surprising that some who know him believe that his parents must have been fairly strict and definitely did *not* shower him with rewards and affection as Lou's parents did. It sounds reasonable to conclude that Lou's parents must have taught him to be so selfish and demanding and produced a ''spoiled'' child, whereas Bud's parents taught him to get along without these things by being more strict and aloof.

Interestingly, Maslow found exactly the opposite in his research on human motivation. People such as Lou, who express a strong need or fixation at the lower levels of physical needs, safety, security, acceptance, affection, are the ones who were *deprived* of need satisfaction in these areas as children. Lou's parents were probably the strict, aloof ones, not Bud's. And people like Bud, who do not show strong needs for satisfaction of these physical, safety, and affection needs, are the ones who were given ample satisfaction of these needs as children.

In other words, if you want to produce a child who has an extreme hunger for affection, or physical pleasure, or whatever, the surest way to do it is to *deprive* that child of satisfaction in these areas, and if you want to produce a child who does not show such strong needs in these areas, then the surest way to do it is to give plenty of satisfaction (comfort, affection, support, recognition, etc.) in these areas. Only by *satisfying* a need can one grow beyond that need.

5. *Self-actualization.* "Refers to man's desire for self-fulfillment, namely, to the tendency for him to become actualized in what he is potentially. This tendency might be phrased as the desire to become more and more what one idiosyncratically is, to become everything that one is capable of becoming."*

Maslow felt that his interpretation of motivation based on level of needs led to important ideas about human behavior that were often overlooked by other psychologists. For example, in his model an excessive amount of gratification of a need would be the surest way to get the child beyond that level, while withholding gratification would have the effect of encouraging the very behavior that is not wanted. (The child who receives an abundance of affection will not show a strong need for affection later, whereas the child with strong affection-seeking behavior is the one who did *not* receive ample affection early in life.)

The example, you probably noticed, is the opposite of what we would predict if we simply applied basic conditioning theory. The child who has been reinforced repeatedly for some behavior, such as affection-seeking acts, should exhibit more and more of this behavior as a result of the conditioning. The child who is not reinforced for such behavior, meanwhile, should experience extinction of such responses. Maslow thought it was important to note that the best basis for self-actualization later in life was the generous satisfaction of the deficiency needs, especially love and belongingness, early in life and that *too little* gratification of the need was the cause of the "spoiled" child rather than *too much* gratification.

Maslow's Hierarchy and the Teacher's Role

A mistake that is sometimes made when Maslow's hierarchy of needs is applied to the profession of teaching is to concentrate primarily on the level of self-actualization, the goal of developing fully functioning, self-actualized persons. Although this is a worthy goal, and one of the loftiest in humanistic psychology, teachers need to remember that self-actualization is a level that is not reached until adulthood, and even then only a small percentage of adults attain it to any great degree. For the child or adolescent, the teacher must be content to work toward self-actualization as a future goal, yet recognize that the child is currently functioning at the level of deficiency needs. The teacher's role, in other words, is primarily one of helping to satisfy the child's needs at the levels of (1) physiological needs, (2) safety and security, (3) love and belonging, and (4) self-esteem.

*From *Motivation and Personality,* 2nd Edition, by Abraham H. Maslow, pp. 36, 46, 59. Copyright © 1970 by Abraham H. Maslow. Reprinted by permission of Harper & Row, Publishers, Inc.

In doing this, it helps to think of the level of need that is important to the child right now, but at the same time to look back at the levels below that need and ask if they have been satisfied. For example, if the child is working on a project that the teacher feels is important in building the child's self-esteem, the teacher must think not only in terms of satisfying this need but also in terms of such questions as, Does the child feel accepted, part of the group, or does the child feel rejected? The child will have to satisfy his or her need for love and belonging before the teacher can do much to build self-esteem.

Going back still farther, does the child have a basic feeling of safety and security? If the child feels essentially threatened and insecure, then this is a need that must be satisfied before the child can move on to feeling accepted and a part of the group. In the primary grades, the teacher will spend considerable time in trying to satisfy the pupils' needs at the levels of physiological and safety and security. The teacher will also be working at introducing the children to the level of love and belonging, but many will just be starting to function at that level. This would probably be as far as the primary teacher could go with Maslow's hierarchy, as a true sense of self-esteem and achievement will not come until later.

In the upper elementary grades, the teacher should still be concerned with physiological needs and safety and security, but a much greater effort should be expended on the levels of love and belonging and self-esteem. In other words, as we move up the grade scale from early elementary to upper elementary, to junior high to high school, we expect to move up Maslow's hierarchy, but not in a simple, clear-cut way. There is no one grade level at which love and belonging or self-esteem suddenly become important needs. It is more a question of degree of attention to these different levels of deficiency needs. The important point is that teachers at all levels from kindergarten through high school *must* devote considerable thought and effort to the satisfaction of deficiency needs, always adapting to the level of physical, social, and intellectual maturity of their students, and keeping in mind that self-actualization is a long-term goal that the teacher works toward but never really reaches. If successful at satisfying the deficiency needs and moving students up the ladder, the teacher is also contributing to an increase in the number of self-actualizing adults in our society.

Description of Self-actualized Persons

The part of Maslow's hierarchy that has received the most attention is the top level: "self-actualization." Note also that expressive, aesthetic, and enlightenment needs are listed in Figure 7.2, but these tend to be outcomes of self-actualization rather than qualitatively different stages. Maslow also acknowledged that there are *some* exceptions, such as the person who has not satisfied the deficiency needs but is highly creative anyway or the neurotic scholar, but for our purposes we focus on the usual case where self-actualization is a process necessary to attaining these higher motives.

Maslow studied productive, healthy human beings and described the characteristics of self-actualization. Keep in mind that these are the results of empirical research and not imaginary traits. One of the conclusions of his research, which is a little sobering, was that only about 5% of adult Americans appear to be functioning at the being motivation level of self-actualization.

Self-actualization is a process, never completed, rather than a static state or product. According to Maslow, self-actualized people exhibit the following tendencies:*

1. More efficient perception of reality and more comfortable relations with it.
2. Greater acceptance of self, of others, and of nature.
3. Spontaneity, simplicity, naturalness.
4. Problem centering.
5. Detachment and a need for privacy.
6. Autonomy and independence of culture and environment.
7. Continued freshness of appreciation of life experiences.
8. Greater capacity for peak experiences.
9. Identification and sympathy with humanity.
10. Deep and profound interpersonal relations.
11. Democratic character structure.
12. High ethical sense.
13. Unusual sense of humor.
14. Creativity, originality, or inventiveness.
15. Resistance to enculturation.

While such a degree of completion and maturity would be unexpected in children and youths, and even rare in adults, it seems reasonable that we should strive for a climate in the schools that would enhance movement toward such eventual personality development. Maslow also pointed out that his research in no way represented a search for perfect human beings and that self-actualized people have their faults, just like anyone else.

Because of their accurate perceptions and keen ethical sense, Maslow reported that "self-actualizing people are not well adjusted" (Maslow, 1970, p. 171). By this he meant that they see the flaws and shortcomings in society and do not show high approval and identification with the culture. They adjust to conventions, but can discard them easily, and al-

*Derived from Maslow, A. *Motivation and Personality,* 2nd ed. (New York: Harper & Row, 1970), pp. 153–174.

ANATOMY OF A PEAK EXPERIENCE

Fred was having an absolutely fantastic night on the basketball court. He knew his shots would fall in as soon as he released the ball, and he also knew he was dribbling, faking, passing, and defending better than ever before. His entire body seemed to be working effortlessly, more coordinated than usual, and he seemed to know just where each defender was at all times. He had the feeling he could see everything around him, as if there were eyes in the back of his head.

Fred scored thirty points that night, but in his memory of that game, the number of points or rebounds is not what stuck in his mind. It was the feeling of joy, of elation that he had, the sense of being more alive and aware than ever, "having it all together" as his teammates called it. Ordinarily, Fred found such things as "getting position" and "taking a charge" by the offensive man as very difficult. He was usually poor at this, and he also feared getting hurt, as he often ended up on his back when he did take a charge. Tonight, establishing a position and taking a charge was easy, and his positive, elated mood rubbed off on the rest of the team as well. The general feeling of assurance, awareness, joy, and well-being lasted for several hours after the game.

This experience is typical of the "peak experiences" reported by self-actualizing persons studied by Maslow. Although sports is only one of the many areas in which peak experiences can manifest themselves, it is an area in which the results of the experience are often obvious and amazing to both the athlete involved and the spectators.

though not rebels or radicals, they will not hesitate to work for change *if* there is reasonable likelihood their work will have some effect.

The Phenomenon of "Peak Experiences"

An unusual finding of Maslow's research, and one that he concluded was a common characteristic of self-actualizing persons, was their increased ability to have "peak experiences." A peak experience is a somewhat mystical phenomenon in which a person feels far more alive, aware, perceptive, and able than he or she is ordinarily. Although they are very rare occurrences for most people, these "moments of highest happiness and fulfillment" can occur in any area of living. Maslow found such experiences to be characteristic of self-actualizing persons, but *not at all* typical of the rest of us.

In studying the peak experiences of self-actualizing persons, Maslow found that the experience tends to be seen as a whole and is detached from purpose or usefulness. The peak experiences were felt as self-validating, self-justifying moments, with their own intrinsic value. He also reported a characteristic disorientation in time and space and the learning of important insights about self and the world for those having these experiences. Maslow also concluded that a peak experience is good and desirable and is never experienced as evil or undesirable.

The Imperfections of Self-actualizing Persons

As presented here, self-actualization would appear to be a worthy goal of education, and certainly the self-actualization of the teacher must be a crucial part of it. As is true of all human beings, however, self-actualizing persons have their faults as Maslow found in his research.

The imperfections of self-actualizing persons seem to stem primarily from the strength of their personalities and their independence of mind (Maslow, 1970). They can act in a cold and almost ruthless fashion, carrying out a decision with such force that it strikes others as selfish or cruel. They can appear to be oblivious to others' feelings at times, and their detachment could strike others as heartless. Their independence from others' thoughts might seem insulting, and at times they appear deliberately to alienate people they see as ''stuffy'' or close-minded. They become ''absent-minded or humorless and forget their ordinary social politeness'' or ''use language or behavior that may be very distressing, shocking, insulting, or hurtful'' (Maslow, 1970, p. 175).

Such characteristics are not universal or inevitable in self-actualizing persons, however, and their increased objectivity should help them to see and control such rough edges when they do occur. Maslow also reported that some of his subjects were teachers, and he felt that it was very important for a teacher to strive for self-actualization and very helpful for the students if the teacher did.

SUZIE FINDS A DIFFERENT TYPE OF TEACHER

When Suzie enrolled in Mr. Richard's class, it did not take her long to see why he was so popular with the students. He started by taking pictures of the whole class and learning their names in less than a week. He had a real knack for getting everyone to participate and always made them feel good about their contributions. He listened with full attention to everyone who spoke and didn't interrupt or devalue what they had to say.

Mr. Richards obviously loved to teach, and the class members had the feeling that, for right now at least, they were his favorites. He was the most flexible teacher Suzie had ever had and yet obviously well prepared and clear on what his goals were. The small-group discussions, individual projects, student leadership, and responsibility were greater than in any other class. Suzie found that she knew and liked the students in this class, and quickly became close friends of several—more than in any other class. Mr. Richards obviously felt good about himself and about teaching, and he made the students feel good about themselves and about learning.

While not realizing the terminology, what Suzie was perceiving in Mr. Richards was a classic example of the self-actualized teacher as described by Maslow. With more teachers like Mr. Richards, the school could become an effective place for growth motivation toward self-actualization and a healthier society.

Deficiency Motivation and Growth Motivation

One final area of Maslow's work of interest is that of differences between two types of motivation—deficiency motivation, or the "D-needs," and growth motivation, or the "B-needs" ("B" here standing for being). For example, a person who has grown beyond the deficiency needs of safety, security, affection, and esteem and has moved on to the growth or being needs of self-actualization, creativity, and enlightenment is *seeking* these motives in a positive way rather than getting *rid of* deficiencies. Also, Maslow maintained that pleasure results from the tension of being needs, whereas D-motivation involves escape from tension; satisfying B-needs leads to pleasure and a desire for fulfillment, whereas satisfying D-needs leads to a sense of relief and satisfaction.

DIFFERENCES BETWEEN DEFICIENCY NEEDS AND BEING NEEDS*

1. A person acts to get *rid* of deficiency needs but *seeks* being needs.
2. Deficiency motivation leads to a reduction of disagreeable tension and restoration of pleasurable tension. Being motives maintain a pleasurable form of tension.
3. Satisfying deficiency needs avoids illness. Being needs produce positive health.
4. Satisfying deficiency needs leads to a sense of relief and satiation. Satisfying being needs leads to pleasure and a desire for further fulfillment.
5. Deficiency needs gratification tends to be episodic and results in consummation (eating three meals a day). Being gratification is continuous and never ending.
6. Deficiency needs are shared by all members of the human species. Being needs are idiosyncratic because each person is different.
7. The fact that deficiency needs can be satisfied only by other people leads to dependency on the environment and a tendency to be other-directed. Being needs are satisfied more autonomously and tend to make one self-directed.
8. The deficiency-motivated person is more dependent on others, whom he or she sees primarily as need gratifiers rather than as individuals in their own right. Consequently, the deficiency-motivated person is limited in interpersonal relations. The growth-motivated person is far less dependent upon others and may actually be hampered by them.
9. The deficiency-motivated person tends to be self-centered. The being-motivated person is capable of being problem centered and of perceiving situations and people in a detached way.
10. The deficiency-motivated person must depend on others for help when he or she encounters difficulties. The being-motivated person is more able to help himself or herself.

*Derived from Maslow A. *Toward a Psychology of Being,* 2nd ed. (New York: D. Van Nostrand, 1968) pp. 27–41.

What Humanistic Psychology Is Not

Having looked at these two views of humanistic psychology, you should now have an understanding of what humanistic psychology is. To emphasize this, we need briefly to stress what it is *not*. This is extremely important in view of the current attacks on humanism.

Humanistic psychology has been criticized as being antireligious. But this is inaccurate, as humanistic psychology is *not* a disbelief in the supernatural replaced by belief in reason and science. Although it does not specifically espouse religion, humanistic psychology is not inconsistent with religion. It is reasonable to claim to be both a Christian (or some other religion) and a humanist. It is inaccurate to summarize humanistic psychology as an "interest in human concern rather than divine concern."

It is oversimplified and inaccurate to describe humanism as "a devotion to human welfare." Humanistic psychologists do express concern for human welfare, but this is not a definition of the approach. It is not the study of the humanities or human culture, nor is it the rejection of Jesus as a supernatural being, the embracing of altruism, or a form of communist conspiracy.

Now that you have a clear understanding of humanistic psychology, we explore several key terms from the affective domain, namely values, moral development, and belief systems.

Values: Some Leading Approaches

The study of values, or those things in life that truly matter to people, those ends that are deemed important, is a very popular and active area in education. Many different approaches—the behaviorist or conditioning approach, value sharing, value clarification, and value process approaches—are currently being used.

The Behaviorist Approach

One approach that is spelled out clearly and logically, although not widely known among teachers, is that of Klausmeier and Ripple (1971). It is essentially a behaviorist approach, and it stresses stability, scope, subjectivity, significance to self, and significance to society.

In this approach, *tastes* are seen as temporary and changing throughout life. Tastes are specific to the object and a result of simple conditioning. You like Mozart, you don't like pizza, and you don't really care about milk, based not on any internal conviction but simply on the object and

Values are taught in schools in many ways such as in the ''Pledge of Allegiance.'' (Bernie Weithorn/SIUC Photographic Service.)

your experience with it. Tastes are not significant to the self, not a part of your ego strength, and probably of not much importance to others either. There is no real value involved in whether you prefer Coke over Sprite or slacks over dresses.

An *attitude*, in Klausmeier and Ripple's model, is another step toward generalization, internalization, centrality to self, and significance to self and society. "Attitudes are learned, emotionally toned predispositions to react in a consistent way, favorable or unfavorable, toward a person, object, or idea" (Klausmeier and Ripple, 1971, p. 518). Attitudes contain feeling tone, either rational or irrational, and this feeling influences acceptance or rejection of anything connected with the attitude. A cognitive aspect is also included, with internalized views toward the object, person, or idea, and an action aspect or predisposition to certain types of behavior. For example, one may have an attitude of opposition toward autocratic persons or situations. One may resist autocratic tendencies in others, refuse to comply, argue the wrongness of autocratic views, and do all in one's power to combat autocratic tendencies.

Attitudes, then, are directional rather than neutral and are more stable than are tastes or preferences. A liberal attitude will have wide application across a variety of life situations and will be far more continuous over time than will a taste or preference. It is internalized and conceptualized more deeply, is more subjective, is more a part of the individual's self-concept, and is more apt to be defended. Attitudes are also usually of more significance to society. Developed through imitation and conditioning, attitudes become internalized and take on increased significance over time, with the attitude being reinforced further each time it is expressed.

217

Farther along the continuum, *values* are internalized further, and generalized further, and are even more important than attitudes. Values affect entire ways of life (Klausmeier and Goodwin, 1975). They help to determine what one considers moral or immoral and thus contribute to what is often called character.

A value system is the final result of conditioning that has become internalized and, it is hoped, has become the basis around which one builds one's whole life. It is values that form the central core of what we call character. Thus, the character of Christ might be said to center around the value of compassion, that of Caesar on conquest, that of Confucius on wisdom, and that of Einstein on knowledge.

Value Sharing

Value Sharing: A Creative Strategy for American Education (Brandt et al., 1969) is a remarkable book because it describes a careful long-term experiment in a value-oriented approach to the entire curriculum of a public school, carried out in a cluster of mainly poor schools in Chicago in the 1960s. It is one of relatively few instances in which a teacher education institution has had the opportunity (and the funding) to test its philosophy and beliefs on a whole population of students on a long-term basis. This particular example of what is usually referred to as "action research" was based on a philosophy of *value sharing*, as elaborated by Harold Lasswell (1962).

The value framework behind this project was based on the central concept of human dignity, defined as "a state where no participant pursues his value objective in such a way as to seriously overdeprive or overindulge the pursuit of the value objectives of others in the process" (Brandt et al., 1969, pp. 7–8). Lasswell reduced all the possible value goals in life to a list of eight universal values in a democracy. These eight values are affection, enlightenment, power, rectitude, respect, skill, wealth, and well-being.

It was Lasswell's belief that all human societies must provide the equivalent of these values in some degree to their members to survive. The degree of sharing of these values depends on the objectives and social order of each society. For example, is the society oriented toward privileged possession by a few or toward the greatest dignity and worth of any and all members of the society? In a totalitarian nation, the masses of people are deprived of basic values in favor of monopoly or concentration in the hands of the privileged few. In a democratic society, the goal is the widest possible sharing of values, for such a society strives to accord dignity and worth to all its members.

With this in mind, Lasswell saw education playing a crucial role in assuring that the widest possible sharing of values really did take place. For this to happen, he also concluded that considerable modification of educational institutions as we know them is needed for schools to play this strategic role.

Briefly, the eight values in Lasswell's (1962) model are as follows:

1. *Affection.* Liking and being liked by others. Being accepted as one is. Caring and being cared for. Includes love relationships also but is not limited to these.
2. *Enlightenment.* Any outcome that is concerned with the clarification of meaning. Learning, knowledge, understanding about the world and one's place in it. Includes not only school learning but other types as well.
3. *Power.* Having control over important influences in one's life. The process of decision making, the control over policy. Human relationships in which there are implied or real consequences for nonconformity. The degree to which a leader influences a decision that affects others determines the weight of his or her power.
4. *Rectitude.* Right and wrong, personal and social responsibility. Concern with ethics, morality, fairness, and equity. Includes religion, but it can also exist separate from it.
5. *Respect.* One's reputation, prestige, and value in terms of society and its standards. Thus, people respect themselves in terms of how they see their value in society. Includes both respecting and being respected by others.
6. *Skill.* Proficiency in any practice whatever. Includes arts and crafts, trade or professional skills, school abilities, social skills, athletics, music. A skill tends to be valued by the person in relation to its value to society.
7. *Wealth.* Being comfortable in terms of goods and services. Warmth, clothing, possessions, food, care, anything contributing directly or indirectly to goods and services. Correlated only vaguely with money.
8. *Well-being.* A psychological feeling of assurance, safety, security. Absence of anxiety. Closely related to other values.

In studying these values, Brandt et al. (1969) found that certain commonly used adjectives tended to describe them. For example, a "knowledgable" person (enlightenment); "competent" individual (skill); someone who is "admired" (respect); a "healthy" person (well-being); someone who is "trustworthy" (rectitude); an "influential" person (power); an "affluent" family (wealth); and a "popular" child (affection). Various studies were done that indicated that these basic values are indeed an important part of our lives.

In looking at society, it is easy to see that each social institution has a primary concern with a certain value. For example, consider the following:*

---

*Based on E. R. Brandt et al. *Value-Sharing: A Creative Strategy for American Education.* (Evanston, Ill.: National College of Education, 1969), p. 10.

Institutions	*Primary Value Reflected*
Schools, the media	Enlightenment
Occupations, sports	Skill
Honors, awards	Respect
Family, fraternal groups	Affection
Church, home, courts	Rectitude
Psychiatry, social services	Well-being
Banking, business	Wealth
Government, lobbying	Power

In the value-sharing approach, it is important that the schools strive for the sharing of these eight basic values by all members of the school—students, teachers, administrators, and others. The schools involved in the study based on Lasswell's model planned their entire curriculum on this concept and explored and developed ways to carry out such a value-oriented curriculum. Those involved in the study concluded that a value-laden approach could indeed serve as a basis for curriculum in our schools.

Value Clarification

A prominent area in the affective domain today is that of values as they relate to education. Somewhat different from the value sharing approach of Lasswell is the *value clarification* approach advocated by such enthusiasts as Raths et al. (1978). They believed that a value must be chosen freely and that values must be explored and discussed freely so that individuals may understand their value choices. The valuing process they described consists of seven steps, as follows:

Choosing one's beliefs and behaviors.
  1. Choosing from alternatives.
  2. Choosing after consideration of consequences.
  3. Choosing freely.
Prizing one's beliefs and behaviors.
  4. Prizing and cherishing.
  5. Affirming publicly when appropriate.
Acting on one's beliefs.
  6. Acting in one's daily living.
  7. Acting with a pattern, consistently and repeatedly.

According to Raths et al., nothing reaches the deep level of value in life unless it proceeds through these seven steps. Obviously, if this is the case, then attempts to protect children or to indoctrinate them by exposing them only to the "right" values work against this valuing process. The child must be free to choose and explore values before he or she can really cherish them and live by them. The goal of the values clarification ap-

Role playing and dramatization may help teachers, parents, and children understand their own as well as others' values. (CEMREL, Inc.)

proach is to help students utilize the seven-step process in their own lives and to apply this process to already formed beliefs and behavior patterns and to those still emerging.

To do this, teachers must use materials and methods that encourage students to consider alternative modes of thinking and acting. Students must learn to weigh the pros and cons and the consequences of the various alternatives. Teachers must also help students to consider whether their *actions* match their own stated *beliefs* and, if they don't, help them bring the two more into congruence. Teachers must try to give students options in and out of class, if they are following this approach, as the steps make it obvious that it is only when students make their own choices and evaluate the consequences that they actually develop their own values.

In addition to the valuing process itself, Raths et al. have suggested strategies for helping students to explore their values. Informal discussions outside of class contribute toward this goal. In addition, anecdotes may be presented to which students can react in terms of their values. Value sheets, on which students systematically explore alternatives and their consequences, can be employed. Role playing may be used. All sorts of group processes, word games, puzzles, cooperative ventures, brainstorming, and interaction processes have been developed to allow for such value clarification. Two examples of these are presented in the box in detail.

There is no end to the strategies such as those in the box that have been invented, many of which have been around for years and are now

221

PLAYING VALUES GAMES

In an interesting book, *Values Clarification: A Handbook of Practical Strategies for Teachers and Students* (1972), Simon et al. collected a valuable assortment of strategies or "games" that help to bring about value sharing, value enhancement, and value clarification. Take, for example, the following.

The teacher passes out paper and asks the students to write the numbers 1 through 20 down the middle of the sheet. The teacher then says, "And now will you please make a list of twenty things in life that you love to do." The teacher tells them these might be little things and that the students can list more or less than twenty if they prefer. When the lists are completed, the teacher tells the students to use the left-hand side of their papers to code their lists as follows:

1. A dollar sign ($) is to be placed beside any item that costs more than $3 each time it is done.
2. The letter "A" is to be placed beside those items that the student really prefers to do alone, the letter "P" next to those activities that the student prefers to do with other people, and the letters "AP" next to activities that the student enjoys doing equally alone or with other people.
3. The letters "PL" are to be placed beside those items that require planning.
4. The coding "N5" is to be placed next to those items that would not have been listed five years ago.
5. The numbers 1 through 5 are to be placed beside the five most important items. The best loved activity should be numbered 1, the second best 2, and so on.
6. The student is to indicate next to each activity when (day, date) it was last engaged in.

Students can study their own lists in attempting to explain their entries and how they feel about them. It is usually helpful to pair the students to explore each other's list in detail and to answer questions about them. All class members can discuss their lists, which serves as a self-analysis, and gain greater understanding of each other and a sharing and clarification of their values.

A second example of a value clarification strategy presented by Simon et al. (1972) is seen in the following *rank order* assignment. The teacher explains to the class that they are going to be asked some quesitons that will require them to look deeper into themselves and make a value judgment. In each set of three, the student is to rank order the alternatives according to his or her own preferences.

1. Where would you rather be on a Saturday afternoon?
   _____ at the beach
   _____ in the woods
   _____ in a discount store
2. How do you learn best?
   _____ through lectures
   _____ through independent study
   _____ through seminars

in the "public domain." Teachers can also invent strategies of their own that accomplish the goal of getting students to discuss their values, to share and clarify them, and to learn to understand and respect the values of others.

To carry out such strategies effectively, teachers must have a positive, humanistic, and flexible classroom climate. Children must feel free to hold values that are different from those of the teacher or of other children. The validity of one's position on a value is determined by how carefully one has proceeded through the seven steps.

Value Process

An approach with several similarities but also some differences from Raths et al.'s approach is that of Jack Fraenkel. Central to his approach is a concern over how values are learned in school. If not learned in a planned and systematic way, they will be learned accidentally. Obviously, Fraenkel (1977) is not concerned with the question "Should values be taught?" since he believes they definitely are taught, intentionally or accidentally. Instead, he asks "What values do we want in our students, and how can they be developed?"

Since we live in a pluralistic society, with many subcultures and thus

223

a variety of values, it is important for the school to allow for this. Thus, Fraenkel is very concerned with the validity or *representativeness* of any set of values that are advocated by the school. How well do these values reflect the values of our society, and how well do they allow for the differences in subgroups that exist? In doing this, Fraenkel believes that we must go beyond the value as stated and look at specific behaviors that would be shown by a student who had that value. As an example, note the behaviors that might be shown by a student who valued the dignity and worth of others:

waits until others have finished speaking before speaking himself (does not interrupt others);
encourages everyone involved in a discussion to offer his opinions (does not mo-
   nopolize the conversation with his arguments);
revises his own opinions when the opinions of others are more solidly grounded
   in, and supported by, factual evidence than his own (does not blindly insist
   on his own point of view);
makes statements in support of others no matter what their social status (does not
   put others in embarrassing, humiliating, or subservient positions). [Fraenkel,
   1969, p. 458]

There is much research to be done to validate behaviors such as these as true indicators of the value in question—recognizing the dignity and worth of the individual. However, Fraenkel's approach has a certain ring of authenticity and common sense to it that is compelling, and in the absence of any contradictory evidence, seems to be a worthy model for teachers to follow. Fraenkel advocates stories in class that are as realistic as possible, with the children encouraged to identify with the characters and discuss the values involved. Such stories should have two or more conflicting alternatives, so that the children can discuss value alternatives and the reasoning behind them. Fraenkel calls this his "value developing strategy."

Milton Rokeach: Survey of Values

A most interesting and worthwhile contribution in the field of values is that of Milton Rokeach. Rokeach (1973) concluded that probably the most important concept in all of psychology is the term *value*. What does a person really value in life, in what is a person really interested? "Show me a person's values, and I'll understand that person and know what to expect from him."

Rokeach concluded that people are more interested in this, in their personal lives, than in anything else in the social sciences, and he commenced to study it with great intensity in the mid-1960s. He was interested in pinpointing what cultural and societal factors cause certain values to emerge and also in what the results of holding specific values would be.

In studying values in real life, Rokeach concluded that they could be defined with two essential and related meanings, both as ends and as means.

1. Values are *end* states of existence that one desires in life.
2. Values are descriptive ways of behaving or *means* of attaining these ends.

Rokeach challenged two traditional beliefs about values, as he pursued his goal of understanding the nature of human values. First, it had always been assumed that values were extremely difficult to measure, and second, it had also been accepted as fact that values were highly difficult to change. Rokeach ignored these two cherished beliefs and forged ahead in trying to find an easy but effective way to measure something important about human values.

The result was an instrument consisting of eighteen nouns (value ends, or ends in life) and eighteen adjectives (value means, or ways of attaining those ends). The subject merely has to rank order each list from 1 to 18, in order of importance in his or her own life, and the measure is completed. This simple but powerful instrument tells many things about an individual's values, what behaviors can be expected, and whether or not the individual is likely to change.

ROKEACH VALUE SURVEY*

Directions: Arrange the eighteen value nouns in order of their importance to *you*, as guiding principles in *your* life. Then do the same with the eighteen value adjectives.

Value Nouns (ends)	*Value Adjectives (means)*
A comfortable life	Ambitious
An exciting life	Broadminded
A sense of accomplishment	Capable
A world at peace	Cheerful
A world of beauty	Clean
Equality	Courageous
Family security	Forgiving
Freedom	Helpful
Happiness	Honest

*From Milton Rokeach. *The Nature of Human Values* (New York: The Free Press, 1973), pp. 358–361.

225

Value Nouns (ends)	*Value Adjectives (means)*
Inner harmony	Imaginative
Mature love	Independent
National security	Intellectual
Pleasure	Logical
Salvation	Loving
Self-respect	Obedient
Social recognition	Polite
True friendship	Responsible
Wisdom	Self-controlled

In *The Nature of Human Values* Rokeach explained the theory behind his value scale, the statistical research work that was required in developing it, and many of the findings from research utilizing the scale. Rokeach found that values are *not* extremely difficult to measure, as you would realize if you took the time to order the eighteen nouns and adjectives supplied. Anyone who knows how to read, regardless of age, should be able to perform this task. He also found that values are *not* so difficult to change, the major requirement being that subjects must see some dissonance between the things they say they value and the way in which they are living. A feeling of dissatisfaction on the part of a subject after completing the scale and looking at results is the best predictor that values will change later.

Just a few key values predict certain specific behaviors in life. For example, if you want to know whether a friend (or yourself, for that matter) is likely to give up smoking, you simply look at two values—broadminded and self-controlled. The person who ranks broadminded high and self-controlled low is not likely to stop smoking, and in a workshop for those desiring to give up smoking, the best chance for this person to stop smoking would be based on whether he or she could change the relative values of broadminded and self-controlled.

Likewise, the person who ranks self-controlled high and broadminded low is likely to be a good candidate for giving up smoking. Obviously, if one wanted to help people stop smoking, efforts should be designed around these two values—to increase the value of self-control and decrease the value of broadmindedness. Although you may not find yourself in the position of directing stop-smoking clinics as a teacher, the example is presented to show how specific values relate to certain specific behaviors. Much of Rokeach's research has been directed toward finding which value rankings are correlated with which specific behavioral changes, to better understand how our values are basic to what we do.

Another example of specific values and their relationship to behavior is in the area of politics. To tell where a person is in terms of his or her political behavior, we need to look at just two values and their rankings—

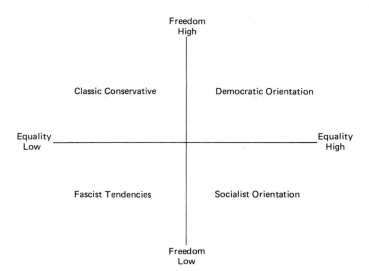

Freedom
High

Classic Conservative   Democratic Orientation

Equality _____ Equality
Low   High

Fascist Tendencies   Socialist Orientation

Freedom
Low

Figure 7.3
Political outlook as reflected by ranking of values of freedom and equality.

freedom and equality. If both of these are ranked very high, the person has true democratic ideals. If freedom but not equality is high, the person is a classic conservative. If equality but not freedom is high, the person is a believer in socialistic ideals. And if both equality and freedom are low, the individual has totalitarian or fascist tendencies. If the rankings for these two values are somewhere in the middle, then the person is probably a moderate or "middle-of-the-roader" politically (see Figure 7.3).

Rokeach's theory about change in values hinged on an idea of conflict, discrepancy, or dissonance. To change behavior, one must first change the values underlying behavior. For this to happen, there must be a *self-confrontation,* a dissonance in which the individual does not like what he sees in himself. He has not really discovered something "new" about himself; it is more a matter of "catching oneself red-handed," asking why this is so, and then concluding that one is inconsistent with one's own beliefs and must change. Rokeach referred to this as X (the self) and Y (the perceived behavior). X and Y cannot be too discrepant, or the individual will experience conflict and the desire to change. If X and Y are consonant, the individual is comfortable with himself as he is.

It is easy to see how Rokeach's value survey, and the ideas behind it, fit right in with the value sharing, value clarification, and valuing process theories of Raths et al., Lasswell, Simon et al., and Fraenkel. Rokeach sees some differences, however, the key difference being that value clarification, in his eyes, is too neutral a strategy. He believes that teachers must work *actively* and *intentionally* to change values, that this is really the major part of their jobs. He is fairly similar to Fraenkel in this regard. In spite of this active outlook, Rokeach cautions that he is in favor of value *change* but *not* in favor of *manipulation.*

227

Lawrence Kohlberg: Moral Development

A different approach from any that we have been exploring is Lawrence Kohlberg's theory of moral reasoning. Unlike most theories of morality, Kohlberg focuses on the *process of reasoning* behind the behavior rather than on the behavior itself. For example, if a child breaks the cookie jar, the important judgment to be made concerns *why* the child broke the cookie jar—was the child stealing cookies, getting cookies for someone else, washing the jar, or what? Kohlberg (1966, 1975) found that there were several levels and stages of such moral judgments, closely paralleling Piaget's stages of cognitive reasoning, that could be isolated as follows:

Level I. Preconventional Morality. At this level, the child makes moral decisions based on egocentric concerns. The immediate consequences of his or her behavior determine moral decisions. There are no internalized, abstract concepts of morality. Level I consists of two stages:

Stage 1. Punishment and obedience. The child behaves morally based on a desire to avoid punishment and seek rewards instead.
Stage 2. Instrumental relativism. The child adapts a pragmatic or "what's in it for me" attitude, with moral decisions based on "you scratch my back and I'll scratch yours."

In both these level I stages, no moral code has been internalized from outside, and the child is behaving based on preconceptual cognitive reasoning, similar to Piaget's preoperational thought. This is perfectly appropriate for a child until about age 8 or 9 (there appears to be a slight lag between cognitive stages and moral stages).

Level II. Conventional Morality. At this level, the child makes moral decisions based on concepts that others have taught him or her, primarily his or her parents. There is logical reasoning involved as in the stage of concrete operations in Piaget's model. The child tries to live up to the moral code that has been internalized. Many adolescents and adults are at this level of moral reasoning.

Stage 3. Interpersonal concordance. The child seeks to behave morally according to what "good boys" or "nice girls" do. The child has internalized a conventional code of morality from parents and society. No abstract concepts of morality are involved.
Stage 4. Societal maintenance or "law and order." The child has extended his or her concepts of conventional morality to include the rules and regulations of society as a whole. However, this tends to follow the letter of the law more than the spirit, and no general concepts of moral equity are involved.

In both of these stages, moral judgments are made on the basis of what *others* say is right rather than on a true understanding of moral concepts.

Level III. Postconventional, Autonomous Morality. At this level, which co-incides with Piaget's stage of formal operational thought, the individual makes moral judgments based on high-level concepts of fairness, equity, and justice. The individual is no longer other-directed but, instead, is directed by his or her own concepts of right and wrong.

Stage 5. Social contract, legalistic. The individual is oriented toward individual rights and general standards agreed upon by the society. Legalistic-type reasoning is often involved. Stage 5 goes beyond stage 4, in which the letter of the law was followed, to the concepts and principles underlying the law. The Constitution and By-laws of the United States reflect this stage.

Stage 6. Universal ethical principle. High-level, abstract ethical principles are the basis for moral decisions. These principles tend to be universal, transcending time and location, and are based on the dignity of the human being. Justice, reciprocity, and equality are included, at a high level of logical comprehensiveness, universality, and consistency. At both stages, the individual is inner-directed rather than other-directed and is utilizing formal logical reasoning based on abstract moral concepts.

To illustrate the six stages, let us look at several situations and how the different stages of moral reasoning would look in regard to those situations.

In the cookie jar example presented in the box, if Caroline chooses option 1, she is fairly obviously reasoning at Stage 4: the law and order stage. She does what is right according to rules and regulations, the letter of the law, without any time wasted on moral principles or concepts. In

---

THE COOKIE JAR

Caroline sees her little brother, Jamie, take some cookies from the cookie jar, something that they both know he is *not* supposed to do. At what level and stage is she in Kohlberg's model if she

1. runs immediately and tells her mother, as she knows this is against the rules and it is wrong for Jamie to be stealing cookies?
2. tells her mother because she fears that she'll be punished, if her mother finds out that she knew Jamie did this and didn't tell her?
3. makes a deal with Jamie that she won't tell about the cookies if he in turn won't tell about the dishes that Caroline broke?
4. tells Jamie that it just isn't nice to take cookies from the jar and that a good boy would ask his mother for permission?

option 2, she is behaving at stage 1—punishment and obedience. Her first concern is that of the immediate consequences to herself, and her behavior is designed to avoid punishment, without any real concern for Jamie or for moral ideas.

In option 3, she is reasoning at stage 2—instrumental relativist. Her concern is pragmatic, what's in it for me, and she turns the situation into one in which she has something to gain; she makes a deal with Jamie.

Finally, in option 4, Caroline is reasoning at stage 3—interpersonal concordance, or the "Good boy, nice girl" stage. She really has no high-level moral principles on which to base her behavior, but simply the straightforward idea that "nice boys don't steal cookies." She probably could not explain exactly why this is so, but she is willing to take it on faith, primarily faith in her parents, who have told her that this is so.

The example of Tom the carpenter cited in the box provides quite a long list of options to work with, but each should fit somewhere in Kohlberg's hierarchy. In option 1, he is clearly at stage 1—punishment and obedience. His only thought is the possible immediate result of getting caught and going to jail, so he decides not to desert. What is interesting here, however, is that it is *not* the fact that he doesn't desert that places it in stage 1 but, rather, the reasoning behind the decision. Notice that, in option 2, he follows the same kind of reasoning, that of fear of immediate negative consequences, but in this case he *does* desert his family. The punishment he is avoiding here is that stemming from his wife, family, and neighbors' disapproval.

In option 3, he is operating at the pragmatic stage 2—instrumental relativist. His major concern is "What's in it for me" and he sees the opportunity to take care of his family and at the same time enjoy himself. Thoughts of right or wrong, or even of punishment, don't enter his mind. Note, however, that this same reasoning could have led to the opposite decision, to stay, perhaps for the adulation of being a hero and perhaps because of other schemes for getting the money more easily.

In option 4, he is basing his decision on stage 3 reasoning—the interpersonal concordance or "Good guy, nice girl" orientation. It just isn't right for a good father to desert his family. In option 5, we see an example of stage 4—law and order—reasoning. His devotion is to the letter of the law, rather rigidly and without other considerations. He can't break the law, even when there are extenuating circumstances.

In option 6, he is reasoning based on the law also, but is now getting into abstract ethical principles, the spirit of the law. In option 7, he examines principles of fairness and equity in relation to his duties as a father, contrasts these to the meaning of the legal restrictions involved, and decides that the principle of human rights and dignity of individuals is more important than the technical details of the law. Note that he does *not* decide that it is a clear-cut question of right and wrong but, rather, that a behavior that he doesn't really like to do and knows is wrong under ordinary circumstances is best in this unusual situation. He makes his decision based

TOM THE CARPENTER

Tom, a carpenter, was fixing his roof when he fell and broke both wrists. Now he will be unable to work for several months, and he has no insurance or other financial benefits. He is extremely worried about his wife and six children. The youngest has a severe neurological problem that is greatly aggravated whenever the mother is not present and lapses into seizures. Besides, his wife is pregnant, so there is no possibility of her working. Tom is absolutely desperate to get money to feed his family.

Tom's cousin, who works for HEW, tells him it is no problem. All Tom needs to do is "desert" his family, and they will qualify immediately for Aid for Dependent Children. Furthermore, he doesn't *really* need to desert, but only pretend to, so that the family can qualify. If he wants to, he can hide out at a friend's apartment during the day and visit his wife at night. What should Tom do in this situation?

1. He decides not to desert his family since he might get caught and go to jail.
2. He decides to desert his family because if he stays he will be nagged by his wife, his kids will complain constantly, and his neighbors will shun him for failing to support his family.
3. He deserts, without a moment's hesitation, because his family can get the money it needs, and he can have an enjoyable vacation at the same time.
4. He refuses to desert, saying it just wouldn't be the proper thing to do. Decent fathers just don't desert their families.
5. He says he cannot do it because it's against the law. It is illegal to get funds in this way, and regardless how much he needs them, he just can't break the law.
6. He decides that ADC is for needy families and that his family is surely needy. It is only a bureaucratic problem that causes the long delay in getting funds, and his "desertion" would be entirely in the spirit of what the law intends.
7. He deserts, but only after careful examination of the principles involved. A man's highest duty is that of caring for his family, he decides, and the only way he can do this is to gain the financial help needed. The ADC funds are meant for needy family such as his, and the technical fact that he is breaking the law is far less important than his duty to care for his family.

on high-level principles of human dignity and individual rights as compared with society and the law.

Some Important Considerations for Teachers

Several relevant facts about Kohlberg's model are noteworthy for teachers to consider. First, this is not a rigid stage theory, and some exceptions to the normal progression through stages can be seen. People's reasoning vacillates at different levels at different times, sometimes running the whole gamut of the six stages. While it is impossible for an individual to reason beyond the stage of which he or she is capable, it is certainly possible for someone to utilize all the stages *below* his or her maximum level of reasoning.

A second fact about moral reasoning is that teachers who rigidly stress rules and regulations are not helping children to progress through these stages but, instead, are helping to fixate them at the lower levels. Overly enthusiastic use of punishment and obedience in discipline tends simply to fixate children at stage 1, whereas slavish adherence to law and order tends to keep the children at the conventional level, not encouraging any advance beyond stages 3 and 4.

Of course, stressing law and order might be beneficial to a young child who is still in stages 1 and 2 and needs encouragement to move on to the conventional level, but for older children the goal is to get the child to move on to a level of autonomous morality, to reasoning from internal standards that are based on true ethical principles. Children must see a continuous model of such reasoning in the teacher if they are ever to develop it themselves.

A third fact that is yielded by research on Kohlberg's stages is that a child cannot really understand more than one stage above his or her own stage of moral reasoning. Thus, to discuss ethical principles at a stage 6 level with young children who are in stages 1 and 2—punishment and obedience and instrumental relativism, respectively—is really equivalent to speaking a foreign language. Instead, teachers must start at the level of the children—that of preconventional morality, stages 1 and 2—and lead them to no more than one stage above if their understanding is to be maintained. Thus, a Sunday school lesson that stressed the "Good boy, nice girl" reasoning level is fine for a group of 7-year-olds who are mainly at the preconventional level, even though this would not make sense for a group of adolescents. In like manner, a group of adults who are primarily at stage 4—law and order—might not profit much from a lesson at stage 6 but could follow an argument at stage 5—social contract, legalistic—quite nicely.

Kohlberg and Piaget

Another fact about Kohlberg's stage model of moral reasoning is that it closely parallels Piaget's stages of cognitive development. Table 7.1 shows how moral stages are related to cognitive stages. Note that there is no stage of moral reasoning that parallels Piaget's sensorimotor stage. The child at this level is not engaged in any type of moral reasoning.

Kohlberg's level I—preconventional morality—coincides with Piaget's stage of preoperational thought. Note, however, that, whereas Piaget estimates this stage covers approximately ages 2 to 7, we see in Kohlberg's theory that the ages are roughly 3 to 9. This is because there is a slight

Piaget / Cognitive Development	Kohlberg / Moral Reasoning
Sensorimotor period (ages 0–2)	

Preoperational, intuitive thought (ages 2–7)	I Preconventional level
	  1. Punishment and obedience
	  2. Instrumental relativism
	    (approximately ages 3–9)

Concrete operations (ages 7–11)	II Conventional level
	  3. Interpersonal concordance
	  4. Law and order
	    (approximately ages 9–14)

Formal, logical operations (ages 11–15)	III Postconventional, autonomous, principled level
	  5. Social contract, legalistic
	  6. Universal ethical principle
	    (approximately ages 14–?)

Table 7.1
Piaget's Stages of Cognitive Development as Compared with Kohlberg's Stages of Moral Reasoning

lag between the point at which the child has the cognitive capacity for a given type of moral reasoning and the point at which the child actually starts to demonstrate such moral reasoning. This same fact is true throughout the table, with a slight lag of level II following the onset of concrete operations, and the lag reaching a magnitude of several years by the time we are looking at level III, moral reasoning. By consulting this table, a teacher or parent can readily see the stage of cognitive development that is essential for any particular type of moral reasoning and the approximate age levels for the different types of reasoning.

Another point that should be obvious after looking at this table is that moral reasoning at any level can only emerge *after* the stage of cognitive development has appeared. In other words, until clearly consolidated in preoperational thought, the child will be unable to exhibit preconventional level moral reasoning. Only after concrete operations are clearly established can the child exhibit any conventional level moral judgment, and formal operations are a prerequisite for the autonomous, principled level.

The Need for Discussion

It seems readily apparent that the child cannot develop a particular pattern of moral reasoning without experience with that type of reasoning. This means that, in following Kohlberg's model, proper behavior by itself is *not* the goal. The child might be behaving properly, as nearly as one can tell, on a daily basis, and still functioning at stage 1 of moral reasoning. The implication here is that teachers and parents (and other adults) must find ways to get children to *discuss* their moral reasoning. An open discussion of the reasons underlying behavior in a story the children have read, a discussion of the reasons behind a rule or regulation and the causes of violations of that regulation, a comparison of reasons why different chil-

Discussion of rule violations such as "No smoking on school property" can help develop moral reasoning. (Arkansas State Department of Education.)

dren would behave differently in a hypothetical situation—all these are examples of discussions of moral reasoning that would be beneficial in developing the students' moral reasoning processes.

One interesting finding from research on Kohlberg's model is the fact that the majority of adult Americans are at level II—conventional morality (Kohlberg, 1975). Many of these are still functioning at the "good boy, nice girl" reasoning of stage 3, with still more at stage 4—law and order. Just what explains this is not clear, although it probably indicates that (1) many adults fail to reach formal operational reasoning, which is essential to level III morality; (2) most adolescents cannot be expected to function beyond level II; and (3) there may be various forces in our culture that discourage people from operating at level III in moral reasoning, particularly at the autonomous stage 6, universal ethical principle, level. Perhaps teachers are in a position to do something about this, to work toward the long-term goal of having more people eventually reach stages 5 and 6 in moral reasoning.

One thing that is clear from the research is that those persons who are functioning at stage 6 in their moral reasoning are very independent and are much more apt to carry through on the results of their reasoning than are persons lower down in the hierarchy. Thus, a stage 6 reasoner who decides that something is morally wrong and demands action is much

MR. PETERSON'S DILEMMA

Mr. Peterson taught social studies in high school. He was highly student oriented and very proud of the excellent rapport he had with students. This rapport was an important part of his teaching success, he believed. He trusted the students, and they trusted him.

He was teaching about democracy and had just finished several days of discussion about such things as freedom of speech, the right to dissent in a democracy, and the effectiveness and legality of peaceful protest. After class, several students stayed to talk with him and proceeded to describe their plans to hold a peaceful protest. The school lunchroom was serving "nonunion" lettuce and grapes, and they felt that this was wrong and unfair to migrant workers. They planned to organize a boycott of the school lunchroom next week, complete with pickets, signs, and all the trappings of a peaceful protest. They hoped to force the school lunchroom to use only union grapes and lettuce.

Mr. Peterson tried to talk them out of it, but they insisted that they would do it. They wanted his help, and at the very least they wanted him to keep quiet about it. If the administration found out, they would surely fail.

Mr. Peterson's dilemma was that he knew that school policy, as spelled out in his contract, required him to report *anything* that might cause any disruption of the school day. But if he reported this to the administration, he knew that he would lose the respect and rapport he had with students. He also knew that if he didn't report it, he would be violating school policy and might even lose his job. What would *you* do in Mr. Peterson's shoes, and why?

Kohlberg used anecdotes such as this to get students to express their moral reasoning. It would matter little whether the student said he would or would not report the incident; what determines the student's level and stage is the reasons he or she gives for taking a particular course of action.

more apt to take that action than is a stage 3 or 4 thinker. This is probably viewed as problematic or even dangerous behavior by many conventional thinkers. Leaders in dissident and protest movements are many times sincere stage 6 moral reasoners (although some are also clearly in stages 1 and 2). It is clear that many of the great leaders and thinkers in history were people who consistently operated at stage 6, fully believing and following universal ethical principles, wherever this might lead them.

Belief Systems of Children and Adolescents

A rather delicate area that teachers should recognize regarding children's behavior is that of the belief systems of children and adolescents. Children below the age 12, and many adolescents also, do not reason logically and abstractly, which means that they do not understand cause and effect in the same way as adults do. The child sees magical connections between his or her thoughts and events in the world and jumps to the conclusion that thoughts cause events to happen. This leads to guilt feelings, and it is important for the teacher to help the child to see that a thought is *only* a thought; even a "bad" thought cannot cause a "bad" event to happen, and good thoughts do not directly cause good consequences.

Since the child's mind, being unable to reason logically and abstractly, is so vulnerable to misinterpretations, the teacher must help the child to understand his or her beliefs and to continually test those beliefs against reality. Some things in life are strictly subjective opinions, but most beliefs can be tested in some way to see if they are realistic. Gradually, the child will develop an independent ability to subject beliefs to reality testing, especially as he or she moves into concrete and finally into formal operational thought as an adolescent. Often, the emotions of the child are closely interwoven with the belief systems that he or she holds.

Obviously, one of the best ways in which to understand beliefs and to subject them to reality testing is to discuss them publicly. The teacher can provide numerous opportunities for this in the classroom, by guiding classroom discussions in the direction of what the children believe and what these beliefs lead to logically. Critical examination of beliefs, in an atmosphere of respect and kindness, is invaluable to the students in developing a basis for their own beliefs. The teacher must be careful that such discussions do not become embarrassing, threatening, or in other ways damaging to students emotionally. An attitude of highest respect on the part of all participants is required in such discussions, with critical thought focused on thought processes but not on criticism of the children as individuals.

Adjusting to a Changing World

It is painfully obvious that many things have changed in the last twenty years. The baby boom that followed World War II, the period of unprecedented affluence and economic growth, the moon shots, a world of cheap energy—all these are things of the past. Teaching in the schools is different in today's world, where budget cuts and declining enrollments are commonplace, and living in today's world is also different. It is most difficult to adjust to a declining standard of living, something that many citizens cannot believe can be taking place in the United States. As inflation eats away at the value of the dollar, and the family eats food they wonder how they can continue to afford, a mood of pessimism and nastiness spreads easily. Nobody likes to give up something that has been taken for granted.

In difficult times such as these, which most experts predict will continue and in some ways worsen through the 1980s, the teacher is in an excellent position to model constructive behavior in the affective domain. When values are in flux, it is helpful to view a mature model who has solid values and to explore and clarify one's own values in a nonthreatening atmosphere. A strong sense of ethical behavior and moral judgment takes many years to develop, and consistent models in the form of parents and teachers are a great help in this process. As teachers demonstrate both a sound and stable set of attitudes and beliefs of their own, coupled with tolerance and openness toward those of others, children will find it easier to adjust to life in a difficult and changing world.

Summary

There are three important domains in relation to what is taught in the schools: the cognitive, the affective, and the psychomotor. A taxonomy of objectives for the first two of these domains has been developed in detail by Bloom and Krathwohl and their colleagues. The third domain, the psychomotor, has not been explored or developed to this extent and is not a concern of this book.

The focus of this chapter is on the affective domain. Feelings, emotions, attitudes, values, appreciation, and interest are all components of this domain, and they are important in relation to classroom teaching, whether or not the teacher wants to acknowledge this. Attitudes and values are internalized through a continuum of receiving, responding, valuing, organizing, and characterizing. Each affective term that is used—adjustment, value, attitude, appreciation, and interest—covers part of the taxonomy, with considerable overlapping. This makes it difficult to distinguish a value from an attitude or appreciation from interest, but these are still useful concepts for describing the affective domain.

Humanistic psychology is a type of psychology that tries to focus on the healthy aspects of human nature rather than on the sick. Humanists believe that the nature of human beings is positive, that each person has an inner nature that will develop in a positive fashion if not thwarted by society. This inner nature or core of personality is delicate and subtle, but it is still there, even in the sick person.

In believing that everyone is born to be a wholesome, productive, healthy human being, humanists also believe that a major goal of psychology should be that of freeing up each individual to find his or her own inner self. In doing this, psychologists must focus on individuals and maintain positive beliefs about human nature.

The ideas of two humanistic psychologists are explored in this chapter. First, Carl Rogers and concepts emanating from his person-centered therapy are presented. Rogers is critical of American educational institutions for focusing so intently on ideas that they have produced "education from the neck up." Rogers sees this narrowness of focus as the cause of serious social problems, causing students to deny an important part of themselves, that part connected with feelings. Rogers stresses the importance of educating the whole person.

Abraham Maslow has provided us with a "psychology of the healthy." In his famous hierarchy of needs, each level must be satisfied before the individual can move on to the next level of needs. Needs in the areas of physiological, safety, security, acceptance, belongingness, and self-esteem are all deficiency needs, which means that the individual acts to correct a shortcoming or deficiency and ceases to feel a need in that area as soon as the deficiency is removed. Such needs can be handled fairly well with concepts and theories from traditional psychology.

Maslow saw another level of need, however, which he called growth needs. In this type of need, the individual is pursuing growth and change in a positive sense rather than eliminating deficiencies. A growth need is not satiated as a deficiency need is but, instead, leads to further growth and change. The individual is free to become more and more that which he or she is capable of becoming.

In studying self-actualization and growth motivation, Maslow found a number of characteristics that made self-actualized people different from the average. For example, self-actualized persons were found to have more realistic perceptions, a greater acceptance of self and others, autonomy and independence, a democratic character structure, and a greater capacity for peak experiences. They also tend to possess creativity, originality, inventiveness, and an unusual sense of humor.

Maslow spent considerable time studying the phenomenon of "peak experiences." This is a somewhat mystical occurrence in which a person feels far more alive, aware, perceptive, and able than usual. Such experience is common in self-actualized persons, but not as common in the rest of us.

Several different approaches to studying values are described. Klausmeier, in his conditioning approach, distinguishes taste, attitudes, values, and finally value systems in a step-by-step continuum. Klausmeier sees values as the central core of what we call character. All steps in the continuum are the result of conditioning.

Lasswell, on the other hand, focuses on value sharing. Eight basic values in life—affection, enlightenment, power, rectitude, respect, skill, wealth, and well-being—are seen as essential to all persons, and the sharing of these values is crucial for human dignity to flourish in a democracy. Lasswell's value sharing ideals were used as the philosophical framework for an entire curriculum in an experimental program in several schools, and the results supported the notion that a curriculum *could* be established and function successfully based on a value sharing model.

Other educators, such as Raths et al., stress the importance of value clarification. They describe a valuing process in which one must proceed through a number of steps before something can become a value. Choosing freely from alternatives, after considering the consequences; prizing, cherishing, and publicly affirming the belief; and acting consistently and re-peatedly are all steps in this process. Unless allowed to proceed through these steps, the child is not really developing his or her own values. When beliefs are imposed, the child may act as if these beliefs are his or hers, but beliefs imposed from without cannot really become values.

Fraenkel focuses on how values are learned in school. He advocates a planned and systematic approach in teaching values, for otherwise they will be learned accidentally. Fraenkel believes that teachers are teaching values whether they realize it or not, so that it makes sense to consider what values the teacher wants students to develop and to do everything possible to foster these values. In this approach, the representativeness of the values is important, and the teacher must be careful to teach those values that are broadly accepted in our culture. Techniques for developing values, such as stories with conflicting alternatives, are part of Fraenkel's approach.

Still another approach to values is that of Rokeach, who believes that the particular values that a person holds are the central core of personality. Rokeach ignored the prevailing belief that values were extremely difficult to measure or to change and developed an instrument for measuring an individual's hierarchy of values. This list of eighteen nouns and eighteen adjectives reveal important points relating to the means and the ends that a person sees as important in life. Rokeach also found that people who experience dissonance in looking at their values are likely to change to resolve this dissonance.

Differing from all these models is Kohlberg's model of the development of moral reasoning. In studying moral behavior, Kohlberg concluded that it was not the behavior itself, but the process of reasoning behind the behavior, that was important. Kohlberg identified three levels of moral reasoning—preconventional morality, conventional morality, and post-conventional morality—and six stages of reasoning, with two stages in each level. As the child's cognitive ability proceeds to higher stages, the child's moral reasoning would be expeced to follow. Teachers should keep these stages in mind as they try to foster moral development.

1. Is there a conflict between the ideals of humanistic psychology and the goals of the classroom teacher? Can a teacher be humanistic and still maintain conrol in the classroom? How can this be done?
2. In this text, the primary goal of the schools is seen to be the goal of cognitive development. Would Carl Rogers agree that this should be the school's primary goal? What do you think Rogers would see as the primary goal of the schools?
3. Humanistic psychology has been seen by some as antireligious. What is it about humanistic psychology that some religious leaders object to? What are the authors' views on humanistic psychology and religion?

4. Do you think that the principles of Rogers's client-centered therapy apply in the classroom? List several ideas from Rogers's work that you believe are relevant for the classroom teacher as well as some that are not.

5. How can Maslow's hierarchy of needs be of help to the classroom teacher? What levels of the hierarchy will the teacher most likely be dealing with in elementary school? in junior high school? in high school? What about the teacher's *own* needs—where are they on the hierarchy?

6. Why is the affective domain significant in teaching? Why has it received less attention than the cognitive domain? Why do you suppose the "experts" have been unable to delineate a psychomotor domain in similar fashion as the cognitive and affective domains?

7. What are the essential differences among attitudes, values, beliefs, and tastes? Why would it seem more appropriate for a teacher to try to change *beliefs* than it would to change *tastes?* Would there be different strategies involved in changing an *attitude* than in changing a *value?*

8. What are the eight basic values that Lasswell presented as essential to life in a democracy? How could a school curriculum be built around these values? Can you think of any important changes that would need to occur for the schools to reflect these values?

9. Why might it be a mistake to try to indoctrinate or "brainwash" children with the "right" values? What do Raths et al. claim is necessary before an idea or belief can become a value?

10. What two values would you focus on that would be crucial in getting someone to give up smoking? Can you suggest any reasons why these two values are related to smoking? How would you go about changing them?

11. Kohlberg found that only a small percentage of adults in our culture exhibit moral reasoning at the level of stage 6, universal ethical principle. Why do you suppose this is? Are there pressures in our culture that prevent individuals from reaching stage 6?

References

Bloom, B. S., et al., eds. *Taxonomy of Educational Objectives. Handbook I. Cognitive Domain.* New York: David McKay, 1956.

Brandt, E. R., Moore, A. P., Broadbeck, A., and Troyer, W. L., eds. *Value Sharing: A Creative Strategy for American Education.* Evanston, Ill.: National College of Education, 1969.

Combs, A. W., et al., eds. *Florida Studies in the Helping Professions.* Gainesville, Fla.: University of Florida Press, 1969.

Combs, A. "The Human Side of Learning." *National Elementary Principal,* 52(4), January 1973, pp. 38–42.

Fraenkel, J. "Values Education in the Social Studies," *Phi Delta Kappan,* 50(8), April 1969, pp. 457–461.

————. *How to Teach About Values: An Analytic Approach.* Englewood Cliffs, N.J.: Prentice-Hall, 1977.

Harrow, A. J. *A Taxonomy of the Psychomotor Domain: A Guide for Developing Behavioral Objectives.* New York: David McKay, 1972.

Kibler, R. S., Barker, L. L., and Miles, D. T. *Behavioral Objectives and Instruction.* Boston: Allyn & Bacon, 1970.

Klausmeier, H. J., and Ripple, R. E. *Learning and Human Abilities: Educational Psychology,* 3rd ed. New York: Harper & Row, 1971.

Klausmeier, H. J., and Goodwin, W. *Learning and Human Abilities: Educational Psychology,* 4th ed. New York: Harper & Row, 1975.

Kohlberg, L. "Moral Education in the Schools: A Developmental View," *School Review,* 74(1), Spring 1966, pp. 1–30.

———. "The Cognitive-Developmental Approach to Moral Education," *Phi Delta Kappan,* 56(10), June 1975, pp. 670–677.

Krathwohl, D. R., Bloom, B. S., and Masia, B. B. *Taxonomy of Educational Objectives. Handbook II. Affective Domain.* New York: David McKay, 1964.

Lasswell, H. D. *Power and Personality,* 2nd ed. New York: Viking Press, 1962.

Maslow, A. *Toward a Psychology of Being,* 2nd ed. New York: D. Van Nostrand, 1968.

———. *Motivation and Personality,* 2nd ed. New York: Harper & Row, 1970.

Piaget, J. *Intelligence and Affectivity: Their Relationship During Child Development.* Palo Alto, Calif.: Annual Reviews, Inc., 1981.

Raths, L., Harmin, M., and Simon, S. *Values and Teaching: Working With Values in the Classroom,* 2nd ed. Columbus, Ohio: Charles E. Merrill, 1978.

Ringness, T. *The Affective Domain in Education.* Boston: Little-Brown, 1975.

Rogers, C. R. *On Becoming a Person: A Therapist's View of Psychotherapy.* Boston: Houghton-Mifflin, 1961.

———. *Freedom to Learn.* Columbus, Ohio: Charles E. Merrill, 1969.

———. *A Way of Being.* Boston: Houghton Mifflin, 1980.

Rokeach, M. *The Nature of Human Values.* New York: Free Press, 1973.

Shaffer, J. B. P. *Humanistic Psychology.* Englewood Cliffs, N.J.: Prentice-Hall, 1978.

Simon, S., Howe, L., and Kirschenbaum, H. *Values Clarification: A Handbook of Practical Strategies for Teachers and Students.* New York: Hart, 1972.

Motivation and Classroom Instruction

8

PREVIEW

How is motivation defined by psychologists?

Why is it important to see that motivation comes from within?

What are the three levels of motivation?

What is the nature of physiological drives?

What is the homeostatic model?

What is deficiency motivation?

Why is it important for the teacher to be aware of physiological drives?

What are stimulus needs?

What are the needs for tactual comfort and stimulation?

How do stimulus needs compare with physiological drives?

How do stimulus needs function in the classroom?

What are learned motives?

How do learned motives compare with physiological drives?

What is a motivational hierarchy?

What is the certainty motive?

How does motivation to achieve affect the individual?

How does motivation to avoid failure affect the individual?

What are the motives of affiliation, anxiety reduction, dissonance resolution, competition, and cooperation?

What are the motives for power and aggression, approval, dependence and independence, and altruism?

How can teachers move students toward self-actualization?

What is the difference between intrinsic and extrinsic motivation?

How can a teacher model motives?

Why are positive aspects of motivation so important?

What dangers are inherent in avoidance learning?

What are the negative effects of anxiety as a motivator?

How can anxiety be an aid in learning?

Does failure have a function in learning?

Can learning itself act as a motivator?

Why is empathy important?

How do unconscious motives affect behavior?

How can dissonance be used constructively in the classroom?

What does it mean to say that there are side effects of motivation?

Why is feedback so important in classroom learning?

What are the strengths and weaknesses of informal classes?

What are the dimensions of effective praise?

Is there such a thing as *too much* motivation?

Probably no other term used in discussing teaching problems is as over-used, or as misused, as the term "motivation." Not only teachers, but administrators, counselors, parents, and even students can be heard with the perennial explanation for failure to learn, "Oh, Johnnie just isn't mo-tivated" or "Suzie isn't really dumb; she'll learn if she's motivated." A look at ways in which motivation is defined by teachers, and then a com-parison with psychologists' views on motivation, points out some inter-esting and consistent differences.

The "Hypodermic Needle" Model

Teachers generally define the concept of motivation as "something *you* do to *another* person to get *him* to learn what *you* want *him* to learn." In this sense, motivation is an active verb, as the teacher ponders such questions as "How do I motivate him?" "What can I do to motivate this class?" or "Did they do poorly because I failed to motivate them?" Many times a teacher will design a lesson plan, with a very clever, unusual, or puzzling opener (the motivator) followed by the lesson itself and some discussion. Such procedures elicit an image of a giant hypodermic needle, filled with this mysterious stuff called motivation, that arouses curiosity, enthusiasm, interest, and a desire to learn immediately following inoculation. The teacher's job when motivation is perceived in this way is to find ways in which to administer repeated shots of motivation, and learning will follow almost automatically. Such a view of motivation is inconsistent with the way in which psychologists view motivation. The remainder of this chapter is devoted to clarifying the concept of motivation as seen by psychologists and presenting a series of suggestions for the classroom teacher to utilize what is known about this topic.

Motivation Comes from Within

Perhaps the most obvious difference between motivation as an everyday term and motivation as a psychologist sees it is that motivation is *a force originating within the individual* rather than something the teacher does to the student. Dictionaries of psychological terms define motivation as "the nonstimulus variables controlling behavior; the general name for the fact that an organism's acts are partly determined in direction and strength by its own nature" (English and English, 1958). Such a definition clearly implies that the key to motivation lies within the individual, as some internal drive or need, rather than outside in something that is done to "motivate him." In fact, the statement "Johnny isn't motivated" is immediately dismissed as untrue by the serious student of psychology, since all persons have internal needs or drives. The teacher's statement "He just isn't motivated" could only mean, "He isn't motivated to do the things I want him to do" or "I can't seem to tie in to his drives and needs."

Teachers must realize that motivation comes from within. (Bernie Weithorn/SIUC Photographic Service.)

Level 1: Physiological Drives

We have all experienced thirst, and, even without the extreme of being shipwrecked or lost in the desert, we know what a powerful motivation thirst can be. Hunger and its all-consuming power after severe food deprivation also is easily understood by most people, even if they've never faced imminent starvation. Both these are examples of physiological drives, and both have the characteristics of being universal (everyone gets hungry and thirsty), of being innate or built in, and of being essential to life itself. These three characteristics—universality, innateness, and life-sustaining capability—plus a fourth characteristic that we'll look at shortly are the distinguishing clues to physiological drives.

Examples of other physiological drives are *pain avoidance, breathing, elimination, temperature maintenance, sleep,* and last, but not least, *sex.* In addition to being innate, universal, and life-sustaining, these drives satisfy a fourth characteristic of physiological drives, that of fitting a *homeostatic model.*

To understand the term "homeostatic," think of the thermostat in our home that keeps the temperature within certain boundaries by turning the furnace on whenever the temperature drops to the lower boundary and by turning it off as soon as it reaches the upper boundary. In the physical sciences, the term homeostasis is defined as "balance within the system." It has been employed for years to explain many physiological processes of the body, and psychologists use the term to explain many psychological processes as well.

*Hunger and thirst are powerful motivators. (*Darrell Barry/Little Rock School District.*)*

What do these drives have to do with teaching? At first glance, perhaps nothing at all, if you are contemplating employing them in the classroom to "motivate students." (One doesn't threaten youngsters with starvation, physical abuse, or deprivation of air.) However, they must be taken into account by the schools, since physiological drives will take precedence over all other forms of motivation if not satisfied, and they can indirectly subvert classroom goals. Anything the schools can do to assure that the child has proper nutrition, health care, and minimum satisfaction of physiological drives is not only humane but it also helps to free the child from concern about these physical drives so that he or she can go on to higher levels of motivation.

Another aspect of physiological drives is seen in a classroom that demands too much physical inactivity. Adults know they cannot sit still and listen without periods of muscular activity, that it's very difficult to concentrate when they have to go to the bathroom, and that no speaker can hold their attention when they are sleepy. Yet children, who if anything should be inferior to adults in these areas, are often expected to do what adults cannot tolerate and are punished if they protest. We are not suggesting classroom anarchy but, simply, that physical movement, break periods, relief of physical needs, proper lighting, temperature, and humidity are all important. If a student cannot sit still, the teacher should wonder why—it may be that the teacher is not allowing for simple physiological requirements, or it may be that the student has a special problem needing attention.

A third way in which physiological drives affect classroom learning is seen in the junior high classroom, where the emerging sex drive becomes very important. We are not advocating sexual initiation rites or any other of the oft-repeated jokes about sex in the classroom. We *do* suggest, however, that the junior high teacher recognize the strength of this drive and, rather than fighting it, acknowledge it and even utilize it in classroom strategies. Psychologists tell us that sex at this age level is important primarily as a way of defining the self in line with one's own sex and in contrast with the opposite sex. At the seventh to ninth grade level, this implies ample opportunity to talk to the opposite sex, individually as well as in groups; it is also important to talk about sex and behavior. The teacher can assist in these needs without operating a sex clinic in the classroom.

To summarize, the term "drive" in this breakdown has the following characteristics:

1. Essential for survival.
2. Innate—does not require specific learning.
3. Universal—everyone has them, in similar form.
4. Satisfies the model of homeostasis or "balance in the system."
5. Illustrates what is called "deficiency motivation" (i.e., the organism acts whenever a deficiency is felt and restores equilibrium).

247

ALAN AND HIS PROBLEMS IN PAYING ATTENTION

Mrs. Hamilton could not understand what was bothering Alan. He never listened, behaved in a hostile and sullen manner, and seemed to defy her at every turn. Having taken a psychology course, she was convinced that he was rejected by his parents and had regressed to an infantile stage. This being the case, she arranged an appointment with Mr. Valdez, the counselor, to discuss Alan's case.

Mrs. Hamilton was surprised at what the counselor told her. Alan was the third of six children from a nice family. His parents were fine people, and he had excellent relationships with his entire family. He had an IQ of 116 and had never been in trouble at school.

Mr. Valdez pointed out that Alan's family were migrant farmworkers and that they lived in a very small house and worked long and difficult hours through most of the year. Alan had never spent an entire year in one school. When he went home after school, he worked in the fields until dark and then often baby sat while his parents ran errands. He had no place where he could study in private even on the rare occasions when he did have time. His look of hostility and sullenness was understandable when she found out that he seldom got a full night's sleep and his noon lunch at school was his only hot meal of the day.

As a result of the interest aroused by teachers such as Mrs. Hamilton, the school was able to work out a special program for migrant students, including close cooperation with schools 1,500 miles away where the migrant workers spent the winter. Students like Alan improved greatly in school once their problems of fatigue and nutrition were solved.

Level 2: Stimulus Needs

Stimulus needs are similar to physiological drives in that they are innate or built in and also in that they are universal—everyone has these needs, regardless of the type of family background or experience. They are different from physiological drives insofar as they are not necessary for survival and do not fit into the homeostatic model. A brief look at stimulus needs will clarify their importance in influencing human behavior.

Sensory Stimulation

Imagine yourself alone in a soundproof, lightproof, vibrationproof room, so absolutely isolated that you literally hear your bones creak and want to grab at the blackness and pull it away from your eyes. Such a room or "deprivation chamber" has been employed by psychologists in numerous experiments to study the effects of sensory deprivation (Suedfeld, 1975). In addition to experiencing feelings of confusion, uneasiness, and panic, subjects in these experiments report hearing sounds and seeing lights, even though none is present. Actually, if one stays in such a deprivation room very long, one begins to hear voices and may even carry on a conversation with the nonexistent person behind the nonexistent colored lights.

This is not meant to imply that a soundproof room will drive you crazy; rather, it is meant to illustrate the very basic need for sensory stimulation. The human brain in normal circumstances is bombarded with millions of stimuli in all the sense modalities and is busily processing some, ignoring others, and giving directions to the body's muscles for responding to those stimuli judged important. If the brain is deprived of stimulation from without, the system literally *creates* its own stimuli to replace the nonexistent sounds, lights, smells, and vibrations.

Other psychological experiments show that subjects seek out sensory stimulation, enjoy visual and auditory input even when it is *not* related to reward or learning, are easily distracted by any stimulation that is stronger than the stimuli they are attending to, and see situations as unpleasant when sensory stimulation is low. Subjects who are deprived of sensory stimulation show decreased intellectual functioning, shifts in mood, and auditory and visual hallucinations (Cofer and Appley, 1964).

Implications for teaching should be obvious. We do not expect teachers to employ deprivation chambers as part of classroom discipline, but we do expect them to provide adequate stimulation to encourage learning and to be aware of the effects of sensory deprivation, overload, and interference.

WHAT HAPPENS TO YOU WHEN NOTHING IS HAPPENING

The room had absolutely no light, no sound, not even any vibrations or magnetic field. I had volunteered to be locked in this "deprivation chamber" to find out what it felt like to be without sensory stimulation. The first thing I noticed after the heavy door slammed was that it was darker than anything I had ever seen (or more accurately, *not* seen). The darkness seemed to cling to my eyes and I felt like grabbing at it and tearing it away with my hands.

Soon after the clinging blackness, I noticed that my body was making noises—I could hear every breath, my heart beating, bones creaking and scraping, and I could swear I heard my hair growing. I had never realized my body made so much noise.

The first light appeared after about half an hour. It was like a large flashlight, appearing to the left and moving across in front of me. After following several of these flashlights, I also started seeing colors.

The voices didn't start talking until several hours had passed. They were from a distance and garbled, but gradually they became louder and clearer. I thought I clearly heard "hello" repeated a number of times. There were also sounds of whistles, bells, birds chirping, rustling, and rumbling. For quite a while I sang, whistled to myself, talked, laughed, and in fact felt quite giddy. It was becoming a noisy place. I decided I had had enough after five hours and tapped on the door to signal to get out.

This account was given by an instructor who spent some time in a "deprivation room" in a psychology laboratory several years ago. Actually, he was in the room for a little over an hour but thought it was five hours. Notice how the brain, in the complete absence of sensory stimulation, produced some completely on its own.

Stimulus Variability

In addition to the need for sensory stimulation in a simple quantitative sense, we see stimulus needs illustrated in human behavior in a variable sense also. Subjects who experience a high level of stimulation for a while will actively seek a lower level, and vice versa. Just as the student enjoys a few days of "doing nothing" after a semester of sensory stimulation at school, the same student returns to school early because the lack of stimulation in doing nothing, while at first enjoyable, soon becomes boring. Even newborn infants evidence the need for stimulus variability in that they will look at curved forms longer than they will straight ones (Fantz and Miranda, 1975).

As pointed out earlier, the need for stimulus variability is both innate and universal, so that the teacher knows that *all* children need changing levels of stimulus input, *all* children become uncomfortable if the stimulus level remains constant, and *all* children will want to create their *own* sensory stimulation and variability if the teacher fails to provide them.

The need for stimulus variability in the classroom should be as obvious. This applies not only to a change of subject, such as math to English to history, but to changes in other dimensions. Even without an exhaustive analysis, the reader can probably list quite a few dimensions, such as (1) type of activity, (2) degree of student participation, (3) level of anxiety, (4) tempo or pace, (5) amount of structure, (6) domain (cognitive, affective, psychomotor), (7) rigidity versus flexibility, (8) formality versus informality, and (9) cooperation versus competition. These are just a few of the dimensions that can be varied, and the imaginative teacher can find almost endless permutations and combinations for satisfying the students' needs in this area.

*Motivation requires
sensory stimulation and
variability. (*Darrell
Barry/Little Rock
School District.*)*

TOM CLARK LEARNS ABOUT STIMULUS VARIABILITY

Several of Tom Clark's seventh grade students had been causing him trouble. He thought of himself as a good teacher, since he knew biology well and had worked out what he thought of as a successful routine for teaching it, consisting of fifteen minutes of lecture, five minutes of question and answer, ten minutes of slides or a film, and ten minutes of free discussion each day. As the handful of students began to misbehave, he tried sticking more carefully to this routine, but their minor antics soon turned into major classroom disruptions.

Being by nature a perfectionist, Tom turned to Dick Kellogg, known to be both successful and popular, for advice. Dick did not have any advice, but he welcomed Tom to watch him teach and see if he could discover anything about his own teaching. Observing Dick was a revelation to Tom. Dick did not follow a routine, and the students were never sure what to expect next. Rather than strict time intervals, he had basic goals in mind each day and a number of ways to work toward these goals. His entire lesson plan was open ended insofar as the duration of time spent on anything depended on how it was progressing and what he did next also was flexible. Tom found that Dick spent considerable time planning his classes, but not in the rigid, routine way that Tom was accustomed to. In fact, Dick always had twice as many strategies planned as he had time for, knowing that he could always use them later, and he professed that he enjoyed his classes immensely even though he was "rather disorganized."

After observing several of Dick Kellogg's classes, Tom concluded that Dick was not really disorganized and had, instead, found a secret to classroom organization that had eluded Tom.

From that day on, Tom always had in mind several different strategies for each class, and he forced himself to break away from his predictable routine. He consciously kept his planning open ended, and was delighted to find that, whenever he did something that surprised the students, they seemed to enjoy it every bit as much as he did. One other byproduct of his new approach to planning was that the students who had previously misbehaved adjusted quickly to his new techniques and even helped him by suggesting projects and activities to make biology more interesting. Tom had learned the meaning of stimulus variability in the classroom.

Stimulus Complexity

The stimulus needs discussed have been described in a quantitative sense and must be related to needs in a qualitative sense also. Children need varying *types* of sensory stimulation, and some of the dimensions are not so obvious. In addition to needing a change from the verbal stimuli of reading to the auditory stimulation of music to the numerical stimuli of math, the child reacts to the *complexity* of sensory stimulation in predictable ways (Munsinger et al., 1964). A math lesson can vary from highly complex levels of abstract reasoning to simple numerical operations, just as an English class can vary from a highly complex discussion of hidden sym-

251

bolism in a story to a discussion of the simple facts in the events of the story.

Studies of human behavior in relation to stimulus complexity indicate that we become uncomfortable whenever stimuli are too simple or when they are too complex; that is, each of us has certain limits of stimulus complexity, although these change over time (Haith et al., 1969). The trend of change is in a series of waves, as illustrated in the box following, with the learner pushing repeatedly to the limits of stimulus complexity that he or she can tolerate, then backing off to a less complex level, then moving ahead farther.

The implications of these findings for teachers lie not only in the fact that students will be utterly bored if the level of stimulus complexity is too low and utterly confused if it is too high, but also in the scallops or rollercoaster effect shown in the box. These scallops indicate that students enjoy being pushed to the limit of stimulus complexity and even slightly

CURVE DEPICTING CHANGES IN
STIMULUS COMPLEXITY OVER TIME

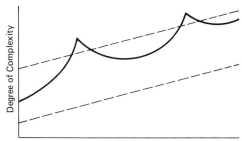

The chart depicts how stimulus complexity changes over time in relation to its effects on motivation. The dashed lines show the upper and lower ranges of acceptable complexity and how these gradually increase over time. The solid line, which follows a cyclical or scalloped effect, shows how a teacher might manipulate complexity in relation to these limits. Notice how the teacher starts at a comfortable level within acceptable limits, but then pushes the students to the upper limit or even beyond. This is only temporary, however, as the challenge of exceeding the top limit can soon lead to confusion or anxiety as the students desire a return to a more comfortable level. The pushing to the upper limit, then backing off, is apparently more stimulating and interesting to the student than is a straight ascending line within the limits and suggests that a type of deliberate varying of stimulus complexity is beneficial to motivation in the classroom.

Teachers are advised to vary the level of stimulus complexity in order to enhance motivation. (Arkansas State Department of Education.)

beyond, *if* it is only for a little at a time and they are allowed to back off to a comfortable level below their maximum to consolidate their gains. The teacher is advised then *not* to proceed by staying at the maximum level of complexity, *not* to stay in the center or at the bottom of this band, but to push to the limit, back off slightly, push to the limit again, and back off. Learning over time would proceed best, if this principle of stimulus complexity is followed, in the pattern of gradually ascending waves or a rollercoaster effect.

There are some problems in the suggestions just outlined. The ideal level of complexity varies considerably from person to person, and even from one task to another for one individual. The teacher facing a class of thirty can hardly tutor each and every student, yet will surely lose some of the students if these differences are ignored. The solution lies in the familiar compromise between responsibility to the class and to each individual, which seems to be the basis of most suggestions concerning individual differences. Teachers must provide a sufficiently broad spectrum in what they do so that it encompasses the complexity tolerance of most of the students in the class, while at the same time offers special aid to those outside this spectrum. Teachers must allow time for review and consolidation periodically and not forge ahead continuously. Subgrouping within classes, if flexible, can help, as can students tutoring others, use of programmed materials, remedial assistance, special projects, a "learning laboratory" approach, breaking content down into specific modules, small-group interaction, and competitive games.

253

Tactual Comfort and Stimulation

Another important stimulus need, of special interest within our culture, is the need for tactual comfort (the need for physical contact, need to touch or be touched, including both living things and inanimate objects). Our (American) culture sets many limits on the conditions when touching, being touched, feeling, holding of persons and things are allowed, so much so that psychologists sometimes describe ours as a "touch-starved" culture. As evidence of this, they point to the "no, no—don't touch" messages that bombard the young child, the punishments for touching oneself and others, and the "taboos" assigned to such behaviors as the following: (1) two members of the same sex holding hands; (2) two members of the same sex hugging, kissing, or in fact touching in any way; (3) fondling of the parts of another's body; (4) fondling of the parts of one's own body; (5) carrying around one's favorite blanket, pillow, or teddy bear; (6) kissing someone you don't love; (7) standing closer than two feet apart during a conversation; (8) handling your food with your fingers; and (9) deliberately brushing up against others while passing in public. These behaviors are determined culturally, since they are allowed or even openly encouraged in some cultures (Montagu, 1971).

The widespread popularity of the various sensitivity and encounter groups is interpreted as evidence of a touch-starved culture by proponents of this "touching taboo" thesis. Whatever variation the group illustrates, touching and being touched is nearly always a part of such group proce-

Touching is important.
(Arkansas State
Department of
Education.)

dures. The way in which customers will line up and literally "feel to death" the objects in carnival attractions that feature paying for the privilege of passing through a tent and touching various everyday objects is another illustration. But perhaps the most interesting observations in support of the "need to touch" proponents center on the research with Harlow's monkeys.

Harry Harlow, founder of the laboratory for research on primates at the University of Wisconsin, began in the 1940s wih a few Rhesus monkeys and a makeshift laboratory. Some of his research focused on raising monkeys from birth under certain specific conditions. In one experiment, the young monkey had no contact whatsoever with peers. In another, the monkey had contact only with a wire mesh surrogate mother. In yet another, the young monkey had contact with a cloth blanket surrogate mother (Harlow and Mears, 1979).

Harlow found that a monkey raised with everything he needs but who is not allowed physical contact with other monkeys is hopelessly maladjusted upon reaching adulthood. If placed with other monkeys after such upbringing, he will be socially withdrawn, afraid and confused, and unable even to learn his basic sexual role. The lack of contact with other monkeys while growing has irreversible effects, and the lack of physical contact with peers, of touching and being touched by other monkeys, is every bit as important as the lack of maternal contact. Probably the most widely known of Harlow's findings was the fact that a monkey raised with access to both a wire surrogate mother *with milk* and a cloth surrogate mother preferred the cloth surrogate *even though* he never received milk from it. The importance of cuddling up to the cloth blanket was thus seen as being every bit as important as satisfying the basic physiological drive of hunger.

Teachers at all levels should be aware of the importance of tactual stimulation and comfort. Not only children but adults also need to handle things, manipulate objects with their hands, even when it is not an obvious learning device. The sympathetic hand on the shoulder or the pat on the back might be more important than any words. Touching and being touched, manipulating things as well as people, should be modeled as normal and acceptable as long as rights are not violated. Physical contact with objects can be encouraged by including concrete objects and their manipulation whenever it is relevant in a lesson. Children must be allowed contact not only in "horsing around" occasionally but in expressing anger, affection, excitement, sympathy, and all the other human emotions. Teachers must also be willing to do this, even if they must struggle with their own taboos.

The problem in all these suggestions, of course, is in where to draw the line, how to distinguish between an inappropriate behavior or violation and reasonable exercise of the needs for stimulation and tactual comfort.

Since teachers seem generally to lean toward the inhibition or "don't touch" orientation, we suggest that the following criteria be employed: if it seems appropriate, go ahead and do it, or allow it, because it probably is all right; but if it seems questionable, examine it closely, and if you can't find anything wrong with it, go ahead and do it! This would tend to allow for the satisfaction of these needs that psychologists tell us are so important and yet provide a reasonable check on overdoing it.

PLEASE TOUCH

Miss Gregg was by nature somewhat reserved and by upbringing most polite and proper. When she accepted a position in the Second Street School as her first teaching job, she was not thinking about social class or upbringing, however; she was just very happy to find a job. It took her only a few days to realize that something was wrong; she did not seem to have rapport with her fourth grade class, and it was much different from her semester of student teaching in the Butterfield Hill School. After two weeks of school she had the opportunity to observe Mrs. Lorenz and her fifth grade, since all the fourth grades were on a field trip that day.

Mrs. Lorenz had a completely different classroom atmosphere. It was somewhat noisy, and certainly a little "disorganized," but the students obviously liked her, and she enjoyed them. Miss Gregg noticed also that Mrs. Lorenz moved around a lot and talked and joked with the youngsters individually as well as in groups. And Miss Gregg noticed something else; Mrs. Lorenz touched her students. A hand on the shoulder, tossle of a kid's hair, pat on the arms, just plain sitting close to a student she was helping. The students seemed to touch her, lean on her, rub up against her naturally. Only once during the morning that Miss Gregg observed did she see what appeared to be an emerging discipline problem, when one of the students who had done her homework assignment wrong was arguing with another that she was right and stubbornly refused to change it. When Mrs. Lorenz talked with her, it looked like she was definitely ready to defy her and even unleash all her pent-up anger on Mrs. Lorenz. But Mrs. Lorenz did not argue or defend the rightness of the assignment and the wrongness of the student's mistake. Instead, she placed her hand on Janet's shoulders, just looked at her until Janet returned the gaze, then smiled warmly and said, very softly, "I'll help you start on it; I'm sure we can have it finished in record time." Janet's anger suddenly seemed to subside, she held onto Mrs. Lorenz's arms for a few seconds, and then the two of them sat right on the floor and started to redo the assignment.

Miss Gregg remembered her methods instructor reminding her class again and again that accepting students was more than an intellectual exercise. She now realized that her prim and proper approach implied a lack of true acceptance and went out of her way the next week to "touch" her students with eye contact, active listening, smiles, and physical contact whenever it seemed appropriate, and her classroom atmosphere changed from one of uncomfortable stiffness to something more like Mrs. Lorenz's class, even though she remained more formal and more organized. She had learned a valuable lesson in observing her colleague that day.

To summarize this section on level 2, stimulus needs motivation, stimulus needs are

1. innate—they do not require specific learning.
2. universal—everyone has them in similar form.
3. not essential for survival, nor do they fit the homeostatic model of "balance in the system."
4. an illustration of "deficiency motivation" in that the organism is usually reacting to some deficiency in stimulation.

Level 3: Learned Motives

We come finally to the third level of motivation, a level in which motives are *not* innate, *not* universal, *not* essential for survival, and definitely *not* explained by homeostasis. These motives are a result of experience and thus vary considerably among individuals, even though once internalized they do satisfy the definition of "nonstimulus variables."

Motives at this level are defined as "a specific personal . . . factor controlling behavior" (English and English, 1958). It is at this level that many of the individual differences implied in the term "personality" are found. An important aspect of these differences is a result of the organization of learned motives into a hierarchy for each individual.

A Motivational Hierarchy

Before going on to examples of learned motives, it is necessary that the reader understand a motivational hierarchy. This concept allows for the fact that an individual has many motives but that they are organized into a hierarchy, with the "stronger" motives near the top and the "weaker" motives lower down. "Stronger" and "weaker" are defined in terms of probability—if John's certainty motive is stronger than his achievement motive, then the probability of his seeking certainty in a particular situation is higher than the probability of his seeking achievement. If we looked at John in a variety of situations, we would see the certainty motive affecting his behavior more often than the achievement motive, but it is important to note that we *would* see both.

The motivational hierarchy concept explains why individuals are different, and predictably so, even though the same motives are evident. If Tom, Dick, and Harry each have the motives of certainty, achievement, and affiliation, but each in a different order within their hierarchies, then we have some ideas of what behaviors to expect from each. If we look even closer and see what *types* of situation trigger particular motives in Tom versus Dick versus Harry, we are well on our way to describing the kind of person each is.

EACH THE SAME, YET EACH DIFFERENT

Taking a closer look at the hypothetical Tom, Dick, and Harry, just how do we mean each is different because of the ordering of achievement, certainty, and affiliation in their respective "motivational hierarchies"?

First, take Tom. One of his most predictable behaviors is that he likes structure, likes to know what is expected and what to expect in any new situation. Partly because of this, Tom is an accountant for a large firm, works very regular hours, follows a routine every day that includes an exact order for the many little tasks of getting up and off to work, parking, eating lunch, and so on. He plays bridge every weekend and enjoys the company of his circle of friends very much. One of his friends usually has a party for his group twice a month, and he always attends and enjoys it. He keeps his checkbook balanced, deposits $400 in savings every month, and has no thoughts of advancement since he "enjoys the job he has." The three motives in Tom's hierarchy are ordered certainty first, affiliation second, and achievement third.

Dick, on the other hand, is constantly busy with his social life, and even though he would like to improve his skills as a salesman and win more in terms of recognition, bonuses, trips, and the other incentives that his company offers, he just cannot bear dropping out of any of the groups of which he is a member. His bowling takes every Wednesday night, he sings with the Barber Shoppers on Thursday, Fridays invariably end with a party he just couldn't miss, he eats lunch almost every day at the diner where so many salesmen eat, and even though these time-consuming activities limit his sales, he doesn't know how he could change it. Besides, he doesn't want to get into a rut, and he is always ready to drop what he is doing to have coffee with a friend, make a new acquaintance, or do something completely spontaneous like taking off for the horse races. The three motives in Dick's hierarchy are ordered as follows: affiliation, achievement, certainty.

Harry's chief concern is usually his next case. An outstanding student, he went to graduate school in speech and communications. A first-rate debater, he became debate coach in graduate school and his team compiled the best record ever for his school. Following his master's degree, he enrolled in law school, earned his law degree in record time while working thirty hours per week, and is now an expert defense lawyer, specializing in legal services for the disadvantaged. Harry was too busy to get to know many people in school, and he is too busy now, but he is very proud of the number of cases he has won and the changes in law to which he has contributed. He spends what little "spare" time he has studying the latest cases in his area and planning his next defense in scrupulous detail. The order of Harry's three motives is achievement, certainty, and affiliation.

Additional facts about the three are that they are each age 35, married, with three children, belong to the same church, have the same annual income, and all voted the same ticket in the past three elections. Unusual? Not at all. While hypothetical, Tom, Dick, and Harry illustrate the fact that all of us have much in common as human beings, even to the point of amazing coincidence, and yet each one of us is unique and different. In the case of this trio, a key to their differences lies in the ordering of learned motives within each of their motivational hierarchies.

Certainty

Most people like to know what is coming next, to count on events and expectations in their daily lives, to know "where they stand." This is probably the motive underlying such suggestions as the importance of the teacher "structuring the situation" for the students, and it also explains children's tendencies to ask questions, to test limits, and to want to know "where they stand."

A closer look, however, shows several aspects of the certainty motive that are easily overlooked. First, we see that some individuals display a remarkably high degree of this demand for certainty, whereas others evidence little of this motive or even seem to thrive on *not* knowing what's coming—a sort of "surprise me" attitude toward life that implies an "uncertainty" motive in contrast to certainty.

Second, we find that the strength of the certainty motive is related to the types of experiences of the individual, particularly in early family life. The similarities in motives of father-son, mother-daughter, and brother-sister comparisons are often mistaken for proof of the predominance of heredity over environment, but actually these similarities prove neither side of the heredity-environment question, since they demonstrate an interaction of both factors.

Third, we see that an individual's certainty motive is very obvious in some situations, somewhat noticeable in others, and not at all apparent in still others. This is a characteristic of any learned motive, since an individual has a large repertoire of drives, needs, and motives that make up his or her personality and no one motive will predominate all the time. One aspect of the certainty motive that we see is the fact that it is obvious in new situations, particularly social situations and those involving achievement and competition.

Achievement Versus Failure Avoidance

Achievement is a term that is well known to most Americans, since it is linked to the idea of upward mobility and the "Protestant ethic." Closer scrutiny of the motive has brought out a number of interesting facts and misconceptions.

Achievement motivation can be defined simply as the positive desire to excel, to do well, to accomplish something on one's own. As studied experimentally, achievement is almost always linked to standards recognized by others, so that achievement motivation might be labeled more precisely "competitive achievement." Several findings concerning achievement motivation are presented here, since this is an area of much interest to teachers.

In the 1950s and early 1960s, David McClelland (1961) studied achievement motivation in a variety of laboratory situations that included different age groups and even different nationalities. One of his first findings was that behavior that is actually influenced by other motives is often mistaken for achievement motivation. The child who strives valiantly to

259

The desire to excel motivates practice. (Darrell Barry/Little Rock School District.)

prepare for an exam in school *might* be achievement motivated, but if a closer look indicates that his chief concern is fear of losing the approval of parents and teachers, we are probably witnessing the approval motive in action. Likewise, if another child is struggling through all the calisthenics and routines of conditioning so that he can make the football team, he might be achievement motivated, but if his major goal is friendship and acceptance into the "in" group of athletes, the affiliation motive might describe his behavior more accurately. The positive desire to do well, to achieve because it "feels so good," is the essence of the achievement motive.

A look at some of McClelland's research dramatizes characteristics of achievement motivation and contrasts these to another motive that is often mistaken for achievement, namely, avoiding failure. McClelland (1958) played a game with five-year-olds in which each child was brought into a room, handed several rope loops, and told that the game was to toss the loops on a wooden peg in the middle of the room. The child could stand anywhere in the room and was to estimate how many loops he could successfully toss on the peg.

One of the findings in this study was that M_S (achievement-motivated) children stood at a medium distance from the peg, whereas M_{AF} (avoid failure) children stood either right on top of the peg or else way back at an extreme distance. McClelland explained that the M_S child wants the task to be a challenge but, at the same time, wants a reasonable chance of doing well. Thus, he compromises between the high payoff of an extremely difficult task and the higher probability of success at an easier task and stands a medium distance from the peg. This tendency to balance probability of success with amount of payoff has been found in a wide variety of tasks and across age groups, including achievement motivated adults as well as children (Atkinson and Feather, 1966).

The M_{AF} children, rather than balancing probability of success and payoff, were concerned chiefly with avoiding failure and all the negative feelings related to it. It appears that one way of doing this is to make the task so easy that there is little chance of failure by standing up close. Another strategy is to stand so far back that there is little chance of success: Who would possibly expect a child to ring the peg from 20 feet away? Both these strategies, while successful in avoiding the accusing finger of failure, do *not* result in the M_{AF} child's feeling good, however, since there is no positive sense of achievement in either strategy. This tendency to set goals that are either too easy or extremely difficult is one of the major shortcomings of avoidance motivation.

Another finding from McClelland's research was the difference between M_S and M_{AF} subjects in reacting to failure. An M_S subject, if he sets a goal and falls short, will modify it slightly but in a reasonable fashion and try again. In the loop toss game, this would result in his standing a little closer to the peg or lowering his estimate slightly (he said he would make five but only makes three, so on the next series he estimates four), or perhaps setting the same goal (I think I have the hang of it—I think I can make five this time). If he succeeds the first time, he'll set a slightly higher but realistic goal.

The M_{AF} subject, however, makes extreme and unrealistic adjustments to failure (Atkinson, 1974). If he estimates five loops and makes only three, he may set a goal of one on the next try. If he falls short at 20 feet, he may move up to 1 foot on the next try. He may even fall short of his goal and set an *even higher* goal next time. These maladaptive reactions to failure tend to assure that the M_{AF} child will *not* receive the positive feelings of success on a challenging task, or we might say his attempts to avoid failure are almost a guarantee of avoiding success also.

Other characteristics of the M_{AF} child, such as a tendency to blame other persons and things for failure, all add up to the conclusion that achievement for positive satisfaction, rather than to avoid failure, is the type of motive to develop in the classroom. Critics of traditional education maintain that it is avoidance rather than achievement that governs most school behaviors. The child conforms to the behavioral requirements in school to *avoid* punishment, guilt, remorse, ridicule, rejection, and various other negative consequences. Positive satisfactions of achievement, these critics contend, are rare and are limited to a handful of students with high ability, and even these students in many cases are motivated by the desire to avoid failure. You can see this by announcing a test in your class and noting the reaction of students. A truly achievement-motivated student would welcome the test as another opportunity to succeed and demonstrate how well he or she is doing.

Affiliation

The need to be accepted by others, to belong to groups and to identify with peers, is a strong motive in almost all members of modern civilization, even though the ways of satisfying this motive are many and varied. The so-called "nonconformist" could more accurately be labeled a counter-conformist, since it is usually found that such a person conforms extensively to the standards of nonconformists. Adolescents are concerned with demonstrating their nonconformity to parents and other adults but in doing so often show slavish conformity to values, tastes, styles, and behaviors of other adolescents.

The affiliation motive is seen at all ages, but it becomes particularly strong in early adolescence, as anyone who has spent time at a junior high school can attest. At the same time that the "teenagers" are asserting their uniqueness and desire for independence from adults, they become more concerned with peer approval and conformity than at any other time in life. Adult approval, achievement, and any other motive that may have been predominant yesterday take a back seat today as they seek affiliation with their peers.

Anxiety Reduction

In explaining motivational behavior such as peer conformity, the favorite model of many psychologists is found in the dynamics of "drive reduction." The basic outline of this can be seen in the sequence of *drive-cue-response-reinforcement* described by Dollard and Miller (1950). A drive, such as hunger, emanating from within, alerts the person to anything in his or her environment that has to do with food. The individual reacts to any food-type stimulus as a "cue" to alert feeding responses, and if his or her response to some food cue results in *reducing* hunger, drive reduction has taken place because the individual's response has been reinforced. In this model, we learn to do those things that lead to drive reduction and to avoid doing those things that do not reduce our drives.

This simple model can be extended to the level of learned motives by substituting a learned motive for the hunger drive (Hebb, 1955). The type of learned motive most commonly studied in this light is in the general area of avoidance of unpleasant feelings. Guilt, shame, anger, fear, remorse, jealousy, and other feelings are familiar to all of us as feelings that are unpleasant and thus are to be avoided whenever possible. A key element in any of these feelings is that they make us anxious. Nobody likes to be anxious, and any time we feel anxious, we look for something to do that reduces the anxiety. If what we do in an anxious situation is rewarded by a lowering of our anxiety level, we'll do the same thing in that situation in the future.

Even though this idea of anxiety reduction as a major motive in human behavior can be extended to almost any situation, there are some problems for the person who commonly behaves in this fashion. In avoiding anxiety, children may also be avoiding doing things that they really should be doing. If mathematics makes Johnny anxious, and he in turn avoids mathematics as much as possible, he may be slipping steadily farther behind in an important area. His avoidance of anxiety in this fashion may lead to much bigger anxieties in the near future. A more constructive way in which to reduce his anxiety about math would be to provide the necessary help and practice to improve his mathematics skills.

Another negative aspect of anxiety reduction is that it can function as a self-fulfilling prophecy. The child who is extremely anxious about being rejected may avoid social situations and intimacy as a way in which to avoid rejection. One's anxiety about being unpopular is thus confirmed, since one who avoids and mistrusts others can hardly be popular. The more one avoids others because of anxiety, the more one is convinced that one's anxieties are well founded.

A similar problem can be seen in the dynamics of frustration tolerance. The ability to tolerate frustration, to adjust constructively to those obstacles that keep us from reaching our goals, is one of the most important characteristics of personal and social adjustment. This is not an inborn ability but, instead, is learned over numerous experiences with frustration. If the child finds frustration so damaging that he or she does anything to avoid it at all costs, then the child is avoiding the very experience that is needed to develop frustration tolerance. By avoiding those situations that could cause frustration, the child is guaranteeing that he or she will *not* learn constructive ways to handle frustration.

Cognitive Dissonance

Picture yourself volunteering to serve as a subject in a psychological experiment. After filling out a questionnaire concerning your political beliefs, you are told that you will be participating in a discussion group and that your role is to read and defend the views listed on the sheet handed to you just before joining the group. You find, however, that the views listed are exactly opposite to your actual beliefs, and you are very uncomfortable as you try to defend these views in the group discussion.

After the discussion session, you again complete a questionnaire concerning your political beliefs. Do you think they would change as the result of such an experience? Would they change in the direction of the views you were forced to read and defend, or would you become even firmer in your opposition to such views? Would it make a difference if the experimenter *paid* you for participating?

Most readers will insist that their views would *not* change as the result of such an experience, but the research on this and similar situations by Leon Festinger (1957) suggests that their views *would* change. Subjects in an experiment similar to that just described moved toward the views they were forced to defend, but when subjects were paid for participating, they showed less movement toward the opposing views (Festinger and Carlsmith, 1959).

Festinger's explanation for this was that reading the opposing views and defending them caused dissonance in the subjects, since this behavior was inconsistent with their views of themselves as honest, intelligent, and reasonable. To resolve this dissonance, these subjects unconsciously saw some reason and merit in the views they had to defend and moved in the direction of those views. Those subjects who were paid to participate showed less change in their views on the posttest, and Festinger explained that this was because the experiment did not arouse dissonance in these subjects. Reading and defending views that they did not believe was *not* dissonant to their image of themselves as honest, intelligent persons because they were paid for it, whereas the other subjects had no such rationale on which to fall back. This explanation, that we will behave unconsciously in ways that reduce the dissonance that often arises in life, is the basis of Festinger's cognitive dissonance theory of motivation.

In similar experiments, Festinger set up a situation that caused a discrepancy or "dissonance" between subjects' perceptions of themselves as reasonable, intelligent people and behavior that seemed to contradict this. In each case, subjects unconsciously changed their perceptions of the situation to resolve the dissonance. This has important implications for teachers, since children they teach will also find ways of resolving the cognitive dissonance they perceive. Perceiving the teacher as mean and unfair causes less dissonance than admitting the wrongness of one's own behavior, just as seeing math as a stupid and useless subject reduces the dissonance of making a "D" on the test. The parent who spanks his child as he explains that "this hurts me more than it does you," the child who cheats because "everyone else was cheating," the adolescent who gives into her boyfriend's sexual demands because "in the eyes of God we're married already" all illustrate ways in which cognitive dissonance is resolved. Teachers must learn to recognize their own mechanisms for reducing cognitive dissonance as well as the myriad ways in which students resolve theirs, and teachers must monitor their own behavior to see if they are providing healthy channels for the resolution of cognitive dissonance rather than contributing to negative and maladaptive behavior.

Competition Versus Cooperation

How many times have you heard the expression "competitive instinct," or "kids thrive on competition," or "he's just naturally competitive." Such sayings illustrate the widespread belief that competition is part of human nature, that it is as natural as eating and sleeping. On the other hand, we

Competitive behavior is learned and motivating. (Darrell Barry/Little Rock School District.)

have also been told about the importance of "learning to share," the difficulty of "making people cooperate," and the fact that cooperation goes against the child's "competitive instincts." Such phrases illustrate that, while competition is accepted as inborn and natural, cooperation is not usually seen as inborn. This view asserts that it is very difficult to teach children, competitive by nature, the difficult and self-sacrificing skills of cooperating with others.

Competitive behavior is *not* inborn or part of human nature; on the contrary it is a learned motive just as is cooperation. It only *seems* that competition is an inborn characteristic or "human nature" when one views it from the midst of a culture that teaches this motive at an early age and continues to reward it throughout life.

Much has been written about the evils of stressing competition in our society, to the extent that some critics even espouse the elimination of all competition within our schools. Individuals learn by succeeding, not by failing, so we should develop "schools without failure" to maximize learning for all (Glasser, 1969). Competition develops a few winners and mostly losers, so instead we should encourage cooperation and make everyone a winner.

Since competition is instilled so strongly in most children even before they come to school, it makes sense to avoid adding to this and creating an extremely competitive classroom climate. On the other hand, it is unlikely that teachers can eliminate all competition from the classroom regardless how hard they try, and, besides, the idea of a completely noncompetitive classroom is probably both impractical and undesirable in the midst of a highly competitive society.

265

THE MANY FACES OF FAILURE

Charles was descended from Cherokee Indian parents. Liberty Bell School was about 60% Indian and 40% white, if you counted anything above one quarter Indian ancestry as Indian. It was one of the poorest schools in one of the poorest counties in Oklahoma, once Indian territory, and its pupils scored far below national averages on almost everything.

Miss Barth knew these facts when she came to Liberty Bell School, although she didn't really understand the underlying reasons, and she came with the zeal of a missionary determined to help these children and raise their scores.

A typical scene two months later illustrates just one of the problems. Miss Barth is working on a math lesson. She calls on Charles, who she knows is good at math, and fully expects him to get the right answer so she can praise him as a model for the rest of the class. When she calls on him, he doesn't answer at first. After some probing and some helpful hints, he still seems completely unable to work the problem. Puzzled, but determined that this little Indian boy should serve as an example of success and her intention to teach *all* the students, she proceeds to attack the problem step by step, seeking an answer from Charles on each step. (After all, this always worked in methods class and in student teaching.) She is amazed that he is unable to do a single part of it and somehow seems to be determined not to try. She feels irritation, anger, even some bitterness, which is reflected in her voice, and the rest of the class looks at her noncommittally.

This scene is not unusual in this type of school and contributes to the feeling that these Indian children cannot learn, that they refuse to try, and that they might just as well be left alone. What Miss Barth doesn't realize is that Charles is being loyal to his peers, that in his culture it is shameful to show up your friends publicly, and that in this situation Charles really *cannot* do the problem even though he knows exactly how! In a competitive white middle-class situation, Charles literally cannot win, even if he knows how, and failure to understand such background differences may be fatal to a teacher's classroom career.

It is possible, however, for the teacher to try to develop *both* competition and cooperation in the classroom by creating situations that foster both and by finding ways to reward both. It is also possible to develop other types of competition than the familiar "I win, everyone else loses" approach. Competition of group against group, a student against his or her own past record, the class against grade norms, and scores based on amount of improvement are all ways in which to break away from "cutthroat" competition and encourage cooperation at the same time.

Power and Aggression

In a book which attempts to explain human behavior by comparing it to animal behavior, Lorenz and Leyhausen (1973) have presented an impressive argument for the notion that the individual's tendencies toward violence, aggression, and war are a basic part of human nature. Modern attempts to subdue these cannot succeed completely because the basic nature of man still lies beneath—the "naked ape" is only covered, but not changed, by all those clothes (Morris, 1969).

The violence of modern societies is certainly impressive, especially since it is directed so often not only toward our own species, but even toward those closest to us: our own families and friends. Psychologists believe, however, that aggression is essentially a learned motive, even though our hereditary potential may be such that this motive is easily learned. The basis of this belief lies in close observation of aggressive behavior within our culture, laboratory research in which aggressive behavior is both conditioned and extinguished, and cross-cultural studies that find both the degree and the types of aggression vary considerably from culture to culture. The fact that aggression is a learned motive has important implications for the teacher, since this means that he or she can influence the amount of the aggression motive developed in students and also develop healthy outlets for aggression. Research tells us that children learn aggression through a modeling process; that is, by observing it in others, and through rewards for their own aggressive behavior (Bandura et al., 1961). Teachers should monitor their own behavior to see how much and what kinds of aggression they are modeling ("how many times have I told you not to hit people" as you paddle a student's behind) and try to provide healthy outlets for aggression (beating someone in handball is better than punching the person in the hallway).

It is not necessary to portray violence to model aggressive motives for children. If adult behavior indicates that "might makes right," or that "winning at all costs" is crucial, or that "the strong make the rules and the weak must follow," then the child learns that aggression is justified as a way to satisfy his or her needs. Respect for others and an awareness of how one's behavior affects others are probably the most important traits to foster if the goal is to keep unhealthy forms of aggression in check.

Some psychologists see aggression as an expression of even more basic motives in life. Alfred Adler, for example, presents an analysis of human behavior in which the "power" motive is the basis for much of human behavior (Adler, 1930). We do not like to feel inferior, but instead we have a strong desire to feel superior, so we are motivated to do those things that give a sense of control, dominance, a sense of "power." Adler's famous "inferiority complex" idea explained how individuals who acted superior, rude, domineering, or insulting were actually doing these things to cover up basic feelings of inferiority. Even such neurotic states as depression and obsessive-compulsiveness are explained in terms of feelings of powerlessness and attempts to gain power.

Although modern psychologists see power motives as learned rather than as part of "human nature," we would have to agree that children as well as adults learn to do those things that give them feelings of superiority,

267

power, and control and to avoid those things that lead to feelings of inferiority and helplessness. The teacher can avoid modeling the power motive through dominance of others and, instead, help children to find ways of gaining feelings of power through achievement, affiliation with others, and democratic processes.

Other Learned Motives

The list of learned motives is much longer than those we have discussed, although we have included some of the most important. One that has not been discussed, but one that is certainly well known to teachers, is the *approval motive.* The young child is strongly motivated to gain the approval of parents and to avoid their disapproval, since this is the primary source of status in the preschool years. Once in school, the child discovers a whole new arena for gaining approval and avoiding disapproval. Teachers, classmates, older children, and in fact anyone with whom the child has contact in school is a potential source of approval. It is not surprising then that the influence of parental approval begins to fade even in the elementary grades.

By age 12 to 14, or roughly the junior high level, the need for approval swings so strongly toward peers that parents and teachers are sometimes alarmed. Although young adolescents go out of their way to show their loyalty to peers and criticize or reject adult values and authority, it is a mistake to conclude that the approval motive has swung 100% to peers. Approval of adults, including teachers, is still important, even though the adolescent might not appear to be affected by it. Teachers should try to

*There is a very strong need for peer group approval during the early teens. (*Bernie Weithorn/ SIUC Photographic Service.*)*

utilize peer approval toward constructive ends, add their own approval as much as possible, avoid situations in which the adolescent is forced to choose between peer approval and adult approval, and work toward developing judgment and standards that are internalized so that the adolescent becomes less dependent on the approval of any outside source. The approval motive becomes maladaptive when it is so strong that it supersedes all other motives or when it leads a child to destructive, immoral, or illegal behavior, or when it becomes the only source of satisfaction.

Some motives seem to exist along a continuum in which both ends develop concurrently and appear to be pitted against each other. This was noted in the certainty-uncertainty dimension and in competition-cooperation, and it is definitely the case in the dependence-independence continuum. We all start life far out on the dependence end, our feelings of "infantile omnipotence" as we demand our parents' attention notwithstanding. That we are dependent in childhood is so obviously the case that it is easy to forget that dependent behavior is learned. The child who is strongly rewarded for dependence and ignored or even punished for attempts at independence becomes an expert at being dependent, and this can extend even into adulthood. The child whose dependence is accepted as necessary but not overly encouraged, and whose attempts at independence are encouraged and rewarded, demonstrates a much stronger independence motive even in childhood and has a headstart toward becoming an independent adult.

One psychologist, Otto Rank, was so impressed with the conflicting and vacillating motives of dependence versus independence during adolescence that he concluded this was the basis of adolescent personality development (Rank, 1932). The natural position of the child is one of dependency, and dependent behavior is normal, encouraged, and rewarded. The basis of adulthood is independence, and an adult whose dependency motives predominate is not really an adult, in Rank's view. But during adolescence, both motives are strong, since adolescence is the transition from childhood to adulthood. The moodiness, vacillation, clumsiness, embarrassment, guilt, and unpredictable behavior so common in adolescence is a result of these two motives, dependence and independence, both functioning as important determinants of behavior as the adolescent struggles for independence but also clings to the familiar rewards of dependent behavior. The sometimes amusing insistence on "Please, mother, I want to do it myself," in the face of slavish loyalty and obedience to peer pressures, is interpreted by Rank as a result of dependence and independence conflicts.

Another important learned motive that should be mentioned is that of *altruism*. Altruism, or the doing of kind or generous acts without expecting any recognition or reward, is certainly not an inborn or universal trait. Some psychologists, such as Piaget, believe that it can only come in those who are fairly advanced in cognitive development. But children as young as 3 years old act in a fashion that certainly appears to be that of being kind or generous without expecting any recognition or reward. Obviously, such a young child must learn from somebody to act this way, and the most likely somebody would be the parent.

But teachers too are in a position to develop altruism in students. It is probably one of our most neglected learned motives. By being an altruistic model, teachers can instill a desire for this most worthy form of behavior in their students.

Learned Motives in the Classroom

If there is any one principle that finds universal acceptance, it is the notion that motivation leads to learning and that without proper motivation, learning will either not occur or be minimal. The first place to look then, if a teacher's attempts to foster learning lead to insufficient results, is in the area of motivation. The "hypodermic needle" model described at the beginning of this chapter is then drawn upon as a teacher does everything but stand on his or her head trying to motivate so that learning will occur.

There are several shortcomings in emphasizing the motivation-learning relationship. Motivation *does not* always lead to learning. It may lead only to anxiety or confusion if the task is beyond the child's readiness or is not understood. It also may lead to rote memory rather than to the teacher's goal of insight or understanding. There are obviously many ways in which good, strong motives can fail to accomplish the desired results.

But a relationship different from the motivation-learning model is so often overlooked by teachers and writers that it deserves special emphasis. This is the relationship of learning to motivation, exactly the opposite of what is so commonly stressed. Laboratory research as well as careful observation demonstrate that *learning is itself a motivator,* that the simple fact that one is improving on a task, or learning something new, can act as an incentive for further learning and improvement.

This principle suggests that teachers need not exhaust their repertoires of motivational devices or give up when the necessary motivation is not evident. They may, in fact, be wasting time straining to create what is not there as a necessary prerequisite for learning. If reasonable attempts to tap the students' motivational hierarchy have failed, we suggest that the teacher approach it from the opposite direction, namely, "Is there some way (short of outright evil) in which I can con, trick, manipulate, deceive, maneuver, or shock this student into *learning,* so that learning will then provide the motivation that is now absent?" We wish merely to dramatize the fact that the motivation-learning relationship works both ways and that the teacher should be constantly aware of the reciprocal relationship instead of focusing on one direction only.

The remainder of this chapter deals with suggestions as to some reasonable motivational techniques that may be tried before resorting to trickery or shock.

270

Intrinsic and Extrinsic Motivation

To begin, teachers should recognize and utilize both intrinsic and extrinsic motivation. Intrinsic, referring to motivation within the task itself, is stressed so highly as the "ideal" that one easily forgets that this is often insufficient. A self-examination by the reader should yield the confession that the sheer joy of knowing, satisfying curiosity, and just plain doing what is right was not enough when we were in school either. Recall, also, that many motives must be learned before gaining any internal function, and it is not surprising that extrinsic (from outside the task) motivation is necessary also. Getting a child to learn multiplication through the use of team games is not bad; it is only when it becomes the total way of motivating, or when such motives as fear, shame, jealousy, or revenge are widely used, that it becomes counterproductive. Teachers will usually need to encourage both intrinsic and extrinsic motives to get the job done, but they should try to maintain a healthy balance.

Teachers should also be aware that they cannot *provide* motivation. They can only capture or trigger motives from within the learner. Until a

*Teachers should realize that the task itself may or may not be motivating. (*Darrell Barry/Little Rock School District.*)*

271

DANNY'S HUNGER FOR ATTENTION

Danny spoke out of turn, laughed at some of the strangest times, pestered students around him, invariably asked questions when Mr. Smith had just finished giving directions, and never had his work done on time. Mr. Smith tried to combat this by verbal chastisement and sarcastic comments, making Danny sit in the corner, bawling him out, sending him to the principal, and even making fun of him. The more he tried to curb Danny's behavior, the more Danny misbehaved. He decided that Danny must be one of those "hyperactive" kids he had heard about and referred him to the school psychologist.

Once the psychologist convinced Mr. Smith that Danny was normal, intelligent, and in fact a highly motivated child, the cure to his irritating behaviors was easy. Mr. Smith learned to call on Danny often and to respond to any of Danny's questions that were not out-of-turn interruptions. He also used projects, and even errands, as ways to heap attention on Danny. When Danny pestered other students or spoke out of turn, he ignored it. Danny did not become a model student, and he was still somewhat irritating at times, but by recognizing his strong need for attention and feeding it as much as possible in constructive ways, Mr. Smith was able to utilize an important motive in Danny's hierarchy as a stimulus to classroom learning.

new motive, such as "intellectual curiosity" becomes part of the child's motivational hierarchy, the teacher will need to link it to an already existing motive. It should also be noted that any motive that works (within reason, obviously) should be employed. For example, if the child has strong need for attention, utilize this to accomplish the goals of your teaching; the same goes for peer approval and competition. The saying "if you can't lick 'em, join 'em" describes the situation as far as the child's inner motives are concerned. In the example in the box, Mr. Smith learned to utilize Danny's need for attention rather than fight it.

Modeling Motives

A principle about teaching that is easily forgotten is the fact that feelings, attitudes, beliefs, yes, even motives are taught in school. Students must learn to have motives such as cooperation, respect, achievement, altruism, and intellectual curiosity, to name a few, and the most important way in which these motives are learned is by modeling. The child will consciously strive to be like an adult (imitation) and will also unconsciously behave like someone he or she admires and/or loves (identification). If you want your students to "share," then you had better model this behavior, as well as reward its occurrence. If you intend for students to show a keen desire to know, to learn new ideas as an end in itself, then you need to model this behavior on a daily basis. On the other hand, if you practice such

Cooperation must be learned.

approaches as "we must learn this because it's on the test," "do it because I say so," or "I'll teach you not to be a bully" (as you paddle the student's behind), you are modeling a different set of motives.

Accent the Positive

If any theme stands out in the conclusions that are popular about motivation and its implications for teaching, it is the message "accent the positive." Positive desires to do things, achieve, solve problems, help others, satisfy curiosity, or have new experiences are more effective, safer,

---

AVOIDANCE LEARNING IN ACTION

Peter plays the clarinet in the grade school band. Since his band director gets upset and corrects him whenever he plays a wrong note, miscounts, holds his instrument incorrectly, sits in the wrong position, or taps his foot to keep time, Peter tries hard to *avoid* doing these things. The anxiety, embarrassment, and failure that he feels are effective in getting him to *try*, but try to do what? To *avoid* doing anything wrong. As a result, Peter is very cautious, does not play any difficult part, and lags farther behind in learning to play his instrument. In addition to the detrimental effect on his skills, Peter may develop such a negative feeling about band that eventually he drops out.

and have fewer side effects than do the negative incentives of avoiding pain, anxiety, shame, embarrassment, and failure. Negative motivation, which at times appears to be very effective, tends to inhibit behavior, retard future growth, and cause damaging side effects. Some of these side effects might not be obvious, since they often lie in the domain of emotions, attitudes, and feelings, but they are important and often outlive the original or "constructive" effects of the negative motive.

Combatting Anxiety

One of the most widespread misconceptions about anxiety is that it interferes with learning. A survey of studies of anxiety and learning reveals that the relationship of anxiety to learning in a wide variety of tasks is that of an "inverted U" function (see the box following) (Malmo, 1959). A low level of anxiety is related to mediocre performance, and as anxiety increases, performance improves *up to a point*. Beyond that point, as anxiety increases, performance declines. In other words, a *moderate* degree of anxiety is best for learning most tasks.

The teacher's job, then, is not to eliminate anxiety from the classroom (which is probably impossible anyway) but, instead, to keep it within moderate limits. These limits vary somewhat depending on the task at hand—a lower level is needed for abstract or creative tasks, for example—

EFFECT OF ANXIETY ON LEARNING OVER A VARIETY OF TASKS

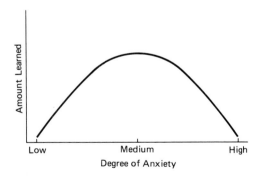

This figure shows the relationship of anxiety to learning over a wide variety of learning tasks. Notice that with a low degree of anxiety, the amount learned is low, whereas with a higher degree of anxiety, the amount learned increases. The increase in learning continues only through moderate levels, however, and as anxiety becomes high, the amount learned again is low. This relationship is referred to as an "inverted U" function, and the implication for teachers is that a moderate anxiety level is best for many learning tasks.

and even more so from child to child. The teacher's dilemma is to find ways to increase anxiety for those students whose level is too low, yet decrease the anxiety for those students whose level is too high.

Even more basic than the need to hold anxiety as a motive within healthy levels is the need for the teacher to provide ways in which the student can *reduce* anxiety. Whenever anxiety acts as a motivator, the learner wants to do something that will make him or her feel less anxious, not *more* anxious. If attempts to solve a problem, follow directions, try something new, and ask questions serve to *reduce* anxiety, the student will continue to use these tactics. But if such attempts lead to *more* anxiety, the student is likely to drop such tactics and turn instead to apathy, withdrawal, horsing around, or even cheating. So the two messages are clear: keep anxiety within healthy boundaries and provide constructive ways in which to *reduce* anxiety.

One other point that is sometimes overlooked is the importance of teachers keeping their *own* anxieties within healthy limits. A teacher who becomes so blasé about his job that he feels little if any anxiety has probably become stale or "in a rut," and the teacher who feels highly anxious is not likely to perform well either. In addition to affecting one's own performance, anxiety is contagious, so that a teacher who doesn't seem to care fosters lack of caring in students, and a teacher who is highly anxious and defensive fosters these behaviors in students also. Teachers must find ways to avoid either extreme of anxiety and must also learn to recognize their own anxieties and look for constructive ways to reduce them.

THE MOTIVATION TIGHTROPE

Phil Harper noticed on the first day that he taught eighth grade French that Jack was extremely anxious. Since it was a small class of only eight students, Phil felt that he should apply some of the principles of learning that he had studied. He remembered that high anxiety interfered with learning, so from that very first day he did everything he could to reduce Jack's anxiety. This included an informal atmosphere, joking with the class, reassuring Jack about his grade, postponing quizzes at the request of any student, ignoring student tardiness, and allowing work to be turned in whenever the class got around to it. Jack's anxiety subsided, but to Phil's chagrin, the class scored extremely low on a standardized test that the school had participated in for years (this same group had been in the top 10% last year), and several parents came in to complain that their son or daughter was not getting anything out of the class. When Sam, one of his top students, dropped the course after the midterm, Phil realized his mistake; in his well-meant attempt to reduce Jack's anxiety, he had failed to provide a reasonable level of challenge and anxiety for the rest of the class. He had experienced the "motivation tightrope," the dilemma in which the teacher must *raise* the anxiety level of those students whose anxiety is too low, yet at the same time *lower* the level of those who are too anxious.

The Importance of Failure

The effects of positive reinforcement for correct responses has been advertised so thoroughly in the educational literature that the word "failure" is almost taboo. If students learn by success, then let us construct classrooms where success is maximized, with the ideal being described by the popular title *Schools Without Failure* (Glasser, 1969). If we can eliminate failure in school and thus have a school of winners rather than losers, this will surely lead to a nation of winners, stimulate the gross national product, and wipe unhappiness from the face of the earth.

This description is obviously exaggerated and is not really intended to discredit Glasser's book, which contains many worthwhile ideas. But it is aimed at some overzealous enthusiasts who look at research that indicates that, in general, success is more effective and safer than failure and conclude that the most success possible and the least failure possible is the only reasonable goal of the schools.

We do not advocate a reversal of this view, eliminating success and maximizing failure; we are merely calling attention to the fact that failure is not necessarily bad and that *failure is sometimes a necessary and effective step in the learning process.* This means that errors play an important role in learning; one must know what something *is not* as well as what it is.

Learning to set goals that are reasonable and yet challenging and working effectively toward meeting these goals is not easy; indeed, it takes years of experience for a person to develop productive goal-setting behavior. A key ingredient in learning how to set realistic goals, make reasonable attempts to reach them, and modify goals or try new strategies is the ingredient of *failure.* A child without sufficient failure experience cannot possibly assess these goal-setting abilities, just as a child without sufficient success experience cannot either. In other words, it appears that considerable experience with both success and failure is necessary in developing constructive and intelligent goal-setting behaviors.

Another important point for the teacher to keep in mind is that it is not failure itself that is important but, rather, the child's interpretation of that failure. In this respect, we are *not* suggesting that children should be conned into believing that failure is success or that they develop such a relaxed attitude that failure no longer bothers them. On the contrary, an accurate perception of failure, and the desire to improve and succeed, are seen as necessary attributes. We believe that the teacher should model healthy reactions to failure, help the child to overcome failure when possible, modify goals when necessary, and attempt to develop tolerance for failure at times when it must be accepted. In addition to his or her own attitude about failure, which should imply that it is a normal part of the learning process, the teacher should avoid being overprotective, and as the child proceeds through school his or her tolerance for failure should increase, just as his or her years increase. In this way, failure can act as a motivator rather than as a restrictor of behavior.

The Need for Empathy and Acceptance

Empathy, or the ability to see, feel, and understand from within another's experience, is a crucial factor in understanding motivation. Unlike sympathy, in which we are aware of anothers' feelings, empathy involves actually sharing the others' cognitive field. The teacher who can empathize with students is in a position to understand their motives and teach them accordingly.

A second step, after developing the very difficult and sensitive ability to empathize, is perhaps even more difficult—the respect for *all* motives. This is not to say that we expect you to value all motives equally, because this would be both illogical and impossible. But it is saying that the motives that you see in children's behavior are real, normal, and important and cannot be rejected, ignored, or dismissed as unreasonable. If you see a child whose needs for security and acceptance are so strong that he will not risk anything to achieve and grow and he avoids all competition, you must accept this as a fact about this child's motives and not a reason to devalue or reject him. At the same time that you accept him as he is, you also help him to learn and grow into all he can be.

Be Aware of Unconscious Motives

In addition to the need for empathy and acceptance of the child's motives, it is also important to remember that human beings are not completely aware of their own motivations. Keeping in mind that some behavior is the result of unconscious motivation can be very helpful in deciphering behavior that is otherwise disappointing, infuriating, or even shocking. The child who is doing failing work and never meets a deadline in spite of high potential may not be aware that this is attention-seeking behavior, or that he is getting even with parents, or that his self-concept demands that he behave in a way that contrasts him to his perfectionist older brother. The bully (both verbal and physical) may be unaware that feelings of inadequacy and fear of rejection are the basis of his behavior, and the gifted female whose work is slipping in senior high is probably aware only vaguely, if at all, that she is functioning as a result of fear of success that has been identified in some females in our culture (Horner, 1972).

Becoming aware of unconscious motives not only aids in understanding behavior of others but also provides an important element in monitoring one's *own* behavior. Contrary to some of the popular descriptions of "teacher," which paint a picture of a saint who loves all children equally and models all good things, it is essential that teachers remember that they are human and reflect all the failings of human nature. It is much better to admit that you like some youngsters more than others, that you see some children as downright obnoxious, and that your motives in enforcing rules and dispensing punishment are not always noble.

277

As we stress the importance of empathizing and accepting motives as they exist in others and in ourselves, we must at the same time highlight the hazards involved in inferring motivation (an interior state) from behavior (an observable event). Even while practicing the skills of "putting yourself in the child's shoes," you must remind yourself that the inferences you make from behavior are only *informed guesses* at best and that sometimes these guesses are highly inaccurate. Even though the conclusions you reach make eminent good sense, they still may be wrong, and the best way to avoid some of these errors or identify them in time to form a new hypothesis is to become a good listener. This is a very difficult suggestion to make to teachers because the very nature of teaching tends to lead to compulsive talking, not listening.

Creating Dissonance and Resolution

Cognitive dissonance is useful as a guide in planning classroom strategies as well as an interesting research activity. A recurring cycle of dissonance-exploration-discovery-solution-resolution is an excellent pattern to follow since it leads to self-regulated learning, a sense of satisfaction, a high level of motivation, and long-term memory of concepts learned.

The teacher's function in this area is to try to create problem situations that arouse dissonance in the students as they try to find answers. Recalling that dissonance includes a certain degree of anxiety, the teacher should expect students to show signs of impatience, frustration, and restlessness and to indicate that the task is too difficult or to cajole the teacher into giving the answer. *Don't give into such attempts.* One common mistake in teaching is to make it too easy. The arousal of dissonance is a good thing, provided that there are avenues for reducing the dissonance. Students who wrestle with a problem and finally find a solution on their own will feel pride and success; students who are helped by the teacher may be robbed of these positive feelings.

Be Alert for Damaging Side Effects

As teachers manipulate the classroom environment attempting to stimulate growth and learning, they must look beyond the immediate effects for more subtle or delayed effects, which we label "side effects." These side effects can be good, bad, or indifferent, depending partly on the subjective areas of values, goals, and philosophy. The most important point, however, is to remember that *all* classroom strategies have side effects, which often are not immediately apparent. Only by knowing the side effects of method A versus method B can the teacher make an intelligent decision regarding which method to employ.

WHAT HAPPENED TO THE OTHER DOLLAR?

Mr. Kelly began his sixth grade math lesson with the following problem:

Joe, Dave, and Bill rented a hotel room, which they thought cost $21. While Dave and Bill were cleaning up for supper, they sent Joe to the desk to pay for the room, each of them giving Joe $7 as his share of the cost. At the desk, the bellboy took the $21 that Joe gave him, but then gave $2 back, saying that the room cost $19. Actually, it cost only $18, and the bellboy pocketed the other dollar.

When Joe returned to the room, he decided to keep the $2 and not tell Dave and Bill about it. Now, we have a situation in which Dave is out $7, Bill is out $7, Joe is out $5 (he pocketed the other $2, remember), and the bellhop has $1. This totals $20, but we started with $21. What happened to the other dollar?

In discussing the problem, students argued vehemently about how to account for the other dollar. Every time they asked Mr. Kelly to settle it, he refused, and the class finally traced the money by sending one student to the board and listing all the ways to tally it. Mr. Kelly then went on to similar problems about golf balls, colored hats, and forks in the road, with similar hot discussions, on successive days.

Mr. Kelly was forcing the students to think logically and to solve problems, to do this on their own, and to have some fun while doing so. This attitude carried over into all aspects of the math class, and hardly a day went by that his class did not have a vigorous argument over a problem that the students were trying to solve. Mr. Kelly rarely provided an answer or was even asked to as time went on. The students had developed the ability to solve problems on their own and then review their own thinking to verify its accuracy, one of the most important aspects of logical reasoning.

The Need for Feedback

If there is anything on which psychologists agree, it is the principle of feedback. Several implications of the importance of feedback in motivation are apparent.

First, of course, feedback should be built into virtually everything that the student does. Without feedback, the tendency is to lose interest in the task, whether from anxiety, frustration, confusion, or just plain boredom. The only exceptions to this rule are cases where the teacher withholds feedback for some special reason, such as creating dissonance, testing a student's confidence, or trying to encourage more independence.

Second, teachers should include *all* types of feedback in their teaching, but accent positive knowledge of progress, as it is knowledge of progress plus the "pat on the back" that says that this progress is good that serves as the best motivator. Knowledge of mistakes, wrong answers, and incorrect moves can be motivating also, as can information that a student is

279

EDGAR AND HIS MIND BENDERS

Mr. Russell, fondly referred to as "Edgar," had taught math in Central High for over thirty years. He was so thoroughly immersed in the Socratic method that some students really believed that he did not understand math. He would ask students so many questions, without answering them, and force the class to solve all problems themselves, that a common statement was that "Edgar is a tremendous teacher, but he just doesn't know any math."

One of his many techniques involved what appeared to be a gross violation of the principle of immediate feedback. He would present the class with an unusual problem and then claim that it was unsolvable. He would do this near the end of class, often on Friday, with the challenge that if anyone could figure out a solution, that person would receive ten bonus points toward his or her grade.

Edgar always pretended that he knew of no way the problem could be solved. Somehow, word always made the rounds before class concerning who thought they had it solved and just what the solution was. Invariably, the problem would be solved and there would be a big argument in class over who had the best solution and how to prove it was best. Edgar always forced the class to settle the argument themselves, feigning complete ignorance and surprise that there was a solution. His delayed feedback technique appeared to work just right in arousing and holding student interest in his many "mind benders" showing that the principle of immediate feedback, as does any rule, has important exceptions.

not doing well or should be doing better. But these latter types often lead to a motive to give up, withdraw, blame somebody, or get even rather than the desired positive motives. Research also tells us that feedback is best when it is highly specific, not vague or general.

Third, feedback, regardless what type, should be immediate, since any delay in feedback (with a few exceptions) tends to weaken its effect. So, if the teacher hopes that knowledge of success will "turn on" an apathetic student, the knowledge should immediately follow the behavior. Likewise, if some kind of negative feedback is to jolt a student into acting or impress him with the inaccuracy of his attempts, it should be immediate.

Remember That Enjoyment Is a Good Motivator

Even though the idea that human beings operate strictly on the basis of the "pleasure principle" (hedonistic motivation) is one that is easily dispelled by both research and casual observation, teachers must be careful that they do not revert to the opposite extreme of seeing enjoyment as bad. The description of the classical Puritan as one who thinks that "somewhere there is somebody having some fun, and I'm going to find him and put a stop to it" unfortunately describes more than a few teachers. Regardless of what religion or philosophy of life one holds, we must admit that pleasure is a powerful motivator, that there is nothing wrong with pleasure per se, and that it should be encouraged consciously in school.

We are *not* joining those writers who seem to advocate turning everything into "fun," since many of the most important things in life are not really fun. What we *are* saying is that teachers should really enjoy most of what they do, and so should students—that the business or work of the school, while sometimes routine, mundane, frustrating, or even drudgery, should lead in general to pleasure or enjoyment for *both* teacher and students. In fact, some of what happens in school should be justifiable on the basis of this alone, that it is pleasurable. If what you are doing in school is not enjoyable for you and most of the students most of the time, then change what you're doing.

The Determinants of Effective Praise

Probably no other word used in relation to teaching is abused more often than the word "praise." To some teachers, if some praise is good, more praise is better, and lots of praise is best.

A number of observed facts about praise lead to the advice that teachers should be very careful in the use of praise (Farson, 1972). Surely the reader has observed (and has probably exhibited) some of the common reactions to praise, namely, suspicion, embarrassment, denial, hostility, or clumsy

Some of what happens in school should be enjoyable. (Arkansas Gazette.)

attempts to return the praise. Why would such a good and valuable commodity as praise bring about such reactions? Rather than dismiss it as simply a cultural peculiarity, we suggest that these responses are the result of the motives that often underly praise and the ways in which praise is given.

Some examples of praise given for ulterior motives are (1) as an opener, fully expecting praise in return (I tell you your dress is beautiful so you'll tell me how great my new fur coat is); (2) to soften the receiver for the kill (I tell you how brilliant you are as I am about to borrow your notes to cram for a test); (3) to establish superiority (''My, that's a nice painting'' means I am an expert who can judge the humble efforts of a novice); (4) to patronize or make fun of (''That's a very clever question'' means only a moron would ask such a thing); (5) as a logical extension, if praise facilitates progress then praise everyone all the time (once you become known for this, anything you say is ignored automatically).

If these examples are accurate then, must we eliminate praise from the teachers' repertoire of behaviors? Not entirely, although it would help if we could eliminate praise as in the five examples cited. Instead, we suggest the following guidelines to constructive praise:

1. Praise should be earned; it should not be the result of something in which the recipient had no part. If we are praised for something we have done or have had a part in, we feel pretty good, but if the praise is for something completely beyond our control, we do not have this good feeling. The child who is complimented whenever his relatives visit for how much he's grown hardly feels a sense of accomplishment, since he scarcely had anything to do with his being two inches taller. But, if he is complimented for his skill at a game, or something he made, or anything else that he can actually take credit for, he's apt to appreciate this since he has earned this praise.

2. Praise must be sincere; dishonest praise can be worse than none at all. The child who is told that he is doing a terrific job when in reality he is doing poorly will see through this, either now or later, and will feel hurt and resentment. If he doesn't recognize the insincerity, the result is still unfavorable, since he has been misinformed and is basing further actions on inaccurate feedback. The teacher must constantly look for opportunities to give praise that is really deserved, honestly and accurately, if it is to enhance future behavior.

3. Praise should be specific; vague generalities are of little use. If Bob has just performed a difficult piece of music and you tell him "Gee, that was really swell," he will probably interpret this as a polite remark, customary behavior that does not offend but hardly excites him. If, however, you tell Bob, "I really liked your interpretation of the third movement; your tone in the Andante was just right, and you certainly must have worked hard to memorize such a difficult piece," then he is apt to believe that you listened closely, noticed something important in what he did, and are giving honest feedback that is most satisfying. Teachers must be constantly on the lookout for something specific to praise, even in cases where the performance in general is not outstanding. Specific praise helps not only because it makes the recipient feel good but also because it is accurate feedback and helps to pinpoint other areas in which improvement is needed.

4. Effective praise requires a frame of reference. The old joke about the man responding to the question "How's your wife" with "Compared with what?" is relevant here. The recipient needs to know whether he did well compared with others his age or compared with all the students you ever taught, or whether he has improved compared with last week. Praise that has no frame of reference tends to be dismissed in the same fashion as praise that is too vague and general.

5. Praise should be immediate. Research on learning implies clearly that feedback of all types is more effective if immediate rather than delayed. One reason is that the recipient may have forgotten precisely what he

did to deserve praise. Another is that the boost in motivation that one gets from sincere, specific, earned praise may be too late to do much good if the praise is delayed. Praise has the biggest payoff in terms of both motivation and learning when it follows immediately after the behavior being praised. A further point is that other students can profit vicariously from praise if they know specifically what is being praised.

Some Final Suggestions

Psychological theory and research yield many suggestions in addition to what has been discussed here. Here are a few additional suggestions:

1. Ego involvement (the degree to which a person's self-esteem is affected by an activity) is an important aspect of motivation. Democratic participation increases ego involvement. Thus, pupil participation in planning, setting guidelines, and carrying out activities are constructive strategies.
2. Motivation is contagious! Teacher enthusiasm and interest tend to rub off on students; so do teacher boredom and apathy.
3. It is important for students to see a purpose in what they do. However, this does *not* need to be the same purpose that the teacher has in mind. In fact, it is probably impossible in some instances for the student to understand the teacher's purpose, and in other instances knowing the purpose would cause resistance.
4. Although motivation is basically a stable characteristic, the level of motivation fluctuates and depends on situational variables. The child with a strong need to achieve does not always demonstrate that need, and an occasional aggressive act does not prove a strong aggressive need. Teachers should expect day-to-day variability in student motivation.
5. High motivation is not always helpful. The learner can literally try so hard or care so much that it interferes with learning. This applies not only to anxiety as discussed earlier but to virtually *any* motive. We must remember that cheating, fighting, and truancy are sometimes results of *high* motivation.
6. Students tend to study what they *think* will be on the test. A teacher may think that something is highly important, and yet if the students don't believe they'll be tested on it, they won't study it. On the other hand, if the students have zealously studied some material and it is *not* on the test, they feel let down or cheated. Teachers should make an attempt to test students on those things that they deem most important; teachers should also try to inform the students in a general way about what they will be tested on and in what fashion. The test should not be a game in which the teacher tries to "fool" the students.

7. Above all, "know thyself." A teacher who does not understand or cannot admit his or her *own* motives can hardly be expected to understand students' motives.

Summary

In this chapter, motivation was defined as "the nonstimulus variables affecting behavior" or that part of behavior coming from within the learner. This was contrasted to the tendency for teachers to think of motivation as "something you *do* to someone else to get them to learn something you want them to learn."

The principle that motivation comes from within was then illustrated in a discussion of three levels of motivation: (1) physiological drives, (2) stimulus needs, and (3) learned motives. Physiological drives are innate or "built into" all humans as well as animals. They are essential for survival, and they can be explained by the homeostatic model of maintaining balance within the system. Although physiological drives are *not* learned, it is obvious that learning is involved in the ways in which different individuals satisfy the drives. These drives can affect classroom learning in a negative way if they are not met.

Stimulus needs are not essential for survival, nor do they fit a homeostatic model. They *are* innate and universal, however, just as are physiological drives, and they do not require specific learning. Some of these needs, such as the need for sensory stimulation, stimulus variability, and stimulus complexity and the need for tactual comfort and stimulation, were presented in detail. It is possible that this level of motivation is sometimes overlooked by teachers, and it is reasonable to suggest that it is an important level in relation to the classroom. The teacher must assure that there is an adequate level of stimulus input to keep the students from being bored. Also, stimulus variability enhances learning. It is possible to provide such variability in type of activity, degree of student participation, level of anxiety, tempo or pace, amount of structure, flexibility, degree of formality, competition and cooperation, and many other dimensions.

Stimulus complexity is important also. The teacher must be careful not to present a level of complexity that is beyond the students' ability but also must gradually increase the level of complexity over time. Sometimes this requires individual attention, adequate time for review, subgrouping within classes, the use of programmed materials, and special projects.

The need for tactual comfort and stimulation also enters into classroom instruction. All children enjoy touching things and doing things with their hands. Teachers can help to satisfy these needs by including concrete objects and their manipulation whenever it is relevant in a lesson. Occasional "horsing around" can be allowed also, so long as it does not get out of hand, and touching is sometimes a natural part of expressing any emotion.

Intrinsic motivation, or that which is part of the task itself, is the ideal, but the teacher often needs to add extrinsic motivation. This is normal and natural. Before students can develop some of the learned motives that have been presented, they often need to fall back on extrinsic motivators. Although teachers cannot really provide motivation, they can capitalize on the motives that are already there.

Teachers must also be aware of the fact that they are models of motivation. Students *learn* to have such motives as cooperation, respect, achievement, altruism, and intellectual curiosity, and one way they learn them is through modeling the teacher.

Another worthy idea is for the teacher to accent the positive. Positive desires to do things, achieve, solve problems, and gain approval are better than are negative reasons such as fear, anxiety, embarrassment, and anger. The positive motive to succeed is better than the negative motive to avoid failure, even though both might work in getting the student to achieve.

Anxiety reduction is a common way in which students learn. A moderate degree of anxiety is best for most tasks, with too little anxiety being almost as bad as too much. Of course, one of the most important considerations is to make sure that the student has some means by which to reduce the anxiety. One of the most difficult problems is that of reducing anxiety for those students whose anxiety level is too high, while at the same time increasing it for those whose level is too low. Teachers also need to keep *their own* anxiety within reasonable limits.

Although failure is usually seen as something undesirable in teaching, failure can be a useful learning experience also. Failure at some task can lead the student to set more reasonable goals, try new strategies, and develop frustration tolerance. It is not really failure itself that is damaging but, rather, the student's attitude about failure. The teacher can help the student to accept occasional failure as part of life.

One aspect of motivation that is often overlooked is the fact that learning can result in motivation, just as motivation leads to learning. Everyone knows that motivation leads to learning, so that teachers often focus on motivation as the key to learning. But it is also true that, if a student learns something, for any reason, that learning can be a motivator for further learning. The simple fact that one is improving on a task, or is learning something new, can act as an incentive for further learning.

Other aids are empathizing with the students so that one can understand their motives, respecting all types of motives, being honest about motivation, and being aware of subconscious motivation. In the last instance, teachers must always be aware that their conclusions are only hypotheses and that they may be wrong.

The concept of cognitive dissonance can be useful in planning instruction. Creating dissonance, allowing exploration that leads to discovery and resolution of the dissonance, can be very effective in the classroom.

The side effects of any particular form of motivation must also be considered, since the most "effective" method in terms of results is not necessarily the best method. A method with damaging side effects will often be rejected by the teacher, and another method with fewer damaging side effects will be employed. Another important consideration is that of the need for feedback. Knowledge of results along the way is one of the most important forms of feedback. Positive feedback is of course preferable to negative, but both types can be motivating, especially when they immediately follow some behavior.

Enjoyment or pleasure can be a good motivator as can praise. Teachers must take care, however, that the praise is effective rather than counterproductive. Effective praise is earned, sincere, and as specific as possible, has a relative frame of reference, and is as immediate as possible.

Some final notes are that ego involvement is a motivator, motivation can be contagious, students must see a purpose in what they do, the level of motivation fluctuates from day to day, there is such a thing as "too much" motivation, and teachers must strive constantly to understand their own motives.

Study Questions

1. What is the crucial difference between the way in which many teachers see motivation and the way in which psychologists define it? Would it make any difference which model you accepted in relation to how you would behave as a teacher in the classroom?

2. What is the principle of homeostasis, and how does it explain some aspects of human behavior? At what level of motivation is it an appropriate explanation, and at what levels does it fail to describe the dynamics of motivation accurately?

3. What ideas for teachers follow from what you have read about sensory stimulation? stimulus complexity? stimulus variability? How do these needs sometimes interfere with what the teacher is trying to accomplish in the classroom?

4. What is the significance for classroom teachers of Harlow's research on monkeys? Is touching or being touched physically an important part of classroom interaction? What sort of limitations should be placed on such touching?

5. What is the concept of "motivational hierarchy" as used in this chapter? How does this concept help in understanding the differences in personality from one student to another? How would you expect the motivational hierarchy of a twelfth-grader to differ from that of a third-grader?

6. What are the essential differences between achievement motivation and motivation to avoid failure? What can a teacher do to help students to strive to achieve rather than to avoid failure?

7. Why are physiological drives important in the classroom? Can you describe several ways in which physiological drives interfere with learning in the classroom? Are there any ways in which the teacher can use physiological drives in a positive way?

8. What does it mean to say that a lesson plan is "open ended"? How does an open-ended lesson plan allow a teacher to provide for stimulus needs in the students? Can you see any disadvantages in using open-ended lesson plans?

9. What is the difference between intrinsic and extrinsic motivation? Why is it often necessary for teachers to add extrinsic motivators to the tasks that are required in school? Do teachers function entirely on the basis of intrinsic motivation in doing their job, or do they need some extrinsic motivation also?

10. What is the relationship of anxiety to learning? Should the teacher attempt to eliminate anxiety from the classroom? What level of anxiety should teachers aim for in many classroom tasks if they want the anxiety to facilitate rather than to interfere with learning?

11. What are some healthy reactions to failure? How can failure lead to further learning? Do you believe that teachers should at times deliberately engineer failure in the classroom?

References

Adler, A. *The Education of Children.* New York: Greenberg, 1930.

Atkinson, J. W. "The Mainsprings of Achievement-Oriented Activity." In J. W. Atkinson and J. O. Raynor, eds., *Motivation and Achievement*, pp. 13–41. Washington, D.C.: V. H. Winston, 1974.

Atkinson, J. W., and Feather, N. T., eds. *A Theory of Achievement Motivation.* New York: John Wiley, 1966.

Bandura, A., Ross, D., and Ross, S. "Transmissions of Aggression Through Imitation of Aggressive Models," *Journal of Abnormal and Social Psychology*, 63(3), November 1961, pp. 575–582.

Cofer, C. N., and Appley, M. H. *Motivation: Theory and Research.* New York: John Wiley, 1964.

Dollard, J., and Miller, N. E. *Personality and Psychotherapy: An Analysis in Terms of Learning, Thinking, and Culture.* New York: McGraw-Hill, 1950.

English, H. B., and English, A. C. *A Comprehensive Dictionary of Psychological and Psychoanalytic Terms.* New York: David McKay, 1958.

Fantz, R., and Miranda, S. "Newborn Infant Attention to Forms of Contour," *Child Development*, 46(1), March 1975, pp. 224–228.

Farson, R. "Praise Reappraised," in D. E. Hamachek, ed., *Human Dynamics in Psychology and Education*, 2nd ed., pp. 146–155. Boston: Allyn and Bacon, 1972.

Festinger, L. *A Theory of Cognitive Dissonance.* Stanford, Calif.: Stanford University Press, 1957.

Festinger, L., and Carlsmith, J. "Cognitive Consequences of Forced Compliance," *Journal of Abnormal and Social Psychology*, 58(2), March 1959, pp. 203–210.

Glasser, W. *Schools Without Failure.* New York: Harper & Row, 1969.

Haith, M. M., Kessen, W., and Collins, D. "Response of the Human Infant to Level of Complexity of Intermittent Visual Movement," *Journal of Experimental Child Psychology*, 7(1), February 1969, pp. 52–69.

Harlow, H. F., and Mears, C. *The Human Model: Primate Perspectives.* Washington, D.C.: V. H. Winston, 1979.

Hebb, D. O. "Drives and the CNS (Central Nervous System)," *Psychological Review*, 62(4), July 1955, pp. 243–254.

Horner, M. S. "Toward an Understanding of Achievement-Related Conflicts in Women," *Journal of Social Issues*, 28(2), 1972, pp. 157–175.

Lorenz, K., and Leyhausen, I. *Motivation of Human and Animal Behavior: An Ethological View.* New York: D. Van Nostrand, 1973.

McClelland, D. C. "Risk-Taking in Children with High and Low Need for Achievement," in J. W. Atkinson, ed., *Motives in Fantasy, Action, and Society*, pp. 306–321. Princeton, N.J.: D. Van Nostrand, 1958.

———. *The Achieving Society.* Princeton, N.J.: D. Van Nostrand, 1961.

Malmo, R. B. "Activation: A Neuropsychological Dimension," *Psychological Review*, 66(6), November 1959, pp. 367–386.

Montagu, A. *Touching: The Human Significance of the Skin.* New York: Columbia University Press, 1971.

Morris, D. *The Naked Ape.* New York: Dell, 1969.

Munsinger, H., Kessen, W., and Kessen, M. I. "Age and Uncertainty: Developmental Variation in Preference for Variability," *Journal of Experimental Child Psychology*, 1(1), April 1964, pp. 1–15.

Rank, O. *Modern Education: A Critique of Its Fundamental Ideas.* New York: Knopf, 1932.

Suedfeld, P. "The Benefits of Boredom: Sensory Deprivation Reconsidered," *American Scientist*, 63(1), January-February 1975, pp. 60–69.

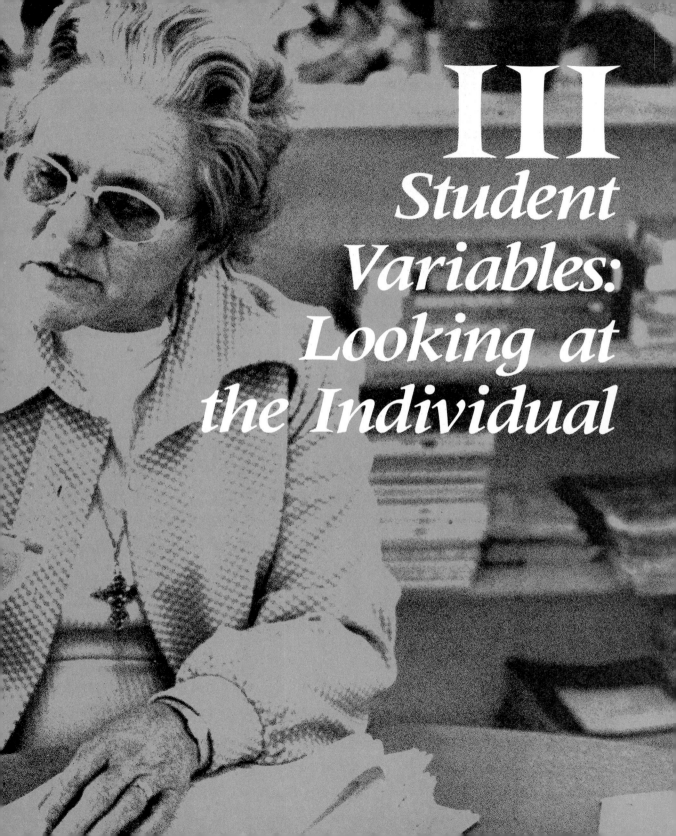

III
Student
Variables:
Looking at
the Individual

Humanistic educators are concerned with the fact that their students are human beings. They would like to see all the human beings they teach maximize both their achievements and their freedom of choice to become what they are capable of becoming. To accomplish this goal, the humanistic teacher must be prepared to deal with the many differences that exist among people. In this part, some important areas of individual differences are explored.

In Chapter 9, intelligence and intelligence testing are presented. One of the major points of this chapter is that the information provided by intelligence tests is thought of more accurately as an indicator of scholastic potential than of innate intelligence. Along with intelligence, Chapter 9 explores creativity, which may be thought of as an individual's ability to think in noncustomary ways. It is often stated that schools devalue creativity in favor of more customary thinking. If this is true, we may be placing severe limitations on the ability of an individual to deal with new and unique problems.

Social backgrounds of students and teachers are discussed in Chapter 10. While most teachers in the United States reflect traditional middle-class values, their students come from a broad range of social classes. This means that values of the teacher and the student can be different and may even be in conflict. The classroom teacher must be prepared to cope with these differences.

Sex and gender role are examined in Chapter 11. Females and males in American culture have long been taught that they have different roles to play and that they should reflect different personality characteristics. This enculturation of gender roles into students places serious limitations on their ability to develop into whole, self-actualizing adults. A discussion of psychological androgyny in which each student is encouraged to adopt appropriate characteristics of both traditional males and traditional females is presented in Chapter 11.

Part Three closes with a discussion of exceptional children. As a result of recent federal legislation regarding special education, each child is expected to be taught in an environment as close to the normal classroom as possible. Each teacher must now be prepared to work with students who have various mental and physical handicaps. Chapter 12 discusses present requirements for special education and characteristics of different categories of exceptional children.

Intelligence and Creativity

PREVIEW

What is the meaning of the word "intelligence"?

When was the first modern intelligence test developed, and how was it constructed?

What does deviation IQ mean, and why is it important?

How did two world wars contribute to the understanding of intelligence and IQ testing?

What is the g factor in intelligence testing, and why is it so important?

What are the s factors in intelligence, and why have they become increasingly important?

What did Thurstone contribute to intelligence testing?

What was Guilford's structure of intellect, and why was it so important?

What does a modern IQ test look like?

What are some of the specific tasks in the most popular tests of mental ability?

What are some strengths and weaknesses of group versus individual intelligence tests?

What are some current controversies concerning intelligence testing?

What are some sex differences in intellectual performance?

How do IQ scores affect teacher expectancy?

What are some reasonable guidelines for teachers in using tests of mental ability?

What does it mean to see IQ as a functional score?

What is a score band, and how is it used?

What other data do teachers need in addition to the specific scores?

What is a subgroup norm, and how can it be useful?

How can teachers help to educate the public concerning IQ scores and what they mean?

What is the meaning of the word "creativity"?

What is the learned behavior approach to explaining creativity?

What is the traits approach to explaining creativity?

What do creative people have in common?

What personality characteristics do creative persons have in common?

Why is internal locus of control important in relation to creativity?

How are creativity and intelligence related?

What is the nature of the process of creativity?

What are some of the attempts at measuring creativity?

What are the shortcomings of creativity tests?

What can teachers do to encourage creativity in their classes?

If your friend told you that his new girlfriend was "really bright," "sharp," "a brain," what would you think he meant? What about the student who makes straight "A's" in math but has "no common sense"? Or the friend who can build anything or make any motor run, but is just no good at "book learnin'." In everyday conversation, we use expressions repeatedly that imply a belief in some sort of mental powers or abilities called "intelligence." These expressions usually imply that intelligence is a "good thing" and frequently indicate that there are different types. In this chapter, the meaning of the concept of intelligence is explored along with the history of attempts to measure it, its relationship to creativity, and the implications of this for classroom teachers.

Galton's Inquiry

Modern ideas about intelligence, and attempts to measure it scientifically, have their roots in the work of Sir Francis Galton. This brilliant younger cousin of Charles Darwin noticed that individuals and families differed from one another in intellectual achievements and occupational eminence. Galton (1869) noted that successful men were known for "originality of conception, for enterprise, for activity and energy, for administrative skill, for power of literary expression, for oratory. . . ." He very ambitiously examined the lives and achievements of the families and relations of four hundred eminent men from various periods of history and found that an unusually high proportion of fathers, sons, and brothers of these men also demonstrated outstanding achievements. Galton's definition of eminence

Table 9.1. *Eminent Kinsmen of Eminent Relatives**

	Judges	Statesmen	Commanders	Literary	Scientific	Poets	Artists	Divines
Father	26%	33%	47%	48%	26%	20%	32%	28%
Brother	35	39	50	42	47	40	50	36
Son	36	49	31	51	60	45	89	40
Grandfather	15	28	16	24	14	5	7	20
Uncle	18	18	8	24	16	5	14	40
Nephew	19	18	35	24	23	50	18	4
Grandson	19	10	12	9	14	5	18	16
Great-grandfather	2	8	8	3	0	0	0	4
Great-uncle	4	5	8	6	5	5	7	4
First-cousin	11	21	20	18	16	0	1	8
Great-nephew	17	5	8	6	16	10	0	0
Great-grandson	6	0	0	3	7	0	0	0
All more remote	14	37	44	15	23	5	18	16
Number of families each containing more than one eminent man	85	39	27	33	43	20	28	25
Total number of eminent men in all the families	262	130	89	119	148	57	97	75

*From F. Galton, *Hereditary Genius: An Inquiry into Its Laws and Consequences* (London: Macmillan, 1869), p. 308. Reprinted with permission.

was stringent—a man was eminent if he ranked first among 4,000 individuals on a scale of merit. Table 9.1 presents some of Galton's findings as published in 1869. The data in Table 9.1 indicate that the percentage of eminent men in each category who had eminent kinsmen was strikingly high. This percentage declines with increasing distance of relationship from the original person. (For example, 26% of eminent judges had eminent fathers, 35% had eminent brothers, 36% had eminent sons, but only 2% had eminent great-grandfathers.) Note also how the 43 families of eminent scientists contained a total of 148 eminent men, the 39 families of eminent statesmen contained 130 eminent men, and so on.

Findings such as Galton's supported the belief that there was some general mental ability trait, passed on genetically, that determined outstanding achievement. This doctrine was applied rather broadly to a wide range of social phenomena, such as social class, income, occupation, and education, in a theory later called "social determinism." This theory proposed that almost all things in life, including social class structure, were a result of genetic potential: the rich were rich because they had more ability and the poor were poor because they were genetically deficient. The social structure of society, and those persons occupying the different levels, was the result of natural selection, "the survival of the fittest," just as in Darwin's evolution of species.

295

Early attempts to measure the intelligence factor that Galton believed was basic to such eminence focused on perceptual skills. The intelligent person, in this approach, should also be one whose seeing, hearing, and sensing in general was sharper and quicker than the average person's. Although this belief was predominant for several years, attempts to find perceptual skills in which "bright" persons were actually superior failed miserably and finally faded away.

As the twentieth century began, the general belief was that there were several traits or skills that correlated highly with one another to form a group that could be called intelligence. Intelligence was very important to success in life. At that point, nobody knew what traits or skills were in the intelligence group or how to measure it.

The First Modern Intelligence Test

Shortly after the turn of the century, the beginning of intelligence testing as we know it today took place in Paris, France. The minister of public instruction, desiring to distinguish normal children from those who would be unable to profit from regular classroom instruction, commissioned Alfred Binet and Theodore Simon to devise some simple test to identify these below-average children. In seeking to make such a differentiation, Binet and Simon experimented with numerous tasks. They found that tasks involving vocabulary, counting, and reasoning as well as pictures, cartoons, and puzzles were effective in separating those children who were likely to do well in school from those destined to do poorly.

Binet and Simon soon realized that the tasks they were developing for identifying below-average students at the different age levels were also useful in determining the relative abilities of other students. Older students performing the same task tended to get more right than did younger students, so that a bright student of age 5, for example, would score the same as an average student of age 7. Binet labeled the student's performance on the tasks as "mental age" and by comparing this mental age with chronological age, he coined a ratio called the "intelligence quotient," or IQ.* The set of tasks for each level that Binet and Simon developed allowed the tester to determine the child's mental age, then divide by chronological age, and multiply by 100 to compute IQ (e.g., Dan scores like a 7-year-old, but is only age 5, so his IQ is $7/5 \times 100 = 140$).

---

*Binet's choice of the word "intelligence" in relation to this score was probably an unfortunate accident of momentous proportion, considering the agony, harm, misunderstandings, and general pain that the term has caused over the years. It is interesting to ponder what might have happened if this original IQ test had instead been called a "scholastic ability" or "verbal aptitude" test. But he did call it intelligence, and teachers cannot escape the term or its implications, regardless of how many movements there are to stamp out IQ testing.

The Binet test was translated into English and revised for use in America by Lewis Terman in 1916. IQ testing quickly became the leading area of measurement in the United States. World War I was a tremendous boost to the testing movement, since thousands of recruits had to be classified quickly and economically regarding their suitability for military service. Those with exceptional ability had to be identified as well as the average and the retarded. Two famous tests—Alpha and Beta—were designed by the Army, the Alpha test being for literate English speakers and the Beta test for illiterates and non-English-speaking subjects. Both tests were believed to measure general intelligence, and the various nonverbal performance tasks on the Beta test supported the argument that intelligence was more than verbal knowledge. Unlike previous IQ tests, which were administered to one person at a time, the Alpha and Beta tests could be administered to a large group of recruits.

A general factor that seemed to underlie scores on all types of intellectual tasks was dubbed the "*g* factor" by Charles Spearman in 1927. He noted that intercorrelations among various subtasks on IQ tests was high, and he claimed that each subtask tapped an "*s* factor" or specific area of IQ, but that an underlying general or *g* factor was reflected in all these scores and their intercorrelations.

Deviation IQ

From its beginning until the 1930s, IQ was seen and computed as a proportion, a ratio of mental age to chronological age. This caused problems, however, in comparing persons of different ages and also in knowing just where a person stood in relation to others his or her own age. For example, was an IQ of 125 at age 7 really as outstanding as an IQ of 125 at age 12?

To solve this problem, David Wechsler (1939) introduced the concept of the *deviation IQ* in the 1930s. This approach stated that a person's intelligence at any given time is defined by his or her relative standing among his or her age peers. In other words, the performance of a 7-year-old was compared with that of other 7-year-olds, and if he scored twenty points better than the average 7-year-old, his IQ was reported as 120. A 10-year-old with a 120 IQ was in exactly the same place, in relation to other 10-year-olds, as the 7-year-old with an IQ of 120 was in relation to other 7-year-olds. The mean on Wechsler's IQ scale was set at 100 (i.e., theoretically, if everyone in the United States were sampled, their average score would be 100) and the standard deviation (variability) at 15.

The percentage of people scoring within certain limits on this deviation IQ is constant regardless of age (i.e., an IQ of 115 is above 84% of others for any age, and 13.6% of people of any age score between 70 and 85).

THE MEAN AND STANDARD DEVIATION

A set of scores can be described by concentrating on two aspects of the distribution. The first is to describe the typical or average score in the set. A statistic frequently used for this is the mean. The second is to describe the dispersion that exists in the scores or to indicate how variable the scores are. A statistic frequently used to describe variability is the standard deviation. The following is an example of how the mean and standard deviation of a set of ten scores are calculated.

Score (X)	Frequency
120	2
119	1
118	4
117	1
116	2
	$n = 10$

MEAN ($\overline{X}$)

$$\overline{X} = \frac{\Sigma X}{n}$$

$$= \frac{120 + 120 + 119 + 118 + 118 + 118 + 118 + 117 + 116 + 116}{10}$$

$$= \frac{2 \times 120 + 119 + 4 \times 118 + 117 + 2 \times 116}{10}$$

$$= \frac{240 + 119 + 472 + 117 + 232}{10}$$

$$= \frac{1180}{10}$$

$$= 118$$

STANDARD DEVIATION (SD)

$$SD = \sqrt{\frac{\Sigma (X - \overline{X})^2}{n}}$$

$$= \sqrt{\frac{\begin{array}{c}(120 - 118)^2 + (120 - 118)^2 + (119 - 118)^2 + (118 - 118)^2 + \\ (118 - 118)^2 + (118 - 118)^2 + (118 - 118)^2 + (117 - 118)^2 + \\ (116 - 118)^2 + (116 - 118)^2\end{array}}{10}}$$

$$= \sqrt{\frac{\begin{array}{c} 2 \times (120 - 118)^2 + 1 \times (119 - 118)^2 + 4 \times (118 - 118)^2 \\ + 1 \times (117 - 118)^2 + 2 \times (116 - 118)^2 \end{array}}{10}}$$

$$= \sqrt{\frac{2 \times (2)^2 + 1 \times (1)^2 + 4 \times (0)^2 + 1 (-1)^2 + 2 (-2)^2}{10}}$$

$$= \sqrt{\frac{(2 \times 4) + (1 \times 1) + (4 \times 0) + (1 \times 1) + (2 \times 4)}{10}}$$

$$= \sqrt{\frac{8 + 1 + 0 + 1 + 8}{10}}$$

$$= \sqrt{\frac{18}{10}}$$

$$= \sqrt{1.8}$$

$$= 1.34$$

Thus, the set of ten scores has a mean of 118 and a standard deviation of 1.34. We can say that the average score in the set is 118 and that, typically, other scores differ from that average by 1.34 score units.

When we say that the mean IQ is 100 and that the standard deviation is 15, we are saying that the average IQ for a group is 100 but that the typical person can be expected to fall within 15 IQ points of the mean of 100.

Figure 9.1 shows how this looks on the normal curve and the location of various scores in terms of standard deviations from the mean. The normal curve shown depicts standard deviation units and the percentage of any normal population that will fall between these units (e.g., about 34% lie between the mean and one standard deviation above the mean with 34% also lying between the mean and one standard deviation below the mean).

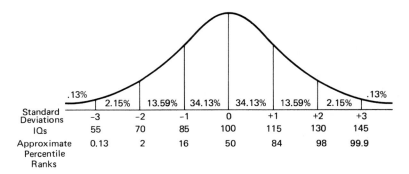

Figure 9.1
The normal curve.

IQ scores are shown in relation to standard deviation units (e.g., about 68% of the normal population have IQs between 85 and 115).

From the beginnings of modern IQ testing until World War II, the focus was on the product of intellectual functioning (what does the child answer, not what is the thought process) and on estimating the general or "*g* factor" underlying the answers. Indeed, we might say that intelligence *was* the *g* factor! After World War II, however, a new idea emerged—the idea of the importance of specific mental abilities. Attempts to identify and measure these specific factors were a major focus of IQ testing in the 1950s and 1960s, along with an attempt to look at some aspects of the *process* of thinking.

Guilford's Structure of Intellect

During the 1930s L. L. Thurstone began to identify and measure specific factors of intelligence. In 1938, he identified twelve "primary mental abilities" such as perceptual speed, numerical facility, verbal comprehension, and general reasoning (Thurstone, 1938). As a result, the idea of going beyond the measurement of the *g* factor of intelligence to the measurement of *s* factors became popular.

J. P. Guilford developed the idea of specific intelligence factors into a very detailed model beginning in the 1950s. Guilford (1967) conceives of intelligence as being a combination of three dimensions—operations, contents, and products—with each specific intellectual ability being one specific combination of these three factors. Since there are 5 operations, 5 contents, and 6 products in Guilford's model, as shown in Figure 9.2, this means that there are 150 different mental abilities that could conceivably be measured! Although only about 100 have been measured to date, Guilford's model is an important advance in understanding intelligence.

The *operations* in Guilford's model are major intellectual processes. These are knowing or discovering or being aware (cognition), retrieving from storage (memory), the generation of multiple responses (divergent thinking), arriving at a specific, accepted solution (convergent thinking), and judging the appropriateness of information or decisions (evaluation).

The *contents* in Guilford's model refer to the types of information on which the operations are performed. The types of content are visual, auditory, symbolic, semantic, and behavioral. Visual content is information in visual form such as shape or color. Auditory content involves information in auditory form, such as spoken words or music. Information in signs such as numbers and codes is included in symbolic content. Semantic content gets into word meanings and verbal inference. Behavioral content is nonverbal, involving such things as feelings and emotions.

300

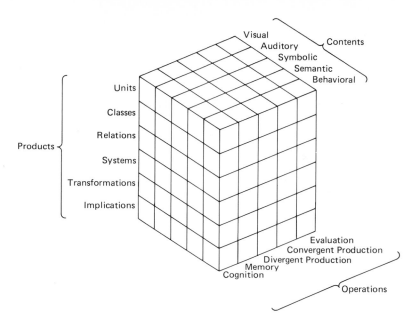

Units

Classes

Relations

Products

Systems

Transformations

Implications

Visual
Auditory
Symbolic
Semantic
Behavioral
Contents

Evaluation
Convergent Production
Divergent Production
Memory
Cognition
Operations

Figure 9.2
Guilford's structure of the intellect. From J. P. Guilford, Way Beyond the I.Q. *(Buffalo, N.Y.: Creative Education Foundation, 1977). Reprinted with permission.*

The *products* in Guilford's model are the results of applying an operation to a content, the form that information takes once it is processed. These are single, segregated items of information (units), sets of items grouped by virtue of their common properties (classes), connections between items of information (relations), organizations of information (systems), changes of information (transformations), and prediction from information (implications).

By locating the specific cube in the three-dimensional block, based on just which operation, content, and product one is focusing, it should be possible to identify and measure each of the 150 distinct abilities. For example, if the concern is with *memory* of specific *units* of *semantic* material, this is one specific cube, as distinct from *memory* of specific *units* of *behavioral* material.

Although Thurstone's claim of 12 primary mental abilities or Guilford's model of 150 mental abilities had powerful historical significance, from a practical viewpoint they have failed to yield powerful results. In most cases, measuring *s* factors fails to predict future intellectual performance with any greater accuracy than does the general IQ score. This is due in part to the fact that the *g* factor score, being based on a *group* of subtests, provides scores that are more consistent (reliable) than any subtest score. The term "reliable" refers to the extent to which a person can be expected to maintain the same relative position in relation to his or her comparison group if the test is given more than once or if different forms of the test are given. The *s* factors or subtest scores, then, are interesting to look at

Table 9.2
Profile Showing Scatter
of Subtest Scores on an
IQ Test

Subtest	Score	IQ Approximation
Information	12	110
Comprehension	15	125
Arithmetic	9	95
Similarities	7	85
Vocabulary	18	140
Picture completion	6	80
Picture arrangement	7	85
Block design	10	100
Object assembly	13	115
Coding	15	125

to find out more about a student's intellectual makeup, but they do not predict such things as school performance as well as the overall score. Furthermore, a "scatter" in subtest scores such as that presented in Table 9.2 does *not* really tell as much about the student as one might think. Experts such as Cronbach (1970) have warned repeatedly that "scatter" in subtest scores is a natural thing, part of the random variation in measurement, and that the subtest scores are *not* reliable enough to have any deep interpretation based on them.

Validity and Reliability

Before placing faith in the scores resulting from any educational test, we should consider the quality of that test. Two indices that indicate that quality are validity and reliability.

Validity is the most basic concept. A test is said to be valid if it "measures what it purports to measure." While this sounds simple enough, it should be noted that educational tests are never completely valid or invalid. Rather, validity exists in degrees with some tests doing a better job of measuring what they are supposed to measure than others. In addition, validity is dependent upon the situation in which the test is to be used. For example, a test may be reasonably valid if used in an all-white suburban high school but may possess little validity if administered in a school on an Indian reservation.

Reliability refers to the consistency with which a test measures. An index of reliability is basically a correlation coefficient that indicates the relationship between two sets of scores. With respect to reliability, these may be the scores that individuals receive on two different administrations of the same test, administration of two different forms of the same test, or the scores that a person receives on different parts of one administration of a test. If a test has high reliability, it means that a person taking the test will tend to be in the same relative position in one score distribution from the test as he or she is in the other. Both validity and reliability are discussed at length in Chapter 14.

A reasonable way of looking at it is to keep in mind that there are a variety of intellectual functions, that a high IQ score does *not* mean that the student should do well in every area. Two students with the same IQ may have considerably different cognitive strengths and weaknesses. At the same time, the teacher must keep in mind that specific subtest scores cannot be relied on as highly accurate predictors of success in those areas and that the child's *general* intellectual ability is correlated with *general* success in school. Beyond this, the teacher must depend on professionals such as psychologists, psychometrists, and counselors to interpret any important aspects of the child's performance in different cognitive areas compared with his or her overall IQ score.

Summary of Popular Intelligence Tests

One fact that cannot be overemphasized is that intelligence, as is true of most other psychological terms, is a hypothetical construct that cannot be measured or observed directly. Consequently, there may never be agreement as how to define it or measure it. As a result, one must be very careful as to how one interprets an IQ score.

Even though IQ scores are often thought to be indicators of the evasive construct of intelligence, they are viewed better as indicators of scholastic aptitude. That is, they do provide an indication of how well one may be expected to achieve in school in comparison with others who take the test. They are probably not an indicator of innate ability or intelligence since we are not even sure what that is as you have seen in the preceding discussion. With this caution in mind, we will look at several examples of scholastic aptitude or IQ tests presently being used in schools.

Individual Tests

IQ tests are designed to be administered to one person at a time (individual tests) or to be administered to several different people at the same time (group tests). In this section, we examine several individual tests and then, in the next section, look at popular group IQ tests.*

Wechsler Intelligence Scale for Children–Revised (WISC-R)
The most widely used individual IQ test is the Wechsler Intelligence Scale for Children-Revised. This test, developed as a downward extension of the

*Additional information regarding individual and group tests discussed here as well as others may be obtained from Oscar K. Buros, ed., *The Eighth Mental Measurements Yearbook* (Lincoln, Neb.: University of Nebraska, Buros Institute of Mental Measurements, 1978).

Wechsler-Bellevue Adult Intelligence Scale (WAIS), was designed to focus on children from about ages 6 to 16. The ten subtests comprising the verbal and performance scales of the WISC-R as well as two optional subtests, with an example of an item from each subtest follow:

1. *General information.* "What makes water boil?"
2. *General comprehension.* "What should you do if a boy (girl) much smaller than yourself tries to start a fight with you?"
3. *Arithmetic.* "A milkman had 25 cartons of milk and sold 14 of them. How many bottles did he have left?"
4. *Similarities.* "In what way are a plum and peach alike?"
5. *Vocabulary.* "What is the meaning of 'nuisance'?"
6. *Picture completion.* (Child is shown picture of a comb with tooth missing, or a door with a hinge missing, and asked to tell what is missing in the picture.)
7. *Picture arrangement.* (Child is given frames from a cartoon and told to put them in order to tell a story.)
8. *Block design.* (Child is given colored blocks with geometric configurations and told to arrange them so as to get the same designs as in each picture.)
9. *Object assembly.* (Child is given a puzzle problem that requires assembling a cut-up man, horse, face, auto.)
10. *Coding.* (Child has to follow key and record correct figure below each number or at earlier age correct simple entry within each figure.)
11. *Digit Span* (Optional Verbal Test). "Repeat after me: 8 - 4 - 2 - 3- 9."
12. *Mazes* (Optional Performance Test). (Child traces his or her way out of mazes with a pencil.)

In the WISC-R the examiner scores the child as he or she answers each question, proceeding until the child misses several and cannot proceed any higher, the items in each subtest being arranged in order of increasing difficulty. The child's raw score is then compared with the norms for his or her age and is converted into a "scaled score" based on an average of 10 and a standard deviation of 3 (e.g., 13 is one standard deviation above the mean on every subtest, 7 is one standard deviation below, etc.). The examiner, after administering the test and scoring the child on each task, can then add up scores and consult a table that gives an overall verbal IQ (based on the five verbal tasks), a performance IQ (based on the nonverbal tasks), and an overall IQ (or *g* score based on all tasks). The examiner writes a verbal report of the test, noting characteristics of the child, rapport, and any observations beyond the scores themselves. Thus, the WISC-R actually serves as a carefully controlled and structured interview in which the examiner can observe the child closely, assure that rapport is established, score the child's performance on standardized tasks and compare him or her with other children of the same age, and report anything important that has been noticed in this child.

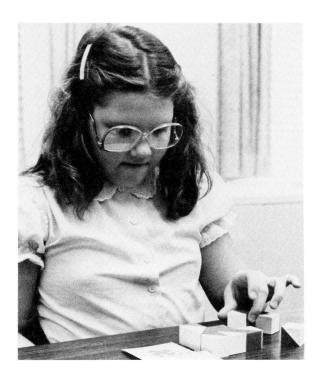

A child works on the block design section of the WISC-R. (Bernie Weithorn/SIUC Photographic Service.)

The WISC-R has high reliability, is valid particularly in predicting school performance and diagnosing cognitive areas of weakness, and is helpful in pinpointing learning disabilities, social disadvantage, dyslexia, aphasia, and various other clinical problems.

Wechsler Preschool and Primary Scale of Intelligence (WPPSI)
The Wechsler Preschool and Primary Scale of Intelligence (WPPSI) is designed for use with children from ages 4 to 6J and is a special group of tasks for this age level rather than a downward revision of the WISC-R. It is similar to the WISC-R in form and content, but it has a separate and distinct set of IQ norms. These were based on a stratified sample of both white and nonwhite children, in line wih the 1960 census. This test is excellent for estimating intellectual potential of children before school through about the first grade level.

Stanford-Binet Intelligence Scale
Another commonly used individual intelligence test in America today is the Stanford revision of the Binet IQ scale, first published in 1916 by Lewis Terman and his associates at Stanford University. Although based on Binet's work, it was new and unique enough to be considered virtually a new test. This was the first test to be based on a standardization sample of Americans (1,000 children and 400 adults), and it was the first test to

SCALED SCORES

It is easier to make comparisons between scores from two different tests if these tests have the same mean and standard deviation. For example, if Billy's score on a math test is 21 and his score on spelling is 39, we really don't know which score indicates a better performance. If we find that the maximum score possible on math was 25 and on spelling 100, we have a better idea of his relative performance in math and spelling.

Another way in which to compare Billy's performance in math and spelling is by looking at the scores in relation to the performance of the rest of the class—statistics that indicate that performance are the mean and standard deviation. If the mean score on math was 22, with a standard deviation of 2, we see that Billy performed below the average in math. If the mean score on spelling was 35 with a standard deviation of 4, we see that Billy scored above the mean in spelling. In relation to the rest of the class, Billy did better in spelling than in math. This type of comparison across subjects would be easier if math and spelling had the same mean and standard deviation. This can be done by calculating a scaled score as follows:

$$
\begin{array}{cc}
\textit{Math} & \textit{Spelling} \\
\overline{X} = 22 & \overline{X} = 35 \\
SD = 2 & SD = 4 \\
\end{array}
$$

$$
\text{Scaled score} = \frac{X - \overline{X}}{SD} \qquad\qquad \text{Scaled score} = \frac{X - \overline{X}}{SD}
$$

$$
= \frac{21 - 22}{2} \qquad\qquad\qquad = \frac{39 - 35}{4}
$$

$$
= -.5 \qquad\qquad\qquad\qquad = +1
$$

In this case, we see Billy scored .5 standard deviation below the mean on math and 1 standard deviation above the mean in spelling. The mean of this distribution of scaled scores is 0 and the standard deviation is 1. We can change the mean and standard deviation to other values by first converting to the scaled score and then multiplying by the desired standard deviation and adding the desired mean. For example, if we want to convert the scaled scores to a mean of 10 and standard deviation of 3, we would proceed as follows:

$$
\begin{array}{cc}
\textit{Math} & \textit{Spelling} \\
\text{Scaled score} = -.5 & \text{Scaled score} = +1 \\
\text{New scaled score} = (-.5) \times 3 + 10 & \text{New scaled score} = (+1) \times 3 + 10 \\
= -1.5 + 10 & = 3 + 10 \\
= 8.5 & = 13 \\
\end{array}
$$

This is essentially what is done in calculating scaled scores for the WISC-R.

employ the IQ, since Binet's early tests had used mental ages as the basic yardstick.

A brief look at some tasks from the Stanford-Binet illustrates a basic point of disagreement that comes up in almost any standardized IQ test. The tasks obviously are related to experience, but the test supporters insist that this is as it should be and that they do *not* reflect specific learnings available to only a few (i.e., almost any child growing up in America will have enough exposure to his or her culture that the tasks represent general potential and learning ability rather than specific training). Meanwhile, critics insist that the tests are unfairly biased against lower-class, nonwhite, rural, and disadvantaged children.

SAMPLE BINET ITEMS—AGE 13

1. *Plan of search.* Child is shown diamond-shaped figure with a small gap in it and is told that it is a big field where he has lost his purse. The child is asked to take a pencil, start at the gap, and show how he would proceed to hunt for his purse until he found it.
2. *Abstract word.* "What is a connection? What do we mean by compare? What is revenge?"
3. *Memory for sentences.* "The airplane made a careful landing in the space which had been prepared for it." (Child repeats.)
4. *Problems of fact.* (Child tells what he thinks happened after hearing a situation described.)
5. *Dissected sentences.* (Child has to rearrange sentences presented on cards in scrambled order.)
6. *Copying a bead chain.* (Examiner strings a chain made from three types of beads and then asks child to do this from memory.)
7. *Paper Cutting (alternate).* (Examiner folds piece of paper, cuts it, and then asks child to draw how it will look when unfolded.)

In looking at the Binet examples presented here, and the WISC-R examples presented earlier, notice the heavy loading of verbal ability involved in the tasks. Remember that the tests' original goal and major use even today is in identifying and predicting success at *school-type tasks.* Most readers will agree that school is loaded with verbal tasks, so in this regard the tests are appropriate. As a direct index of genetic endowment, in this or any other area, however, they are not appropriate.

Peabody Picture Vocabulary Test–Revised (PPVT-R)

Children with special problems, such as the physically handicapped or the deaf, would have considerable difficulty in performing the tasks of the Stanford-Binet or WISC-R. A typical example of this would be the child with cerebral palsy, who could be anywhere on the IQ scale and yet who could not respond adequately on WISC-R tasks without modifications by the examiner. The Peabody Picture Vocabulary Test-Revised gets around this problem by requiring no reading or verbalizing, no response at all really, other than indicating which of several pictures is appropriate. The PPVT-R assesses "use" vocabulary or how well a person understands the meaning of words (without having to describe or explain). This skill has a high correlation with overall IQ scores.

The PPVT-R is simple to administer, involving the showing of a series of plates and asking which of the four pictures on each plate fits the verbal description given. It takes ten to twenty minutes to administer, can be scored quickly, and does not require a trained examiner. This test was widely used in Head Start research, because its speed and economy lead to a quick estimate of IQ for large numbers of people and also because of its relative freedom from verbal skills and middle-class bias. The scores from the PPVT-R are reported as percentile scores and standard scores rather then traditional IQ scores. The PPVT-R has norms ranging from ages $2\frac{1}{2}$ to 18.

To summarize, the major strengths of individual intelligence tests are their accuracy, precision, rapport with subjects, assurance of an appropriate testing situation, de-emphasis on reading, and the diagnostic and clinical value of the one-to-one interview. The major disadvantages of individual IQ tests are that they are time consuming and expensive, there is a shortage of qualified examiners, and they are not practical for large groups or quick estimates of IQ level. They are used primarily to get an accurate and legally acceptable score on an individual.

Group Intelligence Tests

The majority of students at any grade level, when tested for intellectual ability (often referred to as scholastic aptitude, mental maturity, or learning potential, but essentially testing the same basic skills as an IQ test) are tested with some type of group test. Such paper and pencil tests are more economical and easier to administer and score than are individual tests. They give a reasonable estimate of intelligence, which is usually all that is desired. In many cases, the test is really a battery of tests, with a different one for each grade level. The list of several widely used test batteries given in Table 9.3 along with grade levels covered is a vivid example of just how many terms are employed to describe what is essentially the same variable.

Group tests such as those in Table 9.3 cover a relatively restricted range of difficulty. Items geared to a particular grade level are the focus of these tests, and they are especially suitable for use in the schools, where continuity and comparability across grade levels is needed, and where time and expense considerations are important. Each test in the battery typically includes no more than three grades, and yet the entire battery usually covers a broad grade span, with the same scales, reporting figures, sampling, and testing procedures used.

In addition to a total, global score, most multilevel batteries also yield

Table 9.3
Group IQ Tests
Currently Available

Test Battery	Grade Levels Available
Cognitive Abilities Test (CAT)	K–12
Otis-Lennon Mental Ability Test	K–12
Developing Cognitive Abilities Test (DCAT)	2–12
Cooperative School and College Ability Tests (SCAT)	4–14
SRA Short Test of Educational Ability	K–12
Short Form of Academic Aptitude	1.5–12
Analysis of Learning Potential (ALP)	1–12

separate verbal and quantitative, or linguistic and nonlinguistic scores. Some tests, such as the Analysis of Learning Potential, are based on specifically predicting academic performance, whereas others give a number of subtest norms. The teacher should be cautious in using these subtest norms since they may not be reliable enough for specific prediction.

Some group tests provide special forms for testing students who have low functional reading ability. These are often designed to be administered to groups, with instructions and questions read by the examiner and the students responding on answer sheets. However, scores on these tests are not directly comparable with the regular form, and a close look at the correlation of the two forms is necessary. Group tests are really not practical any earlier than the kindergarten or first grade level; if you need an IQ score for anyone younger than 5 years of age, you must use an individual test administered by a trained examiner. Even at the 5- or 6-year-old level, the group test can be administered to no more than ten or fifteen children, and the examiner must give considerable individual attention to ensure that directions are followed, pages are turned properly, and other procedural details are followed. Until grade four, the intelligence test should be nonverbal, since the children cannot read or write. These should not be confused with "nonlanguage" tests, which require no language at all, written or spoken. Such nonlanguage tests are suitable for foreign-speaking and deaf children as well as for the nonliterate. The designation "nonverbal" for primary level tests is thus misleading, although commonly employed, and it would be more accurate to call them "nonreading" tests.

A glimpse of a typical group test at the high school level is given in Anastasi's comments about the School and College Ability Tests (SCAT):

In line with current trends in testing theory, SCAT undertakes to measure developed abilities. This is simply an explicit admission of what is more or less true of all intelligence tests, namely that test scores reflect the nature and amount of schooling the individual has received rather than measuring "capacity" independently of relevant prior experiences. Accordingly, SCAT draws freely on word knowledge and arithmetic processes learned in the appropriate school grades. In this respect, SCAT does not really differ from other intelligence tests, especially those designed for the high school and college levels; it only makes overt a condition sometimes unrecognized in other tests. [Anastasi, 1982, p. 313]

309

Another example of a group test is the Developing Cognitive Abilities Test (DCAT). Published in 1980, the DCAT is one of the newest scholastic ability tests on the market. The DCAT takes about fifty minutes to administer and can be administered to a large group with ease. The DCAT does not provide an overall IQ score. Rather, the test provides verbal, quantitative, and spatial subscale scores as well as subscale scores for five levels of cognitive skills (knowledge, comprehension, application, analysis, and synthesis). The teacher is advised to consider DCAT scores, as other group tests, as a reasonably accurate estimate of scholastic ability in the designated areas and not as a measure of innate intelligence. Further, remember that scores from any one test such as the DCAT are not directly comparable with scores from another test such as the SRA Short Test of Educational Ability. Extreme caution should be used in comparing scores from one scholastic ability (IQ) test with another.

Strengths and Weaknesses of Group Tests

Strengths and weaknesses of group intelligence tests are in direct contrast to those of individual tests. Where the individual tests are the most precise and accurate available, the group tests are less precise and accurate. Likewise, the assurance of an appropriate testing situation, rapport with the subject, opportunity for individual clinical observations, and less dependence on reading are all advantages of *individual* tests that are missing in group tests. If a child scores extremely low on a group IQ test or fails to complete a task, the examiner really has no idea what happened; all the examiner has to go on is the *product* of the test (i.e., the answer sheet). In an individual test, the close contact and chance to observe the child gives the examiner some idea at least as to social, emotional, motivational, perceptual, or other problems that might contribute to a low score. The difference here is analogous to a teacher examining a student individually on his knowledge of a book he has read as compared with looking at his answers on an objective test.

But these advantages of individual over group tests are counterbalanced by the advantages of group tests. The latter tests are far less expensive and time-consuming to administer, and they do not require a specially trained examiner; a large group or entire grade level can be tested in one place in one or two hours, and they provide a general estimate of scholastic ability and that is all that is needed in most cases.

DCAT ITEMS*

The following are several items from the Developing Cognitive Abilities Test. These items, taken from a form intended for grades seven and eight, illustrate the types of items included on verbal and nonverbal ability group tests.

1. A long race is called a
   a. pabulum   b. smorgasbord
   c. marathon   d. tambourine
2. The opposite of an *appointee* is
   a. an elected official
   b. a designated leader
   c. a person given a position
   d. a person drafted for a position
3. A train can travel at 70 miles per hour. How many miles can it travel in $4\frac{1}{2}$ hours?
   a. 280 miles   b. 315 miles
   c. 300 miles   d. none of these
4. When the figure on the left is folded, which of the objects on the right will it look like?

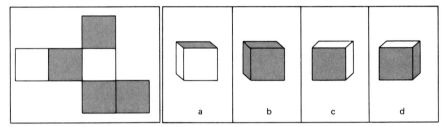

5. The figures in the top row are in order from left to right. Find the figure in the bottom row that comes next.

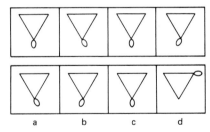

6. The figures in the top row are alike in some way. Find the figure in the bottom row that belongs to the group in the top row.

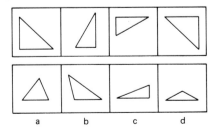

*From D. L. Beggs and J. T. Mouw, *Developing Cognitive Abilities Test* (Glenview, Ill.: Scott, Foresman, 1980). Reprinted with permission of authors and publisher.

Given the interpretation that IQ tests measure innate intelligence, a view that prevailed in the United States since Terman first adapted the Binet test for use here in 1916, there is little wonder that IQ testing is plagued with emotional controversy. The ninety minutes that a student spends taking a group IQ test as a third- or fourth-grader has consistently been thought to result in a single score that labels him or her for life as smart or dumb, gifted or retarded, above average or below. In reality, IQ tests are not intended to assess the construct of intelligence. Rather, they measure something that we call *scholastic potential,* and even with this modification we must be cautious in the interpretation of the results. You may recall that, at the very beginning, Binet was charged with the responsibility of developing a test of academic potential. He just happened to use the term "intelligence quotient" for the score resulting from his test. A quick review of the titles of tests in Table 9.3 demonstrates that test publishers have now dropped the term IQ from their tests of scholastic ability.

Another reason that these tests do not label a student for life is the unreliability and invalidity of measurement. The results of tests of scholastic ability for any given student are subject to change. Research has shown that, upon repeated testing, a student's IQ score can be expected to increase. In fact, most test publishers state in their testing manuals just how much you can expect the average student's score to increase if he or she is given the same test a second time.

Presently, the use of scholastic ability tests in schools is viewed with a great deal of healthy skepticism stemming from a number of highly emotional controversies that have arisen in recent years. The skepticism is healthy in that it helps to prevent overinterpretation and overuse of the test results by parents, teachers, and other school officials. The controversies are instructive in that they shed considerable light on the meaning and appropriate use of scholastic ability tests and they demonstrate clearly the emotions that are involved in the assessment of IQ.

Heredity Versus Environment

No other issue in the history of IQ testing has caused as much emotional reaction as that of the heredity-environment question. With the realization of the tremendous effects of environment in the early 1900s, followed by the far-reaching behaviorist movement, anyone speaking of the importance of heredity is seen as a virtual heretic, returning us to the Middle Ages. Meanwhile, as data are amassed to support the genetic argument, anyone ignoring it is seen as naïve and unscientific. And since all this comes at a time when the young, women, minority groups, and disadvantaged persons on all sides are seeking equal opportunity, the controversy becomes bitter as political implications are raised.

A famous example of this controversy and the emotions surrounding it centers on the work of Arthur Jensen, a developmental psychologist. In the *Harvard Educational Review* (1969), Jensen presented an impressive body of statistical findings in support of his conclusion that approximately 80% of what we call intelligence is determined by genetic endowment. Since only 20% remains to be influenced by environment, Jensen argued, children who score low on IQ tests do so mainly because of heredity. The final blow, and probably the part that caused such a furious reaction, was that Jensen suggested that his data indicated that these genetic differences are related to race. It was Jensen's contention that whites are different from blacks in the distribution of what he called "Level Two IQ," mainly reasoning, understanding, and problem solving. (Critics claim that Jensen said that blacks were inferior to whites, but Jensen denies this.)

Jensen's conclusions hinged on the findings of a number of studies of twins, particularly those of identical twins separated at birth and reared apart. Even in differing environments, high correlations were found between the IQs of the twins, so that it appeared that the IQ of these twins was determined primarily genetically. When compared with fraternal twins, siblings, cousins, and unrelated children, the correlations dropped in direct line with genetic similarity; that is, siblings reared apart showed lower correlations than did twins, and cousins lower than did siblings.

Jensen also noted that blacks score an average of 15 points lower on IQ tests than do whites, and the difference was almost all accounted for in his Level Two IQ—abstract reasoning and problem solving. He also observed that there were differences in the intellectual functioning of a retarded child with an IQ of 70 and a socially disadvantaged child with an IQ of 70.

A number of psychologists present arguments that are counter to Jensen's, notably James McVicker Hunt (1969). While agreeing with much of Jensen's statistical analysis and findings (e.g., the lower scores on Level Two IQ differences related to race and social class), Hunt's major point of disagreement has to do with the source of these IQ differences. Jensen pointed out in his work that, by age 4 or 5, IQ scores correlate about .70 with IQ at age 17. Hunt's reaction to this fact was that this could show the results of consistency of environment as well as results of heredity, and it could also be interpreted as dramatizing the profound effect of environment in the first four years of life.

Hunt found Jensen's distinction between Level One—associative learning—and Level Two—cognitive learning—of interest. Jensen had reported that blacks and/or lower-class children scored the same as middle-class whites on associative learning but were significantly below them on cognitive learning. Jensen concluded that the differences in IQ scores of black and lower-class children, when compared with middle-class white children, was in this "Level Two," cognitive learning, realm and that it was mainly a genetic difference. Hunt disagreed and saw the difference as being caused by the backgrounds of the children. The results of environmental

313

deficit, said Hunt, are seen in abstract performance such as Jensen's "cognitive learning" but not in the more concrete "associative learning." Hunt also pointed out that there were probably many other areas of difference and that Jensen had barely scratched the surface with these two types of learning. Finally, Hunt argued, all the tasks tended to reflect immediate learning of small bits or tasks rather than the long-term learning of large bodies of material and complex tasks.

Since all IQ tests measure the interaction of heredity and environment, or in other words measure performances that are neither purely hereditary nor purely environmental, the debate over interpretations of people such as Jensen and Hunt cannot be settled at the present time. We don't really know what percentage of IQ can be influenced by the environment, or just how much heredity limits IQ change. For a teacher, however, the statement by Paul Woodring seems particularly pertinent:

> Whether differences in inherited intellectual endowments are great, small, or non-existent is not the vital question for educators. Whatever the answer to that question may be, nothing can be done about the inherited capacity once the child is conceived. A great deal can be done to improve the educational opportunities that result from differences in the environment, in school and out. The educator's job is to make the most of what talent is available. [Woodring, 1966, p. 80]

Discrimination

Since so much is in the news these days about discrimination, and so many laws are highlighted in resolving problems in this area, we cannot neglect the meaning of this word in relation to IQ testing. An IQ test is not *bad* because it discriminates! On the contrary, this is precisely what the test is supposed to do—discriminate those with high IQs from those with average IQs from those with low IQs, discriminate high verbal from high performance, and discriminate one type of profile from another. Social scientists work continually on the precision with which IQ tests can discern such discriminations, and the more discriminating the test is in relation to these questions, the better the test it is.

It is only in relation to unfair discrimination that this word becomes something "bad" in IQ testing. If the test says that the child is average on this type of task, when in reality the child is outstanding, if it tends to identify a particular type of child as retarded far more often than is really the case, if it predicts that someone will do poorly on a task when that person actually will do well, then the discrimination is inaccurate or unfair. In a way, one might say that the test itself never really discriminates unfairly, but rather the test user does, since it is up to the user to make sure that the test is being employed appropriately, with the proper normative comparisons, and that it is interpreted reasonably.

Test developers today are hard at work trying to find ways in which to eliminate inaccurate and unfair discriminations based on IQ tests, primarily discrimination against minority groups. This is not an easy problem to resolve, but the major focus today is on the use of appropriate subgroup norms and the use of specific validity studies (i.e., data on the test for the specific task and subgroup that is being studied). For example, if an IQ test is being used to screen applicants for a job, you must have data showing how that test actually does predict success for this type of applicant on this type of task. If you don't have such data, you cannot use the test appropriately.

An intriguing area of findings in relation to IQ testing is that of differences in performance based on sex. It is true that boys score higher than girls on some math tasks, spatial visualization, and analytical reasoning and that girls score higher on some verbal tasks and on tasks involving speech and reading.

Such differences fail to tell us much about *innate* differences in intelligence, however. Boys are treated differently from girls in our culture, so we don't really know if superiority in math and inferiority in grammar is hereditary or environmental. Likewise, the more rapid verbal development of girls doesn't really prove genetic superiority.

On the opposite side of the coin, because the distribution of IQ scores for males at any age is indistinguishable from females and because the sexes are so nearly identical on nearly every IQ task doesn't prove anything either. One must keep in mind that the tests were developed in this way *deliberately,* with any tasks that showed a large discrepancy between males and females eliminated from the test. In other words, those developing the tests *assumed* the absence of sex differences in intelligence and then made sure that the tests came out "asexual." One must note also that sex differences in intellectual performance observed in elementary school often disappear later on.

There are *probably* no really important inherent differences in male and female IQ—that is, human intelligence is asexual—and it is *individuals* that differ, not male versus female, blacks versus whites, or blondes versus brunettes. The fact that male students may tend to do better in math and science, females in grammar and literature, and males are more "analytical" and females more "intuitive" should *not* lead to stereotyping of the sexes. Each individual should be encouraged to develop all areas to the fullest, and cultural expectations should be resisted.

Teacher Expectancy

All teachers form expectations as to the way in which they expect a student to behave in certain situations or the likelihood that the student will be successful academically. Once these expectations are formed, teachers will

315

behave in ways that communicate these expectations to the student. As a result, the student develops self-expectations that are consistent with the teachers' and tends to perform in ways that are consistent with the teachers' expectations.

This argument was presented originally by Rosenthal and Jacobson in 1968 in *Pygmalion in the Classroom: Teacher Expectations and Pupils' Intellectual Development.* Rosenthal and Jacobson reported on a study in which they led elementary school teachers to believe that certain of their students could be expected to make large gains in academic achievement over the year (late bloomers). In fact, there was no reason to expect the students so identified to perform differently from other students in the classes. However, at the end of the year, students in the first and second grades who had been identified to their teachers as "late bloomers" showed greater gains in general academic ability and reading achievement than did their classmates. While students in grades three through six who had been identified as "late bloomers" did not outgain their classmates, Rosenthal and Jacobson concluded that the gains of the first- and second-graders demonstrated that teachers' expectations do influence their students' academic performance.

The publication of Rosenthal and Jacobson's work brought about a flurry of emotional and scientific response. A number of attempts to replicate their study were unsuccessful, leading to arguments that the effects of teacher expectancy had been overstated (Claiborn, 1969; José and Cody, 1971). Other researchers, however, were successful in demonstrating aspects of the teacher expectancy effect described in *Pygmalion in the Classroom* (Braun, 1976).

Despite the mixed findings with respect to teacher expectancy, Good and Brophy concluded that "the past five years' work by a large number of investigators using a variety of methods has established unequivocally

Research suggests that a teacher's expectations may affect student achievement.
(CEMREL, Inc.)

that teachers' expectations can and do function as self-fulfilling prophecies'' (1980, p. 260).

While a number of factors such as appearance, sex, and social class seem to influence teacher expectations with respect to students, one factor that clearly affects teacher expectations is test scores (Braun, 1976). This effect may be positive, but teachers appear to be more influenced in their expectations by low scores than they are by high scores. In other words, if a student scores low on an IQ test, this information could well lead to his or her teacher expecting low academic performance. The teacher expectation itself could become a self-fulfilling prophecy leading to poor achievement on the part of the student. This possibility has led to great concern over the use of IQ tests in schools throughout the country. It emphasizes again the need for accurate interpretation and cautious use of tests of IQ (scholastic ability) by teachers.

Recommendations for Teachers

The field of intelligence testing is difficult to discuss without going into great detail. It is confused further by the emotional arguments of the ''stamp out IQ testing'' enthusiasts. IQ tests are neither made in heaven nor the root of all evil but, instead, tools of some usefulness that require a great deal of caution in implementation due to the extremely sensitive area involved.

The following suggestions are *not* meant to be the ''final word'' on intelligence testing; rather they are guidelines that might be helpful to teachers in maintaining sanity and common sense in the midst of emotionalism and controversy. By trying to be as well informed as possible in this area, proceeding sensibly and objectively, you can avoid adding to the many abuses of IQ tests.

1. *See IQ as a functional score.* One of the best ways in which to avoid many of the pitfalls of heredity versus environment, misinterpretation of scores, and unreasonable expectations is to emblazon on your mind, never to be forgotten, that an IQ score is nothing more, and nothing less, than a *functional* score. If Joan scores 13 in block design on the WISC-R, she is functioning one standard deviation above average, or better than 84% of others her age, on that task. We don't know why she is functioning at that level; she may have had some unusual interests and experiences that developed her skill, she may have inherited a high potential for that type of learning, or she may have been extremely lucky. Likewise, if Freida scores 7 on the same block design task, all we really know is that she scores one standard deviation below the mean; in other words, below about 84% of her age group, on that task. We really don't know if Freida is disturbed, wasn't trying, comes from a very poor background, or is just not good at that type of task.

317

It would be analogous to testing children on how far they can jump. If Fred can jump farther than anyone else, this may be useful information, especially in relation to any activities where jumping pays off. But one test is not a perfect indicator of Fred's jumping potential, it certainly is not a perfect estimate of Fred's overall athletic ability, and it probably has nothing to do with Fred's math ability.

By sticking to the "functional score" interpretation, the teacher may note how a student scores on specific IQ tasks and how he or she scores in general. While the teacher knows that this gives some idea how the student will most likely do in many school tasks, the teacher is free to entertain hypotheses as to why the test score may be either too high or low. The teacher must allow the child the chance to prove the test wrong by performing differently from the test predictions. Likewise, if the child scores very low in a given area, the teacher may guess that the child probably needs help in this area but must avoid making assumptions about inherited intelligence, environmental influence, or social class stereotypes.

2. *Don't overinterpret.* Many of the abuses in IQ testing come from overinterpreting the scores. When a child scores 125, about the ninety-third percentile, a very high score on an intelligence test, this does *not* mean the child can be expected to do extremely well in every subject or that the child is the same as the next one with an IQ of 125. It means that the child functions pretty well on some IQ tasks and should do pretty well on some school tasks, but we aren't sure of that. Teachers must keep in mind that the score is useful, but *not* infallible, *not* rigid; it is only an approximation. It is a direct index of neither heredity nor environment but the result of numerous factors interacting. Just as weight or height or number of cavities should be used sparingly as indices of a child's physical health, so IQ scores must be used very cautiously as useful but limited indices in the cognitive area.

3. *The scatter of individual profiles.* "Scatter," or a spread on subtest scores in one's profile (see Table 9.2), should be treated with extreme caution. Interpretation of the scatter on subtest scores is a prime example of overinterpretation implied in suggestion 2. The subtests are almost always *not* reliable or valid enough, and the meaning of the subtest not clear enough, to make much out of them. If a child scores 87, 93, 99, 106, and 112 on various subtests, the variation could be due to sampling error as much as to anything else. You can have a greater degree of assurance, however, that the child's overall IQ level is about average, somewhere around 98, or even better, in the 93–103 range (assuming a standard error of measurement of 5). Beyond that, the teacher should be alert for further data that support the possibility the child is stronger in one area than another, without thinking of the test score as any sort of proof.

In addition to making very little of "scatter" in subscores, teachers should look with skepticism at any such emphasis on the significance of scatter by psychologists or counselors. Be skeptical about claims in this area, regardless who is making them.

INTERPRETING IQ SCORES

Mrs. West was very upset as she looked at the test results for her children that the school had given her. Billy had scored 114 on the test, and Sally had only scored 107. And yet Sally was making mostly "A's" in school whereas Billy made mostly "B's." She decided that she would really have to get on Billy and made him work harder. Billy definitely should be making better grades than Sally; he must be loafing. She would have to get on him especially for getting a "C" in English while Sally got an "A." Obviously, Billy should be making an "A" in English, since he was brighter than Sally.

What really irked Mrs. West was the fact that Donald, the boy who lived across the street, scored higher on the test than her two children, a fact that her neighbor made sure to mention. Donald had scored 116 on the test, which meant that he was smarter than either Billy or Sally. Mrs. West hated to face this fact, but there it was in black and white. However, it was comforting to know that Donald made "B's" also, so that he was even more of an underachiever than were her Billy and Sally. This was small consolation, though, for the neighbor's kid was definitely smarter than her two kids.

Can you see the fallacies in this situation? First, we have the fact that IQ scores of 107, 114, and 116 are not really different. The safest thing to say is that all three are probably slightly above average in intelligence. Furthermore, many factors in addition to IQ interact in determining grades, and we can't say which one should be making the highest grades. Finally, these students will differ from subject to subject, regardless of general IQ score. If we looked at a profile, we might find that Billy had high aptitude for math, average aptitude for history, and low aptitude for English. Mrs. West is definitely naïve and guilty of misinterpreting IQ scores in a way that could be damaging to her children.

4. *Think of a score width or score band.* To eliminate one serious problem in interpretation, the idea that an IQ score is fixed or a precise estimate, it is recommended that teachers employ the idea of score limits. If you think of Fred's 115 score instead as "he scores about 111–119, but we're not sure exactly what his true score is," this helps to get across the idea that the IQ is just an estimate of a functional score. Then, if Frank is reported as "he scores in the 109–117 range," we can see that Fred and Frank are about the same and we're not sure who scores higher. If we report that Fred scored 115 and Frank 113, many will believe that Fred is two points smarter than Frank, which we really don't know at all.

As test developers, examiners, and teachers get used to the idea of reporting test scores as score bands, many of the misinterpretations and overinterpretations in testing can be avoided.

For example, the standard error of measurement (i.e., how reliable the score is) for the WISC-R verbal scale is about 4 and the standard error of measurement for the performance IQ scale on the WISC-R is about 5. We know from the normal curve in Figure 9.1 that a student who has a verbal IQ of 110 from the WISC-R has a 68 percent chance of having a true verbal IQ between 106 and 114. Likewise, if that student's performance IQ is 113, then there is a 68 percent chance of the true IQ being between 108 and 118. In other words, we are viewing the obtained IQ score as the mean of a normal distribution of possible scores for the student in question with the standard error of measurement being considered the standard deviation. The score band gives us a much more accurate (we have a 2 to 1 chance of being correct) picture of what the student's true IQ scores are. In addition, Anastasi (1982) states that so long as the score bands for verbal and performance IQs overlap, they should not be considered as different. In comparing two scores, only when the score bands *do not* overlap can one be certain that the scores are different.

5. *Be realistic, but keep an open mind.* In such a delicate area as intelligence testing, this suggestion is difficult to follow, partly because it is difficult to discern just what "realistic" is. No test of an hour or so is going to tell you everything about a child's intellectual functioning, and no test can tell you anything with perfect reliability or validity. Thus, any test score should be viewed with healthy skepticism, knowing that it is an estimate that could be inaccurate for numerous reasons.

Students are limited by individual differences in intelligence, temperament, motivation, and background. While it makes one feel warm and cozy inside to hear of the powers of positive expectations, in reality the expectations of the teacher are limited in how much influence they can have on students. Just as positive expectations cannot improve a student's hearing or eyesight, they cannot magically change a slow learner into a gifted child. The teacher is advised to have realistic but positive expectations for children and to keep an open mind, allowing for the possibility that expectations might be very inaccurate. The tests might be wrong, the child might perform much better—or worse—than the test predicts, and the child might change significantly, even though the test at the time was highly accurate.

Teachers are also limited in just how much they can help a student. With five or six classes of thirty or forty each, teachers have little time available for individual students. Even when the teachers know that the child's learning problems are primarily the result of social disadvantage, or a specific cognitive deficit, there are realistic limitations as to just how much they can help. Ideally, such problems will receive the attention of a specialist, but there is no way that a specialist can help each individual child, since *every* child could profit from such special help.

6. *Insist on more than a score.* Whenever a child is referred for special testing, which quite often involves an individual intelligence test, the teacher should insist on receiving adequate feedback from such a referral. A test score by itself is usually not adequate. If the school has gone to the expense of having the individual tested in the first place, then the teacher, who will most likely be working with the child in his class, deserves a detailed explanation of what the referral yielded. What are the child's strengths and weaknesses, what are the subjective observations of the examiner,

what sort of hypotheses and suggestions does the examiner have for helping the child? The teacher should receive not only a written report, but also have a conference with the examiner to explore strategies and ideas. Ideally, this would be followed up with another conference and a progress report in a continuing effort to aid the teacher in understanding and helping the child.

Counseling and school psychologists are busy people and usually have a backlog of children with problems that need attention. In addition, they often have the impression that classroom teachers lack the time, the interest, or the sophistication to understand the findings of individual tests. By making an active effort to counteract this impression, the teacher can improve the working relationship of teachers and auxiliary personnel and develop a professional rapport that is mutually beneficial to both parties as well as far more helpful to the child.

7. *Combine IQ with other predictors.* An IQ score should never be used as the sole predictor of school performance. By combining all the information available, the teacher will have a much better basis on which to estimate the child's potential. Such information as past grades, emotional maturity, social adjustment, social class background, interests, physical health, and many other factors all interact in determining a child's school performance. While useful, any test score, IQ or otherwise, should be seen as just one of many possible predictors of school success.

Instructional groupings should not be done on the basis of IQ alone. (Bernie Weithorn/SIUC Photographic Service.)

While IQ scores may do a good job if you want to look only at how well a single factor can predict school performance, keep in mind that *no* single factor predicts school performance very well. The best predictor of school performance is the judicious combination of all available data.

8. *Don't group classes based on IQ alone.* We don't want to get into an involved discussion of all the pros and cons of ability grouping, but one must honestly admit that almost all teaching involves groups. Unless you are tutoring every child, or lecturing to the whole student body en masse, then students are being grouped, by chance, by age, by interest, by sex, by grade, or by ability.

It should be clear by now that IQ scores are not absolute, not completely reliable, and must be combined with other information. Thus, it doesn't make much sense to ignore all other variables and group by IQ alone. Such grouping tends to be detrimental to the average and below-average students, not only in fostering feelings of inferiority but also in how much they learn. Meanwhile, above-average or superior students seem to do as well in homogeneous as in heterogeneous grouping.

In grouping classes, the primary goal should be to allow for the maximum probability of learning for the students involved, without troublesome and negative side effects. A realistic goal that is actually just about as important and probably tends to facilitate the first is that grouping should make it easier for the teacher to get the job done. If the teacher feels more comfortable, secure, and effective in a class where some of the variability on relevant factors has been reduced, this may contribute to more effective teaching.

The mainstreaming movement has helped to eliminate some of the abuses of overly rigid and unidimensional ability grouping. The trend today is for a more heterogeneous mixture in the classroom, with a wide IQ range included. While there is no simple answer to the question "How should we group these students?" you should be aware that research has failed to show straight ability grouping to be effective. When grouping students into sections, teachers should have in mind basic reasons for the grouping and what the classes are trying to accomplish and consider many variables in deciding on a good mix.

9. *Use subgroup norms.* Whenever they are available, the teacher should look at subgroup norms in interpreting a test score. The child's fifty-ninth percentile score based on national norms takes on a different meaning when seen as the seventy-eighth percentile for her community. The black child's 90 IQ looks low until it is compared with appropriate norms for black ghetto children and the child is seen as above average in intelligence. The 70 IQ of an extremely disadvantaged rural child may be seen as average when compared with appropriate norms.

We could go on and on with such examples. The important thing to keep in mind is that the test score *always* compares the child with other children. It is important to be very careful as to just which other children are used as the basis for comparison. Whenever an appropriate subgroup can be identified, and normative data are available, the child should be compared with this subgroup to make a sensible interpretation of the score.

10. *Educating the public.* The misuses and abuses of IQ tests have led many critics to demand the elimination of such testing. This "help to stamp out tests" approach is based on the view that you can't have abuses of IQ testing if you don't have IQ testing! The key question to ask any advocate of this approach is "What will you use in place of the tests?" The ways of discriminating unfairly against a group or individual are almost endless, and stamping out IQ tests in no way guarantees that such abuses will stop.

Another strategy for dealing with misuses of IQs has been the "secrecy" strategy. This approach sees intelligence testing and IQ scores as such a sensitive and explosive area that as much information as possible must be kept confidential. If a child and his or her parents do not know the child's IQ score, then it can hardly lead to misinterpretation, hurt feelings, or unreasonable expectations. Even the teacher may be kept in the dark in this approach.

A somewhat different and far more acceptable answer is that of giving considerable information, but getting away from the label "intelligence quotient" and its dynamite implications. In this approach, the test is one of "cognitive ability" or "school ability" or some such label that reflects accurately what is in an IQ test and what the scores mean, without using the term IQ with all its negative connotations. In such an approach, parent, child, and teacher are given considerable information as to how the child performed compared with others of his or her age level, but the test is described more accurately in terms of its function, that of estimating scholastic or cognitive ability. At present, this approach seems to be gaining numerous supporters as a way to puncture some of the IQ myths and take some of the threat out of the testing of mental ability.

The Right to Know

Traditionally, IQ scores have *not* been revealed to those who take IQ tests, and they are often not revealed to parents or even teachers. The reason for this secrecy about IQ scores is the fear that the test results will be misinterpreted and damage the child. Currently, the "sunshine laws" or "the right to know" challenges this secrecy, and teachers are sometimes at a loss as to just what information is confidential and what must be released, even though federal law is clear on this point. The following is presented as a clear statement of guidelines in this area:

Two principles and one verbal technique seem to us to provide a sound basis for communicating the information obtained from testing. The two "commandments" are absolutely interdependent—without the second the first is empty, and without the first the second is pointless.

The first: PARENTS HAVE THE RIGHT TO KNOW WHATEVER THE SCHOOL KNOWS ABOUT THE ABILITIES, THE PERFORMANCE, AND THE PROBLEMS OF THEIR CHILDREN.

The second: THE SCHOOL HAS THE OBLIGATION TO SEE THAT IT COMMUNICATES UNDERSTANDABLE AND USABLE KNOWLEDGE. Whether by written report or by individual conference, the school must make sure it is giving *real* information—not just the illusion of information that bare numbers or canned interpretations often afford. And the information must be in terms that parents can absorb and use. [The Psychological Corporation, 1959, pp. 1–2]

Creativity

Throughout the discussion of intelligence, we stressed that a better name for IQ is scholastic ability. We also indicated that individuals who score high on IQ tests tend to be those who have learned the types of behavior that are considered important in school. This means that IQ tests tend to concentrate on convergent rather than on divergent tasks. In convergent thinking, one integrates what is already known in a way that is consistent with existing knowledge. In divergent thinking, one moves into the unknown or the original (Haimowitz and Haimowitz, 1973). It is when we move from that part of intelligence represented by convergent thinking to consideration of divergent thinking that we move into the part of intelligence known as creativity.

Consider, for example, Susan and Sarah who are the same age and even look quite similar. They are from middle-class backgrounds, both have the same IQ score, and both make the same grades in school. There is one thing noticeably different about them, however. Susan is predictable and orderly, always has her work done on time, and always does a good job. But somehow Susan's work is never unique, unusual, or unexpected. Her work always has the touch of the customary, the expected, the routine, even though it is well done. She likes structure and planning, wants to know what to expect, and does not appreciate sudden changes or surprises.

Sarah thrives on the unexpected, can tolerate considerable uncertainty, and even in the simplest tasks her work has a touch of the unusual or unique. Sarah does not like deadlines and gets engrossed in tasks and loses track of time; her work ranges from outstanding to mediocre or even incomplete. She asks unusual questions, which sometimes irritates her teachers, and often comes up with strange ideas and solutions to problems. She loves to be surprised as well as to surprise others.

The difference between Susan and Sarah lies mainly in the area of creativity. Sarah has several characteristics found to be common in "creative" persons; Susan is more like the rest of us, more "customary."

Creativity: What Is It?

While creativity has been defined in many different ways, these definitions can be grouped into two categories: the *traits* approach and the *learned behavior* approach. In the traits approach, creativity is defined as a set of characteristics and tendencies that is part of one's nature. This implies that creativity is innate or inborn, that different persons are endowed with different amounts of this trait just as they are endowed with varying amounts of musical talent or athletic ability. The traits approach does not deny the influence of environment but, rather, sees it primarily as the incubator in which inborn creative potential or tendencies are realized.

The learned behavior approach defines creativity as the result of experience, a set of skills and behaviors that have been conditioned into the individual. In this approach, everyone is potentially creative. Differences in creative achievement among people are explained as the result of conditioning. Applied to the example of Susan and Sarah, Susan has learned how to be organized, routine, and structured; Sarah has learned to be unusual, unique, and imaginative. Given the right experiences, Susan can learn to be just as creative as Sarah.

We are not concerned with a precise definition of creativity. The simple idea that there is some process that leads to unique, imaginative results that have some value will suffice. People who are good at this process, who have more of the skills or behaviors that facilitate these unique results, are called creative. People whose thinking, problem solving, and other behaviors lead to more usual results (most people most of the time) are labeled as being low on creativity.

Some people are more creative than others. (Darrell Barry/Little Rock School District.)

SOME DEFINITIONS OF CREATIVITY

Creativity has been defined as the capacity to innovate, to invent, to place elements in a way in which they have never been placed, such that their value or beauty is enhanced. [Haimowitz and Haimowitz, 1973, p. 197]

Creativity is an infinite phenomenon. A person can be creative in an endless number of ways. The outcomes of creative behavior are inexhaustible. [Torrance, 1971, p. 35]

Problem-solving and creativity are complex, little-understood processes, and any conclusions we draw from what is known are subject to cancellation without notice. [Owen et al., 1978, p. 283]

What then is creativity? . . . First, the product must be novel if it is to be called creative. The second criterion is value. A creative product must reflect value by being judged correct (a technical solution works) or good (the music is satisfying). [Good and Brophy, 1980, p. 520]

Creativity is that special quality in students that *other* teachers in *other* classrooms stifle. [LeFrancois, 1979, p. 271]

Personalities of Creative People

The personality characteristics of creative individuals is probably the best documented area of research on the topic. Creative persons are self-directed, can tolerate ambiguity, display a bulldog tenacity, are somewhat free from conventional mores, are spontaneous, usually display a sense of humor, are flexible, are *not* neat, are often intuitive rather than logical, and may be seen as disorganized. They often appear playful, radical, or eccentric and marginal to the society, and they dislike tradition or authority, abhorring routine and organized tasks (Torrance, 1962). In other words, creative persons tend to be unique and different.

The personality characteristics associated with creativity, when compared with practices in the schools, is certainly a cause for discomfort on the part of teachers. For example, how many teachers in the reader's background were inflexible, demanded neatness, and stressed structure and certainty rather than ambiguity? How many were slaves to the clock, stressed logic over all else, and were rather unaccepting of unusual ideas or strange humor? It appears that many of our classrooms do not tend to encourage the type of personality characteristics that are associated with creativity.

Of all the personality characteristics identified, the most important in relation to creative achievement is probably that of high self-esteem. It is not clear just where or how they get it, but creative persons somehow end up with self-confidence and a sense of their own personal worth. There certainly appears to be no absence of problems in the life of the creative individual. Instead, creative people apparently do not allow problems to interfere with their creative production.

A popular area of study in recent years is that of *internal* and *external* locus of control. A person with internal locus of control is self-directed, has his or her own set of standards and values, looks within for judgments and decisions, and in general is his or her own source of authority and evaluation of his or her efforts. External locus of control, on the other hand, connotes awareness of others' beliefs and values, social conformity, concern for others' opinions, and a looking outside for standards, values, and evaluation of self. The majority of people, particularly young people, respond to an external locus of control; you might say that they are "other-directed."

As with so many of the characteristics of creative persons, their inner-directedness can cause problems for the teacher. As you envision the creative child as described here, consider how that child might act and how a defensive teacher might react in the classroom. Certainly, the creative child may be seen as a threat by the teacher.

Intelligence and Creativity

Considerable controversy has arisen concerning the relationship of intelligence and creativity. On the one hand, critics complain that intelligence tests do not reflect the many facets of creativity and that they discourage the creative individual; on the other hand, an argument rages over whether intelligence has any relationship at all to creativity.

Before engaging in such an argument, however, keep in mind a clear conception of the two constructs. The analytic thought and convergent reasoning inherent in IQ tests certainly appear to be different from the divergent and imaginative processes of creativity. As a result, intelligence may be viewed as a variable quite separate from creativity.

If one reviews research that compares intelligence and creativity scores, the finding is that there is usually little correlation between the two variables. A closer look, however, shows that, in most of these studies, the subjects all had average to above-average IQ scores. In other words, slow learners and retarded children are not usually a part of such studies. There are also disagreements about the design of such studies and the types of IQ tests employed.

Anyone who peeks over the fence into this field is apt to be astonished at the visible chaos. The definition of creativity is confounded by the diversity of subareas within the field, the criterion problems are far from licked, and so little is known about the creative process that measuring instruments are, seemingly, chosen on a trial-and-error basis. [McNemar, 1964, p. 876]

327

One finding that makes sense concerning the relationship of intelligence to creativity is that the correlation differs depending on the field of endeavor being studied. Painters and sculptors, for example, show little relationship between their artistic success and their IQ level, whereas creative writers and novelists show a much higher relationship. And, although no clear correlation was established, outstanding architects were found invariably to possess high IQs as were creative scientists.

Creative writers may have an average IQ of 140, with none below 120, but an IQ of 180 is no better a predictor of creativity than is one of 150. This means that "a high IQ is a necessary, but not sufficient, condition for outstanding success as a writer" (McNemar, 1964, p. 878). It appears that a minimum IQ, which varies some from field to field, is necessary for creative success for writers, architects, scientists, and researchers, but beyond that minimum level, higher IQ does not contribute to higher creativity.

Obviously, if this is the case, then *below* a certain minimal cutoff, creative achievement becomes increasingly unlikely. Exploits of "creative" painters such as Congon the chimpanzee notwithstanding, studies of creative persons seldom if ever find creative achievement in the feeble minded, and the chances of someone with a borderline retarded IQ succeeding as a novelist or creative researcher are slim.

Although most studies report low correlations of creativity and IQ (studying samples above the minimum IQ cutoff), a few studies report much higher correlations. For example, the Project Talent study of over 7,000 adolescents found that creativity correlated .67 with IQ (Shaycroft, et al., 1963). In other words, those with higher IQs tended to be more creative. This is certainly inconsistent with claims that creativity and intelligence are unrelated.

Teaching Creativity

Another finding, one that should be the cause of increased optimism, is that it is indeed possible to teach children to think creatively (Torrance, 1972). While there is concern about the validity of research demonstrating that creativity can be taught (Mansfield et al., 1978), Torrance's finding may indicate that children do those things that are rewarded in school, responding with a critical, analytical set, and showing little signs of creativity. But when taught to do so, they can shift gears and perform in a more creative fashion. While children at all levels can probably increase their creative performance if encouraged to do so, specifically, this finding among high-IQ children is particularly important. It may be sobering to ponder the reason why such children see creativity as useless or unrewarding in the first place, but it is at least encouraging to know that potentially creative children *can* be released from such limitations.

Possibly the most important area of research on creativity, the process itself, is also the area most in need of research. Although several creativity enthusiasts have expressed the belief that this is the area on which research will increasingly focus, there is presently not much evidence as to the nature of the process of creation. Hypotheses abound, with vivid descriptions of events inside the creative person, but little in the way of proof of these hypotheses is available. The major reason for this is that empirical study of such a process, especially while it is happening rather than in retrospect, is extremely difficult to carry out.

Given this concern, the creative process, as understood at present, may be summarized in the following ten steps:

1. *Perceiving problems.* The creative person is able to see problems that do not occur to others, to see unusual problems in simple, everyday things, to focus on these without the usual limitations and restraints that most of us impose on ourselves. Seeing things in a different light, perceiving unusual relationships, toying with problems in a playful and even childish fashion are all part of this first step.

2. *Modifying the problem.* Rather than seeing problems in the usual ways, the creative person can see problems from a different view, change the problem into something other than the obvious. This is done in many ways, such as *expanding* the problem (extending it far beyond its original boundaries), *reversing* the problem (seeing it as its exact opposite, turning it inside out, seeing it in a different cause and effect relationship), *compacting* the problem (reducing it to much smaller proportions, seeing it in microcosm), *transforming* the problem (changing it into a different form or emphasis), and *elaborating on* a problem (embellishing it, adding new details). In being able to modify problems in ways such as these, the creative person is able to see all sorts of possibilities that would not otherwise be apparent.

3. *Suspending judgment.* The ability to suspend judgment is very difficult for most people in a society that compares and judges almost anything and encourages conformity to public standards. But the creative process demands that one ignore such restrictions and limitations, try out ideas that may in the end prove frivolous, and consider all possibilities that come to mind. Along with this, creativity requires a playful attitude and the ability to fantasize, in the spirit of fun and invention.

4. *Incubation effect.* This refers to the way in which progress on a problem takes place when one is *not* working on it! For example, the writer struggles with a problem, sees no good solution, and then drops it. Two days later several possibilities are seen that were not seen before. Somehow, unconsciously perhaps, the problem has been "incubating" in the back of the writer's mind, and progress has been made without conscious thought. Although difficult to study empirically, this incubation effect has

been described repeatedly by creative people when asked to explore their own creative process, and it is apparently an important part of creative problem solving.

5. *Sticking with an idea.* Sometimes striking others as stubbornness, there is a tenacity apparent in the creative process that enables creative people to bring possible alternatives to fruition that others would discard. One wonders what the teacher might have thought of Tom Edison, who seemed so obsessed with the crazy idea of passing electricity through a metal filament and producing light. Most other people would have gone on to various other problems (and routine solutions), but Edison refused to abandon this one idea so fixed in his mind.

6. *Envisioning results.* Early in the process of creation, the individual must be able to envision possible results of what he or she is doing. Such envisioning is a sort of fantasizing and indeed is not always realistic. The important dimension does not appear to be the accuracy of one's projection but, rather, the question of whether or not the person *can* dream of possible results.

7. *Selecting the best conclusion.* A step often overlooked in describing the creative process is the critical faculty, the ability to eliminate all but the most promising solution and then execute that solution. The nature of this self-critical faculty is not clear, and it may be quite similar to the critical and evaluative judgments made in analytic thinking. The big difference, however, is that in creative accomplishment such critical judgment is *postponed* until many possible solutions are considered, rather than being part of the process at the start. Somehow the creative person is able to tolerate ambiguity, uncertainty, and confusion until a richer field of possibilities has emerged and then to make the critical judgments at the last possible moment.

8. *Willingness to facilitate a decision.* Regardless of how creative one's fantasies or imagined solutions are, they lead to nothing unless put into practice. The truly creative individual has an intense desire to convert his or her creative ideas into actual practice and will do so in spite of strong opposition from others or from the inanimate world. One does not always win such battles, however, and the creative individual seems able to tolerate occasional or even fairly frequent losses at such attempts, possibly because of a strong sense of basic self-esteem as well as the satisfactions of those times when he or she *is* able to put the creative solution into practice.

9. *Acceptance of uncertainty.* Being comfortable with ambiguous and uncertain situations is an essential part of creativity, and the individual must be able to tolerate such ambiguity throughout the creative process. In fact, a situation that is too clear and structured does not appeal to a creative person; it takes all the fun out of it.

10. *Hazards of systematizing the unsystematic.* Ironically, this statement contradicts the others on this list. There is no way that the process of creating can be converted to an orderly, rigid, dogmatic set of rules. The

very essence of any creative act is that it is unique, different, and unusual
and therefore does not fit normal order of rules. Time and again, when outstanding creative individuals have been interviewed, they have concluded that they don't understand how it works, but they know it doesn't fit some clear-cut, orderly, and scholarly explanation. The best advice to the teacher seeking rules for creativity might be: "there are no specific rules—creativity is the escape from rules, the transcending of limitations, the discovery of infinity."

Tests of Creativity

As we pointed out at the beginning of this discussion of creativity, IQ tests are generally thought to measure those aspects of intelligence that involve convergent thinking. In such thinking, there is one accepted correct response. Creativity, on the other hand, involves divergent thinking. Because such thinking involves the production of noncustomary responses, there are many possible answers to any problem. Tests of creativity, then, present difficulties for test writers and especially for test scorers.

Many tests of creativity have been developed, but most are of questionable value for the classroom. To a large extent, this lack of usefulness results from an inability to determine what creativity is. One test, generally accepted as being more appropriate for school use than others, is the Torrance Tests of Creative Thinking (Kindergarten to adult). The tests are designed to measure four aspects of creativity: fluency, flexibility, originality, and elaboration. Fluency refers to the ability to come up with several ideas. Flexibility refers to the approaching of problems in different ways. Originality refers to the uniqueness of responses. Elaboration refers to the ability to expand upon ideas.

Probably the major drawback of creativity tests such as the Torrance Tests is that they seem to have low relationships with actual creative achievement. This, combined with extreme complexity in scoring makes them of questionable value for classroom teachers (Gronlund, 1981).

Suggestions for Promoting Creativity

The lists of do's and don't's for teachers in relation to creativity seem endless. The following suggestions are presented to stimulate the reader's thinking regarding the role of teacher and its interaction with the creativity of students.

1. *Don't overvalue the customary.* While it may help to preserve the sanity of teacher and students alike to require conformity, conventionality, and predictable behavior, teachers must be careful that they do not communicate the message that "customariness is next to Godliness." This is not meant to imply that it is *wrong* to be customary; it only suggests that the

331

Teachers can actively encourage creativity in the classroom. (Arkansas State Department of Education.)

first step toward encouraging creativity in students is that of making it clear that you really do respect and value creative students. This is not easy to do, as creative children are not always the easiest to work with and sometimes say "the most unheard of things" at the oddest times. The teacher must somehow get across that conventional, predictable, routine, structured behavior is good in a general sense but that the gems of unusual, unique, imaginative, and unpredictable behavior are highly valued.

Such an attitude requires more than lip service. You probably will never encounter a teacher who *says* that he or she is opposed to creativity; teachers invariably *say* that they are much in favor of creativity in students. And yet the actions of a teacher often make it unmistakably clear that such behavior is frowned upon; that what is valued is the usual, not the creative. Ask yourself at least twice a day, "What have I done to encourage creativity in my class today?" Then be sure that you can cite several things in answer.

2. *Be willing to lose time.* Slavish attention to the clock works directly against creativity, even though there are many times in a teacher's day when attention to the clock is important. By deliberately setting aside certain times when the clock no longer rules, and by being willing to drop time constrictions and get behind schedule occasionally, the teacher can help to foster creative ideas in students.

The very nature of the teacher's job seems to be that it encourages obsessive-compulsive behavior. Perhaps a teacher could never meet all the requirements of the job without being somewhat compulsive. But rigidity, compulsiveness, and fear of such sins as "wasting time" work directly against the development of creativity in students. A conscious effort to escape such restrictions is necessary, along with a willingness to look at classroom activities and say, "I guess that was a waste of time, but so what? Much of school is a waste of time. Tomorrow, when I waste some time, something creative might happen."

3. *Encourage unusual questions.* For some reason, questions that lead off on tangents, draw laughter, are puzzling, or require a shift of gears seem to irritate teachers. The teacher may respond to such questions with, "That's an interesting question," accompanied by a look that says, "Don't you dare ask such a question," or perhaps "You really are a smartass, aren't you?"

Sometimes unusual questions *do* throw a teacher; they certainly can waste time, and they are often difficult even to fit into the discussion. But such questions are the stuff from which creativity comes. At least part of the time, when such a question is asked, the teacher should drop everything and pursue the question, show that such questions are valued, and seize the opportunity to tease out a creative idea. If the question was meant strictly as a joke, nothing is really lost anyway. The class might even discover something creative in a question that was meant to annoy the teacher and will end up respecting the teacher more because of his or her response.

In addition to valuing and pursuing unusual questions by students, encouraging follow-up questions and explanations, and rewarding such questions, the teacher should try to come up with unusual questions to *ask* the class as a model of this type of behavior. Sometimes a question that the teacher asks, only half serious or in jest, can result in a most creative discussion. Encouraging, formulating, and responding to such questions enhances creativity.

4. *Demonstrate testing of ideas.* One of the most damaging ideas that students have is the image of school being the pursuit of correct answers to specific questions. The textbook, the encyclopedia, and the teacher are all potential sources of such answers, and it is amazing to see the look of satisfaction that crosses a student's face after having found that be all and end all of learning, the one correct answer.

How do you break away from such a conception of schooling? Not easily, obviously, because such views have been reinforced in students over a period of many years. But somehow the teacher must get across the tentativeness of ideas, the possibility that some questions have many answers and that other questions have no known answers. An idea that comes up in class discussion, that is planted deliberately by the teacher, that does not have one "correct" answer is valuable material to explore if creativity is desired. Often, the pursuit of an idea leads nowhere, but this is not important. The important point is that students see a model of "let's try out that idea, let's think it through and see what happens," which encourages them to follow up on their *own* ideas, to pursue what might be creative in their own lives.

5. *Treat all ideas with respect.* The dangers of hurting a student by failing to respect a well-intended idea more than offset anything that may be lost when a teacher respects a poorly intended idea. It is unlikely that a teacher can automatically distinguish between a strange but creative question and a joke. There is probably little to be gained by such a skill anyhow. However, disrespect for a student idea has a stifling effect on creative thinking, not only for the student involved, but for any other students listening or observing.

It is best, then, to treat *all* ideas with respect, no matter how offbeat, bizarre, or obtuse they might appear at first. If a suggestion turns out to be unworkable, the student will figure that out in time, and nothing is lost. Some ideas that sound ridiculous at first become valuable ideas. The crucial lesson for students is that any ideas they might have, regardless of how strange, will be treated with respect by the teacher.

This suggestion is *not* intended to discourage questions of fact or to argue that any idea is as good as any other. A student can be corrected on a factual error, if this happens to be relevant, or alerted to re-examine his or her thinking, without communicating disrespect. Evaluative judgments can be made, based on sound criteria. Students can see that some ideas are better than others, that some solutions are quicker, more effective, or more economical. The key to this suggestion is the respect for students and the respect for thoughts and ideas that are an essential part of freeing up anyone for creative endeavor.

6. *Vary assignments and activities.* As useful as structured, routine, daily activities can be, disciplined organization can extinguish creativity. We have all had teachers whose carefully organized and systematic teaching drove us up the wall, whose attempts at constructive habits went too far and took all the joy out of learning. Plan to vary your assignments, invent new and unusual ones, change the pace of activities and procedures often.

Varying of assignments and activities does *not* necessarily increase learning in the classroom, and it does not automatically increase classroom control (although it *does* sometimes have such results). The suggestion is made here strictly in terms of its effect on creativity. Routine, habitual, structured sameness tends to work against creativity. The unusual, the different, changes, and varying of approach tend to enhance creativity. The teacher should be willing to sacrifice other goals in teaching, such as classroom order or control, at times for the sake of encouraging creativity. Be aware of the occupational hazards that we all face as teachers, the tendency to become overly compulsive, organized, routine, and habitual.

7. *Avoid perfect examples.* Being in awe of masterpieces, worshipping great creators from the past, admiring heroic examples are *not* prescriptions for encouraging creative behavior. The problem is that, in looking at a perfect example, students consciously or unconsciously compare it with their own work, find their own wanting, and become discouraged.

Instead of examples of perfect outcomes (the perfect poem, play, novel,

Varied assignments and activities will encourage creativity. (Arkansas State Department of Education.)

picture, sculpture), the teacher should stress the creator's efforts, the problems encountered along the way and the shortcomings and flaws that are almost always a part of any creative outcome. The disappointments and dissatisfactions that some artist, writer, or musician has faced serve as encouragement to creative students, as they see that they are normal and that their work is not *supposed* to be perfect. Instead of stressing Michelangelo's fantastic work on the Sistine Chapel, stress the fun and value of the students painting a mural in the gym or building their own model of Shakespeare's theater. Being in awe, overwhelmed, incredulous at the work of others is of very limited use in developing one's own creative abilities.

8. *Informality and flexibility.* Two characteristics of classroom atmosphere that stand out clearly as stifling creativity are those of the overly formal and rigid classroom. Conversely, a classroom that maintains an atmosphere of informality, flexibility, and experimentation tends to encourage creative ideas and exploration.

Somehow, having a healthy flexibility and informality in the classroom does not come easily for many teachers. Perhaps this goes against the natural desire for structure, control, and order. Or perhaps it is only a function of teachers unconsciously wanting to teach in the same way that they were taught themselves.

One way to approach this is to escape from the all-or-none dilemma by starting with just a portion of each day that is especially informal and flexible. For example, the teacher might preserve one hour each morning that is different from the usual structure and routine, where the major goals are those of encouraging creativity and imagination. Or there might be natural points at which the usual restrictions can be dropped and time devoted to creative endeavors.

Remember, the classroom that is more informal and flexible *in general* tends to bring out creative and imaginative behavior. Any teacher should be able to find ways of providing enough informality and flexibility in the classroom while at the same time satisfying content and analytical subject matter needs. Each teacher must experiment to find what works in relation to his or her own particular classroom personality.

9. *Tolerance of ambiguity.* Throughout the writings on creativity, a term that crops up incessantly is "tolerance of ambiguity." What this means is the ability to accept uncertainty, to live with tentativeness, to overcome the need for absolutes, and to live with possibilities and a certain degree of vagueness. This is one personality characteristic of creative persons. It may be due partly to genetic endowment, but it is certainly affected by learning. It is essential that it be part of a classroom environment that intends to promote creativity.

If the students are to develop a tolerance of ambiguity, the teacher must model this characteristic. Ask yourself: Do your questions always lead to one correct answer? Do you spell out all details of an assignment so that absolutely nothing is left to chance? Are the rules and regulations in your classroom so clear that nobody could possibly misinterpret any of them? Is everything that happens in your class so clear, ordered, and expected that a good student could follow all the prescriptions and earn an "A" almost in his sleep? If so, you may have a very successful prescription for conformity and conventionality but a very poor model for encouraging tolerance of ambiguity and other creative characteristics.

The answer, of course, is not a whole-scale change so that your classroom becomes vague, confused, ambiguous, and tentative to the point of constant uncertainty. Mischief in the name of creativity is inexcusable. Instead, the answer is that the teacher must be careful not to overstructure, not to eliminate all food for thought and decisions, and leave some room for the type of tentativeness and uncertainty that encourages creative problem solving.

10. *Positive criticism.* Contrary to popular opinion, creativity does not abound automatically in situations devoid of criticism. If all criticism squelched creativity and all encouragement caused it to blossom, the answer would be simple—don't criticize, give only positive feedback; reward, encourage, and watch creativity grow.

A closer look at the research yields the commonsense fact that there are different types of criticism and that it is only certain types that squelch creativity. Is the result being criticized, or is it the child's effort that is disparaged? Is the work in need of improvement, or is the student himself or herself being rejected? Is the criticism constructive or destructive? Is the criticism associated with strong general approval, or given in an atmo-

Positive criticism enhances creativity. (Darrell Barry/Little Rock School District.)

sphere of disapproval? Is the criticism depersonalized, or is it highly personal?

Although not yet understood fully, it seems fairly clear that children achieve confidence in the value of their ideas beginning in early childhood. Parents obviously play a large role, but teachers are also important in this process. Two keys to helping students learn to value their ideas are (1) to encourage all efforts at creative achievement regardless the outcome and (2) to encourage internalized, self-criticism rather than dependence on an external judge.

In writing about ways of rewarding creative thinking in children, Torrance points out that the teacher should *tie in evaluation with causes and consequences:*

In criticizing defects in ideas or in punishing naughty or dangerous behavior, explain the response in such a way as to foster the ability to see causes and consequences of behavior. Do not say, ''This is good'' or ''This is bad.'' Say, ''I like this because . . .'' or ''This could be made better . . .''. [Torrance, 1965, p. 319]

337

Objective criticism, focusing on outcomes while strongly encouraging efforts, always leading to internal standards and self-criticism, seem to be the basic guidelines in criticism as it relates to creativity. Criticism that is negative, too personal, discourages effort, devalues one's own ideas, and implies "goodness" and "badness" seems to be the formula for squelching creative effforts.

11. *Show how to resist peer pressures.* Consider the following:

The great thinkers of the world have had to have confidence that their own thoughts were valuable. Otherwise, they would not have been willing to spend most of their lives bringing into being the great advances in our civilization. Often, this struggle has been without financial profit and in opposition to the established ideas of the day. [Torrance, 1965, p. 235]

It would be foolhardy to suggest that a teacher set out to destroy peer influence as a way of enhancing creativity. From about seventh grade on through senior high, the peer group is number one for determining thoughts, tastes, and standards of its members. But a teacher *can* encourage students to resist peer pressures when it comes to creativity, to value their own ideas. One way is for the teacher to model internal standards and resistance to outside pressures, thus demonstrating the self-confidence and self-evaluation required. The teacher must also take care not to unwittingly reward peer conformity or punish independent behavior in the quest to mantain order and sanity in the classroom.

Teachers can help students to discover that resistance to peer standards and conformity lead to respect and peer *approval* in the long run. Thus, the student who sticks his neck out and pursues his own creative bent can receive not only the approval of teachers, but the support and approval of peers. Open-ended assignments, individual projects, thought-provoking questions, and discussions of slavish conformity are all ways of developing resistance to immediate peer conformity for the sake of greater rewards in the long run.

12. *Encourage self-initiated learning.* Thoreau's oft-quoted statement that "If a man does not keep pace with his companions, perhaps it is because he hears a different drummer" is relevant here. Studies of highly creative persons indicate that freedom to engage in self-directed activities and learning are essential to creative achievement. Sometimes it appears that our society's emphasis on the well-rounded person works against such self-initiated learning. When a curriculum forces students to take exactly the same program as everyone else, when standards are set so rigidly that sameness is implied, when the bulk of time is spent on developing deficient areas rather than advancing in an outstanding area, creative individualism is hardly the likely result.

Instead, teachers must constantly look for ways to individualize assignments, to encourage students to develop areas in which they are already above average, to focus on unique skills and ideas that are *not* the

BRAINSTORMING TECHNIQUES

Every reader has undoubtedly taken part in a "wild blue yonder," "pipe dream," or "rap session" discussion. These sessions have received a great deal of attention in the creativity literature and have proven effective in devising new and imaginative solutions to problems (Osborn, 1963). The official name for such a procedure is *brainstorming;* the relevant guidelines are as follows:

1. *Deferred evaluation.* This is the most important requirement in a brainstorming session. All participants must agree that no criticism, no critical judgments, no evaluation of "good" or "bad" will be permitted.
2. *Nonthreatening situation.* Every possible effort is made to set up a relaxed, positive, encouraging, cheerful, and friendly situation. The threat of competition is removed, since there is no winning or losing, and cooperation is the order of the day.
3. *Positive, enthusiastic leadership.* To set the stage for the relaxed, positive, nonthreatening situation and to assure that deferred evaluation is the mode, a positive and enthusiastic group leader is required. Such a leader must understand and be committed to the efficacy of brainstorming techniques, and his enthusiasm and relaxed manner aid the rest of the group in adapting to the special conditions of the brainstorming session.
4. *Unrestricted generation of ideas.* Every idea, no matter how silly or trivial it may seem, must be listed or mentioned. The rationale is that by devising every solution imaginable, without any criticism, the best solution can emerge. Criticism and elimination of unrealistic solutions can come later, but it is usually not a part of a brainstorming session.
5. *Encouragement of far-out solutions.* Not only are weird, unusual, unconventional, odd, eccentric, and irregular ideas allowed in brainstorming sessions, they are actively encouraged. Participants are told that it is not just the obvious, safe, and sensible idea (which everyone is probably familiar with anyway) that is being sought, but all the other ideas that might seem far-out or inappropriate. In other words, here is an opportunity to let your imagination soar and come up with the craziest ideas imaginable!
6. *Embellishment of ideas.* A brainstorming session does far more than develop a long list of possible (or impossible) solutions to a problem. A number of systematic ways to expand on or revise a proposed solution have been developed. For example, several ideas can be combined into one larger solution. A proposed solution can be modified into something else. An idea can be expanded or augmented into a much larger idea, or it can be reduced into a much smaller dimension. Whether the group develops such techniques systematically or just "plays around" with ideas that come up, the basic creative skills of fluency, divergence, flexibility, originality, and elaboration are much in evidence.

norm, to reward nonconformity as well as conformity. A searching, inquiring attitude on the part of the teacher, accompanied by freedom, courage, independent thinking, and discipline on the part of the students, implies a high valuing and rewarding of self-initiated learning.

Summary

Intelligence is a hypothetical construct that is difficult to define. Definitions of intelligence speak of learning quickly, reasoning logically, adapting to the environment, perceiving, and solving problems.

Modern ideas about intelligence, and attempts to measure it scientifically, have their roots in the work of Sir Francis Galton. His studies of eminent men concluded that intelligence was primarily an inherited characteristic.

Alfred Binet, working in France, published the first modern intelligence test. From its beginning, intelligence testing has been linked closely to school performance. The term "IQ" originally referred to a ratio of mental age to chronological age. Later, the standard way of computing IQ became that of finding how far the child deviated from the norm for his or her age level.

At first, IQ tests attempted only to measure the general or *g* factor. In the 1930s, Thurstone hypothesized twelve "primary mental abilities" and the idea of measuring specific or *s* factors became popular. Guilford conceived of intelligence as being a combination of three dimensions—operations, contents, and products—with each intellectual ability being one specific combination of these three factors.

There are many controversial issues in relation to IQ tests, the most emotional one being the question of heredity versus environment. For many years, social scientists focused on the effects of environment on intellectual performance, but in 1969 Arthur Jensen concluded that only 20% of IQ can be influenced by environment and that the other 80% is determined by heredity. Jensen also raised the question of whether IQ, particularly abstract reasoning ability, was distributed differently in black as compared with white populations. J. McV. Hunt disagreed with Jensen's conclusions on the grounds that the differences in IQ scores among such groups as lower class versus middle class, blacks versus whites, can be explained just as easily as the result of environmental differences.

Other controversies in IQ testing focus on the question of general versus specific IQ. Teachers should keep in mind that there are a variety of intellectual functions, that a high IQ score does *not* mean that the student should do well in every area, and that two students with the same IQ may have considerably different cognitive strengths and weaknesses. The general success of the child in school is predicted better by the child's *general* IQ score than by specific subscores.

Although differences in male and female performance have been observed in various intellectual tasks, it is unclear whether these differences are innate or the result of environment. In terms of general IQ score, the tests are constructed so that male and female distribution of scores are the same.

The results of IQ tests can influence teacher expectations of students' academic performances. Because these expectations might become self-fulfilling prophecies, the teacher must interpret IQ test scores cautiously.

Discrimination is a problem in IQ testing only when the tests discriminate unfairly. The test is supposed to discriminate the different levels of cognitive functioning.

Several popular IQ tests—the WISC-R, the Stanford-Binet, and the PPVT-R—as well as information about group tests are presented and discussed. Strengths and weaknesses of individual and group tests are discussed, and a list of recommendations for teachers in using and interpreting IQ tests is presented.

Defining creativity is not easy, but all the different definitions can be reduced to just two approaches: the *traits* approach and the *learned behavior* approach. The traits approach sees creativity as an inborn talent. The learned behavior approach describes creativity as the result of conditioning or experience. This text defines creativity as a process that leads to unique and imaginative results that have value.

Creative individuals are described as being self-directed, tolerant of ambiguity, tenacious, generally free from conventional mores, spontaneous, and flexible and as having a sense of humor. They often appear eccentric or "marginal" to their culture. However, stereotyping must be avoided, since creative persons are each unique and unusual.

Probably the most important personality characteristic of creative persons is high self-esteem. These individuals usually have a high degree of self-confidence and personal worth. Although not free of hardships or problems in their lives, creative individuals apparently do not allow problems to interfere with their creative production. They have also been described as responding to an *internal* rather than to an *external* locus of control.

Although theories and research concerning the creative process have been advanced, there is as yet no clear picture of the creative process. Hypothesized steps in the process are presented in this chapter. In that step-by-step description, the conclusion is that creativity cannot be reduced to a set of orderly, rigid, and dogmatic rules.

There are differing opinions of the relationship of intelligence to creativity, but most studies report only low correlation of these two variables. Beyond a certain minimal IQ level that is required, there appears to be little relationship. The relationship also varies depending on the specific field and type of endeavor.

Another important relationship is the particular combination of creativity and intelligence within the individual. The high-creativity–high-intelligence student fares much better than does the high creativity–low-intelligence student, for example. Another important problem in studying creativity is that of measuring it. One attempt to measure creativity is presented.

The chapter ends with twelve suggestions for encouraging creativity in the classroom. These should be studied carefully by the teacher who hopes to promote creativity.

341

1. Can you define intelligence in your own words, and explain why yours is a good definition?

2. Suppose that the term "intelligence quotient" had never been used in relation to what we know as IQ tests and instead that they were called "scholastic aptitude" tests. What sort of problems would be avoided by not calling them IQ tests? Would anything be lost by not linking the tests to the term "intelligence"?

3. Suppose you are told that Tim has an IQ of 130 and Ben has an IQ of 85. What differences can you assume probably exist between the two? Do you know anything about their personality, looks, size, or honesty?

4. Define the terms operations, contents, and products as used in Guilford's three-dimensional model. Do these terms add anything to your concept of intelligence? Can you think of specific examples that fit into this model from your teaching field?

5. How much do you know about your scores on intelligence tests? Would you like to know more? What are the dangers in giving a student all the results of an IQ test? Are all these problems solved simply by calling the tests something else?

6. Which of the several definitions of creativity presented in this chapter do you like best, and why? Can you give a definition of creativity in your own words and explain why this is a good definition?

7. What is it about a creative child in the classroom that is sometimes upsetting to the teacher? Why do such children at times disrupt the class rather than act as leaders? What can the teacher do with a creative child to help keep the creativity channeled in the right direction?

8. How many ways can you think of for a teacher to encourage creativity? Why are these things not done more by teachers, if creativity is a valued trait?

9. Why is creativity so difficult to measure? In everyday life, what kind of evidence do you accept as evidence that someone is creative?

10. Twelve suggestions for encouraging creativity are presented at the end of this chapter. Which of these do you see as the most practical? Are any unlikely to be carried out because of the various pressures on the teacher in the regular classroom?

References

Anastasi, A. *Psychological Testing,* 5th ed. New York: Macmillan, 1982.

Braun, C. "Teacher Expectation: Sociopsychological Dynamics," *Review of Educational Research,* 46(2), Spring 1976, pp. 185–213.

Buros, O. K., ed. *The Eighth Mental Measurements Yearbook.* Lincoln, Neb.: University of Nebraska, Buros Institute of Mental Measurements, 1978.

Claiborn, W. L. "Expectancy Effects in the Classroom: A Failure to Replicate," *Journal of Educational Psychology,* 60(5), October 1969, pp. 377–383.

Cronbach, L. J. *Essentials of Psychological Testing,* 3rd ed. New York: Harper & Row, 1970.

Galton, F. *Hereditary Genius: An Inquiry Into Its Laws and Consequences.* London: Macmillan, 1869.

Good, T. L., and Brophy, J. E. *Educational Psychology: A Realistic Approach.* New York: Holt, Rinehart and Winston, 1980.

Gronlund, N. E. *Measurement and Evaluation in Teaching,* 4th ed. New York: Macmillan, 1981.

Guilford, J. P. *The Nature of Human Intelligence.* New York: McGraw-Hill, 1967.

———. *Way Beyond the IQ.* Buffalo, N.Y.: Creative Education Foundation, 1977.

Haimowitz, N. R., and Haimowitz, M. L. "What Makes Them Creative?" in M. L. Haimowitz and N. R. Haimowitz, eds., *Human Development.* New York: Thomas Y. Crowell, 1973, pp. 197–207.

Hunt, J. McV. "Has Compensatory Education Failed? Has It Been Attempted?" *Harvard Educational Review,* 39(2), Spring 1969, pp. 278–300.

Jensen, A. R. "How Much Can We Boost IQ and Scholastic Achievement?" *Harvard Educational Review,* 39(1), Winter 1969, pp. 1–123.

José, J. and Cody, J. J. "Teacher-Pupil Interaction as It Relates to Attempted Changes in Teacher Expectancy of Academic Ability and Achievement," *American Educational Research Journal,* 8(11), January 1971, pp. 39–49.

LeFrancois, G. R. *Psychology for Teaching: A Bear Sometimes Faces Front,* 3rd ed. Belmont, Calif.: Wadsworth, 1979.

Mansfield, R., Busse, T. V., and Krepelka, E. J. "The Effectiveness of Creativity Training," *Review of Educational Research,* 48(4), Fall 1978, pp. 517–536.

McNemar, Q. "Lost: Our Intelligence? Why?" *American Psychologist,* 19(12), December 1964, pp. 871–882.

Osborne, A. F. *Applied Imagination: Principles and Procedures of Creative Problem-Solving,* 3rd ed. New York: Charles Scribner's Sons, 1963.

Owen, S., Blount, H. P., and Moscow, H. *Educational Psychology: An Introduction.* Boston: Little, Brown, 1978.

The Psychological Corporation. *Test Service Bulletin No. 54.* New York: The Psychological Corporation, 1959.

Rosenthal, R., and Jacobson, L. *Pygmalion in the Classroom: Teacher Expectations and Pupils' Intellectual Development.* New York: Holt, Rinehart and Winston, 1968.

Shaycroft, M. F., et al. *Studies of a Complete Age Group—Age 15. Technical Report to the U. S. Office of Education, Cooperative Research Project No. 566.* Pittsburgh: Project TALENT Office, University of Pittsburgh, 1963.

Spearman, C. *The Abilities of Man: Their Nature and Measurement.* New York: Macmillan, 1927.

Terman, L. M. *The Measurement of Intelligence: An Explanation of and a Complete Guide for the Use of the Stanford Revision and Extension of the Binet-Simon Intelligence Scale.* Boston: Houghton Mifflin, 1916.

Torrance, E. P. *Guiding Creative Talent.* Englewood Cliffs, N.J.: Prentice-Hall, 1962.

———. *Rewarding Creative Behavior: Experiments in Classroom Creativity.* Englewood Cliffs, N.J.: Prentice-Hall, 1965.

———. "Creativity and Infinity," *Journal of Research and Development in Education,* 4(3), Spring 1971, pp. 35–41.

———. "Can We Teach Children to Think Creatively?" *The Journal of Creative Behavior,* 6(2), 2nd quarter 1972, pp. 114–143.

Thurstone, L. L. *Primary Mental Abilities.* Chicago: University of Chicago Press, 1938.

Wechsler, D. *The Measurement of Adult Intelligence.* Baltimore: Williams and Wilkins, 1939.

Woodring, P. "Are Intelligence Tests Unfair?" *Saturday Review,* 49(16), April 16, 1966, pp. 79–80.

343

Social Class, Race, and the Disadvantaged

10

PREVIEW

What is the history of social class in America?

How is social class defined?

Why is it better to define social class in terms of attitudes and values?

What is the traditional stereotype of a lower-class child?

What are the beliefs and values of a middle-class teacher?

Why is it difficult for a middle-class teacher to understand a lower-class child?

What does a typical lower-class child look like?

How does a teacher misinterpret data concerning a lower-class child?

What can the teacher do to help lower-class students?

Why is it important for lower-class children to adopt some values that are thought of as middle-class?

Why is the concept of race actually a myth in today's world?

What is the favored race in America?

What groups tend to be at a disadvantage in America?

How did the Reconstruction period contribute to racial problems?

What was the ''separate but equal'' doctrine?

What was the signficance of the *Brown* v. *Board of Education* ruling?

Why has there always been opposition to integration?

What progress has been made since 1954?

What differences in performance have been observed among racial groups?

What is the genetic argument concerning observed differences in performance?

345

What is the environmental thesis concerning observed differences in performance?

Why is it impossible to settle conclusively the heredity versus environment argument regarding racial differences?

What does the term "disadvantaged" mean?

How do many factors interact in the case of the disadvantaged child?

What are the seven groups of disadvantaged in America?

How do child-rearing patterns differ in various social groups?

What are the characteristic outlooks of the very poor?

What can the teacher do to help the disadvantaged?

What is compensatory education?

What are the strengths of compensatory education?

What shortcomings can be seen in compensatory education?

"We hold these truths to be self-evident: That all men are created equal." These oft-quoted words from the Preamble to the Constitution of the United States may be true in an ideal sense, but they are *not* true when one looks at social class in America. Everyone is born into a social class framework in which the social classes are *not* equal.

America has always been a class society in spite of democratic ideals and in spite of the glorification of the "middle-class American." The early settlers in the United States, despite the desire of many to escape from societies that enforced rigid social class distinctions, had no intention of developing a classless society. Perhaps it is human nature that any society, regardless how egalitarian its beginnings, will produce social class distinctions. In colonial times, it was clear that some citizens were from the "privileged" classes, some were from more average backgrounds, some were rather low on the scale as common workers, and some were slaves. With the exception of attempts at communal-type living (most of which failed, although communal experiments have always been part of the American experience), the early settlers probably would have laughed at the idea that America was a classless society.

The Industrial Revolution expanded social class differences by making a clear distinction between the managers and the workers, as well as different levels of management, skilled versus unskilled workers, the wealthy owners, those outside the industrial system, and so on. These distinctions have carried over into the twentieth century and are still with us, with only minor variations, today. Even with social, economic, attitudinal, and life-style changes since World War II, and especially since 1960, America still has lower, middle, and upper classes. One aspect of American society that may be unique among nations is that there is upward mobility among classes. Education seems to be one of the chief sources of that mobility.

Social Class

Every reader has heard the terms "lower class," "middle class," and "upper class," but just what do these terms mean? Defining social class in terms that are acceptable to the experts and yet meaningful to the layperson is no easy task.

One solution to the problem is that of defining social class strictly in economic terms. For example, a figure such as $10,000 a year is arbitrarily established as a minimum cutoff, and any family making less than this amount is considered "lower class." Those families with more than $10,000 a year of income, but less than some other cutoff, say, $50,000, are considered "middle class," and any families above the $50,000 level are dubbed "upper class."

Many problems arise with this economic definition of social class, however. What about the minister, or the school teacher, or the author who earns less than $10,000 a year? Is this a lower-class family? And what of the truck driver or junkdealer who might earn $10,000, $20,000, $30,000, or more a year? Is a $50,000-a-year junkdealer upper class, but a $5,000-

---

TO WHAT SOCIAL CLASS DOES DOUG BELONG?

Doug is 17 and a senior in high school. He attends mass every Sunday at the Roman Catholic church. His father is a construction worker who earns $40,000 a year.

Doug's parents did not attend college, but they live in one of the nicest sections of town. Doug wears his hair long and has a beard. He wears old, tattered clothes to school and is generally rather disheveled and in need of a bath. Cleanliness is definitely not one of his virtues.

Doug thinks nothing of using four-letter words, which is something that bothers his teacher. He has no idea what he wants to do in life and seems to live strictly for immediate pleasure. Nevertheless, he makes good grades in most of his classes. He also drives a late-model car to school, and earns his spending money by working at the hairpin factory during the summer.

Doug does not always get along with his peers, and he has been involved in several fistfights on the school grounds. He seems to express himself physically instead of verbally. He is known as being compulsive and emotional. Several of his closest friends have dropped out of school.

Based on this information, to what social class does Doug belong? It is easy to see the difficulties that arise when traditional stereotypes are used in attempting to classify people. Doug has characteristics of both the lower class and the middle class. He could not really be placed in one class or the other on the basis of the information provided here.

a-year person from the same field lower class? What if an author earns $5,000 one year and $50,000 the next? A plumber might earn far more than a white-collar worker or teacher, yet we would be hard pressed to prove that the plumber is from a higher social class.

For reasons such as these, a purely economic distinction of social class fails to hold up as a reasonable definition. A second possibility is to define social class by level of education. In this approach, if the parents have had less than a high school education, the family is lower class, with high school to college education qualifying for middle class, and education beyond college, such as law school or medical school, meaning an upper-class family.

The reader is probably aware of many cases that challenge such a definition of social class. The highly successful insurance agent with an eighth grade education, the unemployed college graduate living in the slums, the store manager who dropped out of high school at age 15, all cast doubt on the meaning of the term. In what social class do we place these persons? Sometimes the economic is combined with education level— for example, a college graduate earning beyond $10,000 a year is definitely middle-class—but this is far from a perfect solution and sheds little light on what is really meant by social class.

Other simple and arbitrary ways of defining social class have been attempted, ranging from the location of one's residence (do you live in a middle-class neighborhood?) to the degree of affluence (what kind of life-style do you follow?) to the types of groups one belongs to. None of these, alone or in combination, holds up very well as a definition of social class, and none sheds much light on the meaning of this elusive term.

Importance of Beliefs and Values

At this point, the reader may be tempted to conclude that social class is a useless concept for teachers to study. However, the term does have meaning for the teacher and is an important consideration in understanding children. The point is that the economic background of families, or the amount of education parents have had, or the neighborhood in which they live, or the type of church they attend, or their level of conspicuous consumption are *not* characteristics of social class that really matter for the classroom teacher. The important consideration for the classroom teacher is that children from different social class backgrounds tend to have different beliefs and values that are important variables in determining school behavior and success. Furthermore, teachers and school systems tend to espouse a system of values and beliefs that can be labeled "middle class" that are not consistent with the beliefs and values of many of their students.

McCandless (1967) has spelled out the differences between the values of the middle-class teacher and the scores of students who do not express

Teachers need to understand that their values and those of their students may differ and cause communication problems. (Darrell Barry/ Little Rock School District.)

such values. Although many changes have taken place since the 1960s, the stereotype of the middle-class teacher and the lower-class child that is presented in Table 10.1 still accounts for much of the misunderstanding and difficulty in communication that occurs when a middle-class teacher works with children who are essentially lower class in socioeconomic background.

McCandless has pointed out that the differences in attitudes and values that are summarized in Table 10.1 are a constant source of conflict between the middle-class teacher and the lower-class student. Estimates are that at least one third, and perhaps one half or more, of the students in our schools have essentially a lower-class outlook. Meanwhile, even though some teachers come from lower-class and many from lower-middle class backgrounds, virtually all teachers reflect a middle-class outlook, it is argued. This is because an individual adopts the values of a social group toward which he or she aspires (the teacher becomes middle class in outlook even before getting there) and because the schools are based on predominantly middle-class values.

McCandless sees the gap in values between the middle-class teacher and the lower-class child as enormous and advocates getting middle-class teachers to understand and appreciate lower-class values. In doing so, he believes that these teachers will become more accepting of lower-class children and their families and will modify some of their own values and beliefs.

The case study of Benny presented in the box on p. 352 should illustrate some of the problems that a middle-class teacher could encounter if she failed to exhibit any understanding of lower-class children.

349

Table 10.1
*A Stereotype of Middle-
Class and Lower-Class
Values**

Middle Class	Lower Class
1. Believes in God, attends church, usually Protestant.	1. Is not as likely to belong to a church; more often Catholic or fundamentalist if they do.
2. Believes in personal cleanliness.	2. Sees cleanliness as unimportant.
3. Values thrift and security.	3. Says "If you get any money, spend it!"
4. Values intellect and reason, not emotion.	4. Desires immediate action.
5. Frowns on open sex and aggression.	5. Believes that aggression makes sense; tolerates more open expression of sex.
6. Represses emotions.	6. Expresses emotions physically.
7. Uses gossip, sarcasm, verbal aggression.	7. Frowns on gossip and sarcasm; uses more direct, physical aggression.
8. Uses clean and correct language.	8. Uses action language, considered crude by middle class.
9. Is upwardly mobile.	9. Has little hope for upward mobility.
10. Supports the idea of equity and fairness.	10. Values a different form of honesty, but *not* a hypocrite.
11. Exhibits social responsibility.	11. Has little respect for white-collar or professional workers.
12. Believes that education is power.	12. Sees education as a pain in the neck.
13. Sees clothes, cleanliness, and grooming as important.	13. Sees clothes, cleanliness, grooming as sissy.
14. Is compulsive about rules and regulations, organization, good uses of time.	14. Is poor at rules and regulations, orderliness, or attention to the clock.
15. Sees life as *future* oriented; is trained in deferred gratification.	15. Sees life as *present* oriented; has no experience in deferred gratification.

*Stereotypes such as these typify a group but are not descriptive of individuals within the group. [Derived from B. R. McCandless, *Children: Behavior and Development,* 2nd ed. (Hinsdale, Ill.: Dryden Press, 1967), pp. 586–593.]

An Interpretation of Benny's Record

The description of Benny is, of course, hypothetical and may appear artificial and contrived. It is useful, however, in illustrating some of the differences between the middle-class teacher and the lower-class student.

A step-by-step look at the facts about Benny yields some interesting interpretations about him, his school, and his teachers. Benny is now attending school in a nice suburb twenty-five miles from a large city. The students regularly score high on achievement tests, and most plan to go to college. This strongly suggests that Benny is attending a middle- or upper-middle-class school, with middle-class students, many of whom do very well in school. But what kind of student is Benny?

WHICH TYPE OF PARENT DID YOU HAVE?

Consider the case of Walter. He has come home with a note from the teacher to his parents, asking them to come and see her. Both parents go at the appointed time and talk with the teacher, finding that Walter has been involved in several fights on the playground. The parents are very concerned, and they listen to the teacher and then express their desire to help Walter get over whatever problems he has. They tell the teacher about their desire that Walter should earn high grades, even now at the age of 10, so that he can go to a good college. They have discussed this with Walter many times and have encouraged him to think about what he will be when he grows up. They go home, determined to have a long talk with Walter and get across to him that he cannot fight with other boys on the playground.

Meanwhile, consider the case of William. He, too, has come home with a note from the teacher, but he threw it away instead of giving it to his parents. After several tries, the teacher was able to contact William's mother by telephone. She explained that William had been involved in several fights on the playground, and she would like to meet with the parents and discuss this. William's mother said she would tell his father and he would whip William.

The teacher explained that she didn't want this. She merely wanted to talk with the parents, so they set a date for the next day.

When William's mother told her husband about the fight, the first question he asked was "did he win?" He felt some pride in the fact that William was a "chip off the old block." She could not talk him into seeing the teacher, as William's father had never liked school himself. Eventually, his mother met with the teacher, and she told him she had no idea why William didn't like school and got into trouble. She looked puzzled when the teacher asked what William's future plans were. It was obvious that William had no future plans, other than that of quitting school as soon as he was old enough.

This episode dramatizes part of the stereotype of the lower-class as compared with the middle-class family. Walter's parents are middle-class, very concerned about school, desirous that Walter make good grades and go on to college. They believe it is wrong for Walter to be involved in fights on the playground, and they will take immediate steps to stop such behavior. They constantly try to teach Walter to plan for the future, to achieve, and to defer immediate pleasures for a bigger payoff later.

William's parents, on the other hand, are lower class. They are not concerned very much about school, because they did not do well in school themselves. A call from the teacher is not very important to them, and they consider William's fighting on the playground to be fairly normal. The father especially thinks that school is a place for "sissies" and is proud of his son's ability to defend himself. They have not taught William the importance of planning for the future, because their life is one constant battle with present problems. Although stereotypes such as these tend to be somewhat exaggerated and unrealistic, they do shed some light on the differences among children from different family backgrounds.

BENNY—A TROUBLESOME CHILD

Mrs. Pearson teaches sixth grade in Yorkville, a nice suburb twenty-five miles from a large city. She is proud that her classes generally perform well on the Iowa Test of Basic Skills, and of the high percentage who go on to college.

Mrs. Pearson's initial encounter with Benny was on the first day of school. She was going through her orientation procedure, in which each student stood up, told the class his or her name and address, how many brothers and sisters they had, what their father did for a living and so on. Benny didn't seem to be paying attention—he didn't stand up when it was his turn, so she had to prod him. He was not very cooperative, she noted, and she wrote in her anecdotal record that he was "surly and has a bad attitude."

After this encounter, Mrs. Pearson looked up his cumulative record. She noted the following facts:

1. He lives at $227\frac{1}{2}$ Sherman Avenue.
2. His father is a janitor, his mother a checker at the supermarket.
3. He has two brothers and four sisters, ages 2 to 14.
4. He passed the school health exams, including vision and hearing.
5. His IQ scores were:
   a. 93 on the Stanford-Binet, in first grade.
   b. 66 on the California Test of Mental Maturity, language portion; and 96 on the nonlanguage portion, third grade.
   c. 77 on the Otis Intelligence Test, fifth grade.
6. She averaged the above test scores and concluded that he is a slow learner, but not mentally retarded.
7. She was puzzled by the fact that Benny was 13 years old and also there was no phone listed.
8. She notes that Benny moved to New York from Kentucky two years ago and that he had better grades in his first few years of school. Since third grade, his marks had taken a nose dive. Last year, his only "C's" were in science and math, and the remaining grades were "D's" and "F's."
9. She also noticed that he has been tardy and absent quite often.
10. His sister, Pam, who is 14 and in eighth grade, has a much more favorable cumulative record, with numerous "A's" and "B's."

Mrs. Pearson concluded that Benny was not too bright and that the bad attitude she noticed on the first day was certainly supported by his cumulative record. She decided to be nice to him and not expect too much in class, but he has continued to be difficult. She decides to ask others what they think of him, and receives the following responses:

Gym Teacher: "Benny is cooperative and does very well in gym. I wish I had more like him."

Fifth Grade Teacher: "Benny is one of the most obnoxious kids I've ever had. I'm glad they let me promote him."

Music Teacher: "Benny has a nice soprano voice but refuses to use it. I tried to make him an angel in the Christmas play, but he said some awful things and I kicked him out."

Principal: "Benny who?"

School Counselor: "Benny is experiencing an identity crisis. I am building his ego strength. Whenever he causes a disturbance, send him to me. He loves to play chess."

Social Worker: "Benny is an ambitious child and adjusts well to home and neighborhood life. I don't know why he fails in school."

Reading Teacher: "I never did figure out why Benny was a poor reader. It's a shame we don't have remedial reading for sixth graders."

Mother: "Benny's sister does real good in school. I don't know what's wrong with Benny. He never has any homework. Why don't the teachers make him work harder?"

A number of facts in his record indicate that Benny is *not* a middle-class child. This being the case, the orientation procedure Mrs. Pearson followed, with each student telling about his summer, father's job, and so on was probably embarrassing to Benny. Other children could speak with pride of where they lived, what their parents did, where they went on vacation, while Benny had nothing like that to tell. Thus, he was reluctant to stand up and be embarrassed, and Mrs. Pearson misinterpreted this as evidence that "he was surly and had a bad attitude."

In looking at Benny's cumulative record, Mrs. Pearson failed to see how this record adds up to the fact that Benny is from a lower-class background, is in a middle-class school, and is having a hard time. Although it is not unusual for teachers to misinterpret cumulative records, some of Mrs. Pearson's conclusions are inexcusable. How might she have interpreted each item more realistically and put them all together to an obvious conclusion?

1. He lives at $227\frac{1}{2}$ Sherman Avenue. Such an address may mean a multiple-family dwelling, a makeshift apartment of some sort.
2. His father is a janitor, his mother a checker at the supermarket. So both parents are working, in spite of the large number of children, and apparently at rather mediocre jobs.
3. He has two brothers and four sisters, ages 2 to 14. Seven children in the family, all of school age and some even preschool. The family lives in what is probably inadequate housing, and both parents must work to support them.
4. He passed the school health exams, including vision and hearing. This doesn't really eliminate the possibility of vision or hearing problems. Such exams usually prove only that the person is not blind or deaf. He could still have various perceptual problems or other learning disabilities.
5. His IQ scores are very revealing. His 93 on the Stanford-Binet in first grade tells us he was probably already having problems, since the Stanford-Binet is an individual test, expensive to administer, and is usually only given for some type of problem, or for research purposes. The score of 93 tells us he is of about average IQ and is a more reliable score than the other group test scores.

The California Test of Mental Maturity, a group test, supports the idea of an average IQ since he scores 96 on the nonverbal portion, but raises the possibility of a reading problem, since he scores only 66 on the language portion. Also, it is not unusual for a disadvantaged child to score higher on the nonlanguage portion.

The 77 on the Otis, another group test, seems to indicate that his IQ is below average. But the Otis, a group test, requires reading ability, so this score supports the idea of a reading problem and is probably a low estimate of his true IQ.

6. Mrs. Pearson's averaging of the test scores and concluding that Benny is "a slow learner, but not mentally retarded," is very poor practice, showing a lack of sophistication on her part. A more reasonable interpretation is that he is about average in IQ, with scores dropping because of poor background and some type of reading problem.

7. Benny is 13 years old, and no phone is listed. The lack of a telephone is further support of the low social class hypothesis. Being behind in school (13 years old, but only in sixth grade) is not unusual for lower-class children, who sometimes need to repeat grades due to poor performance or lack of attendance.

8. He moved to New York from Kentucky two years ago, and he had better grades until third grade. Perhaps he is from a small, rural setting in Kentucky (this could be checked easily) and was in a lower-class setting. After third grade, his family moved to a middle-class suburban setting, which was probably very difficult for Benny. Also, after third grade, any type of reading problem begins to create severe difficulties for a child.

9. His tardiness and absences are not uncommon for a lower-class child and support our basic hypothesis. They also indicate that he is probably very unhappy with school and would rather not attend.

10. His older sister does much better in school. This is not unusual in lower-class families, where it is accepted as feminine for the daughter to do well in school, but the son is expected to be more manly. A sister who makes better grades tends to discourage any desire to compete.

Mrs. Pearson's conclusions show little awareness or sensitivity to the plight of lower-class children. She really has little evidence that he is "not too bright," and the "bad attitude" phrase frequently means "I don't like him." Her "being nice and not expecting too much in class" is a condescending attitude, typical of those middle-class teachers who look down on lower-class students, and Benny probably resents this. (Children are usually very much aware of this condescension.) The "bad attitude" perception on the teacher's part can easily become a self-fulfilling prophecy.

Reactions of the Other Teachers

Are the reactions of the other persons with whom Mrs. Pearson talked consistent with our hypothesis of a lower-class child in a middle-class school? These reactions show that

1. Benny does well in gym, a more manly, macho pursuit, more in line with his desire for masculinity. Also remember that gym activities do not rely on reading ability and maximize physical skills.

2. Last year's teacher, also middle class, probably had no understanding of Benny's problems either. She and the gym teacher were seeing two different facets of his personality, which is not at all unusual.

3. It was a mistake for the music teacher to try to make him an angel in the Christmas play. This would be very embarrassing to a child such as Benny, who wants to prove he is tough, a man, not a sissy. Remember, he already has many reasons to feel out of place.

4. The principal has obviously not been involved with Benny or his problem.

5. The counselor uses jargon, which does not help much. But the fact that Benny plays chess supports the hypothesis that he is at least normal in intelligence.

6. The social worker supplies information that shows that Benny adjusts well in his own environment. His problems seem to center on his being maladjusted in an upwardly mobile, middle-class setting.

7. Apparently, the school never really pursued his reading problem very successfully in his two years in New York. They have now ceased to make any attempt, which is most unfortunate. Remedial reading programs should continue beyond fifth grade for any child with a reading problem.

8. The chat with Benny's mother implies that the mother does not see the parental role that she might play and fails to understand the problem. Lower-class parents, who have often had poor experiences in school themselves, often fail to be sympathetic or enthusiastic about school.

Thus, all the data hang together and support the hypothesis that Benny is a lower-class child, in a strange environment, probably one of only a small number of lower-class children in a middle-class school. He is unhappy about school, not doing well, and his teacher expresses a negative attitude toward him. He is a poor reader, failing in the most basic tool of school, and unless he receives some help, his performance and related problems will continue to deteriorate until he becomes another casualty—a school dropout. But what should teachers *do* about lower-class children such as Benny? The American educational system is intended for *all* children from *all* backgrounds. Schools and teachers should make every possible effort to adjust to the cultural diversity of the students. Specific suggestions as to how this might be done are addressed in the discussion "What Can the Teacher Do to Help?"

A final point to be made here is that a child *must* adhere to certain "middle-class" values if he or she is to go to school at all. It is to the child's benefit to learn to respect other people's property, to develop the ability to work toward long-term goals, to become somewhat compulsive about paying attention to the clock, to learn to settle differences amicably rather than through violence, and to learn to control (not repress, however) emotions. While learning to accept and understand the values of the lower-class child, the teacher at the same time must strive toward instilling these so-called "middle-class" values, which are values shared by many of the social institutions in our democratic society.

The Myth of Race

The topic of race, not only in education but in our society in general, is highly controversial. Deprivation, discrimination, prejudice, hostility, and conflict have been a part of race relations throughout American history. The schools have had to assume a considerable portion of the attempted solutions to racial strife in our society.

Any theories of the purity of race become very difficult to apply in today's world. The three fundamental racial stocks of Caucasoid, Mongoloid, and Negroid have become so intermixed over hundreds of thousands of years that geneticists tell us that purity of race is a myth. And yet people talk of blacks, whites, Mexicans, Indians, and Puerto Ricans as if each of these were some sort of pure racial stock!

The meaning of race in the United States is easy to discern. Anyone who is, or appears to be, white is of the favored race. Anyone who is black, red, brown, or in any way separate from the preferred white race is in trouble. Although Hispanic-Americans, American Indians, Puerto Ricans, and various other "unpreferred" persons have their share of problems, we focus on the most widespread racial problem in America, problems of black Americans, as illustrative of the dificulties still to be resolved in the area of race and the schools.

Historical Background of Black-White Relations

The roots of racial problems in America date back far before the establishment of the country. The black race was introduced into the United States as slaves and continued to live under inhumane conditions for some two hundred years. An entire social structure and economy, that of the southern states, depended on a large labor force of slaves, and the United States is still paying for this most unfortunate part of its history. Although the Civil War officially brought an end to slavery, it did not bring an end to the plight of the black person in America.

Part of the basis of the slave-supported economy was the belief that blacks were inferior, less sensitive, less intelligent, a lower form of humanity. Psychologically, such a belief was necessary to assuage the guilt that would otherwise surely follow from the mistreatment of human beings. As inferior creatures, slaves obviously could not learn in the same fashion as their white counterparts, and formal schooling for slaves was forbidden. This clearly was a way also of assuring that "inferior" slaves remained inferior slaves.

The Failure of Reconstruction

After the Civil War, it would seem that blacks should have had the opportunity to join in the benefits of American life, including the benefits of public education. But that was not the case. Reconstruction was a sad time in the life of the South, and the former slaves found themselves free in theory, but not in reality. The few blacks who received any education

---

SO YOU WANT TO BE EDUCATED

Imagine yourself living in a rundown shack, with a leaky roof, an old wood stove for heat, no running water or electricity, no privacy as you share the shack with your parents and six brothers and sisters. Your family has no money and can barely get enough to eat, as they work for the owner of the farm on which they are tenants. Your parents have never known any work other than that of field hands, and nobody in the family can read. From this background, you want to go to school and learn to read.

There is a school just a mile and a half down the road, where all the white children are educated. But you cannot go there because you are black. You must go to a school six miles away in a building every bit as dilapidated as your own home. The one teacher in this school can barely read herself. The school has no money, no heat, no supplies, and very few books. Your chances of learning much here are slim, and after several years of attending this school, you will be far behind the white children in their much better school. The fact that you are so far behind will make it impossible for you to continue in high school and college, as the white children do.

This is typical of the education opportunities for black children during Reconstruction, the period from 1865 to about 1885, although, theoretically, the blacks were now free and had the right to pursue an education.

This picture did not change much during the first half of the twentieth century. In 1950, buses of black students still drove right by the school where everyone else was educated to an all-black school down the road. Although these schools were supposed to be equal as well as separate, they tended to be very separate and not very equal. The cry of "busing" as some sort of evil was not heard in those days. Blacks had to wait until after the landmark case of *Brown* v. *Board of Education* in 1954 before such "separate but equal" schools could even begin to be phased out. By 1981, full integration of the schools had still not become a reality, although much progress has been made, especially in the South.

were forced to attend grossly inferior, all-black schools, and in many cases, the poor black sharecroppers were no better off than they had been as slaves. Most black Americans continued to find themselves outside the broader white society and certainly outside any opportunity for a sound education. The achievement of blacks, despite these restrictions, is one of the truly amazing facts of American history.

The "Separate but Equal" Doctrine

From the seeds of the Reconstruction sprung an approach to education that was to hamstring black Americans for the next seventy years. This was the "separate but equal" doctrine, legitimized by the Supreme Court in 1896, which stated that it was fair and reasonable to maintain separate (but equal) schools for black and white children. Such schools effectively kept black children out of the mainstream of American education, in violation of the common school idea, and helped to keep black society separate from white society also.

The separate but equal doctrine continued as the law of the land until 1954. In that year, the Supreme Court ruled in *Brown* v. *Board of Education* that separate educational systems were inherently unequal, no matter how much was done to make them equal, and a violation of the intent of the Constitution. The court ruled that such segregation in schooling must end, and the results of that decision are still taking effect in our schools. This case did not lead to an immediate solution to the problems of blacks in education, however, and many American cities still have essentially seg-

In many cities, integration in schools has been achieved through busing. (Bernie Weithorn/SIUC Photographic Service.)

regated schools. The segregation in our schools today tends to be a "de facto" rather than "de jure" segregation; that is, it is not supported by law but rather, is a result of housing patterns and school district lines. If a school happens to be in an all-black neighborhood, and thus have all-black children, it is a de facto segregated school.

The effects of decades of deprivation, prejudice, discrimination, poverty, ignorance, and cruelty could not be erased easily by simply ending segregation in the schools. Black students continued to perform poorly in school, score low on standardized tests, and found it difficult to adjust to the new integrated school setting. Both black and white students felt hostility and uneasiness in many of the newly integrated schools, and the anger and violence of some parents is well known. Opposition came not only from racists, but also from well-meaning parents who feared for the welfare of their children and from some educators who worried about the school's goals being lost in a socially tense situation.

Opposition to Integration

In addition to the classic racist, who objects to the very idea of integration, many other sources of opposition to integration in the public schools have emerged. Usually, such opposition purports *not* to be against integration itself but, instead, to be against the way in which it is carried out. Thus, some citizens object to the idea of busing students to achieve racial balance, believing that such busing takes the child away from his or her neighborhood, is dangerous, and is inconsistent with American ideals of choosing where to live and go to school (St. John, 1975). Parents who have deliberately chosen a home because of the schools in the area feel they are cheated by busing. On the other hand, defendants of busing point out that children were bused great distances (especially blacks) to perpetuate segregation in earlier days, and little opposition was expressed.

Parents seem to object especially to any type of "unnatural" or mandated integration, claiming instead that integration should be a natural, not a forced, undertaking. The term "quotas" has taken on an odious meaning in this regard, with critics claiming that *any* kind of quota is a form of discrimination based on race. If I am placed in a school, so this argument goes, for the simple reason that I am white and more whites are needed to achieve "racial balance," then this is obviously discrimination based on race. American parents apparently approve of the idea of integrated schools and of eliminating prejudice and discrimination, but balk at specific ways of carrying this out.

Amidst the arguments about busing, quotas, reverse discrimination, and quality education (which some feel is threatened by integration), there is considerable evidence of the success of integration in our schools since the landmark *Brown* v. *Board of Education* decision in 1954. With the exception of school systems in some large cities, schools throughout our

359

I THINK IT'S FINE, BUT . . . !

Two mothers, we'll call them Mabel and Anna, were discussing problems in the school system. It seems that their neighborhood school, formerly all white, was now part of a program designed to integrate the schools. Their daughters were fifth graders, and all fifth-graders were being bused to another school to achieve integration. Their school, meanwhile, was going to have all the third graders in the system, again to achieve integration.

"I'm all for integration," Mabel said, "but why do they have to bus children all over the city? My daughter will have to ride on a bus for forty minutes to go to school, when there is a perfectly good school right here in our neighborhood."

"I agree, and it's dangerous to ride buses like that. Putting all the fifth-graders together in one place can cause all sorts of problems," Anna responded.

"The reason we moved here was that we wanted our kids in a good school. It isn't fair for them not to allow our kids to attend our own school."

Anna shook her head. "It just doesn't make sense. Kids should go to school in their own neighborhoods. White kids don't want to go to black schools any more than black kids want to go to white schools. This busing will cause nothing but confusion, and our kids won't learn what they need to learn. It doesn't make sense to disrupt a whole school system because of a few black families."

"I'm worried about my daughter being harmed or picking up all sorts of bad language riding on a bus like that. I hear they deal dope and all sorts of things go on in those buses," Mabel replied.

"I'm in favor of integration in the city schools, but not in suburbs like ours. It will lead to nothing but trouble here. They'll have to have police patrolling the halls. Our own school won't be ours anymore."

"I don't know about you, but I know what we're going to do. We're going to send our kids to a private school until this blows over. After a few years, they'll see that it doesn't work, and our kids can go to their own school with their own kind."

Conversations such as this were not uncommon in the 1970s. Some parents came right out and said that they were against integration, while many more objected simply to the way in which it was being done. It was said that integration was all right for others, but not for *my* kids. The most hated form of integration was that brought about by busing for racial balance. Critics of this called it "forced busing" and felt that it was clearly un-American. Much progress has taken place in integrating the public schools, but many problems are yet to be solved.

country have managed to achieve integration of the races with a minimum of problems. In the South, where segregation was the legally supported norm in 1954, it is difficult to find a school system that has not satisfied minimum requirements of integration. The forefront of school integration has now moved to the college level, and excellent progress is being made.

This does not mean that all racial problems in the schools have been solved, however. Controversy still exists in many schools, accompanied

Great strides have been made toward school integration since 1954. (Darrell Barry/Little Rock School District.)

by tension, hostility, and even occasional violence. Some white parents have removed their children from public schools and have sent them to private schools to escape integration. Parents have a harder time adjusting to integration than do the children themselves.

Racial Differences in Performance

A further problem that integration has not solved is that of the actual academic performance of black children in school. Although Stephan (1978) cites cases of improvement in academic achievement by blacks, Coleman et al., in discussing performance of various racial groups on standardized achievement tests, stated that "the average [black] pupil scores distinctly lower on these tests at every level than the average white pupil" (Coleman et al., 1966, p. 21).

In a more recent discussion of the academic performance of blacks in school, Craig et al., said:

In the metropolitan North and West, black students are three times as likely as white students to drop out of school by the age of sixteen or seventeen. . . . Unfortunately, most drop out before they are exposed to occupational and vocational information and skills that could aid them in their search for a new identity. It is hardly surprising that the nonwhite high school dropout is at the bottom of today's job market. [Craig et al., 1975, p. 88]

361

Thus, even with integration, many black children remain outside the mainstream of American education. While integration in the schools is legally required, much more than this is needed to bring about total integration of blacks in a predominantly white, middle-class society.

What is the reason for racial differences in performance, now that school integration has been the law of the land for more than twenty-five years? One explanation already explored in Chapter 9 is the genetic thesis, which sees differences in black performance as the result of genetic differences in intelligence. Just as study after study finds black children scoring an average of fifteen points lower than white children on standardized IQ tests, so, too, do studies find black children scoring lower on achievement tests and other indices of school learning. The genetic argument is that such differences are mainly hereditary, the result of genetic selection:

Different races have evolved in somewhat different ways, making for many differences among them. A few of the many physical characteristics found to display genetic variation between races are body size and proportion, hair form and distribution . . . Among various behavioral traits, intelligence is perhaps the most strongly influenced by genetic factors. The relative importance of genetic factors will inevitably increase as the environmental factors that influence mental development are made more equal for everyone. [Jensen, 1981, pp. 198 and xiii]

Although it may be impossible to settle the genetic argument with conclusive scientific evidence, it is accurate to state that most social scientists do *not* support this view. Even though the inheritability of intelligence and other aptitudes has received increasing interest in the last decade, most social scientists would still support the conclusion expressed by Jerome S. Kagan, that "it is erroneous to suggest that genetic differences between human populations could be responsible for failure to master school related tasks" (Kagan, 1969, p. 277).

Some facts that are lost in the emotional reaction to the genetic argument are that even with genetic identity, IQs can still vary widely (by as much as twenty-five points in identical twins), that a much broader assessment of abilities and potentials is needed, and that the genetic theory really has no meaning when applied to an individual student. Also, we must remember that, regardless how important the genetic component might be, it cannot be affected by the teacher, so that the teacher's goal is to allow each student the opportunity to develop by manipulating the only thing she or he can manipulate—the environment.

For many years, differences in performance between black and white children have been explained by differences in environment. This viewpoint argues that family background, especially in regard to child-rearing practices, is an important determination of school performance. It argues that such variables as malnutrition, poor health care, poverty, and inadequate schools are a part of the background of most black children in America. In addition, backgrounds and child-rearing practices of blacks are different from those of whites.

SYDNEY TAKES A TEST

Sydney was black, and he lived in the section of town where most of the blacks lived. He had no idea what school was like and had no desire to attend when he was abruptly taken to school by his mother and enrolled in the first grade. Most of the other children in the class had already attended kindergarten, and they were not shy and afraid like Sydney was.

Sydney did not do well in school, and after a month had passed, he was sent to the counselor for some testing. Sydney had never played any games like those found in this test. The fact that it was a Stanford-Binet Intelligence Test meant nothing to Sydney.

The man giving the test was white, and he talked kind of funny. Sydney was very scared and tried to be very careful not to get into trouble. His major goal was to escape from this room as quickly as possible, and meanwhile he tried to be very quiet and not get into trouble. The man kept asking strange questions, and then smiling at Sydney. Since he did not know what he was supposed to do, Sydney said nothing on some of the questions and answered in a very soft voice on others. After what seemed like an awfully long time, the white man put his cards, puzzles, and books back into his little suitcase and took Sydney back to his classroom. Sydney breathed a sigh of relief, even though he didn't like his classroom too much either.

Is it surprising that Sydney scored 80 on the Stanford-Binet? Or that he took the test again a year later, after changing schools, and scored 90? Or that, still later, a black researcher gave him the same test and he scored 100? As Sydney experienced more of the school environment and learned the language and how to play the games, his IQ climbed. Also, as he got accustomed to taking IQ tests, his IQ magically increased each time. Critics of testing as it relates to black students feel that black children score unreasonably low on these tests for reasons such as those described here and that, therefore, most standard IQ tests do not give a fair estimate of the average black child's potential.

Another key point in the environmental argument is that language is an important area of experience for any child. The school happens to be built on language patterns familiar to the white child but not to the black child. Thus, the school environment itself is stacked against the black child. Discrimination in all its forms from early on in life is presented as part of the environmental argument also, since a child growing as part of a disadvantaged and discredited minority in a culture in which another race predominates can hardly have the same environment as a child who happens to be a member of the preferred race.

There is also the claim that the tests that indicate the various differences in performance between black and white children are themselves biased. In other words, if the test itself is oriented toward a particular group and discriminates against another group, then apparent differences will be indicated by the test even when no real differences between the groups exist.

The environmental argument concludes with what may be the most important point: the differences in attitudes and values of blacks and whites. This argument is presented here as part of the broader discussion of differences between middle-class and disadvantaged children of any race.

Race, Social Class, and the Disadvantaged

Years ago, textbooks spoke about "underprivileged" children. Then the phrase was changed to "culturally deprived" and later to "culturally different." Some authors simply spoke about the poor. In each case, the previous term (underprivileged, deprived, etc.) was abandoned as snobbish, condescending, and not entirely accurate.

In the search for a neutral term that described more accurately all of those to whom the generalizations applied, the term "culture" was dropped entirely. Regardless of one's background, nobody is deprived of a culture. The term that is used today is really a catchall to describe all those who, for any reason, are at a disadvantage in developing, adjusting, and competing in our society. The term today is "disadvantaged."

There are many ways in which a person can be disadvantaged in America. The term covers (1) economic factors, including both rural and urban poor; (2) racial factors, with blacks, Puerto Ricans, Hispanic-Americans, and American Indians being four of the leading disadvantaged groups; and (3) educational background, occupational factors, and even sex, with females in our culture considered disadvantaged in certain ways because of sexual discrimination. In other words, the term "disadvantaged" includes numerous possibilities of being denied full access to the fruits of the American dream.

In most cases, the disadvantaged child is suffering from the interaction of several factors rather than from just one. For example, a black child is quite often poor, from lower-class background, living in an undesirable neighborhood, and in a family with insufficient education. It would be difficult to determine which aspect perpetuates the problem—whether it is being from a minority group, being poor, having insufficient nutrition and health care, lacking an education, living in a bad neighborhood, or what. But a teacher does not have to settle this question. What a teacher needs to realize is that there are many disadvantaged children in our schools (about one fourth to one third by most estimates) and that they need special help in adjusting to the requirements of school. Let us take a brief survey of several of these types of disadvantaged children as discussed by Craig et al. (1975).

1. *Urban whites.* Many disadvantaged urban children are from Caucasian families, some who are recent immigrants from Europe, others who have migrated from rural areas, and still others who are second- and third-

generation urban poor. In the case of the urban poor, they often still think of themselves as "Italian," "Polish," or "Jewish" rather than as fully assimilated into American culture. Such families perpetuate many "Old Country" attitudes, values, and behaviors.

This segment of the disadvantaged population is often referred to as the "invisible poor," as they are not obvious on the basis of color or geographic area. These poor whites are less aware of their limitations, less organized, and less aware of opportunities than are other disadvantaged groups. Although the percentage of disadvantaged whites is relatively small (10% to 20%) in comparison with the percentage of poor in minority groups (about 75%), in terms of actual numbers, disadvantaged urban whites constitute the largest single group of disadvantaged.

2. *Urban blacks.* The prime inhabitants of the urban ghettos, most of these are children of rural migrants to the big cities. Harlem, Watts, Chicago's South Side are all examples of such hard-core areas of black disadvantaged. Although *not* the largest group in terms of numbers, this is the best known of the disadvantaged groups. While they are aware of their plight, it is very difficult for children to escape from their disadvantaged situation. Unlike urban whites, who might fade into another segment of society without being noticed, black children cannot hide their blackness. Discrimination in housing, jobs, and education have, in effect, kept blacks in these ghettos. Large numbers of these children are from families that migrated to large northern cities from the rural south following World War II and on into the 1960s (as are many of their white counterparts), and the disillusionment and despair felt by these families is a major social problem of our times.

3. *Rural blacks.* Although most rural blacks live in southern states, a few can be found in northern states also. They represent only a small portion of the disadvantaged, but their plight is very real, and in most cases, nothing is being done to improve their situation. Both the rural black and the rural white groups might be classified as the "forgotten poor" in terms of attention and programs for helping them. Many of these children go to no school at all and are not reached by government programs.

4. *Rural whites.* The other half of the "forgotten poor," rural whites probably total more than rural blacks. They are divided about evenly between southern and northern states. The best known group of poor rural whites is that in the former coal mining states of Appalachia, and attempts to change the roots of their poverty have failed for the most part. However, many other states, both in the north and in the south, have significant populations of rural white disadvantaged, and in most cases, little is being done to help them. Among such groups, the average adult has a sixth grade education and only one in four ever completes high school.

5. *Mexican-Americans.* There are presently some $3\frac{1}{2}$ million to 4 million disadvantaged Mexican-Americans in the United States, with some estimates much higher than this. Most of these disadvantaged children are

found in the southwestern states of Texas, New Mexico, Colorado, Arizona, and California. They are one of the poorest of the disadvantaged groups, and since many of them belong to migrant worker families, they present unique problems for the public schools. They are probably the most rapidly increasing group of disadvantaged in America, primarily since more are migrating from Mexico every day in search of a better life.

6. *Urban Puerto Ricans.* These disadvantaged families live primarily in a few large northern cities, such as New York and Chicago. They have had a greater degree of economic and social mobility than do the black poor, but they constitute one of the major ethnic groups of disadvantaged. Leaders of this group, as of the black poor, believe that prejudice and discrimination are major factors in perpetuating their life of poverty. Since they are congregated in so few cities, a teacher may not encounter these children in most schools but will face them in large numbers if teaching in these cities.

7. *American Indians.* Descendants of the native Americans who lived here thousands of years before our European ancestors "discovered" America, this may be the saddest of all disadvantaged groups. Although there are probably less than 1 million disadvantaged American Indians,

A traveling museum provides an educational experience for children of migrant workers. (SIUC Photographic Service.)

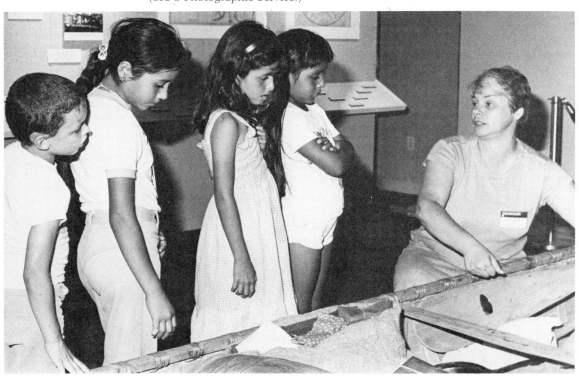

the extent and hopelessness of their situation seems to be far worse than that of other disadvantaged groups. Surrounded by a hostile culture that has effectively eliminated their own, many Indian children live in shacks, adobe huts, brush shelters, or worse. Statistics on disease and life expectancy are appalling, and most programs to help the Indians have been dismal failures. The average American Indian completes five years of school, the worst record of any minority group. The plight of these native Americans is indeed a blot on the social conscience of Americans.

Scholastic Performance

Craig et al. present the following conclusions about the scholastic performance of these groups of disadvantaged:

In tests of scholastic achievement, blacks score significantly below the average for whites and Orientals. The American Indian, Puerto Rican, and Mexican-American score below whites but above blacks on tests of school achievement. The achievement gap remains fairly constant throughout the elementary and secondary school periods. During the 10-month school year, low-income students as a group generally progress 7 months in reading. By eighth grade, lower-class youth are typically 2 to 3 years behind grade level. [Craig et al., 1975, p. 87]

All these disadvantaged groups suffer from high school dropout rates that are sometimes two or three times that of average whites. Those who drop out usually have a history of poor performance and failure dating back to early elementary school. Only a small percentage of disadvantaged children go on to college, and, of course, most disadvantaged children are in no position to qualify for the better job opportunities in our society.

Child-Rearing Patterns

An important area of differences between disadvantaged and average children, which teachers must understand in working with these children, is that of child-rearing patterns. The way in which a child is treated by parents obviously affects the child's values and behaviors and especially the way in which the child reacts to teachers. Table 10.2 compares the child-rearing pattern of the poor and the child-rearing patterns considered to be adaptive to American society.

It is not difficult to see how differences in family background as illustrated in Table 10.2 could affect a child's attitudes and behavior in school. A fatalistic attitude, orientation toward the present, and "keep out of trouble" outlook hardly encourage the risk, exploration, and effort required to succeed academically. Lack of a parental model of educational achievement, conflict in the family, and low self-esteem all contribute toward the

367

Table 10.2
Child-Rearing Patterns of the Poor as Compared with Patterns Adaptive to American Society*

Patterns Reported to Be More Prevalent Among the Very Poor	Patterns Conducive to Adaptation to Today's Society
1. Inconsistent, harsh physical punishment.	1. Mild, firm, consisent discipline.
2. Fatalistic, personalistic attitudes, magical thinking.	2. Rational, evidence-oriented, objective attitudes.
3. Orientation in the present.	3. Future orientation, goal commitment.
4. Authoritarian, rigid family structure.	4. Democratic, equalitarian, flexible family structure.
5. "Keep out of trouble," alienated, distrustful approach to society outside family; constricted experiences.	5. Self-confident, positive, trustful approach to new experiences; wealth of experiences.
6. Limited verbal communication; relative absence of subtlety and abstract concepts; a physical action style.	6. Extensive verbal communication; value placed on complexity, abstractions.
7. Human behavior seen as unpredictable and judged in terms of its immediate impact.	7. Human behavior seen as having many causes and being developmental in nature.
8. Low self-esteem, little belief in one's coping capacity; passive attitude.	8. High self-esteem; belief in one's own coping capacity; an active attitude.
9. Distrust of opposite sex, exploitive attitude; ignorance of physiology of reproductive system and of contraceptives.	9. Acceptance of sex; positive sexual expression within marriage by both husband and wife valued as part of total marital relationship; understanding of physiology of reproductive system; effective use of contraceptives.
10. Tendency not to differentiate clearly one child from another.	10. Each child seen as a separate individual and valued accordingly.
11. Lack of consistent nurturance with abrupt and early granting of independence.	11. Consistent nurturant support with gradual training for independence.
12. Rates of marital conflict high; high rates of family breakdown.	12. Harmonious marriage; both husband and wife present.
13. Parents have low levels of educational achievement.	13. Parents have achieved educational and occupational success.

*Adapted from R. Craig, W. Mehrens, and H. Clarizio, *Contemporary Educational Psychology* (New York: John Wiley, 1975), pp. 96–97.

child's distrust of the teacher and school and also toward the teacher's finding this type of child hard to work with or to help. The disadvantaged child, thus, is often poorly adjusted in school, where his or her values and orientations toward life are out of step with the prevailing culture, while the child may be well adjusted to life outside school.

The disadvantaged child will encounter adjustment difficulties if he is expected to adapt a set of values, beliefs, and mores different from what he has acquired. When evaluated according to the standards of his particular cultural group, he is very well adjusted. Teachers trained to work with the middle-class child may be puzzled by behaviors that only reflect differences between the values of the lower-class culture and those of the middle-class culture. It is difficult for the middle-class teacher to empathize and to communicate with youngsters whose style of life is so different from theirs. [Craig et al., 1975, p. 97]

The story of Benny, the troublesome child, and Mrs. Pearson, his teacher, earlier in this chapter illustrates the difficulties that disadvantaged children face if they have teachers who fail to understand their problems. The prognosis for a child like Benny is that he will probably stay in school, with his achievement slipping every year, until he is old enough to drop out, and then join the ranks of unskilled and often unemployed adults.

Understanding the Disadvantaged

Asking the middle-class teacher to understand the disadvantaged student is no easy assignment. One mistake often made is that of *sympathizing* with such students or feeling sorry for them. This is a form of condescension, of looking down one's nose at one's inferiors. Much more than sympathy, the disadvantaged child needs *empathy,* or the ability to put oneself in their place and see how the world looks through their eyes. Such an ability to walk a mile in the shoes of another is a rare but valuable commodity in today's world.

A disadvantaged child is *not* without experience and, in fact, has often had far more experience than the teacher in many aspects of life. The disadvantaged child is in many ways tough and realistic, and in turn tends to see school as unrealistic and "sissy." While failing to understand the game being played, the flowery language, deferred goals, planning, structure and careful use of time, the quiet concentration and studying, such children nevertheless realize that they are doing poorly at the game of school. They see the school as being unfair to them, the teachers as disliking them, picking on them, and favoring other children. They may resent middle-class children who know how to play the game and gain the rewards of school. Their belief that the teachers dislike them and that they are doing poorly can easily become self-fulfilling prophecies.

This child's honesty, straightforwardness, active approach to life, direct expression of emotion, lack of repression, and ability to adjust to tremendous hardships in life should not be denigrated by the teacher. While middle-class values and habits are certainly different from those of the lower class, they are not really better. Teachers must strive to accept the fact that their value system is different from that of the disadvantaged and work with that difference.

Remember, also, that this disadvantaged child whom you are struggling to reach has much to be angry and distrustful about. The repeated failures in his past have had a cumulative effect, thus, teaching him that the way

369

to adjust is *not* to try, *not* to stick his neck out. One solution is to make fun of school, even to become the class clown. He easily becomes the classic failure-avoidant, rather than achievement-oriented, student. The lower-class, disadvantaged child reacts very poorly to criticism, punishment, and any form of negative feedback. It is an understatement to say that "he has a strong need for positive reinforcement."

What Can the Teacher Do to Help?

There are no magical solutions to the difficulties described in the preceding pages. We offer here some possibiliies that may be helpful. These suggestions certainly are not easy to carry out, but they are consistent with what is known about the disadvantaged child in school.

1. *Find out all you can about these children.* Not only from textbooks and professional journals, but also from magazines, newspapers, films, and above all personal experience, carry on a long-term campaign to acquire an understanding for the disadvantaged child. This is, of course, what the

Teachers should treat each child as an individual. (Darrell Barry/Little Rock School District.)

teacher should be doing continually in trying to understand *all* children, but it takes a special effort to gain the information to understand disadvantaged children. Some experts feel that nobody who has not been disadvantaged himself or herself can possibly achieve such understanding, but this argument would tend only to serve as an excuse for the average teacher.

2. *Treat each child as an individual.* Again, this is a general suggestion that applies to all children, but it takes on a special significance in relation to the disadvantaged. A child resents being treated as part of a category of "poor kids," "black kids," "lousy students," or some other similar grouping. The disadvantaged child must be seen and reacted to as a unique and worthwhile individual, and the teacher may have to put forth some extra effort to get to know the child in this way.

3. *Avoid the self-fulfilling prophecy.* Disadvantaged children are especially vulnerable to this labeling effect. With nothing in their backgrounds to make them expect success in school, the teacher is easily perceived as carrying the familiar message of failure. Sometimes it appears that a silent deal is made—you don't bother me, and I won't bother you—and the disadvantaged child sits quietly in the back of the room and learns nothing, as expected. Teachers must make a special effort to break away from such self-fulfilling prophecies.

4. *Try to provide opportunities for improvement of self-concept.* Although not necessarily true for their entire life situation, disadvantaged children almost invariably have poor self-concepts in relation to school. Because of their outlook and their values and habits, they very easily appear to be a threat to what the teacher is trying to accomplish. This leads easily to the teacher taking immediate steps that in effect knock down the self-concept of the child. Teachers should avoid such negative attacks and, instead, find ways of building the much needed positive self-concept.

5. *Provide opportunities for success.* Unfortunately, such success is sometimes difficult to arrange, since the child must perceive that he or she has been successful at some important task and may be reluctant to take the teacher's word for this. Don't make the mistake of deliberately giving the child something "easy" to do to assure success. The child will probably see through this and dislike you for it, in addition to feeling a failure. It is only by setting up real tasks and helping the disadvantaged student to succeed at these tasks that such a feeling of success can be achieved.

If success can be achieved, it is also important that the child *knows* that he or she has succeeded. Disadvantaged children need large amounts of feedback. They also need a variety of activities with which to maximize their opportunities for success. This single factor—a feeling of success—is probably the most important variable in dealing with a disadvantaged child.

6. *Avoid condescending, patronizing views.* Teachers must strive to see the disadvantaged child as different from themselves, perhaps, but not of less value or importance. Seeing such children as "poor, dirty, ignorant kids"

371

and showering them with affection as you look down at them as inferiors is *not* the answer to getting them to develop positive self-concepts and the feeling of success in school. It would be wiser to see them as interesting and worthwhile children with great untapped potential for school achievement.

7. *Be honest and admit the shortcomings in your own background and experience.* Each of us has only a limited view of life, a limited range of experience. This is true also of the teacher, who is usually limited by middle-class background, outlook, and experiences. Although there is nothing shameful about middle-class values (they have certainly helped to build and staff our schools), there is nothing particularly wonderful about them either. Psychologists point out many ways in which middle-class values can become hangups and sources of psychological problems. Remember this as you look at the disadvantaged child with his or her different set of values and experiences.

Teachers must also remember that disadvantaged children have often experienced events and hardships in their lives. A teacher has often led a "sheltered life" in comparison with some of these children. Keep this in mind and try to understand how the disadvantaged child can look on the *teacher* as strange or inexperienced or even as innocent and naïve.

8. *Provide structure, organization, and security.* Disadvantaged children, perhaps more than average children, need order and security in their lives. The teacher can provide this order and security by being organized, systematic, and predictable in his or her behavior, by making clear what is expected, and by establishing a comfortable and consistent routine. Clear and consistent discipline is part of this, as are established guidelines for behavior and clear expectations of what follows misbehavior. In an orderly

The teacher should provide plenty of structure when working with disadvantaged children. (Darrell Barry/Little Rock School District.)

and predictable world, some of the anxiety and confusion that is part of the disadvantaged child's reaction to the school gradually disappears, and his or her chances for some realistic successes are maximized.

9. *Ignore much of what you've heard about lower-class children.* Much of what is known as "the facts" about the disadvantaged is either inaccurate or subject to change in the right circumstances. Erroneous beliefs can act as barriers or self-fulfilling propecies that keep the teacher from relating to the child as an individual person and allowing the child to become all that he or she is capable of being.

As an example, parents of disadvantaged children tend to have poor attitudes about school. Numerous studies have reported such attitudes in one form or another—the lower-class parent does not value school, fails to see the importance of education, will not support the school, does not trust school officials, or had a poor experience with school himself or herself. Yet these views can be changed dramatically if parents of disadvantaged students realize that the school *really is* doing their children some good. In these cases, uninterested and uninvolved parents suddenly become typical middle-class parents, involved in what the school is doing, asking questions, criticizing, taking on all the chracteristics that they supposedly do not reflect. It appears that the determinant of whether or not lower-class parents will support their child's school and become interested and involved is simply whether the school is *really* doing some good for the child in a way that is apparent to the child and/or the parents.

10. *Don't expect to be a hero.* The conditions that produce disadvantaged children take years to develop, and the child comes to you after years of exposure to scores of factors. Don't expect to work miracles. Don't expect to undo all these factors. Don't expect it to be easy, and don't expect any medals for what you do accomplish.

The successes you have with disadvantaged children will probably be outnumbered by those cases where you feel you have made no progress. This in no way negates the importance of the successes. The teacher must consistently, repeatedly, and with patience offer the disadvantaged child the opportunity to succeed in school and accept failure on his or her part just as the child must learn to accept his or her failures. But failure must not lead to giving up, neither for the student nor for the teacher.

These thoughts were implied in the statement of a teacher who had taught for twenty years in the inner-city schools of Detroit. "The only experts on the disadvantaged are those who have never worked with the disadvantaged." He went on to explain that there are no easy answers in working with these children, and those who think that there are magic solutions are ivory-tower theorists who do not have to work with these children on a daily basis.

11. *Get all the help you can.* The school counselor, psychologist, psychometrist, reading consultant, social worker, principal, and all other professionals who might have some input that would assist you in working with a disadvantaged child should be sought. These auxiliary personnel

373

cannot be used as ways to get rid of a problem but, instead, as ways to help you solve problems. Don't be afraid to talk with these people about disadvantaged children in general and ones in your class in particular. Also, don't be afraid to read about these problems, attend workshops and lectures—participate in any activities that might give you some new thoughts and insights. At the same time, exercise a healthy skepticism about what you are told and insist on proving it yourself rather than accepting it blindly. As with any other educational problem, that of working with the disadvantaged must be approached in an experimental frame of mind, ready to try things and see what works for you.

12. *Avoid invidious comparisons.* It is probably very rare for a teacher to compare one child with another with malicious intent, but it is very common for teachers to compare children either intentionally or unintentionally. The result of such comparisons for the disadvantaged child is often a feeling of inferiority, embarrassment, jealousy, bitterness, or resentment. The child fails to see the teacher's positive intent of encouragement and providing a goal to work for and instead sees only the negative connotations of being compared with other children.

The case of Benny earlier in this chapter illustrates an invidious comparison. By asking all the children to stand up, introduce themselves, tell about where they lived, what their parents did for a living, what they did last summer, the teacher, perhaps unconsciously, was making Benny feel embarrassed and ashamed at how his family compared with the families of his more affluent classmates. When it came Benny's turn to participate, he would not stand up and allow himself to feel demeaned.

13. *Don't be afraid to interact with the disadvantaged child.* All the teacher's words of acceptance and good intentions can be offset by the unconscious drawing away from a child who is a little bit dirty, sweaty, poorly clothed, and so on. Teachers sometimes also unconsciously avoid talking with students who are from a different background or who don't talk "quite right." It is almost as if there were some fear that letting one's hair down and rubbing elbows with a lower-class child will somehow rub off, that the nice, clean, middle-class values will be spoiled by interaction with the lower class.

Unless a true and complete acceptance, which includes physical closeness, a touch on the arm, or pat on the back when appropriate, is provided, middle-class teachers cannot really expect acceptance and understanding in return from such children.

Compensatory Education: Boon or Boondoggle?

Compensatory education, or "education to 'compensate' for real or perceived lacks in the total environment of many children" (Evans, 1975, p. 6) is a most controversial topic in American education. Beginning in the early 1960s, especially in "Project Head Start" for disadvantaged pre-schoolers, the programs were later expanded to include aid throughout the entire K–12 sequence and to provide help for the potential school dropout. Dramatic innovations in curriculum, tutoring, expanded vocational development, personnel training programs, bilingual-bicultural education experiments, alternative schools, and special admissions programs and special services at the college level are all forms of compensatory education.

Arthur Jensen (1969) began his famous *Harvard Educational Review* article with the statement that compensatory education had been tried and had failed. He was probably referring to only one form of compensatory education program, the Project Head Start programs for 3- to 5-year-olds. Even in this setting, the statement is debatable, since research results from Head Start programs are far from being consistent. Some programs were more successful than others, notably full-year programs, programs in the southeast, and programs for black children, at least in the variables that were mentioned. Most gains that were measured tended to disappear within the first two or three years of regular school, but this may indicate the need to follow through rather than the fact that the programs were useless.

Head Start programs, as a group, apparently have not lived up to their original promise, but they have given an impetus to preprimary education. The year-long programs, as well as those that are highly structured and cognitively oriented, have yielded the best results. Even though the results have not been altogether glowing, we should not be unduly disheartened, for these were our first efforts and some of them were hastily conceived and implemented. It should also be remembered that the amount of time that children spend in summer Head Start programs constitutes less than 2% of their waking hours from birth to age six. [Craig et al., 1975, pp. 113–114]

For some, the whole idea of compensatory education places the emphasis in the wrong place by focusing on the presumed deficiencies of the poor and culturally different instead of making a critical evaluation of school practices. This has been called "institutionalized racism," the belief that children from poor homes or minority groups are inherently inferior to middle-class children.

Other compensatory education programs that have been attempted are followthrough programs (continuation of Head Start into the primary grades), pre–Head Start programs, Piagetian preschools, educational day care centers, diversified staffing, use of teacher aids, inner-city internship programs, parent and community involvement programs, and adult education programs. One area that deserves special attention is that of nonintellectual factors, such as motivation, attitudes, interests, and values, which some psychologists believe might be more amenable to change at a later age than are intellectual factors. In reality, it is too early to make a judgment of how compensatory education has worked, but there is no doubt that it will continue to be an important part of innovation in education.

HEADSTART TO WHAT?

Marvin had the misfortune of being born into a very poor family. Because of this, he would be not at all ready to start school at age 5. Marvin, however, also had the good fortune of being selected to participate in a Project Head Start program. Beginning at age 3, and continuing until he entered first grade at age 6, he reported every weekday to be stimulated by games, drills, field trips, coaching, tutoring, playing, and all the things that a good Head Start program does. He liked this very much, and he liked the leader and the other people that were all part of this, most of these being graduate students, a factor that was unknown to Marvin. All he knew was that there were several people that were like new mothers and fathers to him, and he decided that he liked school very much.

At age 6, Marvin entered the regular public school. He had just one teacher and thirty-five classmates, and the teacher did not seem to be very happy. He didn't get to know her like he had the adults in Head Start. His classroom was an old, dilapidated room that was very gloomy, and they didn't play any of the games, talk about any of the things they had in Head Start, or take any field trips. The teacher got mad if anyone talked out of turn, and she acted as if she wished she was somewhere else. Marvin felt that she did not know who he was and that she probably didn't like him. Second grade was even worse, and Marvin started to get into trouble. He decided that he didn't like school at all.

By third grade, Marvin's performance was no better than those in the class who had not been part of Head Start. He and several other children had participated in this program, and it appeared that they had made great gains and were ready for school. But this Head Start experience was not accompanied by any followthrough, and Marvin's case is illustrative of what happens to the gains from a preschool Head Start program when it leads to inferior classes and experiences in first, second, and third grades. By about the third grade, in cases such as this, any gains that had been made in the Head Start experience have disappeared.

If Marvin's Head Start experience had been followed by improved climate and instruction in his early years of regular schooling, the gains he had made may not have disappeared so easily.

Summary

America has always had social class differences, as have other societies. To date, the classless society remains a dream and, to many, a nightmare.

Social class differences in the early decades of U.S. history were expanded as a result of the Industrial Revolution. Clear-cut differences between the managers and the workers were evident as were differences between levels of management, skilled versus unskilled workers, type of profession, and owners versus employees. Today, America still has the lower, middle, and upper classes as it did in 1900, although there is some mobility among classes. Education represents the most promising source of mobility in American society.

Defining lower-, middle-, and upper-class characteristics is not easy.

Definitions based strictly in terms of economic, education, neighborhood, income, life-style, or job criteria have all fallen short. In this text, the lower and middle classes are our concern, and the most important differences between these classes lie in the areas of attitudes and values.

The stereotype of lower-class children describes them as not valuing cleanliness, valuing emotion over reason, living in the present, tending toward immediate action, being sexually open and physically aggressive, and not valuing self-discipline or learning for its own sake.

The stereotype of middle-class children describes them as valuing cleanliness and thrift, valuing intellect over emotion, expressing hostility verbally or indirectly, valuing sexual restraint, and exhibiting clean and correct language and moderation. Most of all, the middle-class child is taught to value deferred gratification, to work toward a future goal, and to believe in the importance of learning.

Although all stereotypes contain exceptions, they do shed some light on the problem of the lower-class child functioning in a school based on middle-class attitudes and values, with middle-class teachers. The case of Benny, a troublesome child, who is a lower-class child in a middle-class school, illustrated some of these problems.

A second area of importance in the classroom is that of race. Although the idea of race in any "pure" sense is a myth in the modern world, people still speak of blacks, whites, Hispanics, Indians, Orientals, and Puerto Ricans as if each of these were some sort of pure racial stock. The meaning of race in the United States is easy to discern, with those varying from white to any degree being seen as inferior. Even though considerable progress has been made regarding the rights and equal treatment of minorities, race continues to be a problem in American society.

Although technically freed from slavery during the Civil War, blacks in America continued through Reconstruction and after to have less than full participation in the American dream. The "separate but equal" doctrine, legitimized by the Supreme Court in 1896, stated that it was fair and appropriate to maintain separate schools for blacks and whites. It was not until 1954 that this doctrine was eliminated and integration became the law of the land. Segregation has continued in many schools, however, as a result of housing patterns and school district lines. Even those who say that they favor integration still object to such practices as busing to achieve racial balance, quotas, and other terms that have arisen in this conflict. Nevertheless, there is considerable success in the integration of our schools throughout most of the country.

Another area of concern is that of standardized test scores. In tests of scholastic achievement, blacks consistently score lower than whites. Many educators believe that this is the result of differences in background and experience and that the tests are biased in favor of white, middle-class children. Such factors as family background, child-rearing, nutrition, health care, financial security, schooling, and differing language patterns have been advanced to explain these differences in test scores.

"Disadvantaged" is the term being used currently to describe *any* child who is in a difficult position in developing, adjusting, and competing in our society. In most cases, the disadvantaged child is suffering from the interaction of several factors. For example, a black child is often poor, from lower-class background, and living in an undesirable neighborhood and in a family with insufficient education. Specific disadvantaged groups that are discussed are urban whites, urban blacks, rural whites, rural blacks, Mexican-Americans, urban Puerto Ricans, and American Indians. The important area of child-rearing patterns is described in detail. The disadvantaged child is often poorly adjusted in school, where his or her values and orientations toward life are out of step with the prevailing culture; still, he or she may be well adjusted to life outside school.

Working with disadvantaged children requires empathy rather than sympathy and the ability to lead this child through real achievement. The teacher must learn to see the child's good points, while at the same time help the child to adjust to the requirements of school. Honesty, straightforwardness, an active appraoch to life, direct expression of emotion, lack of repression, and ability to adjust to hardships are all characteristics that are often seen in the disadvantaged child. Thirteen suggestions are given regarding what the teacher can do to further the success of disadvantaged children.

Compensatory education programs, such as Head Start, followthrough, pre–Head Start, Piagetian preschools, educational day care centers, diversified staffing, and many other programs have been attempted in the goal of helping the disadvantaged. These programs have had mixed results, but the reader is reminded of the humanistic goal of "Let each become what he or she is capable of and desires to become."

Study Questions

1. From what social class do *you* come? What criteria did you use to determine your social class? Would these criteria work as an indication of social class membership, in general?
2. What does it mean to say that the description of a type of person is a stereotype? Are stereotypes good or bad? In what ways can stereotypes be useful?
3. Why does a lower-class child usually have difficulties in the typical middle-class classroom? What characteristics of the lower-class child are particularly damaging to the child in school?
4. Why is the separate but equal doctrine inherently unfair to *all* races, regardless of how good the facilities are? Does integrating the schools guarantee an equal education to all?
5. Can you think of characteristics of the environment that would account for white children scoring one standard deviation (fifteen points) higher than black children on IQ tests? Is there a hereditary argument that explains this difference? Which explanation do you accept, and why?
6. In the case of Benny, the troublesome child, what would *you* do if you were in Mrs. Pearson's place as Benny's teacher? What were Mrs. Pearson's biggest errors in interpreting the information she had about Benny?

Coleman, J. S. et al. *Equality of Educational Opportunity.* Washington, D.C.: U.S. Government Printing Office, 1966.

Craig, R., Mehrens, W., and Clarizio, H. *Contemporary Educational Psychology.* New York: John Wiley, 1975.

Evans, E. D. *Contemporary Influences in Early Childhood Education,* 2nd ed. New York: Holt, Rinehart and Winston, 1975.

Jensen, A. R. "How Much Can We Boost IQ and Scholastic Achievement?" *Harvard Educational Review,* 37(1), Winter, 1969, pp. 1–123.

———. *Straight Talk About Mental Tests.* New York: Free Press, 1981.

Kagan, J. S. "Inadequate Evidence and Illogical Conclusions," *Harvard Educational Review,* 39(2), Spring 1969, pp. 274–277.

McCandless, B. R. *Children: Behavior and Development,* 2nd ed. Hinsdale, Ill.: Dryden Press, 1967.

St. John, N. H. *School Desegregation Outcomes for Children.* New York: John Wiley, 1975.

Stephan, W. "School Desegregation: An Evaluation of Predictions Made in *Brown v. Board of Education,*" *Psychological Bulletin,* 85(2), March 1978, pp. 217–238.

Sex Differences and Gender-Role Development

11

PREVIEW

What are sex differences?

What is gender role?

What is the role of sex hormones in biological sex differences?

How do sex hormones affect human behavior?

What are the roles of reinforcement and punishment in gender-role development?

What is the role of modeling in gender-role development?

What is a cognitive theory of gender-role development?

How does Kohlberg describe gender-role development?

How do behaviorism and cognitive theory interact in determination of gender role?

What is the traditional male stereotype?

What is the traditional female stereotype?

What stereotypical differences between males and females have basis in fact?

What are limitations of traditional sex-role stereotypes?

What is psychological androgyny?

How do teachers contribute to gender-role stereotyping?

What is happening in education to help eliminate sexism?

What are some ways in which the teacher may help develop psychological androgyny?

What impact will changes in the American family have on the role of the teacher?

Fred is age 19. He is strong and athletic as well as independent and assertive. He is forceful in expressing his opinion and is known to be reliable and cool in a crisis. While dominant and aggressive, he is also known for his honesty and objectivity. He is somewhat detached and unemotional, but his analytical mind and ease at making decisions make him desirable to work with. In all, he is a typical male and an ideal leader. At present he is attending college and has not yet decided on a major but is considering architecture, engineering, and mathematics as possibilities. Whatever he does, he plans to be his own boss, achieve highly, and earn a good income.

Fran is also 19. She is very understanding, compassionate, and good at soothing the hurt feelings of others. Warm and friendly, she is also gentle and soft-spoken and even a bit shy. She believes in giving in rather than arguing or fighting and thinks a woman should be neither aggressive nor domineering. She is easily hurt, gets emotional in a crisis, and prefers to trust her feelings rather than logical analysis. Her friends enjoy her childlike nature and naïve charm as well as her patience and loyalty. She is almost always cheerful, loves children, and has always wanted to be either a teacher or a nurse. She makes good grades but has no real concern about great achievements or earning a high income.

How do these descriptions seem to you: far fetched or fairly typical? If the names were reversed, if Fran were linked to the first description and Fred to the second, would it still seem typical? This chapter explores masculinity and femininity in our culture and how the role of a teacher influences behaviors and values in this area.

Sex and Gender Role

Before proceeding with a discussion of masculinity and femininity as they exist in the United States today, it is necessary to distinguish between two terms: *sex* and *gender role.* Sex refers to the biological differences that exist between men and women. Gender role refers to the psychological associations that one makes with maleness or femaleness and the enactment of the association. In this section, we elaborate the distinction between these two terms and discuss the effect that each has on the development of the masculinity and femininity of an individual.

Sex

The most basic differences between men and women are biological. Some of these biological differences are obvious. A man has a penis and testes. A woman has a vagina, clitoris, ovaries, and breasts. These obvious differences are necessary for the differential roles that males and females play in the reproductive cycle of humans.

Underlying these obvious biological differences are differences that are not easily determined but that form the basis for the development of male or female sexual organs. The most basic distinguishing characteristic between the sexes lies in the chromosomes. A normal man has an X chromosome and a Y chromosome; a normal woman has two X chromosomes. It is this genetic difference, established at conception, between embryos that determines whether a fetus develops male or female reproductive organs.

If everything functions normally, the Y chromosome present in the male triggers the release of male hormones known as androgens. These androgens determine the development of the penis and testes. The X chromosomes of the female trigger the release of female hormones known as estrogen and progesterone. In the presence of these female hormones and in the absence of androgens, the fetus develops female reproductive organs. Occasionally, there is some abnormality in the genetic structure of the fetus or in the amount of male and female hormones present in a fetus. Excess androgens in a fetus that is genetically female or insufficient androgens in a genetic male may lead to the development of external sex organs that cannot be identified clearly as male or female. These individuals are called hermaphrodites, as they have the genitals and secondary sex characteristics of both sexes.

It has been shown in recent years that hormone levels in the fetus also affect the development of the brain. In particular, high levels of androgens in a male or female fetus tend to masculinize that part of the brain known as the hypothalamus. The hypothalamus triggers the release of male and female hormones at puberty (O'Leary, 1977).

Male and female hormones have been shown to affect the behavior dispositions of laboratory animals (Ward, 1974; Goy, 1975). The effects of these hormones on human behavior have been much more difficult to determine because of the ethical restrictions on modification of human beings to perform carefully controlled experimental research studies. Ehrhardt and Baker (1974), however, studied a number of genetic females and genetic males who had a condition known as AGS, in which the glands of the fetus released too many androgens. In the genetic female, this excess of androgens causes masculinization of the external genitalia but does not affect the internal reproductive organs. Excess androgens in the male fetus has no affect on the sexual organs.

Ehrhardt and Baker found that males with AGS showed more intense energy in play and sports than did males without AGS. Otherwise, the behavior of AGS males could not be differentiated from non-AGS males. In comparing AGS females whose sexual organ abnormalities had been corrected by surgery to non-AGS females (in this case, sisters and mothers), it was found that the AGS girls tended to be much more tomboyish.

383

That is, they showed much more energy in outdoor play, a preference for boys to girls as playmates, *low* interest in playing with dolls, and little rehearsal of the maternal role. However, these AGS girls were clearly identified in the female role, and their behavior was not considered abnormal. Ehrhardt and Baker concluded that it was unlikely that these AGS girls would show any more tendency toward lesbianism as adults than did their non-AGS sisters and mothers. A major conclusion reached as a result of this study was that "If it can be documented that prenatal hormone levels are among the factors that account for the wide range of temperamental differences and role aspirations within the female, and possibly also within the male, sex, a great variety of adult roles should be available and can be adequately fulfilled by both women and men, and they should be equally acceptable and respectable for either sex" (Ehrhardt and Baker, 1974, p. 50).

After puberty, sexual hormones also have some effect on human behavior, with females again being more affected than males (O'Leary, 1977). O'Leary based this conclusion on research that demonstrated that the administration of the female hormone, estrogen, had been effective in the treatment of depression experienced by women after childbirth and during menopause (Kane et al, 1969; Klaiber et al., 1971). Even with the cautious interpretation that hormones may affect female behavior at these critical periods in their lives, O'Leary stated that "at the human level . . . biologically based behavior dispositions may be modified by social factors" (1977, p. 29). In other words, the behavior of men and women at any point in time may be influenced by biological factors, but it is certainly influenced (probably more so) by learning.

Gender Role

As soon as a baby is born, the doctor examines its genitalia and calls it a boy or a girl. From that point forward, its gender is determined. As adults, we see important differences between the baby called "boy" and the one called "girl." These differences occur in dress, expressions, attitudes, values, and personality characteristics. The development of these differences in gender role begin much earlier than many people realize and continue throughout the life of the individual. We examine two different explanations as to how this development progresses. The first is an explanation of gender-role development from a behaviorist (S-R) viewpoint; the second is a cognitive developmental theory.

Before proceeding, however, we must point out that the terms "gender role" and "sex role" are used interchangeably in literature regarding differences between males and females. We also use the two terms as synonyms in the remainder of this chapter.

Behaviorism

There are two important aspects of the behaviorists' explanation of gender-role development. The first is that parents, teachers, and other adults in any culture have expectations as to how a boy or girl should behave. By communicating their expectations to a child, positively reinforcing desirable behaviors and punishing undesirable behaviors, adults strengthen behaviors in a child that are consistent with their understanding of male and female roles in the culture.

The reinforcement and establishment of sex-role behavior begins in infancy and continues throughout childhood. The first signs of differential expectations are seen in the fact that parents see female infants as more fragile than males (O'Leary, 1977). This differentiation is demonstrated in a tendency to be more concerned about illness in girls and in restrictions placed upon the physical activity of girls as they begin to walk, climb, and engage in other physical activities. These restrictions seem to result from a fear on the part of the parents that little girls are more subject to injury than little boys.

The reinforcement of gender-role behavior is also seen in the selection of clothing, toys, and other articles for infants and toddlers. Girls have traditionally been dressed in pink, red, or yellow, while boys are dressed in blue, green, or brown. Boys are dressed in pants; girls wear dresses (Lewis and Weinraub, 1974). Girls are given dolls and toy dishes to play with; boys get baseballs, footballs, and toy tools. Friends and strangers alike clearly expect to be able to identify a boy or girl baby by its appearance. They may even express negative feelings to the parent who dresses a child in a way that is considered inappropriate. We express embarrassmnt to the parents of a child when we mistakenly call their daughter "a little man" or call their son "a sweet girl." All these behaviors of parents and others communicate to the child that which is male and female. They also reinforce behaviors in the child that are consistent with the adults' conception of appropriate sex role.

Research attempts to establish positive reinforcement as an explanation of gender-role development beyond infancy have been largely unsuccessful. In fact, Maccoby and Jacklin (1974) concluded that there was no more tendency for parents to reinforce positively independence and aggression, behaviors typically believed to be male, in boys than in girls. The use of punishment, on the other hand, has been demonstrated clearly. The use of punishment in sex-role development occurs primarily in attempts to weaken certain behaviors in boys that are viewed as inappropriate for males (Fling and Manosevitz, 1972). "Be a man!" or "Don't be a sissy!" are typical negative statements made to boys in attempting to weaken undesirable behavior.

Punishment is not used to weaken behaviors in girls nearly as frequently as it is with boys. It seems to be all right for a girl to be a "tomboy," for we know she will outgrow it. Boys are never allowed to be sissies.

The adequacy of reinforcement theory as an explanation for sex-role development has been questioned consistently by psychologists, even though it does play a role. Probably more important in establishing sex role, however, is the second aspect of the behaviorists' explanation, modeling. The role of modeling is usually explained in terms of an identification between a child and the parent of the same sex. According to this explanation, a child will have firmly established itself as a boy or girl by about 3 years of age as a result of differential treatment and reinforcement as an infant. Once its gender is established, the child will identify with the parent of the same sex. Such identification will lead to the imitation of the behaviors of that parent; in other words, the child will model the same-sexed parent. These imitations occur without direct external reinforcement. Rather, they seem to be reinforcing in and of themselves.

The modeling of adult behavior is evidenced especially in the things that children say. You have only to listen to a portion of a conversation involving children before you begin to hear highly accurate reflections of the modeled parent's language patterns. This can be embarrassing when a 4-year-old imitates with the use of such words as damn, hell, or worse. How many times have parents said, "now, where did she learn that?" in an attempt to hide the embarrassment that results from hearing their child use some choice expression in the most inappropriate setting?

This same-sex identification theory seems to explain with accuracy a part of adult sex roles. But other parts of the adult sex role also come from modeling behaviors of other adults important to the child such as a grandparent, teacher, or neighbor (Bandura, 1969). In addition, modeling behavior continues into adulthood, and we see adults imitating the behaviors of friends, television and movie personalities, and others. But, at least part of the adult sex role of an individual is the result of identification with the parent of the same sex as a child (Brophy, 1977). However, considerable evidence suggests that the parent of the opposite sex also has a great influence on the adult sex role (O'Leary, 1977). In addition, Hetherington (1975) found that in some families one parent is dominant over the other. In these situations, the identification of the child will tend to be with the dominant parent who may or may not be the same sex as the child. In any case, the adult sex role of individuals can be explained, in part, as a modeling of adults who were important to the child.

While modeling of adult behavior can be used as a partial explanation of adult sex roles, it is inadequate as an explanation of childhood sex roles (Brophy, 1977; O'Leary, 1977). There is little question that boys do not act like men and girls do not act like women. Brophy concluded that "modeling does not involve watching and imitating the same sexed parent. Instead, it involves watching and imitating other children and same sexed models on television, in books, or in other media" (1977, p. 253). In other words, the sex-role behavior of children is partially the result of modeling, but it is not modeling the behavior of the same-sexed parent so much as the modeling of behaviors of members of the peer group.

Cognitive Theory

In contrast to the reinforcement and social learning theory explanations of sex-role development is the cognitive theory of Lawrence Kohlberg (1966). In this theory, Kohlberg, as a cognitive psychologist, is not concerned with reinforcement or imitation; rather, he views sex roles as concepts. This emphasis on concept reflects the cognitive aspect of Kohlberg's theory as it indicates that he is concentrating on the child's mental image or understanding of sex role and not just on observable behaviors. It is Kohlberg's contention that, since sex roles are understandings or concepts, they should go through developmental transformations that are consistent with Piaget's stages of cognitive development.

According to this theory, conceptions of sex roles are extremely important for two reasons. The first is that sex typing is universal. That is, it occurs in all cultures. To be sure, the nature of that sex typing is culture specific, but it does occur in all cultures. The second reason that sex-role concepts are important is that gender is the single category into which a child can place himself or herself that is unchanging. No matter how old a child gets, the child can depend on remaining male or female even though all other aspects of its identity will change. Kohlberg and Ullman (1974) state that in cases where gender reassignment has occurred, such as in the surgical and/or hormone modification of AGS females described earlier, the transformation had traumatic psychological effects. The only exceptions to this occurred if the child was reassigned before the ages of about 2 to 4. This seems to be clear evidence that gender identity is not fixed before that age. Once gender identity is established and the child has a self-concept in the only unchanging category possible, any change will have profound psychological implications.

By age 6, according to Kohlberg, gender identity is established firmly. While a child can identify its gender correctly as early as age 3 or 4, it is not until age 6 that this gender identity is clearly based on genital differences. At this point, the child will recognize that a girl cannot be a boy and a boy cannot be a girl. As the child develops this fixed gender identity, it also develops attitudes and preferences for sex roles. A boy cannot be a mother; neither would he want to be a nurse nor a secretary since these are girl jobs. A girl cannot be a father; neither would she want to be a doctor nor a fireman since these are boy jobs. A boy prefers playing with other boys because they are like him; girls prefer other girls because they are similar. Boys like fathers more than mothers, and girls prefer mothers because they are female. The preference even runs to toys and play activities. As 6-year-old Danny said when he refused to accept a girl's bike as a birthday gift, "A boy has to have boy things and a girl has to have girl things."

One aspect of sex typing in 6-year-olds that Kohlberg sees as being universal to all cultures is that distinctions are based on perceived physical attributes of men and women. Boys and girls alike see men as more pow-

KOHLBERG INTERVIEWS A 6-YEAR-OLD BOY*

Q. What are ladies like?
A. Ladies have long hair and men don't.

Q. How else are they different from men?
A. They wear lipstick and men don't.

Q. Why do girls get hurt more easily than boys?
A. Because the boys have tougher skin.

Q. Who should have a harder job?
A. The man. Because the woman wouldn't be that strong to do a hard job.

Q. Who should be the boss in a family?
A. The man. He is smarter because he works. If the lady was, then the lady wouldn't know what to do so very often.

Q. Could a man be a nurse?
A. He could still be in the hospital because the doctor is almost like a nurse. He could wear the stuff, but he would still be called a doctor.

*From L. Kohlberg and D. Z. Ullman, "Stages in the Development of Psychosexual Concepts and Attitudes," in R. C. Friedman et al., eds., *Sex Differences in Behavior,* pp. 214–216 (New York: John Wiley, 1974). Reprinted with permission.

erful, aggressive, authoritative, and smarter than females. This difference appears to result from the fact that the 6-year-old does not distinguish between physical and psychological attributes.

As children grow older, their conceptualization of gender role begins to change as their level of cognitive functioning changes. By the time children are 10 years old, they have at least two major characteristics that distinguish them from 6-year-olds. The first is that gender is no longer based strictly upon physical differences but can now be attributed to psychological differences as well. We see here that the child is able to categorize males and females on more than one characteristic, which, according to Piaget, cannot occur until the child develops decentration. According to Piaget, decentration begins to develop during the preoperational stage (ages 2–7) but is not completely present until concrete operations (ages 7–11). Thus, we see the consistency between Kohlberg's theory of sex-role development and Piaget's theory of cognitive development in that it isn't until about fifth grade that children are able to define sex role on more than a single characteristic.

The second major distinction between 10-year-olds and 6-year-olds in defining sex roles is that, for the 10-year-old, male and female are defined by the social role each plays. Whereas a 6-year-old defines sex role on the

basis of physical characteristics, the 10-year-old defines sex role on the
basis of social function. For the 10-year-old, a sex role is dependent upon
what society says it ought to be. In the 10-year-old's view, a mother stays
home and takes care of children because society says that is the way it is
supposed to be and she is expected to do it. Apparently, the 10-year-old
does not question whether or not there is moral justification for what
society expects. The only important concern is that it does have expectations and men and women must comply. In the words of a fifth-grader,
"Men should act like men and ladies like ladies. They should act like they
should" (Kohlberg and Ullman, 1974, p. 218).

As children begin to move into Piaget's stage of formal operations,
about age 11 and above, they begin to understand internal psychological
differences between men and women. Sex roles are no longer dependent
strictly upon physical differences and societal expectations. The individual
is free to choose to be masculine in some ways and feminine in others.
To be sure, the traditional sex-role stereotypes (we examine these in detail
in the next section) of a culture are present. For example, the 13-year-old
sees women as gentle and emotional and men as independent and aggressive. But the individual is now seen as determining the extent to which
he or she chooses to reflect these stereotypical characteristics. In other
words, the inner psychological makeup of the individuals can determine
just how masculine or how feminine the person is. This inner determination of sex roles is seen clearly as being distinct from society's expectations. However, the early teenager has no sex-role alternatives to the
ones that exist in society. As a result, the 13-year-old's conception of sex
roles is still based largely upon societal expectations.

*Sex Differences and
Gender-Role Development*

KOHLBERG INTERVIEWS A 10-YEAR-OLD*

Q. How come girls like to stay home and do the housekeeping?
A. I don't know, maybe they like to do what their mother does. Because they are going to be mothers.

Q. Who is smarter in general, men or women?
A. Men, because they have to do a lot of things, like thinking. They have to think a lot and they have to work and they have to figure things out.

Q. Could a man be a nurse?
A. It is okay because they can do what they want. But I still think a boy should become a doctor because I think a doctor's job is mostly for men, not women.

*From L. Kohlberg and D.Z. Ullman, "Stages in the Development of Psychosexual Concepts and Attitudes," in R.C. Friedman et al., eds., *Sex Differences in Behavior,* pp. 217–218 (New York: John Wiley, 1974). Reprinted with permission.

While the 13-year-old is seen as being in a transitional stage in which psychological differences determine sex roles but, in the absence of alternatives, sex role is still defined by society, college students recognize that sex roles are not innate. They are defined by society and are internalized by individuals within the society. College students can define ideal sex roles. In these definitions, they attempt to balance physical and psychological commonalities between men and women. There is an attempt to define sex roles based on a concept of equality between the sexes. Yet college students recognize that their ideal definitions may be in conflict with the societal expectations that they have internalized. Therefore, their personal behavior and emotional reactions to violations of long-standing sex role definitions may be inconsistent with their own idealized definition. According to Kohlberg, the ways in which the conflict is resolved are unclear. Certainly, current events and recent history regarding changing roles of men and women in the United States indicate that the conflicts exist. Ways of resolving the conflicts may not be completely clear, but one factor that many believe will have a significant impact is the elimination of sex-role stereotyping that occurs in schools. We examine recommendations as to how this may be accomplished later in the chapter.

As we pointed out with respect to other developmental stage theories, Kohlberg's stages of psychosexual development are not rigid. Individuals may reflect characteristics of several stages at one time and may fluctuate between one stage and another in their thinking. Also, what is learned in any stage is culture specific. In many cultures, what is clearly defined as masculine in the United States is considered more appropriate for females. Sex-role development does occur in all cultures, and children will tend to learn the prevailing definitions of sex role in the culture during the period in which they are growing.

Interaction of Behaviorism and Cognitive Theory

Kohlberg's theory is based upon the belief that gender-role development occurs through maturation. While consistent with Piaget's stages of cognitive development, Kohlberg's theory fails to explain exactly how gender identity and gender role are learned. It also fails to explain how change in gender role may be brought about.

In reality, gender-role development is the result of a complex interaction of reinforcement, modeling, and maturation. The exact nature of this interaction and the degree to which each of the various modes of learning influences that interaction have not been specified. It is only important to recognize at this point that, as a teacher, you will influence a child's conception of gender role through communication of your expectation as to appropriate gender-role behaviors, through use of reinforcement and punishment, and through serving as gender-role model. It is also important to realize that children's conceptions of sex role at any given time depend on their level of cognitive functioning. If you keep this in mind, it will not surprise you that a 6-year-old boy is more of a male chauvinist than any man you have ever known. The child's chauvinism results from his inability to define sex role on more than the single characteristic of physical differences and his tendency to identify with those who are like him. You can rest assured that maturation and learning will temper this chauvinism.

391

Gender-Role Stereotypes

Males and females in American culture have traditionally had distinctive gender roles. These have been with us for so long that we frequently forget that gender roles are not innate differences but primarily learned behaviors. In this section, we examine stereotypes of masculinity and femininity that have been traditionally held in the United States, point out which characteristics have foundation in fact, and discuss limitations of sexual stereotyping.

Traditional Masculinity

A close look at traditional masculinity as seen in early American life, and still hanging on in twentieth century, finds a composite of traits not all of which are consistent with each other. The traditional male is a source of power and toughness, reacting with courage in dangerous situations. He is tight-lipped and controls his emotions, preferring action to words. He doesn't cry or show fear, and he is cool and level-headed in a crisis.

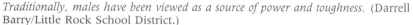

Traditionally, males have been viewed as a source of power and toughness. (Darrell Barry/Little Rock School District.)

Characteristics	Masculine Traits
I. Physical	Virile, athletic, strong
	Sloppy, worry less about appearance and aging
	Brave
II. Functional	Breadwinner, provider
III. Sexual	Sexually aggressive, experienced
	Single status acceptable; male "caught" by spouse
IV. Emotional	Unemotional, stoic
V. Intellectual	Logical, intellectual, rational, objective, scientific
	Practical
	Mechanical
	Public awareness, activity, contributor to society
VI. Interpersonal	Leader, dominating
	Disciplinarian
	Independent, free, individualistic
	Demanding
VII. Other personal	Aggressive
	Success oriented, ambitious
	Proud, egotistical, confident
	Moral, trustworthy
	Decisive
	Competitive
	Uninhibited, adventurous

Table 11.1
*Traditional Masculine Traits as Seen by American College Students**

*Adapted from Janet Saltzman Chafetz, *Masculine, Feminine, or Human,* 2nd ed. (Itasca, Ill.: F. E. Peacock, 1978), pp. 38–39. Reproduced by permission of the publisher, F. E. Peacock Publishers, Inc., Itasca, Illinois.

Problems are solved through logic, reason, and force, if necessary. Such a man finds his identity through career and achievement, primarily through competing with other men, and a large part of his everyday life is absorbed in "making it in a dog-eat-dog world." He is the financial provider for his wife and family, the authority on matters financial or logical, and the head of the family (Brenton, 1966).

More specific aspects of masculinity in modern times were identified by Janet Chafetz. She asked a group of college students to list the words that they thought Americans would use in describing masculinity. The results of that survey of masculinity are outlined in Table 11.1.

Along with the characteristics described in Table 11.1, males are also seen as being the more important sex in terms of careers, achievement, running things, and making decisions. This image of the man as more important than the woman except in the area of bearing and raising children is claimed by many to be nature's way since it is found not just in America but in most, if not all, cultures.

Even before the dawn of history, scientists believe, man became the ruler of the roost, establishing the design for living that generally prevails today. Everywhere, even if women are highly regarded, the activities of men are valued more than those of women. It matters not a whit how a society allocates roles and tasks between the sexes; those that belong to men inevitably count for more in the eyes of the whole community. [Swerdloff, 1975, p. 9]

Traditional Femininity

If the traditional view depicts males as independent, assertive, strong, aggressive, competitive, and responsible for pursuing a career and supporting a family, then what about females? Why, of course, the woman's role is in the home: as mother, cook, housekeeper, supporter, and companion to her husband.

In this traditional view, woman is not only tied to "home and hearth." She is also tied to certain traits such as sensitivity, emotionality, and feeling for others. Her dependency and other-directedness make her ideal for roles that involve serving others, and she is seen as submissive, cheerful, helpful, affectionate, loyal, and sympathetic. Table 11.2 presents the terms that college students used to describe femininity in Chafetz's study.

These requirements for being feminine in the traditional sense lead to a conception of "the woman as an ornament." This means that the attractive, well-groomed, clean, and pretty woman is displayed by the proud father, husband, or boyfriend. The little girl who is to stay clean and pretty for her parents and teachers grows into the perfumed and pretty adolescent wanting to attract a boy and then becomes the attractive and fashionable wife. The cosmetics, clothing, and accessories industries attest to the strength of these demands.

One of the first things I found out in working with women and health is that absolutely every woman, no matter what she looks like, thinks something about her is ugly. . . . We show our best friend a photo of the two of us taken last

Traditionally, females have been viewed as mothers, cooks, and housekeepers. (Arkansas State Department of Education.)

Characteristics	Feminine Traits
I. Physical	Weak, helpless, dainty, nonathletic
	Worry about appearance and aging
	Sensual
	Graceful
II. Functional	Domestic
	Maternal, involved with children
	Churchgoing
III. Sexual	Virginal, inexperienced; holds to double standard
	Must be married; female "catches" spouse
	Sexually passive, uninterested
	Responsible for birth control
	Seductive, flirtatious
IV. Emotional	Emotional, sentimental, romantic
	Can cry
	Expressive
	Compassionate
	Nervous, insecure, fearful
V. Intellectual	Scatterbrained, frivolous, shallow, inconsistent, intuitive
	Impractical
	Perceptive, sensitive
	"Arty"
	Idealistic, humanistic
VI. Interpersonal	Petty, flirty, coy, gossipy, catty, sneaky, fickle
	Dependent, overprotected, responsive
	Status conscious and competitive, refined, adept in social graces
	Follower, subservient, submissive
VII. Other personal	Self-conscious, easily intimidated, modest, shy, sweet
	Patient
	Vain
	Affectionate, gentle, tender, soft
	Not aggressive, quiet, passive
	Tardy
	Innocent
	Noncompetitive

Table 11.2
Traditional Feminine Traits as Seen by American College Students*

*Adapted from Janet Saltzman Chafetz, *Masculine, Feminine, or Human,* 2nd ed. (Itasca, Ill.: F. E. Peacock, 1978), pp. 38–39. Reproduced by permission of the publisher, F. E. Peacock Publishers, Inc., Itasca, Illinois.

summer; she is lean and beautiful in her bikini. "What a terrible picture!" she cries, and tears it up. "I'm going on a diet!" Nothing we say can persuade her that she is already svelte and slim. [Friday, 1977, pp. 139, 148]

Documented Differences

Obviously, some of the stereotypical differences presented in Tables 11.1 and 11.2 are pure myths. On the other hand, others seem to have some basis in fact. Maccoby and Jacklin (1974) attempted to distinguish between fiction and fact in male and female stereotypes. They concluded that there is no basis for such conclusions as girls are more socially oriented than boys, girls are more influenced by peer groups than boys, and girls are better at simple rote learning or repetitive tasks than boys. Maccoby and Jacklin (1974) also concluded that boys are not more analytical than girls, boys are affected as much by heredity as girls, and boys are not more achievement motivated than girls. Finally, boys and girls are equally adept at using the auditory and visual senses.

Some differences between males and females have been well documented by research studies (Maccoby and Jacklin, 1974). Boys are better than girls in mathematical skills. Girls are better than boys in tasks requiring verbal ability. Boys have more ability than girls in tasks requiring spatial ability. Boys do appear to be more aggressive than girls.

It should be noted that, even though these differences have been documented in research, they are based on averages. They may or may not hold for any individual girl or boy. In addition, documentation of differences does not mean that the reasons for the differences are known. We cannot conclude that the differences are innate or that they are the result of learning simply because we know they exist. Our previous discussion on the limited effects of biological determination of behavior may indicate that the differences are more the result of learning than of biological factors.

Limitations of the Stereotypes

The disadvantages of the traditional view of masculinity and femininity are becoming increasingly obvious, although the view still has very strong defenders. *Probably the biggest disadvantage, if adhered to rigidly, is that a stereotype limits both males and females to being only partial persons.* The man who is tough, competitive, unemotional, and hardworking might be a success on his job but may be missing a lot in life because of his inability to express emotions and his insensitivity to others. An avoidance of personal involvement, reluctance to enjoy leisure time, and a compulsion to get ahead in a career may be additional manifestations of the "manly" role. The woman who is a devoted wife and mother, submissive, sensitive, and emotional may be happy with this role, but she may also resent the fact that she was never encouraged to grow, achieve, compete, and to develop in the world outside the home. The little boy who strains to act tough, hide his feelings, compete, and be the "strong silent" hero may be inhibiting part of his personality, as does the little girl who limits her horizons in life to being a helpful supporter of men. It may be that little girls should be encouraged to dream of being not only teachers, nurses, or secretaries, even though these are important occupations.

The differences in male and female outlooks and how these differences become part of the crises that adults face in their lives have been detailed in books on adult personality development by Roger Gould (1978) and

Gail Sheehy (1976). They paint a picture of the male, raised to compete and achieve, wrapped up in his career in his twenties, uneasy and aware that something is missing in his thirties, and experiencing a "midlife crisis" in his forties. This crisis is resolved with a different outlook toward work and achievement and probably renewed interest in interpersonal relationships and aspects of life other than work. If it is not resolved, the midlife crisis leads to a stagnation or deterioration of the individual. According to Gould and Sheehy, the woman is completely wrapped up in her home and family in her twenties, becomes aware that something is missing in her thirties, and may turn to work, career, and other pursuits *outside* the home by age 40. These changes in orientation cause considerable strife in marriages because the man and woman are obviously going in different directions.

Although the "typical boy" as described by stereotype probably does not exist, let us examine a hypothetical boy, we'll call him Mark, who epitomizes all the traditional male characteristics.

We immediately note a number of problems. Mark is constantly comparing his performance with that of other boys to judge whether he is acceptable. Being a "chicken" is about the worst fate that could befall him. He learned not to cry, even when hurt, long ago, and now he has learned to hold back anger, affection, and anxiety also. He shies away from music and art, even though he has obvious talents in these areas because they are not manly. He can't stand to be called a sissy. He'll talk about sports, cars, and even sexy jokes, but seems either incapable or just uninterested in talking about personal matters. Everything he does, even in asking a girl for a date, is couched in terms of competition. He gets along great with the other guys but has no one to whom he can reveal his deepest thoughts. He has not shown much interest in studying until now, but at age 16 he is starting to realize that the most important thing is to do well in college and become a lawyer to be a success in life. Just as being a success in athletics has made him a worthwhile adolescent, he believes that any problem can be solved by attacking it physically. Even girls are seen as a challenge for him to conquer to prove his manhood to the other guys.

Would it not be better for Mark to temper his competitiveness and toughness with expressions of feelings and acceptance of emotions? Would he not profit from closer interpersonal relations, better understanding of others, freedom to pursue art and music without embarrassment, less concern about competition, a wider view of all those things in life that are important besides competitive success and a career? In other words, wouldn't he be a better and happier person if he could *combine* the best of both stereotypes in his makeup rather than being so painfully and self-consciously "male"?

Look now at the "typical girl" as described by the traditional stereotype. We'll call her Grace. Grace is a darling girl, always bubbly and cheerful. She goes steady with the varsity quarterback and was elected homecoming queen this year. She has always made excellent grades but has no long-term educational plans other than possibly teaching for a few years before marrying and having a family. She loves art and literature, is close to her parents and family, and is a little embarrassed that she was awarded an "A" in algebra. She carefully avoids being labeled "brain" and would deliberately get poor grades if necessary to be popular and have dates. She loves high school, especially her friends and the social life. She can talk for hours with her friends, the main topic being other adolescents. When a crisis occurs, she usually cries. On occasions when she has competed vigorously and won, she has felt a little worried and embarrassed at what others would think of her. At this point in life, she is very happy because she has close friends and a steady boyfriend and is popular and having fun. Her main ambition in life is to fall in love and get married.

Once again, the reader might ask "So what's wrong with this? Here is a happy, nice girl who will make a good wife and mother. Why not leave well enough alone?" And once again, the humanist answers that this is too limiting, too dehumanizing a model. Should not Grace be free to achieve and compete without fear of "not being feminine"? Wouldn't it be better if she could express anger, hostility, and aggression as freely as boys? Wouldn't it be better for Grace to be an athletic, strong, independent, logical, leader and winner *as well as* sensitive, lovable, understanding, and all the characteristics already described? And why shouldn't she plan for careers and life work along with marriage and a family? Shouldn't her dreams go on beyond marriage, just as Mark's do?

There is no reason why a woman cannot be attractive and competitive. (SIUC Photographic Service.)

The Advantages of Psychological Androgyny

The idea of an individual, regardless which sex, having a well-rounded combination of *both* masculine and feminine traits (in terms of the traditional model, that is) is not really new. The psychologically androgynous person is someone who enjoys the best of both worlds, you might say—the best of masculinity and the best of femininity, as defined earlier. An androgynous woman would be "feminine" in terms of sensitivity, attractiveness, understanding, patience, artistic, and with good personal relations, or some such combination of "feminine" traits, but would also be able to compete, strive to win, assert herself, use logic and reason, and be independent—in other words, add a number of useful "masculine" traits to her personality. In like manner, the androgynous man might be strong, independent, aggressive, and successful but also sensitive, understanding, able to accept and express emotion, in tune with his feelings, supportive of others, and close to his family.

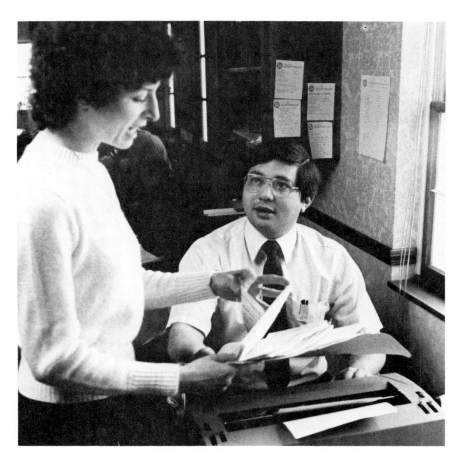

Reversals of traditional sex roles in the world of business are becoming more common. (Bernie Weithorn/SIUC Photographic Service.)

Student Variables:
Looking at the Individual

The point is *not* to advocate that this is how everyone should be but, instead, to note that the restrictions of the old stereotypes must be removed so that *each person* is free to develop whatever combination of traits suits him or her. It would be naïve to believe that many males would exhibit feminine but not masculine traits in complete reversal of the old model or that many females would reject all feminine traits in exchange for masculine, but even this should be possible. And an old-fashioned "John Wayne" male or "Ginger Rogers" female is perfectly all right as long as the cards are not stacked so that this is the *only* thing they can be. There happens to be special significance in certain "masculine" traits, such as assertiveness, independence, and achievement because these are important for career success in our culture. The point is that personality traits such as these should be valued for their usefulness in society rather than the sex of the individual displaying them.

NOT ONLY SUGAR AND SPICE

Natalie is an unusual girl. She loves sports and at age 10 she can hold her own against any boy in football, baseball, basketball, wrestling, or any other sport. She is not a sissy and she refuses to cry even when injured. When a game is organized on the playground, Natalie is usually in the midst of things, and she is almost always captain of one of the teams. She loves to compete, especially to win, and stay cool and in control in the toughest situation. She is a good student, but sometimes gets into trouble for challenging the rules. When she grows up, she would like to be a professional athlete, but barring this, she thinks she'll go into some branch of engineering. She is very good at math and science.

But this is not the total picture of Natalie, for she also expresses her emotions openly, and although she holds back the tears if injured in a game, she cries in situations where her feelings are hurt. She has many close friends of both sexes, and she is looking forward to dating boys when she is old enough. She loves art, and also plays the violin in the school orchestra. Although she'll argue and stand up for her rights verbally, she doesn't believe in fighting physically like the boys do. She loves her parents and her close friends very much, and she is very good at empathizing with the feelings of others. In addition to her plans of a career in athletics or in engineering, she also plans to fall in love, get married, and have children. In spite of her "tomboy" behavior, she looks forward to being a woman and wants to be attractive to males.

Is Natalie unusual? Not really, since many girls today could be seen to fit this description. Often called "tomboys," these girls are generally healthy and do well later in adolescence and adulthood. Natalie is merely an androgynous female, which means that she has many of the characteristics and behaviors of both sexes. Most writers believe that such a combination of the traits of both sexes is healthy, both for males and females, and that it is an improvement over the stereotyped masculine and feminine roles of the past.

In our culture today, there is an ever-increasing need for women to work outside the home. Many families' financial security requires both the husband and wife to have income-producing jobs. A woman who is strongly imbued with the traditional views of femininity not only has a difficult time in being aggressive, assertive, and competitive in the world of work, but also feels a failure in a feminine sense. Somehow, she feels, she is not a good wife, mother, and homemaker because of her job outside the home and the masculine characteristics it requires. An androgynous female is able to adjust to the demands of both the competitive job outside the home and her homemaker's role of wife and mother, without feeling that it decreases her stature as a woman.

Can Teachers Help?

Teachers are in a position to aid in freeing children from the restrictions of the old stereotypes, but unfortunately teachers sometimes only add to the restrictions. When teachers encourage boys to be active leaders and girls to be followers, they are reinforcing the old stereotype. When we use examples of males as leaders, achievers, adventurers, and thinkers and females as submissive, flighty, dependent mothers and homemakers, we are encouraging the old restrictions. When a school has all female teachers, but all male administrators (true especially of some elementary schools), the school is supporting the old tradition. When books depict males as active and courageous doers and seekers, workers, doctors, pilots, truck drivers, as well as husbands and fathers, while depicting females as helpless victims, talkers, obedient daughters, wives, and mothers, with the only careers ever mentioned those of teacher, nurse, and secretary, they are supporting the old restrictions. Studies of elementary textbooks find that the majority of the characters and almost all heroes are male (Britton and Lumpkin, 1977).

What teachers do to perpetuate the old stereotypes does not stop in the classroom. The stress on male athletic achievement with females watching, supporting, and cheerleading falls right into the old stereotype. So does the *expectation* that males will be good at, and therefore interested in, math, science, and mechanical and physical things, while girls are interested and good at English, art, and the humanities. The type of advice given to high school students in regard to courses, programs, career plans, and life goals often supports traditional male-female gender typing.

When history is taught as a male subject, virtually ignoring any but the more amusing female figures, when physics is seen as a "male" subject and poetry as "female," when the important leadership roles go automatically to boys, when misbehaving is seen as masculine and conforming

401

as feminine, when a teacher shifts gears in speaking to a male versus a female versus a mixed group, when sex education is offered in classes segregated by sex—all this implies support of the old traditional stereotypes of masculinity and femininity.

What Is Happening Today?

Title IX of the "Education Amendments," passed by the federal government in 1972, states that

> No person shall, on the basis of sex, be excluded from participation, be denied the benefits of, or be subjected to discrimination under any education program or activity receiving federal assistance. [Public Law 92-318, 86 STAT. 373].

Title IX was implemented beginning in 1975. Its effects have been observable in the tremendous growth in women's athletics since that time. Beginning at the elementary school level, all schools receiving federal funds must provide equal facilities for females and males. While many would argue as to whether or not equality has been achieved, women's athletic programs have certainly expanded tremendously at all educational levels since 1975.

Changes in other aspects of the school's curricula have not been as dramatic. Yet some advances seem to have been made toward equality. We see women's studies programs emerging in colleges, secondary schools, and elementary schools. The major purpose of these programs is to achieve psychological androgyny (McClure and McClure, 1977). In elementary schools and secondary schools, women's studies refers to curricular, extracurricular, and indirect teaching activities designed to help students recognize the role of women. According to McClure and McClure (1977), women's studies may include such things as

1. A discussion in eighth grade about careers in science and math.
2. A discussion about sexist language.
3. A library display of books about women in mathematics.
4. A bulletin board about the changing roles of men and women.
5. A lesson in psychology class about men and women and attitudes toward success.

While this is a very limited set of examples regarding activities that could be included in women's studies, it provides an indication that most activities of the teacher and school can be used to help eliminate sex-role stereotyping.

> This integration is not likely to occur for some time. After all, the problem of stereotyped sex roles touches upon all our lives, male and female. Changes in these roles affect the cognitive structures around which we have organized most of what we know about humanity. . . . The task before us is immense. [McClure and McClure, 1977, p. 11]

Recommendations for Teachers

One of the first constructive things that teachers can do in this area is to be aware of and try to minimize the use of sexist examples in textbooks, films, and other materials. By sexist examples, we mean males and females presented in ways that rigidly support the traditional stereotypes. Research on textbooks and classroom material has found them loaded with blatantly sexist outlooks and examples, and they can easily go unnoticed since we are so deeply immersed in our own culture. If your textbook is the only one, or perhaps the best one available, and yet presents mostly male heroes, an image of "male" as the independent doer and "female" as the dependent follower, or any of the other traditional views, you can at least point this out and add more balanced examples of your own. You can also look for a textbook that gives a more balanced picture.

Boys in sewing and cooking classes are becoming common. (University of Arkansas.)

An analysis of 2,760 stories in 134 books found two and a half times as many stories about boys as about girls. These books suggested 147 career possibilities for boys while mentioning only 26—mothers, nurses, librarians and the like—for girls. Moreover, the male characters seemed to have a monopoly on personality traits considered desirable in late 20th century America. [Swerdloff, 1975, p. 161]

Sometimes it helps to present examples *deliberately* that conflict with the traditional model. To talk about a doctor or lawyer and deliberately make the example a female (but avoiding the term ''a woman doctor,'' since you wouldn't qualify ''a man doctor'' in the same apologetic fashion) helps to alert students to the fact that males don't ''own'' these professions. In the same way, examples of a male telephone operator, cook, or secretary help to jolt old stereotypes. When students are daydreaming about the future, girls should be encouraged to daydream about being pilots, athletes, scientists, or world travelers right along with boys, and both sexes should also dream about being spouses and parents. Both sexes need to be aware of the infinite possibilities in life.

A second way in which teachers can help concerns the question ''What kind of model are you?'' The obviously strong and athletic male teacher who also shows sensitivity and understanding and expresses feelings is helping children to learn that being ''masculine'' can include all these things. The charming and pretty female teacher who can be assertive, competitive, and cool and logical is showing children that you can still be ''feminine'' and possess these characteristics. The teacher can help children to see that each individual is different and that each can have a combination of so-called ''masculine'' and ''feminine'' characteristics and still be very much a man or a woman. By avoiding the perpetuating of old myths as well as opening up the possibility of androgyny, you are not ''brainwashing'' the students but instead doing exactly the opposite—freeing them from possible brainwashing.

In the long run, education probably will be the most effective force in establishing an equitable balance between the sexes. For generations are now being brought up that no longer subscribe to the old stereotypes. The behavioral changes that were initiated in the '60's and '70's are still gathering momentum, and only history will be able to say how profound their effect will be on the relationships of men and women. [Swerdloff, 1975, p. 161]

In the area of adult roles, which are being molded from kindergarten on, it is not just a question of allowing students to see career possibilities as open to both sexes. It is important also to stress that personal relationships and domestic roles apply to both sexes. Males become husbands and fathers just as often as females become wives and mothers, and interpersonal and social skills are just as important to both sexes. It is wrong to define either male or female solely on the basis of the job they do (''I'm a doctor's wife,'' ''a minister's father,'' ''a con man's brother''). Teachers must consistently emulate the humanist sentiment, ''Let each become what each is capable of and wants to become.''

Girls athletics has grown rapidly since 1975 when Title IX was implemented. (Gerald Updike.)

It is not always easy to do these things, since it means that you must show respect and understanding for all. The little girl in the dainty pink dress with the sweet, shy smile who would do anything to please the teacher is just as deserving as the girl in the next row who has learned to be aggressive, competitive, and independent. The fellow in back who is all wrapped up in proving how tough he is and how much pain he can stand cannot be condemned. The teacher is part of the school's function of offering the opportunity to grow and change, but the teacher does not determine the specific results for each student. Two key areas are to help boys to learn how to be tender and express emotions and to help girls to get over their fear of competition and success.

Although there is nothing automatically wrong with establishing all-boy or all-girl groups for instruction, it sometimes is done in a way that perpetuates traditional stereotypes. Does it really make sense to have homerooms that are all male or all female? When sex education is dispensed to one sex at a time, isn't this missing an important part of the subject? Is having babies really of interest only to girls? Can segregated physical education classes really be justified, outside of actual contact sports? Should industrial arts be taken by boys only—or even mostly—and home economics limited to girls? It is hoped that we have come a long way from the days when it was permissible for a boy to take typing with all those girls for one semester if he insisted, but something must really be wrong if he wanted to take a *second* semester.

Another point that should not be overlooked is that of encouraging students to *talk about* problems in this area. Even though they might be adjusting to the new ways better than their parents and teachers, students

405

U.S. Supreme Court Justice Sandra Day O'Connor provides a successful role model for females.

are bound to have some misconceptions, differences, and concerns. Discussing these with members of both sexes helps to increase awareness and insight into self as well as others. Discussions of this sort can be worked into almost any subject.

Finally, balancing males and females in the different areas of the teaching profession would help. Children need to have male as well as female teachers at all levels, even kindergarten, and in all subjects. This includes females in math, science, shop, agriculture, and coaching, as well as males in lower elementary, art, music, literature, and commercial subjects. It also means a better balance of males and females in counseling, administrative positions, and auxiliary personnel (such as psychologists and social workers) and even in such jobs as bus driver and custodian. Only when these are present as natural parts of the environment can children feel free to explore all the possibilities available to them in life.

A final note: some of the worst perpetuators of blatant sexist models are the students themselves, particularly adolescents. Sexism in textbooks and role models have been discussed in detail in the literature relating to the elementary school years, but the adolescent peer culture as a bastion of traditional masculine and feminine stereotypes has not received much attention. Those of you who intend to teach at the secondary level should be aware of this problem and think of ways in which to combat it.

What is the traditional view of an American family? A substantial homestead, with a father and mother together for life, a number of children created by that marriage, various possessions as symbolic of family history and success, and some tie-in with grandparents, cousins, aunts, and uncles? Both parents clearly present, with mother running the home on a day-to-day basis and father as the breadwinner and head of the family? This family is seen as a unit, with values and traditions in common and the members gaining not only physical succorance but also psychological, social, and even recreational support within the family. In this view the family is clearly an important influence in one's life.

But how accurate is this picture when compared with statistics of what is currently happening to American families? Nearly half the nation's mothers work outside the home today, with 40% of the mothers with children below school age being so employed. Thirty-five percent of all children grow up in situations where only one parent is present during a significant portion of their childhood, and one in nine is raised in homes where one or both parents are not the biological parents. As a typical example, 1,182,000 divorces were granted to Americans in 1980 (National Center for Health Statistics, 1981). Data from previous years tells us we can safely assume an average of one child per divorce indicating that more than 1,000,000 children were affected by divorce in 1980. More and more, children grow up in what may be labeled "broken homes," if the criterion used is that of both biological parents present in the home, and an untold number live in unhappy homes with no close family ties.

In addition to divorces, single-parent families, and "broken" homes, the figures on child abuse, wife abuse, and desertion are also discouraging. No figures are available on psychological and verbal abuse, but the reported figures of physical abuse are staggering. What kind of image of masculine and feminine can a child internalize in a home where mother, father, or children are beaten physically? We also have figures on runaway children (both figurative and literal), runaway wives, and runaway husbands. A picture of a besieged family, falling apart under the pressures of modern life, easily emerges from these statistics. Each member of this family is going his or her own way, little if any communication is taking place, and the home becomes a place to sleep and eat only. The parents have lost control of the family, and their values are not predominant.

Pictures such as those just cited have been painted in numerous articles tabulating the many ways in which the family is crumbling in modern America. One could easily get the idea that the situation is hopeless, that the teacher can count on no help at all from the family.

What are the facts? For one thing, such concerns over the demise of the American family are as old as the country itself. This institution has *always* been under pressure, but it has survived. Second, the traditional

407

family painted earlier is becoming rare, with a much more mobile and limited family replacing it. Grandparents, aunts, uncles, and cousins are rarely a crucial part of daily family life nowadays. Third, it is true that there are more divorces and hence more families without biological parents present. Fourth, more women *do* work outside the home today, and the roles of mother and father are not as clear as they once were. And it seems clear that the old picture of children being "seen and not heard" or afraid to question parents out of respect for authority is less common also.

The effects of these changes are debatable, however. Repeated instances of strong family ties under unlikely conditions in which quality of a family's time together seems more important than the quantity can be found. Children from single-parent families are not necessarily neurotic or unhappy, and mothers who work often have closer contact with their children than do mothers who stay home. The mobility of modern life can draw families closer together instead of separating them further, and the family can become a place of safety in a world of flux. For the teacher, it is important to recognize the variety of family situations, the high number of children who come from situations other than the so-called "normal" family, and the fact that the circumstances at home are sometimes horrible, with obvious effects on the child in school. Beyond this, a true tolerance for differences in family backgrounds, and an awareness that the teacher can provide a nurturing adult model that may be missing at home, can be helpful to the teacher.

Summary

Sex refers to the biological aspects of the human body that determine an individual's role in the reproductive cycle. The external sexual differences between individuals, which are obvious, are based upon genes and hormones. The sexual hormones of an individual do have some influence on behavior disposition but probably not as much learning.

Gender role refers to the psychological association that one makes with male or female and the enactment of those associations. It is in gender role that we see the values and personality characteristics of masculinity and femininity.

There are two important aspects of the behaviorists' explanation of gender-role development. The first is the use of reinforcement theory to strengthen behaviors considered appropriate for a given sex. Research has been unable to document the use of positive reinforcement in gender-role development, but it has demonstrated that punishment is used to suppress undesirable behaviors in boys. The second aspect of the behaviorists' explanation of gender-role development is modeling. The adult gender role is explained in part as a modeling or imitation of same-sexed parents, opposite-sexed parents, or the dominant parent. Modeling of other important individuals in a child's life and adult peers also explains part of the adult gender role.

Kohlberg presented a cognitive theory of gender-role development that is consistent with Piaget's stages of cognitive development. In this theory, Kohlberg indicated that the important factor in explaining gender role is one's conception of that role. This conception changes as one matures and becomes capable of decentration and formal operations. Actual gender-role development can be thought of best as a complex interaction of reinforcement, modeling, and maturation through cognitive stages.

Traditional stereotypes of males and females are presented in this chaper. Instilling these stereotypes in children is not consistent with humanistic ideals. Males would be better off if they could temper their competitive natures with expressions of feelings and acceptance of others. Females would probably be happier if they could express aggression and independence as freely as males.

The idea of combining the best of both sexes into a complete and well-rounded individual is called psychological androgyny. The point is not to advocate that this is how everyone should be but, instead, that the restrictions of the old stereotypes must be removed so that each person is free to develop whatever combination of traits suits him or her. Teachers should encourage each individual to be and become all that each is capable and desirous of being.

Specific things that teachers can do in the classroom are to minimize the use of sexist examples in textbooks, films, and other materials; present examples that conflict with the traditional models; be a model of a well-rounded, self-actualizing individual; encourage girls to pursue all career possibilities; stress the importance of home and family roles to the male; and encourage all children to be themselves. The teacher must also combat the extent to which children and adolescents themselves perpetuate blatant sexist models.

An additional area of change is that within the American family. The traditional model of father at work and mother at home with the children is rapidly breaking down. In addition to both parents working, the effect of divorce and other forms of broken homes are widespread. The teacher must learn to adapt to and to work with all the variations of family and home situation that children face.

1. What is the earliest event in your life in which you remember realizing that you were male or female? What did your parents do to develop your sex-appropriate behavior? Was your conception of masculinity and femininity in line with the traditional stereotypes?
2. What should the teacher do if a boy in his or her fifth grade class displays extreme behaviors of the opposite sex (e.g., a real "sissy")? Is this the same situation as a girl who displays extreme behaviors of the opposite sex (e.g., a "tomboy")? How do you explain any difference in reaction to these two individuals?

76

2

3. How much have the conceptions of masculinity and femininity changed since you were a child? Do these changing conceptions present problems for the teacher in the classroom? What is the role of the teacher in regard to the changing view of what is masculine and what is feminine?
4. Much has been made about how the traditional view of femininity is demeaning to the woman and in many ways puts her at a disadvantage. Can you suggest a number of ways that the traditional views of masculine are bad for the male?
5. What is it about the traditional view of femininity that causes women to fear success? Are there any ways in which modern views of femininity can create new problems for the female?
6. What kind of problems might you run into if you were in a very traditional school and were trying to encourage androgyny in your students? How might you resolve some of the misunderstandings that this might cause among colleagues and parents?

References

Bandura, A. "Social Learning Theory of Identificatory Process," in D. A. Goslin, ed., *Handbook of Socialization Theory and Research,* pp. 213–262. Chicago: Rand McNally, 1969.

Brenton, M. *The American Male.* New York: Coward, McCann, 1966.

Britton, G., and Lumpkin, M. *A Consumer's Guide to Sex, Race and Career Bias in Public School Textbooks.* Corvallis, Ore.: Britton & Associates, 1977.

Brophy, J. E. *Child Development and Socialization.* Chicago: Science Research Associates, 1977.

Chafetz, J. S. *Masculine, Feminine, or Human?* 2nd ed. Itasca, Ill.: F. E. Peacock, 1978.

Erhardt, A. A., and Baker, S. W. "Fetal Androgens, Human Nervous System Differentiation, and Behavior Sex Differences," in R. C. Friedman, R. M. Richart, R. L. Vande Wiele, and L. O. Stern, eds., *Sex Differences in Behavior,* pp. 33–51. New York: John Wiley, 1974.

Fling, S., and Manosevitz, M. "Sex Typing in Nursery School Children's Play Interests," *Developmental Psychology,* 7(2), September 1972, pp. 146–152.

Friday, N. *My Mother, My Self.* New York: Delacorte, 1977.

Gould, R. L. *Transformations; Growth and Change in Adult Life.* New York: Simon and Schuster, 1978.

Goy, R. W. "Early Hormone Influences on the Development of Sexual and Sex-Related Behavior," in R. L. Unger and F. L. Denmark, eds., *Woman: Dependent or Independent Variable?,* pp. 448–472. New York: Psychological Dimensions, 1975.

Hetherington, E. M. "A Developmental Study of the Effects of Sex of the Dominant Parent on Sex-Role Preference, Identification, and Imitation in Children," in R. L. Unger and F. L. Denmark, eds., *Woman: Dependent or Independent Variable?,* pp. 263–274. New York: Psychological Dimensions, 1975.

Kane, F. J., Lipton, M. A., and Ewing, J. A. "Hormonal Influences in Female Sexual Response," *Archives of General Psychiatry,* 20(2), February 1969, pp. 202–209.

Klaiber, E., Kobayashi, Y., Broverman, D., and Hall, F. "Plasma Monoamine Oxidase Activity in Regularly Menstruating Women and in Amenorrheic Women Receiving Cyclic Treatment with Estrogens and a Progestin," *Journal of Clinical Endocrinology and Metabolism,* 33(4), October 1971, pp. 630–638.

Kohlberg, L. "A Cognitive-Developmental Analysis of Children's Sex-Role Concepts and Attitudes," in E. Maccoby, ed., *The Development of Sex Differences*, pp. 82–173. Stanford, Calif.: Stanford University Press, 1966.

Kohlberg, L., and Ullman, D. Z. "Stages in the Development of Psychosexual Concepts and Attitudes," in R. C. Friedman, R. M. Richart, R. L. Vande Wiele, and L. O. Stern, eds., *Sex Differences in Behavior*, pp. 209–222. New York: John Wiley, 1974.

Lewis, M., and Weinraub, M. "Sex of Parent X Sex of Child: Socioemotional Development," in R. C. Friedman, R. M. Richart, R. L. Vande Wiele, and L. O. Stern, eds., *Sex Differences in Behavior*, pp. 165–189. New York: John Wiley, 1974.

Maccoby, E. E., and Jacklin, C. N. *The Psychology of Sex Differences*. Stanford, Calif.: Stanford University Press, 1974.

McClure, G. T., and McClure, J. W. *Women's Studies*. Washington, D.C.: National Education Association, 1977.

National Center for Health Statistics, "Births, Marriages, Divorces, and Deaths for 1980," *Monthly Vital Statistics Report*, 29(12), March 1981, pp. 1–11.

O'Leary, V. E. *Toward Understanding Women*. Monterrey, Calif.: Brooks/Cole, 1977.

Sheehy, G. *Passages: Predictable Crises of Adult Life*. New York: Bantam, 1976.

Swerdloff, P. *Men and Women*. Alexandria, Va.: Time-Life Books, 1975.

Ward, I. L. "Sexual Behavior Differentiation: Prenatal Hormonal and Environmental Control," in R. C. Friedman, R. M. Richart, R. L. Vande Wiele, and L. O. Stern, eds., *Sex Differences in Behavior*, pp. 3–17. New York: John Wiley, 1974.

Special Education and Exceptional Children*

12

*The original draft of this chapter was written by Elizabeth C. Thomas, Ph.D.; University of Arkansas.

413

What are the forms of speech impairment in children?

What are the consequences of speech impairment?

What are common multiple handicaps?

What are some recommendations for education of the multiple handicapped?

What is a gifted or talented child?

How are gifted children identified?

How should the gifted be educated?

What are some general recommendations for the education of exceptional children?

Our History of Education for All

Early in American history, the blind, the deaf, the insane, and the "idiots" were placed in poorhouses, out of the way. By the midnineteenth century separate educational institutions were established for the blind, the deaf, and the mentally retarded. Although these schools were few, they started a trend toward providing education for the handicapped. When state legislatures began enacting compulsory school attendance laws in 1840, public school teachers were faced with the problem of what to do with children whose physical and/or mental disabilities interfered with their ability to learn.

While the need was present throughout the latter half of the nineteenth century, it was not until the first half of the twentieth century that state governments took an active role in the development of special education. Through supportive legislation that provided financial aid to local school districts, states began to encourage the development of segregated special education classes. In the 1950s, the federal government also began to take an active role in the development of special education. Public Law 85-926, passed in 1958, provided grants to colleges, universities, and state agencies to educate teachers for the mentally retarded. In 1963, Public Law 88-164 extended federal appropriations to the education of teachers for mentally retarded, hard of hearing, deaf, speech impaired, visually handicapped, seriously emotionally disturbed, crippled, and other health-impaired children. This 1963 legislation also provided funds for special research into the education of exceptional children. In 1966, Public Law 89-750 set up the Bureau of Education for the Handicapped (BEH) and a National Advisory Committee on Handicapped Children.

The most recent and most powerful law, Public Law 94-142, was passed in 1975. Known as the "Education for All Handicapped Children Act," PL 94-142 ensures free and appropriate public education for all handicapped children between the ages of 3 and 21. This law commits the federal government to pay an increasing percentage of the costs for special education. It says that each state must submit a plan to the commissioner of education and that each local agency must submit a plan to the state government. These plans must include

1. assurance of full educational opportunity for all handicapped children along with a detailed timetable for accomplishing this goal;
2. assurance of an individual education plan for each handicapped child;
3. assurance that special education is provided to all handicapped children in the least restrictive environment;
4. maintenance of comprehensive personnel development or in-service training programs; and
5. provision for an annual evaluation of special education programs.

This act transfers the authority for educating the handicapped from the state to the federal government. Also some children who were not allowed to attend school before must now be included. Placing the child in the *least restrictive environment* means placing the child in the most normal setting possible. This new approach is based on a philosophy that assumes that a special class is better than an institution, a resource room is better than a special class, and a regular classroom is better than a resource room when the capabilities of the child permit.

It should be noted that each of the laws cited applies only to handicapped children. The gifted are not included. At present, there is no federal legislation or funding comparable to PL 94–142 for the education of the gifted.

Dangers of Labeling

As a result of PL 94-142, every classroom teacher is faced with the responsibility of providing education for exceptional children. In the remainder of this chapter, we provide descriptions of various characteristics of different categories of exceptional children. Before beginning that series of descriptions, a word of caution is necessary.

The labels attached to different classifications of exceptional children are used as a means of communication among educators. They allow special educational services to be obtained and provided for children. The labels aid a school system in reporting to federal and state agencies. They allow institutions of higher education to identify and establish teacher training programs directed at particular physical and mental disabilities. Unfortunately, these same labels applied to an individual may have serious damaging effects.

Suppose you were told that Billy is mentally retarded. As we see in the section on mental retardation, this labeling is intended to communicate certain specific facts about him. There are at least four problems with this process. First, many children labeled as mentally retarded have been classified incorrectly. Second, Billy is an individual. He may or may not demonstrate any given characteristic of the classification "mentally retarded." If a teacher assumes that, because he is classified as mentally retarded, Billy is indeed mentally retarded and that he must possess all the characteristics that label is intended to communicate, the potential for seriously mistreating Billy is present. It may well be that Billy was misclassified or that he demonstrates only some of the characteristics of mental retardation. We urge you to view the following descriptions as generalities only. They should not be interpreted as absolute or as necessarily applying to any given individual.

Third, the label that is attached to Billy, or any other child, may become a self-fulfilling prophecy (Cohen, 1977). The label that communicates certain characteristics of a child to the teacher also communicates information to the child. Billy, classified as mentally retarded, sees himself as a dumb kid. Sally, classified as emotionally disturbed, sees herself as a crazy kid. A negative view of self sets limits on the expectations for success that a child has for himself or herself. And the child will then tend to perform in a way consistent with these limited expectations. Therefore, teachers must attempt to avoid having a label become their basis for deciding what a child can be expected to do. If they do not, they will strengthen the ability of the label to become a self-fulfilling prophecy.

Fourth, labels stigmatize a student. Stigmas are disturbing to anyone so marked, but they can be particularly damaging to children. Elementary teachers have long recognized this problem and have attempted to avoid stigmas by calling the subgroupings for instruction in their classrooms by such names as Fiesta and Panorama or Redbirds and Bluebirds. Students, however, know which group includes the good students and which has the slower ones. Being in the slow group, whatever it is called, automatically means that a student is dumb and that every student in the class knows it. Being classified as mentally retarded means that a student is dumb and that everybody in school, and maybe in town, knows it.

Educators have attempted to eliminate the problem of stigma attached to special education classifications by changing the names for the various classifications as the negative connotations attached to a given set of labels become too great. For example, the terms idiot, imbecile, and moron have been replaced by such terms as "educable mentally handicapped" and "trainable mentally handicapped." Unfortunately, students and others soon learn the associations that exist between the old labels and the new. The new labels then take on all the negative connotations of the old.

The problem of stigma is one that a student in special education may not outlive. That is, once Billy is labeled mentally retarded, he will always be considered to be mentally retarded by those who know him.

Procedural Safeguards

The drafters of Public Law 94-142 recognized the inherent dangers in labeling students as exceptional. In attempting to avoid capricious assessment and assignment of students, the law placed several requirements into the process for determining special education placement. A school system, when it decides to perform an assessment of a student for possible special education placement, must notify and obtain the consent of the parents. Along with this notification, all records of the school with respect to the student must be made available to the parents. If the parents refuse to give consent, the school may go to court to obtain an independent and impartial judgment as to whether such assessment is necessary and justifiable. In other words, the law provides for the involvement of parents from the very beginning of the special education process for the protection of the student. In addition, should it be determined that a child is to be placed in a special education program, PL 94-142 requires that any proposals to change that placement and the planning of the yearly educational program of the student must include the parents as equal partners in the decision-making process. Should the parents be dissatisfied with the process at any time, they have the right to file a complaint with the school district and must be awarded a hearing. They have the right to have a lawyer or other representation of their choosing accompany them in that hearing.

Exceptional Children

The exceptional child is defined as "the child who deviates from the average or normal child (1) in mental characteristics, (2) in sensory abilities, (3) in neuromotor or physical characteristics, (4) in social behavior, (5) in communication abilities, or (6) in multiple handicaps" (Kirk and Gallagher, 1979, p. 3). To develop to maximum capacity, these children require a change in school practices or special educational services. Exceptional children include the gifted, the mentally retarded, the learning disabled, the mentally ill, the physically handicapped, the deaf, the blind, and the multiple handicapped.

The largest percentages of handicapped children in descending order are speech impaired, learning disabled, mentally retarded, mentally ill, crippled or health impaired, deaf or hard of hearing, visually handicapped, and multiple handicapped. Gifted children can be defined as the top 3% to 6% of the population.

The drafters of PL 94-142 made very specific provisions for the process of identifying exceptional children. Once parental consent has been obtained, the assessment of a child being considered for special education placement must include the following:

1. Tests must be in the primary language of the student.
2. Tests and other evaluation materials must have been validated for the specific purposes for which they are used in the assessment process.
3. Tests and other materials used in the assessment process must be recommended by their producers for the purpose for which they are used.
4. The evaluation materials must assess specific areas of educational need rather than just general intelligence.
5. The tests and evaluation materials must be tailored to the needs of the students so that they do indeed assess intelligence and achievement and not the sensory or physical impairment of the child.
6. No test or other evaluation instrument may be used as the *sole* criterion for special education placement.
7. Information from other than aptitude and achievement tests must be used. Such information would include home background, physical condition, adaptive behavior, and so on.

After the assessment information is gathered, the determination as to whether or not to place a student in special education becomes the responsibility of an educational planning and placement committee (EPPC). While the members of this committee may vary from state to state, the EPPC generally includes a member of the administrative staff of the school district, a member of the instructional staff, a member of the diagnostic staff that conducted the assessment, and the parents of the child. The EPPC decides whether the child should be placed in special education. PL 94-142 mandates that, in the presence of information from ability and achievement tests that shows that a student, despite a handicap, is not in need of a special setting, the EPPC may not place that student outside the regular classroom. In this mandate, we clearly see the philosophy that pervades PL 94-142: that is, the least restrictive environment for a student is the closest approximation to the normal classroom in which he or she is capable of functioning.

Mentally Retarded Children

To be classified as mentally retarded, an individual must have low intellectual ability and poor adaptive behavior. Intellectual ability is determined by an individually administered IQ test. The cutoff score now is 70. Allowing for measurement error, this cutoff score actually represents a score band of 65 to 75. Poor adaptive behavior means that these children are not as independent or socially responsible as normal children of the same age.

Table 12.1 describes the potential functioning of mentally retarded children.

Mental Retardation	Educational Potential	Adult Functioning
Mildly retarded: IQ 50–70	"Educable"; capable of third to sixth grade academic achievement; can read, write, and calculate.	Able to be an independent self-supporting adult, blend into normal population and lose their EMR identity.
Moderately retarded: IQ 35–49	"Trainable"; capable of academic work up to second grade; most do not read or write.	If supervised, can work in unskilled occupation; cannot be self-supporting and typically do not marry.
Severely retarded: IQ 20–34	May acquire some self-care skills; may use telescopic language; unable to acquire academic skills; ambulatory.	Need permanent care; may perform very simple chores; need lifelong supervision and care from family and society.
Profoundly retarded: IQ 20 and below	May be unable to walk; may remain bedridden throughout life.	Require total nursing care for life.

Table 12.1
*Potential Functioning Among the Mentally Retarded**

*Based on American Psychiatric Association, *Diagnostic and Statistical Manual of Mental Disorders,* 3rd ed. (Washington, D.C.: APA, 1980), pp. 39–40.

Etiology of Mental Retardation

The vast majority of mentally retarded children are cultural familial cases. The small number of cases that remain are clinical in origin.

Most retarded children show no organic symptoms. This is especially true of the mildly retarded or educable mentally handicapped. The source of their retardation is familial. This means that mental retardation is passed on genetically from parents who have low intellectual abilities themselves. Usually children who score low on IQ tests are also culturally deprived. Their home environments offer little stimulation. Hunger, malnutrition, poor housing, and limited encouragement to read all contribute to the problem. Retardation in some children is caused by pathological factors. Phenylketonuria and galactosemia, inborn problems with metabolism, can be treated with proper diets. Down's syndrome, which stems from a child being born with an extra chromosome, cannot be treated. High-risk parents can know early in the pregnancy if they will have a Down's syndrome child. If the mother gets German measles in the first trimester of pregnancy, this child too may be retarded or have other defects. A vaccine has now been developed for this virus. If parents have incompatible Rh blood types, their children can develop blood problems that cause retardation. These children need to be treated at an early age. Anoxia or lack of oxygen to the brain during birth can cause retardation. Encephalitis and meningitis are the most common postnatal causes of mental retardation. Both diseases cause damage to the brain.

419

Educational Programs

Most "educable" and "trainable" mentally retarded children receive their education in the public schools. Teachers need special strategies to deal with the special problems these children have. Retarded children have very short attention spans. They also have problems focusing. Teachers need to present learning materials in an interesting way so that the children don't get distracted.

One of the most noticeable characteristics of retarded children is their speech. They tend to talk at a delayed rate, and the quality of their speech is poor. Therefore, language training is a very important part of their curriculum.

Menally retarded children are afraid of failure and ridicule. Often they try to avoid failure much more than they try to achieve success. Prolonged failure is a source of great emotional pain for these children. Fights and other disruptive behavior occur when peers confront the retarded with failure. Adults are also seen as recognizing and confronting them with failure. Such feelings may be transferred from parents to teachers. Teachers need to try to build self-esteem in these children. Teachers also need to be extraordinarily patient.

ERIKA

Now 13 years old, Erika is ready for the seventh grade. She lives with her parents who have an elementary school education and who are on welfare. She has an older brother who is a trainable retardate and goes to a special school. Erika, who has a WISC-R Full Scale IQ of 56, attends the public school segregated class for educable mentally handicapped (EMH) children. She was identified as EMH when she was 6.

Erika made little progress in her first four years of school. She could not add two-digit problems. Her teacher for her fifth and sixth years of schooling worked with her on a one-to-one basis. She was very slow in grasping ideas but developed a strong positive relationship with her teacher who began first-grade level work. Over the last two years, Erika made considerable academic progress as a result of the individual attention and is now functioning at about the third grade level in arithmetic and second grade level in reading.

In her peer group, Erika is reasonably well accepted. However, she is having difficulty learning how to be a friend. For a few days she gets along well with one girl. But when a new girl joins the group and talks about her boyfriend, Erika starts a fight. Her teacher must spend time consistently restoring good relations and teaching interpersonal skills.

Also Erika constantly tries to get attention. She makes excessive demands on her teachers. She loves her teacher but wants constant reassurance. She has experienced failure daily and thus has felt rejection in school. Her recent academic success made her feel proud for the first time. These are strange new feelings and the teacher must help her deal with them.

Retarded children have difficulty understanding what they are expected to learn in a given learning situation. Often they are outer-directed, which simply means that they look for cues in their environment to help them solve problems since they don't trust their own thinking. Some teachers refer to this style of problem solving as distractibility. Because of their dependence on the environment, retarded children may be influenced by suggestions from others more than normal children. To help combat negative influences from the environment, teachers need to provide retarded children with many situations in which they can be successful.

Retarded children have limited capabilities in short-term and long-term memory. Convergent, divergent, and evaluative thinking are very limited as well. An effect of these limitations is rigidity. Because of their tendency to be inflexible, the mentally retarded enjoy monotonous and repetitive tasks.

Learning Disabled Children

According to the 1975 Education for All Handicapped Children Act, the term "learning disabilities" means "a disorder of one or more of the basic psychological processes involved in understanding or in using language, spoken or written." This condition can include perceptual handicaps, brain injury, minimal brain damage, dyslexia, or developmental aphasia. In the absence of a known etiology, a good technical definition of learning disability is not possible.

At present, learning disability is understood to mean a major discrepancy between expected and actual achievement. (CEMREL, Inc.)

In dealing with this lack of specificity in PL 94-142 regarding the nature of a learning disability, the U.S. Office of Education called upon experts in education, psychology, and medicine for assistance. "The office concluded that it is not possible to specify all the components of a learning disability except to say that such a disability is evidenced by a major discrepancy between expected achievement and actual achievement" (Bersoff and Ysseldyke, 1977, p. 78). That is, learning disabled students are underachievers. There is no universally accepted explanation for the discrepancy between achievement and ability or why these children fail to learn. However, some studies report that as many as 20% of students in school may exhibit learning disabilities in the form of difficulty with listening, speaking, writing, spelling, adding, or subtracting. This figure may be misleading in that learning disability is not well defined or understood.

One attempt at specifying learning disabilities was made by Rabinovitch in 1959. Rabinovitch identified two groupings of learning disability. The first group was called primary learning retardation and included students whose problems with learning were biological. The second group was called secondary learning retardation and included students whose learning problems resulted from other than other biological factors.

Primary Learning Retardation

With primary learning retardation, the cause is biological. As a result, there is an inability to learn symbols such as letters or words. This is called dyssymbolia. For example, a child could not connect the word "cat" with the idea of the animal cat. All symbolic material prresents problems for these children. This includes reading, writing, spelling, arithmetic, foreign languages, and musical notation. These children also have difficulties with abstract concepts such as time, distance, and height. No amount of teaching seems to help children with dyssymbolia to read, write, or calculate at the expected grade level even though they may have average or above-average intelligence.

The long-term effects of dyssymbolia were examined in a longitudinal research study conducted by Frauenheim (1979). In that study, forty adult males who had been identified as having dyssymbolia were surveyed regarding their academic achievement, educational attainments, occupational status, and general adjustment characteristics. The conclusions of Frauenheim's study are presented now. Keep in mind as you read this that all the male subjects had average to above-average intellectual potential.

Academic Achievement. As adults, the subjects of this study still had severe learning disabilities. They read and did arithmetic at about the third grade level. Word and letter reversals were common. They had problems hearing and understanding words as well as reading and writing them (see Figure 12.1).

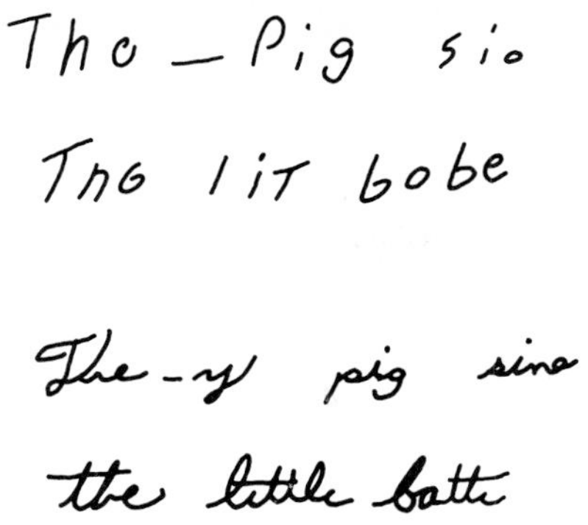

Tho _ Pig sio

Tho lit bobe

Figure 12.1
Written responses to the
dictated sentence "The
yellow pig saw the little
baby." (Adapted from
Frauenheim, 1977, p. 3.)

The _y pig sine
the little batte

Educational Attainment. Some of these youngsters managed to finish high school and even to attend trade schools. However, the percentage who quit school was significantly larger than the overall dropout rate. A majority of these children also failed one or more grades in grammar school. They never saw repeating a grade as a good idea. These children felt ambivalent at best or negative toward school and teachers. As adults,

---

DOUG

Thirteen-year-old Doug has average intelligence. He had received the usual public school education for his age but had not been able to profit from it. All this remained an enigma to his teachers and parents. He was referred to the reading clinic where he was found unable to read first-grade-level material. His sight vocabulary was almost nil. Speaking vocabulary was low for his age, but not nearly so low as his reading vocabulary. He could hold a reasonably good conversation, but his language use was quite concrete. In arithmetic Doug scored at the second grade level. On the Wechsler Intelligence Scale for Children-Revised, his verbal IQ was 90 and performance IQ was 110, a discrepancy of 20 points. His previous history indicates that, as is true for other children with the same problem, this difference had been small at first and had increased with age. His lowest subtests were vocabulary, arithmetic, and similarities. Doug expressed concern over his academic achievement to the examiner. When asked to estimate the examiner's height, he said "about $10\frac{1}{2}$ feet." He did not know the present month of the year. When asked what is the hottest month of the year, he said, "November." When asked what is the coldest month, he said "July." When asked how many days in a month, he guessed "75." He said the distance from Detroit to Chicago was 10 miles. He could not print the word *dog* or write numbers correctly from dictation. Doug was diagnosed as having a concept symbolication problem; he had a true learning disability.

Four years of individual tutoring in language and arithmetic skills was provided by the clinic, but Doug made only limited gains (about third-grade-level achievement). His future is dim. His job aspirations must be revised, and it is hoped that he will be able to learn a trade.

many still blamed the school for their reading problems. However, there was a positive relationship between the age at which special reading intervention was begun and the last grade completed in school.

Occupational Status. As adults, the learning disabled surveyed usually worked as semi- or unskilled laborers. Most of them realized that their reading problems prevented them from getting better jobs.

General Adjustment Characteristics. As adults the learning disabled still tended to project the causes for their problem to school, teachers, or others. Many went great lengths to hide their problem. As a result they married less often. The demands of a literate society were very frustrating for them. They rarely had checking accounts since they couldn't write checks. They also had problems reading menus, the newspaper, *TV Guide*, road signs, and maps.

Secondary Learning Retardation Children

Since these children do not have dyssymbolia, their future in school is bright. They are children who *can* learn. The cause of their learning disabilities is environmental. All kinds of factors may be involved. These include (1) failure to develop necessary internal controls and ego strength, (2) poor self-concept, (3) fear and embarrassment, (4) poor motivation, (5) poor home environment, (6) poor parenting, and (7) poor teaching, among others.

Special reading intervention is very helpful for these children. A large proportion of these children are boys. Boys seem to have a lack of readiness for school that girls don't have. Boys as a group develop more slowly neurologically than do girls. It may be that our traditional teaching methods force boys to learn before they are ready to do so.

Beyond special reading, there is considerable question as to how to deal with secondary learning retardation, since its specific causes are not known. The teacher must recognize that these students have unique problems. Brief assignments made at the readiness level of the student may be helpful. Opportunities for success and review should be frequently used teaching strategies. By all means, be patient!

Children with Mental Disorders

In 1980 the American Psychiatric Association published the third edition of the *Diagnostic and Statistical Manual of Mental Disorders.* Referred to simply as DSM-III, this manual provides a description of the etiology and diagnostic criteria for a broad range of mental disorders. The manual is intended to aid clinicians in diagnosing, treating, and communicating about the various mental disorders described. While the diagnosis of these mental disorders is a professional decision made by practicing clinicians, mature teachers with a knowledge of normal behavior patterns at certain ages can be very helpful to the clinician in making appropriate diagnoses.

While DSM-III is intended for clinicians, many of the mental disorders included are of concern to teachers because they occur during childhood and adolescence. We discussed one such classification in the section on mental retardation. We now provide a brief description of several other classifications of mental disorders that affect children and adolescents as presented in DSM-III.

Attention Deficit Disorder. While all children and adolescents have trouble paying attention at times, about 3 percent of children in the United States have difficulty in the area beyond what is considered developmentally appropriate. A child with this disorder will have trouble completing assignments, listening, concentrating, and sticking to play activities. He or she will also tend to be very impulsive. That is, he or she will often act before thinking, shift quickly and excessively between activities, and will have difficulty organizing work.

The Attention Deficit Disorder may be present with or without *hyperactivity*. Hyperactivity refers to excessive gross motor activity. This may include climbing, running, fidgeting, and "always on the go."

Since learning requires the ability to attend to the learning task at hand and since most classrooms place restrictions on the physical activities of students, it should be clear that a student with an attention deficit disorder may be expected to have trouble in school. Such individuals frequently fail academically and may develop conduct disorders. The attention deficit disorder frequently is not discovered until a child enrolls in school even though it may be present much earlier.

Conduct Disorder. Children and adolescents can be expected to engage in a certain amount of mischief and any student might cause a problem in a given classroom on a given day. However, a consistent pattern of violation of rules or the rights of others may indicate that a student suffers from a conduct disorder. DSM-III lists four specific types of conduct disorders: Undersocialized, Aggressive; Undersocialized, Nonaggressive; Socialized, Aggressive; and Socialized, Nonaggressive. *Undersocialized* types of conduct disorders result from an inability to establish normal relationships with others. As a result, the individual shows a general lack of concern for the feelings of others. *Socialized* types do show attachment to others but will demonstrate a general lack of concern for anyone to whom he or she is not attached. The *Aggressive* types demonstrate a consistent pattern of physical violence such as rape or assault. This physical violence may be against property rather than people such as in robberies. *Nonaggressive* types demonstrate a lack of physical violence but do demonstrate a con-

425

sistent violation of rules such as in truancy or in running away from home.

All four conduct disorders are common in the United States. The age at which the conduct disorder is first seen may vary widely. Many students who demonstrate this disorder achieve reasonably normal adjustment as adults.

Anxiety Disorder. If a child or adolescent demonstrates excessive worrying and fearful behavior, he or she may be suffering from an anxiety disorder. If the worry and fear are not specifically directed, it is called an *overanxious disorder.* The overanxious disorder is generally characterized by unreasonable worry about the future, appropriateness of past behavior, or competence and by a constant need for reassurance. This disorder is not common, but it can be incapacitating for those who have the disorder.

If an anxiety disorder is specifically related toward separation from individuals with whom close attachments have been formed, it is called *separation anxiety disorder.* Characterized by unreasonable fear of separation, this disorder may be accompanied by refusal to attend school. It may occur as early as preschool age but most severe forms are usually seen around ages 11 or 12. Fortunately, the separation anxiety disorder usually lasts only about two weeks.

A third anxiety disorder presented by DSM-III is the *avoidant disorder.* In this disorder, the student is so afraid of meeting strangers that normal social functioning is interrupted. The disorder will appear after normal stranger avoidance should have passed. It can be expected to last at least six months.

Specific Developmental Disorders. If a child demonstrates delay in the development of a specific area well beyond what is considered normal, he or she is said to have a specific developmental disorder. ''For example, a delay in language development in an otherwise normal child would be classified as a Specific Development Disorder whereas a delay in language development in a child with Infantile Autism would be attributed to the Infantile Autism'' (American Psychiatric Association, 1980, p. 92). DSM-III describes Specific Development Disorders in reading, arithmetic, language, and articulation. The age at which these disorders appear is, of course, dependent on when the specific skill would typically be expected to develop. Developmental reading and language problems are quite common in the United States.

Mental Disorders and Education

The mental disorders just described represent only a small portion of the disorders described in DSM-III. They are indicative of the large number of different problems with which a teacher may have to deal. Teachers of children with these disorders must be trained in teaching academic skills,

426

KIMBERLY

Ten-year-old Kimberly has had a history of deviant behavior. She is beautiful, quiet, and seemingly well disciplined. Kimberly was adopted at age $2\frac{1}{2}$. Her foster mother reported that Kimberly had "spells." Kimberly showed no concern about leaving her foster mother. When corrected, Kimberly turned her head and pretended not to hear and went her own way. More and more the mother, who was a junior college English professor, came to realize that Kimberly was manipulative, unattached emotionally, and difficult to control.

During preschool life, Kimberly was noted by her mother and teachers to be inattentive, unaffectionate, strong willed, and a "loner." Her mother displayed affection toward the child, but Kimberly seldom, if ever, returned it. She never seemed to fear anything and became more manipulative. She eventually developed into an uncontrollable child who had frequent temper tantrums. At this time the mother sought professional help in raising the child, but little change was seen in Kimberly's behavior.

After two years of nursery school and one year of public school kindergarten, Kimberly entered first grade in the neighborhood school. Three months later she was transferred to a self-contained classroom for emotionally disturbed children. The only girl and the only white child in a class of six children, Kimberly was in an environment foreign to her socioeconomic class. The team teachers were nonacademic in their curriculum, functioned as therapists, and avoided the culturally expected role of a teacher. This experience brought further insecurity and confusion to Kimberly and her behavior deteriorated. Temper tantrums increased, and it became impossible for the mother to control her in the home. The child had repeated nightmares, insomnia, and excessive intake of food. She began to wander off through heavy traffic far from her home. She seemed less attached to everybody and everything. A severe relationship problem was obvious.

In the second grade Kimberly was moved to a private church school where she was backward in all her academic skills. Although this school provided better structure and better academic instruction, Kimberly failed to grow emotionally, socially, and academically. The psychiatrist feared that her capacity to relate to others was much more severely impaired than previously thought. When the church school eventually refused to keep her as a student, she was returned to public school. Three months of private tutoring followed, after which she completed the second grade in a regular classroom.

The mother and child moved to another state, and Kimberly was placed in the third grade. Her mother continued private tutoring in the basic skills. Her behavior was at best borderline, requiring much attention from the teacher. Kimberly continued to evade the teacher's requests, to do as she pleased, and to act in an undisciplined manner. She had no friends and, indeed, manipulated other children in a thoroughly despicable way. Her temper tantrums continued. Although the school provided special help in reading and math, Kimberly, who has average intelligence, still remained below grade level.

curriculum, and behavior management. These children need contact with their peers since an important part of their education is learning how to live and to work with people.

Children with Physical Disorders

A physical health disorder is "an impairment of normal interaction with society to the extent that specialized services are required" (Cross, 1981, p. 256). This category includes physical handicaps, orthopedic handicaps, neurological impairments, chronic illnesses, disabling illnesses, and chronic physical disorders.

Chronically ill children and their families face many problems. There is a threat to health and life as well as to psychosocial development. Since young children do not understand why they are sick, they tend to give subjective reasons for their disabilities. They view pain, hospitalization, treatments, and separation from parents as punishments. Many avoid talking about their illness and keep the hurt inside. It is important for professionals, teachers, and parents to try to correct these misconceptions and to view these children's illnesses objectively.

Research (Pless and Roghmann, 1971) comparing the psychological adjustment of children who were chronically ill with those who were not shows that

1. except for delinquent boys, chronically ill children are more often truant, troublesome in school, and socially isolated;
2. chronically ill children have a much higher incidence of psychiatric disorders;
3. the risk of psychological maladjustment is directly related to the length of the illness;
4. the risk of psychological and social maladjustment is greater if the illness is more severe; and
5. psychological and social maladjustment is more frequent among children with permanent illnesses than among children with temporary illnesses.

Common Physical Health Disorders of Childhood

Cerebral palsy is a crippling condition of the central nervous system. Commonly, there is neurological motor dysfunction due to brain damage. Such brain damage can affect the child's intelligence, but this is not generally the case. Cerebral palsy cannot be cured, but physical therapy and surgery can sometimes improve mobility and muscular coordination.

Epilepsy is a disease of the neuromuscular system. The symptoms include repeated losses of consciousness, convulsions, or disturbances of feeling and behavior. Anticonvulsant drugs are used to control seizures. Although some mentally retarded individuals suffer from seizures, the seizures themselves do not cause mental retardation.

Special services provide wheelchair students with recreational activities. (SIUC Photographic Service.)

Spina bifida is a congenital defect of the spinal column. Children with severe forms of the disease will definitely be paralyzed in their lower limbs unless they receive surgery. Although the lives of these children can usually be saved by surgery, many still have considerable physical and intellectual disabilities.

Muscular dystrophy involves a progressive degeneration of the muscles. Usually these children need wheelchairs as the disease gets worse, but their intelligence is not affected.

Limb deficiencies are caused by genetic birth defects or by amputations due to disease or accidents. Although mechanical limbs can sometimes be fitted, children usually need a great deal of training and emotional support to learn to use them.

Cystic fibrosis is the most deadly hereditary disease of children in the United States. The specific cause of the disorder is not known. There is no known cure, and the illness is inevitably fatal. However, many patients survive into adolescence and young adulthood. The symptoms include dysfunction of the exocrine glands, very high salt concentrations in the sweat, and chronic pulmonary dysfunction with pneumonia often occurring. An extensive respiratory therapy program is required at home. Excessive mucous excretions, chronic coughing, and breathing difficulties often make these patients feel emotionally inhibited. However, these chil-

429

dren have no physical restrictions on their behavior, so they are encouraged to lead active lives. These children have normal cognitive abilities and stay in regular placement at school.

Leukemia is the most common form of childhood cancer. It is characterized by sudden increases of white blood cells in the bone marrow and blood. Recent advances in chemotherapy have made cures or at least long disease-free periods possible. However, the child and family have to deal with the fear of death. Providing a normal environment and stressing the positive aspects of living are important countermeasures.

Asthma is a psychophysiological illness. Children with this disease find it difficult to breathe due to narrowing of their bronchial airways. Asthma involves severe attacks of wheezing that may cause death because the patient cannot breathe. Drug therapy and aerosols can prevent and control attacks. Parents tend to be overprotective because the breathing attacks are very frightening to the child.

Diabetes is a dysfunction of the pancreas that prevents sugar from being stored in the blood. Symptoms include loss of weight, excessive thirstiness, and frequent urination. Diabetes can be controlled with insulin therapy and a proper diet. If not, there is a risk of diabetic coma.

Mainstreaming and Special Education

Previously many children with physical health problems could not attend regular schools. For example, many children in wheelchairs could not function in regular classrooms because school buildings were not equipped for them. Now more of these children are mainstreamed into regular classes because of the Education for All Handicapped Children Act of 1975 (PL 94-142). Most children with normal or better intelligence are placed in regular classrooms, and most school districts have special schools or special classes for crippled and health-impaired children.

Children with Visual Impairment

The first medical-legal definition of blindness was provided by the American Medical Association in 1934. There are two basic criteria for determining legal blindness. These are visual acuity and field of vision. Visual acuity is a measure of how accurately a person can see compared with someone with normal vision. If a person's vision is less than 20/200 in the better eye with a corrective lense, that person is considered legally blind. (A person with 20/200 vision can see things only at a distance of 20 feet whereas a normal person can see the same things at 200 feet.)

Field of vision is the other criterion. If a person's angle or field of vision is 20 degrees or less, that person is considered legally blind. This is called "tunnel vision."

Partially sighted individuals are also defined. They have visual acuity of between 20/70 and 20/200 in the better eye with a corrective lense.

Educational Classification

Legal blindness does not mean total blindness. Many people who are legally blind still have some sight. Some of these persons can even read print. The way people use the vision they still have is called *functional visual efficiency*. A child's functional visual efficiency is very important in determining that child's educational program. In fact, it is probably more important than whether or not the child is legally blind.

Educationally blind children cannot use vision for learning. These children must rely on touch and hearing in order to learn. They are usually taught braille so they can read.

The standard English braille is a system of 63 alphabetical, numerical, and grammatical characters. Each character uses a six-dot cell. The cells are embossed on paper, and the points are read by touch. There are two types of braille: type I braille uses letters to spell words; type II braille is a shorthand for words and phrases. Braille can be written on a braille writer, which is like a typewriter. Students can write on a slate and stylus, which is like paper and pencil for sighted persons.

Good braille readers can only read about as fast as a sighted person can read aloud. Moreover, braille materials are very bulky and cumbersome and are paced much more slowly than are sighted reading materials.

An alternative to braille is "reading with the ears." Records and tapes are important educational tools. The Library of Congress maintains a large collection of braille and recorded materials for the blind.

Partially sighted children can use vision for learning, although they may be legally blind. The educational goals for partially sighted children stress using as much of the residual vision as possible. Magnification, illumination, and large-print books are good teaching aids for these children. Eye exercises can also help to improve functional visual efficiency.

Etiology

There are many different causes for severe visual impairment. Problems can stem from hereditary factors (cataracts), prenatal factors (drugs, radiation, rubella, syphilis), perinatal factors (retrolental fibrophasia), and postnatal factors (accidents, infections, inflammation of the eye, tumors, and vascular disease).

Factors in the Development of Blind Children

Sometimes blind children show signs of early retardation in motor development even though they are neurologically intact otherwise (Scholl, 1973). Their lack of vision interferes with self-initiated activity. Blind children don't explore their environment as normal children do because they can't see it. This delay doesn't necessarily affect overall motor development, but it may affect the child's personality. Blind children who have been immobilized for long periods often have a strong desire to be left alone.

431

In general, blind youngsters are less outwardly mobile. Instead they wave their arms, sway from one foot to the other, or turn and twist their bodies. These rhythmic yet directionless movements are called *blindisms.* Visual imagery is the basis of much of our language. Since blind children lack visual experience, it takes them much longer to build useful vocabularies. Also blind children are unable to learn through imitation of what they see (Caton, 1981). In spite of these problems, school-aged blind children talk a great deal. They often speak confidently about things they never really experienced. This is called *verbalism.* The blind, however, miss most nonverbal communication because they cannot see it.

A common belief is that blind people have a better sense of hearing and touch to make up for their lack of sight. This is known as sensory compensation. This belief, however, is not supported by research (Hare et al., 1970). Also the belief that blind persons are better listeners than are sighted persons is not necessarily true. In general, when the effects of blindness are controlled, the range of intelligence for blind children is similar to the range for normal children. However, the blind are usually two or three years behind their peers in academic achievement.

ANN

Although blind, Ann, who is 7 years old, will go into the second grade next year. Born prematurely, she had to be given oxygen to save her life. Blindness resulted from retrolental fibrophasia. Ann and her parents lived in one of the most backward areas of the country. Her parents, both uneducated and poor, appeared unable to cope with the situation. The father abandoned his wife and baby, who moved in with the maternal grandparents, who were also poor and had less than third grade educations.

Fortunately, a member of the board of trustees for the School for the Blind lived in the grandparent's neighborhood. He advised the mother and grandparents about Ann's rearing and education. Ann's family insisted that they didn't want her to grow up uneducated. During Ann's preschool years, the family received constant help from their benefactor. They dealt with the problems of "rocking," temper tantrums, blindisms such as eye rubbing, and erect posture. This and much more had to be taught to prepare Ann for school and for life with her peers.

At age 5 Ann needed preparation for formal education. Money was scraped together to send her 200 miles to the state school for the blind. Ann's mother took domestic employment and lived in an apartment across the street from the school. Ann profitted greatly from this year. On the Blind Learning Aptitude Test (BLAT), she scored an IQ of 120, which is quite good.

Ann and her mother returned home for Ann to enter first grade in the local school. PL 94-142 was just going into effect. The school teachers felt very insecure about their ability to teach Ann. She went to a resource room teacher for one half day and to the regular first grade for the other half day. Both teachers had to learn braille from Ann's benefactor. At the end of the first grade, Ann scored above grade level in all subjects. This is a real accomplishment for Ann, for her family, and for her teachers.

Children with Hearing Impairment

A deaf person is one whose hearing is not functional for ordinary educational and social purposes. A hard-of-hearing person is one whose hearing is disabled but functional with the use of a hearing aid (Telford and Sawrey, 1981). The educational distinction is that the deaf must be taught spoken language. Otherwise, they remain without oral language skills. On the other hand, the hard-of-hearing child can acquire spoken language by watching and listening to others speak.

Hearing loss is measured by an audiometer, in decibels which indicate degrees of loss. For the deaf, loss of hearing is over 70 decibels; for the hard of hearing, loss is between 20 to 69 decibels. With hearing aids, some children can decrease their decibel loss from the deaf range to the hard-of-hearing range.

Hearing losses may be conductive, neural, or both. In a conductive loss, sound vibrations are not conducted from the outer ear to the middle ear and finally to the inner ear. A neural hearing loss is caused by defects of the inner ear or of the auditory nerve. A conduction loss can be helped with a hearing aid; a neural loss cannot.

Etiology

It is often difficult to pinpoint the reason for deafness. Three common causes are heredity, rubella, and meningitis. Hereditary deafness is the most common cause of early-childhood deafness. Deafness can be carried

Hearing loss is assessed by an audiometer. (SIUC Photographic Service.)

by a dominant gene, but more than 90% of inherited deafness is recessive. Each parent has normal hearing but is a "carrier" for deafness. Most children with hereditary deafness are normal physically and mentally.

Approaches to Deaf Education

Historically, educators haven't agreed on the best methods for teaching the deaf. There were two major methods: *oral* and *manual.* With the oral approach, children are taught to communicate by spoken words; with the

---

JIM

At 22 months of age, Jim was found to have a severe hearing loss in both ears. He had not learned to talk. When first fitted with a body aid, he stamped his feet on the carpet. Then he stamped again, recognizing that the noise came from his feet. His face lighted up, and he ran off the carpet and jumped on the hardwood floor. At age 2, Jim heard his first sounds.

Jim's parents realized that they must now become both parents and teachers. The mother enrolled 2-year-old Jim for half-day sessions in a preschool for hearing-impaired children. There Jim learned to speak, learned self-discipline and self-control, and learned about social encounters with others. His parents had daily feedback from the teacher and weekly conferences during the three years of preschool. The parents commented that the words of help and encouragement from his teacher helped them to complete the difficult job of carrying through the school program in the home.

At the school, Jim's program was carried out with eye-to-eye contact with his teacher. He was first encouraged to babble and then to say single words connected to concrete objects. Following this stage, adjectives were placed before nouns (red ball), then came telescopic speech, and finally complete sentences. Articulation practice accompanied his work. He learned to lip read beautifully. But he was also forced to use his residual hearing. Auditory training was carried out back to back with his teacher and at home with his mother.

At home as well as at school, discipline and self-control had to be learned. It was necessary to be certain that Jim understood what was right or what was wrong before correction or punishment was administered. The parents had to communicate with only a limited vocabulary when they potty trained Jim and taught him table manners and other tasks. Jim mastered the tasks of early childhood at a reasonable rate.

At the completion of three years of preschool, Jim tested above age level in all skills except language. Although his language age was $2\frac{1}{2}$ years, this represented a real achievement for a severely hearing-impaired child. He was found to have above-average intelligence. He has been promoted to kindergarten. Teachers must learn how to talk to Jim, however, and not accept "I know" as a response; they need to ask him *what* he knows.

Jim does not know that he has a handicap. His parents are now planning for how they will manage the crisis that will occur when he realizes he has a defect. They want Jim to have self-confidence and a positive self-concept. Their ultimate plan for him is a university education that will make him economically independent.

The reasons for hearing loss have been difficult to pinpoint. (Courtesy of Charles C. Cleland and Jon D. Swartz.)

manual approach, children are taught manual communication or "signing."

The *oral approach* uses incomplete lip information and as much sound as the child can hear. It emphasizes speech and speech reading. Reading and writing are the primary means of teaching language with this method. Manual communication is generally forbidden, but some natural gestures are allowed. Oralists argue that they teach the deaf the skills needed to deal with general society. However, critics think that the oralists limit the deaf to inaccurate oral and slow written communication. They think this is frustrating for the deaf as well as intellectually restrictive. They say that it doesn't produce rapid, natural understanding of language.

The *manual approach* is usually used in combination with speech. It uses a visual mode of communication. Finger spelling is the spelling of words with the manual alphabet. Signs are visual representations of concepts. These are complete in themselves with no grounding in the written

435

or spoken language. This method makes it easy for children to communicate before they can speak or read or even if they can't learn to speak. Critics of manual techniques argue that they don't force children to depend on speech and speech reading and that they do not give a good foundation for verbal language.

Recently there has been a dramatic shift in the methods used in classrooms with deaf children. Total communication is now used in most programs at all levels. Total communication includes speech, speech reading, residual hearing, finger spelling, signing, and body language.

Technical advances have greatly helped severely hearing-impaired children. Children can now use more of their residual hearing because hearing aids are better fitted.

Children with Speech Impairment

There are many different forms of speech disabilities in children. These include delayed onset of speech, speech usage below age expectations, peculiar usage of language, odd articulation, unusual intonation, paucity of speech, inability to recall or use appropriate words, poor self-expression, or total absence of speech (Chess and Rosenberg, 1974). All speech disabilities are impairments of effective verbal communication. This reduces the intelligibility of spoken language.

Speech disabilities fall into four major groups: (1) articulation disorders, (2) timing disorders, (3) voice disorders, and (4) language disorders.

Articulation disorders include omitting and distorting sounds, substituting one word sound for another, and adding sounds. For example, lisping is substituting one word sound (*th*) for another (*s*). Children have many articulation problems during the developmental period (Milisen, 1971). But these articulation inaccuracies are not cause for concern, unless they continue past the child's eighth year. Other children often ridicule those who speak incorrectly. This can be damaging to the child's self-esteem. Articulation disorders should be treated early.

Timing disorders include stuttering and cluttering. Stuttering is a pattern of speaking in which the rhythm is disrupted or broken. There are excessive or inappropriate prolongations, repetitions, hesitations, and/or interjections of sounds, syllables, words, or parts of sentences. This is usually accompanied by struggle and avoidance behavior (Van Riper, 1971). Cluttering is a rhythmic disorder. It involves (1) speaking rapidly, (2) omitting syllables, (3) pausing in the wrong place in a sentence, and/or (4) occasionally emitting slurred, garbled, and unintelligible speech. The clutterers are unaware that people can't understand their speech, but stutterers are painfully aware of their problem. Often when children are excited or trying to say something too fast, their normal speech patterns are broken.

Voice disorders are problems with the quality of the voice. The voice may be too loud or too soft or too high or too low pitched or have a stereotyped inflection. Some of these problems happen during normal developmental periods. For example, a boy's voice can jump to high pitch and embarrass him. If these problems are constant, the speaker must work to control the voice.

Language disorders involve a dysfunction of the central nervous system. Such problems impede the comprehension or use of words (Myklebust, 1971). Aphasia is a general term for a disability in the use of words. Receptive aphasia occurs when the person cannot comprehend spoken language. Expressive aphasia occurs when the person cannot find the correct word to communicate verbally. The same individual can have both problems at the same time. Also these disorders can occur without the person being aware of it. Severe language delay in children is called developmental aphasia. This type of aphasia implies brain injury.

This system of classification is not exhaustive. Severe social deprivation or physical disabilities can cause speech problems. Many mentally retarded and mentally ill children have speech disorders. Hearing-impaired children also have speech problems.

Developmental and Social Consequences of Speech Impairment

The consequences of a speech problem depend on the nature of the problem and its severity. For example, a language disorder associated with cognition can cause extreme difficulty in the developing child. On the other hand, problems with articulation or rhythm might only have a slight effect, or none at all. Language delay and expressive aphasia not only limit the language a child uses to think with, but also prevent cognitive development. Children with such problems seem to fall behind in school more and more each year. Research shows that expressive language delay is associated with delay in nonverbal as well as verbal abilities (Stevenson and Richman, 1976).

Rhythmic, articulation, and voice problems do not necessarily affect learning and educational progress in a negative way. But these problems usually make children feel anxious and inferior. Either directly or indirectly, these children get negative feedback about their speech problems from others. This inhibits their ease in social situations. Teachers need to help children deal with their feelings of inadequacy and incompetence.

Children with Multiple Handicaps

The Education for All Handicapped Children Act of 1975 makes it mandatory for public schools to educate all children. This has brought about considerable change for multiple-handicapped children. The common groups of multiple-handicapped children who need special planning are (1) the

437

hearing-impaired child who is also visually impaired (deaf-blind), mentally retarded, or mentally ill; (2) the cerebral-palsied child who is also mentally retarded, visually impaired, or hearing impaired; (3) the mentally retarded who is also mentally ill; and (4) the severely and multiple-handicapped child who is also mentally retarded.

Educational Programs

The nature of the combinations of handicaps of a child with multiple handicaps causes the needs and abilities of each child to vary widely. Therefore, each child requires an individualized educational program (IEP). Generally, the educational programs for multiple-handicapped children include teaching basic social, self-help, and communication skills. Normal children generally acquire these same skills by age 5. The essentials of the curriculum for the multiple-handicapped are

1. self-help training, including dressing and undressing, using the toilet, eating, and maintaining personal hygiene;
2. movement, posture, and manipulation to overcome or compensate for motor defects;
3. teaching of receptive and expressive language. Nonverbal children are taught sign language;
4. social interaction with peers and adults, to minimize the tendency to withdraw or to have violent outbursts;
5. occupational skills taught in sheltered workshops;
6. basic academic skills, including reading a few words, possibly writing one's name and address, and learning such arthmetic skills as counting change; and
7. special-interest skills, including music or general information.

Gifted and Talented Children

The concept of giftedness has always been linked closely with IQ scores, the earliest definition being that a gifted child was one who had an IQ above 140. In 1978, Congress passed the Gifted and Talented Children's Education Act. This law defines the gifted as having "demonstrated or potential abilities that give evidence of high performance capability in areas such as intellectual, creative, specific academic, or leadership ability, and in the performing and visual arts." The law obviously has a much less restrictive definition, but IQ scores are still generally used in identification of the gifted. Such an emphasis on IQ implies that, in practice, gifted refers to students who are excellent in language skills.

The term "talented" is used to refer to students who have special abilities in the creative or recreative arts. However, there tends to be considerable overlap between students identified as gifted and those considered talented.

Characteristics of Intellectually Gifted Children

A thirty-five-year follow-up study of 1,528 intellectually gifted children was conducted by Terman and Oden (1959). These children were identified by teacher nominations and group intelligence tests. Gifted underachievers and those with problem behaviors were eliminated. The mean IQ for this group was 151, and these children were from the higher socioeconomic levels.

At birth these children were heavier than normal. Their heights, strengths, physiques, and general health were far superior to that of other children. They maintained this superiority throughout the years. About half of these children learned to read before the age of 6. In school, these children achieved at least two full grade levels above the one in which they were enrolled. Some 90% of the men and 86% of the women attended college. The gifted participated in extracurricular activities much more than the average students. They maintained their intellectual superiority when tested as adults.

These gifted individuals were much more interested in abstract than in practical subjects in school. Approximately 80% of the gifted men had professional, semiprofessional, or business occupations as compared with 14% in the entire population. Their incomes were considerably higher than the national average.

Terman and Oden's overall conclusion was that gifted children became gifted adults.

Identification of the Gifted

Gifted and talented children can be identified best by using both objective and subjective evaluations. In addition to IQ scores, rating scales for leadership, creativity, and superior learning and motivation can be used. These ratings should be done impartially by those in the school who are well acquainted with the student's strengths and weaknesses and the strengths and weaknesses of various assessment procedures.

Education of Gifted and Talented Children

A program for the gifted should extend from the kindergarten level through high school. Three components in an adequate program are (1) the product component, (2) the process component, and (3) the affective component. The product component consists of new knowledge. Gifted students

JONATHAN

Jonathan is an 8-year-old who has a WISC-R Full Scale IQ of 150. He comes from a middle-class home in a rural community. His father and mother completed high school and both work to support the family. The parents have taken a great interest in their child and are very concerned with his social and academic performance.

Since no program for gifted children exists in his school, Jonathan is in the second grade classroom. He functions as a well-motivated child in all subjects. When given an opportunity to work in areas of special interest, Jonathan is fascinated. He can spend an indefinite amount of time making discoveries and discussing and evaluating them. He loves to look at the globe and spends much time locating various places. He has his own atlas, which he studies at home. He is fascinated with his own environment as well. He asks countless questions about why the crops grow, why the birds fly, and why the leaves change color in the fall.

He often draws the things in which he is interested. Jonathan spends hours drawing the horses on a neighbor's farm. He gets so engrossed that he loses his sense of time and is often late for dinner, which doesn't please his mother. He watches an older brother play chess and is very excited about the game. He already knows how all the pieces move. Almost everything he sees is interesting to him.

Jonathan enjoys his peers as well as his teachers. He is very popular and a leader in academic activities. On the playground he behaves like the other children. He has good relationships with his teachers and respects democratic authority. He enjoys conversing with his teachers on appropriate topics. Jonathan's teachers believe that he needs a special curriculum in order to perpetuate his intrinsic joy of learning.

are generally well above grade level so they find advanced subject material stimulating and fascinating. Process refers to the mental operations an individual uses to think. Guilford (1977) defines mental operations as (1) cognition or comprehension, (2) memory, (3) convergent thinking or organizing, (4) divergent thinking or imagination, and (5) evaluation. These need to be developed. Affective growth means emotional growth. Flexibility and emotional comfort make higher conceptual processes easier. The gifted need to integrate their mental and emotional functioning.

Educational Programs

The education of exceptional children may require specially adopted teaching techniques in the regular classroom or special learning environments. As pointed out previously, the present philosophy is to place exceptional children in the least restrictive environment possible, but some special students require alternatives. A description of various educational settings and services for exceptional children is provided now.

Mainstreaming

As a result of PL 94-142 with its least restrictive environment philosophy, handicapped children whose academic ability and achievement are not affected by their handicap must be placed in the regular classroom. This procedure is called mainstreaming. As a result, all teachers now need to learn how to integrate these children into their classrooms. Physical close-

At present, exceptional children are placed in the least restrictive environment. (Courtesy of Charles C. Cleland and Jon D. Swartz.)

ness does not necessarily produce psychological acceptance (Johnson, 1950). Psychological acceptance by teachers and peers is essential for the classroom to be a therapeutic learning environment. Therefore, the teacher needs to help evolve feelings of acceptance (Shane, 1980).

Many normal teachers and children don't know how to act around handicapped students. Normal persons feel unsure of themselves and ambivalent. They are afraid to show their negative feelings, so they become inhibited. Their behavior becomes more formal because they are in an unfamiliar situation and they don't know what to do (Voeltz, 1980).

There is a widely held attitude that normal persons should be kind and considerate to others who are less fortunate. Normal people tend to tell the handicapped what they think the handicapped want to hear (Kelly et al., 1960). Research shows that, when normal persons meet handicapped persons, the normal persons displayed the following behaviors: (1) more distortion of opinion, (2) less variability in the opinions offered, and (3) shorter responses to questions (Kleck et al., 1966). This means that handicapped children often get inaccurate feedback. Inaccurate feedback makes it difficult for handicapped children to develop social skills and to learn what others really think of them.

There are three characteristic stages in the development of an accepting social relationship between handicapped and nonhandicapped persons. The first stage is *fictional acceptance.* This is an attempt to act normally and equally. Everyone pretends that the handicap doesn't exist even though it is very obvious. The second stage is the *break through.* Here the normal person forgets the handicap and just reacts to the handicapped child's personality. The third stage of acceptance is *amending the normal relationship.* This happens when the normal person is aware of the handicap and takes it into account but doesn't let it get in the way of the friendship. Both teachers and students need to pass through these stages. Teachers must set good examples since children tend to imitate them.

A number of services available to classroom teachers to help them meet their responsibilities are described briefly now.

Consultant services. Consultants are available to regular classroom teachers to help with special materials or teaching methods. These include special teachers, psychologists, social workers, and medical personnel.

Itinerant personnel. Special personnel may travel to the school at regular intervals. They work with children individually and consult with teachers. These include speech pathologists, social service workers, school psychologists, and learning disability teachers. This arrangement is especially good for rural schools.

Resource rooms. Resource rooms are small, appropriately equipped classrooms. Children go there on a regular basis to do remedial work with special teachers.

Part-time special classes. Children can receive a half day of special instruction with a special teacher. The rest of the day is spent in regular class.

Specialized Settings

If the educational and evaluation planning committee determine that the results of the comprehensive assessment of a student indicate that he or she cannot function successfully in a normal classroom, the child may be placed in a special setting. Some of these special placements for exceptional children might be self-contained classes, special day schools, residential schools, or hospital and homebound services.

Self-contained special classes. More severely handicapped children are put in separate classes. Specially trained teachers handle these special classes.

Special day schools. These schools are organized by private groups or by school districts for a specific type of handicap. The mentally ill and trainable mentally retarded are frequently educated in day schools.

Residential schools. These schools provide living facilities as well as classes for the more severely handicapped children. School programs are designed for each child individually. Residential schools are usually for severely mentally retarded, delinquent, deaf, blind, and mentally ill children.

Hospital and homebound services. If children are confined to hospitals or to home, special homebound teachers can visit and help these children with their lessons. Larger hospitals have full-time teachers.

Individual Educational Plan

A key idea in special education is individualization. The Education for All Handicapped Children law (1975) states that each child shall have an individual educational plan. An IEP should include

1. the present levels of educational performance for each child that include intelligence and achievement test scores;
2. the annual goals and short-term instructional objectives for that child;
3. the specific educational services to be provided to each child and the extent to which a child can participate in regular educational programs (mainstreaming); and
4. the expected dates for starting and continuing the use of such services and the evaluation criteria and procedures for determining whether instructional objectives were met (*The Illinois Primer on Individualized Education Programs,* 1979).

The IEP is developed by a committee that generally consists of the teacher with major responsibility for the child, the building principal, the school psychologist, and the child's parents. This committee must use all the information available to determine the student's needs, develop the

Figure 12.2
Individualized Educational Program. (Reprinted from Learning Disabilities: Systemizing Teaching and Service Delivery *by D. Sabatino, T. Miller, and C. Schmidt by permission of Aspen Systems Corporation, © 1981.)*

Individualized Educational Program

I. STUDENT INFORMATION   Date ________

STUDENT NAME ______________________________ SEX ______
Last   First   Initial   M–F

BIRTHDATE ____________ PARENT ____________ PHONE ________
Mo.   Day   Yr.

ADDRESS ______________________________ ZIP ________

DISTRICT OF RESIDENCE ____________ RECEIVING SCHOOL/AGENCY ________

II. MEDICAL INFORMATION

A. VISION SCREENING ____________ ________ ________
Mo.   Day   Yr.   Examiner   Results

B. HEARING SCREENING ____________ ________ ________
Mo.   Day   Yr.   Examiner   Results

COMMENTS ______________________________

III. LEVEL OF CURRENT PERFORMANCE (Based upon achievement, diagnostic, criterion-referenced testing and teacher observation)

A. ACHIEVEMENT:		
SPELLING LEVEL	TEST	DATE
MATH LEVEL	TEST	DATE
READING LEVEL	TEST	DATE
B. MENTAL ABILITY:	TEST	DATE
C. PSYCHOMOTOR:	TEST	DATE
D. SOCIAL BEHAVIOR:	TEST	DATE
E. SPEECH/LANGUAGE:	TEST	DATE
F. OTHER (self-help, vocational, etc.):		

Figure 12.2
(Continued)

IV. PROGRAM ELIGIBILITY [check appropriate item(s)]

___ a. EMH		___ h. Deaf D	
___ b. TMH		___ i. Hard of Hearing HH	
___ c. BD		___ j. Deaf/Blind DB	
___ d. LD		___ k. Physical Handicap PH	
___ d. Speech Impaired SI		___ l. Educ. Handicap EH	
___ f. Visually Impaired VI		___ m. Early Childhood EC	
___ g. Autistic AUT		___ n. Other (Specify)	

V. PROGRAM PLACEMENT (enter information in columns following listing)

	DATE	DURATION	EXTENT OF PARTICIPATION IN PERCENTAGES
a. Regular Class			
b. Reg. Class w/Consult.			
c. Reg. Class w/ Supp. Tchng. Treatment			
d. Reg. Class w/ Res. Room			
e. Part-time Spec. Class			
f. Full-time Spec. Class			
g. Residential School			
h. Special Day School			
i. Hospital School			
j. Hosp./Treatment Center			
k. Alternative School			
l. Homebound			

VI. SUPPORTIVE SERVICES [enter item(s) in columns following listing]

	DATE	DURATION	EXTENT OF PARTICIPATION IN PERCENTAGES
a. Counseling			
b. Indiv. Psych. Counseling			
c. Group Psych. Counseling			
d. Speech Therapy			
e. Occup. Therapy			
f. Hearing Aid Evaluation			
g. Adaptive P. E.			
h. Regular P. E.			
i. Parent-Infant Education			
j. Remedial Reading			
k. Social Work			
l. Braille/Large Print			
m. Orientation/Mobility			
n. Adaptive Equipment			
o. Barrier-free Environ.			
p. Diagnostics			
q. Physical Therapy			
r. Audiological Therapy			
s. Hearing Therapy			
t. Vision Therapy			
u. Phys. Hand./Ment. Hand.			

445

Figure 12.2
Individualized
Educational Program.
(Cont.)

	DATE	DURATION	EXTENT OF PARTICIPATION IN PERCENTAGES
v. Behavior Therapy			
w. Supportive Materials			
x. Other (Specify)			

VII. PRIMARY LANGUAGE _____

VIII. PLACEMENT COMMITTEE

IX. ANNUAL GOALS: _____

X. PARENT INVOLVEMENT

I have been involved in the preparation of this Individualized Plan and:

_____ I am in agreement with it.

_____ I disagree with its contents.

I realize that this is an educational plan and not a binding legal contract.

_____
Signature of parent/guardian

XI. INSTRUCTIONAL OBJECTIVES   EVALUATION   DATE

446

IEP, evaluate the educational program, and monitor the procedures specified to protect the rights of the student. The committee is expected to meet annually to conduct its evaluation of the educational program and to make appropriate modifications in the IEP. In addition, a complete reassessment of the child and his or her special education placement must be performed at least once every three years. These reassessments must follow the same guidelines that were followed in the initial screening and may be found on page 418.

Figure 12.2 provides an example of a recommended IEP form. It should be noted that the IEP must be completed annually but PL 94-142 does not specify a particular format. Rather, PL 94-142 specifies the necessary components of an IEP and local districts must design or adopt their own form. The IEP form in Figure 12.2 is a particularly good example because it includes all the information that the law requires be included in the planning for a student placed in special education.

Summary

Special education has grown rapidly since the Education for All Handicapped Children Act (PL 94-142) was passed in 1975. This law requires that all handicapped children between the ages of 3 and 21 be educated in the least restrictive learning environment possible.

Exceptional children include the mentally retarded, the learning disabled, those with mental disorders, the physically handicapped, the visually impaired, the hearing impaired, the speech impaired, the multiple handicapped, and the gifted. Educational programs for these children are influenced by the type of handicap and the degree of its severity.

Psychological assessment must be carried out by qualified professionals. Children can be taught in a number of differing learning environments ranging from resource rooms to hospitals. A program must be planned individually for each handicapped child. Exceptional children are now more frequently a part of the regular classroom. As a result, all teachers must adapt to meet the needs of exceptional children in their classrooms.

Study Questions

1. What significant changes in the regular classroom teacher's job does the Education for All Handicapped Children Act (PL 94-142) make?
2. Compare and contrast the different types of behaviors a teacher could expect from a learning disabled child, a mentally retarded child, and a child with a mental disorder.
3. Does a hidden handicap, such as deafness, have an advantage over an obvious handicap such as blindness or a speech disorder? Would a deaf child be easier to mainstream than a blind child? Consider the social, emotional, and academic dimensions of this problem.
4. What is an IEP? Why are they formulated? What should each include?
5. What are the different learning environments for an exceptional child? Under what conditions would each be used?

6. How do the normal react to the handicapped? What strategies could you employ to nurture the acceptance process?

References

American Psychiatric Association. *Diagnostic and Statistical Manual of Mental Disorders*, 3rd ed. Washington, D.C.: APA, 1980.

Bersoff, D. N. and Ysseldyke, J. E. "Non-discriminatory Assessment: The Law, Litigation, and Implications for the Assessment of Learning Disabled Children," in S. Jacob, ed., *The Law: Assessment and Placement of Special Education Students, Final Institute Report*, pp. 65–92. Ann Arbor: Michigan Department of Education, 1977.

Caton, H. R. "Visual Impairments," in A. E. Blackhurst and W. H. Berdine, eds. *An Introduction to Special Education*, pp. 206–252. Boston: Little, Brown, 1981.

Chess, S. and Rosenberg, M. "Clinical Differentiation Among Children with Initial Language Complaints," *Journal of Autism and Childhood Schizophrenia*, 4(2), March 1974, pp. 99–109.

Cohen, J. S. "Litigation and Psycho-Educational Services," in W. C. Rhodes and D. P. Sweeney, eds., *Alternatives to Litigation: The Necessity for Parent Consultation, A Final Institute Report*, pp. 1–24. Ann Arbor: Michigan Department of Education, 1977.

Cross, D. P. "Physical Disabilities," in A. E. Blackhurst and W. H. Berdine, eds., *An Introduction to Special Education*, pp. 255–298. Boston: Little, Brown, 1981.

Frauenheim, J. G. "A Follow-up Study of Primary Reading Retardation Cases," *Hawthorn Center Bulletin*, 4(2), Winter, 1979, pp. 3–4, 8.

Guilford, J. P. *Way Beyond the IQ*. Buffalo, N.Y.: Creative Education Foundation, 1977.

Hare, B. A., Hamill, D. D., and Crandell, J. M. "Auditory Discrimination Ability of Visually Limited Children," *New Outlook for the Blind*, 64(9), November 1970, pp. 287–292.

Johnson, G. O. "A Study of the Social Position of Mentally Handicapped Children in the Regular Grades," *American Journal of Mental Deficiency*, 55(1), July 1950, pp. 60–89.

Kelley, H. H., Hastorf, A. H., Jones, E. E., Thibaut, J. W., and Usdane, W. M. "Some Implications of Social Psychological Theory for Research on the Handicapped," in L. H. Lofquist ed., *Psychological Research and Rehabilitation*, Report of a Conference of the American Psychological Association, Miami Beach, 1960, pp. 172–204.

Kirk, S. A., and Gallagher, J. J. *Educating Exceptional Children*, 3rd ed. Boston: Houghton Mifflin, 1979.

Kleck, R., Ono, J., and Hastorf, A. H. "The Effects of Physical Deviance Upon Face-to-Face Interaction," *Human Relations*, 19(4), November 1966, pp. 425–436.

Milisen, R. "The Incidence of Speech Disorders," in L. E. Travis, ed., *Handbook of Speech Pathology and Audiology*, pp. 619–634. New York: Appleton-Century-Crofts, 1971.

Mykelbust, H. R. "Childhood Aphasia: Identification, Diagnosis, Remediation," in L. E. Travis, ed., *Handbook of Speech Pathology and Audiology*, pp. 1181–1202. New York: Appleton-Century-Crofts, 1971.

Pless, I. B., and Roghmann, K. J. "Chronic Illness and Its Consequences: Observations Based on Three Epidemiologic Surveys," *Journal of Pediatrics*, 79(3), September 1971, pp. 351–359.

Rabinovitch, R. D. "Reading and Learning Disabilities," in S. Arieti ed., *American Handbook of Psychiatry*, Vol. I, pp. 857–869. New York: Basic Books, 1959.

Sabatino, D. A., Schmidt, C. R., and Miller, T. A. *Learning Disabilities: Systemizing Teaching and Service Delivery*. Rockville, Md.: Aspen Systems Corporation, 1981.

Scholl, G. T. "Understanding and Meeting Developmental Needs," in B. Lowenfeld, ed., *The Visually Handicapped Child in School*, pp. 61–92. New York: John Day, 1973.

Shane, P. "Shame and Learning," *American Journal of Orthopsychiatry*, 50(2), April 1980, pp. 348–355.

Stevenson, J., and Richman, N. "The Prevalence of Language Delay in a Population of Three-Year-Old Children and Its Association With General Retardation," *Developmental Medicine and Childhood Neurology*, 18(4), August 1976, pp. 431–441.

Telford, C. W., and Sawrey, J. M. *The Exceptional Child*, 4th ed. Englewood Cliffs, N.J.: Prentice-Hall, 1981.

Terman, L., and Oden, M. *Genetic Studies of Genius: The Gifted Group at Midlife. Thirty-five Years' Follow-up of the Superior Child*. Stanford, Calif.: Stanford University Press, 1959.

The Illinois Primer on Individualized Education Programs. Springfield, Ill.: Illinois State Board of Education, 1979.

Van Riper, C. *The Nature of Stuttering*. Englewood Cliffs, N.J.: Prentice-Hall, 1971.

Voeltz, L. M. "Children's Attitudes Toward Handicapped Peers," *American Journal of Mental Deficiency*, 84(5), March 1980, pp. 455–464.

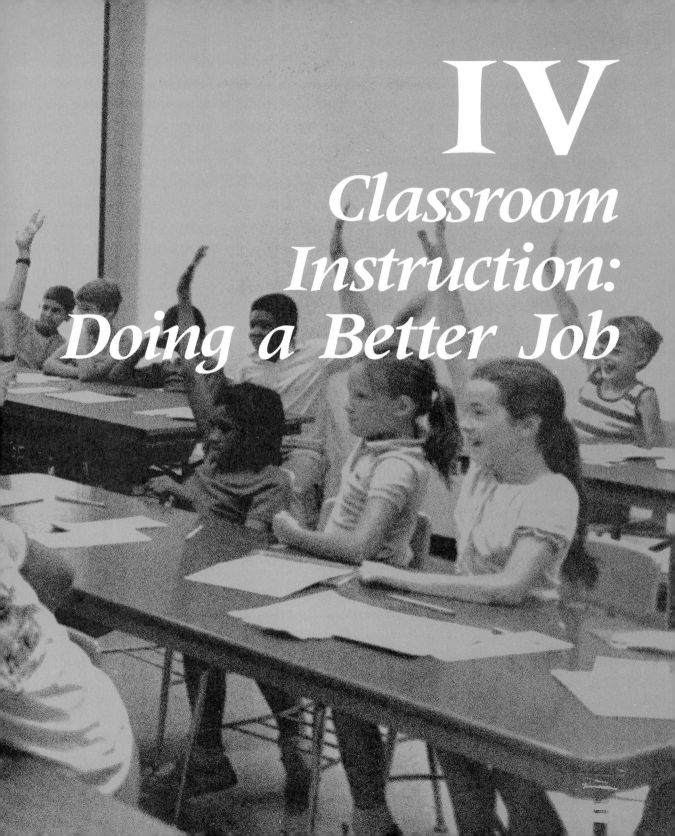

IV
Classroom Instruction: Doing a Better Job

In teaching, there are many important functions to perform in addition to the actual presentation of a lesson. In this part we present some of these other aspects of teaching along with suggestions as to how they might be performed.

A number of alternative environments might exist in a classroom: autocratic, democratic, or completely without structure. The classroom environment best suited for any given teacher is dependent upon his or her personality. Chapter 13 presents a discussion of these and other variables that might determine the effectiveness of a teacher in the classroom. In addition, Chapter 13 presents some ways in which teachers may gather information regarding their actual teaching and classroom performance. These evaluation procedures are necessary to help bring actual teaching strategies into line with teachers' perceptions as to what they should be.

Chapter 14 discusses the important area of using educational objectives in the planning of instruction. Particular emphasis is given to objectives in the cognitive domain that constitute the primary function of the school. Standardized test, particularly achievement, results are also presented with the view that this information should be incorporated into the planning of classroom teaching.

A major role of the teacher is to evaluate students. This evaluation results in the assigning of grades that provide feedback both to students and to their parents. Chapter 15 discusses methods of student evaluation and grading. The preparation and use of teacher-made tests in the evaluation process is stressed in Chapter 15.

All classroom teachers, regardless of how long they have been teaching or how good they are, face situations in which students behave in unacceptable ways. Chapter 16 presents a historical and psychological perspective on dealing with discipline problems. An extensive list of suggestions for dealing with behavior problems also appears in Chapter 16.

Teacher Characteristics and Classroom Climate

13

PREVIEW

Is it possible to define "good" teaching?

What are some approaches to studying teaching?

What is the ultimate criterion of successful teaching?

Why is it difficult to measure the effects of teaching?

What is the *global* approach to evaluating instruction?

What is the *specific* approach to evaluating instruction?

How does Flanders's interaction analysis categorize teaching?

What is the rationale behind Flanders's interaction analysis?

How can Flanders's matrix be used to improve instruction?

What approach is used in the Ryans's teacher characteristic schedule?

What three basic behavior patterns are identified by Ryans?

How do the characteristics of teachers affect classroom learning?

What classroom skills are important for teachers to have?

How can student evaluations be used to improve instruction?

What characteristics have been found for outstanding teachers?

What is classroom climate, and why is it important?

How do democratic, autocratic, and laissez-faire groups affect students?

How do teachers see themselves in the classroom?

How can teachers evaluate themselves?

How can peers be used in evaluation of teaching?

How can supervisors evaluate teaching?

What can teachers do to develop healthy classroom climates?

Why is it important for teachers themselves to be in the classroom?

After studying development, learning, intelligence, creativity, and all the other factors that affect teaching, we come to some questions. What separates the highly successful teacher from the mediocre?

These questions are not easy to answer. It is often argued that teaching includes such a complex set of activities that it is impossible to decide upon the characteristics of a "good" teacher. Each person has his or her own definition, and his or her own criteria, so that the problem cannot be studied scientifically. If we started to list the characteristics, so this argument goes, we would finish with such a long list of the good things in life that it would be less than helpful in understanding teaching. Furthermore, if any sizable group ever did agree on a definition of "good" teaching, we would have no way of measuring it.

This argument constitutes an easy excuse for ignoring a difficult problem. If the field of education exists, if research and theory on all the topics discussed in this book exist, if thousands of professionals are trained and paid every year to perform this task, then certainly effective teaching *can* and *must* be defined and measured. Approaches to doing this are explored in this chapter with the goal of helping you to develop an image of the kind of teacher you want to be and how you will measure your success in the classroom.

Are Teacher Characteristics an Important Variable?

Before proceeding in our analysis of teacher characteristics, it appears reasonable to address the question "Does *anything* teachers do really matter anyway?" It is fashionable these days to look on *all* research on teaching from a negative point of view, to point out its shortcomings, and to argue that nothing much has been shown to matter to date. For example, Wallen and Travers concluded in 1963 that "teaching methods do not seem to make much difference" and that "there is hardly any evidence to favor one method over another" (p. 484). Getzels and Jackson (1963) reported that "very little is known for certain . . . about the relationship between teacher personality and teaching effectiveness" (p. 574). And Withall and Lewis (1963) concluded that "until very recently, the approach to the analysis of teacher-pupil and pupil-pupil interaction . . . has tended to be unrewarding and sterile" (p. 708). These conclusions were all given widespread dissemination in the *Handbook of Research on Teaching* (Gage, 1963). Published in 1963, this *Handbook* was the first reference work of its kind, and it helped to spread the belief that research on teacher behaviors and characteristics had yielded only negative results. This belief is still with us today (Gage, 1978).

Such pessimism is unwarranted, however. A closer look reveals that much is known about the importance of teacher behavior and character-

454

istics, and the research can be looked at much more optimistically. As
Gage points out,

The disparaging statements about the yield of past research may reflect the fact
that research workers are inveterate critics. Their reflex on hearing about positive
findings is to look for flaws in rationale, design, sampling, measurement, and
statistical analysis. Only when such a quest for error is unsuccessful are research
workers willing to grant credence to positive findings. [Gage, 1968, p. 401]

A large-scale study often used as evidence that little that schools or
teachers do really matters is the Coleman et al. report on *Equality of Educational Opportunity* (1966). The report concluded that, while family background did explain some of the differences in student achievement, such
things as per pupil expenditures, books in the library, and other facility
and curricular variables were related only slightly to achievement. What
was often overlooked was that the report stated that *teacher characteristics*
explained more about the variability in student achievement than did all
other aspects of the school combined with the exception of student body
characteristics (Coleman et al., 1966). A close look across numerous studies yields the unmistakable conclusion that certain characteristics and behaviors of teachers in the classroom *are* important to the attitudes and
learning of the students.

Approaches to Studying Teaching

It seems difficult to argue with the claim that the ultimate criterion for
assessing successful teaching lies in what the students learn. This is the
reason we have schools and teachers; this is the final outcome for which
the public pays. And one would certainly appear foolish in claiming outstanding teaching if his or her class learned nothing. Just as we hail the
maestro if the orchestra plays well, or the farmer if the crop or cattle are
outstanding, so too we think of the outstanding teacher as one who has
fostered outstanding learning.

Unfortunately, this clear-cut and reasonable approach is loaded with
problems (Millman, 1981). How much students learn must be compared
with the potential that the students possess. One could hardly fault a
special education teacher if his or her students failed to learn as much as
an average or gifted class. The conditions in which the teacher operates,
motivation of students, available materials, course goals, ability of students, support from administration or community—all are variables that
are important in determining how much students learn. In some classes,
the students' zeal and potential are such that almost anyone can succeed
with any method; in other classes, Christ, Socrates, and Mark Hopkins

455

A FAMOUS STUDENT AND HER TEACHER

The impact of a dedicated teacher is illustrated vividly in the story of Helen Keller and her teacher, Anne Sullivan. Early in her life, Helen was stricken both deaf and blind. Her parents were ready to give up all hope for Helen, but her governess, Anne Sullivan, refused to give up. Day after day she worked with Helen, trying to get some feedback that indicated that Helen understood and could learn sign language. (Eventually, she learned to speak also.) The day on which the major breakthrough came, Anne was trying to get Helen to associate objects with words, and she finally got her to associate water with the word "water" by running water on her hands and then spelling out the word "water" on her hand. The excitement of both Helen and her teacher as Helen suddenly realized that there was a word "water" that corresponded with the cold liquid running over her hands is described vividly in the biography of Helen Keller. Anne Sullivan, who demonstrated great dedication and bulldog tenacity as she worked so patiently with the unfortunate but extremely eager student, provides a model for all those who have chosen teaching as a career.

combined would have almost insurmountable obstacles in getting the class to learn anything.

In addition, it is difficult to measure how much students learn in a course. It requires an accurate pretest to assess what the students already know, then a posttest. How much is learned in a course would be shown by just how much the students gained from pretest to posttest, assuming that we could rule out other factors such as maturation or outside experiences. This practice is seldom followed, both because of the lack of suitable tests and also because of such things as deliberate faking once students are aware of what is happening. In almost every case, students are graded on their performance in a course (usually compared with other students), and no claim is made that this is an accurate indication of how much they have learned.

A second approach to studying and defining successful teaching is that of looking at the broad picture, taking into account as many general factors as possible, and then identifying outstanding teachers based on these global criteria. Identifying the teacher who is highly regarded by peers, or supervisors, or students as an "all-around good teacher" represents a global approach. Rank ordering a group of teachers, giving an overall evaluation, telling a teacher that his or her rating is 8 on a ten-point scale are all examples of this approach. The reputation of a teacher is usually based on an informal and global assessment of total teaching effectiveness. While notorious in some circles for being inaccurate or unfair, the reputation factor is often surprisingly consistent with more precise measures.

The biggest flaw in the global approach to defining and measuring teaching lies not in its susceptibility to error (which is certainly a problem) but in its failure to identify strengths, shortcomings, or suggestions for

Table 13.1. *Evaluation of a Famous Teacher**

Teacher: Socrates

A. Personal Qualifications

Rating—high to low

	1	2	3	4	5	
1. Personal appearance	__	__	__	__	X	Dresses in an old sheet draped about his body
2. Self-confidence	__	__	__	__	X	Not sure of himself—always asking questions
3. Use of English	__	__	__	X	__	Speaks with a heavy Greek accent
4. Adaptability	__	__	__	__	X	Prone to suicide by poison when under duress

B. Class Management

	1	2	3	4	5	
1. Organization	__	__	__	__	X	Does not keep a seating chart
2. Room appearance	__	__	__	X	__	Does not have eye-catching bulletin boards
3. Utilization of supplies	X	__	__	__	__	Does not use supplies

C. Teacher-Pupil Relationships

	1	2	3	4	5	
1. Tact and consideration	__	__	__	__	X	Places student in embarassing situation by asking questions
2. Attitude of class	__	X	__	__	__	Class is friendly

D. Techniques of Teaching

	1	2	3	4	5	
1. Daily preparation	__	__	__	__	X	Does not keep daily lesson plans
2. Attention to course of study	__	X	__	__	__	Quite flexible—allows students to wander to different topics
3. Knowledge of subject matter	__	__	__	__	X	Does not know material—has to question pupils to gain knowledge

E. Professional Attitude

	1	2	3	4	5	
1. Professional ethics	__	__	__	__	X	Does not belong to professional association or PTA

Table 13.1. *Evaluation of a Famous Teacher* (Cont.)*

Teacher: Socrates

E. Professional Attitude (Cont.)

	1	2	3	4	5	
2. In-service training	—	—	—	—	X	Complete failure here—has not even bothered to attend college

	1	2	3	4	5	
3. Parent relationships	—	—	—	—	X	Needs to improve in this area—parents are trying to get rid of him

RECOMMENDATION: Does not have a place in education. Should not be rehired.

*From John Gauss, "Socrates Evaluation," *Saturday Review,* July 21, 1962, p. 47. Copyright © 1962 by *Saturday Review.* All rights reserved. Reprinted with permission.

improvement. To be told that a global assessment of your teaching is 3 on a scale of 10 is not only a crushing blow but one that is particularly frustrating in that it fails to tell you what you are doing wrong.

A third approach to studying teaching is to define particular elements of teaching and gain objective measures of each element (see Table 13.1). Measuring the teacher's ability to organize a lecture, present it effectively, ask questions, lead a discussion, construct a test, and evaluate students are examples of more specific factors in teaching. While not necessarily any easier than the global approach, many specific aspects of teaching have been defined and measured, some with an amazing degree of precision, and have contributed to the understanding of teaching.

Categorizing Teaching with Flanders's Matrix

Probably the most famous system for categorizing teaching through direct observation of teacher behavior is that devised by Ned Flanders (1970). This system, called *interaction analysis,* focuses on verbal communication in the classroom, which Flanders believes is central in classroom behavior. The objective is to categorize, objectively and systematically, two types of teaching behaviors: direct influence and indirect influence. The rater uses a score sheet with ten categories (illustrated in Table 13.2) and simply makes a tally in one of those ten categories every three seconds to indicate what the teacher is doing. For example, the teacher might be praising a student, showing that he or she accepts a student's feelings, accepting or using a student's ideas, or asking a question. All these are indirect influences, and a mark is made in category 1, 2, 3, or 4. The mark is made quickly, without pondering or deliberating, and the fact that the tally is sometimes inaccurate is no problem, since the picture becomes clear across a large number of tallies.

Many times the teacher will be involved in direct influence, such as lecturing, giving directions, criticizing, or justifying authority. These are all

458

traditional activities in teaching, particularly at the higher grade levels. Research on Flanders's system indicates that indirect teaching behaviors are frequently found paired with better achievement, motivation, and attitudes on the part of students (Dunkin and Biddle, 1974). While this pairing does not necessarily mean that indirect teaching causes improved achievement, Flanders's technique can be used to determine whether the teacher is engaging in too much direct influence and neglecting indirect influence. Not all classroom behavior is teacher talk or influence, however.

Categories 8 and 9 in Flanders's interaction analysis are "student talk" categories. (Category 10 is not talk by teacher or students.) Perhaps it is appropriate that only two categories refer to student talk, while seven reflect teacher talk, since research has shown that the vast majority of teachers in standard classrooms are direct in their approach (Dunkin and Biddle, 1974). The student may be answering a question, asking a ques-

Table 13.2. *Ten Categories in Flanders's Interaction Analysis**

Teacher Talk	
Indirect Influence	*Direct Influence*
1. *Accepts feeling.* Accepts and clarifies the feeling tone of the students in a nonthreatening manner. Feelings may be positive or negative. Predicting or recalling feelings are included.	5. *Lecturing.* Giving facts or opinions about content or procedures; expressing own ideas, asking rhetorical questions.
2. *Praises or encourages.* Praises or encourages student action or behavior. Jokes that release tension, but not at the expense of another individual; nodding head or saying "um hm" or "go on" are included.	6. *Giving directions.* Directions, commands, or orders to which a student is expected to comply.
3. *Accepts or uses ideas of students.* Clarifying, building, or developing ideas suggested by a student. As teacher brings more of his or her own ideas into play, shift to category 5.	7. *Criticizing or justifying authority.* Statements intended to change student behavior from nonacceptable to acceptable pattern; bawling someone out; stating why the teacher is doing what he or she is doing; extreme self-reference.
4. *Asks questions.* Asking a question about content or procedure with the intent that a student answer.	

Student Talk	
8. *Student talk—response.* Talk by students in response to teacher. Teacher initiates the contact or solicits student statement.	9. *Student talk—initiation.* Talk by students that they initiate. If "calling on" student is only to indicate who may talk next, observer must decide whether student wanted to talk. If he or she did, use this category.

10. *Silence or confusion.* Pauses, short periods of silence, and periods of confusion in which communication cannot be understood by the observer.

*From N. A. Flanders, *Analyzing Teacher Behavior*, © 1970. Addison-Wesley, Reading, MA., p. 34. Reprinted with permission. Categories 1–4 together indicate the amount of indirect influence, 5–7 indicate direct influence by the teacher, 8 and 9 are student behaviors, and category 10 is separate from these three major divisions.

tion, making a point of some kind, discussing something, or category 10, "silence or confusion." Naturally, we would not expect a high number of tallies in this tenth category during a classroom activity, but there is no reason to conclude that a teacher is "poor" just because some tallies appear here. A certain amount of confusion, along with silence, is indeed appropriate for some classroom purposes.

When compared with an observation following the global approach, in which the observer looks at anything he or she wants to and then gives the teacher general impressions, Flanders's approach proves to be much more helpful. For one thing, it is objective, eliminating questions about the observer's biases or motives. For another thing, it is specific, showing the teacher some of the things he or she is and is not doing. Because anyone who is teaching is of necessity so immersed in what he or she is doing that it is extremely difficult to notice details, the extra pair of eyes and ears of the observer are invaluable in providing the teacher with specifics as to what is going on in the classroom.

Gage (1968), in discussing research on Flanders's category system combined with research on other systems, summarized results by stating that three underlying dimensions of successful teaching emerge from this instrument. These are (1) warmth (tendency to approve, support, speak well of, like and trust their students), (2) indirectness (permitting students to explore, discover, make decisions on their own, ask questions, try solutions), and (3) cognitive organization (the teacher's intellectual grasp of

Classrooms do not have to involve only communication between teacher and student. (CEMREL, Inc.)

what he or she is trying to teach and how this relates to students' experience). Flanders's interaction analysis should help teachers to determine the extent to which their teaching reflects these characteristics.

Learning to use Flanders's interaction analysis technique is not difficult, and almost any untrained person, regardless of background, can become proficient in this system in about eight hours. (One researcher commented jokingly that undergraduates learn it with ease in a few hours, teachers or graduate students take longer, and professors find it difficult. His point was that the system is designed for people with no special backgrounds and that motivation and adaptability are the key to learning a new technique such as this.) Flanders comments that, in teaching teachers about this technique,

Special emphasis is given to the idea that any teacher, regardless of his style, may benefit because the feedback consists of an analysis of teacher statements, and we are sure that all teachers talk. We also point out that it is the job of the inservice staff to provide the feedback. It is the teacher's job to decide whether this information is consistent or inconsistent with his own intentions. He must decide what changes, if any, are desirable. [Flanders, 1970, p. 57]

Supporters of Flanders's technique point out that such interaction analysis should *not* be used in an attempt to "force teachers to alter their teaching approaches." As with any analysis of teaching style, interaction analysis can be useful only if the teacher *wants* to know more about his or her teaching behavior, wants to improve, and feels free to explore and change.

Ryans's Teacher Characteristics Schedule

Another approach to understanding teaching is to look at how teachers respond to a series of questions that have been shown to correlate with what a teacher does in a classroom. A well-known example of this, with solid research support, is that of D. G. Ryans (1960). Ryans began by having observers rate teachers on a list of twenty-five dimensions of behavior after observing a class for about fifty minutes. Each dimension was explained in detail to the observers. Note that, in this approach, the assessment is intended to provide a recollection or general impression, a judgment based on a number of factors, rather than the specific, objective tallying of Flanders's technique. As a result, Ryans identified three basic behavior patterns among teachers:

1. Warm, understanding, and friendly versus aloof, egocentric, and restricted.
2. Responsible, businesslike, and systematic, versus evading, unplanned, and slipshod.
3. Stimulating and imaginative versus dull and routine.

461

As Gage (1968) pointed out, there is a great similarity between these three factors and the three underlying factors of successful teaching identified by Flanders. This leads us to conclude that teachers do differ from one another in areas considered to be desirable characteristics of teachers.

Characteristics of Outstanding Teachers

When students are asked to describe their most outstanding teachers, certain terms appear repeatedly. Piecing together these descriptions over a large number of students begins to produce a fairly detailed description of an outstanding teacher. Table 13.3 presents fifteen characteristics most often used when ten groups of college students were asked to describe their "best" and "worst" teachers.

The findings in Table 13.3 indicate a strong emphasis on such qualities as decent, caring, and understanding. These characteristics, as we indicated in Chapter 7, are descriptors of humanistic psychology. Thus, one conclusion that can be drawn from the information in Table 13.3 is that good teachers, as seen by students, are decent humanistic people who also possess considerable competency in their academic area.

MY FAVORITE TEACHER

The assignment was to write an essay on the topic "My Favorite Teacher." The choice of which teacher to write about was easy—Mr. Barclay, my ninth grade social studies teacher, came immediately to mind.

The first thing I remembered about Mr. Barclay was that he was always fair and always interested in the students. He had a good sense of humor, and it was clear that he loved to teach. His style was to talk to the class informally, like someone telling a story, and to get the students involved in telling that story. He was always well prepared, and he appeared to "know his subject cold."

Mr. Barclay was not an easy teacher as he expected the best from his class, and he usually got it. He did not "talk down" to students but, instead, always treated them with respect. He was willing to listen to students and seemed to understand their problems better than the other teachers. He seemed to be able to make each of us feel like a decent human being, and I always felt a little smarter in his class than I did in any other. This was probably because Mr. Barclay was definitely a decent human being who sincerely liked students, and we felt like decent human beings in his presence. As a result, he had very few discipline problems; students simply did not misbehave in his classes.

I could go on all day in describing Mr. Barclay, my favorite. What I don't understand is, why are there not more Mr. Barclays in our schools?

Best Teacher	Worst Teacher
Sincere	Unfair
Patient	Negative
Flexible	Rigid
Good discipline	Moody, irritable
Caring, helpful	Overly critical
High expectations	Cold, impersonal
Friendly toward students	Unfriendly toward students
Fair, honest	Dislike of teaching
Consistent	Poor discipline
Students seen as individuals	Classroom engenders "bad feelings": guilt, fear, jealousy, resentment, anger
Enthusiastic, likes teaching	Dull, boring
Understanding	Distracting mannerisms
Good planning, organization	Punitive
Sense of humor	Distrust of (lack of respect for) students
Knowledgable in subjects	Not knowledgable in subjects

Table 13.3
*Fifteen Characteristics of "Best" and "Worst" Teachers as Described by College Students**

*This information was gathered by Robert Reilly at the University of Arkansas.

A second source of information about successful teachers may be found by contrasting outstanding teachers and mediocre teachers. Don Hamachek conducted research by identifying those teachers seen as outstanding by students and colleagues and comparing them to a group of less successful teachers. He also looked at the results of other such studies and concluded that three major factors distinguish outstanding from ordinary teachers: (1) certain classroom behaviors or characteristics, (2) attitudes toward and acceptance of self, and (3) attitudes toward and acceptance of others.

CHARACTERISTICS OF OUTSTANDING TEACHERS*

A. In the classroom
  1. Flexibility
  2. Empathy
  3. Personal touch
  4. Experimental attitude
  5. Skill in asking questions
  6. Knowledge of subject
  7. Well-established exam procedures
  8. Provision of definite study helps
  9. Appreciative attitude toward students
  10. Informal, conversational style
B. Ways of viewing self
  1. Identification with people
  2. Basic feeling of adequacy

*Based on Hamachek, 1969.

Students consider empathy and concern for them as individuals to be characteristic of outstanding teachers. (Bernie Weithorn/SIUC Photographic Service.)

      3. Self-concept as reliable, trustworthy
      4. Appreciated
      5. Worthy
  C. Ways of viewing others
      1. Positive view of others
      2. Trusting, accepting of others
      3. More favorable view of democratic procedures
      4. Willingness to share other's point of view
      5. View of students as individuals, exhibiting trust and respect.

    Hamachek placed the ten items under "In the classroom" in rank order with flexibility most important, empathy next, and so on. This category seems to consist of skills and characteristics that are at least in part trainable, suggesting that a teacher can develop these. Categories B and C lie more in the personal and social adjustment areas. Once again, these findings support the humanist's contention that a good teacher is a decent human being, with positive attitudes toward self and others and with certain classroom skills that are consistent with humanistic beliefs. When compared with the description of "best" and "worst" teachers given by students in Table 13.3, similarities can be noted. The sincere, patient, flexible, fair, and knowledgeable teachers the students described are similar to the outstanding teachers described by Hamachek.

One final look may help you to summarize the characteristics of a good teacher. Employing a careful analysis of what goes on in classrooms, Good and Brophy concluded that four special skills were crucial to a teacher's success:

1. Skill in communicating respect and belief in children's ability to perform academically.
2. Skill in modeling desirable language, social skills, and problem-solving abilities.
3. Managerial skill in organizing and maintaining effective learning environments.
4. Skill in grouping students, enabling students to learn from each other, and allowing the teacher time for both remedial and enrichment activities [Good and Brophy, 1973, p. 296].

Good and Brophy believe that these skills are all teachable and that the ability to conceptualize what goes on in the classroom is a starting point. Teachers must have concepts and principles concerning classroom interaction to understand their own behavior and that of their students. In this view, teachers can help each other to identify what is going on in their classrooms and use this insight to improve their teaching.

Dimensions of Classroom Climate

Classroom climate refers to the various psychological and social dimensions in the classroom, such as degree of formality, flexibility, structure, anxiety, teacher control, activity, and stimulation. Wilbert McKeachie focused on this area for several years at the University of Michigan, producing some intriguing findings. He was interested in a cluster of such factors, which he called the "traditional class," as compared with another group of factors, which could be labeled "progressive." The traditional classes were formal, dominated by the instructor, rigid, and structured, as in the typical large lecture section. In other classes, McKeachie experimented with more flexible, democratic, relaxed, informal, personal groups, even including settings outside the classroom, eliminating tests, and letting students plan the course. To his surprise, some of McKeachie's (1951) early findings did *not* support the superiority of the "progressive" sections, but found instead that students often did as well and had favorable attitudes in large, traditional lectures. This led to the realization that students

465

Classrooms vary greatly in the degree of formality and teacher control. (CEMREL, Inc.)

who are accustomed to rigid, structured, autocratic classes do not adjust to a different approach overnight, nor do they like the new approach better until they have learned to adapt to it. But if the teacher builds a bridge whereby students are weaned away gradually from their dependence on the various parts of the traditional climate, McKeachie found that they adapted quite well to such classes and came away with much better attitudes toward the subject, themselves, and what they were learning.

Another famous series of studies involved the experimental manipulation of classroom climate by group leaders to find outcomes of each type of climate (Lippitt and White, 1952). The investigators delineated three basic types of climate—autocratic, democratic, and laissez-faire—and trained group leaders so that they could conduct their groups of boys in one of these three ways. The characteristics of each type of group are as follows.

Autocratic Groups

In the autocratic groups, the leader expected immediate acceptance of all orders, maintained rigid discipline, kept a constant check on the group's behavior, dispensed very little praise, did not trust students, and in general, made all group decisions. There was no question as to who was in charge, and if the group members did as they were told, they would learn or achieve the group's goals. These goals, of course, were determined by the leader.

Group members were submissive but tended to dislike the leader. "Passing the buck" to escape blame was a common defense, and members in these groups did not tend to form close personal friendships. Achievement in these groups was good while the leader was present but slipped markedly when the leader left the room. Lippitt and White (1952) concluded that such groups were orderly and allowed learning to take place but lacked individual responsibility and initiative and resulted in poor attitudes toward the subject and the group.

Democratic Groups

In the democratic groups, planning and decision making were shared with all group members. The leader gladly gave help and guidance to individuals, dispensed praise freely, and supplied criticism if requested. The leader encouraged as much individual and group responsibility and participation as possible and tried to be a helper and facilitator with goals determined by the group under his guidance.

Group members liked their work, each other, and the leader better than in the autocratic groups. The quality and quantity of work were good and did not decline when the leader left the room. Such groups had few motivational problems and developed a high sense of responsibility for what they were doing.

Laissez-Faire Groups

In the laissez-faire groups, the leader was neither rigidly in charge nor strongly supportive but, rather, tended to ignore the group. There were no clear-cut goals and no advice or criticism, and group members were free to proceed any way they wished. Responsibility was not guarded jealously by the leader nor was it given to the group. The leader was more like a baby-sitter who allowed the group the freedom to do anything it wished without guidance or advice.

The work of the group was haphazard and of poor quality, and morale was low. There was considerable irritability, buck-passing, and scapegoating among group members. Rapport was not good, and teamwork or cooperation failed to develop. Since nobody was sure what to do, group members tended to waste time. When the leader left the room, the situation did not improve.

One of the most important points to note from this research is that it

467

THREE DIFFERENT CLASSROOM CLIMATES

Jodi, Julie, and Dan all taught ninth grade English. In Jodi's classroom, Jodi was clearly the queen and the classroom was her castle. She decided what was done, how it was done, and when. Classroom discussions were run with an iron hand, always completely under Jodi's control. They were really more like recitation sessions, with Jodi asking questions and calling on students to answer.

Jodi maintained discipline by being rigid and tough. She laid out the rules and the students followed them, or else. She had few discipline problems because the students were afraid to do anything in her class. Her rigid control of the class did let students know exactly where they stood, but it also fostered the goal of avoiding trouble rather than of sticking one's neck out to learn something.

Julie, meanwhile, ran a much more informal class in which the students participated in decisions about what was done. Julie did not treat the classroom as her castle, nor was she the queen, but, instead, made each student feel that he or she was important. Once they decided on a course of action, Julie tried to make sure that the students lived up to their responsibilities. It was a class in which the teacher was a helper or facilitator, but the students themselves determined much of what went on in the class.

This did not lead to an ''anything goes'' atmosphere, however. Julie was very careful to outline the acceptable alternatives and then let the students choose from those alternatives. Everyone in the class felt a part of the group and had some opportunity to influence what was done in class. Students gladly brought their problems to Julie because they knew she would listen and encourage them to solve the problem.

Dan's class was organized very loosely and often appeared to be in a state of chaos. Dan believed in turning the students loose and letting them find their way. The students felt that ''anything goes'' in his class, which led to a lot of social interaction. Dan scrupulously avoided making decisions or telling students what to do. He claimed that his method was a ''discovery learning'' technique, with the students learning what they needed to learn on their own. Although they had fun in his class, many students claimed that they weren't really learning anything.

It was interesting to see what happened when these three teachers left the room. Jodi's class, which behaved well and paid attention while she was there, did little when she was not. It seemed that learning could take place only when Jodi was in charge. In Julie's class, there didn't appear to be much of a change when she left the room. Students continued with their projects and went right on learning whether she was there or not. Julie sometimes wondered if she was really needed at all.

Dan's class was the most startling of the three in this regard. Things were confusing and disorganized when he was there, but when he left, the situation degenerated completely. There was real danger of someone getting hurt when he was not there.

was not the autocratic groups that achieved the least but, rather, the laissez-faire groups. Both in quality and quantity of work, and in feelings and attitudes toward self and others, the laissez-faire groups were definitely in last place. It is important for teachers to realize that giving students freedom without guidance, criticism, and responsibility is not an effective alternative to traditional autocratic methods.

Another interesting fact here is that the democratic groups did not learn more or produce higher-quality work than the autocratic groups. The advantage of the democratic groups was that their performance remained high when the leader left the room. This suggests that students are dependent on the teacher in an autocratic classroom and do not develop the initiative and responsibility to carry on without the teacher's domination. The usual interpretation of the Lippitt and White studies, when applied to classroom teaching, is that they support the value of democratic teaching in terms of the attitudes and responsibility of the students, that they indicate that democratic teaching is not actually superior to autocratic teaching in terms of the amount learned, and that the worst thing the teacher can do regarding both achievement and attitudes is to adopt the detached laissez-faire attitude.

Evaluation of Classroom Teaching

From the previous information, you may have decided upon the type of characteristics that you would like to demonstrate as a teacher and the type of climate you would like to have in your classroom. We all have some perception of ourselves as teachers. As it turns out, however, there is often considerable discrepancy between what we see in ourselves and what others see in us.

It is not easy to see oneself accurately in a complex role. Teachers will describe themselves as democratic and then proceed to conduct class as authoritarians. Teachers describe themselves as dynamic and enthusiastic and then teach in a boring and stultifying fashion. Teachers describe themselves as strict disciplinarians and then run a disorganized and undisciplined class.

These discrepancies are not difficult to understand. The task of teaching is complex. Engineering the daily learning tasks for scores, sometimes hundreds, of young people is not an easy job. It seems to take all our energy just to get through it, without taking the time to seriously scrutinize what we are doing. It is easy to ignore information that is contrary to our own perceptions.

You will recall that cognitive dissonance is the process of deciding on what we believe is true, accepting and internalizing information that is consistent with our perception, and ignoring or rejecting data that are inconsistent with that perception. This discounting of inconsistent information is not necessarily a conscious act, so we may not even be aware that it is happening.

469

WILL THE REAL MRS. BROWN PLEASE STAND UP

Mrs. Brown thought of herself as an outstanding teacher. She believed that she was creative, well organized, innovative, and student oriented. She encouraged responsibility in students, made individualized assignments, and maintained high standards in her classes. She also believed that she was an expert both in English literature and in teaching grammar.

With this in mind. Mrs. Brown did not feel threatened at having her students evaluate her. She was confident that she would score high in the eyes of students.

But Mrs. Brown was jolted by the results of the students' evaluation. The students saw her as disorganized and also as expecting too much. They complained of feeling like guinea pigs in her classroom experiments. They rated her as aloof and cold and as having little patience. They complained further that she was not a fair grader and that she favored certain students at the expense of others.

The evaluation was quite an eye opener for Mrs. Brown. It made her realize that the way in which one imagines oneself to be is not necessarily the way in which one is seen by students. It caused her to re-examine her teaching and to find ways to be truly innovative and student oriented. It also taught her the importance of structuring class requirements clearly for students, so that they would not feel confused or ill at ease. Mrs. Brown continued to use the evaluation forms at the end of each semester and was gradually able to be the type of person she wanted to be in the classroom and to be seen this way by her students.

In view of the difficulties of self-perception in the role of teacher, a teacher must attempt to be as objective as possible in evaluation of what is really happening in the classroom. He or she must systematically go about the job gathering information that can objectively be studied when there are not a hundred other things happening. This process of evaluation can help us to see ourselves as our students, our peers, and our superiors see us. This input can be a valuable aide in bringing our actual teaching into line with what we would like it to be. In the remainder of this chapter, we look at various types of input that you can get to help you evaluate your own teaching.

Self-evaluation

An excellent source of information regarding your behaviors as a classroom teacher is self-evaluation. A number of strategies are available to assist you in self-evaluation; for example, self-evaluation forms, audiotapes, and videotapes. Remember that, in any technique you decide to use, your purpose is to get as objective a picture as possible of your actual teaching practices. To do so, you must be prepared to overlook the fact that it is yourself that you are evaluating and attempt in every way possible to be objective.

Self-evaluation is often formalized through the use of a self-evaluation questionnaire, checklist, or rating scale. In each of these, the teacher examines the behaviors that he or she exhibits in teaching to assess the extent to which he or she practices desirable and undesirable behaviors. These forms tend to require substantiating evidence for each rating. For example, in the area of using student feedback in developing lesson plans, the form requires the teacher to provide examples of specific student feedback and the ways in which it was incorporated into subsequent lessons. This requirement serves the purpose of verifying ratings and of forcing the teacher to be even more objective in his or her assessment.

Following the assessment of present teaching characteristics, the teacher must prepare a set of goals for improvement of desirable teaching practices or reduction of undesirable ones (Manatt et al., 1976). During subsequent time periods, the teacher can work toward these goals and then perform a re-evaluation.

A portion of a self-evaluation form demonstrating these characteristics is presented in Figure 13.1 (we have not included the complete form because of its length). With this form, a teacher is asked to conduct a self-evaluation in each of the following areas: (1) diagnosis of student strengths and weaknesses, (2) preparation of long-term and specific objectives, (3) facilitation of instruction, (4) evaluation of student performance, (5) classroom management, and (6) involvement in professional responsibilities outside the classroom. You will note in the instructions for the self-evaluation form in Figure 13.1 that the teacher is expected not only to evaluate himself or herself but also to have another person or persons conduct an assessment. The second person helps the teacher to be objective about the process and to provide an independent and perhaps different interpretation of the data gathered. The other person may be another teacher, the principal, or some other professional staff member in the school. The role of other persons in the evaluation of teaching is discussed in the sections that follow.

The teacher may also evaluate his or her performance in the classroom through the use of audio- and videotapes. All the analysis in the world may fail to pinpoint a problem that is painfully obvious upon hearing or seeing yourself teach. Such tapes can be very short and need not focus on any particular aspects of teaching as long as something is happening that the tape can record. Many teachers have had excellent results in having a portable videotape recorder in their classrooms and turning it on at will. In utilizing this method, start by taping some of your best or favorite lessons, listening to them at your leisure, then move on to more critical aspects of your teaching. You may want to go so far as to complete an observation checklist similar to those discussed under peer and superior evaluation to help you objectify your analysis of these tapes.

471

Diagnosis of Critical Work Activities

* *

Evaluator _____ ☐

Evaluatee _____ ☐   Person completing this form

Date _____ / _____ / _____
     Mo.   Date   Yr.

Directions:

    Using a copy of this inventory form, evaluatee and evaluator will independently diagnose the status of the evaluatee's current performance. It is to be used to assist in the identification of areas indicating performance strengths or those in which improvement is needed. (Qualitative Rating). It is also to be used in prioritizing those areas in which improvement is needed. (Priority Rating).

* * * * Legend * * * *

Qualitative Rating	Priority Rating
1 = area of strength	1 = high, must be an established job target
2 = area of acceptable performance	2 = low-high, established as a job target but requires less time and resources
3 = area needing some improvement	3 = high-low, may be improved by establishing job target if time allows
4 = area needing considerable improvement	4 = low, to be included after high priority areas have been achieved appropriately

When the status of current performance and priorities has been determined, those areas identified as needing considerable improvement with a high priority should be given first consideration in preparing job targets.

472

Priority Rating				Performance Areas/Activities	Qualitative Rating			
1	2	3	4		1	2	3	4
				III. FACILITATING INSTRUCTION				
				1. Uses vocabulary and content appropriate to the student's instructional level. Verification: _____ _____ _____				
				2. Develops and utilizes instructional materials appropriate to the instructional goals. Verification: _____ _____ _____				
				3. Utilizes community agencies, groups, and individuals to supplement the instructional program. (Should be consistent with instructional goals.) Verification: _____ _____ _____				
				4. Calls on a child by name before asking a question and insures that all pupils are given an equal number of opportunities to answer questions; i.e., don't call on just "pets" or "problems". Verification: _____ _____ _____				

Figure 13.1
(Continued.)

473

Figure 13.1
(Continued.)

JOB TARGETS

JOB IMPROVEMENT TARGETS

Setting job targets is the central theme and major thrust of this evaluation system. It is a task which requires time and thoughtful reflection. It is expected that evaluator and evaluatee will work together in identifying and stating targets.

INSTRUCTIONS: EVALUATEE

1. Write one goal on each work sheet. The word (TO) is often used to start the goal statement.

2. Write a specific job target which will help you in achieving the goal. The word (BY) is often used to start the job target statement. Additional worksheets are to be used for other job targets. REMEMBER, 4–6 TARGETS ARE ENOUGH!

3. Section C includes a brief outline you intend to use to accomplish your job target. A projected date to complete the job target should be identified.

4. In Section D include indicators or measures illustrating the successful completion of the job target. Remember to distinguish between an activity and an indicator.

INSTRUCTIONS: EVALUATOR

In Section E indicate an estimate of accomplishment or status of the goal or job target at the end of the evaluation period. Include commendations and/or recommendations.

Figure 13.1
(Continued.)

VII.   JOB TARGETS WORKSHEET

A.   Goal No. ____: Long-range, fundamental, on-going

B.   Job Target No. ____: (criteria—specific—challenging—realistic—
                        manageable—measurable)

PRIORITY RATING   /   /

C.   How: Include means, methods, activities, processes, materials,
            personnel by which specific objective will be achieved

TARGET DATE   /   /

D.   Evaluatee Comments: Include
      indicators or methods for
      measuring achievement of job
      targets

E.   Evaluator Comments:

Evaluatee _____

Date ___ / ___ / ___

Evaluator _____

Date ___ / ___ / ___

475

Peer Evaluations

Potential sources of information regarding the actual teaching practices you employ in the classroom are your peer teachers. As noted under self-evaluation, one of your peers may look at the information you gather in the process of self-evaluation and provide an independent assessment of that information. This process would serve as a check on your own ratings. In addition, one of your peers might observe one or more of your classes with the idea of providing specific feedback about your teaching. If this is done, the observer usually completes an evaluation checklist or rating form such as that presented in Figure 13.2. Sometimes, however, the evaluator simply provides a written description of what he or she observes along with an assessment. Peer evaluation might also take the form of having a colleague view videotapes or listen to audiotapes of your teaching with you. The two of you can then analyze your teaching together.

A major criticism of peer evaluation advanced in the literature on teacher evaluation is that teachers are not trained evaluators (*Evaluating Teachers,* 1974). Many teachers believe, however, that their peers are more competent to evaluate them than anyone else (*Evaluating Teachers,* 1974). Confidence in the person doing the evaluating tends to make peer evaluation less threatening to a classroom teacher than evaluation by a supervisor. With anxiety and threat removed from the evaluation, the possibility exists for the process to provide meaningful results.

Peer evaluation is not a common practice in public schools for a number of reasons, the most obvious being that, to observe another's class, the teacher has to leave his or her own class or other responsibilities. A number of school districts across the country do make provisions for substitute teachers to support peer evaluation, but this is generally limited to districts in which peer evaluation is a mandatory part of the teacher evaluation process.

Another reason for its infrequent use seems to result from the unwillingness of some teachers to judge their peers (*Evaluating Teachers,* 1974). We believe that teachers who do not participate in peer evaluation for this reason are making a serious error. Not only can teachers provide valuable feedback to other teachers as the result of observing another's classes, but they can gain a great deal of information regarding their own teaching as well.

If you are concerned that you might not be a good observer, consult the references and programs that are available to help you develop such skills. Generally, these are directed toward principals and other administrators responsible for teacher evaluation, but they will serve to train peer evaluators as well. For example, Richard P. Manatt of Iowa State University provides a *Handy Pocket Reference to Teacher Appraisal Procedures.* Manatt suggests that before visiting a class, you ask of the teacher you are to observe:

PORTLAND PUBLIC SCHOOLS
TEACHER EVALUATION FORM

TEACHER'S NAME _____   Number of Observations _____

Social Security No. _____   Total time of Observations _____

Date _____   Was there a pre-conference? _____

Assignment _____   post-conference? _____

School _____   Employee Status: ____ Probationary
                                                                   ____ Tenure

INSTRUCTIONS

It is essential that the teacher and evaluator be familiar with the "Process" booklet, *Evaluation*, and the State bulletin on *Standards of Competent and Ethical Professional Performance*.

HOW TO EVALUATE PERFORMANCE . . . . .
- The principal should indicate whether the teacher meets minimum standards in each of the eight major peformance sections. This judgment is to be based upon a review of each of the practices listed within a section. Performance may be regarded as meeting minimum standards even if mild deficiencies exist in every practice in the section. Conversely, a single practice, if seriously deficient, can result in an unsatisfactory rating for the entire section.

- If performance is judged to meet minimum standards, the principal should simply check (✓) the practice on the line at the left. No supporting documentation is necessary.

- If performance does not meet minimum standards or is in any way deficient, the principal should put an "I" on the line to the left of the practice(s) in question.

- A teacher who meets minimum standards is a very competent professional teacher (see State bulletin). If a teacher makes a major contribution to a school or consistently exceeds expectations, the principal may make a "C" on the line wherever appropriate and describe the commendatory practice.

HOW TO DOCUMENT DEFICIENCIES . . . . .
- Principals are required to document deficiencies in any section or practice rated as not meeting standards. This is done by checking "I" (improvement suggested) on all deficient practices and recording comments below. Such comments should have two parts: (1) a description of observed deficiencies and (2) suggestion(s) for improvement. The back of the sheet should be used if necessary.

- In making comments on each section, reference must be made to any previous evaluation on file for the teacher being evaluated, and special care must be taken to note the result of any previous suggestions for improvement.

YOU MUST RECOMMEND FOR OR AGAINST EMPLOYMENT . . . . .
- On page four the principal is required to make a recommendation for or against continued employment. He should draw a line through "do" or "do not" or "shall" or "shall not" to leave the wording desired. Note that the principal marks either the first line or the second line, not both.

Figure 13.2.
A portion of the Portland public schools teacher evaluation form. [From Teacher Evaluation *(Arlington, Va.: Educational Research Service, 1978), pp. 67-71. Copyrighted 1978 by Educational Research Service, Arlington, Va. Reprinted with permission.]*

TEACHER EVALUATION FORM   Teacher's Name _____

                                 Date _____

THEN SIGN AND SEND TO AREA OFFICE
   • The evaluation form must be signed by the teacher, principal, and vice principal (when involved in the evaluation), then the original must be forwarded to the area office with copies retained by
the teacher and principal.

Complete in triplicate: *Legend:*
   original for Personnel Services   ✓ = Meets minimum standards
      via Area Office   I = Improvement suggested
   one copy for teacher   C = Commendation for consistently
   one copy for principal   exceeding minimum standards

1. PROFESSIONAL PREPAREDNESS AND GROWTH

	Performance Meets Minimum Standards	Performance Does Not Meet Minimum Standards

_____ 1.   Instruction reflects well-planned and effective methodology.

_____ 2.   Instruction reflects adequate and current knowledge of subject.

_____ 3.   Works to improve professional skills and knowledge.

_____ 4.   Bases professional growth program on priority needs identified
            through cooperative planning with principal or designee.

Comments:

2. PLANNING

	Performance Meets Minimum Standards	Performance Does Not Meet Minimum Standards

_____ 1.   Has plans that can be clearly understood and used.

_____ 2.   Can clearly communicate the way any instructional activity
            relates to the goals of the course of instruction.

_____ 3.   Contributes to team planning or other coordinated planning
            as needed by the teaching assignment.

Comments:

Figure 13.2. (Continued.)

TEACHER EVALUATION FORM Teacher's Name _____

           Date _____

_____ 3. Keeps room properly lighted, ventilated, and free of hazards to health and safety
     (to degree teacher can influence).

Comments:

6. USE OF RESOURCES

Performance Meets Minimum Standards	Performance Does Not Meet Minimum Standards

_____ 1. Procures, uses and takes proper care of such materials and equipment as are
     appropriate and avialable in the school and district.

_____ 2. Uses library, media, students, and personnel of the school and school system as
     learning resources.

_____ 3. Uses natural and human resources of the community as learning resources.

_____ 4. Uses cultural and business-industrial resources of the community as learning
     resources.

Comments:

7. EVALUATION

Performance Meets Minimum Standards	Performance Does Not Meet Minimum Standards

_____ 1. Maintains and uses cumulative records of student progress in planning instruction.

_____ 2. Uses tests and/or other evaluative information in planning instructional units and
     after instruction to determine if goals have been met.

_____ 3. Consults principal, specialists, other teachers in the school, and students in evalua-
     ting own plans, methods, and results.

_____ 4. Uses instruments and methods that effectively measure the students' attainment of
     learning goals.

_____ 5. Makes clear to students how success in learning will be judged.

Figure 13.2. *(Continued.)*

479

TEACHER EVALUATION FORM   Teacher's Name _____

                                 Date _____

_____ 6. Communicates effectively with parents and students regarding student
            achievement, behavior and attendance.

Comments:

8. ORGANIZATIONAL RESPONSIBILITES

Performance Meets Minimum Standards	Performance Does Not Meet Minimum Standards

_____ 1. Cooperates with and supports other faculty members.

_____ 2. Observes the spirit and intent of rules and regulations of the school and school
            system.

_____ 3. Provides complete and accurate data to the school, area, and district as requested
            for management purposes.

_____ 4. Assumes necessary non-instructional responsibilities.

_____ 5. Shares the responsibility with all other employees for promoting the educational
            goals and developing public acceptance of the school system.

Comments:

9. OTHER:

I (do, do not) recommend this permanent teacher for another year
of service in School District No. 1.

If this probationary teacher's work continues to be of its present
quality, I (shall, shall not) recommend election for another year
of service in School District No. 1.

_____ _____   _____ _____
Principal's Signature   Date   Vice-Principal's   Date
                                    Signature

I have read the above report consisting of four pages:

_____ _____
Teacher's Signature   Date

Received and Contents Noted
_____ (Area Office) Date: _____
_____ (District Office Personnel Services) Date: _____

Figure 13.2. (Continued.)

1. Where are you in the course?
2. What teaching and learning activities will take place?
3. What skills, attitudes, and knowledge will be taught?
4. How are you going to do it?
5. Are there particular teaching behaviors you want monitored?
6. What special characteristics of students should be noted?

Manatt also suggests that you ask yourself how you would teach the same lesson before observing. Such a process of preparation for observation can serve to improve the quality of observation, since it helps to provide *specific* things to be observed.

Supervisor Evaluation

In 1978, the Educational Research Service reported that, of 362 school districts surveyed in the United States, 97.9% required some sort of formal teacher evaluation. The service reported further that 46.4% of those surveyed districts required an annual observation of tenured teachers and that 80.9% required at least two observations of teachers who had not yet earned tenure. In most districts, these observations are conducted by members of the administrative staff, primarily the principal of the building to which a teacher is assigned. While the primary reason given for these observations is to help teachers improve, the results are also used to decide on renewed appointment of probationary teachers, to recommend dismissal of tenured teachers, and to decide upon salary increments (*Evaluating Teacher Performance*, 1978). With such important decisions influenced by the outcome, evaluation by a supervisor can obviously be very threatening to a classroom teacher. To compound the threat, many teachers do not believe that their supervisors are qualified to assess their teaching.

There is little doubt that evaluation will continue to be used in making the personnel decisions just described. But teachers should be aware that recent legislation in New York, California, and New Jersey, for example, should prove to be a real asset to the evaluation process. According to Richard Hyman, "what these laws and court decisions do is require supervisors to be more judicious, more careful, more sure of their data, more precise, more helping" (Hyman, 1975, p. 9). As a result, many school districts across the country have undertaken extensive training programs in the evaluation of teaching for the supervisors. While this will not eliminate all the anxiety from supervisor evaluations, the teacher can probably expect more extensive and much improved feedback from his or her supervisor. Supervisor evaluation should, under these conditions, be an extremely valuable source of information for the improvement of teaching.

Certainly, a major part of the evaluation by supervisor process will

Person Observed _____   Observer _____

Date: _____   Time: _____

Tuckman Teacher Feedback Form

1.	ORIGINAL	___: ___: ___: ___: ___: ___: ___:	CONVENTIONAL
2.	PATIENT	___: ___: ___: ___: ___: ___: ___:	IMPATIENT
3.	COLD	___: ___: ___: ___: ___: ___: ___:	WARM
4.	HOSTILE	___: ___: ___: ___: ___: ___: ___:	AMIABLE
5.	CREATIVE	___: ___: ___: ___: ___: ___: ___:	ROUTINIZED
6.	INHIBITED	___: ___: ___: ___: ___: ___: ___:	UNINHIBITED
7.	ICONOCLASTIC	___: ___: ___: ___: ___: ___: ___:	RITUALISTIC
8.	GENTLE	___: ___: ___: ___: ___: ___: ___:	HARSH
9.	UNFAIR	___: ___: ___: ___: ___: ___: ___:	FAIR
10.	CAPRICIOUS	___: ___: ___: ___: ___: ___: ___:	PURPOSEFUL
11.	CAUTIOUS	___: ___: ___: ___: ___: ___: ___:	EXPERIMENTING
12.	DISORGANIZED	___: ___: ___: ___: ___: ___: ___:	ORGANIZED
13.	UNFRIENDLY	___: ___: ___: ___: ___: ___: ___:	SOCIABLE
14.	RESOURCEFUL	___: ___: ___: ___: ___: ___: ___:	UNCERTAIN
15.	RESERVED	___: ___: ___: ___: ___: ___: ___:	OUTSPOKEN
16.	IMAGINATIVE	___: ___: ___: ___: ___: ___: ___:	EXACTING
17.	ERRATIC	___: ___: ___: ___: ___: ___: ___:	SYSTEMATIC
18.	AGGRESSIVE	___: ___: ___: ___: ___: ___: ___:	PASSIVE
19.	ACCEPTING (People)	___: ___: ___: ___: ___: ___: ___:	CRITICAL
20.	QUIET	___: ___: ___: ___: ___: ___: ___:	BUBBLY
21.	OUTGOING	___: ___: ___: ___: ___: ___: ___:	WITHDRAWN
22.	IN CONTROL	___: ___: ___: ___: ___: ___: ___:	ON THE RUN
23.	FLIGHTY	___: ___: ___: ___: ___: ___: ___:	CONSCIENTIOUS
24.	DOMINANT	___: ___: ___: ___: ___: ___: ___:	SUBMISSIVE
25.	OBSERVANT	___: ___: ___: ___: ___: ___: ___:	PREOCCUPIED
26.	INTROVERTED	___: ___: ___: ___: ___: ___: ___:	EXTROVERTED
27.	ASSERTIVE	___: ___: ___: ___: ___: ___: ___:	SOFT-SPOKEN
28.	TIMID	___: ___: ___: ___: ___: ___: ___:	ADVENTUROUS

Figure 13.3
The Tuckman Teacher Feedback on classroom climate. [This form was published by Bruce Tuckman of Rutgers University and appears in Hyman (1975, p. 32).]

continue to be observation of the teacher in the classroom. If supervisors follow the suggestions of such writers as Hyman (1975), their observations will concentrate on more specific aspects of the instructional process than is frequently the case. For example, Hyman provides specific suggestions and techniques for observing classroom climate, interactional patterns, cognitive processes, student groupings, and teaching strategies. Certainly, a teacher can use the feedback of a trained observer in each of these important areas. To illustrate the specificity of Hyman's suggestions, the Tuckman Teacher Feedback form is presented in Figure 13.3.

Unfortunately, every school district and every supervisor will probably not commit the effort and resources to teacher evaluation that is implied in this discussion. We believe, however, that teachers who teach in a school system that does make this commitment will find their supervisor to be an excellent resource for improvement of teaching. Teachers who do not work in such a system may have to help their supervisors see and accept their responsibility.

Student Evaluations

Evaluation of teachers by students in colleges and universities is a very popular practice. The results of these evaluations may even be published in the school newspaper or in special evaluation of teachers brochures so that all students are aware of which teachers students think are good and which not so good. Just because student evaluations are commonly used does not mean they are generally accepted as being a good technique. The following quotation illustrates what some college teachers think about student evaluations:

Students are not competent to judge the merit of either the process or the results of teaching. They are, it is alleged, incapable of distinguishing between indoctrination and good teaching. . . . It is a democratic fallacy that the teaching is best which pleases the majority. 'If the teacher's promotion is to depend upon student ratings, student prizes should be awarded those who graduate precisely in the middle of the class.'. . . Students are immature, superficial, mistaken, and prejudiced. . . . Student ratings tend to disrupt the morale of the faculty. . . . Student ratings tend to have a disruptive effect on the morale of the students. . . . The cost in time and money is frequently urged as an objection to teacher rating by students. [Remmers, 1939, pp. 230–231]

While Remmers's statement was written in 1939, the view of many regarding student ratings is not really different today. Yet student evaluations of teachers appear to be an increasing trend in the public schools. Secondary schools tend to use student evaluations more frequently than elementary schools, but it should be noted that student evaluations have been documented as being used even with kindergarten students. Because of this increasing trend, you should be aware of a number of points regarding student evaluations that do gain general agreement.

1. Student rating scales do seem to be a reliable indication of something. Exactly what that something is seems to be debatable, but at least they tell the teacher the extent to which students like or dislike his or her teaching.
2. Students tend to be lenient in rating teachers. They are reluctant to use the low end of the scale.

3. The best and most defensible uses of student evaluations of teaching is for teacher self-evaluation. They should be combined with other sources of data and should never be used as the "only" criterion for effective teaching.

4. There does not appear to be a relationship between intelligence test scores and student ratings of instruction. However, there does appear to be a positive relationship between student achievement and their ratings of teachers in such areas as clarity, enthusiasm, use of student ideas, and variability of presentation.

5. Student ratings do have an effect on the behavior of teachers, but it is not always a constructive effect.

6. Student ratings of teachers seem to suffer from a halo effect. That is, if the teacher is seen as being good in one area, he will also be seen as being good in other areas (Follman, 1982).

With these thoughts in mind, you might want to use this important area of feedback in the evaluation of your teaching. Just be careful to recall each time you look at the results that we are not sure what it is that student rating scales measure. Sample student rating forms from an elementary and secondary school are presented in Figure 13.4.

Figure 13.4
Sample student rating of teaching form. [The K–3 form is from Sullivan County Schools in Blountville, Tennessee. The secondary school form is from Berea City Schools in Berea, Ohio. Both appeared in Teacher Evaluation *(Arlington, Va.: Educational Research Service, 1978, pp. 51-52, 65). Copyrighted 1978 by Educational Research Service, Arlington, Va. Reprinted with permission.]*

STUDENT EVALUATION OF TEACHER
Grades K–3

DIRECTIONS: The teacher will read the questions orally to the students. The students will mark the sheet by drawing a circle around "yes" or "no" in response to each question. The students should mark only one answer to each question.

1. Does your teacher give you work that is too hard?	Yes	No
2. Does your teacher give you enough time to finish your work?	Yes	No
3. When you don't understand something, are you afraid to ask your teacher a question?	Yes	No
4. Is your teacher interested in the things you do at home?	Yes	No
5. Does your teacher help you with your work when you need help?	Yes	No
6. Does your teacher like some children better than others?	Yes	No
7. Does your teacher yell at the children too much?	Yes	No
8. Does your teacher give you work that is too easy?	Yes	No
9. Does your teacher try to make school interesting to you?	Yes	No
10. Does your teacher care about you?	Yes	No
11. Do you get as many chances as other children to do special jobs in your classroom?	Yes	No
12. Does your teacher treat you fairly?	Yes	No
13. Do you wish your class could have this teacher next year?	Yes	No
14. Is your teacher often too busy to help you when you need help?	Yes	No
15. Do you like your teacher?	Yes	No

Figure 13.4
(Continued.)

Secondary Teacher Self-Improvement Form

Teacher's Name _____

What is your opinion concerning this teacher's:

Key: 4 — The very best; 3 — Good; 2 — Average; 1 — Below Average

1. KNOWLEDGE OF SUBJECT: Does he or she have a thorough knowledge and understanding of his or her teaching field?   4   3   2   1

2. CLARITY OF EXPLANATIONS: Are assignments and explanations clear?   4   3   2   1

3. FAIRNESS: Is he/she fair and impartial in treatment of all students?   4   3   2   1

4. CONTROL: Does he/she keep enough order in the classroom? Do students behave well?   4   3   2   1

5. ATTITUDE TOWARD STUDENTS: Is he/she patient, understanding, considerate and courteous?   4   3   2   1

6. ABILITY TO STIMULATE INTEREST: Is this class interesting and challenging?   4   3   2   1

7. ATTITUDE TOWARD SUBJECT: Does he/she show interest in and enthusiasm for the subject? Does he/she appear to enjoy teaching this subject?   4   3   2   1

8. ATTITUDE TOWARD SUBJECT OPINIONS: Are the ideas and opinions of students treated with respect? Are differences of opinion welcomed even when a student disagrees with the teacher?   4   3   2   1

9. ENCOURAGEMENT OF STUDENT PARTICIPATION: Do students feel free to raise questions and express opinions? Are students encouraged to take part?   4   3   2   1

10. SENSE OF HUMOR: Does he/she see and share with students amusing happenings and experiences?   4   3   2   1

11. PLANNING AND PREPARATION: Are plans well made? Is class time well spent? Is little time wasted?   4   3   2   1

12. ASSIGNMENTS: Are assignments (out-of-class, required work) sufficiently challenging without being unreasonably long? Is the weight of assignments reasonable?   4   3   2   1

13. AVAILABILITY: Is he/she available to the students who need help?   4   3   2   1

14. INDIVIDUALITY: Does the teacher recognize individual differences and provide for them?   4   3   2   1

Please name two or more things that you especially like about this teacher/course.
Please give two or more suggestions for the improvement of this teacher or course.

Establishing a Productive Classroom Climate

In making use of what is known about teacher characteristics and student reactions to them, it is reasonable for teachers to ask how to go about constructing a "good" classroom climate. This is not an easy question to answer for several reasons. First, there is no one "good" climate but,

485

rather, an almost endless number of possibilities. Second, classroom climate involves the interaction of numerous variables so that any one factor can be judged only in relation to other factors and the total picture that emerges. Third, each teacher is a unique individual, as are students, and the type of classroom that is effective and comfortable for one teacher may not be so for another.

The first step in developing a healthy climate is to "know thyself." Only by facing your own strengths, weaknesses, goals, personality, and idiosyncracies realistically can you hope to have an effective and enjoyable classroom. If you have a strong need for structure, you must find ways of structuring your class but not inhibiting or restricting important goals in so doing. If you are democratic by nature, you must find ways of using this without allowing your class to fall into the rudderless mold of the laissez-faire model. Above all, you must experiment and find a climate that is enjoyable and rewarding for *you,* since a class in which you feel bored, threatened, or anxious can hardly be one that facilitates effective learning and positive attitudes.

A second step in developing a healthy climate is to "know thy students." An informal, nondirective class with much student participation and the teacher in the background might work fine in one setting with a

---

TEACHING IN THE GOOD OLD DAYS

The following rules for teachers, posted in 1872 by a principal in the City of New York, demonstrate our cause to rejoice that "times have changed."

1. Teachers each day will fill lamps, clean chimneys, and trim wicks.
2. Each teacher will bring a bucket of water and a scuttle of coal for the day's session.
3. Make your pens carefully.
4. Men teachers may take one evening each week for courting purposes or two evenings each week if they attend church regularly.
5. After ten hours in school, the teacher should spend the remaining time reading the Bible or other good books.
6. Women teachers who marry or engage in unseemly conduct will be dismissed.
7. Every teacher should lay aside from each payday a goodly sum of his earnings for his benefit during the declining years so that he will not become a burden on society.
8. Any teacher who smokes, uses liquor in any form, frequents pool or public halls, or gets shaved in a barber shop will give good reason to suspect his worth, intentions, integrity, and honesty.
9. The teacher who performs his labor faithfully and without fault for five years will be given an increase of twenty-five cents per week in his pay, providing the board of education approves.

certain type of group, but fail miserably in another. You must gauge the climate of the class to the maturity, needs, personalities, and abilities of the students as well as your own needs. Every class is different, so that some portion of the classroom climate should be left open rather than predetermined.

Along with knowing the students, it is important to recognize the nature of their *past experience* also. Students with a long history of formal autocratic classes will not adapt immediately and smoothly to an informal, democratic class. The more cautious approach of starting where they are and then gradually building the climate you want is probably more effective and less dangerous in the long run.

As in so many aspects of teaching, having your goals clearly in mind is very important. It is only through blind luck that you can hope to achieve the most suitable climate if you are unaware of your goals. For

---

SUGGESTIONS FOR FIRST-DAY PROCEDURE IN THE CLASSROOM

1. Be on hand early. See that you have a definite assignment for each class, something that requires preparation for the next day. See that all your plans are made so that each recitation goes off in a systematic manner. Order and method lead to effective work.
2. Have and follow a very definite pattern, especially the first few days. You may be more flexible later, but at first be definite and decisive.
3. Have plenty of work ready and try to open up some class or group problems the first day that will carry over to succeeding days. Motivate your pupils from the first.
4. Insist on good working habits from the first. Have things done properly. Keep everyone busy.
5. Keep yourself in the background as director and master, but be in control from the first. Avoid talking too much and too fast, but get the pupils so busy at work that they will not want to do the talking.
6. Keep yourself cheerful, natural, and human; see the funny side of things with the pupils. Expect an acceptable degree of perfection in both conduct and work.
7. Remember that the pupils have just come in from a long vacation and that both they and you are working at a problem of adjustment.
8. Watch your own habits of work and determine whether they are such as you would wish your pupils to imitate.
9. Make a note of special problems that come to you during the first day to be discussed in faculty meetings later.

This advice, from a high school teachers' handbook, is typical of handbooks and textbooks on teaching. The central message seems to be to get on with it in as orderly and as systematic a way as possible, be well prepared, keep students busy, then things will go all right.

example, a relaxed, informal, unstructured climate might work well if an important goal were student interaction, awareness of others' opinions, and the examination of personal values. But that climate would most likely be ineffective and confusing if major goals were the understanding and application of basic facts and concepts.

A question that often arises is "How do I begin?" Student teachers are sometimes so concerned with maintaining discipline and authority that they try to impress the class with their meanness at the start and thereby undermine the very climate they would prefer. Advice to "Start out tough" and "Don't smile until Christmas" tends to encourage this early overkill. The advice to start right in working toward the climate you want, ready to meet tests of authority but not seeking them, seems more appropriate. Begin by being as natural as possible, without overstructuring the situation, and get right into teaching activities to reduce your anxiety.

Finally, in line with the humanistic viewpoint, the real "you" must emerge in the classroom. Only by being sincere, authentic, secure, and confident can you hope to really enjoy your task. In this way, too, your students will learn and feel good about themselves and the subject. Thus, the pursuit of classroom climate becomes one of understanding yourself and your goals, planning strategies to achieve these, testing out different approaches until you find those that work, and keeping at it until you get the type of climate you want.

Summary

The characteristics that separate outstanding teachers from average or mediocre teachers are difficult to pinpoint, but it is possible to identify some differences. Although the ultimate criterion of successful teaching lies in what students learn, there are various reasons why it is difficult to assess teaching in this fashion. One approach to studying teaching is the *global* approach. This amounts to looking at the broad picture, taking into account as many general factors as possible. For example, the reputation of a teacher is usually based on an informal and global estimate of his or her total teaching effectiveness.

But the global approach, even when it is accurate, fails to identify specific teacher shortcomings and thus fails to indicate what it is that needs improvement.

Specific approaches to measuring teaching effectiveness attempt to define particular elements of teaching and develop objective measures of each element. The most famous example of this is that of Flanders and his interaction analysis for scoring classroom behavior. Flanders breaks down teaching into ten observable categories, the two major headings being direct influence and indirect influence by the teacher. He also has categories for student behavior and a final category for silence or confusion.

Findings with the Flanders model include the fact that many teachers

488

exert direct influence on the students most of the time, even though indirect influence may be more effective. Also, most of the activity in a classroom is teacher talk rather than student talk. Flanders's matrix provides an objective measure of what is going on in a teacher's classroom, with some idea of what to change in order to improve.

Another example of an objective approach to studying teaching is Ryans's teacher characteristics schedule, in which he identified three important dimensions in teaching: (1) warm, understanding, and friendly versus aloof, egocentric, and restricted; (2) responsible, businesslike, and systematic versus evading, unplanned, and slipshod; and (3) stimulating and imaginative versus dull and routine.

Critics of systems such as Flanders's and Ryans's argue that research has failed to support the idea that teaching can be accurately defined and measured. Reports such as the Coleman et al. *Report on Equality of Educational Opportunity* are cited as proof that what the teacher does really doesn't matter. However, Gage and others argue that research really does tell us a lot about teaching.

In their study of teaching, Good and Brophy concluded that four special skills were crucial to success in the classroom: communicating, modeling, managing, and grouping. Good and Brophy also claim that these skills are teachable. They encourage teachers to become skilled observers and to help each other to see what is going on in their classrooms.

Many different approaches to evaluating teaching have been tried. Peer evaluations are a promising but little-used technique. When teachers observe and evaluate each other, both the observer and the teacher being observed profit from it. Video- and audiotapes can be used to help the teacher to see how he or she appears from the student's point of view. Evaluations by superiors are the most common form of teacher evaluations and can be helpful if done systematically and thoroughly, with detailed feedback to the teacher.

Evaluation of teachers by the students themselves has become popular, but there remains considerable controversy about such evaluations. Research has shown that student evaluations are a reliable indicator of *something*, but there is disagreement about just what that "something" is.

Student evaluation of teaching yields considerable agreement as to what is "good" and "poor" teaching. Terms such as sincere, patient, flexible, caring, good discipline, liking students, and fairness emerge repeatedly when students describe their best-liked teachers; terms such as unfair, negative, mean, rigid, cold, and disliking emerge when they discuss their worst-liked teachers. Hamachek, in studying characteristics of outstanding teachers, found three distinct areas of importance: (1) behavior in the classroom, (2) ways of viewing themselves, and (3) ways of viewing others.

In comparing three types of classroom climate—the democratic, the autocratic, and the laissez-faire—it has been found that both the democratic and the autocratic atmosphere lead to the same amount of subject matter learning but that the democratic climate is superior in such dimensions as attitudes, feelings, and self-esteem.

Study Questions

1. Several different approaches to identifying successful teachers are presented in this chapter. What is *your* definition of a good teacher? Can you think of one of your favorite teachers and enumerate those qualities that made him or her successful?

2. What are the strengths and weaknesses of the global approach to studying teaching? What are the strengths and weaknesses of the specific approach? Which approach do you prefer, and why?

3. In employing Flanders's matrix, it has been found that most teachers spend the majority of classroom time in teacher talk, leaving very little time for student talk. What are some ways that the teacher can increase the amount of student talk in the classroom? Why do so many teachers fail to do these things?

4. Using Ryans's checklist, it has been found that good teachers tend to be warm, understanding and friendly, responsible, businesslike, stimulating, and imaginative. Do you think that teachers can be taught these characteristics, or are they qualities a person either has or doesn't have? Are good teachers made, or are they born?

5. Why is it so important for the teacher to be a good observer? How can observing skills be developed? Is it helpful for teachers to observe each other?

6. When you become a teacher, it is almost certain that you will be observed and evaluated. What type of instrument, and what type of observation, would you prefer? Whom would you like to do the evaluating, and why?

References

Coleman, J. et al. *Equality of Educational Opportunity.* Washington, D.C.: U.S. Government Printing Office, 1966.

Diagnosis of Critical Work Activities. Carbondale, Ill.: Carbondale Elementary Schools, 1978.

Dunkin, M., and Biddle, B. *The Study of Teaching.* New York: Holt, Rinehart and Winston, 1974.

Evaluating Teachers for Professional Growth: Current Trends in School Policies and Programs. Arlington, Va.: National School Public Relations Association, 1974.

Evaluating Teacher Performance. Arlington, Va.: Educational Research Service, 1978.

Flanders, N. A. *Analyzing Teaching Behavior.* Reading, Mass.: Addison-Wesley, 1970.

Follman, J. *Basic Questions Regarding Evaluation of Teaching. Technical Report.* Tampa, Fla.: College of Education, University of South Florida, 1982.

Gage, N. L., ed. *Handbook of Research on Teaching.* Chicago: Rand McNally, 1963.

Gage, N. L. "Can Science Contribute to the Art of Teaching," *Phi Delta Kappan,* 49(7), March 1968, pp. 399–403.

Gage, N. L. *Scientific Basis of the Art of Teaching.* New York: Teachers College Press, 1978.

Gauss, J. "Socrates Evaluation," *Saturday Review,* July 21, 1962, p. 47.

Getzels, J. W. and Jackson, P. W. "The Teacher's Personality and Characteristics," in N. L. Gage, ed. *Handbook of Research on Teaching*, pp. 506–582. Chicago: Rand McNally, 1963.

Good, J. L., and Brophy, J. E. *Looking in Classrooms*. New York: Harper & Row, 1973.

Hamachek, D. "Characteristics of Good Teachers and Implications for Teacher Education," *Phi Delta Kappan*, 50(6), February 1969, pp. 341–345.

Hyman, R. T. *School Administrator's Handbook of Teacher Supervision and Evaluation Methods*. Englewood Cliffs, N.J.: Prentice-Hall, 1975.

Lippitt, R., and White, R. K. "An Experimental Study of Leadership and Group Life," in G. E. Swanson, T. M. Newcomb, and E. L. Hartley, eds., *Readings in Social Psychology* Rev. ed., pp. 340–354. New York: Holt, Rinehart and Winston, 1952.

Manatt, R. P. *Handy Pocket Reference to Teacher Appraisal Procedures*. Ames, Iowa: R. P. Manatt, undated.

Manatt, R. P., Palmer, K. L., and Hidlebaugh, E. "Evaluating Teacher Performance with Improved Rating Scales," *NASSP Bulletin*, 60(401), September 1976, pp. 21–24.

McKeachie, W. J. "Anxiety in the College Classroom," *Journal of Educational Research*, 45(2), October 1951, pp. 153–160.

Millman, J. "Student Achievement as a Measure of Teacher Competence," in J. Millman ed., *Handbook of Teacher Evaluation*, pp. 146–166. Beverly Hills, Calif.: Sage, 1981.

Remmers, H. "Appraisal of College Teaching Through Ratings and Student Opinion," *National Society of College Teachers of Education Yearbook*, pp. 227–240. Chicago: University of Chicago Press, 1939.

Ryans, D. G. *Characteristics of Teachers, Their Description, Comparison, and Appraisal*. Washington, D.C.: American Council on Education, 1960.

Wallen, N. E., and Travers, R. M. W. "Analysis and Investigation of Teaching Methods," in N. L. Gage, ed., *Handbook of Research on Teaching*, pp. 448-505, Chicago: Rand McNally, 1963.

Withall, J. and Lewis, W. W. "Social Interaction in the Classroom," in N. L. Gage, ed., *Handbook of Research on Teaching*, pp. 683–714. Chicago: Rand McNally, 1963.

491

Objectives, Planning, and Evaluation

14

PREVIEW

Why study a taxonomy of educational objectives?

What are some examples of items from the taxonomy?

What are the components of the cognitive domain?

How many different dimensions of knowledge are there?

How many different dimensions of comprehension are there?

Why is it important to include application objectives in teaching?

What are the differences between analysis and synthesis?

Why is analysis understood more easily by teachers than some of the other dimensions of the taxonomy?

Can a teacher learn to think in terms of different levels of the taxonomy?

Why is the cognitive domain not the only taxonomy that is important for teachers?

What are learning outcomes, and why are they important?

Why does a teacher need both general objectives and specific learning outcomes?

What are the criteria for a good objective?

What are the differences between a goal and an objective?

What guidelines are helpful in setting goals?

Why is it important to plan strategies?

How can the teacher build feedback into teaching?

What are some of the ways to assess results?

Why is it important to revise goals and try again?

What are some guidelines in reporting progress?

What are some strengths and weaknesses of lectures and discussions?

When should a teacher plan a lecture or a discussion?

What does reliability mean?

What are some guidelines for carrying out a good discussion?

In what situations are lectures superior to discussions?

What are three types of reliability?

What is the standard error of measurement?

What are score bands, and how are they helpful in interpreting scores?

What is the concept of validity?

What are four types of validity?

What are some reasonable guidelines in using standardized tests?

What is a norm-referenced test?

What is a criterion-referenced test?

What are the areas in which standardized tests are used in the schools?

What are some examples of widely used standardized tests?

What are some possible reasons for rising grades and declining test scores?

In Chapter 7, Humanistic Psychology and the Affective Domain, we introduced the idea of a taxonomy of educational objectives. A taxonomy is a detailed set of principles that are used to place things into categories. Taxonomies have been used widely in botany and zoology for the classification of plants and animals. In education, the taxonomy of educational objectives first places each objective into one of three major categories: (1) cognitive, (2) affective, or (3) psychomotor. Each of these categories is then broken down into subcategories that start with low-level skills and move on to the more complex skills. Thus, the taxonomy not only categorizes objectives but also establishes a hierarchy of categories based upon the degree of complexity reflected in each category.

Using this taxonomy of objectives can be very helpful to a teacher. It helps us to be aware of the broad areas into which objectives fall, which, in turn, allows us to be certain that we concentrate not only in the cognitive domain but also recognize that there are objectives from the affective and psychomotor domains as well.

The taxonomy also helps in reviewing objectives within a given domain. There is a tendency for teachers to concentrate on lower-level skills within a domain to the exclusion of higher-level skills. In other words, we may be more inclined to ask students to remember a specific date from the Civil War period than to ask them to analyze causes for the war. Since it is important to get beyond these lower-level skills in teaching, the classification of objectives in the taxonomy allows a check to see that we have objectives at the various levels of complexity. In this regard, the idea of a hierarchy of objectives and the determination to use it in planning objectives are far more important than the specific hierarchy being used. Teachers may adopt the cognitive hierarchy of Bloom et al. (1956) or the affective hierarchy of Krathwohl et al. (1964) or they may create their own hierarchy. The important point is that objectives reflecting higher-level cognitive and affective skills should be involved in one's teaching.

Those who have tried know that it is difficult to categorize objectives precisely and clearly. Several teachers judging independently will sometimes place the same objective in several different categories. But this is not really important. What is important is that the teacher think and plan in terms of a taxonomy that goes beyond simple knowledge or memory of facts. A teacher may well spend most of his or her time with low-level skills unless he or she makes a conscious and systematic attempt to incorporate other levels into his or her teaching.

The Cognitive Domain

As we have seen before, the cognitive domain is the domain concerned primarily with learning of subject matter. The teacher concerned with the development of healthy well-rounded students will state objectives in the affective and psychomotor domains as well as in the cognitive domain. However, the majority of objectives reflected in tests and grades fall into the cognitive domain. For this reason, we will analyze the cognitive domain in some detail. The following listing presents the cognitive domain as it was laid out by Bloom et al. in 1956.

The Cognitive Domain of Educational Objectives*

1.00 Knowledge. (The recall of specifics and universals, the recall of methods and processes, or the recall of a pattern, structure, or setting.)

    1.10 Knowledge of Specifics. (The recall of specific and isolable bits of information.)

        1.11 Knowledge of Terminology

        1.12 Knowledge of Specific Facts

    1.20 Knowledge of Ways and Means of Dealing with Specifics (Knowledge of the ways of organizing, studying, judging, and criticizing.)

        1.21 Knowledge of Conventions

        1.22 Knowledge of Trends and Sequences

        1.23 Knowledge of Classifications and Categories

        1.24 Knowledge of Criteria

        1.25 Knowledge of Methodology

*From *Taxonomy of Educational Objectives: The Classification of Educational Goals: Handbook I: Cognitive Domain* by Benjamin S. Bloom et al. Copyright © 1956 by Longman, Inc. Reprinted by permission of Longman, Inc., New York.

1.30 Knowledge of the Universals and Abstractions in a Field (Knowledge of the major schemes and patterns by which phenomena and ideas are organized.)

   1.31 Knowledge of Principles and Generalizations

   1.32 Knowledge of Theories and Structures

2.00 Comprehension. (A type of understanding or apprehension such that the individual knows what is being communicated and can make use of the material or idea being communicated without relating it to other material or seeing its fullest implications.)

   2.10 Translation. (Comprehension as evidenced by the care and accuracy with which the communication is paraphrased or rendered from one language or form of communication to another.)

   2.20 Interpretation. (The explanation or summarization of a communication.)

   2.30 Extrapolation. (The extension of trends or tendencies beyond the given data to determine implications, consequences, corollaries, effects, etc.)

3.00 Application. (The use of abstractions in particular and concrete situations.)

4.00 Analysis. (The breakdown of a communication into its constituent elements or parts such that the relative hierarchy of ideas is made clear and/or the relations between the ideas expressed are made explicit.)

   4.10 Analysis of Elements. (Identification of the elements included in a communication.)

   4.20 Analysis of Relationships. (The connections and interactions between elements and parts of a communication.)

   4.30 Analysis of Organizational Principles. (The organization, systematic arrangement, and structure which hold the communication together.)

5.00 Synthesis. (The putting together of elements and parts so as to form a whole.)

   5.10 Production of a Unique Communication. (The development of a communication in which the writer or speaker attempts to convey ideas, feelings, and/or experiences to others.)

   5.20 Production of a Plan, or Proposed Set of Operations. (The development of a plan of work or the proposal of a plan of operations.)

   5.30 Derivation of a Set of Abstract Relations. (The development of a set of abstract relations either to classify or explain particular data or phenomena or the deduction of propositions and relations from a set of basic propositions or symbolic representations.)

6.00 Evaluation. (Judgments about the value of material and methods for given purposes. Use of a standard of appraisal.)

   6.10 Judgments in Terms of Internal Evidence. (Evaluation of the accuracy of a communication from such evidence as logical accuracy, consistency, and other internal criteria.)

   6.20 Judgments in Terms of External Criteria. (Evaluation of material with reference to selected or remembered criteria.)

To illustrate this hierarchy of the cognitive domain, let us look at how representative learnings for students in a beginning psychology course would fit into the different categories.

1.00 *Knowledge.* The student can recall the basic steps in the scientific method.

   1.10 *Knowledge of specifics.* The student states that Freud discovered the unconscious.

   1.11 *Knowledge of terminology.* The student can recall the meaning of ego, superego, and id.

   1.12 *Knowledge of specific facts.* The student states that Wundt had the first experimental psychology laboratory in Leipzig in 1876.

   1.20 *Knowledge of ways and means of dealing with specifics.* The student knows that humanistic psychologists focus much more on introspective data than do behaviorists.

   1.21 *Knowledge of conventions.* The student explains that the .05 and .01 levels of probability are commonly used to accept or reject a hypothesis.

   1.22 *Knowledge of trends and sequences.* The student recognizes how psychology became increasingly obsessed with the environment during the behaviorist era and how it more recently moved toward an interactionist approach.

   1.23 *Knowledge of classifications and categories.* The student can describe the fields of social, industrial, educational, clinical, physiological, and experimental psychology.

   1.24 *Knowledge of criteria.* The student states the criteria by which a psychologist judges a "good" or "poor" experimental study.

   1.25 *Knowledge of methodology.* The student describes the steps in carrying out a correlational study.

   1.30 *Knowledge of the universals and abstractions in a field.* The student recognizes that the psychoanalytic approach is based on the importance of early experience and that adult behavior has its roots in the first five years of life.

   1.31 *Knowledge of principles and generalizations.* The student describes the major principles involved in learning.

   1.32 *Knowledge of theories and structures.* The student recalls that there are classical conditioning theories, instrumental conditioning theories, Gestalt theories, and cognitive theories.

Notice in each of the elements of the hierarchy that nothing is said about the student's being able to *carry out* the basic steps in the scientific method, or *understanding* the meaning of the unconscious, or *explaining* the difference between ego and id, or *approaching* material from a humanistic point of view, or *carrying out* a correlational study. The entire knowledge section of the taxonomy refers to knowing, remembering, and knowing about things but not applying, understanding, explaining, or any other abilities beyond the level of knowledge. This does *not* mean that this category is somehow inferior or worthless, however, since every field has numerous items of knowledge that must be known.

2.00 *Comprehension.* The student learns how to distinguish between examples of learning and of other forms of changes in behavior.

2.10 *Translation.* The student is able to take a list of statements of an emotionally disturbed person and convert these into an explanation, in his or her own words, of just what these statements mean in terms of psychological symptoms.

2.20 *Interpretation.* The student is able to convert a list of symptoms into an explanation of just what is bothering a person and just what life means from his or her point of view.

2.30 *Extrapolation.* The student, after translating the patient's statements into symptoms, interpreting these in terms of their meaning in the life of the patient, is now able to go on and predict how this patient is likely to react to a particular type of treatment.

Notice in each category of the comprehension section that it is not enough to remember or know about certain things. The student must go beyond this to doing something with the material, be that translating it into another form, interpreting its meaning in some way, or extrapolating beyond the material and realizing its significance. This is undoubtedly a large part of what the teacher tries to get across in almost any course and a part that is often unsatisfactory in terms of what the students actually learn. At the level of comprehension, the student must go beyond the memorization of facts, catch phrases, names, dates, and terminology. Teachers must make a special effort to see that students really are satisfying the requirements of learning at the level of comprehension, and not merely memorizing or making lucky guesses.

3.00 *Application.* The student can apply what he or she knows about the principles of adolescent development to several case studies of specific adolescents.

Don't be fooled by the fact that the application category has only one section. It is still every bit as important as any other category of the taxonomy. Application gets very much into the question of transfer of what is learned, and no question is more important than that of transfer. Students must continuously apply what they learn in school to other situations, both inside and outside of school, and it is this category that focuses on such transfer. Needless to say, transfer is often grossly neglected in teaching, perhaps because teachers sometimes take it for granted.

4.00 *Analysis.* The student is able to take a statement of a client and analyze it into its component parts, understanding the meaning of each part.

4.10 *Analysis of elements.* The student can label the elements and parts of a patient's communication.

4.20 *Analysis of relationships.* The student can show how the different elements and parts of the patient's concerns are related to each other and how several statements of a patient are related.

4.30 *Analysis of organizational principles.* The student is able to view a typical example of an advertising commercial and recognize the general propaganda techniques used in the materials.

For some reason, the category of analysis is more readily apparent to teachers as an important part of school learning than are some of the other categories. Perhaps this illustrates why breaking down into parts and converging on the one best solution are stressed in school. In spite of such awareness on the teacher's part, many students display inadequate skills at this level of the hierarchy. Analysis takes practice, and students probably rarely receive the necessary time and encouragement for practicing this skill. Many things learned at the knowledge level could probably be discovered by the student independently at the analysis level.

5.00 *Synthesis.* The student is able to combine numerous elements of what he or she has learned in the course and write a brief autobiography, describing himself or herself from a psychological point of view.

    5.10 *Production of a unique communication.* The student is able to construct and deliver a speech on constructive ways of motivating students.

    5.20 *Production of a plan or proposed set of operations.* The student, upon reading a psychologist's work, is able to propose ways of testing a hypothesis.

    5.30 *Derivation of a set of abstract relations.* The student is able to study lists of symptoms and classify them into categories of neuroses and psychoses.

The synthesis category implies a new skill on the part of the student, that of *putting things together*, choosing and combining to form a new whole. It is this category that comes closest to describing creativity, and it is also the category that is most neglected in teaching and especially in classroom tests. In attempting to measure synthesis, a situation that allows it, such as a project or essay, is required, rather than the traditional multiple-choice test.

6.00 *Evaluation.* The student can read a research article and say whether or not this is a satisfactory study based on research criteria.

    6.10 *Judgments in terms of internal evidence.* The student can listen to a psychological explanation and evaluate its logical accuracy, consistency, and exactness.

    6.20 *Judgments in terms of external criteria.* The student can compare the major theories of learning and point out strengths and weaknesses of each theory.

In this category, the student is using all the preceding levels, his or her knowledge, comprehension, application, analysis, and synthesis, but not as ends in themselves, and is applying all his or her skills of judging based on criteria and standards that have been learned. These judgments may be qualitative or quantitative, based either on the student's own standards or on those that are provided. This category is not only a capstone of the cognitive domain; it also provides a link to the affective domain in which valuing, liking, and enjoying become important.

Rather than proceeding through the hierarchy and then concluding with evaluation, the categories work more often in a cyclical form. The student reaches the evaluation level, which leads to seeking new knowledge or understanding at a lower level of the hierarchy. Thus, the pursuit of learning is never ending.

Before leaving Bloom et al.'s taxonomy, we emphasize again that this particular hierarchy is presented as an illustration of what can be done in analyzing one's teaching objectives. If you find it too detailed or too complex for your own use, modify it, devise your own taxonomy, or look for another that may be better suited for you. The important point is to spend time in your planning to be sure you get beyond knowledge-level skills in your teaching.

Goals and Objectives

To understand what is involved in teaching and testing what is taught, it is necessary to differentiate between goals and objectives. A *goal* is a general, long-term target of teaching, which can be stated in such broad terms as understand literature, appreciate the classics, or interpret Shakespeare. Goals cannot be observed specifically ("appreciating" or "understanding" are not specific behaviors), but they are highly important in planning, teaching, and testing. The broad, general, long-term goals must be thought out carefully before proceeding to plan the steps whereby these goals are reached.

An *objective,* on the other hand, is the more specific *learning outcome* that a teacher pursues on the way to achieving the long-term goals. Objectives should be stated in specific behavioral terms, such as to state, describe, explain, demonstrate, recognize, solve, complete, or list. In such behavioral terms, the teacher can readily observe whether or not specific behavioral objectives are being reached as he or she pursues his or her long-term goals in teaching. Whether or not a student "appreciates the American Indian" cannot be observed directly, but the teacher *can* observe whether the student lists or describes things in such a way that it is safe to conclude that the student "appreciates the American Indian."

Criteria for a Good Objective

The most important criterion for a good objective is that "it describe an important learning outcome." Unless an important outcome is being described, a beautifully stated objective may be of little use.

In addition, an objective must be stated clearly, as succinctly as possible, avoiding vague or confusing terms, and stated in terms of observable behavior. Thus, "interpreting Shakespeare" would qualify as a long-term instructional goal, but not as an objective. Objectives such as listing, specifying, recalling, or describing all relate to learning outcomes that demonstrate whether or not the student can interpret Shakespeare. To say that "The student shall recite the multiplication tables through 12 times 12" is a good objective because it is clear and succinct and because it is stated as a behavior that can be observed and measured. Words such as recite, state, write, design, recall, and identify are all effective verbs for classroom objectives because they each refer to a behavior that is observable and thus can be measured. On the other hand, words such as appreciate, feel, believe, understand, know, and value, while useful in stating long-term goals, are ineffective for stating classroom objectives, because in each case the word is ambiguous and cannot be observed and measured directly.

In addition to wording objectives in clear and unambiguous terms, other criteria of a good objective are that it must be realistic, reasonably achievable, and not so broad as to be unmeasurable. Whereas goals are long term, it is best to state objectives that can be achieved in a fairly short time, so that feedback and further planning can take place.

A Two-Step Process

The stating of goals and objectives in teaching is essentially a two-step process. First, the teacher states long-term teaching goals, for example, understanding basic principles. Then the teacher goes on to describe basic steps in understanding a principle, such as "identifies an example of the principle," "states the principle in his or her own words," recognizes a description of the principle," "uses the principle correctly." By stating the major instructional goals first, and then the specific behavioral objectives, the teacher contributes to the integration and transfer of learning, rather than just learning bits and pieces.

Evaluation in the Classroom

Every teacher is involved in the process of evaluation, regardless of the subject taught, regardless of what system of grading is used, and regardless of the grade level. Rather than fitting a common conception of evaluation as something that is done at the end, after everything else has been carried out, evaluation is actually a more continuous process, encompassing all stages of teaching, and having as much to do with an attitude or state of mind as with specific operations. Let us take a look at this never-ending evaluation cycle.

501

Setting Goals

The first step in the evaluation cycle is that of setting goals. Even this is not purely a "first" step, since the goals themselves are the result of previous experience, previous evaluations and decisions based on feedback from previous teaching attempts.

Each goal must be an important, long-term outcome of instruction. The goals taken together describe the general picture of what the teacher is trying to achieve.

Stating Objectives

Once goals are stated, the teacher goes on to describe specific objectives related to each goal, either in terms of student behaviors or as statements that can be converted readily into observable behaviors. They should be stated in the teacher's own words, as simply as possible, and preferably in writing. It is best to state modest but achievable objectives, because other objectives can easily be added later. It is also wise to set a deadline for achieving objectives.

Note, for example, the goals and objectives of a band director for his first month of lessons with the beginner's band. His overall goals are respect for the instrument, care in using the instrument, alertness and a positive attitude about playing in the band, and understanding the rudiments of musical performance. For achieving these goals, he has outlined the following specific objectives for the first month:

1. Students will be able to assemble and take apart their instruments properly and with reasonable speed by the second week.
2. Students will hold their instruments properly in both playing and at rest positions by the end of the second week.
3. Students will make some sort of sound on their instruments by the second lesson.
4. Students will play whole notes, half notes, and quarter notes, counting them properly, by the third week.
5. Students will be able to finger and play all notes in keys of C, G, and F in middle octave of their instruments by the fourth week.
6. The band will play together, with reasonable sound and intonation, the songs "Mary Had a Little Lamb," "Twinkle Twinkle Little Star," and "My Bonnie Lies over the Ocean" by the end of the fourth week.

Planning Teaching Strategies

After goals have been stated and converted into descriptive behavioral objectives, the teacher is ready to plan teaching strategies. What classroom experiences will bring about the desired behavioral changes? Teaching

Teachers need to spend time planning the strategy most appropriate for a given objective.
(CEMREL, Inc.)

strategies are planned for the specific objectives that were declared originally. Unless the strategy will lead logically to the behaviors as stated in the objectives, it cannot be justified as a teaching strategy. In this way, the teacher plans economically and straightforwardly for the specific objectives he or she has in mind, and the teaching has a clear focus. In everyday language, there is no "dilly-dallying around."

Building Feedback into Teaching

An important component of teaching as an evaluation cycle is that feedback is built into everything the teacher does. If the goals are stated as behavioral objectives, strategies are planned to reach these objectives, and these strategies are carried out, it stands to reason that evidence is needed for deciding how well goals are being met. The teacher has this in mind when he or she builds feedback into what he or she does. This feedback can be formal—in the form of tests, papers, and such—or informal, in the way of discussions, observing what students are doing, and listening closely. The important point is that there must be evidence available for the evaluation cycle to continue, and there must be behaviors and activities in order to provide this evidence.

The band director planned demonstrations, had students put together and take apart their instruments five times each day before starting to play, had them inspect each other doing this, used a stopwatch to time them at the end of the week, and had individual students stand up and explain how their instrument is assembled and disassembled. All these activities were designed to satisfy the objective that "Students will be able to assemble and take apart their instruments properly and with reasonable speed by the second week." During the second week, he merely observed them doing this at the beginning and end of each rehearsal, occasionally giving a student a tip or showing someone how to improve on this task. The goal was satisfied so well by all the attention and feedback devoted to it in the first two weeks that all students assembled and disassembled their instruments properly after that, with only the occasional lapse due to hurrying or carelessness that one might expect. By watching closely at the beginning and end of rehearsal, the director was able to gauge when it was time to review the rudiments of instrument care and perhaps remind the band of its importance.

Assessing the Results

Assuming that the teacher has set goals, converted them into behavioral objectives, planned strategies to meet these objectives, and then carried out these activities with ample opportunity for feedback, the next step in the evaluation process is to assess the results. Even in the most precise and systematic approach, this involves a fair amount of subjective judgment. What does it mean when half the class scores below 80 on a test? Or when ten students fail to finish their essays on time? Or when two thirds of a class complains that the work is too hard? Such items of feedback have no magic meaning in and of themselves, but only in the context of how they relate to the objectives at hand. The best way to relate feedback to objectives is already to have a standard in mind. For example, if the teacher has established the objective of half the class scoring 85% or above on a classroom test by a certain date, then it is known that the teacher has not yet reached the objective when 50% score below 80. Unfortunately, it is not always so easy to set such an objective, because the teacher often does not really know how easy or difficult a test is until it has been tried out.

In other words, the advice here is to have as much in mind as possible about the evidence that is being gathered and how this will be interpreted, but still leave ample room for flexible subjective judgment of what the evidence means. By putting together test data, assignments, reactions of students, personal impressions, and even gauging the looks on students' faces, the teacher can make a decision as to how all of this stacks up in relation to the objectives.

In some ways, the band director has an easier time of it than some other teachers, since all sorts of activities and opportunities for feedback are built into the subject. Unlike the "think system" made famous in the hit show "Music Man," no band director would seriously consider teach-

A band director has many opportunities to assess progress toward objectives such as the judging of a marching band in a parade. (SIUC Photographic Service.)

ing band by lecturing or explaining some theory. Band is a subject that is taught primarily by doing, and the director's senses, especially hearing, give him or her considerable feedback as to the progress being made on objectives. A band director doesn't have to test formally whether the clarinetist understands embouchure (the proper formation of the mouth in playing) but can tell by simply watching the student play. The director can hear if a student understands a fingering or is reading the music incorrectly. If so many are making mistakes that one cannot hear what is what, this feedback is used to decide that the piece is too difficult.

Revising Objectives and Trying Again

What do teachers do when they fail to reach an objective, or when an objective is reached way ahead of time? Most objectives are only educated guesses, and some are purely shots in the dark. This in no way detracts from the importance of stating objectives as specifically as possible and

505

planning strategies to bring about the desired changes in behavior. It just means that the cycle goes on and on endlessly, with the teachers setting goals, specifying objectives, planning strategies, getting feedback, assessing the results, going back to the drawing board and revising some objectives, dropping others, and happily concluding that others have been met. It highlights the fact that evaluation is a continuous process and that in some ways it is as much an attitude or state of mind as a technique. The attitude is an empirical one, that of converting everything that is done to observable behavior, an attitude of insisting on evidence and basing one's decisions on empirical evidence logically gathered and interpreted.

We hope that you will approach teaching with just such an empirical, experimental attitude. Remember that many goals are not reached the first time (some never) and that you will often have to revise and try again. But you do not want to be like the pilot who was lost in the clouds and reported "I don't know where we're headed, but we're sure making good time getting there." Without objectives and the major goals to which they lead clearly in mind, teachers are no better off than the pilot, for they have no way of knowing whether or not they are reaching their goals.

Reporting Progress

Students as well as the teacher need feedback as to how well they are reaching objectives. The best type of feedback is that built right into the task, such as the feedback a football player receives when he kicks the ball and can see exactly how far and how high it goes. Whenever possible, the teacher should build such automatic feedback into the learning activities of students.

But it is rare in teaching that adequate feedback can be intrinsic to the task itself. The teacher must add external feedback in the form of verbal advice, praise, suggestions, criticism, and, of course, *grades.*

Grades in some form appear to be here to stay, and most teachers regularly give grades as part of their jobs. By making clear what the objectives are, providing ample opportunity to reach those objectives, and giving numerous items of feedback all along the way, students will know when they receive a grade just what it means and on what it is based. Also, it is much better to receive a "B" as a culmination of a dozen assignments with grades given on each than it is to receive the "B" at the end of the marking period with no other grades leading up to it.

We see, then, that evaluation is a continuous process, an approach, an attitude toward teaching. With this approach in mind, teachers will continually find new ways to state objectives, plan strategies, carry them out, obtain feedback, assess the results, report progress, and repeat the process continually in their teaching.

In planning for classroom teaching, the objective the teacher has in mind is an important consideration in deciding on the type of classroom activity. For example, using the categories in Bloom's taxonomy, teacher presentation works quite well for most of the knowledge objectives, not quite as well for comprehension objectives such as translation or interpretation, rather poorly for application and analysis, and poorly in achieving objectives at the synthesis and evaluation levels.

In discussions, however, the picture is almost exactly the reverse. Discussions are excellent (if conducted properly) for achieving objectives at the level of interpretation, not so good when it comes to translation, and poor for achieving objectives at the knowledge level. One can easily see that a discussion would be appropriate if the teacher were concerned with synthesis or evaluation but that this would be a waste of time if the objective were the mastery of terminology, facts, names, or knowledge about anything.

Lecturing to a class to impart knowledge and understanding should not be taboo in teaching and can be a most effective and economical way in which to foster learning. For one thing, it is economical in time, money, facilities, equipment, and space. It is a flexible and repeatable experience that can be reinforcing to both teacher and student. It gives the student a feeling of security in knowing just what is expected and tends to make the teacher feel secure also. Research (McKeachie and Kulik, 1975) to date seems to indicate that lecturing is about as effective, in general, as most other methods of instruction. Retention of material learned in a lecture is good for a few days or weeks, which is what is usually measured on a classroom test.

But these facts do not in themselves tell us when a lecture presentation is appropriate. In deciding when to lecture to a class, Gage and Berliner (1979) suggest that lecturing is appropriate to consider as a form of instruction:

1. When the purpose is to dispense information.
2. When material is not available elsewhere.
3. When the specific structure and group is set.
4. When there is a need to create some interest.
5. When long-term recall is not necessary.
6. When the lecture leads to other learning activities.

On the other hand, there are many times when an activity *other than* a lecture is the appropriate thing to do. Gage and Berliner suggest that an alternative to lecturing should be considered in the following situations:

507

1. If application, analysis, synthesis, or evaluation is the objective being pursued.
2. To strengthen long-term retention.
3. With very complex or abstract material.
4. If learner participation is an essential part of the goal.
5. If students have inadequate backgrounds or learning levels.

There is some agreement among researchers (McKeachie and Kulik, 1975) that discussion is especially useful in developing critical thinking and in appraisal of ideas. This suggests that teachers should encourage students to support their opinions with reasoning based on facts, definitions, concepts, and principles. Obviously, they must have *some* knowledge base to do this. Thus, the knowledge gained through presentations and reading can be expanded into higher steps in the taxonomy in discussion sessions.

Discussions are recommended also for such goals as socialization, participation, respect for others, developing listening skills, and value clarification. Sometimes teachers do not see these as part of the subject they teach, but they are certainly important goals of the school in general, and it seems reasonable to expect *all* teachers to aid in reaching these goals.

Another claim made by researchers (Gage and Berliner, 1979) is that discussion is more appropriate in "low-consensus" fields, such as the so-

*Some objectives require
learner participation and
cannot be achieved by
lecture.* (Bernie
Weithorn/SIUC
Photographic Service.)

Discussion groups are important for objectives such as socialization, participation, and value clarification. (Bernie Weithorn/SIUC Photographic Service.)

cial sciences, literature, the humanities, and the arts. In fields such as math, physics, and chemistry, it is easier to defend a higher proportion of time spent in learning facts and techniques and working on problems and projects.

Necessities for Discussion Teaching

Some teachers make the mistake of believing that teaching through discussion is easy. This, of course, is not true, and there are probably just as many discussion sessions that are a "waste of time" in terms of any meaningful learning as there are lectures or any other method of instruction. For one thing, discussions require just as much planning as any other method of instruction. The specific goals of the discussion must be clear in the teacher's mind, and the teacher must also be very careful in the choice of topic and plan of attack.

One of the first steps in leading a discussion is to establish some common ground for the group. What is it that the participants have in common that will enable them to interact and profit from the discussion? The physical setting is important also, since the type of open, relaxed climate that encourages participation is difficult in a rigid, formal setting. Even such subtle factors as lighting are important, with extremely bright lighting tending to inhibit discussion.

A certain amount of conflict tends to stimulate discussion, but the teacher must be careful not to overdo this. With younger groups, with groups in which members do not know each other, or with large groups, conflict beyond a minimal degree may tend to inhibit rather than encourage discussion.

To be an effective discussion leader, the teacher must relinquish some responsibility to the group and refuse to be the sole leader or to serve as an ''answering service.'' Unless successful at this, the discussion easily lapses into monologues by the teacher or dialogues between the teacher and specific individuals. The teacher can ignore some mistakes in fact and interpretation and delay some corrections of important facts until after the discussion, but the teacher must also step in at times and correct serious errors of fact on the spot. This should be a rare occurrence, however, and teachers probably err on the side of overdoing rather than on letting unimportant errors go uncorrected.

Finally, above all, the teacher needs to take great pains to assure that a discussion class is more than just a warm, cozy group churning happily away. Just because students are involved in a discussion does not necessarily mean that any important goals are being achieved. It is up to the teacher, who should have specific objectives clearly in mind, to oversee the discussion and lead it toward those objectives, and this is not always easy to do.

There is fairly clear research available on the type of teacher who makes a good discussion leader. Above all, this type of instruction requires a tolerance of low level structure and organization. The teacher who cannot tolerate ambiguity and needs to control a clear, highly structured situation will find it difficult to adjust to the discussion situation.

Discussion sessions require a high degree of patience and intellectual agility (Gage and Berliner, 1979). The teacher must allow students to explore various pathways and yet must also have the ability to steer the discussion back to the objectives and topic at hand. This means a willingness to relinquish authority, to turn over some of the responsibility to the students. It also suggests a true desire to actually sit back and *listen* to what the students have to say.

Guidelines for a problem-solving or discovery lesson were presented in Chapter 5. It is important that students know what the problem is, what they are supposed to be trying to solve. Although a problem-solving activity generally involves considerable motion and noise, it is important that this be goal directed. An informal situation, with the teacher roaming around and helping students individually or in groups, is usually best.

In one of the best reviews of lecture teaching as compared with dis-

cussion teaching, McKeachie and Kulik (1975) summarized the results of
thirty-seven separate studies and concluded that

1. The lecture method was found to be superior for "factual examination."
2. Discussion techniques were superior for "retention and higher-level thinking."
3. Discussion techniques proved superior for developing "attitudes and motivation."

Thus, one can easily see that the choice of lecture or discussion as the means of achieving teaching objectives depends very much on the type of objectives the teacher has in mind. If it is important to get across facts at a particular point in teaching, the lecture method would be better; if long-term retention, higher-level thinking, or developing attitudes and motivation are important, the discussion format is more appropriate.

In discussing the many different methods that teachers use and how they select and combine these methods for different objectives in the classroom, Gage and Berliner (1979) employ the apt analogy that the teacher's use of method is similar to the composer's use of *orchestration*. Just as the composer blends the sounds and characteristics of woodwinds, brasses, strings, and percussion to achieve different musical effects, so also does the teacher blend the different settings and methods in the classroom to achieve different educational effects.

Teachers and students have more than one objective that they intend the students to attain in any unit of instruction. And for any kind of objective, some methods are more appropriate than others. Further, students differ in the objectives and the teaching methods that are most suitable for them. It follows that classroom teachers should use a combination of methods.

In our view, this combination of methods is what constitutes classroom teaching. This kind of teaching may be regarded as flexible enough to be made appropriate for much of the formal teaching that goes on in schools—teaching conducted with groups of students, numbering between 20 and 40, who differ in all the ways we have noted. [Gage and Berliner, 1979, p. 594]

Objectives and Homework Assignments

Too much homework seems to be assigned because this is what is expected of a teacher, with the hope that somehow it will "pay off." It is as though a teacher expects the student to learn through homework what the student is failing to learn in class.

When homework assignments are made, it should be with specific objectives in mind, such as described by the categories of Bloom's taxonomy. If the teacher is striving for understanding at this particular point in his or her teaching, then the homework assignment should clearly lead to better understanding. If, on the other hand, it is knowledge of terminology that is sought, the assignment should clearly lead to improved knowledge of terminology. Application activities for purposes of transfer should definitely require students to apply what they know and expand their learning to a variety of situations. Needless to say, the assignments should be no longer than necessary to achieve the desired objective, and feedback must be provided either within the assignment or as soon after as possible, preferably by going over the homework the next day in class. Both common sense and research findings indicate that it is important for teachers to give assignments that can be done *without* the aid of the teacher. Dependence on "someone else" to help students who have difficulties with homework is unrealistic.

Gage and Berliner (1979) summarized research findings regarding ways in which to maximize the learning that occurs from individual work on the part of the student. First, the teacher must help students to devote more time to actual academic activities. While students enjoy games, toys, and machines, research shows that such activities are related to lower academic achievement, whereas activities involving the abundant use of textbooks, workbooks, and other paper-and-pencil activities are associated with higher achievement. Second, instructions should be kept to a minimum. However, the rules and procedures to be followed should be clear enough so that students rarely need to ask for advice or for permission to do something. Third, the teacher should move around the room when students are working individually to monitor work and give whatever advice is needed.

Using Measurement in the Classroom

Since this is not a measurement textbook, references to measurement concepts and terminology have been minimized. It is necessary to review a few basic measurement concepts, however, before describing basic types of standardized tests and their uses, and then going on to the important area of classroom tests constructed by the teacher.

Reliability

The meaning of reliability can be seen in the example of a carpenter measuring a board with a ruler. If he has a good tape measure, one of wood or metal, he can measure the board rather quickly and know that he has an accurate measure. If he took three measures of the board, the measures might come out 6 feet 2 inches, 6 feet $2\frac{1}{4}$, and 6 feet $1\frac{7}{8}$. The board is around 6 feet 2 inches in length.

But what if he is measuring with a cloth measure? One that is old and worn besides? Now he quickly measures the board at 6 feet 2, but a second measure, with the cloth tape stretched tightly, shows the board to be 6 feet 1, while a third measure is around 6 feet 4. He still concludes that the board is around 6 feet 2 inches in length, but now he is not as certain, since the cloth ruler is *not as reliable as* the steel ruler.

This idea of consistency or dependability can be extended to tests and test items. A reliable test score is one that you can be relatively certain is approximately what you measured and would not vary much if measured several times or under different conditions. An unreliable test result would vary quite a bit if measured several times, and in fact you do not know whether you could depend on the score you observed as a representative score.

Three types of reliability are important in testing. One, called the *coefficient of stability* (test-retest reliability), is obtained by administering a test on two different occasions to see how well the scores on one occasion compare with the scores on another occasion. This gives an index of the dependability of the score, of the extent to which each test score observed today would be similar on another day. The second, called *internal consistency reliability,* is an index of how well the test hangs together, how well the items tend to be measuring the same thing. This type of internal consistency is usually determined by giving the test only once and computing its consistency by comparing the score on odd-numbered items with the score on even-numbered items. A student who scores high on half the items should tend to score high on the other half. The third type is *alternate forms reliability*. In this case, two forms of a test are devised. The alternate forms reliability gives an index of how students' scores on the first form of the test compare with their scores on the second form.

All three types of reliability estimates give the teacher an idea of how stable or dependable a score or set of scores is. A high correlation coefficient (.80 or above) is generally required before any standardized test score can be used as a reliable score, and with standardized tests all three types of reliability estimates should be available and high. With teacher-made tests in the classroom, however, it is difficult to attain estimates above .80, and reliability levels considerably lower than this, as low as .50 or .60, are often thought to be satisfactory. Also, classroom tests are not often given twice or in alternate forms to secure a test-retest or alternate forms estimate, so that the teacher will usually have to depend on an internal consistency estimate of the reliability of his or her own teacher-made tests.

Standard Error of Measurement

Reliability is related to what is probably the most important measurement concept for students to understand. This is the concept of *standard error of measurement*. If a student throws a ball for us, we should be able to get an estimate of just how good that student is at throwing a ball. But *one* throw is not a very good estimate, since it might just happen to be an unusually good or an unusually poor throw. Several throws would be better—but how many throws do we need before we can be certain of just how well this student throws? Ideally, as many throws as possible, but this breaks down as the student gets tired and can't throw any more, or starts getting wild due to fatigue, or gets bored and quits trying. Theoretically, we could have the student throw the ball a thousand times under "normal" conditions and find out what the average throw was as well as how much the throws varied from this average.

When assessing a test score, it is just like looking at one throw of a ball and trying to guess how good an estimate that one throw is. A high standard error tells us that the observed scores will tend to fluctuate quite a bit around the "true" score. A "true" score is one that would be obtained if a test were perfectly reliable (Gronlund, 1981, p. 102). The standard error of measurement tells us just how large a range we must take into account to be reasonably certain that the person's "true" score lies within that range. For example, in Table 14.1 Jane scored 75 on a test with a standard error of 5, which means that we can be relatively certain that the range of 70 to 80 includes her true score. Carl scored 18 on a test with a standard error of 6. Thus, we are fairly sure that the range of 12 to 24 includes Carl's true score. Both are fairly large standard errors. In the case of Jan, her score of 65 with a standard error of 3 is more precise, since we can be relatively certain that the range of 62 to 68 includes her true score.

Every time a teacher looks at a score for a student on any task, he or she should have this concept of standard error in mind. Jim scores 94 on an IQ test. But how accurate is that 94? If the standard error of the test is 6, then we should think of Jim's score as a *band* from 88 to 100 rather than as a specific score *point* of 94.

This idea of the standard error of measurement was implied in the discussion of intelligence and IQ tests in Chapter 9. The recommendation that score bands be employed follows directly from the idea of standard error. For example, when Helen scores 78 and Henry scores 74 on a test

Jane	70———75———80	
	Standard error = 5	
Carl	12———18———24	
	Standard error = 6	
Jan	62———65———68	
	Standard error = 3	

Table 14.1
Score Bands of Three Different Students on Three Tests with Different Standard Errors

Helen	73———78———83		Koenia	80———85———90	
Henry	69———74———79		Denise	69———74———79	

Table 14.2
Score Bands Based on
Standard Error of 5

whose standard error is 5, we can see by looking at the score bands (Table 14.2) that we can be reasonably certain that Henry scores between 69 and 79 and that Helen scores between 73 and 83, but we *cannot* be at all certain that Helen will score higher than Henry most of the time. The two scores overlap considerably, if the standard error is taken into account, and we can only say with any certainty that Helen and Henry score within the same score range on the test, with only a slight probability that Helen scores higher. In the second case in Table 14.2, we are on much more solid ground, since Koenia and Denise score in such a way that they are more than two standard errors apart. This means that there is little chance that Denise's true score is really higher than Koenia's, and it is safe to say that Koenia is better on this task than Denise.

Validity

The validity of a test score refers to how well it measures what it claims to measure. For example, the carpenter may have a ruler that measures the length and width of a building reliably, but how well does this measure the *volume* of the building? Measuring the area at the base of a building is probably not highly valid as the estimate of total volume, since buildings differ in shape and height. In the same way, we might have a test that gives a reliable measure of students' IQ, but this test might have only moderate validity as an estimate of math potential and no validity as an estimate of music ability. When asking about the validity of a test, the relevant question is "Valid for what purpose?"

Several different types of validity are described in test manuals. Each type is really looking at different purposes for which the test may be used. For example, in *content validity,* the content of the items themselves are studied to verify that the items measure the particular content being tested. High content validity means that the items are reasonable and relevant and provide a representative example of the material being tested. Items that did not satisfy these requirements have been eliminated.

In *concurrent validity,* a type of *criterion-related* validity, the scores have been compared with a currently existing criterion to see if they correlate as they should. For example, Joyce's Short IQ Test is a quick and easy way of estimating IQ; the scores on this new test can be compared with existing IQ tests. If students who score high on the WISC-R tend to score high on the Short Test and students who score low on the WISC-R tend to score low on the Short Test, then we have established concurrent validity for this test.

In *predictive validity,* another type of criterion-related validity, the test is validated on its ability to predict a criterion in the future. For example, a math aptitude test should be a fair predictor of success in a mathematics course, even though we know it will not be a perfect predictor due to other factors such as motivation, health, and anxiety. If we administer the aptitude test to a group before they take the math course, then compare the scores to the grades they make in the course, we can check the predictive validity of the test. A correlation of .70 between test scores and math grades would indicate that the test is a valid predictor of success in math, whereas a correlation of .15 between aptitude test scores and math grades would indicate this test is not a valid predictor of success in math.

Another type of validity, *construct validity,* has to do with the logic of the underlying psychological variables being tested and the reasoning behind the test. A typical way of testing this is to explain the construct being tested, then compare test scores with a wide variety of other variables, some of which you expect the test scores to correlate with and some not. For example, if you developed a test of "Traditional Masculinity," you should be able to suggest how this test should fit in with a number of other variables. If it is really testing masculinity, it should have a high *negative* correlation with femininity test scores. Likewise, it should have only a slight correlation with a test of androgyny and a moderate negative correlation with a test of artistic interest. You would predict a substantial correlation with a "Playboy Macho" test, a negative correlation with a test of interpersonal sensitivity, no correlation at all with IQ test scores, and a fairly high correlation with a test of athletic interest. In other words, you compare the construct you claim to be testing with a whole network of variables that logically should relate to the construct in various ways.

Figure 14.1 presents an example of such a network, in this case giving excellent support to the construct validity of the "Traditional Masculinity"

Figure 14.1
Construct validity of a test
of traditional masculinity
showing correlations with
seven other tests in a
nomological network.

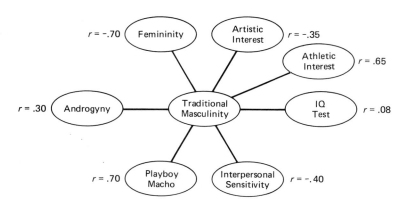

test. The test correlated highly with a "Playboy Macho" test and with an "Athletic Interest" test, as predicted, had a slight correlation with androgyny, which is reasonable, and a high negative correlation with femininity. Although you might have expected somewhat higher negative correlations with tests of artistic interest and interpersonal sensitivity, the negative correlations attained are reasonable, and the nearly zero correlation with IQ is gratifying because a masculinity test should not measure IQ. In all, the way in which the test has correlated with the seven other measures in this network gives strong support to the idea that the construct measured on this test is "Traditional Masculinity."

Standardized Tests

A standardized test is one in which the procedures for administration have been established so that everyone takes the test under the same conditions (Beggs and Lewis, 1975). Generally, standardized tests are thought of as tests that have been published by a testing company, but this is not a necessary condition. The distinguishing characteristics of standardized tests are that instructions, time, and procedures for the test are the same every time and everywhere the test is given. The purpose of this standardization of administration procedures is to ensure comparability of scores that students attain on the test.

Norm-Referenced Tests

Norm-referenced tests are tests in which the student's performance is compared with the performance of other students. In such a test, the student finds out that he or she did better than most other students, or not as well, or just about average in comparison with the reference group. Since the meaning of this comparison is dependent upon how much we know about the reference group, we find that we sometimes know little about the meaning of a norm-referenced test score.

There are two types of norm-referenced tests, one in which the *immediate* peer group is the reference group and one in which a *distant* peer group is used. If Lisa's score is compared with her classmates' scores and we find that Lisa had the second highest score in the class, this is a norm-referenced test in which the immediate peer group is the reference group. We don't know if Lisa's score means that she is truly outstanding in the subject unless we know something else about her peer group. Is this an excellent class, an average class, or a below-average class? Lisa's second highest score might mean she is second from the top in an outstanding class, or it might mean that she is only average in knowledge of the subject but that most of the rest of her class is below average or poor in that subject. Even though a student may be the best or worst student in a particular class in a school, this provides little information about what he or she knows unless we know how the students in that reference group perform with respect to students from other classes or schools.

A second type of norm-referenced test compares the student to some distant peer group. If you score in the seventh percentile on a literature test with national norms, this means that, when compared with the distant peer group of students your age around the nation, 7% score lower than you and 93% score higher than you. You might be in the fiftieth percentile for your own class (immediate peer group), but the national norms show that you are low on this test compared with a broad reference group. In like fashion, you might score at the ninety-third percentile when compared with all students your age but only at the fiftieth percentile when compared with your immediate class. This would mean that most of the students in your particular class are above average when compared with national norms—it is a very strong class.

For norm-referenced measurement to be useful, the reference group must have an experiential background that is similar to that of the student whose performance is in question. For example, a student from a very small high school with a very limited science program may score only at the sixtieth percentile in comparison with the national normgroup. However, the limited science program in that high school may mean that the experiential backgrounds in science of students from that high school and the norm group are considerably different. Therefore, a score at the sixtieth percentile in comparison with national norms may indicate tremendous potential in science. Similarly, a student who scores at the ninety-fifth percentile on a test may not have as much potential as one thinks the score indicates if that student's background includes a great deal of experience with the content being tested while the reference group has had very little experience with that content.

It is important to remember that with norm-referenced measurement the scores obtained from a standardized test will compare a particular student with members of the reference group. Whether the reference group is immediate or distant, the comparison is limited in interpretation to the comparability of that reference group with the student in question. Also to be considered in determining comparability of the reference group are age, sex, experience with the content, geographical location, size of school, economic background, social background, and urban versus rural setting.

Criterion-Referenced Tests

A different type of test used in education, one that has been receiving an increasing amount of attention, is the criterion-referenced test. In a criterion-referenced test, students are not compared with each other. Instead, the student's performance on the test is compared with some domain of content. In this way, the test tells you how well Fred can read materials, or how well he can use a compass, or understand literature and tells us nothing about how he compares with his peers. This is often the goal in the classroom—to help students achieve a certain level of performance rather than to compare them with each other—so that this type of test has enjoyed increasing popularity in recent years. In criterion-referenced testing, students need not worry about competing against each other or about facing comparisions to the other students. Instead, they simply work toward achieving the level of performance that is set for the learning task, and criterion-referenced tests help to monitor their progress toward mastery.

In criterion-referenced testing, a comparison is made, but the comparison is with content assessed by the test rather than with other students. Most frequently, the score that a student receives on a criterion-referenced test indicates the percentage of the items on the test that the student answered correctly. Since the test is designed to be representative of the content that the student is expected to have achieved at the time he or she takes the test, this percentage of items answered correctly is interpreted to be the percentage of the content assessed by the test that the student has achieved. Obviously, the accuracy of this interpretation depends upon the content validity of the test. If the student has had the opportunity to study the content measured by the test, then the interpretation that his or her score is reflective of his or her achievement is appropriate. On the other hand, if the student has had little or no exposure to the content measured by the test, then a low score on the test is indicative of the low content validity of the test for that student rather than poor achievement.

Even though there has been a great deal of enthusiasm for criterion-referenced tests, students and parents are still interested in the question, "How do I compare with other kids?" Teachers should be aware of both types of testing. Incorporate criterion-referenced testing whenever possible, but combine this with both immediate and distant peer group norm-referenced testing. In this way, you can obtain the benefits of each type of feedback and avoid some of the negative consequences of using only one type of testing.

Areas of Standardized Testing

There are essentially four areas in which standardized tests are used in the classroom: (1) achievement, (2) aptitude, (3) interest, and (4) personality. Although there is use for results from each of these areas, most teachers are more interested in achievement testing than in the other three types, as achievement testing corresponds so closely to their usual objectives in the classroom.

Achievement Tests
Although classroom achievement is evaluated most frequently through informal and formal observation by the teacher, and by various forms of teacher-made tests, standardized tests of achievement can be useful for

certain purposes. The primary reason for using standardized achievement tests is to compare the performance of pupils in a given school with the performance of pupils in other schools. This comparison might be based on national norms, state or regional norms, or norms established on some other dimension. In most cases, the purpose is to compare students with a wider population. This is necessary to evaluate the effectiveness of an instructional program and the standing of students relative to a broader peer group.

The advantages of using standardized achievement tests are that they have been prepared by measurement experts; are designed to obtain systematic samples of behavior under uniform procedures; have exact directions for administration, timing, and a fixed set of questions; and are scored objectively and uniformly. This list of advantages is formidable, but it does *not* necessarily mean that standardized achievement tests are better than teacher-made achievement tests. The major disadvantage of such tests is that they rarely reflect the exact goals and classroom activities of any particular school or class, so that the results are often difficult to interpret. If the purpose is to compare students with a broad sample on an array of objectives that many schools might have, then the standardized achievement test is valid. But if the goal is to see how students are progressing in their curriculum or how well they are learning what they are being taught, then it is rare that a standardized test can be found that fits the specific situation. The results of the teachers' own tests are usually more valid for this purpose.

The first standardized achievement test was a spelling test prepared by J. M. Rice in 1895. In 1923, the Stanford Achievement Test was published, representing the first standardized achievement test battery. Since that time, scores of achievement tests and batteries have been developed for almost any topic or level. The vast majority of these, however, assess achievement in reading, English, mathematics, science, and social studies.

Two of the most widely used achievement test batteries are the Metropolitan Achievement Tests and the Iowa Tests of Basic Skills. The former covers all grades from kindergarten through twelfth, allowing comparison of students across all grade levels; the latter covers grades kindergarten through nine. Other excellent achievement batteries are the California Achievement Tests (grades kindergarten through twelve), the Iowa Tests of Educational Development (grades nine through twelve), the SRA Achievement Series (grades kindergarten through twelve), the Sequential Tests of Educational Progress (grades kindergarten through twelve) and the Stanford Achievement Test (grades one through twelve). Each of these satisfies all requirements of expert construction, careful standardization, national norms, objective scoring, and clear directions and can be depended on to tell how a student compares with a large sample of students on general educational goals. They must be looked at very cautiously, however, in terms of telling one anything about the students' strengths, weaknesses, and progress within a specific school or curriculum. Results of a standardized achievement test must *never* be used to determine grades in a course.

Aptitude Tests

Standardized aptitude tests are designed to measure a student's potential for future success in a particular area. While standardized achievement tests are designed to assess what a student knows at a particular point in time, aptitude tests are designed to assess what the student is capable of doing in the future.

In reality, the distinction between aptitude and achievement tests is not as clear cut as it might seem. Because past achievement in a given area is a good indicator of future success, for example, an achievement test may do a better job of predicting future success than an aptitude test. Also, aptitude in a given area at any given time is dependent upon past experience in the area, so an aptitude test must assess achievement. For example, if a mathematics achievement test were to be given at the end of tenth grade, the test designer would assume that all students who take the test will have had fairly standard instruction in mathematics. On the other hand, if a math aptitude test were to be given at the end of tenth grade, the test designer would assume a more varied and general experience in mathematics. Both test designers assume past experience in mathematics. The distinction is in the degree of specificity assumed in that experience. We can see that this is not a clear distinction, and we should expect a student's score on the achievement test to be closely related to his or her score on the aptitude test. Present achievement and present aptitude both depend upon past achievement.

The IQ test is a general aptitude test. The trend among educators is to refer to IQ tests as scholastic ability tests, since IQ tests are designed to assess the capability of a student to perform well in school. The items on a scholastic ability test are designed to minimize the effects of specific instruction and experience. Rather, the test attempts to provide an indication of how well a student can be expected to achieve in school based upon his or her general experience in our culture. This general experience, of course, is not independent of school experiences, so part of what is assessed by a scholastic aptitude test is previous school achievement.

Whereas the IQ test can be thought of as a general scholastic aptitude test, there are tests for specific aptitudes. The most common areas are mechanical, clerical, musical, and artistic. Once again, the approach is to measure the subject's current ability in an area and use this to predict his or her potential for future learning in this area.

Interest Inventories

Although the measurement of interests cannot be separated easily from attitudes, motives, or values, the area that has been chiefly measured is that of interest in relation to vocations. Common sense might suggest that the easiest way to find out about a person's interests in relation to a certain career is to ask. But this approach is clouded by the individual's lack of knowledge about different jobs and careers, difficulty in understanding one's own motivation, unfamiliarity with educational needs, and stereotypes regarding certain occupations. Students make superficial and unrealistic statements if asked directly about vocational interests, since nobody is in a position to know all about their interests in various fields prior to participation in those fields. These problems have led to the development of tests such as the Kuder General Interest Survey and the Strong-Campbell Interest Inventory. The Kuder General Interest Survey provides eleven scores, in the areas of outdoor, mechanical, computational, scientific, persuasive, artistic, literary, musical, social service, and clerical and a verification scale. Although this is an excellent instrument for showing a child's interests, professional help is needed in interpreting it, even though the manual does not specify this. The inventory can survey the strengths of broadly defined interest areas, but it cannot specify an occupation. The manual suggests that it can be used in a group setting and self-scored, but most reviewers doubt this. If using this instrument, you should make certain that a qualified counselor is available for help.

A second widely used instrument is the Strong-Campbell Interest Inventory. This instrument has 325 items with the same form used for both sexes. The test provides general occupational theme scales, basic interest scales, and occupational scales. This may be the best vocational interest inventory available. If you are particularly interested in a person's interests relative to occupations, then this is the instrument to use.

Personality Inventories

Although the area of personality is a delicate one, it is sometimes important to know about certain personality factors in relation to educational decisions. These tests bear titles such as inventories, schedules, records, profiles, checklists, surveys, and even tests. They measure such variables as temperament, personality, problems, preferences, values, and attitudes. Because of the sensitive and complex nature of what is being measured, these tests should always be administered and interpreted by trained psychologists, counselors, or researchers.

Because of concerns about privacy rights, personality inventories are not used nearly as widely in the schools as are the other three types of instruments mentioned. Teachers are not qualified to administer these inventories; neither are most counselors. When the tests are used, they are administered by a school psychologist or clinical psychologist, who is often from an agency—for example, a mental health center.

There are essentially two types of personality inventories: the self-report type and the projective technique. In the latter, such as the Children's Apperception Test and the Thematic Apperception Test, students look at pictures and talk about what they see. They project themselves into the stories they tell to describe the picture.

Self-report inventories are helpful in counseling students about decisions in which it is important to understand more about themselves, such as choices of programs or occupations. The California Test of Personality, the Edwards Personal Preference Schedule, and the Minnesota Counseling Inventory are used for this purpose. Once again, although these are useful instruments, they should only be employed with great care and administered and interpreted by a qualified expert.

The Uses of Standardized Tests

The 1970s were notable for the strong movement *against* standardized testing. The movement was based partly on the claims that standardized tests were unfair to various subgroups and partly on an implied notion that testing in general was evil. In some quarters, humanistic ideals seemed to be interpreted as synonymous with the idea that testing was bad for children and other living things and that any progressive educator should join in the movement to "stamp out tests." It has since been recognized that tests are useful and necessary tools in teaching and can be a constructive part of humanistic teaching.

Guidelines in relation to standardized tests and their uses in education are the following: (1) Standardized tests should be used only when there is specific reason for doing so. (2) Unless the scores from a standardized test are actually *used* for some specific purpose, the test cannot really be justified. (3) Whenever possible, students should be given feedback of the results of any standardized tests that are given.

Many schools have stopped "testing for the sake of testing" and administering various standardized tests every few years because other schools do it or because it has always been done. Standardized tests have been given in some schools without any real purpose in mind. In such a testing atmosphere, the results of the testing frequently were not used.

A school system that plans its testing program carefully will administer the minimum necessary to achieve the goals of the program. Tests at all levels will be coordinated into a total program that makes sense. The results of the testing program will be incorporated into the planning of the curriculum of the school and of the individual student. A testing program not so carefully planned may leave students, teachers, and parents confused about and opposed to the whole idea of standardized tests.

Following is a list of ways in which teachers can use the results of a standardized testing program in their planning:

1. *Checking on content emphasis.* In establishing objectives for a class, a

teacher decides upon certain content areas and levels of complexity within those areas that will be stressed. The results of a standardized achievement test can be used to confirm whether students perform better in those areas or whether the actual areas of strength differ. In addition, a review of student performance on an achievement test can provide information regarding content areas that need to be stressed in future instruction.

2. *Individualizing instruction.* The subtests on an achievement test identify the areas in which student performances may be weaker than in others. Looking at responses to the individual test items within subtests will help to identify the specific causes for a student's low performance in that area and allows the teacher to design instructional activities for the needs of individual students.

3. *Grouping students.* Ability grouping is one of the most common practices in the school. The results of a standardized aptitude and achievement testing program can be useful in helping to make decisions regarding into which group a student should be placed.

4. *Counseling students.* The results of general-interest and vocational-interest inventories can be useful in helping students to make education and career choices. Interest inventory and aptitude test results can give a teacher insight into what may be appropriate or inappropriate choices for a student. For example, a student who shows very low mathematics ability and little interest in science probably should not choose chemical engineering as a career goal.

5. *Identifying special needs.* Certain students differ so markedly from the typical student in a classroom that they require special educational programs. Standardized tests of achievement, aptitude, and personality can help to identify these students.

6. *Measuring academic progress.* Standardized achievement tests are especially useful in measuring the academic gains (or lack thereof) of students over an extended period of time (Gronlund, 1981).

Again, we urge that you use caution in interpreting the results of these tests as they will undoubtedly measure only a portion of the goals and objectives of your school. Also, there are many factors that affect the performance of a student on a standardized test. Therefore, any given test score may be badly misleading regarding that student's achievement, ability, interests, or personality.

Rising Grades and Declining Test Scores

A striking trend in education since the 1960s has been that grades have consistently risen, with more and more students achieving "A's" whereas standardized test scores have dropped. This has been well documented at the college level, with increasing percentages of students achieving 4.0

averages, graduating classes with an average grade point of 3.5, and numerous stories of what has been dubbed "grade inflation." Some universities have even had to raise the criteria for graduating with honors because so many students are now getting higher grades. This same grade inflation has been seen at the high school level, where several students may share the honor of valedictorian because all have straight "A" averages, a phenomenon that was relatively rare in former years.

While grades in school have been getting higher, scores on college admission tests such as the Scholastic Aptitude Tests (SAT) and the American College Testing Program (ACT), have declined steadily since the early 1960s. The drop has been significant and perplexing when one compares it with the steady rise in such scores in the years preceding 1963. Since 1963, the average SAT verbal score for males entering college dropped from 478 in 1963 to 475 in 1970 to 459 in 1978.

Table 14.3 illustrates the decline in average SAT scores that has occurred since about 1963. You will note that, while the average SAT, verbal, and SAT, math, of both males and females has declined, their GPAs' have increased.

Further scrutiny of other standardized test scores indicates that this phenomenon has been widespread, across most grade levels. Interpretations vary, but the evidence favors those who argue that the trend of declining scores has not stopped.

As an example of the size of the decline, one study concluded that scores have been dropping 2–3% of a standard deviation per year. And when comparing test scores in 1978 with those in 1963, differences in specific areas are often one half to one full standard deviation. One critic, Paul Copperman (1978), describes the decline in these words: "On college admissions tests only about a quarter of our current high school graduates attain the level recorded by the average high school graduate in the early 1960s" (p. 15).

What has caused this widespread drop in aptitude and achievement test scores? Many reasons have been suggested: the effects of the media, especially television; faulty methods of teaching reading; the increase in electives in the high school curriculum; a general loss of respect for authority in our society; increased class size; declining teacher morale; lack of discipline in the classroom; a loss of interest in achieving on the part

| Variable | Male | | Female | |
	Recent	Previous	Recent	Previous
SAT, Verbal	475	494	473	504
SAT, Math	526	539	489	501
GPA	2.50	2.15	2.69	2.40

Table 14.3
Mean SAT for Verbal, SAT for Math, and Grade Point Averages by Sex

From I. I. Bejar and E. O. Blew, "Grade Inflation and the Validity of the Scholastic Aptitude Test," *American Educational Research Journal*, Summer 1981, p. 154. Copyright 1981, American Educational Research Association, Washington, D.C. Reprinted with permission.

of students; and the broadening of the base of students taking these tests to include minorities, disadvantaged, and marginal students who would not have taken them in the past. Since no real cause and effect studies are available, it is impossible to "prove" any one of these hypotheses. It is reasonable to assume that there are many interacting causes.

Summary

The importance of establishing specific objectives of instruction is the first important message of this chapter. The cognitive domain of Bloom's taxonomy is presented in detail as an example of a way in which to categorize objectives. Bloom's taxonomy contains six basic areas: knowledge, comprehension, application, analysis, synthesis, and evaluation. Subdivisions of each of these six major areas are described, and examples are presented for a beginning psychology class. Teachers are encouraged to spend the time and effort necessary to develop objectives at all levels of the taxonomy.

Criteria for a good objective are that it must be clearly stated, as succinctly as possible, avoiding vague or confusing terms, and stated in terms of observable behaviors. Words such as relate, recite, state, write, design, recall, identify, and select are effective verbs for classroom objectives; words such as appreciate, feel, believe, understand, know and value are not. The reason for the difference is that words in the first list can be observed and measured; words in the second list do not suggest what behaviors to measure.

Evaluation should be seen as a continuous and never-ending process rather than as an addendum to instruction. Evaluation is part of all phases of teaching and is partly a viewpoint or attitude as well as a set of techniques.

The steps in the evaluation process are setting objectives, planning teaching strategies, building feedback into teaching, assessing the results, revising objectives, and trying again. These steps overlap, however, so that the teacher is often concerned with several at once. Examples of these steps are presented for a hypothetical band director and his class. Another part of the process is that of reporting progress. Feedback to the teacher, to the students themselves, to the parents and others are all important components of reporting progress.

Objectives in teaching are related to the type of instruction that is employed. For example, discussions are good for achieving objectives at the analysis, synthesis, and evaluation levels, but not so good for the knowledge and comprehension levels. Lectures, on the other hand, are excellent for knowledge objectives and fair for comprehension and are increasingly inappropriate for objectives higher up the hierarchy. Criteria for deciding whether a lecture or some other mode of instruction is appropriate are presented. In comparing lecture to discussion methods, the former has been found more effective for "factual examination," whereas the latter is more effective for "retention and higher-level thinking" and for developing "attitudes and motivation."

Homework assignments and their relation to teaching objectives are discussed. Teachers must take care to assure that homework assignments are consistent with classroom objectives and are not given as ritual, for punishment, or for some other inappropriate reason.

In using measurement in the classroom, teachers must understand basic measurement terms. Reliability refers to the stability or dependability of a score: validity refers to how well it identifies or predicts some criterion. The standard error of measurement tells us the extent to which we can depend on a particular score, the boundaries within which we feel confident that the true score lies. This concept is extremely important for teachers to keep in mind when they look at test scores or any other type of measure. Four types of validity—predictive, concurrent, content, and construct—are presented and explained.

Two types of test are presented and explained. Norm-referenced tests are tests in which the student's performance is compared with that of other students, often a large reference group, but sometimes only the student's immediate group or class. Most tests in education are norm referenced. A second type—criterion-referenced tests—are gaining in popularity. In this type, the student's score is compared not with those of other students but instead with a domain of content. Since the goal in the classroom often is that of getting students to a certain level of performance, rather than comparing them with each other, this is potentially a very useful type of test.

In using standardized tests, the teacher cannot help but be aware of controversy over such tests, namely, the "stamp out tests" movement. Some guidelines for using standardized tests are presented, and four types of instruments—achievement, aptitude, interest, and personality—are discussed. The chapter ends with a discussion of the declining test scores that have been observed in standardized achievement tests over the past twenty years.

1. Why do teachers sometimes object to the use of a taxonomy of objectives? What would you tell a teacher on the positive side about using a taxonomy? What could be gained from applying Bloom's taxonomy to one's teaching?
2. Studies of classroom tests have shown that the typical test is loaded with knowledge items but items that measure analysis, synthesis, and evaluation are rare. Why do you suppose this is so? What could be done to get teachers to use more items from the higher categories of the taxonomy?
3. What criteria would you apply to decide whether to use a lecture or a discussion session in your classroom? What objectives can be achieved best in a lecture format? When is it better to hold a discussion? Do such factors as the age of the students and the size of the class make a difference?
4. What is the meaning of the term "construct validity"? What kind of nomological network would you employ to find the construct validity of a test of mathematics aptitude, and what sort of correlations would you expect with the other elements of the network?

5. Why is there so much concern over the use of standardized tests in schools? What can schools and teachers do to overcome these objections?
6. Studies of achievement test scores show that students' achievement has been dropping since 1963. Can you think of any reasons for this? Can you describe a possible relationship between the level of cognitive skill stressed by teachers and the decline in scores?

References

Beggs, D. L., and Lewis, E. L. *Measurement and Evaluation in the Schools.* Boston: Houghton Mifflin, 1975

Bejar, I. I., and Blew, E. O. "Grade Inflation and the Validity of the Scholastic Aptitude Test," *American Educational Research Journal,* 18(2), Summer 1981, pp. 143–156.

Bloom, B. S., et al. *Taxonomy of Educational Objectives Handbook I. Cognitive Domain.* New York: David McKay, 1956.

Copperman, P. *The Literacy Hoax.* New York: William Morrow, 1978.

Gage, N., and Berliner, D. *Educational Psychology,* 2nd ed. Chicago: Rand McNally, 1979.

Gronlund, N. E. *Measurement and Evaluation in Teaching,* 4th ed. New York: Macmillan, 1981.

Krathwohl, D. R., Bloom, B. S., and Masia, B. B. *Taxonomy of Educational Objectives, Handbook II. Affective Domain.* New York: David McKay, 1964.

McKeachie, W. J., and Kulik, J. A. "Effective College Teaching," in F. N. Kerlinger, ed., *Review of Research in Education,* Vol. 3, pp. 165–209, Itasca, Ill.: F. E. Peacock, 1975.

Testing and Grading in the Classroom

15

PREVIEW

What steps should be followed in constructing a classroom test?

What is a criterion-referenced classroom test?

How can we judge the quality of a criterion-referenced classroom test?

What is a norm-referenced classroom test?

How can we judge the quality of a norm-referenced classroom test?

How does a teacher determine internal consistency reliability?

What guidelines govern the construction of multiple-choice items?

What are the strengths and weaknesses of multiple-choice items?

How can true-false items, supply-type items, and matching items be used effectively?

What are the strengths and weaknesses of essay items?

What are some basic guidelines in constructing essay items?

How can essays be graded reliably?

What information can be gained through an item analysis?

What is the difficulty index, and what does it show?

What is the discrimination index, and what does it show?

How can the security problem be minimized?

What are other uses for tests besides grading?

How can the grading procedure be made more objective?

Why is subjective judgment always involved in grading?

What sort of grading practices do students prefer?

Almost every teacher is involved in some way with testing. The most common form of testing is that designed to measure the child's performance on what is being taught in the class. Many different reasons can be advanced for classroom testing. Teachers test students in the subjects they teach to provide feedback, to find out if they are meeting their objectives, to diagnose weaknesses, to decide on what to teach next, or to provide a reward or even punishment. The most common reason for using tests in teaching is to gain information to use in assigning grades.

In Chapter 14, we pointed out that a standardized test is not necessarily more valid than a teacher-made test. In fact, a teacher's own test is often the most valid test for a specific purpose. This does not imply that a test designed by a teacher is automatically a good test. Unless well-established principles of test construction are followed, teacher-made tests are likely to be mediocre, with no information available as to how they can be improved.

The general principles of test construction can be seen in a hypothetical example. Graduate schools all over the country are concerned with screening students for admission and often are not completely satisfied with such tests as the Miller Analogies or the Graduate Record Exam. If a testing company were to develop a new test for predicting likelihood of success in graduate school, the process would be as follows:

1. Establish the *need* for the test, what purpose it is to serve. Pinpoint the shortcomings of tests presently being used and the areas in which a contribution can definitely be made.
2. Clearly spell out broad, general goals and objectives. Convert these general goals to specific behavioral objectives.
3. Construct a detailed table of specifications or a blueprint for the test. Produce a few sample items for each cell in the table, check them for content validity, and try them out on a few subjects.
4. Based on the results of step 3, revise the table of specifications as a final blueprint for the test. Develop a large pool of test items. Review the item pool and eliminate many due to overlap, bad format, and other errors.
5. Assemble several forms based on the remaining items, fitting the table of specifications. Test these out on representative samples of prospective graduate students for whom the test is intended. Analyze standard error, difficulty, and validity.
6. Take the best items from previous screening and test them on representative national samples. Perform careful statistical analyses, checking for reliability, objectivity, variability, standard error, difficulty, and validity. Eliminate all items that do not reach rigorous criteria.
7. Revise further based on the nationwide study, reduce the test to two equivalent forms, test on further samples to develop norms. Have a number of colleges use it experimentally with careful recording of results.

Table 15.1
Table of Specifications*

	Cognitive Level of Objectives		
Content Area	Knowledge	Comprehension	Application
Validity	Items #1, 3, 6	Items #8, 9, 13	Items #17, 20
Reliability	Items #4, 10, 7	Items #2, 12	Items #18, 19
Standard Error of Measurement	Items #5, 11, 16	Items #13,15	Item #14

*A table of specifications is a two-dimensional table in which the level of cognitive functioning of specific objectives constitutes one dimension and the content area assessed the other. The specific test items measuring each cognitive functioning level within a content area are specified in the cells of the table. The table allows a teacher to check that all levels of cognitive functioning in each content area desired to be assessed are indeed measured by the test in about the same percentage as they were stressed in instruction. Such a procedure in test development helps to assure content validity of the test.

8. The final revised version (two forms) can now be sold, complete with manual, norms, directions, and research findings. As it is being used, continue to gather data, revise items, and update norms.

There is no guarantee that the company would earn a fortune on such a test, but it would likely be a good test. You can follow this general outline in designing a test for the classroom. First, be certain of the purpose in testing and that the test is really necessary. Second, check what is available, which in most cases means looking at items from past tests, items that accompany the textbook, and items developed by other teachers. Third, spell out broad, general objectives and convert these to specific behavioral objectives. Fourth, construct a table of specifications for the test (see Table 15.1). Fifth, write a few sample items to verify that each will work, and check for content validity by having a colleague or two examine them. Sixth, prepare an item pool that contains 50% to 100% more items than will appear on the final test. Finally, use the items in the classroom. The class taking the test this semester will serve as a research group for the class next semester. The *only* way a test can be proven to be good is to *use* it and get feedback on how it works.

Evaluating Teacher-Made Test

Teacher-made tests, like standardized tests, may be either criterion referenced or norm referenced. The distinction between the referencing systems is important not only for the interpretation of the scores that result but also because the criteria as to the quality of the two types of tests are different.

Criterion-Referenced Tests

In a criterion-referenced test, the teacher is attempting to determine the extent to which students have achieved a particular domain of content. A standard of performance on the test is typically established. If this standard is achieved by a student, the conclusion is that the student has mastered the content. If the standard is not met, the student has not yet achieved sufficient mastery of the content in question. The only comparison made by the teacher in a criterion-referenced system is the performance of the student against the domain of content to be mastered. For example, the teacher may decide to give a test over a unit on single-digit addition before moving into subtraction with single digits. The standard established for successful mastery of single-digit addition is that 90% of all addition problems must be answered correctly. The results of the test tell the teacher which students are ready to move ahead and which need more practice with addition. Also, the answers to particular addition problems that are causing difficulty for a student can be determined by looking at the response to individual items so that subsequent instructions can be concentrated on areas of weakness.

Criterion-referenced tests are used commonly by teachers when attempting to individualize instruction. The validity of the test is of utmost concern since the results of the tests will determine the subsequent instructional program. In particular, content validity of the test must be assured by the teacher. Content validity of teacher-made tests is assessed most frequently by comparing the test items with the objectives of instruction.

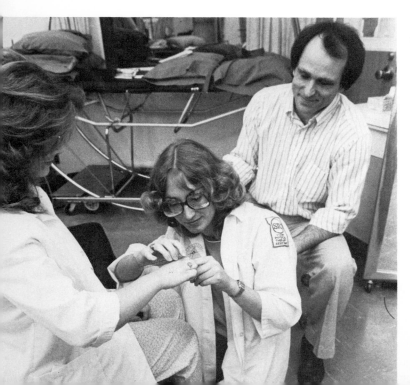

This criterion-referenced test requires the physical therapy student to perform the task. (SIUC Photographic Service.)

If the items appear to measure the objectives, the test may be said to have content validity. This comparison of items to objectives should be done by the teacher who writes the test and by having a colleague or two examine it.

Reliability of criterion-referenced tests for use in the individual classroom is of less concern than validity (Beggs and Lewis, 1975). Traditional measures of reliability are based on an assumption that each item on a test will discriminate between those who know more about the content assessed by the item and those who know less. Under such an assumption, a test item is considered poor if all students get it right or if all students get it wrong. Such items are, therefore, not included in a norm-referenced test. In criterion-referenced testing, the concern is whether students have achieved a domain of content. In this case, some items on a test may be answered correctly by all students and others may be answered incorrectly by 100% of the students. If such an item assesses the content in question, it could still be used on a criterion-referenced test. We recommend, therefore, that the teacher who uses criterion-referenced testing be primarily concerned with the content validity of each item. However, a teacher should be very cautious about making judgments about mastery of an objective on a few (less than 10) test items (Gronlund, 1981).

Norm-Referenced Tests

In norm-referenced testing, an individual's test score is compared with a reference (norm) group. The reference group for a teacher-made test is generally the class to which the test is administered or the combined group of previous classes that have taken the same test. For example, a student gets 25 of 30 problems on an addition test correct. The quality of this score is determined by comparing this score of 25 with the performance of the rest of the class. It might be determined that the mean score for the class was 23 and that the standard deviation was 2. Thus, a score of 25 was one standard deviation above the mean and represented a good score in relation to the performance of the class.

In this norm-referenced system of interpreting teacher-made tests, content validity is of concern. Each item on the test should assess one or more of the teacher's instructional objectives, as with criterion-referenced testing. The determination of content validity is up to the teacher who writes the test but may be assessed by having one or two colleagues examine the items to determine whether they do, indeed, assess the objectives in question.

Reliability of measurement is of concern in norm-referenced teacher-made tests. Reliability, you will recall from Chapter 14, provides an index of the degree to which a test measures consistently. Consistently, in this case, refers to the tendency for a student's score to maintain the same position in the distributions of scores resulting from two administrations of the same test (test-retest reliability), on two different forms of the test (equivalent forms reliability), or on two halves of the same test (internal consistency reliability). Since most teachers do not give the same test over and since most teachers do not use two forms of the same test, internal consistency reliability is of primary concern with respect to teacher-made tests.

Internal consistency reliability is assessed by most teachers by scoring the even-numbered items and odd-numbered items separately. The correlation coefficient between the two groups of scores is then calculated (see Table 15.2). This correlation coefficient is then adjusted using a formula known as the Spearman-Brown correction. This correction is nec-

Table 15.2
Internal Consistency
Coefficient of Reliability

	Score on Even-Numbered Items (X)	Score on Odd-Numbered Items (Y)	$X \times Y$	X^2	Y^2
Joyce	10	15	150	100	225
Jodi	15	13	195	225	169
Julie	13	25	325	169	625
Dan	18	19	342	324	361
Ginger	17	20	340	289	400
Sum	73	92	1,352	1,107	1,780

$$\text{Correlation} = \frac{N\Sigma XY - \Sigma X \Sigma Y}{\sqrt{[N\Sigma X - (\Sigma X)^2][N\Sigma Y - (\Sigma Y)^2]}}$$

$$= \frac{5(1352) - 73(92)}{\sqrt{[5(1,107) - (73)^2][5(1,780) - (92)^2]}}$$

$$= \frac{6,760 - 6,716}{\sqrt{(5,535 - 5,329)(8,900 - 8,464)}}$$

$$= \frac{44}{\sqrt{(206)(436)}}$$

$$= \frac{44}{\sqrt{89,816}}$$

$$= \frac{44}{299.7} = 0.15$$

Spearman-Brown Correction:

$$\text{Reliability on full test} = \frac{2 \times \text{reliability on } 1/2 \text{ test}}{1 + \text{reliability on } 1/2 \text{ test}}$$

$$= \frac{2(.15)}{1 + .15}$$

$$= \frac{.30}{1.15} = +.26$$

essary because the length of the test is actually twice the number of items in either the odd-numbered or even-numbered groups. The result of the correction is the internal consistency reliability index for the full test. An r of $+1$ would indicate that each student had exactly the same position in the even-numbered group of items as in the odd-numbered items. An index of 0 would indicate no tendency to maintain the same relative position with respect to the mean of the two groups of items. Obviously, the index of internal consistency reliability should be as close to $+1$ as possible. However, measurement in education is not perfect, so realistically we might expect the reliability coefficient to be something between $+.70$ and $+.90$. Sometimes teachers are willing to accept a reliability index as low as $+.50$. There are no absolute guidelines for a good index of reliability except to say that the closer the index to $+1$, the more consistently the test measures whatever it measures.

Constructing Test Items

Teachers generally use a variety of items on their tests. This is because each item type has certain advantages and limitations in assessing various cognitive skills. In addition, the various items require different procedures both in preparation and in scoring the results. In this section, we present some considerations for constructing various item types and the limitations and advantages of each.

Multiple-Choice Items

Any item that contains a stem and two or more alternatives from which to choose in completing that stem is a multiple-choice item. Although you are probably most familiar with four alternative multiple-choice items, there is nothing magic about the number 4. In some cases it may be desirable to construct multiple-choice items with two alternatives. Good items can be constructed with as many as five alternatives, but it is difficult both to construct and to answer items with more than five alternatives.

A good multiple-choice item has one answer that definitely can be defended as the best answer and one or more good distractors (incorrect alternatives). The stem of the multiple-choice item should state the problem clearly and be as brief as possible. After having read the stem, it should be clear what has been asked, and the student simply looks for the best alternative to complete the statement or answer the question. Care must be taken to avoid grammatical errors or clues, technical language, and jargon.

535

Each distractor in a multiple-choice item should distract; that is, some students should choose that alternative. An alternative that is never chosen is not a distractor.

Each item should be intended to test particular content, and pains must be taken to avoid testing other factors. Some of those other factors might include reading ability, vocabulary, grammar, test-taking skill, second-guessing the teacher, and acquiescence. In general, short items are better than long ones, and the stem and all the alternatives should relate to the same problem or question. Information should be presented in the stem instead of repeated in each alternative.

Items that test trivia should be avoided (although teachers and students usually disagree on what is trivial). If you have the slightest suspicion that the item is trivial, don't use it.

Negative items should be avoided for the most part, especially when the stem combined with an alternative forms a double negative. However, sometimes the only way to test what you want is by asking "Which one of the following is not such and such," in which case it helps to draw attention to the "not" by underlining.

Keep all responses to a stem approximately the same length or you may be giving away the answer. For example, the student may guess accurately that the one long response is the correct response. Care should be taken to avoid any predictable pattern in the position of correct responses. If not, the student may figure out that an item in which the correct response is in position "a" is generally followed by one in which the correct response is in position "d," or that there is a tendency for the correct response to be in position "b" or "c" and not in "a" or "d."

Alternatives such as "all of these" or "none of these" should be used with great caution. Sometimes this is a dead giveaway, and sometimes it confuses the item. Words such as "always" or "never" also cause problems and should be avoided since most things are generally not "always" or "never" true.

A few examples will illustrate some of the problems frequently present in multiple-choice items:

1. "Clark Hull, a Wisconsin graduate who later became a professor at Yale, and who was originally an engineer, developed an early theory of learning which could be described as (a) A hypothetical-deductive S-R theory, (b) an informal S-R theory, (c) an informal field theory, (d) a formal field theory."

The fault is that there is too much irrelevant material in the stem. The facts that Clark Hull was a Wisconsin graduate, a professor at Yale, and originally an engineer are irrelevant to what the question is asking. In addition to making the item unnecessarily long, they may tend to confuse the student.

2. "A negative correlation is not an undesirable result to encounter in

education because (a) not all useful relationships are positive, (b) we must know which variables are related inversely, (c) truth does not only require establishment of positive facts.

The fault is the negative form of the item, creating double negatives and thoroughly confusing the student. By the time you wade through the "negative correlation . . . not undesirable . . . not useful," you have to shift gears several times to figure out what the statement is. The item should be stated in positive form.

3. "Newcomb found in his study of college students that what seems to most clearly distinguish those who were and those who were not susceptible to community influences in the formation of attitudes appeared to be the kind of adjustments already pretty well set on coming to college, in which two vital areas? (a) Toward the community and life in general? (b) Toward parents and siblings? (c) Toward community life? (d) Toward peers and parents?"

The fault is that the stem is much too long and wordy. By the time you finish the stem, you have forgotten what the question was and will probably need to struggle through it several times. The item may be testing short-term memory or reading comprehension rather than the intended knowledge of psychological research.

4. "The first systematic test of intellectual ability was developed by (a) Alfred Binet, (b) David Wechsler, (c) John Guilford, (d) Ivan Pavlov, (e) John Dewey."

The fault is that some of the distractors are not plausible, and nobody will ever choose them. David Wechsler is a plausible answer, and perhaps even John Guilford, but it is hard to imagine anyone thinking of Pavlov or Dewey as having developed the first IQ test.

5. "A person's attitudes (a) are most affected by the extent of his education, (b) are influenced by his associates, (c) are not related to his intelligence, (d) toward his parents are important."

The fault is that the problem was not stated in the stem so that it really becomes four separate items. After reading "A person's attitudes," one has no idea what is being asked and will be thoroughly confused by the time the alternatives are read.

Multiple-choice items can test a broad sampling of content in a short time. They are good for testing all categories of knowledge and can also be used to test analysis and comprehension. It is more difficult to construct items that test application or evaluation with multiple-choice items, and it may be impossible to test synthesis in this format.

Multiple-choice tests have held up very well, as compared with other types of test, in terms of economy, ease of administration, reliability, and validity. They are easy to score and involve no subjectivity in scoring. When well constructed with good distractors, multiple-choice items hold guessing to a minimum.

537

True-False Items

In writing true-false items, the teacher must avoid loosely worded and ambiguous statements. The best items are those that are absolutely true or false, without qualification or exception. It helps to highlight the central point of the item by placing it in a prominent position or by underlining it. Statements that are partly true and partly false should be avoided. Statements with many qualifying clauses and long and involved statements should be avoided.

In addition to the need for random ordering of answers (so that the student cannot say "the last two were false, so this one must be true"), there is also a need to work hard to produce enough true statements. Somehow, it is easier to produce false statements in most subjects, so that, if the student knows that your true-false items are usually false, the guessing factor is increased beyond 50%. Ebel (1979) suggests, however, that a true-false test should include a higher proportion (up to 67%) of false items.

True-false items can cover a lot of ground in a minimum of time. For example, a 100-item true-false test takes no longer than a 40- or 50-item multiple-choice test. With only two alternatives to ponder, the student just reads each statement and answers true or false. Guessing on true-false items is not as important a factor as it might seem. Although there is a 50% chance of guessing on any one item, the chances of guessing 70% correctly on a 50-item true-false test are 1 out of 350 and 1 out of 10,000 on a 100-item test.

The true-false item can be used to measure reasoning and understanding, but in practice its use is limited mainly to testing information and specific facts. This is because the statements must be absolutely and unambiguously true or false. This eliminates a wide variety of statements that can be made about any subject, since many important outcomes of instruction are generalizations, explanations, evaluations, or inferences. When presented with a statement that is usually, but not universally, true, a student really has no way of knowing how to answer. Statements that are approximately true present a dilemma as the student must guess the degree of untruth that will be tolerated by the teacher. A typical true-false item is as follows:

True-False Item: A major advantage of true-false items is that they are very easy to score.

Matching Items

Matching items are also popular among teachers. Quite often this serves merely as a section of a test that includes several types of items, such as multiple-choice, true-false, and completion. Several different types of items on a test should be included, not only for variety but also to give students a better chance to show their strengths and weaknesses. Some students are just "no good" at multiple-choice items, others freeze on matching, and so on, so that a variety of item formats gives all students a better chance.

In constructing a matching item, you first need a list of homogeneous premises and a list of homogeneous responses. The list of homogeneous terms and responses needs to be kept relatively short, not more than ten or twelve at most. It is better to have two or three matching items of six or eight terms each than to have one long item with twenty terms.

The list of premises and responses should be arranged for maximum clarity and convenience for the student. The longer statements should appear on the left, and the short response alternatives on the right. If possible, the responses should be placed in some logical order, or at least in alphabetical order.

In a matching item, the number of response alternatives should be larger than the number of premises to reduce guessing. The basis for matching should be indicated clearly in the directions. One of the lists should consist of single words or very brief phrases. Note also that a matching section should always be presented on a single page as it is confusing for students to try to match across pages.

The matching item has certain advantages, such as being compact as a result of using the same responses for a whole group of items. A good matching section covers a lot of ground in relatively brief space and testing time. It is particularly good for testing a specific aspect of a field of subject matter or definitions of basic terms. A matching item is difficult to write because several alternatives must be provided for each premise. The problem is similar to that faced in writing multiple-choice items but more complex. In a matching item, each response must serve as a potential distractor for several premises; in a multiple-choice item, each alternative must serve as a potential distractor for a single stem. A typical matching item is the following:

Matching Item: For each phrase in the left-hand column, choose the person in the right-hand column that best completes the phrase. Place the letter of the correct person in the blank beside the phrase.

_____ 1. Gave us the law of effect		A. Pavlov
		B. Watson
_____ 2. Developed the principles of operant conditioning		C. Gagné
		D. Thorndike
_____ 3. Is the father of behaviorism		E. Skinner

Supply Items

In multiple-choice, true-false, and matching items, the student is required only to choose the correct answer from a group of possible responses.

Sometimes the teacher's objective requires that the student produce the correct answer rather than just recognize it. This leads to supply items, in which the student answers a specific question, completes a statement, fills in a blank, or writes a fairly lengthy essay in response to a question. Items that require a relatively short response are generally called *completion items;* items requiring longer responses are called *essay items.*

An advantage of supply items is that they cut down on the possibility of guessing. The student must produce the response. If one does not know the answer, one cannot simply guess from alternatives presented.

A major disadvantage of supply items is the subjectivity that occurs in scoring. In multiple-choice, true-false, and matching tests, a scoring key can be established listing the correct response to each item. Anyone can score the test and if several people were to score it, they would score each item exactly the same, since all they have to do is determine whether the correct response was chosen. Supply items, on the other hand, require the test scorer to make judgments as to whether the response provided by the student is correct. And subjectivity in scoring can lead to one person marking an item correct and another marking it incorrect. While this is less of a problem in completion items than in essays, subjectivity is present in the scoring of both. When a teacher prepares a supply item, care should be taken to ensure not only a good item but also to produce scoring procedures that will minimize the subjectivity of scoring.

Completion Items

Completion items require the student to fill in the blank or to write a short response to a particular question. In fill-in-the-blank items, all that needs to be done is to compose a sentence from which some term can be omitted. The sentence must be constructed carefully so that the student can determine what question is being asked and what term is to be supplied. The sentence must be complete and carry all the necessary information to allow the student to respond correctly. Do not take sentences out of context from textbooks.

Since only single terms must be supplied by the student, it is possible to cover a broad range of content with fill-in-the-blank items. However, this briefness of response limits fill-in-the-blank items to assessment of lower-level cognitive skills. In preparing fill-in-the-blank items, you should consider in what alternative forms the correct response might appear so that the various ways in which students may phrase the correct response can be scored as correct. An example follows.

Fill-in-the-Blank Item: If a test item can be counted as correct by one scorer and incorrect by another, the scoring of the test is said to be

_____.

A short-answer item is one in which the student produces a relatively short response, such as a brief list, summary, or answer to a question. These items are fairly easy to write, but care must be taken to ensure that the item provides sufficient information to prompt the desired response. The less care that is taken in writing the item, the more variable the responses are likely to be. This will increase the degree of subjective judgment that must be made in scoring.

Short-answer questions allow a fairly broad sampling of content and also allow the possibility of testing some higher level cognitive skills. Not only can the item be used to test specific facts but also to ask the student to provide a brief synthesis or generalization. If this is done, the teacher must be prepared for a variety of correct responses. An example follows.

Short-Answer Item: List three (3) ways in which a teacher can make use of the results of a standardized achievement test.

Essay Items
Essay items require the student to prepare a relatively lengthy response to a question. Essays put a real burden on the teacher in that they take considerable time and effort to score, especially in a class of thirty students, not to mention the burden placed on the student. This expenditure of effort is probably justified only when the objective to be measured cannot be assessed with an objective item (Aiken, 1979). This means that essay items should be used to assess such high-level cognitive skills as synthesis, analysis, and evaluation, with other item types used to assess knowledge skills.

It is generally believed that essay items are easy to write. Certainly there is no problem of generating plausible alternatives as with the multiple-choice item or the difficulty of giving away the correct answer as in a true-false item; however, the essay item must be stated very carefully so that the student knows what is expected. The essay item should be stated so as to set limits on the range of possible responses. Don't ask students to write all they know about a topic; instead, ask that a particular aspect of a topic be addressed for some specific purpose. Maintaining a balance between allowing the student freedom of response and structuring the expected response is one of the most difficult aspects of writing essay items.

Other considerations in essay items are to allow plenty of time (usually about double what you think the item should take), to be willing to answer questions to make sure that the class knows what it is being asked, and to have a "model" answer in mind in scoring the essays. Also to be decided is whether or not to permit students a choice among questions to answer. One school of thought holds that it is not the same test unless every student answers the same set of items. On the other hand, the gain in student rapport and reduction of anxiety that comes from allowing some choice may be enough to offset this loss in measurement precision.

541

In grading essay tests, several tips have been found to be helpful. First, read each essay without knowing whose paper it is. If an essay test has several items, it is best to read all the answers to one item, score them, then shuffle the papers into random order and read the next item, never knowing whose paper you are reading. In this way, a student doesn't suffer from having you score his or her entire paper at the beginning, when perhaps your standards are higher, or at a time when you are fatigued. Second, it helps to grade essay items on several different points, rather than just a general reaction. The old method of reading the essay and giving the student a total score on a one-hundred-point scale has been found to be unreliable. If teachers read the essay looking for three separate things, such as originality, clarity, and accuracy, scoring each on a three-point scale, they are much more apt to end up with a reliable score. It goes without saying that students should know what will be scored, whether, for example, they will be graded on sentence structure, spelling, and style.

Third, have the essays read and scored by more than one person if possible. Both graders should, of course, be looking for the same points and with the same criteria. Any papers on which the two graders disagree sharply should be read by a third person or reconsidered by the two who originally read them. An example follows.

Essay Item: Describe the role of teacher-made tests in the evaluation of students.

Item Analysis

To gain feedback from a norm-referenced test and to determine not only how good the test is but specifically which items are worth using, which need revising, and which should be thrown out, requires conducting an item analysis of the test. The rationale behind an item analysis is simple: (1) A norm-referenced test is designed to discriminate between those who know the material very well and those who don't know it quite so well. (2) Each item, then, should contribute toward this discrimination. (3) In a good item, students who know the material will tend to get the item right; those who do not know the material will tend to miss it. (4) A good item should not be too easy or too difficult. (5) Each distractor in a multiple-choice item should be plausible; that is, some students will choose it occasionally.

A statistical item analysis supplies the teacher with two important pieces of information: (1) the *discrimination index*, which tells how well the item correlates with the test as a whole or how well it discriminates between highs and lows, and (2) the *difficulty index*, which tells what proportion of the students in the class answered the item correctly.

The difficulty index of a test item is calculated easily, simply by dividing the number of students who answered the item correctly by the total number of students who took the test (see Table 15.3). Thus, the difficulty index can range from +1 to 0. The closer the index is to 1, the easier the item; the closer the index is to 0, the more difficult the item. In tests designed to discriminate among students, it is a good idea to shoot for an average difficulty index of .50, with the index for individual items ranging from near 0 to near +1. If a test is composed only of multiple-choice or true-false items, the ideal average difficulty index should be closer to .60 than to .50 to compensate for the fact that students may be able to guess some items correctly.

The computation of the discrimination index is somewhat more complicated. The discrimination index is intended to measure the extent to which a test item distinguishes between those who know more and those who know less, that is, the degree to which an item distinguishes between "top" students and "low" students. Top students are defined as the top 27% of the scores on the test; low students are the bottom 27%. The discrimination index is then calculated by subtracting the number of students in the low group who answered the item correctly from the number in the top group who answered it correctly. This difference is divided by the total number in the top 27% to get the discrimination index (see Table 15.3). The discrimination index may range from −1 to +1. A +1 means that all the students in the top group answered the item correctly and that none of the students in the low group answered it correctly. The item,

Table 15.3. Item Difficulty and Item Discrimination Indexes

	Test Item			
	1	2	3	4
Number of students	37	37	37	37
In top 27%	10	10	10	10
In low 27%	10	10	10	10
In middle 46%	17	17	17	17
Number correct responses				
In top 27%	10	8	3	9
In low 27%	0	5	7	2
In middle 46%	4	7	11	5
Difficulty index:				
$\dfrac{\text{Number correct}}{\text{Total number of responses}}$	$\dfrac{14}{37} = .38$	$\dfrac{20}{37} = .54$	$\dfrac{21}{37} = .56$	$\dfrac{16}{37} = .43$
Discrimination index:				
$\dfrac{\text{Correct top 27\% - Correct low 27\%}}{\text{Number in top 27\%}}$	$\dfrac{10-0}{10} = 1.0$	$\dfrac{8-5}{10} = +.30$	$\dfrac{3-7}{10} = -.40$	$\dfrac{9-2}{10} = +.70$

therefore, is a perfect discriminator. A -1 means that all the students in the low group answered the item correctly and none in the high group answered correctly. A discrimination index of 0 indicates that the same number in both groups answered the item correctly and that the item does not discriminate. We do not want items on a test with either a negative or 0 discrimination index. It is not possible to set exact limits on the values of the discrimination index that are desirable except to say that they should be positive and that most items should have a value between $+.3$ and $+.7$.

Test Security

Teachers invariably ask, How can you keep students from gaining unfair advantage by knowing test items in advance? How can you keep one class from informing another class what is on a test? If you have a good test, can you use it over again? How do you eliminate the various forms of cheating on tests?

The best way around the problem of security is to develop such a large item pool to draw from that you won't have to worry about security. For example, if you have 1,000 items for your physics class, rather than worrying about security, it might be better to place the entire 1,000 items on reserve in the library. If students are willing to study 1,000 items with the thought in mind that some of those might be on the test, they well might learn more than they do in class.

It takes time to develop a large item pool. But if teachers will identify items that work well and save them for future use, it is surprising how fast such a pool can be accumulated. Another key to the problem is that you should never give the same test over again. Instead, use items from your pool that cut across a number of previous tests as well as some new items. In this way, students are really not so favored if they have access to a previous test, as the upcoming test may have only a few items on it from the previous test that has been acquired.

As for cheating, teachers adopt a variety of stances. These range from the "master sergeant" approach, which advocates iron-clad security to eliminate all possibility of cheating, to the "laissez-faire" approach, which ignores cheating and suggests that the students "are only cheating themselves." Neither extreme is defensible ethically or practically. First, the tight security approach removes all responsibility from the student and implies that it is the teacher's job to prevent cheating. In addition, there is no way possible to prevent all possibilities of cheating. Students who wonder about the creativity of youth should study some of the research on cheating and see the ingenious ways that have been devised for getting around any system that claims to be cheatproof. Teachers who believe that they can prevent all cheating in their classes are only deluding themselves.

But the other extreme is not only equally impractical, it also represents an abdication of teacher responsibility. While it is true that students themselves have the ultimate responsibility to resist the temptation to cheat, it is also true that a teacher has some reasonable interest in preventing this undermining of the very meaning of education. The student is not cheating "only himself" but cheating other students also, and to ignore it is an abdication of responsibility. Ignoring cheating also contributes to poor student morale, as they see cheating going on without the teacher making any attempt to stop it. This may even cause the student to believe that cheating must be all right since nobody seems to care.

Be realistic about cheating. Admit that it is a widespread phenomenon, yet try to minimize it in your own classes. Make it clear that you stand strongly against cheating, take reasonable steps to maximize security, recognize cheating when it does occur, and do something about it. If students know what is expected of them, believe that you are fair, and have ample opportunity to prepare for each test, the need to cheat will be minimized.

Approaches to and Procedures in Grading

We come finally to that area of student evaluation that bothers teachers more than anything else: grading. As with the weather, everyone complains about it, but nobody seems to be able to do anything about it. Almost every teacher is involved in the activity of pronouncing grades.

But, first, what does a grade mean? Does it indicate one student's performance relative to other students? Is it an indication of progress relative to other students? Is it an indication of progress relative to the student's own past record? Does it tell how well a student is doing in relation to his or her potential? Is it an indicator of attitude, or interest, or effort? Grades have been used for all these purposes, and many more, and no doubt will continue to be even as new reasons for grading are invented.

Making the Procedure Objective

There is no magic solution to the problem of assigning grades. It is probably the area that causes the most agony not only among teachers, but among parents and students also. Many teachers, in fact, describe assigning grades as the most distasteful part of teaching.

A few suggestions are in order, however, for making the whole process easier and more objective.

545

1. *Make clear just what your grades mean and how they are determined.* Regardless what philosophy and what system you are using, it is important that students know this, and as soon as possible. Grading systems that are mysterious or unexplained tend to be the most threatening and encourage cheating. It is probably best to explain your beliefs about grading, what an "A," "B," "C," or "D" means to you, and what is expected of students very early in the course. There is no reason for any secrecy in how test scores and other criteria are combined in determining a grade. Of course, you must also be careful that the information given students about your beliefs and your grading procedures is as accurate as possible.

2. *Use a number of smaller tests instead of one big one.* The fewer tests you use in a course, the more threatening each specific test tends to be. The most threatening situation of all, naturally, is the class in which everything hangs on one comprehensive final exam. Classes in which almost everything depends on a midterm and a final are almost as bad.

It is better to administer a number of smaller tests spread out through the course, each counting only a small portion of the total grade. This not only provides more feedback but also removes quite a bit of the threat of any one particular test. A final exam in this instance can serve as a review of the course without the entire grade depending on it.

3. *Keep complete and detailed records.* Teachers often violate this commonsense principle. Complete and detailed records not only provide a much clearer basis on which to determine grades, but also allow for more feedback to the student as to just where he or she stands. Whenever a controversy arises about a grade (not an uncommon occurrence in our legalistic times), this provides objective evidence to back up the grade that was given. These complete and detailed records should also include notes on just how grades were determined, what factors were combined, and what weightings were used.

4. *Whenever possible, let students participate in the process.* It is usually impractical as well as threatening to turn the job of grading over to the students, but there *are* parts of the process in which students can participate. Determining how many tests to have, when to have them, which types of tests are preferred, and various options in the grading process can profit from student input. Other requirements, such as participation, papers, projects, and other inputs to grades should also be open to some negotiation. Of course, the teacher is still the one who is responsible for what is done and for seeing to it that students live up to what is agreed upon.

5. *Allow for more than one path in achieving a grade.* Requiring every student to do exactly the same thing smacks of a "canned goods" approach to teaching and certainly is not consistent with a humanistic approach. Students sometimes feel boxed in when there is only one route possible for earning a grade and could work harder and learn more if other options were available.

6. *Try to get away from extreme, destructive forms of competition.* It is un-

realistic to suggest that you can have a classroom that is devoid of competition, and probably not practical or advisable in a competitive society. But there are differences in the dynamics of competition. A student competing as part of a group, or against a standard, or against his or her past record is not the same as a student in the cutthroat competitive situation where there is one winner and everyone else loses. Unfortunately, the latter often occurs in the classroom: one student's success is another student's loss or one student is best and everyone else is a loser. Elimination of such individual, negative competition in the classroom will likely lead to a healthier climate and a better student attitude toward the entire grading process.

7. *Don't use grades as a form of discipline.* There are enough other means at your disposal to control classroom behavior without using grades as bribes or punishments. If a student is performing at the "A" level, he should receive an "A," even if he is misbehaving. There are other ways to control or punish his misbehavior. Sometimes the report card uses two grades, one reflecting achievement in the course and the other reflecting an attitude-interest-effort dimension. In this instance, chronic misbehavior in a class might be reflected in the second grade, but not the first.

8. *Give plenty of feedback throughout the course.* This is related to the suggestion to keep complete and detailed records, for one of the uses of these records is feedback to students. A student should know where he stands, what progress he is making, when he is in trouble, throughout the entire course. He should also be given additional feedback in the way of explanations, interpretations, and suggestions whenever he asks for them. It is easy to err in the form of not providing enough feedback to students about grades. It is difficult to conceive of giving too much feedback, provided that it is accurate and given in a way that is not anxiety provoking.

9. *Whatever system you use, remain flexible.* A rigid, unyielding teacher who won't even listen to suggestions is often one of the students' first complaints. But flexibility does *not* mean that you should be easily manipulated. Teachers who have clear, well-established, and organized grading procedures tend to be more successful as well as better liked by students.

It is one thing to agree to change some aspect of grading criteria, or the date of a test, or perhaps extend a deadline for good reason. It is something else to change a grade or to switch criteria to match students. Teachers must be careful that they are clear, organized, consistent, and fair in grading but at the same time not completely rigid and unyielding when it comes to reasonable considerations.

10. *Seventy percent does not have to be the standard for a passing grade.* There is really no more reason for 70 to be the passing grade than 80 or 60 or 50. If you take the suggestion that we made earlier that the average difficulty index for a test should be .50, then the average score expected on a test should be around 50%. You may have to adjust your passing grade to the difficulty level of the test.

11. *The distribution of grades in a class will probably not approximate a*

normal curve. The normal curve is a theoretical distribution based upon an extremely large population. No single group of students, especially students grouped on the basis of ability, should be expected to be distributed normally. It is best to forget about the normal curve when assigning grades.

12. *If criterion-referenced testing is employed by the teacher, grades may be assigned on the basis of an absolute standard.* If norm-referenced tests are used, then grades should be based on the relative performance of the class. The definition of absolute standard is that it is a fixed point, and any student who surpasses that point attains a particular grade. This seems fine when the content being assessed is the frame of reference. However, when the reference for interpreting a score is the performance of other students, the standard must be relative in that the performance of other students affects how any given student's performance is interpreted.

13. *Weighting tests in the determination of grades requires equating their variabilities.* The length of a test does not really determine its weight in the assigning of grades, but its standard deviation does. A hundred-item test with small variability might actually carry less weight than a ten-item quiz if the raw scores are added together as illustrated in Table 15.4.

John, who flunked the exam, but did very well on the quiz, ends up with a "B" in the course, while Joe, who excelled in the exam but flunked the quiz, ends up with a "C." Although this is an extreme case, the same idea applies to tests in general. You don't really know the weight of one test as compared with another unless you consider the standard deviation, and if you want to weight one test versus another, you weight it in relation to common standard deviations. In other words, if two tests have about the same standard deviation, they have about the same effect on the grade. What this really means is that you are getting into the same scale. You are not weighting pounds compared with ounces or meters compared with inches.

Table 15.5 contains a good shortcut formula for computing standard deviation. This gives a very good approximation of standard deviation, adequate for almost any teaching purpose, and can be computed in two minutes or less for most classes. Compute the standard deviation for two or more tests, and if they are close, then use raw scores in weighting the tests. However, if they are discrepant, weight the tests *inversely* to the standard deviations to get them into the same scale, rather than using the

	Quiz	Exam	Total	Grade
Joe	1	100	101	C
	8	100	108	A
	7	98	105	B
	5	97	102	B
John	10	93	103	B
	3	96	99	C
	2	96	98	C

Table 15.4
Scores for Students and Resulting Grades When Variability Is Not Equated

Table 15.5
Shortcut for Calculating
Standard Deviation

Top 17% Scores	Bottom 17% Scores
28	16
27	14
27	12
25	12
24	11
131	65

$$\text{Standard deviation} = \frac{\text{Sum of top 17\% of scores} - \text{Sum of bottom 17\% of scores}}{\frac{1}{2} \text{ the total number of students}}$$

$$\text{Standard deviation} = \frac{131 - 65}{15} = \frac{66}{15} = 4.4$$

raw scores. That is, the scores on the test with the smaller standard deviation should be multiplied by whatever number multiplied times the standard deviation will yield the larger standard deviation. For example, if test A has a standard deviation of 3 and test B a standard deviation of 6, multiply each score in test A by 2, since $3 \times 2 = 6$.

14. *A course grade does not reflect learning of subject matter only.* Whether it reflects competitive performance, individual progress, participation, attitude, or attendance is a matter both of philosophy and of institutional policy. For a course grade to reflect only the learning of subject matter, a pretest would have to be given before the course, followed by a posttest at the end. The difference between the two would estimate how much the person actually learned. In such a case, depicted in Table 15.6, Fred, the student with the biggest increase in score might be said to have learned the most, and thus deserve the "A." Hugo, who has the highest score, has not really shown much of an increase, so he gets a "C." This is seldom done in school at any level, because gain scores are unreliable and because students soon learn that a low pretest score will increase their grades. A grade *usually* reflects a student's performance relative to the rest of the class. The important thing, once teachers are clear on just what the grades are to reflect, is to take every step possible to make sure that the grades really do reflect what they say they do and to make an effort to assure that students know on what the grades are based. You might say that it really is a grading "game," but it is not fair to keep the rules of the game a secret.

Table 15.6
Pretest and Posttest Scores
for a Class in Which Only
Gain Determines Grade

	Pretest	Posttest	Gain	Grade
Hugo	87	98	11	C
Elmer	80	93	13	B
Bertha	78	88	10	C
Erica	70	85	15	B
Fred	52	79	27	A

15. *Quality of teaching is not reflected in the number of high or low grades a teacher gives.* The teacher who gives few high grades does not necessarily have higher standards than the one who gives many. Giving many high grades does not mean the teacher is too easy or so good that his or her students do an outstanding job. You simply cannot tell the quality of teaching by looking at grade distribution.

16. *Remember that, in the final analysis, the grade is always a subjective judgment.* This section began with the statement that there is no magic solution to the problem of grades. Much can be done to make the procedure objective and to use good judgment, common sense, and accepted measurement practices in gathering the data. But in the final analysis, that grade represents an evaluative judgment, an interpretation of what the data mean. Teachers who are unwilling to stick their necks out and make such judgments should probably seek another occupation. And teachers who do not feel some uneasiness, some distress and discomfort, in making these judgments are probably lacking the conscientiousness and sensitivity that make for a good teacher. So do everything possible to gather data intelligently, systematically, and openly and to keep students informed, but never forget that the grade represents a subjective judgment on your part as a teacher.

Student Preferences in Grading

In a recent study, Reilly (undated) asked students at three different universities to indicate what they viewed as the ideal grading system. There was high agreement on a number of points. The students preferred

1. Having a choice among different ways to earn a grade.
2. Setting competition against a standard rather than against the rest of the class.
3. Having grading procedures explained at the beginning of a class.
4. Being involved in determining criteria for course grades.
5. Having the opportunity to raise grades through extra work.
6. Using grading criteria that allow students to estimate their grade early in a course.
7. Providing flexibility in grading criteria to the point that the criteria might change during the course.
8. Being graded on class participation.

While these data reflect only the preferences of university students, elementary and secondary students probably have similar preferences. Interestingly, most of the university students responding in Reilly's studies did *not* see their university instructors as employing the ideal grading practices.

Objections to Testing and Grading

Opposition to both testing and grading practices is widespread in our schools today (Kirschenbaum et al., 1971). Movements that suggest a utopia in which testing and grading are nonexistent and students learn in much more "positive" ways are not difficult to find. And some critics of testing and grading imply that testing and grading are truly two of the evils of our society. Grading has been blamed for almost everything that is wrong with schools.

Grading students' work is not in itself counterproductive or antihumanistic. Grades serve such useful functions as periodic reports of progress, a basis for administrative decisions, reinforcement, and allowing students and parents to determine how a student is doing compared with other students. Instead of cursing grades as evil, or joining a movement toward the unlikely goal of stamping out grades, it seems more reasonable to be aware of what one is doing in the grading process and to take steps to make the grading process as effective and positive as possible.

Summary

Teachers use tests in the classroom for a variety of reasons, but the most common use is that of gaining information to use in assigning grades. The teacher's own test is often more valid for measuring what he or she has taught than are standardized tests. The teacher can follow the same steps, in general, that a professional testing company employs in developing a test.

A criterion-referenced teacher-made test attempts to assess whether a student has mastered a particular domain of content. Content validity is the major concern for determining if a criterion-referenced teacher-made test is good.

A norm-referenced teacher-made test attempts to assess how a given student compares with the rest of the class. The quality of norm-referenced teacher-made tests is assessed through content validity and internal consistency reliability.

Content validity of classroom tests can be determined by comparing the test items with the instructional objectives. If the item assesses the objectives, the test possesses content validity.

A method for determining internal consistency of classroom tests is presented. Classroom tests will generally have lower reliability indexes than will standardized tests.

Guidelines for constructing test items are presented. Strong points and weak points of multiple-choice, true-false, matching, completion, and essay items are discussed. Multiple-choice and other objectively scored items have the advantages of covering a large amount of material and having highly reliable scoring procedures. Essay items allow coverage of types of objectives that multiple-choice, true-false, or matching items cannot tap.

Such goals as application, analysis, synthesis, and evaluation can be measured in essay items; it does not make sense to measure knowledge or comprehension in this fashion, since these can be assessed more readily and quickly by other item types. Guidelines that help to reduce the subjectivity in scoring essay items are presented.

Item analysis is a useful tool in developing test items. The item analysis gives information about such things as the difficulty level of an item, the function of each distractor, and the extent to which the item discriminates among students. By utilizing item analysis data, the teacher can find out how items are actually working as well as gaining ideas about modifying items, thereby developing a file of effective items. Steps for performing an item analysis are given.

The security problem is described, with the best solution being that of maintaining a large file of items and having each test made up of a different combination of items. Essentially, teachers can develop a pool of proven items in the same fashion that a professional testing company does.

To make the whole process of grading easier and more objective, teachers should make clear just what their grades mean and how they are determined. Using a number of smaller tests rather than one big one, keeping complete and detailed records, letting students participate in the process, and allowing for more than one path in achieving a grade all help to improve the process. It is suggested also that the teacher avoid extreme, destructive forms of competition, avoid using grades as a form of discipline, give considerable feedback throughout the course, remain flexible, and remember that regardless how objective the procedure, a grade is still a subjective judgment.

A picture of what students see as ideal grading practices is presented. Students like to have some choice in ways to earn their grade, do *not* like to feel that they are in competition with each other, like to have the opportunity to do extra work, like to know all about grading procedures, and like to have some say in the criteria for grading.

The chapter closes with a brief discussion of current objections to grading and "stamp out tests" movements, with the conclusion that sound procedures in testing and grading are consistent with humanistic ideals. Teachers should know all they can about testing and grading to make it as effective and healthy a process as possible.

Study Questions

1. Why is the teacher's own test often more valid in measuring learning in the classroom than is the use of a standardized test? What can teachers do to make their tests more reliable and valid?

2. Under what conditions would you use a supply-type item instead of a multiple-choice item? When is matching useful? Under what conditions would an essay item be more appropriate?

3. How might a teacher's opinion of student's abilities influence the grading of essays? What steps can a teacher take to avoid the effects of such opinions in grading essay items?

4. How can the teacher get around the security problem in relation to classroom tests? Why is it beneficial to have a large item pool from which to draw?
5. What are the essential differences between norm-referenced and criterion-referenced testing? Under what circumstances would the criterion-referenced test be more appropriate? How does one know where to set the standard for passing on a criterion-referenced test?

References

Aiken, L. R. *Psychological Testing and Measurement,* 3rd ed. Boston: Allyn and Bacon, 1979.

Beggs, D. L., and Lewis, E. L. *Measurement and Evaluation in the Schools.* Boston: Houghton-Mifflin, 1975.

Ebel, R. *Essentials of Educational Measurement,* 3rd ed. Englewood Cliffs, N.J.: Prentice-Hall, 1979.

Gronlund, N. E. *Measurement and Evaluation in Teaching,* 4th ed. New York: Macmillan, 1981.

Kirschenbaum, H., Simon, S. B., and Napier, R. W. *Wad-Ja-Get? The Grading Game in American Education.* New York: Hart, 1971.

Reilly, R. "Student Preferences in Grading," unpublished study.

Discipline: Psychological Approaches

16

PREVIEW

What is a reasonable definition of "discipline"?

What was the meaning of discipline in the "good ole days"?

What are some problems with the practices of punishment and strictness?

What was the meaning of discipline in the progressive approach?

What were some shortcomings in the practice of freedom and permissiveness?

What are current beliefs about discipline as control?

What are the shortcomings of discipline as referral?

What is the philosophy of discipline as prevention?

What is organized sublimation?

What is the conditioning approach to dealing with discipline problems?

How does drive reduction work as a theory about discipline?

What is the behavior modification approach to discipline?

How can reinforcement be used to change behavior?

What is the modeling approach to dealing with discipline problems?

Why are identification and imitation important?

How is reinforcement a part of modeling behavior?

What is the eliciting effect? The inhibiting effect? The disinhibiting effect? The modeling effect?

How are discipline problems seen from a humanistic point of view?

Why is a positive approach to human nature important?

Why are uniqueness and individuality important?

Can a humanist be a good disciplinarian?

Is there a conflict between freedom and responsibility?

Why is it important to establish controls early?

How many rules and regulations should a teacher have?

Why is student involvement helpful?

Why is it important to know students' names?

What is the nature of threats in the classroom?

Is it possible to teach without threatening students?

What is the function of humor in regard to discipline?

Why should the teacher know about policies and practices of other teachers?

What are nonverbal cues, and what is their function in discipline?

How can a teacher discuss misbehavior with a student?

What is the importance of authenticity in the classroom?

How do reason and logic aid in disciplining students?

What is the function of stimulus variability?

Should punishment be immediate or delayed?

What happens when a teacher punishes an entire class?

How does sarcasm affect classroom interaction?

Why should misbehavior *not* be taken personally?

What is a personality conflict, and how does it affect classroom discipline?

How can teachers maximize their advantage over students in the area of discipline?

Discipline is consistently identified in surveys of teachers, parents, and community members as one of the most important problems facing the schools. In fact, the "dropout" problem has been referred to as more of a "stay-in" problem for students and a "burnout" problem for teachers, since so many of the students who stay in school are such discipline problems that teachers drop out! To illustrate the problem further, it is not at all unusual to hear a building principal say in regard to the performance of a teacher, "he knows his subject and is a nice guy, but he just can't control his class."

Discipline, as used here, is defined as having two essential components: *the prevention of and the handling of behavior problems in the classroom.* In this chapter, we describe the causes of behavior problems and present suggestions for preventing them. We also present suggestions for dealing with behavior problems when they do occur.

One approach to understanding discipline is to look at the schools of the past and draw inferences from practices that were followed. As we do this, we will develop synonyms for the word "discipline" that are implicit in the view of teaching and in classroom practices of a particular era.

As we make this survey, you are asked to consider each description in light of your own past experience as well as in relation to your own present beliefs. Are these approaches to discipline a part of the present-day scene, or did they die with the passage of time? Are the underlying philosophies still a part of disciplinary practices today, even if teachers no longer give lip service to them? Which set of synonyms comes closest to describing *your* beliefs about discipline?

The Good Old Days: "Spare the Rod"

A close look at discipline practices in schools of the 1800s reveals practices that can be summarized best with the terms *punishment* and *strictness*. The "discipline means punishment" philosophy of teachers was consistent with the more general view of the 1800s that people were innately sinful. Since all people were viewed as essentially "bad," misbehavior on the part of the child was expected. Discipline referred to the ways in which this misbehavior was punished after it occurred. The single positive aspect of this philosophy of discipline was the apparent belief that, even though each child was basically bad, punishment of misbehavior could modify future behaviors.

The second term that describes discipline in the 1800s—strictness—differed from punishment in that it stressed prevention rather than reaction. The teacher ran such a tight ship that misbehavior could not occur! The basic goal was to prevent misbehavior rather than to punish it. As with the punishment approach, this approach stressed the negative view that threats and anxieties underlying rigid rules and regulations prevented misbehavior.

Punishment and strictness fit well with the predominant view of the learning process in the 1800s. The "mental discipline" approach held that the mind was like a muscle and could be strengthened through rigorous exercise and mental calisthenics. Memorization of large amounts of poetry and prose and the study of Latin, Greek, and the classics were thought to be the best curriculum, since they led to a disciplined mind. The Puritanical tenet that learning must be hard work was an additional underpinning for the strict and punitive practices in the schools.

Although strictness and punishment are based on different rationales and can be separated logically, they tend to overlap in practice. A strict teacher will probably use punishment to back up threats; a punitive teacher

557

MR. STERN'S NO-NONSENSE CLASS

Mr. Stern has taught at P.S. 108 for forty-two years and prides himself on his well-organized classroom. The desks are in neat rows, and the room is clean and orderly. Students sit up and listen when he speaks and do not speak unless called on. "A classroom is a castle, and the teacher is king," says Mr. Stern, with obvious pride. Stories of past indiscretions in his classes are part of the school's folklore, but Mr. Stern is proud that no student dares misbehave in his class today. He is a clear example of the punishment and strictness approach, and he is by no means unusual in the schools of today.

will probably also be strict to hold misbehavior to a minimum. Both approaches are intended to discourage bad behavior. However, we now know that punishing misbehavior is not as effective or as predictable as encouraging desirable behaviors. While punishment and strictness tend to be frowned on today as basic approaches to discipline, prospective teachers are encouraged to ask themselves if these are at all similar to their conception of discipline and that of their teachers.

Progressive Education: "Spare the Child"

Early in the twentieth century, American educators began to ask "Why does the child misbehave anyway?" The answer they supplied was that the child misbehaves *because of* the rigid, punitive system. Place the child in a cold, structured situation, with numerous rules and regulations, force him to learn things that are of no interest to him, and he will misbehave to fight the system. This creates a cycle of the system's becoming more rigid, with more rules and regulations being added in reaction to misbehavior, but with the rigidity, rules, and regulations being the *causes* of the misbehavior.

Progressive education offered a solution to this dilemma. Change the system. Eliminate the rigidity, rules, regulations, and other distasteful requirements that inhibit learning. Break the vicious cycle of bad system-bad behavior-more bad system-more bad behavior by eliminating the cause—namely, the practices of the system that lead to misbehavior. In a permissive and stimulating environment, progressive educators argued, with a learning task that is intrinsically interesting to the child, misbehavior would not occur because there would be no need for it. Freed of the necessity to fight against rigid rules and requirements, to protest being forced to learn what did not interest him, the child would be free to explore, to seek answers to problems that interested him, and to allow his natural curiosity to become the basis for learning.

MISS BLISS'S NO-PUNISHMENT CLASS

Miss Bliss teaches third grade in Washington School, which is considered to be the most progressive in town. A peek into her classroom would reveal an active situation, with lots of talking, movement, and activity. Miss Bliss might be anywhere in the room, but it is almost certain that she would be encouraging students to "do your own thing." She prides herself on the fact that she never uses reprimands or punishment and has no rules or regulations. "The children will learn what they need to know when they are ready," she explains. The children seem to like her, but some of the parents wonder why their children are not progressing in the "Three R's."

Thus, for some educators in the progressive education era, the synonyms for discipline became *freedom, permissiveness,* and *interest.* Place the child in a situation where he is free to explore and learn, surround him with resources and materials, and he will find problems that interest him and work toward their solution. Discipline will automatically follow from the requirements of the problem and from the child since he is now learning what he wants to learn. Since the system will no longer be causing misbehavior, there will be no misbehavior to punish.

The reader will probably agree that freedom and permissiveness are not panaceas for the problems of education. "Please, teacher, don't make us do whatever we feel like doing again today!" illustrates the child's need for structure and direction. A completely permissive class appears to be more anxiety producing than a traditional class, and complete dependence on a child's "felt needs" to determine the curriculum is rarely attempted.

The Present: Building on Our Past

Disposing of one hundred years of discipline practices in a few pages is certainly a bold venture, but before we focus on the present, the reader should ask, Are these practices strictly in the past? We believe they are not and that residues of each can be found in many classrooms today. Teachers demonstrate their real philosophies in what they do rather than in what they say. It is not at all difficult to find teachers whose classroom behaviors are consistent with the belief that discipline equals strictness and punishment. It *is* difficult to find teachers who will admit that this is their belief. Teachers who exhibit a commitment to freedom and permissiveness are harder to find, although it is easy to find teachers who give lip service to such philosophies. These inconsistencies between actual behaviors and

559

stated beliefs are common in any field. In our statements, we reflect what we believe is the prevailing philosophy, but in practice we use what we think, perhaps unconsciously, works.

Discipline as Control

One of the most popular synonyms for discipline in the literature of today is the word "control." Advocates of this approach to discipline argue that controls for behavior must come from somewhere, the alternative being virtual anarchy and chaos. When we have thirty people in a room, each possessing unique interests and experiences and some of them wishing they were somewhere else, how can we expect learning to take place? The answer is that there must be control.

Advocates of the punishment and strictness approaches obviously believe that control must come from external sources and that the child must be coerced into behaving properly and limited to a narrow choice of actions. Advocates of the permissiveness approach, on the other hand, believe that control should come from within. The child will control his own behavior adequately if he is free to learn in response to his felt needs. Other sources of control are the task itself, the peer group, the society and its demands, prestige and authority, humiliation and shame, competition, fear of failure, guilt, and anxiety.

A general hierarchy of beliefs about control is evident in current writings about discipline. Certain controls, such as those coming from within or self-control, are the ideal, and positive means of gaining control are better than negative. The means of control must be consistent with the goals the teacher is trying to reach. Twelve generalizations concerning popular beliefs about control, most of which have considerable research support, follow. Study these in light of your own views on classroom behavior and in relation to your experiences as a student.

A DOZEN POPULAR BELIEFS ABOUT CONTROL AS AN APPROACH TO DISCIPLINE

1. Control from within the child is better than control from external sources.
2. Positive means of control are better than negative.
3. Fear and anxiety can be effective means of control but are unpredictable and have dangerous side effects.
4. Status and acceptance within the peer group are powerful controls.
5. Cooperation can be as effective a control as competition.
6. Humiliation and shame are even more damaging than fear and anxiety.
7. The most effective form of control is not always the best one to use.
8. A child's expectations are an important control, particularly if they are satisfied in the situation.
9. Praise is better than blame, and reward is better than punishment.

10. Control is easier to attain when the child knows what is expected of him or her.

11. Both reward and punishment are most effective when they occur immediately after the behavior that they are intended to control.

12. Control through arbitrary, external force, against the child's will, is one of the least desirable methods.

Discipline as Understanding

Present-day discussions of discipline stress the importance of understanding the child and the reasons for his behaving as he does (Dreikurs et al., 1982). If we understand the child, how he perceives the situation, what his motives are, and how he feels, we will avoid most discipline problems and also know how to handle those that do occur.

Although understanding a child's behavior is certainly a worthy goal, we must point out that understanding does not tell a teacher automatically what to do in a classroom situation or prevent discipline problems from occurring. To understand that a child "is acting out," "has a need for attention," or "lacks peer status" hardly solves the problem or eliminates the behavior. Even though understanding and acceptance might be helpful aids in discipline, they fall far short of defining successful disciplinary practices.

As part of the current emphasis on understanding, there is a strong tendency to describe the misbehaving child as "sick," not "bad." In the strictness and punishment approaches of the 1800s, a child who misbehaved did so because of the innate sinfulness of man. The teacher's job was either to prevent this badness from manifesting itself or to punish it when it occurred to inhibit it in the future. No great effort was necessary to understand a misbehaving child, because he or she was obviously just being bad.

Modern psychology has brought us far beyond this simple explanation of behavior. And yet, if all we add is understanding, we are in danger of saying the child is "sick" rather than "bad" and dismissing it at that. The child misbehaves because of the sickness called cultural disadvantage, emotional disturbance, broken home, or perceptual handicap. And is it really any more flattering to the child to label him "emotionally disturbed" than merely to call him "bad"? We do not mean to imply that these are useless labels; rather, understanding and diagnosis alone do not solve or eliminate the teacher's discipline problems.

Another aspect of understanding that is stressed in modern approaches to discipline is that the child should understand the reasons behind rules, regulations, and disciplinary actions. By understanding the rationale behind these facts, the child can accept them as necessary restraints. An appeal to reason is the basic defense for rules and procedures rather than arbitrary enforcement of superior authority, and the child then has less reason to revolt or question that authority.

The twin aspects of understanding—the teacher for the student and his or her behavior and the student for the teacher and his or her actions—are well established as part of the modern outlook toward discipline. Undoubtedly, such understanding helps even though it does not automatically suggest a course of action for the teacher.

Discipline as Referral

Another synonym for discipline evidenced in today's practices is "referral." The misbehaving child is referred to the counselor for help, to the psychologist for testing, to the remedial reading specialist for instruction, to the social worker, to the school nurse, and to the special education class. The referral tactic fits in very nicely with the "sick not bad" approach, because it is assumed that there is a reason for the child's behavior and that he or she needs help. Referral to an expert will allow the particular source of the "illness" to be labeled and remedied or at the very least will remove the troublesome child from the classroom, and the teacher's problem will be solved.

One of the major shortcomings of referral as a solution is that it is not always clear who should be referred. Teachers and psychologists often disagree as to the symptoms of emotional disturbance and the seriousness of various behaviors. In addition to this, it is often difficult to decide to whom to refer the child or to attain a successful referral even if one knows the sort of expert he or she would like to consult. School systems do not have an unlimited supply of consulting experts, and even when a teacher is convinced that a child should see a psychiatrist, it may be very difficult to arrange.

But the biggest shortcoming of referral as a disciplinary procedure is that the teacher tends to believe that someone else will solve the problem, and this is usually not the case. Even when referral is successful, the teacher usually remains as the key person in working with the child and helping him solve his problems. The expert helps to specify the problem and might even suggest some strategies, but the teacher is still the one "under the gun." If a teacher refers students as a means of gaining information and insight, the referral may be helpful, but if a teacher refers a child as a means of eliminating the problem, that teacher will usually be sadly disillusioned.

Discipline as Prevention

An important characteristic underlying modern approaches to discipline is the belief that most discipline problems can be avoided. Unlike the practices of the 1800s, however, where the goal was to prevent misbehavior through strictness, rigidity, and punishment, the modern approach is that problems are avoided through good teaching. If the teacher understands the students' needs and motives, presents the material properly, gets the students actively involved in learning, and provides adequate rewards, then most discipline problems simply will not develop. The mastering of all the rudiments of good teaching is, therefore, the key to successful discipline, according to this philosophy.

Now, we do not want to destroy completely the basic philosophy behind this approach, since it is true that many discipline problems could be avoided entirely or at least nipped in the bud by a skillful teacher. Good teaching is one key to avoiding discipline problems, but an inherent danger in this approach is that it easily leads to the conclusion that discipline problems are proof of poor teaching practices. The student who is preparing to teach repeatedly hears descriptions of good teaching. If the student asks a question about a possible discipline problem that is worrying him or her, the student is told how the problem could have been avoided if the class has been motivated properly, the situation structured more clearly, or the teacher more sensitive to early signs of discontent. A conspiracy of silence confronts students who seek answers to various problems that they fear might arise, and it is not surprising that they equate good teaching with the absence of discipline problems or see the occurrence of discipline problems as evidence of failure as a teacher.

Behavior is the result of many factors interacting. (CEMREL, Inc.)

A basic psychological principle that must be kept in mind is that complex human behavior is *multiply* caused—many different variables interact to determine an individual's behavior. The teacher is only *one* of the variables in the classroom. The teacher has only limited ability to control most classroom variables and virtually no chance to control or even be aware of some of them. A child's misbehavior might be caused by factors completely outside the school situation, factors that have nothing to do with the teacher, or factors about which the teacher can do nothing.

The "discipline problems do not occur for good teachers" idea is also inadequate because teachers *do* make mistakes. In the classroom day after day, with twenty or more students in a class, it is unrealistic to expect the teacher's interaction with each student to be perfect. On the basis of the numerous variables that are outside the teacher's control, and because it is normal that the teacher will at times contribute to problems in the classroom, a teacher should not feel that he or she has failed simply because discipline problems have arisen. Good teachers prevent many discipline problems but they also have ways of dealing with the problems that do occur.

Avoiding Problems Through Organized Sublimation

Another aspect of the discipline is prevention idea is the practice of "organized sublimation." The word sublimate refers to the psychological mechanism whereby an otherwise unacceptable drive is channeled through an outlet that is socially desirable. Thus Van Gogh sublimated at least part of the time through the outlet of painting, and the angry business executive channels this drive toward business success that is socially beneficial.

By organized sublimation, we mean the planning and scheduling of the school day in such a way that all a student's drives are steered through acceptable channels. Students are so busy that they have neither the time nor the energy to get into trouble. They are under the teacher's thumb not only for classes, but also for clubs, athletics, and extracurricular activities. The break between classes is so short that it can hardly be considered a time for rest or recreation. The provision of acceptable outlets such as band, chorus, gym class, athletics, camera club, computer club, cheerleading, to name but a few, is expected to keep students from expressing aggressive drives and excess energy in ways that are troublesome to the school.

This approach is not the solution to all discipline problems for two reasons. First, although keeping students busy may have some positive relationship to keeping them out of trouble, it is certainly not the only variable and falls far short of a guarantee that misbehavior will not occur. Besides, since activity has a snowballing effect, some behavior problems can be traced to a heavy dose of activity during the preceding class period. Second, the basic idea of "keep 'em behaving by keeping 'em busy" neglects young persons' needs to daydream, think about themselves and their world, and just plain waste time occasionally as part of growing up. Discipline through organized sublimation is an overworked technique whose advantages may be outweighed by its shortcomings.

Discipline as Individualized Instruction

One final idea that is popular in current descriptions of discipline is the idea of individualizing teaching. Since each child is a unique individual, the teacher should recognize this and provide unique learning experiences for each individual. In this way, and only in this way, the needs of each student are met and the major cause of discipline problems is eliminated.

This approach sounds reasonable, but seldom does the advocate of this approach explain specifically how to accomplish it. The teacher with five classes each day plus all the meetings, clerical work, and extra duties can hardly discover what the needs of each individual student *are*, much less satisfy them. Besides, the "state of the art" as to individualizing instruction could only be described as incomplete at best. As a result, the approach of minimizing discipline problems through individualized instruction, while an important educational principle, hardly suffices as a *complete* solution to discipline problems.

ADVENTURES IN INDIVIDUALIZED INSTRUCTION

When David informed his parents that he was on page 60 of the math book and that there were only two months of school remaining, they thought something was amiss. Upon checking with Miss Peterson, his teacher, they found that the book had 400 pages and that David was supposed to be on approximately page 350. Miss Peterson explained that this was the "new math" and that she was taking an individualized approach. Each student was to work on math every day, at his or her own speed, and to see her if any help was needed. Sometimes she gave them some class time, during which she prepared for other classes, but much of the work was to be done outside of class.

David's parents were unfamiliar with such an approach and felt that it was a little unusual for 9-year-olds. His father finally insisted that David sit down with him every night with the math book, while the father worked on his own sketches for the office. David's father ended up spending most of every evening working on David's math with him, and after many tears, frustrations, and even accusations by his wife that he was scaring the boy, he managed to get David through the math book.

At the end of the year, Miss Peterson noted that for some strange reason most of the students had failed to get anywhere in math, but a few such as David did well on the year-end tests. "I guess some students are just not ready for individualized instruction," she concluded, as she made plans to teach reading and science through her "individualized" approach next year. Since she had used it in math, she had eliminated most of the discipline problems she used to encounter when she taught math the "traditional" way.

Causes of Behavior

Three widely used approaches to describing the causes of behavior come from the psychological schools of thought known as behaviorism, social learning theory, and humanism. Behaviorism sees behavior as the result of conditioning, social learning theory explains that behavior is the result of modeling, and humanism sees behavior as the unique core of individuality. In this section, each of these explanations of behavior is explored as a possible basis for disciplinary practices in the classroom.

Behaviorism: The Conditioning Approach

If you were to observe a mother telling her 4-year-old child to "sit down, be quiet, and don't interrupt" and this admonition was followed by these behaviors—(1) the child screams, jumps up and down, and shakes her fists, (2) she then knocks all the magazines to the floor amd climbs onto the table, and (3) she finally lays screaming and kicking, turning bright red while her mother turns white and trembling—how would you explain the causes of this observed behavior? To a behaviorist there is only *one* explanation for this or any other behavior—the child has *learned* to behave in this way as a result of conditioning. (For a review of conditioning principles, see Chapter 4.)

But why would any mother want to teach a child such obnoxious behaviors? The answer, of course, is that the mother undoubtedly did not *intend* for the child to learn such behaviors and was not aware that she was helping in the conditioning. The laws of reinforcement tell us, however, that we learn to do what is reinforced or in plain language, we do *what pays off, is successful,* or *is rewarded.* The child in our example has been reinforced for whining, screaming, crying, and begging and, finally, for "tantrums." The reinforcement was probably in two areas: the attention the child received when exhibiting this type of behavior and the fact that such behavior at times led to her getting her way. Since anything that has been learned can be unlearned, the child's mother must now make every effort to *ignore* such behavior and instead give considerable attention to more desirable behaviors, while making certain that the child does *not* get her way through tantrums.

The Need for Drive Reduction
In conditioning theory, a *drive* (such as hunger) leads to a tendency to *respond* to certain *cues* (such as sounds, smells, pictures), and if the *response* leads to a *reward* that satisfies the original *drive,* an association is learned (Dollard and Miller, 1950). This association or link is actually made between the *cue* and the *response,* even though the reason for the association is that the *reward* satisfies the *drive* that was there in the first place. An

example may help to clarify this model and its applicability to classroom behavior.

How does drive-reduction theory explain Willy's behavior, and what might we suggest for Miss Wells? First, his behavior probably stems from a strong drive for attention. It might seem important to find out why he has such a strong need for attention, but behaviorists don't worry about such things. Since any behavior is a result of conditioning, the important goal is to quit reinforcing it and condition something else in its place.

In Willy's case, his drive or need for attention causes him to respond to any cues that seem to suggest possible rewards for his drive. Sitting still and doing his work do not lead to rewards that reduce the drive, but squirming, pestering others, speaking out of turn, asking questions are all rewarding in terms of providing some "reduction" or satisfaction to the original drive for attention. Miss Wells, although intending to squelch his behavior, is actually rewarding it, and such attempts by his teachers may have been a large part of the conditioning process that has developed his attention-seeking behaviors.

What can Miss Wells do about Willy's behavior?

We have already identified "need for attention" as the underlying drive. Miss Wells should now notice situations in which the attention-seeking behaviors are triggered. She may find that they occur frequently when students are doing in-seat work, during discussions, when she is presenting material, or during certain subjects. She must try to avoid rewarding such behaviors as squirming, pestering, or talking out of turn, which probably means that she as well as the rest of the class must *ignore these behaviors*. She can also provide such cues as questions directed toward Willy, individual or group projects, and other assignments that encourage more constructive attention-seeking behaviors.

Miss Wells can also make a special effort to *reward any behaviors* that represent improvement. Calling on him whenever he raises his hand, complimenting him when he is working, showing him attention for a while when he is *not* squirming, pestering, or interrupting are all examples of rewarding improvement. The crux of this approach can be described in four basic steps:

1. Identify and accept the drive, since it will not change or disappear regardless of your wishes.
2. Decrease the rewarding of behaviors that you want to eliminate.
3. Try to cut down on cues that trigger the undesirable behaviors, yet at the same time provide cues that encourage "better" behaviors.
4. Assure that "better" behaviors are rewarded in ways that satisfy the drive.

If it works, you have changed behavior by encouraging and rewarding improved behavior and ignoring other behavior. The drive of "need for attention" is still there, but it is satisfied in less damaging ways.

How Motives Are Conditioned

Thus far our discussion of drive-reduction theory has focused on accepting the underlying drive and rewarding more constructive ways of satisfying this drive. In fairness to drive-reduction theorists, we should point out that there are other alternatives. One of these stems from the fact that individuals have many different drives (this includes needs and motives, since the drive-reduction theorist lumps all three terms together in what is called "drive"). In any situation, more than one drive is usually involved, and in fact several drives may be rewarded in the same situation, or they might even conflict with one another.

In the case of Willy, this suggests that the teacher might deliberately reward another drive, such as achievement or competition, hoping that this drive would offset the need for attention. It may be that achievement and competitive success can be encouraged to the point that Willy feels more satisfaction than he does in attention seeking, and the end result may include attention also.

Another aspect of drive-reduction theory is that drives can *themselves* be learned. This implies that the teacher can aid Willy in another way— by conditioning drives that are weak or even nonexistent. Children are not born with altruistic motives or needs to cooperate or conform. They literally *learn* these motives, just as they learn such things as taste in clothing or music. Once a motive has been learned, it becomes self-sustaining as a determinant of behavior.

A monkey that is rewarded with food whenever it presses the correct button can then learn to press the button for a poker chip that can be exchanged later for food. If the food is then removed, the monkey continues to perform just for the poker chips. Finally, it exhibits hoarding behavior and apparently has learned to value the poker chips themselves.

Behaviorists see the same dynamics of learned motives in humans. If Miss Wells can somehow get Willy to achieve and she rewards this with attention and approval, Willy will probably develop a desire to achieve and a feeling of satisfaction even when the approval is no longer present. Such an achievement motive obviously is not developed overnight, but the attempt to develop desirable motives rather than cursing their absence makes good sense to the drive-reduction theorist in relation to classroom discipline.

The Behavior Modification Approach

The most popular approach to discipline problems from a behaviorist's point of view is that espoused by the behavior modification enthusiasts. "Behavior Mod" is a collection of concepts, techniques, and procedures emanating mainly from operant conditioning theory that is spelled out in such systematic or "cookbook" form that its direct application to specific problems is obvious. Behavior Mod has been used in hospitals, prisons, schools, mental health clinics, summer camps—any institutional setting in which systematic behavior change is attempted. One does not need to become an enthusiastic Behavior Mod advocate to see that the technique works. We explain briefly how Willy's wiggling problems could be approached from this point of view.

1. Learn how to observe precisely. The first admonishment to Miss Wells is that she must learn to observe carefully and record accurately the behaviors that are occurring in specific situations. To say that Willy is "always horsing around" or "just can't sit still" hardly satisfies this requirement. After all, nobody does any one thing all the time, "bad attitude" is about as general as saying Willy is a problem, and to claim that one really cannot sit still is almost certainly inaccurate. Instead, Miss Wells must pinpoint precise behaviors in specific situations and actually make a *frequency count* of the occurrences. Such a frequency count will give her a *base rate* of behavior so that she can compare that with later frequency counts to find out if behavior is changing; for example, a student who interrupts three times each five minutes compared with a base rate of six times has changed his behavior, even though the casual observer might not notice.

2. *Start with whatever behaviors are available.* An important element of behavior modification is the way in which readiness is acknowledged. The principle here is to start with *whatever behaviors are available*, whatever the child already does, and commence molding and shaping this behavior in the desired direction. In Willy's case, behaviors such as talking, moving around, asking questions, and mimicking others are readily available, even though Miss Wells apparently wishes they were not. Now she must reward such behaviors when they appear in proper context and ignore them at other times. Thus, when Willy describes a movie he saw on television, with a vivid description of the violence and gore, Miss Wells *reinforces* this because he is doing it during discussion and after having been asked to respond. She can worry about improving the quality of his response later; she must first reinforce his responding when called on and ignore his speaking out of turn.

3. *Identify potential reinforcers.* One of the real tricks in Behavior Mod

is that of identifying reinforcers that will work for the particular child or group whose behavior you are trying to change. In the final analysis, you will recall, something is a reinforcer *only* when it leads to an increase in a behavior. Of course, Miss Wells might remain coldly objective and use a purely empirical approach, sampling possible reinforcers until she finds one that works, but this hardly fits the image of an efficient, organized behavioral engineer, which is the behaviorist's definition of a teacher. Miss Wells must know enough about Willy's age group, this class, and Willy in particular to make a good guess as to what reinforcers might work and then look for, or create, opportunities to apply these potential reinforcers.

Looking again at the case of Willy the Pest, Miss Wells was able to identify potent reinforcers in the general area defined as "attention." Not only the obvious smile, nod, word of approval, pat on the back or raised eyebrow, but also the frown, shake of the head, clenched hand, incomplete sentence, and reprimand were all serving as reinforcers to Willy's attention-seeking behavior. Miss Wells must now use these reinforcers at appropriate times to shape Willy's behavior in the desired direction. At first, she focuses only on his speaking when called on, reinforcing this with a smile, nod, word of approval, or a request for him to expand on it.

4. *Raising the stakes and fading the rewards.* Although Miss Wells was quick to reinforce Willy for handraising and for speaking when called on, with little concern for precisely what he said, she very soon requires more than just this slight improvement. This is because of the step-by-step "series of successive approximations" aspect of operant conditioning. She began with a small step—Willy raising his hand—rewarded this, then required a little more until, bit by bit, she had molded his behavior into something different. This "raising the stakes" technique is an important part of Behavior Mod. In Miss Wells's case, she definitely wanted to shape Willy's behavior beyond merely raising his hand, to raising it politely and at appropriate times, responding to questions asked, contributing relevant comments, listening while others speak, and asking appropriate questions.

She also is careful to reinforce Willy as much as possible at first, but then, as he develops the desired behaviors, to "fade" the reinforcement so that eventually he will require only occasional reinforcers. This fading technique not only makes it easier on the teacher, but also leads to a firmly established behavior that is highly resistant to extinction. Fading is also used in a procedure in which she prompts Willy with hints and partial answers at first, so that it is easy for Willy to complete the response, but then gradually removes the prompts until Willy responds completely on his own.

5. *Vicarious reinforcement.* As you read about Miss Wells's attempts to change Willy's behavior, it probably occurred to you that she had twenty-nine other students, all of whom needed some degree of reinforcement, and that it is impossible for her to concentrate so much of her time on individual students. This is true, of course, but fortunately other principles

570

interact to cause her conditioning attempts to extend far beyond one student. One of these is the principle of vicarious reinforcement. As she selectively rewards or ignores Willy's behavior, other students observe this and vicariously experience the same results as Willy; that is, they learn from what Willy does, imitate behavior that is rewarded, feel good if they had the right answer in mind, notice what is not rewarded, and so on. Willy also can learn vicariously, by observing what other students do that leads to rewards and imitating their behavior.

If this sounds like the old idea of "making an example" out of somebody, fine, because there is nothing wrong with examples, they occur all the time. The reason that making an example has fallen into disrepute is that it is done so often in a *negative* sense, the "horrible example" in which the student is punished, ridiculed, lectured, or in other ways held up for public scorn before his or her peers. But Behavior Mod does not advocate such practice, since "bad" behaviors will fade out if not reinforced and "good" behaviors will increase vicariously, if students see that they are reinforced.

Miss Wells can also reinforce groups of students, or even the entire class as a group, and utilize the very powerful factor of students reinforcing one another. Rather than Willy's misbehavior being reinforced by his fellow student's laughter and attention, she can enlist their support in ig-

Desirable activities can be used to reinforce desirable behavior. (SIUC Photographic Service.)

noring such antics and reinforcing more desirable behaviors. She can also use the *Premack principle* (1965), which consists of making one behavior that is already well established contingent on another less frequent behavior. For example, Willy loves to tell stories to his friends, and if this is made contingent on doing his in-seat work, then in-seat behavior will increase as a result of linking it with story telling. One final word on the Behavior Mod approach is that the teacher *must* have other alternatives available if she is trying to eliminate an undesirable behavior. The "don't do that or else" approach is almost certain to fail, while the "do this instead" approach will work if the "instead" behavior is rewarded and the original behavior is ignored.

Social Learning Theory: Modeling

In 1950, Dollard and Miller described drive-reduction theory and related it to *social learning* and *imitation*. Bandura and Walters, writing on the same topic in 1963, stressed social learning through modeling in their book, *Social Learning and Personality Development*. Let us take a close look at some of Bandura and Walters's concepts in relation to classroom behavior.

Identification and Imitation

We see Professor Smith coming across the campus with the peculiar duck walk that is so uniquely his and that allows us to identify him at a great distance. But today we notice something else—four miniature professors following Dr. Smith and looking every bit like little ducklings! These are Dr. Smith's four sons, and the key to their walking, talking, and in so many ways acting just like their father is found in *identification* and *imitation*.

When a child identifies with somebody, he behaves as if he were that person. The emotional tie is so strong that he imagines himself to be the other person. This process is partially or even mostly unconscious, and the child obviously gains status from such an identification. Psychologists stress the importance of the child identifying with the like-sexed parent so that he or she can develop attitudes, values, traits, and behaviors that are appropriate in society. The boy will learn male behaviors and the girl female behaviors in this way.

If a child simply copies another person's behaviors, the term *imitation* is used, since most psychologists see this as more superficial, specific, and intentional behavior than identification. To Bandura and Walters, however, the distinction between identification and imitation is unimportant, since both can be explained as social learning, and the key to social learning is modeling. Hence, the term imitation will be used to cover all modeling, with no distinction between imitation and identification.

HOW JOEY LEARNS THE IMPORTANCE OF MODELING

When little Joey imitates his parents' speech, he learns that the specific words are good, because they are reinforced. But he also learns that imitation *in itself* is good, so he has reason to imitate all sorts of things in the future.

By the time Joey is in fourth grade, he has been trained thoroughly in imitation and therefore learns considerably from observing others. He knows that imitation in general is rewarded and that specific behaviors are rewarded also. He may unconsciously identify with the person he is modeling, but this is not crucial to Bandura and Walters's explanation.

Modeling Effects

Bandura and Walters explain the effects of modeling in terms of reinforcement theory, but with the addition of several key points. The explanation can be summarized in three simple statements:

1. Much human learning is a function of observing and imitating the behavior of others.
2. We learn to imitate because we are reinforced for doing so.
3. In imitating others, we vicariously experience the reinforcement they receive or we imagine they receive. In either case, reinforcement is mediated through observation.

Four Types of Effects

After learning to observe and model others' behavior, we can see a person profiting in several different ways from modeling. The four effects of modeling described by Bandura and Walters are (1) modeling, (2) eliciting, (3) inhibiting, and (4) disinhibiting.

In the *modeling effect,* a child sees somebody else do something, says to himself "that's keen," and copies what he has seen. Clearly this is imitation. It happens all the time in real life, and it is usually straightforward and easy to identify. But if we stop here, we have missed other modeling effects that, while not quite so obvious, are very important in understanding the social learning approach to discipline.

When a child watches Kojak shoot it out with a criminal and then proceeds to tease the dog and hide his sister's toy, he is *not* imitating Kojak's behavior directly. But if observing Kojak's behavior elicits similar types of response (e.g., aggression), even though not the same (he doesn't shoot anybody), we are seeing the type of modeling referred to as the *eliciting effect.* This effect is commonly seen in classroom discipline. George gets away with drawing a cartoon of the teacher, which elicits a wisecrack by Fred, and so on. The behaviors are different, but related, in that they

573

are all forms of disrupting the class. Sometimes the teacher himself or herself is the source of the eliciting effect and is unaware of his or her contribution to misbehavior.

Sometimes the behavior of others does not cause direct imitation or elicit similar responses but, instead, has the effect of stopping or inhibiting behavior. If Max volunteers an answer and is then put down by the teacher, Richard avoids volunteering. If Suzie is reprimanded for chewing gum, Doris decides to save her gum until later. Teachers often *intend* to bring about this *inhibiting effect* only to have their efforts serve one of the other functions (Mrs. Rolf sends Bill from the room and five others misbehave). Also, the effect may be taking place where the teacher did not intend it,

---

FOUR MODELING EFFECTS IN ACTION

Mr. Canaly started his social studies lesson with good intentions, but one thing led to another until finally he "blew his top" and wondered why he ever became a teacher. It all started when Peter (a white student) called Jim (a black) "Toby," and Jim replied "my name Kunta Kinte." At first it appeared to be good-natured horseplay, and Mr. Canaly recognized the name from the show "Roots" that was on TV every night that week.

The horseplay turned into something else, however, when Frank (a white) commented that every black in the class had a slave name and that they were probably all related to him because black women used to sleep with their slave masters. Frank's comment seemed to open up the whole area of black-white relations, and several students who were ordinarily quiet now entered the discussion with comments about their ancestors liking black women, blacks being more inclined toward sex, and the idea that black women prefer white men. When Sam mimicked black speech, several other students picked it up, until Jim, who you will recall was called "Toby" by Peter and had initially responded good-naturedly, called Peter's mother a "whore" and Peter punched him in the arm.

Once the punching and shoving started, it seemed to be contagious, and before Mr. Canaly realized what was developing even his best students were screaming and cursing at each other. While Mr. Canaly stepped out of the room to ask for some aid, many of the arguing students spilled out of the classroom and another class that was passing through the hall joined in the argument.

By the time Mr. Canaly returned with the principal, several blacks and whites were engaged in a slug fest, and several girls of both races were screaming, shouting, and pulling one another's hair. When the principal waded into the pile, Mr. Canaly followed, with the result that school ended early that day. There was an assembly on the next day to warn all students that no references to "Roots" would be allowed. An investigation failed to answer how the whole mess started or whose fault it was. During the next two weeks, there was very little discussion in any classes of any topic whatsoever, and spring vacation was welcomed by all.

as when a teacher intended to discourage speaking out of turn but instead inhibits discussion.

The *disinhibiting effect* has serious implications for discipline, since it so often underlies situations where misbehavior spreads and the entire class "gets out of hand." In this effect, behavior that is normally controlled or suppressed (in other words, inhibited) is *released* from this suppression or inhibition by the behavior of others. One example of this effect is the party at which people do all sorts of unusual things because of the disinhibiting effect of alcohol. (Aunt Matilda, normally quiet and reserved, follows the mood of the party and dances on the table barefooted.) In the classroom, the disinhibiting effect is seen whenever one's behavior serves to release behavior in others that was previously held in check.

Humanism: Unique Individuality

The advocates of humanism insist that it is based on scientific empiricism, although it is often seen as more "philosophical" than the two approaches you have just read. Since the basic tenets of humanism are presented and discussed in detail in Chapter 7, we present only a brief review here, to depict a humanistic approach to discipline.

A Positive Approach to Human Nature

The belief that all persons are born innately good has important implications for the teacher. If one starts with the basic belief that everyone is born innately bad, then the basis of discipline is strictness, punishment, expecting the worst, striving to subdue, control, and stifle the natural inclinations of the child. But the humanist sees such an approach to discipline as the *basic cause* of most discipline problems. To a humanist, by assuming that children are by nature mischievous and expecting the worst, the teacher is maximizing the probability of misbehavior. The arbitrary, strict, and punitive guidelines that emerge in such a situation cause the students to resist, fight back, resent such treatment, and find ways to sabotage such an organization. The teacher spends a great deal of time struggling to stifle the students' inner natures and subdue their behavior, while the students, although they may grudgingly acquiesce to avoid painful consequences, are not at all anxious to learn in such a climate and will readily take advantage of any opportunity to retaliate.

The humanist, proceeding from the basic assumption that everyone is born innately good, expects good behavior from students. This positive assumption allows the humanist to operate in a climate of trust, optimism, and encouragement, which tends to maximize positive behavior. The trust and positive expectations of the teacher are readily felt by the students, and the negative aspects of the traditional approach that were the basic causes of discipline problems are minimized.

575

HUMANISM IN THE CLASSROOM

Mr. Raley's ninth grade social studies class is discussing an outside assignment in which everyone is to bring clippings from a magazine or newspaper and discuss a current event that they found interesting. Helen begins by reading an article about upcoming interviews of former president Nixon. This particular article reviews the Watergate break-in and the trial of the seven who were arrested in the break-in. Helen then proceeds to give her opinion that Mr. Nixon knew about the whole operation and had in fact ordered it.

Bert, who was grinning while Helen read the article, interjects with the claim that this is not a current event. Helen blushes and then reads the date on the clipping, indicating that it came from last night's newspaper. Bert responds that there was an article on the Great Depression in last night's paper also, but that hardly makes it a current event. David comments that Bert is still ashamed because both of his parents voted for Nixon, to which Bert immediately responds "At least they voted." Dick finds the exchange amusing and asks "Are we discussing the Great Depression?" at which point Helen bursts into tears and rushes from the room.

An embarrassed silence falls over the class, but Mr. Raley, who is sitting in the back corner of the room, says nothing. Susan breaks the silence by stating that she read an article on Watergate also and that it is in the papers because of the series of interviews that starts tomorrow. Mr. Raley asks softly "Is this what we should talk about right now?" Susan responds that, since Helen isn't here, the class should probably go on to another article. "Is this what you really want to talk about?" Mr. Raley asks. After a little squirming, Dick speaks up and suggests that what they're all thinking about is why Helen started crying and left the room. Bert, David, and Dick discuss this now in a serious mood, and several others join in.

They focus on how Helen must have felt and the fact that she is shy, not a good student, and seldom participates in discussions. Bert and David both regret what happened, but Susan notes that they all know there was no intention of embarrassing or ridiculing Helen. After some more discussion of Helen's feelings and the fact that the class might make a special attempt to involve her more in the discussions, Susan asks Mr. Raley if he could go and talk to Helen and bring her back to class. He asks if they think that would be the best thing to do.

Several say no, but they think it is important to bring her back into class and discuss her article. Bert then states that, if he were in Helen's shoes, he would want the two who embarrassed him, namely, Bert and David, to apologize and convince him that the class wanted to discuss the article. Mr. Raley then asks if this is related to what they have been reading on communication problems in modern society, and after a brief discussion of how all this ties in with what they have been studying, Bert and David leave the room to retrieve Helen.

While they are gone, several students suggest ideas for involving Helen and others more without embarrassing them, and after Bert and David return with Helen, Bert leads the discussion of Helen's article but manages to draw Helen into the discussion.

Each Child a Unique Individual

The idea of a unique core of individuality is more than a belaboring of the obvious fact that people differ. To the humanist, a key to individual differences is the unique core of individuality that exists deep inside each person and is an inherent part of that person as well as a result of learning or culture. Humanists argue that a major goal of the school is to help the child to find this inner core and let it blossom. Since everyone is born potentially good, there is no fear of helping this inner core unfold, and in fact some degree of misbehavior is easily tolerated along the way as this unfolding takes place.

The Dangers of Repressive Measures

The humanist objects to restrictive, punitive, or coercive measures of control *not* so much because they don't work (after all, we have all been members of such groups and seen that a leader can maintain almost complete control) but, rather, because they stifle and inhibit the true person from emerging. Just as the absence of psychosis does not assure good mental health, in the same way, the absence of visible misbehavior does not guarantee the presence of positive behavior.

Most humanists seem to be consistent with reinforcement theory in that they advocate that the child can learn about behavior by its own natural consequences. No external pressures need be added if the child is engrossed in tasks that are important to him, since he will soon see that frivolous or disruptive behavior is not moving him toward his goal. There is actually another assumption implicit here also, namely, that curiosity, learning, and growth are also part of this inner core, whereas mischief must be learned.

Walking the Tightrope of Humanistic Discipline

It might appear that the humanistic approach is based on the idea of laissez-faire or letting the little darlings do whatever they please. But humanistic discipline is not permissiveness; rather, it emphasizes the dignity of each human being. This emphasis demands respect for the rights of others and frowns on any behavior that undermines the decency and dignity of each human being. In fact, while humanists do not advocate the absence of punishment, they believe that any punishment must be based on the assumptions of innate goodness and humaneness in each child. Punishment itself is not bad, but punishment that violates these assumptions and stifles the inner nature of the child is bad.

Perhaps a look into a classroom that reflects some of these humanistic elements will illustrate the approach much more readily than will further philosophical discussion.

Let us explore some of the ways in which this example illustrates a humanistic approach to discipline.

577

1. The assignment at the outset stressed individual differences, as each person was to find and bring to class current events that he or she wanted to discuss.
2. The emphasis throughout this problem situation was on humaneness—Helen's feelings and those of the class were of utmost importance; improving communication and restoring a positive climate were more important than "covering" material or punishing some "guilty" party.
3. Notice also that there *was* a problem, that the humanistic approach in no way implies an absence of problems but, rather, a different approach to analyzing and solving problems.
4. The class had the responsibility of identifying a problem in interpersonal relations and of finding a way to do something constructive about it. Mr. Raley did not adopt a "laissez-faire" attitude insofar as he gently but clearly reminded the class of this responsibility and did not let them ignore it.
5. Notice also the absence of blame and punishment (although we do not mean to imply that blame and punishment would never be present). In this situation, it was not important to find someone to blame or punish, since this would not have restored the positive climate. Concern rather than blame predominated.
6. The topic of "communication," which is basic to the study of social studies, was being lived in the here and now, which is the ultimate in making learning relevant.
7. The general fact was that this classroom atmosphere was one of decency, openness, trust, and concern and that these variables were able to overcome a problem of communication and hurt feelings that might have mushroomed in a group that did not contain these dimensions.

Freedom Versus Responsibility

A common reaction upon being introduced to humanistic ideas is to conclude that humanism stresses freedom rather than responsibility. This is not at all the intent of the humanists, since they see these two terms as very much interrelated and dependent upon each other. One of the goals of humanistic discipline is that of getting the child to assume responsibility for his or her own behavior, goals, and life. Such responsibility cannot be assumed without the freedom and, in fact, necessity of choosing alternatives and making decisions. This involves a degree of personal freedom that is noticeably absent in the strict, punitive, authoritarian classroom, which stresses, not individual responsibility, but the total responsibility of the teacher. Humanists attempt to change this situation to one in which the student can develop responsibility for his own behavior, which means a focusing on internal choices rather than external coercion. Thus, in the humanistic classroom, we see freedom and responsibility inextricably interwoven—not an absence of problems but a different approach to identifying and treating problems.

Discipline: Suggestions for Teachers

It is impossible to make somebody into a teacher by giving him or her a list of rules to employ in the event of any and all discipline problems. The three approaches to discipline described in this chapter, and the list of suggestions presented now, are intended only as a background or basis on which to build one's own discipline techniques. All teachers are different, all situations are different, and all teachers must be professionals making informed subjective judgments rather than tradespeople applying routine skills. It should be relatively easy for the reader to find exceptions for each of the ''rules'' presented. Rather than invalidating the ideas discussed, we prefer to think that this merely illustrates once again the profound complexity of human nature.

1. *Establish controls early, in the best way available.* For learning to take place in a group of students of all sizes, shapes, and backgrounds, it is necessary that control come from somewhere.

Teachers must have in mind behavioral controls they prefer and the techniques that they will follow to develop such controls. If self-control is the goal, the teacher should have specific steps in mind to get this across. But the teacher had better have backup controls in mind in case the first goal cannot be realized. A major point here is that there is only a certain amount of time, probably just a few weeks or even days, in which rapport

In order for learning to occur, control must come from the teacher.
(Arkansas State Department of Education.)

in a group is established. If unable to institute his or her loftiest ideal of control, the teacher had better be willing to retreat back down the hierarchy until he or she finds something that will work, even if that something is far from the ideal. In other words, arbitrary or negative forms of control are better than the complete absence of control.

Even though we hope that control can be established in a very positive way, the teacher may sometimes have to resort to other means, even including such oldies as punishment and strictness. The method of control that is used depends not only on the situation but also on the goals and the teacher's own personality characteristics. The teacher must find a classroom atmosphere, a type and degree of control that allows him or her to operate comfortably and successfully. A person who is basically autocratic and highly organized can no more have a permissive classroom than a quiet, sensitive person can act like a strict autocrat. Understanding one's own personality and the methods of control that are most suited to it is a major prerequisite of successful teaching.

The suggestion as presented includes the word "early," and for good reason. The teacher cannot afford to allow students to function without behavioral controls for very long, because establishing controls becomes increasingly difficult as time passes. One sixth grade teacher who was well liked and highly successful as a teacher summed it up by saying "you gotta corral 'em early because you'll never corral 'em later on." This teacher rarely employed strict or punitive measures, but he knew the importance of establishing controls early and was willing to take the necessary steps to do so.

2. *Have as few rules and regulations as possible.* This suggestion may sound rather strange on the heels of the "get control early" admonition, but closer scrutiny should make its logic clear. Imposing a long list of rules and regulations seldom leads to behavioral controls all by itself. In fact, most teachers have too many rules and regulations, forgetting that every rule is a challenge to the students. The more rules and regulations you attempt, the more students are encouraged to use their creativity and imag-

HOW MANY RULES ARE NECESSARY?

A teacher who operates successfully with just a bare minimum of rules and regulations is the band director when conducting a rehearsal. He has one very basic rule—when he is on the podium, students must be quiet and pay attention. If he steps down off the podium, almost anything goes. A few minor rules that supplement this one major rule are the requirements that the students snap to attention when he picks up the baton, bring their instruments to playing position when he prepares for the downbeat, and stop playing immediately when the baton stops. Any additional rules are superfluous and might make it more difficult to conduct a successful rehearsal.

ination to find ways to violate them. How many rules and regulations are "too many"? The guideline is easily stated—have only those rules and regulations that are essential in achieving the type of classroom climate you want. Any additional rules and regulations are "too many."

3. *Enforce whatever rules and regulations you make.* A sure way to destroy classroom rapport and undermine your own discipline goals is to establish rules and regulations and then fail to enforce them. Students quickly lose confidence in a teacher who makes a promise (every rule is a promise) and then fails to deliver. Even though we suggest that teachers employ as few rules and regulations as are necessary to get the job done, and that they avoid the "rules for rules sake" approach, those rules and regulations that *are* established must be enforced.

This suggestion is *not* intended to encourage rigid and slavish adherence to the letter of the law. Both humanistic ideals and common sense suggest that rules must be tempered with flexibility, judgment, and compassion. But the suggestion certainly means that if gum chewing is not allowed, then Herman cannot chew gum; or if papers must be in by the final deadline, then Sally's grade suffers if she turns it in late; or if being tardy more than three times requires a paper, then Sam will have to write that paper. In each of these instances, certain mitigating circumstances might justify suspension of the rule, but the circumstances must be special or unusual, and students must realize that rules are suspended only due to extenuating circumstances and *not* because of favorites or scapegoats. Every teacher will face those situations where a rule catches a student who has no intention of causing trouble and yet the rule must be followed.

4. *Involve students in making and enforcing rules and regulations.* If you are ego involved, this means that the outcome is important to you, that success would be a big boost in self-esteem, and that failure would be a blow to the ego. If the teacher can get students ego involved in the classroom, they will work harder and learn more.

This principle of ego involvement applies to discipline also, since people tend to be more ego involved when they have had something to say about the guidelines in a situation. Just watching young children at play illustrates this principle: they love to make up games, with detailed rules, and the child who has had the most to say about the rules is invariably the child who gets most involved in the game. A child who has not contributed to the rules for the game, or whose suggestions have been ignored, tends to play only grudgingly or even attempts to sabotage the game. Whether children or adults, we are reluctant to cooperate when we have had nothing to say about the situation.

5. *Learn the students' names.* This is another of those suggestions that sounds so obvious and logical that it seems trite to mention, yet many teachers fall short of this one way or another. The most beautiful word in the world is your own name, provided that it is in the form that you prefer and is pronounced correctly. This means that Robert should be called Bob if he prefers, Margaret should not be called Peggy unless she really likes

581

this nickname, and Russell has the right to go by his middle name John if he wishes. Students like their names to be pronounced correctly and will forgive several mispronunciations if they know you are trying.

Just because everyone calls Mark "Monk" does not mean that the teacher should follow suit. Also, the temptation to deliberately mispronounce a name because it is cute or funny should be resisted; it is often not cute or funny at all to the possessor of the name. One other hazard is that of accidentally calling a student by the name of a brother or sister, usually older. This is easy to do, since family resemblances are obvious and the former student's name sticks in your mind, but teachers should make every attempt to avoid this. Every child wants his or her own identity as an individual, and calling one by another's name hardly facilitates this.

Why all this nitpicking about names? For the simple reason that being called by your own name, correctly and in its preferred form, implies a personal recognition and builds rapport, while being pointed at, or called incorrectly, undermines rapport and contributes to discipline problems. A student hardly feels a sense of worth and desire to cooperate when the teacher obviously has no idea who he or she is.

Since many classes are large and a teacher might have over one hundred students each semester, getting all the names straight is no easy task. Techniques such as using a seating chart, photographing the class and drilling yourself on names and faces, using name tags the first few weeks, playing games involving names, and many others have been employed. The important ingredient seems to be a real desire to learn names, coupled with finding a strategy that works for you.

6. *Make all threats clear and understandable.* This may sound very strange, in the face of the numerous admonitions of "Never threaten students." But it is well documented that there are many threats inherent in the classroom situation, such as the fact that the student is compelled to be there, that the teacher is in a position of power and authority, and that anything the student does can be judged right or wrong, and be rewarded or punished. The classroom is loaded with possible failure, shame, embarrassment, ridicule, and rejection even if the teacher does everything possible to be "nonthreatening." The compulsory public school is so laden with potential threats to the students that saying "Don't threaten students" is tantamount to saying "Don't send students to school."

Several points in relation to threats in the classroom follow fairly directly from research findings. For example, vague and ambiguous threats are hard to adjust to and may lead to resentment (Deutch, 1973). Threats need not be damaging if there are avenues for constructive action to avoid the negative consequences. In situations in which threats are perceived as vague and ambiguous, the learners' responses may become increasingly erratic and they may exhibit increased anxiety and defensive behavior.

Findings such as these suggest that teachers should (a) make the threats that are inherent in the classroom clear to the students, (b) be certain that there are avenues available for students to *do something* to avoid painful consequences, and (c) avoid adding any additional threats that are not really necessary. The first, making inherent threats clear is probably what psychologists have in mind when they say "Make the boundaries of acceptable behavior clear." Teachers must analyze the classroom situation from the *students'* point of view and pinpoint anything that students see as a threat. They should remove any that are unnecessary, but undoubtedly many threats will still be there. They should give the students a clear picture of the situation, what is expected of them, and what avenues are available for reducing anxiety, gaining rewards, and achieving goals. Again, the basic fact is that vague and ambiguous threats cause anxiety without a clear idea of what to do about them, whereas threats that are clearly defined cause less anxiety and make it easier to decide on a course of action to relieve the anxiety.

As an example, consider a threat that looms larger in the students' eyes than teachers often realize—the threat of tests. The whole idea of taking tests is loaded with threats for the student, even when he or she is an "A" student! What kind of questions will this teacher ask? How will the tests be scored? How will I do compared with the others? Can I get the "A" I must have in this course? How can I prepare? What if I study the wrong things? The best way to clarify these threats is to tell the students just what they are being graded on, how much each test will count, when the tests will take place, and what the general format and content will be and provide suggestions for studying. Telling is not enough, however, since it sometimes serves only to increase the threat. The telling must be followed by an actual test very early in the course. For example, if the first test is given in the second week of classes, students can find out about this instructor's tests—kinds of questions asked, what they are expected to learn—and thus have a much clearer perception of this area of threat. A further step to relieve anxiety constructively is to have the first test "for practice," not for a recorded grade. Or each student may be allowed to eliminate the score on *one* test from his or her total score for the semester, on the assumption that test anxiety will be less if the student knows that he or she can "blow one" and yet not ruin his or her grade. The most anxiety-producing class is not the one in which many tests are given but rather the one in which everything hinges on just *one test* at the very end of the course. This "judgment day" approach is inconsistent with what we know about anxiety and the learning process.

7. *Do not make threats that you cannot carry out.* If teachers choose to add threats to those that are already inherent in the classroom situation, they must keep in mind that every threat is a promise, and regardless of intent they may be called upon to make good on that promise. If they cannot deliver on promises, they lose credibility with the students rapidly, and an important factor in discipline is lost (Deutsch, 1973).

It is surprising how often this rule is violated by teachers. When the teacher threatens to keep the entire class after school in an attempt to put a stop to petty thievery, and the class knows that it would take an act of

Congress to hold up the school buses, the teacher is violating this principle. When the teacher states that nobody passes without completing his or her history notebook, and yet half the class fails to turn it in but they pass anyway, the teacher is violating this principle. When the teacher has clearly established a rule but does nothing when it is broken, the teacher is violating this principle.

8. *Maintain a sense of humor about misbehavior.* This suggestion is not only helpful in maintaining discipline but is also essential in preserving the teacher's mental health. Students can come up with some of the most ingenious forms of misbehavior imaginable, and the events in an average school day, if taken too seriously, could shatter nerves of steel. Teachers do not lose respect when they allow students to see that they are human; on the contrary, such openness leads to better understanding and rapport and thus to better discipline. When teachers show that they appreciate the humor in a situation, they indicate to the students that they can share feelings and laugh with them and at the same time may be able to avert a difficult situation.

A popular myth about humor and discipline is the claim that teachers sabotage any hope for successful control if they allow themselves to smile. Once they have smiled, they cannot possibly reprimand or punish the student, or so the story goes. However, there is no sound evidence or even theory to support this myth. In fact, it is possible that exactly the opposite might occur; the teacher in struggling to deny the humor in a situation might lose control of the situation because of unrealistic behavior.

As an example, look at the ninth grade geometry teacher who was just about to conclude an important point in his lesson when a student asked an irrelevant question—one so grossly irrelevant that it sounded downright silly. Several students laughed and, fearing that he would lose the important conclusion he was approaching, the teacher glared at the culprit without cracking a smile. The sight of this sinister expression in the face of the comical situation was so incongruous that now the entire class broke into laughter, whereupon the teacher flushed and, in a last desperate attempt to maintain the upper hand, he scolded the student severely. This resulted not only in the loss of the point he was pursuing but also in a loss of respect for the teacher as a person and one more step on the road to a bitter and resentful class.

9. *Find out about policies, attitudes, and practices of fellow teachers and administrators.* Not only should the teacher know the official policies and procedures but also the beliefs and actual practices of his colleagues (Curwin and Mendler, 1980). This may not be so easy to accomplish, since officially verbalized policies and those actually followed are often two different things. But if teachers keep their eyes and ears open, they can assemble a fairly accurate picture of these practices and beliefs.

Let's look at the beginning teacher who wanted to use very flexible, democratic procedures in her sixth grade classroom. She jumped right in with informal, nondirective procedures and was appalled when this not only failed to work, but the other teachers complained as well. What she should have realized was that the other teachers utilized a very traditional authoritarian teaching style and the students were adjusted thoroughly to this style. To help them adjust to the climate she wanted, she should have been aware of what they were accustomed to and attempted to build a gradual transition into the new classroom climate. In this way, she would have avoided the confusion and anxiety that led to the breakdown of her democratic methods and saved herself from the wrath of her fellow teachers.

MARGIE

It was Margie Peterson's first time in front of a class. She had memorized the phrase "Don't smile until Christmas" and was determined to establish control in her class no matter what. Being just barely five feet tall and 100 pounds, she had worried the entire summer about how she could teach English to ninth-graders and maintain control. It did not help any when the janitor mistook her for one of the students on her first day at school.

With these thoughts in mind, she stepped in front of the class looking as tough as she knew how, taking a deep breath and standing tall. Her first words were "Allright, I'm Miss Peterson and I'm in charge now," spoken in what she imagined was a no-nonsense voice. She proceeded to list the major requirements for the course on the board, becoming increasingly frightened and using increasingly harsher tones as she did so. She was becoming both scared and angry at the class for making her feel so uncomfortable.

Then a funny thing happened. The class, which had started the period with a look that could be described as general attention and curiosity, grew amused. Smiles and then laughter and comments spread through the room. It suddenly dawned on Margie that here she was, all five feet of her, standing before this class mimicking a dictator, while her hands trembled and her face gave her away. The class could see that she was not a monster, and her attempts to appear tough before the class, in view of what her body, face, and posture said, was so incongruous that they were laughing at her!

At this point, Margie did something that no methods teacher had ever suggested to her but that turned out to be just the right response. She dropped her pretense, laughed along with the class, and then admitted that she was trying to act tough but was really scared to death. She compared her size with several of the biggest boys in the room and reckoned that they could easily throw her out the window. After standing on the chair and saying, "There, now I'm big enough to be your teacher" and a few minutes of joking with the class, she started again with her lesson. This time her body was relaxed, her facial expression one of sincerity, interest, and support, and the lesson proceeded very well. Even though the class nicknamed her "Tiny Tim" after that first day, and occasionally kidded her about her size (one day someone hung a child's chalkboard below the regular chalkboard), she had excellent rapport with the class and found that she liked teaching ninth-graders. She resisted the temptation, after that memorable first day, to pretend to be something that her body language contradicted.

10. *Use your eyes, voice, feet, and posture to communicate nonverbal cues.* Julius Fast, in a best-selling book entitled *Body Language* (1970), presented many entertaining examples of how our bodies carry detailed messages through posture, motion, and facial expression. Although this "language" is far from perfectly understood as a form of communication, the basic ideas certainly apply to teaching; we *do* communicate feelings, moods, attitudes, warnings, and other messages in a nonverbal fashion (Howell and Howell, 1979).

On the positive side, the teacher can convey acceptance, encouragement, reinforcement, and all sorts of humanistic messages through facial expressions, posture, position of hands and feet, tone of voice, inflection. Not only the obvious smile, but also the lifted eyebrow, the quizzical expression, the look of attention, and various other facial expressions convey messages to students. A teacher sitting cross-legged on the floor helping a student with her artwork certainly conveys a message different from the teacher standing over a student with arms folded rigidly across the chest.

On the negative side, warnings, rebukes, even punishments can be dispensed by nonverbal means also. Most readers will remember the "look that kills" that some teacher was able to produce to warn you, without a sound or movement, that you had better get busy immediately! The "moving target" idea is a form of nonverbal cue, as the mere nearness of a teacher can be a warning that he knows what the students are up to.

One final aspect of nonverbal communication: the teacher must be an accurate reader as well as a dispenser of nonverbal communication. By picking up and interpreting students' motions, postures, facial expressions, and tones of voice, the teacher can often decide on what to do or not to do next. One teacher claimed that he always knew when to move on to another topic simply by counting the coughs—when student coughing exceeded the normal boundary of one every fifteen seconds, he knew that the class was getting fidgety and that it was time to move on!

11. *Discuss misbehavior in private with the student whenever feasible.* Teachers should realize that students behave much differently before their peer group than they do in private. When a student is reprimanded or in any way singled out in front of his peer group, he may feel threatened and in need of saving face. Many times an otherwise reasonable, cooperative student has shocked a teacher by his impolite, belligerent behavior when she reprimanded him in class. If she had spoken to him privately, his behavior might have been different; indeed, it is sometimes amazing how easy it is to reason with even a troublesome student when the teacher shows concern and respect and discusses a problem privately. Teachers must also remember that sometimes they are wrong—what may appear to be a blatant example of aggression may turn out to be something entirely different, for the teacher may have seen only part of the episode.

Talking to the student privately when practical extends beyond the realm of misbehavior and blame and even overlaps into the use of praise. Although success and praise before the peer group may be a powerful motivator and reward, it does not always work this way. A student who is singled out for praise in front of his peers might be embarrassed and even fearful of being labeled "brain," "grind," or "teacher's pet," and he may resent the teacher doing this to him. The junior high boy who does a fine job on a poetry assignment might appreciate the teacher's approval, but if she lavished praise on him in front of the class it might serve to guarantee that he'll never do a good job on a poetry assignment again. Praise as well as blame is often best dispensed privately.

12. *Be yourself—only the real you can succeed in the classroom.* The importance of this advice cannot be overemphasized, for the job of teaching requires interaction with other people in ways that are so constant and complex that a teacher cannot afford to waste time attempting to be what he or she is not. Understanding oneself is just as important for successful teaching as understanding the subject matter or understanding children. As was said earlier, teachers cannot shed habits and characteristics that are part of their natures, and they cannot conceal them. Their tasks are to develop a classroom climate that fits their personalities and to find effective ways of teaching that are also in line with their real selves. A basically very gentle, sensitive person, must find ways to control the class and remain a gentle, sensitive person; a compulsive, highly organized, and efficient person, had better find ways to become a compulsive, highly organized, and efficient teacher.

Unfortunately, teacher education programs do not often provide experiences designed to help the students to understand themselves. This leaves the burden for such understanding on the teacher as he or she strives to survive the first few years of teaching. If teachers understand and accept themselves, they will probably survive. But if they attempt to copy others, to be what they think they should be in the classroom, they may run into difficulties that could have been avoided.

13. *Use reason and logic in your behavioral requests and punishment.* The current stress on understanding as a key to discipline cuts both ways— teachers should try to understand the reasons behind student behavior and students should understand the reasons for rules, regulations, requests, and punishment. The need to have a logical explanation for these things increases with age as a natural part of development: the second-grader can accept what the teacher says on faith, but the sixth-grader will be skeptical, and the ninth-grader will demand a reasonable explanation. In keeping with developmental stages of thinking, the explanations for behavioral guidelines must be immediate and concrete for children in the early grades, can start showing some degree of abstraction and generalization from the fifth through ninth grades, and cannot really appeal fully to abstract ideals and principles until about the tenth grade level.

Teachers also encounter the problem of enforcing rules and sanctions

587

that they don't really believe themselves. This can lead to the teacher making up explanations for the rules that aren't really true. Don't do it! If you do not know the reason for some rule or restriction, admit it and attempt to find out the rationale. If you are enforcing a rule simply because the school requires it, admit it. Students can understand the fact that you enforce a strict rule against gum chewing because it is a school rule, so try to make your explanation logical, or the students may not accept it.

14. *Vary classroom activities, with occasional breaks and change of pace.* Despite considerable research on attention span, which indicates that even highly motivated adults suffer boredom and an inability to concentrate on the same activity for more than about forty minutes, teachers sometimes operate as if they were unaware of these facts. The younger child's attention span is shorter than the older child's and in fact the human being does not seem capable of listening intensely to any communication for more than about seven minutes before his or her mind starts wandering. A teacher who allows the same classroom activity to continue unchanged for an hour or more, demanding that the students "pay attention," is probably expecting the impossible.

The need for stimulus variability seems to be a basic human need. After a period of relative quiet, the person needs a higher level of stimulation, and vice versa. Both the type and the amount of stimulation in learning activities may be varied according to the age and capabilities of students by the skilled teacher to satisfy basic human needs and at the same time to avoid discipline problems. (Kounin, 1970).

15. *When you use punishment, make it as immediate as possible.* Psychologists are often accused of creating the commandment "Thou shalt not punish," but it is only fair to point out that there is widespread agreement among psychologists on a number of points relating to punishment, for example, the following: (1) Punishment should fit, but not exceed, the offense. (2) The child should know clearly why he or she is being punished. (3) Punishment sometimes backfires or has unwanted side effects. (4) Although the immediate effects are sometimes dramatic, punishment is *not* the best way to change behavior on a long-term basis. (5) Punishment is best when it can be seen as a direct outcome of one's own behavior. (6) Punishment should be given objectively, without high emotion or personal connotations. (7) To be most effective, both rewards and punishment must ordinarily be immediate.

Although all these factors are worthy of discussion, the immediacy of punishment seems to be the most relevant in this context. Any teacher will employ punishment from time to time, even though we hope positive means of control are used more often. When it is decided to punish some behavior, the punishment should follow the behavior as immediately and as directly as possible (except in a few special cases) (Tanner, 1978). Even a few minutes between the behavior and the punishment numbs its effect, and a lapse of an hour or even days, as sometimes occurs, not only greatly weakens the effect, but also provides increasing probability that the punishment will be linked to something else or misunderstood.

16. *Don't punish the entire class for the misbehavior of a few.* When somebody in the class is guilty of misbehavior—pranks, petty thievery, class disruptions—and the teacher is unable to isolate who it is, the strategy of threatening or punishing the whole class might appear to be the solution. We suggest that you resist this temptation, for punishing the entire class when it is not the entire class that misbehaved is very low on the hierarchy of discipline strategies. And yet teachers often use this approach, on the grounds that it develops a sense of responsibility toward the peer group; it isolates the troublemaker and utilizes the powerful force of peer group pressure to make the disruptive individual behave. If somebody is repeatedly writing obscene words on the blackboard, other members of the class undoubtedly know who the culprit is, and when the whole class has to stay after school because of one person's misdeeds, they will exert direct pressure to change the individual's behavior. The class will be angry at the student and not at the teacher, and thus the teacher need not even know who the culprit is.

In practice, however, when the teacher punishes the entire class when less than the entire class misbehaved, the whole class loses respect for the teacher. Those who were innocent resent being punished unfairly and may make it a point to be guilty next time. Those that are guilty feel that they have forced the teacher to make a fool of himself or herself. Rather than

---

THE MYSTERIOUS GRAFFITI

Miss Jones was shocked to see a series of four-letter words on the chalkboard as she entered her fifth-grade classroom on Monday; but in what she thought was a successful fake, she pretended not to see the board and went right on with her lesson. On Tuesday, the list was longer and in bigger letters, signed at the bottom by "Zorro"; her embarrassment was so great that she complained to the class and asked who did it, but to no avail.

On Wednesday, the words were so big and shocking that she decided to put a stop to it. She ordered all the class members to lay their heads on their desks and close their eyes and said that whoever wrote those words had two minutes to get them erased or else the entire class would stay after school for a week. She didn't care who did it, and she would lay her head on the desk also, she explained, but those words had better be erased or else!

The tiptoeing of little feet ensued, followed by some scratching around and erasing at the blackboard, then footsteps again. When Miss Jones and her class opened their eyes, they now found a blackboard where the words indeed had been erased but replaced by an even more shocking set of obscene terms, concluding with a most risqué poem, and scrawled at the bottom was the signature "Zorro strikes again."

becoming objects of derision, the guilty parties are often seen as heros who have "put one over on the teacher."

What then should teachers do in this situation, when a few students are misbehaving, but they cannot be identified? First, they can use all their knowledge and experience to think of ways of preventing the misbehavior or ways to outfox the culprits. They should realize that there are times when it is better to overlook misdemeanors and not make an issue of them rather than to compound the situation with unjust punishment. This is what old-timers mean when they advise that teachers should not see and hear everything. Third, teachers must "establish controls early, in the best way available." If faced with the unfortunate choice of punishing the whole class or losing any chance of gaining control, the teacher would be better advised to punish the whole class. This predicament can usually be avoided, but the major thesis is that even a poor method of control is better than the absence of any control.

17. *Be careful with the use of sarcasm in the classroom.* Sarcasm—the use of cutting remarks or critical humor—has been singled out in numerous studies and articles as a characteristic that students don't like, a characteristic of the "poor" teacher. This has led some educators to recommend that teachers should never use sarcasm. We do not agree, however, for two reasons: one concerning the nature of personality traits and the other concerning evidence about successful teachers.

The "nature of personality traits" refers to the fact that a person cannot eliminate traits and characteristics that are part of his or her basic personality. One can no more "turn off" a basic tendency to use sarcasm than one can "turn off" one's regional accent. The teacher cannot succeed in the classroom by being a "phony"—a classroom style must be established that fits the teacher's personality. Students can see through a basically authoritarian person who is trying to act democratic, just as they are amused at the attempt of a gentle, sensitive person trying to act tough and autocratic. The teacher has to be seen as a real person to function successfully as a teacher, and the only real person he or she can be is the person that he or she is.

But if we reject the commandment "Thou shalt not be sarcastic," are we ignoring the literature and giving sarcastic teachers the right to attack students? Not at all. What we are saying is that, if sarcasm is part of a person's life-style, it is more reasonable to talk about controlling sarcasm than it is to discuss eliminating it. The teacher can be sarcastic about himself, or herself, or about people in general, but should not direct it at particular individuals. A teacher can even occasionally be sarcastic about students, providing that he or she is not singling out one student and providing that sufficient encouragement is offered to offset it. A teacher who uses sarcasm should also expect sarcasm in return from the students.

The second reason listed, which concerns evidence about successful teachers, is already explained partially in the preceding paragraph. It is a fact that some excellent teachers are sarcastic, just as some poor teachers are not sarcastic. If you are sarcastic by nature, try to make certain that its use enhances rather than detracts from your teaching.

18. *Do not take misbehavior personally.* Although it is natural for teachers to be ego involved in their work and to react to any obstacles or frustrations personally, it is important that they resist the temptation to interpret misbehavior in this way. Even though it is sometimes directed at them personally, teachers are better advised to see misbehavior objectively and react to it in that context.

There are several reasons for this suggestion. First, the teacher is more apt to make an intelligent decision rather than an impulsive act that will be regretted later. Second, the student, when seeing the teacher's fair and objective reaction, is much more apt to see his or her own wrongdoing rather than to blame the teacher or rationalize it. Third, the teacher is making it clear that it is certain behaviors that he or she dislikes, and not the student.

The rule applies even when there is obvious hostility in the student's behavior. Children have many reasons for resenting authority figures, including their hostility at times to the primary authority figures, their parents. If the teacher can see mischievious, hostile, or defiant behavior as an expression against his or her position as an authority figure rather than against him or her personally, this will probably lead to a more effective reaction as well as better mental health for both teacher and student.

This suggestion, while easy to make, is not easy to follow. When faced with a student expression of hostility or defiance, the human reaction tends to be one of hurt or disappointment, followed by anger and a desire to retaliate. But part of the professionalism that a teacher must have is the ability to observe and react to behavior objectively. The point to keep in mind is that *most* student behavior probably has nothing to do with the teacher personally, so the misbehavior that you are tempted to take personally is seldom meant in that way. Remember, talking to a student privately about his or her transgressions is usually the best way to get at both the reasons for and the solutions to behavior problems.

19. *Be aware of personality conflicts and don't feel guilty about them.* A "personality conflict" is the familiar situation in which two people, for no obvious reason, just seem to rub each other the wrong way. These conflicts are far more common than most people realize and certainly more common than most classroom teachers admit. We suggest that teachers face the fact objectively that personality conflicts occur in teaching rather than try to deny them or feeling guilty about them.

Why do personality conflicts occur? The reasons are almost endless. Perhaps you remind the student of an authoritarian father or a rigid mother, as perceived in early childhood. Perhaps you resemble a hated uncle or a big brother, or you just symbolize some bad experience in life. The reason is not really important, and teachers are cautioned *not* to try to delve too

591

MR. SKELTON LEVELS WITH A STUDENT

Rob did not like Mr. Skelton, even though he had not been in a class with him, and he really had never given this feeling much thought. When he found that his tenth grade history teacher was none other than Mr. Skelton, referred to by students as "Uncle Bob," he felt immediately apprehensive about this class. Mr. Skelton had disliked his older brother and harassed him for a semester, he told himself, and he would probably be unfair to Rob.

Sure enough, on the third day of class, just after Mr. Skelton had made a pronouncement about the age of the mummy in the tomb of Ramses II, Rob raised his hand and asked if the statement was inaccurate. Mr. Skelton, somewhat flustered, replied that this was the conclusion of an American archaeologist who had recently studied the mummy, to which Rob responded defensively "Then why does the book say something different on page 23? Are we supposed to believe you or the book?" Mr. Skelton turned red, and immediately sent Rob to the detention room.

As Rob sat in the detention room alone, he bitterly reviewed in his mind how mean and unfair "Uncle Bob" was and how much he had been wronged. He knew that the "old goat" would be in as soon as class ended to browbeat him, and he was prepared to fight back and get in a few good insults of his own. His brother had certainly been right about what a contemptible creature "Uncle Bob" was.

When Mr. Skelton did talk to him, Rob was surprised that he did not berate or harass him at all. Instead, Mr. Skelton was no longer angry, and he began apologizing for losing his temper. He then went on to explain how he felt that there was a "personality conflict" between the two of them that would undoubtedly make it difficult for them to get along. He said that he regretted this conflict, but felt that they must face it and that one solution would be for Rob to enroll in another section of the course if he so desired. He also said that, if Rob chose to stay in this class, he would do his best to be fair with him but that they would still probably face some irritations. He finally got around to the point about the mummy in Ramses's tomb and explained that he had no objections to students challenging him in class, but in this case he felt that it had been done in a defiant and insulting manner and he had reacted accordingly. He promised that he would try not to react in this way in the future, but he hoped that Rob would try also.

The discussion was not a magic solution, and Rob's first reaction was that "Uncle Bob" was just trying to get rid of him. He did stay in the class, however, and although he did not develop an affection for Mr. Skelton, he respected him more as a result of the discussion and had to admit that the idea of a "personality conflict" was an accurate description of the situation. He was surprised that Mr. Skelton understood this, since no other teacher had ever talked about such things before.

far into these dynamics lest you be engaging in the dangerous game of pseudoanalysis. The important idea is to *recognize* these conflicts when they occur and to resist reacting to them emotionally (to the extent that this is possible, for such conflicts obviously arouse the emotions).

Two mistakes may be made in relation to personality conflicts when the teacher attempts to deny their existence. One is the tendency to behave exactly opposite to the emotion. This is the subconscious attempt to say "I couldn't possibly hate this kid, because look how *nicely* I am treating him." Many students have "gotten away with murder" over the years because of such an unconscious attempt to deny a personality conflict.

The second mistake is just the opposite, the tendency to be overly critical and punitive in an unconscious attempt to justify your own negative feelings. In either case, it would be better to recognize and admit the conflict, since neither mistake would be as likely to occur if the conflict were recognized.

20. *Spend time outside of class diagnosing problems and planning strategies.* A strange phenomenon pervades the ranks of teachers, the belief that it is somehow wrong to spend time thinking about discipline problems or planning ways to avoid them. A lawyer would hardly limit his or her deliberations to the courtroom and refuse to spend time outside of court planning a case, nor would a musician perform on stage but refuse to spend time preparing. And yet somehow teachers have concluded that it is a sign of weakness to ponder discipline problems in the evening or on weekends—any time other than during class.

Teachers who follow this thinking are forfeiting one of their largest assets in the game of maintaining discipline in the classroom: their advantage over the students does not lie in their superior intellect or imagination; rather it lies in their years of preparation and experience in dealing with children and in their motivation—they have more at stake than the children. (Contrary to appearances, upsetting the teacher is not a major career goal of the child, whereas controlling the class is a central part of the teacher's life.) If teachers do *not* spend time outside of class analyzing problems, planning strategies, and second-guessing students, they have given up a large part of their advantage.

Teachers who appear to have no problems in the classroom are often found to be those who understand the class and its needs, see discipline problems developing and nip them in the bud, and are not surprised or thrown off by unusual behavior. Nothing takes the wind out of the sails of a student more quickly than seeing a teacher react to the most unheard of act by taking it in stride, completely prepared for it. Indeed, after a few such encounters, the student gets the eerie feeling that the teacher can read his mind, and misbehavior loses its charm because the teacher is not shocked by it.

The teacher who spends time outside class carefully considering the classroom atmosphere, diagnosing problems and their causes, and planning strategies to deal with these problems will probably encounter fewer classroom discipline problems than will the teacher who insists on "playing it by ear."

593

Retrospect and Prospect

After considering these twenty suggestions, you are *not* really expected to possess the magic lantern for avoiding all problems. Of course, we would expect you to see weaknesses and contradictions in the suggestions and to view these proposed rules with a healthy skepticism.

The major points can be summarized very simply as follows. Discipline is a problem inherent in the public school classroom, and no teacher should expect to escape completely problems in this area. The topic can be discussed and analyzed with certain principles emerging, and general suggestions that are helpful to the teacher can be advanced. The best professional judgment of the teacher, in the final analysis, is the best guide for action. Teachers can achieve a positive classroom climate and still maintain discipline without resorting to the false dichotomy of "discipline" (meaning punishment and strictness) versus "humanism" (meaning permissiveness and chaos). Finally all teachers must find the discipline techniques that work best for them in achieving their goals in the classroom.

Summary

Discipline is a topic that is discussed in every educational psychology textbook, although it often comes under other headings such as "classroom management," "problem situations," or "classroom rapport." In this chapter, discipline is defined as *the prevention of, and the handling of, behavior problems in the classroom.*

A brief historical review of discipline and its meaning is presented. In the "good old days," eighty or one hundred years ago, discipline meant punishment and strictness. The teacher was to punish any transgressions severely or else to maintain such a tight ship that no misbehavior was possible. Both punishment and strictness tend to be negative approaches to discipline.

By the 1920s, the progressive education movement saw punishment and strictness to be *causes* of behavior problems rather than solutions. The child was reacting to a bad system, and his or her revolt against that system made it even more strict and punitive. In such a setting, with the system itself as the cause of problems, little hope for solving discipline problems could be seen.

Progressive educators advocated a different approach. Break this negative cycle and, instead, base discipline on positive concepts of freedom, interest, and problem solving. With the child engaged in learning that related to his or her life outside school, in line with the child's interests and needs, there would be little cause for discipline problems. Freedom and permissiveness would actually lead to the elimination of discipline problems.

Neither the punishment and strictness ideas of the old days nor the permissiveness and interest ideas of progressive education proved to be a panacea for eliminating discipline problems. At present, discipline is seen as control (especially self-control), understanding, goal orientation, referral, prevention, and organized sublimation. Techniques such as individualized instruction are seen as ways to eliminate discipline problems. None of these modern ideas serves as a panacea either, and discipline problems, like the weather, continue to occur whether we like it or not.

The conditioning approach to behavior problems sees misbehavior merely as conditioned responses and works toward deconditioning these responses. The drive-reduction theory, another conditioning approach, is another way to look at discipline problems. If the teacher can learn to observe behavior objectively and precisely, utilize the reinforcers that are available, and gradually condition a new response while eliminating the old ones, then the teacher has employed a conditioning approach to discipline. Another concept is that of vicarious reinforcement, that is, the fact that reward or punishment of one student vicariously affects other students also.

Another approach to discipline is modeling. In this approach, the dynamics of identification and imitation are seen as crucial causes for discipline problems. Four modeling effects are identified: (1) the modeling effect, (2) the inhibitory effect, (3) the disinhibitory effect, and (4) the eliciting effect.

A final approach to discipline presented, that of the humanists, is based on the premise that human beings are innately good, that each person has a unique inner core, and that, if this inner core is denied or suppressed, discipline problems may result. The teacher must set up a classroom atmosphere that encourages this inner nature to thrive and develop. Children will learn best, feel good about themselves, and get along better with others in a classroom that has a humanistic climate. The humanistic teacher makes positive assumptions about the students and expects them to behave properly; the humanist does not make negative assumptions and expect students to misbehave.

In spite of the complexity of human nature and the multiple causes of classroom behavior, this chapter includes a number of specific suggestions about discipline, the most important being to get control of the class as soon as possible, in the best way available. It is much harder to get control after several weeks have passed than it is to get control at the outset. We advocate humanistic techniques for doing this whenever possible.

Nobody can tell a teacher exactly how to behave in the classroom to avoid discipline problems. The twenty suggestions in this chapter are meant as guidelines as you adapt to classroom situations and make decisions based on your professional judgment.

Study Questions

1. In the Gallup polls of the past ten years, parents have consistently listed discipline as the number one problem in the schools today. And yet teachers see other problems as more important. How do you explain this discrepancy in how parents see problems as compared with teachers' views?

2. Progressive educators saw many of the discipline problems in traditional schools as the child's reacting against the "bad" system. How many characteristics of "the good old days" can you list that might lead to discipline problems by causing reactions against them?

3. What are your beliefs about control in the classroom? List ten methods of controlling your classroom, beginning with the most desirable and ending with the least desirable.

4. Using the conditioning approach, explain the behavior of a sixth-grader who is frequently tardy, disrupts the class with his offhand remarks, turns in sloppy homework assignments or none at all, and constantly teases the girl sitting in front of him.

5. Describe how you would use the behavior modification approach to change the behavior of a student who finds it difficult to pay attention in class.

6. How would a humanist describe the causes of behavior of a child who is continually angry and acts this out by disrupting the class and defying the teacher? What would the humanist recommend be done with such a child?

7. Discipline is a topic that is often side-stepped in education courses. Why do you suppose this is so? What have you learned about discipline in the courses you have taken in preparation for teaching?

8. One suggestion in this chapter is to "have as few rules and regulations as possible." List the rules and regulations that you believe are essential to having minimal control in your classroom.

9. Another suggestion is to "maintain a sense of humor about misbehavior." Can you think of any instances in your many years of schooling in which a form of misbehavior was funny? How did the teacher handle it? Did the teacher admit that the misbehavior was humorous?

10. In this chapter it is suggested that the teacher find out policies and practices of administrators and other teachers. How many ways can you think of for the teacher to go about doing this?

11. Nonverbal cues are seen as important in classroom discipline. List ten nonverbal behaviors and your interpretation of each. Are some discipline problems a result of misreading of nonverbal cues?

12. It is suggested that punishment be administered as immediately as possible after the behavior. Can you think of any situations when this rule would not hold (i.e., cases in which you would deliberately delay the punishment)?

References

Bandura, A., and Walters, R. H. *Social Learning and Personality Development.* New York: Holt, Rinehart and Winston, 1963.

Curwin, R. L., and Mendler, A. N. *The Discipline Book: A Complete Guide to School & Classroom Management.* Reston, Va.: Reston, 1980.

Deutsch, M. *The Resolution of Conflict: Constructive and Destructive Processes.* New Haven, Conn.: Yale University Press, 1973.

Dollard, J., and Miller, N. E. *Personality and Psychotherapy.* New York: McGraw-Hill, 1950.

Dreikurs, R., Grunwald, B. B., and Pepper, F. C. *Maintaining Sanity in the Classroom: Classroom Management Techniques.* 2nd ed. New York: Harper & Row, 1982.

Fast, J. *Body Language.* New York: M. Evans, 1970.

Howell, R. G., and Howell, P. L. *Discipline in the Classroom: Solving the Teaching Puzzle.* Reston, Va.: Reston, 1979.

Kounin, J. S. *Discipline and Group Management in Classrooms.* New York: Holt, Rinehart and Winston, 1970.

Premack, D. ''Reinforcement Theory,'' in D. Levine, ed., *Nebraska Symposium on Motivation.* pp. 123–180, Lincoln, Neb.: University of Nebraska Press, 1965.

Tanner, L. N. *Classroom Discipline for Effective Teaching and Learning.* New York: Holt, Rinehart and Winston, 1978.

Afterword

Well! You have just about completed this textbook on psychology as it is applied to teaching. You have read about numerous theories, hypotheses, and ideas. You have studied many examples of how these concepts appear in student behavior and classroom situations. You have read many suggestions as to how you might apply these various theories. Now you must look forward to the actual task of application in your own teaching position.

What you are about to read is a guide for survival in your first teaching position. This prescription was written by a classroom teacher, Phyllis Johnson, and contains many suggestions regarding the tasks and responsibilities of a teacher. You may find that not all the things Ms. Johnson suggests will work for you. If so, ignore these points. We believe, however, that you will find this guide a useful advance organizer for *all* the things that you will have to do as a teacher. You may also find it useful to return to this guide from time to time after you have been teaching for awhile for helpful hints and suggestions.

Surviving in Today's Classroom
BY
PHYLLIS JOHNSON*

How well I remember the one statement made by a teacher to me when she learned that I had accepted a teaching assignment. "Well," she said, giving me a penetrating look, "you'll work yourself to death the first year." I was startled at such a frank and discouraging remark, and yet, her statement proved to be much more accurate than I could ever have anticipated. But being forewarned made it somehow easier to cope with the load.

*Phyllis Johnson is presently employed at the College of the Ozarks.

599

Certainly many of the experiences that I and other teachers have encountered will not happen to each of you, but if only twenty percent of what follows is applicable to you during the first year then I will know it was valuable! And believe me I wish there had been such a guide available to enlighten me!

Practice Teaching

All of us (with a rare exception) have an opportunity to "practice teach." Since this is the introduction to most school systems as a practitioner rather than as a student or observer, it is appropriate to discuss this episode first. This experience varies widely according to the policy of the teaching institution, but its primary purpose is to give each novice teacher actual classroom experience while under the supervision of both the classroom teacher and the supervisor from the teaching college. The time span involved can vary from as little as five weeks to an entire semester. Of importance to those of you who are working your way through school is the fact that this semester may force you to beg and borrow, or starve, because it is almost impossible to work while fulfilling this requirement.

Keep in mind that each of you may have a totally different experience. Some will be in complete charge of your cooperating teacher's classes after a brief observation period. Your responsibilities will include lecturing, preparing tests, grading papers, creating bulletin boards, posting grades, and attending faculty meetings and school activities. In other words you will step into the full teaching role. Unfortunately, a few of you will experience your student teaching from the back of the classroom observing, with only an occasional opportunity to test and demonstrate your teaching skills. Keep your eyes and ears open, for you have much to learn and will, even if your actual teaching is limited in scope.

Practice teaching should be exciting and rewarding, and while this is usually true, it can be a frustrating and depressing experience as well. Why? Perhaps because the student teacher finds himself caught between two bosses while fervently wishing he was on his own. The following short list of DO's and DON'T's may help alleviate some of the tension-producing uncertainties and smooth the way for a productive, pleasant experience.

DO'S

1. DO try to find out in advance as much as you can about the school to which you've been assigned. Such things as unwritten school rules, dress expected of teachers, participation expected of student teachers in school activities, use of faculty lounges by student teachers, etc. A good suggestion would be to contact a recent college graduate who did practice teaching at the school to which you've been assigned and ask for helpful hints.

2. DO remember that the cooperating teacher is your boss. This is important and is frequently the source of difficulty because the student teacher feels pulled between his teaching instructors, with their demands, and the classroom teacher, with his or her expectations. You are afforded this opportunity to practice teach because of the classroom teacher's willingness to welcome you, so always respect the teacher's classroom procedures.

3. DO think of your stint at practice teaching as being as important as any job you will hold. Therefore, be on time, dressed appropriately, and prepared! It might help you to know that better than sixty percent of all first teaching jobs are secured as a direct result of the practice teaching experience.

DON'T'S

1. DON'T expect too much of yourself or your teaching position. Even though you've been dying to get "out there" and try out all the methods and ideas you've been learning, remember that the classroom dynamics have been determined. Rather than trying to have everything your way, be considerate of the students and the teacher. Flexibility is an invaluable asset.

2. DON'T come prepared with too little—it's surprising how long an hour can be when you're in charge of the lesson. A good rule to follow is to prepare for class as though it were twice as long as it actually is. Beth's experience is a good example of what *can* happen (and often does). Beth's field was biology, and after observing for two weeks, she was delighted when the head of the science department told her that she would be in charge of the lecture on Monday. She worked all weekend preparing her notes and the accompanying transparencies. Finally the big day arrived. She delivered her lecture in a clear though not too steady voice, and the students, while a bit fidgety, were appropriately attentive. As she turned the page on the last of her notes, she caught the teacher's eye. His look was incredulous, and she didn't know whether to feel good or to be apprehensive. She glanced back at the class and could tell that they were poised, watching her—then (with mounting horror) she stole a quick look at the classroom clock—only twenty minutes had passed! Can you visualize the scramble on the part of the department head to fill up the rest of the class period?

3. DON'T try to be someone that you are not. If you've never taught before, you cannot expect to be an experienced teacher. If you're only twenty-one then don't act as though you're forty and vice versa. If you are assigned to teach a class in which you know very little, be honest and ask for help. Be proud of your regional accent, but be aware that it may cause some barriers. And keep a low profile—if you try to be "superteacher," you may make enemies.

Practice teaching, though very necessary and extremely beneficial, is still just *practice*. It exposes you to the real school world, but remember,

601

it will be different when you are the boss, when the responsibility is all yours. Ask any teacher—the response will be invariable. All are glad they were afforded the opportunity of practice teaching, but they will tell you it cannot in any way be compared with the real thing! In fact, with all due respect for the value of practice teaching, I've never talked to anyone that found it to be an experience they would repeat! Good luck, do your best, and keep in mind that the ultimate goal is farther down the road.

Beginning Fears

You are elated and so filled with excitement that you feel like running around in circles, for you have just heard that the job is YOURS!! After telling all your "closest and dearest" and savoring the thought that now you can buy the tickets, stereo, or whatever it is that you've been postponing, a nagging feeling creeps in—what is it? Ah yes, a "what if" sort of fear begins to displace the initial elation. What if I can't do it—what if I fall flat on my face?

It has been my experience, and in talking with others I have discovered that many have shared the same feeling, that this queasy feeling is perfectly natural. In fact, I believe that it is probably a good emotion to have. How can a negative emotion such as fear be productive? Because anxiety can prod us to prepare, to produce lesson plans, to review, and to study the books we will be teaching. Use this fear to locate additional resources and contact individuals who can give you helpful information.

Collecting milk money is one of the many chores which will make up your day. (Bernie Weithorn/ SIUC Photographic Service.)

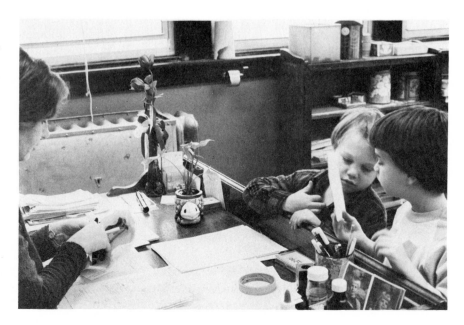

My biggest fear when I started stemmed from the fact that I was to teach two subjects in which I was definitely deficient. If you find yourself in a similar dilemma, remember the only way to overcome a weakness is by studying and doing the very task itself. Find out which courses you are to teach as early as possible, obtain copies of the texts that you will be using (if these are not available, go to the library or a former professor for some materials in the subject area), and then set some specific goals for yourself. Never mind that you are sick and tired of studying—you'll be a lot sicker if you don't prepare while you have the time. One way to prepare is to study the first three chapters of the text and answer the study questions at the end of each chapter. Compile a test, let it rest for a day or two, then take it yourself. You'll learn the material! Typing an outline for each chapter is very helpful, too.

The first few weeks will be particularly hectic; so do have your lesson plans thought out, written out, and established firmly in your mind. A good friend of mine wrote this note after reading the first draft of this guide. "BE PREPARED, this can NOT be stressed enough; believe me, when teaching . . . your students can tell how much you put into your lession plans." If you feel confident about the content of each subject during the first weeks, your entrance into the world of teaching will be a much more pleasant one. But don't be afraid to say, "I'm sorry, I don't know, but I'll be glad to try to find out the answer." It is always better to be honest about information that is hazy or nonexistent than to try to bluff it. The students will respect this type of answer, but they will soon dismiss what you have to say if they discover that you must always give an answer no matter how accurate or inaccurate.

A fear all of us seem to have in common is that of "messing up." Will it help to know that you *will* mess-up and that all teachers still make mistakes? A teacher I know loves to tell this story about himself. He was very prepared in every way but one—his "fly" was unzipped! By the end of the first period he felt so proud—the students had not only listened with rapt attention, but had taken copious notes. He did wonder why there seemed to be so much tittering, though. When a fellow teacher informed him of his state of undress, the glow turned into such embarrassment that the poor fellow could not make the rest of his classes that day. Perhaps the best idea is to set out to deliberately mess up. Then you will no longer have to dread the experience. Most fear is rooted in the unknown, and as each day passes you will know more and more, so relax (if you can) and look forward to the big day.

The Big Day

Finally the days on the calendar are down to two, then one, and you have butteflies so badly that you find it difficult to eat. Of course, to help smooth your entry into the classroom, your school system will have a day or two (in some districts it will be a week-long) program to acquaint you with the basic fundamentals and to give all the teachers instruction for the coming year. You will be welcomed, introduced, and given a grand tour of the facilities. NOTE: if no one volunteers to take you around, explore on your own—nothing is so embarrassing as not being able to locate the restrooms on the first day of classes! In a very few school districts, the attitude is still "sink or swim," so that these first meetings may consist of a perfunctory greeting with a few basic bits of information (such as time schedules). On the other hand, there may be very elaborate instruction with so many meetings and speeches that your head will be swimming. Your stomach will be, too, if there are as many breakfasts, luncheons, and dinners in your district as there are in my former area. Take whatever is offered with the realization that no matter how many details are covered there will be at least five hundred more that will surface.

During these first days of meetings, there will be many forms, lists, schedules, class rules, and grade books distributed, so locate a sturdy brief-case or a large satchel to take with you. Those first few weeks I "lost" something of vital importance every five minutes, but with the foresight of a large container in which to immediately drop everything handed to me, all the lost items showed up later.

An inexpensive folder with pockets in which to keep the class roles, seating charts, class bell schedule, and, if your school is very large, a diagram of the building is also very helpful. In fact, I use one of these folders (a different color for each class) for my class notes, tests, transparencies, and other paraphernalia in addition to the school "info" folder. Since some students seem to come and go rather quickly the first two weeks, I suggest that you DO NOT fill out the grade (record) book until the end of the second week. And rather than keep attendance in the record book, use a separate form. Most schools furnish such a form, but if yours doesn't, try to make you own. It's a lot easier to replace an attendance card than to start over in the grade book. As a matter of fact your grade book is of vital importance to you, and it should be kept in a safe (locked?) place. My story concerning this little matter bears telling.

I stepped into a teaching position with only three weeks left in the semester before Christmas break. After those grueling, hectic weeks ended I heaved a sigh of relief, threw everything in a big box in the back seat of the car, and left for my home, 100 miles away. Three days after Christmas I began to sift through the papers, grade tests, and finally post grades—only, the most sinking feeling imaginable swept over me—I had not seen the grade book. In desperation I began to rummage rapidly through all the papers, folders, bulletins, Christmas cards from students, but to no avail—the *very necessary* green book had disappeared. Panic began to creep in—had I put it in the box? Yes, I remembered carrying it clutched to my chest, along with the last semester tests, out the door. Everyone in the family began to help in the search while I was becoming as green as the missing book, when my sister's voice rang out. In a file folder, where it had slipped, among class notes, lay the essential record book. Now I keep it at home in the top right desk drawer or in my office locked away. Incidentally, in most systems these books become the property of the school, so keep this in mind before you make notes of a personal nature in the book.

The next step is to get the room key, or keys, and to check out the room that you will be using. Make sure that there is a desk and a chair for you. One teacher who was hired at the very last minute discovered to her horror that every desk in the classroom was taken. That couldn't be all that bad *except* in some places where it may take weeks to requisition anything. So do locate everything you think you will need.

How about a fan? Not all schools are air conditioned. If your room gets full sun and the blinds are not functional (or nonexistent), try covering the windows with aluminum foil, shiny side out. This will help to reduce the heat and the glare. What about an overhead projector and a screen? Get acquainted with the librarian, resource room teacher, or whoever is in charge of loan-out equipment. Find out if there is a priority list for equipment and get your name on it. There are several excellent free film sources that you will want to take advantage of after school begins, but if a film arrives and you can't obtain a projector, then your film will be useless. When you do check out the equipment, ask about special instructions regarding their use. The projectors, tape recorders, slide trays, and other equipment that you learned to use in "Audios and Visuals" may be quite different from the equipment at your school.

Don't forget small but essential needs such as pens, paper clips, glue, tape, stapler and staples, thumbtacks, ruler, scissors, and paper for notes. Some schools will furnish these items, but this this is not always the case. Ask the secretary or another teacher about these articles. And last, but far from least, where are the books that the students will be using? In a storeroom perhaps? Who is responsible for issuing them and what procedures are followed? On my first day I distributed all the books to my classes without checking to see what the school policy was. One of the other teachers then informed me that I had to record the number of each book along with the student's name on a special form! What a mess I had on my hands in locating all the books and owners the next day. Locate the teacher's resource book and the keys to tests, too. If these very necessary items aren't found by the end of the second day, place a call to the publisher and request your own copy. Most companies furnish the resource book free of charge and tests may be purchased for a nominal fee. One further essential should be mentioned—the tried but true blackboard. If you have no other props for the first day, find the chalk and an eraser and use your imagination!

You will want to make a good impression as a cooperative, friendly person, but take this advice—don't volunteer for anything! You will be plenty busy without serving on five committees. And never fear, your time will come, and before you know it your expert advice will be requested by several groups. So if someone asks for help, just smile and keep smiling, but keep your hands down and your mouth closed.

Now that the room is all set, bulletin board arranged, calendar turned to the right month, desks in place, and wastebasket handy, turn out the lights and close (lock) the door. Take a deep breath and plan to get plenty of sleep between now and tomorrow.

The First Day

If you are the nervous Nellie type or if ice water runs in your veins, the chances are that the alarm won't be necessary the first morning, but set it anyway! Something magical will happen, and somewhere around 4 A.M. to 5 A.M. you will wake up wide-eyed and apprehensive. This is *normal!* If you're like me, this may be a pattern for the first few weeks. So keep all night activities to an absolute zero for a while, week nights, that is!

There's an old saying about how "clothes make the man." Your first week of school the clothes you wear can make a big difference in the way you feel and act. The students will make a quick note of what you wear; so keep in style yet don't go to extremes. Since you'll be on your feet a great deal, select the shoes to be worn with this in mind. It helps to take along an extra pair and switch off during the day. Being knowledgable about the community and its attitudes toward dress is very wise. A big help for me is to select a week's wardrobe on Sunday, checking to make sure that all the buttons are there, zippers functioning as they should, collars and cuffs clean, etc. By making these selections once a week, I have one less decision to make each day. Since teachers make thousands of decisions in the course of an average day, eliminating even one will be a big help to you.

After dressing, combing your hair, and putting on the finishing touches, don't forget to "put on your attitude." As you look in the mirror keep saying to yourself, "I can do it, and I can do it very well" (the "it" being to tackle the tremendous and wonderful undertaking of teaching!). Your self-confidence will be apparent to your students, your colleagues, the administrators, but most important, to yourself, and what a difference this can make!

Do give yourself plenty of time for the trip to school, whether it be across town by bus or thirty miles in a car pool. It may relieve first-day jitters by letting someone else do the driving, but regardless of your mode of transportation, plan to arrive early enough to cope with any mishaps (such as not having the correct key to the classroom) and be settled in comfortably before the first bell.

What should you do the first day? Everyone has a different style, of course, but I believe that it is wise to use this day to get acquainted. Remember how it was when you were a student? Didn't you want to know something about the course, what you would be studying, and how

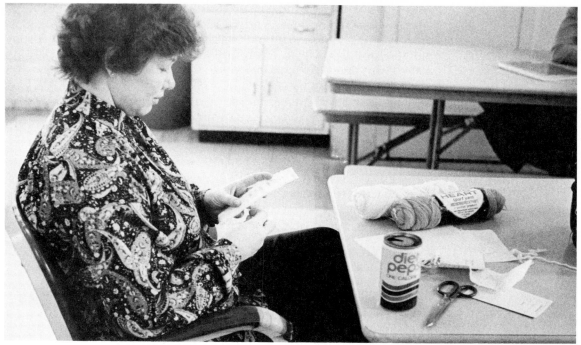

Aides hired to supervise study halls, lunchrooms, and playgrounds have made it possible for teachers to spend free periods planning. (Bernie Weithorn/SIUC Photographic Service.)

you would be graded? How about supplies that are needed for the class? If you tell them that they must have a particular type of protractor, a certain pencil size, a special brand of notebook, or a calculator that has fifty keys, are you certain that these items can be easily obtained in the community? One more thing for you to check out, but this is important. Student pocketbooks are very often slim, so don't insist on the most expensive materials.

An idea that I adopted from other teachers is to have all the students put name, address, and class schedule on one side of a 3″ × 5″ card. On the back instruct them to write a few lines about themselves. For example, what they do in their spare time, their jobs, favorite color or food, or something that they particularly dislike. I have found that this helps me learn their names faster as well as gives insight into each child's individuality.

After asking for information from your students, take time to tell about yourself. You don't have to go into great detail—in fact I advise against doing that—just talk about your favorite things. Tell them how you happened to choose teaching as a career. Describe your family, even your pets. By disclosing a little about yourself, you become more of an individual to

607

your students. Although being a humanistic teacher has come under fire in recent years from some quarters, I am a great advocate of this philosophy. Students who come from walks of life far different from yours are more apt to listen to you when they know that you, too, didn't always make "A's" and "B's" and that your favorite singer (food, color) is also theirs.

How can you be humanistic? It's easy. Be considerate! Learn all you can about your students beginning with the first day. If very few of your students will be going on to college, don't gear all your lectures toward that end. If your students do not have access to newspapers and magazines, remember this when making assignments that require these materials. Don't ask for a "What I Did All Summer" type of paper from students who obviously stayed home and did nothing. You may want to make a lot of assignments that require work outside the regular classroom, but what if most of the class *must* work, either at home with chores or in business? And will it help you to know that Sally falls asleep in class because there are eleven others living at home in three rooms?

I do not mean to imply that you must never bring anything new into your students' lives, for if we don't stretch their horizons, who will? Exciting the child to want to learn is the greatest contribution to a student that a teacher can make. Perhaps my biggest thrill my first year came from a note written by John, who was the smallest in his class and also one of the brightest. The last day of classes my blackboard became a giant notebook with the students writing messages of fond farewell. There, at the bottom, in tiny block letters was John's message. "To Mrs. Johnson, thank you for making me want to learn, the only teacher who has done that!" For John I wish a horizon that stretches around the world.

Don't get discouraged if, at the end of the first day, second day, and thereafter you are frazzled, tense, headachey, and a bit bewildered. All honest veteran teachers will tell you that they feel the same way—in fact the first several weeks leave most of the faculty breathless and worn out. Try to remain calm even though chaos seems to reign and keep remembering that each day gets better.

Putting It Together—The First Weeks

You've heard it before, but I will say it again—the first few weeks are very important with respect to discipline, the students' attitude toward the subject and assignments, and general classroom climate. You as the teacher will influence this atmosphere significantly. What kind of teacher will you be? Democratic, autocratic, or permissive? Most of us are a blend of the three styles, with one dominating the others. You should choose the goals that are appropriate for your classes, then determine the teaching style that will most likely ensure their success, but use a style that reflects your personality. Don't wait until midyear to set the tone of the classes because once the personality has been developed it is very, very difficult to change.

In developing the relationship with the class, remember the line between being friendly and becoming a buddy is extremely fine. Yet too much distance can create a gulf that will never be bridged. My first year as a teacher's aide I tried too hard to be friends, and as a result, I lost control of the class. In their eyes ''good ole'' Ms. Johnson became one of the group, and it was easy to ignore the assignments I gave. It was actually frightening to know that I had made such a mistake, yet there was very little that could be done to rectify the situation. Thank goodness for Mrs. Boswell, the teacher in charge, or those poor students would have had complete control in short order.

Several years ago a psychologist friend made an observation while we were discussing children. He said, ''Children need fences, and although they will be constantly trying to tear them down, they depend on the adults around them to rebuild the fences.'' Being consistent is a good type of fence to build. Tell the students what is expected of them and stick to your expectations. For example, are all the assignments you make of equal importance? Must they all be turned in? And if they aren't, what, if any, are the consequences? If you allow Steve and Joe, the star football players to throw paper wads, will you permit the others to do the same? During my second year of teaching, a vice principal was hired to enforce discipline because the year before near anarchy had reigned. In class discussions during the first week of the new school year, the students expressed their feelings about the new turn of events. Although they didn't particularly like the strict enforcement of school rules, they were much more concerned lest a return to the former situation occur. When I asked them the reason for this worry, all replied that at least now they knew exactly what was expected of them. As one boy said to another (overheard outside my class window), ''last year weren't [sic] no fun anyhow, cause it were [sic] too easy to get away with everythin', and then when you wasn't [sic] expectin' it, they gave ya the double-whammy.'' So have a few rules but stick to them!

Don't be afraid to laugh—particularly at yourself—for a little bit of humor goes a long way. Clearly, if there is one common trait that all first-year teachers share, it is probably taking everything too seriously. Without humor and perspective many teachers never make it back for a second year. Good perspective can help prevent overreaction to a situation. There was a novice teacher who marched half her class off to the principal's office within the first fifteen minutes of the first hour of the first day because two of the boys had thrown paper planes and the others had laughed at the incident. Can you visualize this situation? Ask yourself how you would have handled this episode? Needless to say, this teacher had difficulty with paper projectiles the rest of the year and has not been seen inside a classroom since.

A great aid in the beginning weeks is a seating chart. Ignore all the groans, pleas, and outright griping (and the nagging feeling that a chart is

609

too regimental), and stick to your plan. It is helpful in so many ways that it seems ridiculous not to have one. If, by some stroke of fortune, you find you have a class with only twelve or fourteen students, then a chart may not be necessary. Why a chart? Because you should be able to learn all your students names by using this arrangement. (Don't moan—I've got over 140 students this year, and I learned all their names by the end of the first week using this system).

Remember those cards you had the students fill out the first day? Take them home with you and as you fill out the seating chart, look at the card and find something to help you remember that particular student. Sharon, oh yes, she's so shy that it shows in her eyes, but she loves to embroider so I'll remember to tell her that I love to cross-stitch; Dwayne, he is the oldest of twelve and loves to hunt; and Lavonne, the star basketball player with the motor-mouth. Alphabetical seating isn't the only arrangement to use, but it is easy, so I start with the "Z's" and work backward. This alleviates some of the repetition that students get in other classes. Does this method really help in learning their names? One of the nicest comments I ever received came from a very stout, outspoken student after my first week of class. "Hey, Ms. Johnson, can I ask you a question?" she said very bluntly. When I replied, yes, but I couldn't guarantee an answer, the student went on, "How come you got to know our names so fast? I've still got teachers that have had me in class when I was a sophomore that call me 'hey you.'" Remember when you were only a number or called "Hey, you" or even worse, ignored? That sure told you how important you were to the teacher, didn't it? Show how important you think the students are by learning their names, and I guarantee you that the atmosphere in your classroom will be entirely different from that of Mr. Hallis, where a glass wall exists between his students and his desk from the first day.

Another plus for seating charts is that they help expedite the task of taking attendance, in most schools an everyday, mandatory essential. If you have as many as thirty or more bright shining faces staring at you, it can consume quite a lot of time tracking down all the Jennifers, Marks, and Mikes (still the most popular names in my area). And the fastest way to quell a potential discipline problem is to call "it" by name and give "it" an enjoyable, responsible job. Please don't think that I am locking you into using a seating chart for the entire year or even using the same one— once you feel comfortable with all the students, and IF you believe that they can handle sitting where they choose, by all means throw away that form. Nothing will please your students more, I promise. But a word of caution, for every two classes in which a seating chart becomes superfluous, you will have one in which it will be mandatory to retain one, so reserve the right to reinstate your seating order, if necessary.

Because getting off to a flying start is basically the teacher's responsibility, you may feel as I did at first. When asked by friends and family how I was doing, I would first smile and reply that everything was great.

But if the inquirer was genuinely interested, I would add, "I feel a little like I'm back in college again carrying nineteen hours, and not only do I have to study for classes everyday, but I've been assigned to grade all the student's papers and reports." In other words, I felt swamped, but I was too ashamed to admit this to my fellow teachers. Three times I was so discouraged that I wanted to quit. About the only advice I can give you concerning this feeling is that it, too, is natural and normal. But a word of warning—don't put off doing *anything* because you may wake up one day and discover that you have three weeks of grading to do with report cards due the next day!

And incidentally when grading time rolls around, and in the first year it is upon you before you've caught your breath, the easiest system to use seems to be that of total number of points. That is, assign points to each quiz, major test, and even homework. Reports are also good for using with the point system. At the end of the grading period, total up the number of points possible if a student had made a perfect score on everything. Then total up each student's points and divide by the total possible. This will give a percentage and to this figure you can assign a letter grade. There are other methods, of course, but after many trials and a few errors, this one has worked best for me. I forgot all about the Bell curve after spending more than nine hours trying to get just one typing class to fit it, and after talking with other cohorts, I discovered that they too, have thrown it out the window. Worrying about the grades that you are forced to post on the cards is just part of the job, but this agony diminishes with time. Accept the fact that you just can't reach all of the students all of the time, and the reasons are many, ranging from the fact that the student hates history to the personality conflict that developed the instant the student laid eyes on you.

I do tell my classes that if they received a grade that they truly didn't believe they deserved that they should see me after class. Then I tell them a story that happened to a fellow classmate of mine in general psych a few years back. When our midterm tests were handed back her face went quite pale and she whispered under her breath, "an 'F,' " with stunned disappointment. I started talking to her and finally convinced her that she should see the professor and ask him to at least go over the test with her. The next day she flagged me down in the hall with a huge smile on her face. It seemed that a graduate assistant had graded the tests and had used the wrong key on her test, so instead of an "F" she actually had a "C". There won't be a happy ending for all students, but at least they may understand better why their grade is what it is.

One last item I would like to mention about the first weeks, and that is the state of your health. I am not quite certain what seems to come over first-year teachers, but we do seem very susceptible to every germ that comes along. Perhaps it is the tension that underlies every new job and when this is coupled with all the bugs that fly around schools it is understandable why we are ill so much. Try to eat right and get plenty of rest.

Some sort of exercise is wonderful, if you can find time to squeeze it in between everything else. Expect a few more colds and intestinal viruses with the hope that this will not be as frequent during the years following.

Friendly Relations

I'm not referring to your family, but to the faculty, staff, and administrative personnel that will be an important part of your days for the next nine or ten months. And "friendly" is the best way to develop the relationship you will have with these folks, but to be honest, it's doubtful if all will remain that way. You will, hopefully, be introduced to the other members of the department, and if the school is small, someone will take you around, introducing you to one and all in the space of an hour or two. Unless you've got a photographic memory, you will find yourself in the same predicament that I was—new faces with names that did not match. Oh me, what a mess—Fern looked like Jane, Dennis didn't teach agri, it was science, and Kevin was short, with a potbelly that bounced when he walked, so how could I mistake him for Jack, who was built just like the famous Sprat? At least I got the coaches' names correct, an absolute *must* in some parts of the country.

Faculty meetings will become a part of your routine. (Arkansas Gazette.)

The faculty lounge can be a valuable source of information during the first few weeks, but it will also be an eye-opener!! One of the finest teachers that I ever knew absolutely refused to spend any time in the lounge and fervently wished that he could do away with it. Why? Because it is a great gossip factory, not only about the administration and its latest demands, but also about fellow teachers. Worst of all are the discussions that fly back and forth about students. I much prefer to begin my classes fresh without any suggestive tainting from other teacher's experiences. Then my expectations are my own and not colored by another's prejudice.

My biggest shock in teaching came out of the faculty lounge—I discovered in listening to the teachers that some of them actually *did not like* the students!! They were venomous and ridiculing in their conversation, and I could not understand how someone who despised such an enormous segment of their job would remain. As the days passed I began to realize that for a very few teachers the power of their position had become their only reason for being there. Do not let these few embittered souls influence you! Rather, realize that they would be just as disillusioned no matter what field of endeavor they had chosen—only how unfortunate they picked teaching.

To be philosophical about this situation is to be like my husband, who said, when our youngest son was assigned to one of these types his first year in school. "Every child is entitled to one bad teacher, and Will's getting his early." And wise Will said, "Don't worry Mom, it's only for a school year, I can stand it." But I still protest and maintain that these are the teachers that must be removed from the system. Unfortunately, they

Take advantage of in-service activities to learn new skills and refresh old ones. (CEMREL, Inc.)

are also the very ones who carefully and dutifully fill out every form, on time, who never complain to the staff, except about a fellow faculty member who isn't doing his part. In other words, the teacher evaluations that are so popular these days never seem to weed out these bad apples. No where on those forms does it say, "Does this person really like the students. Does he see them as individuals? Does he respect them for themselves, not for what Daddy does?" Respect is the one key that unlocks the closed relationship that so many teachers have with their students. They are just like you and me, just younger, and even when you are frazzled and downright discouraged, don't ever lose respect for your pupils as humans.

Suggested Readings

The following books and articles have been very helpful to me in teaching; I hope you will seek some of them out and read them.

Campbell, David. *If You Don't Know Where You're Going, You'll Probably End Up Somewhere Else.* Niles, Ill.: Argus Communications. 1974.

Clark, Donald H., and Kadis, Asya L. *Humanistic Teaching.* Columbus, Ohio: Charles E. Merrill, 1971.

Dobson, James. *Dare to Discipline.* Wheaton, Ill.: Tyndale House, 1977.

Ernst, Ken. *Games Students Play.* Millbrae, Calif.: Celestial Arts, 1972.

Hamachek, Don, ed. *Human Dynamics in Psychology and Education.* Boston: Allyn & Bacon, 1977.

"Help! Teacher Can't Teach!" *Time,* June 16, 1980, pp. 54–63.

James, Muriel, and Jongeward, Dorothy. *Born to Win.* Reading, Mass.: Addison-Wesley, 1971.

Lefrancois, Guy R. *Psychology for Teaching.* 3rd ed. Belmont, Calif.: Wadsworth, 1979.

Moustakas, Clark. *Who Will Listen?* New York: Ballantine Books, 1975.

Nirenberg, Jesse S. *Getting Through to People.* Englewood Cliffs, N.J.: Prentice-Hall, 1963 (1980).

Rogers, Carl B. *On Becoming a Person.* Boston: Houghton Mifflin, 1961.

Today's Teacher, all issues.

Weinberg, Carl, ed. *Humanistic Foundations of Education.* Englewood Cliffs, N.J.: Prentice-Hall, 1972.

Index

615

621

627